Prentice-Hall International Series in Management

Athos and Coffey	*Behavior in Organizations: A Multidimensional View*
Ballou	*Business Logistics Management*
Baumol	*Economic Theory and Operations Analysis, 2nd ed.*
Boot	*Mathematical Reasoning in Economics and Management Science*
Brown	*Smoothing, Forecasting, and Prediction of Discrete Time Series*
Chambers	*Accounting, Evaluation and Economic Behavior*
Churchman	*Prediction and Optimal Decision: Philosophical Issues of a Science of Values*
Clarkson	*The Theory of Consumer Demand: A Critical Appraisal*
Cohen and Cyert	*Theory of the Firm: Resource Allocation in a Market Economy*
Cullman and Knudson	*Management Problems in International Environments*
Cyert and March	*A Behavioral Theory of the Firm*
Fabrycky and Torgersen	*Operations Economy: Industrial Applications of Operations Research*
Frank, Massy, and Wind	*Market Segmentation*
Green and Tull	*Research for Marketing Decisions, 2nd ed.*
Greenlaw, Herron, and Rawdon	*Business Simulation in Industrial and University Education*
Hadley and Whitin	*Analysis of Inventory Systems*
Holt, Modigliani, Muth, and Simon	*Planning Production, Inventories, and Work Force*
Hymans	*Probability Theory with Applications to Econometrics and Decision-Making*
Ijiri	*The Foundations of Accounting Measurement: A Mathematical, Economic, and Behavioral Inquiry*
Kaufmann	*Methods and Models of Operations Research*
Lesourne	*Economic Analysis and Industrial Management*
Mantel	*Cases in Managerial Decisions*
Massé	*Optimal Investment Decisions: Rules for Action and Criteria for Choice*
McGuire	*Theories of Business Behavior*
Miller and Starr	*Executive Decisions and Operations Research, 2nd ed.*
Montgomery and Urban	*Management Science in Marketing*
Montgomery and Urban	*Applications of Management Science in Marketing*
Morris	*Management Science: A Bayesian Introduction*
Nicosia	*Consumer Decision Processes: Marketing and Advertising Decisions*
Peters and Summers	*Statistical Analysis for Business Decisions*
Pfiffner and Sherwood	*Administrative Organization*
Simonnard	*Linear Programming*
Singer	*Antitrust Economics: Selected Legal Cases and Economic Models*
Vernon	*Manager in the International Economy*
Wagner	*Principles of Operations Research with Applications to Managerial Decisions*
Ward and Robertson	*Consumer Behavior: Theoretical Sources*
Zangwill	*Nonlinear Programming: A Unified Approach*
Zenoff and Zwick	*International Financial Management*

Prentice-Hall, Inc.
Prentice-Hall International, Inc., *United Kingdom and Eire*
Prentice-Hall of Canada, Ltd., *Canada*
J. H. DeBussy, Ltd., *Holland and Flemish-Speaking Belgium*
Dunod Press, *France*
Maruzen Company, Ltd., *Far East*
Herrero Hermanos, Sucs, *Spain and Latin America*
R. Oldenbourg, *Verlag, Germany*
Ulrico Hoepli Editore, *Italy*

CONSUMER BEHAVIOR:
Theoretical Sources

CONSUMER BEHAVIOR:
Theoretical Sources

Edited by

Scott Ward
Harvard University

Thomas S. Robertson
University of Pennsylvania

Prentice-Hall, Inc., *Englewood Cliffs, New Jersey*

Library of Congress Cataloging in Publication Data

Ward, Scott
  Consumer behavior.

  Includes bibliographies.
    1. Consumers—Addresses, essays, lectures.
  2 Consumption (Economics)—Addresses, essays,
  lectures. I. Robertson, Thomas S., joint author.
  II. Title.
  HB801.W275   658.8'34   73–4306
  ISBN 0–13–169391–3

Printed in the United States of America

10 9 8 7 6 5 4 3 2 1

Prentice-Hall International, Inc., *London*
Prentice-Hall of Australia, Pty. Ltd., *Sydney*
Prentice-Hall of Canada, Ltd., *Toronto*
Prentice-Hall of India Private Limited, *New Delhi*
Prentice-Hall of Japan, Inc., *Tokyo*

Contents

Preface   xi

Acknowledgments   xiii

INTRODUCTION   1

1

Consumer Behavior Research: Promise and Prospects   3
Thomas S. Robertson and Scott Ward

BASIC THEORETICAL AREAS   43

2

Psychological Theories and Interpretations of Learning   45
Michael L. Ray

3

Field Theory in Consumer Behavior   118
Harold H. Kassarjian

4

✕ **Personality and Consumer Behavior**   141

William D. Wells and Arthur D. Beard

5

Theories of Interpersonal Perception   200

Daniel B. Wackman

6

Role Theory and Group Dynamics   230

Lyman E. Ostlund

7

Overview of Economic Models of Consumer Behavior   276

George H. Haines, Jr.

FOCUSED THEORETICAL AREAS   301

8

✕ **Theories of Attitude Structure and Change**   303

George S. Day

9

Cognitive Consistency and Novelty Seeking   354

M. Venkatesan

10

Consumer Decisions and Information Use   385

Steven H. Chaffee and Jack M. McLeod

11

✕ **Theories of Diffusion**   416

Gerald Zaltman and Ronald Stiff

12

Subculture Theory: Poverty, Minorities, and Marketing   469
Frederick D. Sturdivant

13

Stochastic Models of Consumer Choice Behavior   521
David B. Montgomery and Adrian B. Ryans

Preface

Consumer Behavior: Theoretical Sources, intended primarily to meet the needs of graduate students, provides an overview of the various behavioral science topics that have proven to be of particular importance to an understanding of consumer behavior. We hope herein to stimulate conceptual thinking in the formulation of problems for research.

A basic assumption is that consumer behavior research is both an *interdisciplinary* and an *applied* field. That is, the field is built upon several parent disciplines, notably psychology, sociology, and economics, and the primary goal of the field is to apply these disciplines toward the solution of classes of problems, rather than to accumulate knowledge for its own sake. This is not to say that consumer behavior researchers do not, or should not, seek to build theory; rather, our view is that emerging conceptualizations and problem-solving bases for research are complementary. A theoretical basis is a necessary condition for truly useful applied research.

At this point in time, the theoretical literature is not organized so that students and researchers interested in consumer behavior can easily utilize it. The social sciences are too vast to be adequately studied during a consumer behavior course or research project. Readings books and texts on consumer behavior have appeared, but they seldom make explicit the basic theoretical underpinnings, nor are they clearly related to applied problems. Our objective is to provide students with conceptualizations and critical reviews of various behavioral science areas that have proven to be of particular interest in consumer behavior research. To this end, the chapters in this volume are not meant as an attempt to provide a psychology or sociology text; rather each author selectively reviews a circumscribed area of behavioral research and theory, and presents the information in a context designed to point the way toward productive research in consumer behavior.

Taken together, the chapters are not intended to constitute a single theory, or set of theories, of consumer behavior. Our view is that theories emerge from limited, "middle-range" research, and the papers specially prepared for this volume attempt to define and focus problems for such research.

The book can be used in several ways in the classroom. Those teachers who have used the chapters in a mimeographed form have found that they group well into *intra-* and *inter-*individual foci as well as into *basic* and *focused* theoretical areas. The book can also be used in combination with consumer behavior "theory" texts, such as Nicosia, Howard and Sheth, or Hansen, with the chapters being used to highlight parts of the models. The book can further be supplemented by one of the readings volumes now available to enrich the discussion and to provide more research evidence. It is also possible to use the materials in an applied sense by combining them with cases highlighting the various theoretical approaches.

We are indebted to Professor Ronald Frank, Wharton School, University of Pennsylvania, for his careful and critical review of each paper in this volume. We would also like to express our sincere gratitude to each of the authors who contributed so much of their time and effort in the preparation of chapters for this volume. Since the authors represent demonstrated accomplishment in contributing to the field of consumer behavior research, or closely related fields, this investment of time and effort was no small matter. It is our sincerest hope that this book will prove useful in stimulating high caliber, useful, and conceptually-oriented research in consumer behavior.

Scott Ward
Boston, Massachusetts

Thomas S. Robertson
Philadelphia, Pennsylvania

Acknowledgments

The following contributors wish to acknowledge their indebtedness to these sources for granting permission to include certain information in their articles.

Michael L. Ray (Chapter 2)

S. M. Berger and W. W. Lambert, "Stimulus-Response Theory in Contemporary Social Psychology," in *The Handbook of Social Psychology*, Vol. I (2nd ed.), ed. G. Lindzey and E. Aronson. Reading, Mass.: Addison-Wesley, 1968.

D. E. Berlyne, "Arousal and Reinforcement," in *Nebraska Symposium on Motivation, 1967,* Vol. XV, ed. D. Levine. Lincoln, Neb.: University of Nebraska Press, 1967. Reprinted by permission of University of Nebraska Press.

E. R. Guthrie, *The Psychology of Learning* (rev. ed.). New York: Harper & Row, 1952.

Winfred F. IIill, *Learning: A Survey of Psychological Interpretations.* ©1963, 1971 by Chandler Publishing Company, adapted with permission.

J. Howard and J. Sheth, *The Theory of Buyer Behavior.* New York: John Wiley & Sons, Inc., 1969.

C. W. Luh, "The conditions of retention," *Psychological Monographs,* 142 (1922).

N. Miller and D. T. Campbell, "Recency and Primacy in Persuasion as a Function of the Timing of Speeches and Measurements," *Journal of Abnormal and Social Psychology,* 59 (1959). © 1959 by the American Psychological Association, and reproduced by permission.

M. L. Ray and A. G. Sawyer, "Repetition in Media Models: A Laboratory Technique," *Journal of Marketing Research* (February 1971). Reprinted from *Journal of Marketing Research,* published by the American Marketing Association.

M. L. Ray and W. Wilkie, "Fear: The Potential of an Appeal Neglected by Marketing," *Journal of Marketing,* 34 (February 1970). Reprinted from *Journal of Marketing,* published by the American Marketing Association.

E. L. Thorndike, *Animal Intelligence.* New York: The Macmillan Company, 1911.

B. J. Underwood, "Interference and Forgetting," *Psychological Review,* 64 (1957).©1957 by the American Psychological Association, and reproduced by permission.
Herbert Zielske, "The Remembering and Forgetting of Advertising," *Journal of Marketing,* 23 (January 1959). Reprinted from *Journal of Marketing,* published by the American Marketing Association.

Lyman E. Ostlund (Chapter 6)

Harry L. Davis, "Dimensions of Marital Roles in Consumer Decision Making," *Journal of Marketing Research,* 7 (May 1970). Reprinted from *Journal of Marketing Research,* published by the American Marketing Association.
M. E. Shaw, "Communication Networks," in *Advances in Experimental Social Psychology,* Vol. I, ed. L. Berkowitz. New York: Academic Press, 1964.

Frederick D. Sturdivant (Chapter 12)

Marcus Alexis, "Some Negro-White Differences in Consumption," *American Journal of Economics and Sociology,* 1 (January 1962).
Marcus Alexis, George H. Haines, Jr., and Leonard S. Simon, "Consumption Behavior of Prisoners: The Case of the Inner City Shopper," Working Paper Series No. 7012. Rochester, N. Y.: University of Rochester, 1970.
Alan R. Andreasen, "Towards a Model of Structural Dynamics in Inner City Markets," School of Management, State University of New York at Buffalo, 1971 (mimeo.).
Raymond Bauer and Scott Cunningham, *Studies in the Negro Market.* Cambridge, Mass.: Marketing Science Institute, 1970.
Raymond A. Bauer, Scott M. Cunningham, and Lawrence Wortzel, "The Marketing Dilemma of Negroes," *Journal of Marketing,* 9 (July 1965). Reprinted from *Journal of Marketing,* published by the American Marketing Association.
David Caplovitz, *The Poor Pay More.* Reprinted with permission of The Macmillan Company.©1967 by The Free Press of Glencoe, Inc., a division of The Macmillan Company.
Lawrence P. Felman and Alvin D. Star, "Racial Factors in Shopping Behavior," in *A New Measure of Responsibility for Marketing.* Chicago: American Marketing Association, 1968. Reprinted from *A New Measure of Responsibility for Marketing,* published by the American Marketing Association.
Herbert J. Gans, *The Urban Villagers.* Reprinted with permission of The Macmillan Company.©1962 by The Free Press of Glencoe, Inc., a division of The Macmillan Company.
Dennis H. Gensch and Richard Staelin, "Making Black Retail Outlets Work," *California Management Review,* 15 (Fall 1972).
Norval D. Glenn and Charles M. Bonjean, *Blacks in the United States.* New York: Chandler Publishing Company, 1969.
Edward T. Hall, *The Silent Kingdom.* New York: Doubleday & Company, Inc., 1959.
Winthrop D. Jordan, *White over Black: American Attitudes toward the Negro, 1550-1812.* Baltimore, Md.: Penguin Books, Inc., 1969.
Clyde Kluckhohn, *Mirror for Man.* ©1949 by McGraw-Hill, Inc. Permission of McGraw-Hill Book Company.
Elliot Liebow, *Tally's Corner.* ©1967 by Little, Brown and Company (Inc.)
Daniel P. Mannix in collaboration with Malcolm Cowley, *Black Cargoes—A History of the Atlantic Slave Trade: 1518-1865.* All rights reserved. Reprinted by permission of The Viking Press, Inc.
Joseph Barry Mason and Charles S. Madden, "Food Purchases in a Low-Income Negro Neighborhood: The Development of Socio-Economic Behavioral Profile as Related to

Movement and Patronage Decisions," in *Relevance in Marketing: Problems, Research, Action,* ed. Fred C. Allvine. Chicago: American Marketing Association, 1972.

Francis E. Merrill and H. Wentworth Eldridge, *Culture and Society.* Englewood Cliffs, N.J.: Prentice-Hall, Inc., 1952.

David A. Schulz, *Coming Up Black: Patterns of Ghetto Socialization.* Englewood Cliffs, N. J.: Prentice-Hall, Inc., 1969.

James E. Stafford, Keith Cox, and James B. Higginbotham, "Some Consumption Pattern Differences between Urban Whites and Negroes," *Social Science Quarterly,* 49 (December 1968).

Charles Valentine, *Culture and Poverty.* Chicago: The University of Chicago Press, 1968.

David B. Montgomery and Adrian B. Ryans (Chapter 13)

L. A. Foust and J. W. Woodlock, "Early Prediction of Market Success for New Grocery Products," *Journal of Marketing,* 5 (October 1960). Reprinted from *Journal of Marketing,* published by the American Marketing Association.

J. Morgan Jones, "A Comparison of Three Models of Brand Choice," and "A Dual-Effects Model of Brand Choice," *Journal of Marketing Research,* 7 (November 1970). Reprinted from *Journal of Marketing Research,* published by the American Marketing Association.

A. A. Kuehn, "Consumer Brand Choice—A Learning Process?" *Journal of Advertising Research,* 2 (December 1962). Reprinted from the *Journal of Advertising Research,* © 1962 by the Advertising Research Foundation.

David B. Montgomery, "Stochastic Consumer Models: Some Comparative Results," in *Marketing and the New Science of Planning,* ed. R. King. Chicago: American Marketing Association, 1969. Reprinted from *Marketing and the New Science of Planning,* published by the American Marketing Association.

Introduction

1

Consumer Behavior Research: Promise and Prospects

Thomas S. Robertson
University of Pennsylvania

Scott Ward
Harvard University

LOCUS OF THE FIELD: DEFINING "CONSUMER BEHAVIOR"

DEVELOPING INTERESTS IN CONSUMER BEHAVIOR RESEARCH

Users of Consumer Behavior Research. Producers of Consumer Behavior Research.

HISTORICAL PERSPECTIVE

The 1960s. Models: Comprehensive and Limited.

CONTEMPORARY REACTIONS TO CONSUMER BEHAVIOR RESEARCH

APPROACHES TO CONSUMER BEHAVIOR RESEARCH: FORMAL THEORY VERSUS PROBLEM-SOLVING METHODS

Formal Theory. Formal Theory Generation in Consumer Behavior. Problem-Solving Research.

MIDDLE-RANGE THEORY

ISSUE OF BORROWING

Principles of Borrowing.

ACTOR VERSUS SITUATION

METHODOLOGICAL ISSUES IN CONSUMER BEHAVIOR RESEARCH

Methodological Advances. Lack of Replication. Cross-Sectional Surveys. Standardized Definitions and Variable Categories. Validity and Reliability in Consumer Behavior Research.

3

PAPERS IN THIS VOLUME

Basic Theoretical Areas. Focused Theoretical Areas.

CONCLUDING NOTE

REFERENCES

Most research in what has come to be called the field of consumer behavior relies heavily upon concepts, theories, and empirical findings drawn from the various social-science disciplines, notably psychology, sociology, and economics. The purpose of this book is to acquaint the reader with some of the more prevalent conceptual, theoretical, and empirical research traditions, which have been particularly useful to researchers interested in consumer behavior, and to review and illustrate some applications of these traditions in consumer behavior research. It is not our collective purpose to elaborate a "master theory" of consumer behavior, nor to report a listing of disjointed empirical studies. Instead, the focus of this book is on conceptual and theoretical areas of research, which we feel hold the greatest promise for improved understanding of consumption behavior.

The greatest promise for advancing the consumer behavior field resides, in our opinion, in the further development of what have come to be called *middle-range* theories (Merton, 1957). These are theoretical or conceptual frameworks, which do not constitute full-blown theories in and of themselves, but neither are they merely isolated empirical findings. Rather, middle-range theories suggest explanations and predictions concerning some relatively circumscribed areas of inquiry. Middle-range theories are, by definition, developing theories, since re-

The authors are grateful to Raymond A. Bauer (Harvard), Ronald E. Frank (Wharton), Harold H. Kassarjian, (UCLA), Francesco M. Nicosia (Berkeley), and Alvin J. Silk (MIT) for their comments on earlier drafts.

search is carried out in the context of a conceptual structure and should accumulate toward the development of integrated theoretical positions. It is our hope, therefore, that the 13 papers contained in this volume will be helpful to advanced students of consumer behavior who are interested in planning research which is not only useful in the solution of immediate consumer behavior problems, but which is also conceptually rooted and cumulative in nature.

The purpose of this introductory chapter is to provide perspective on the development of consumer behavior as a field of inquiry. Additionally, we shall discuss various approaches to the conduct of consumer behavior research, and analyze some important issues associated with these approaches.

LOCUS OF THE FIELD: DEFINING "CONSUMER BEHAVIOR"

At first glance it would seem to be straightforward enough to specify what is meant by the term consumer behavior. From a role-theory viewpoint, consumer behavior is a subset of human behavior focusing on the consumption role, that is, the activities and conduct attendant with the positions of buyer and consumer and the relations between these positions. Thus *the objective of consumer behavior as a field of inquiry is to understand, explain, and predict human actions in the consumption role.*
This definition, however, begs a number of questions:

1. What is the *consumption role*? The act of being a consumer would seem to consist of sets of behavior associated with the consumption of goods and services. Should, however, the field of consumer behavior be limited only to material transactions, or should the field's domain include transactions of other commodities, such as ideas?

2. What is meant by *buyer* and *seller*? Does seller mean the neighborhood grocery store, a major corporation, a political candidate? Do we mean to limit study to the actual buyer of commodities, or to the buying unit—for example, the distinction between the mother as decision maker and purchaser or as merely purchasing agent for the family?

3. Do we mean to limit the field of consumer behavior to only the activity of buying per se, or should the domain of consumer behavior research also include interest in the cognitive processes that precede and follow various kinds of consumer activities, such as attitudinal development and change and information seeking?

Debate over defining the scope of the consumer behavior field is paralleled by a more general, but similar, controversy concerning the scope of the field of marketing. Some authors express the view that marketing should be considered only as a business technology, limited to concern with buyers, sellers, and economic products and services (Luck, 1969). Other authors, however, argue that marketing concepts and practice can and should be applied to a broad range of transactional phenomena. Kotler, for example, takes the position that "marketing's core idea is transactions, and therefore marketing applies to any social unit seeking to exchange values with other social units" (1972, p. 53).

To a certain extent, this difficulty in defining consumer behavior is merely a semantic argument. The argument becomes important, however, when individuals begin to aspire to a theory or a discipline of consumer behavior, since the domain of theories and disciplines must be delineated.

For a variety of reasons, which will be discussed shortly, there is no "theory" of consumer behavior, if one defines theory formally, according to the criteria of philosophy of science. Consumer behavior may, however, be called a science in the sense that the field has centered around empirical research, which has (usually) been gathered by means of scientific methods. Moreover, consumer behavior research generally meets the criteria that distinguish science in general from other kinds of inquiry (Westley, 1963):

1. Science is general and conceptual.
2. It is founded on controlled observation.
3. It is predictively oriented.
4. It seeks causal connections.
5. It strives for parsimonious explanations of events and closure.

Suffice it to say at this point that consumer behavior is an extremely broad area of research, defined not by a formal, unified theoretical position, nor even by a set of coherent, unique concepts, but rather by the common interests of users and producers of consumer behavior research.

DEVELOPING INTERESTS IN CONSUMER BEHAVIOR RESEARCH

The market for consumer behavior research has expanded rapidly in recent years. It may be of interest to discuss both the "consumption" and the "production" of consumer behavior research findings.

Users of Consumer Behavior Research

The most prominent users and potential users of consumer behavior research are marketers. This seems perfectly logical, but some questions can be raised about just why marketers should be interested in consumer behavior research. As a management function, after all, marketing is a reasonably advanced art. Better understanding and prediction of consumer behavior can provide some answers to the general question of why and how marketing works. But practitioners may not be as interested in the whys and hows as are academic researchers. Despite this, there are perhaps three reasons why marketing practitioners increasingly find consumer behavior research useful.

1. Even if we accept the proposition that marketing is a relatively advanced art from the practitioner's point of view and that research is simply "fine tuning," marketing practice is still open to improvement. Indeed, if consumer behavior research is useful in marketing strategy decisions resulting in only a one or two percentage point shift in market share, this, nevertheless, can be a meaningful contribution to profit in many industries.

2. Marketing practitioners are increasingly called upon by critics and government officials to explain the bases and implications of their actions. Consumer behavior research may be helpful in this regard by providing some understanding of the hows and whys of marketing practices.

3. A competitive environment encourages marketers to improve the quality of information used in decision making. In this regard, marketers are discovering that traditional descriptive marketing research describes the existing state of nature and little else. What is needed is an understanding of market events, and this comes only with explanation of such events. There is, moreover, a growing feeling among businessmen that there is a better way to understand market behavior than the accumulation of discrete, descriptive market studies which are useful for only a limited set of decisions at particular points in time. The complexity and pace that characterize the context for contemporary marketing decisions make purely descriptive, situational market studies somewhat anachronistic. Thus consumer behavior research has emerged partly as a response to marketing management needs for an improved information base regarding the dynamics of market behavior.

The other user group for consumer behavior research findings includes government and social-action agencies interested in establishing or in affecting public policy decisions relevant to consumer affairs. This is particularly true of the Federal Trade Commission, and such privately based organizations as Action for Children's Television, which seeks changes in children's television programming and advertising policies. In 1971, for example, the Federal Trade Commission held public hearings on the impact of advertising on consumers. The primary areas of concern, as discussed by Commissioner Mary Gardiner Jones (1971), were as follows: "(1) the impact of television advertisements addressed to children; (2) the extent to which TV ads may unfairly exploit desires, fears, and anxieties; (3) the extent to which technical aspects of the preparation and production of TV commercials may facilitate deception; and (4) the consumer's physical, emotional and psychological responses to advertising, as they may affect the standards by which advertising is judged" (p. 5). Explicit in these hearings was the understanding ". . . that the Commission must not waste its resources by mandating industry action which is unlikely to have any significant impact on consumer behavior" (Jones, 1971, p. 3).

Producers of Consumer Behavior Research

Perhaps consumer behavior can be aligned most readily with marketing, since this is the field with which most practicing "consumer behaviorists" identify and since this is where the consumer behavior literature as such is developed most fully. It is within the marketing academic community that most responsibility has been taken for the *structuring* of the consumer behavior field and where most consumer behavior courses are taught.

There appears, however, to be a trend toward broader membership and involvement in the consumer behavior community and toward more widespread usage of consumer behavior findings. Consumer behavior may evolve as an interdisciplinary field with separate status and joint academic and professional standing, such as that generally enjoyed by the field of communications. The year 1970, for example, witnessed the formation of the Association for Consumer Research, which represents in its membership a substantial number of lawyers, economists, and consumerist advocates, although it is dominated by marketing academicians.

Consumer behavior also has a certain, admittedly limited, degree of legitimation in its parent disciplines, particularly in psychology. The Division of Consumer Psychology of the American Psychological Association is a case in point, although the membership of the Division is primarily marketing academicians and commercial researchers, rather than psychologists.

In general, however, researchers in established behavioral science disciplines have tended to ignore consumer research. Sociology, for example, has refrained from analysis of the consumption role, despite pleas from Lazarsfeld (1959) and Glock and Nicosia (1963). Cursory review of sociological journals and major texts reveals only passing concern with consumption processes as a social event, with the notable exceptions of Blood and Wolfe's (1960) analysis of husband-wife interaction and Gans's (1962) chapter analyzing consumer behavior in *The Urban Villagers*.

HISTORICAL PERSPECTIVE

Consumer behavior is characterized by studies that make use of theories and concepts borrowed from established behavioral science disciplines. Moreover, the field is multidisciplinary in the sense that it draws from several different fields of study. It also serves diverse user groups, including marketers, consumer advocates, and government regulatory agencies.

Consumer behavior is an applied field in two senses. First, it applies concepts and variables from behavioral-science disciplines toward understanding human behavior in the consumption role; and, second, it intends to increase useable knowledge that can lead to the design of more efficient marketing or social-action programs. Analysis of the historical development of consumer behavior reveals to what extent consumer behavior researchers have been successful in applying behavioral variables to consumer problems and in producing useful knowledge.

The subject of consumer behavior—how and why people buy and consume—has been implicit in marketing since the founding of the discipline. Economic models of consumer actions have constituted an integral part of the marketing literature. The classical utility model, for example, is essentially a statement of how consumers will behave, given a stringent set of assumptions. Veblen's (1899) ideas of conspicuous consumption tempered the harshness of economics doctrine by introducing the social dimension as a very real determinant of consumption. Nor is the application of psychological principles a new development in the field of marketing. As early as 1903, Walter Dill Scott of Northwestern was propounding in *The Theory of Advertising* some notions that he viewed as "a simple exposition of the principles of psychology in their relation to successful advertising." For example, "The attention value of an object depends on the number of times it comes before us, or on repetition" (p. 24).

The emergence and recognition of consumer behavior, however, is primarily a phenomenon of the 1960s. This seems to be a consequence of a number of factors:

1. As a response to the adoption of the *marketing concept* in the 1950s, with its thesis of understanding and satisfying consumer needs.

2. As a response to more sophisticated management and the desire for better data inputs to planning and programming.

3. As a consequence of the growth of behavioral-science disciplines and the subsequent training of marketing doctoral students in the behavioral sciences and behavioral methodology.

4. As a response by business schools to the growing emphasis within universities on conducting original research.

5. As an outgrowth of the acceptance and merging together of a number of research traditions in the 1950s, perhaps most notably *motivation research.*

6. As a consequence of *operations research, simulation,* and *formal models,* which created pressure for greater understanding of phenomena included in models and for more explicit measurement (Ray and Sawyer, 1971).

It is difficult to identify exactly the major thrusts that led to the burst of consumer behavior interest and research which emerged in the 1960s. Nicosia (1969) is inclined to give most credit to the Katona and Lazarsfeld schools of thought, although he also extends credit to Bauer. Katona and his colleagues at the University of Michigan Survey Research Center emphasized the importance of expectations and attitudes on the consumption function (Katona, 1960). Lazarsfeld and his colleagues at Columbia University's Bureau of Applied Social Research focused on information dissemination and the particular role of interpersonal influence (Katz and Lazarsfeld, 1955). The contributions of Bauer at Harvard were focused on theories of communication and on consumer response under conditions of uncertainty (Bauer and Bauer, 1960).

Another major precursor of consumer behavior was *motivation research*. This research was frequently rooted in Freudian concepts and attempted to fathom the "real reasons" why people buy. Its most famous founder was Ernest Dichter, and its research techniques were depth interviews and projective tests. The promise of understanding and manipulating consumer motivations caught the fancy of marketers for a few brief years before motivation research was placed in proper perspective as a research tool of limited predictive ability. It was soon recognized that motivational concepts play only a limited role in explaining consumer behavior and that a broader range of constructs must necessarily be considered.

The 1960s

The field of consumer behavior came into its own in the early 1960s. An emerging concern within marketing for more comprehensive accounts of consumer behavior coincided with a growing interdisciplinary trend within business schools and the hiring of "pure" behavioral scientists for management school faculties.

A consumer behavior literature emerged and research was conducted across a variety of constructs, although very little integrative research was done. Howard (1963) and Kuehn (1962) were instrumental in advocating *learning theory* approaches to consumer behavior; *personality* and *social character* were studied by a host of researchers, including Evans (1959) and Kassarjian (1965); *cognitive dissonance* was pursued by Engel (1963), Kassarjian and Cohen (1965), and many other researchers; Bauer (1960) introduced the idea of *perceived risk* and generated a brief research tradition culminating in the publication of Cox (1967); Stefflre (1968) and Green (1969) focused attention on *perception preference* mapping; Levy (1959) was instrumental in advocating a *symbolic-interactionism* point of view; *attitude* was given explicit treatment by Day (1969) among others; Bourne (1957) and Stafford (1966) focused attention on *reference groups;* King (1963) and Zaltman (1965) studied *interpersonal communication* and diffusion; Levy (1966) and others at Social Research Incorporated related *social class* to consumer phenomena; Wells (1966) furthered the concept of *life style;* and Bauer (1965), Sturdivant (1969), and others focused attention on *subcultures,* such as blacks and ghetto consumers.

The 1960s also saw the emergence of formal models of marketing and consumer behavior. Some models focused on relatively limited aspects of market and consumer behavior, such as those posited by Kuehn (1962) and Frank (1962), whereas others were more comprehensive, dealing with broad ranges of buyer behavior (Howard and Sheth, 1969; Nicosia, 1966).

These models represented a significant departure from the traditional practice of building an area of research on the basis of a specific behavioral concept, such as social class or reference groups. Models represented a new way of viewing consumer problems, as well as a methodology for approaching behavioral phenomena.

Nevertheless, the bulk of consumer behavior research in the 1960s was based on individual behavioral concepts. One result of this tradition has been a need for improved integration of concept-related research and findings. For example, Chapanis and Chapanis (1964) and Oshikawa (1969) lament the point that although a certain set of data may support dissonance-theory applications to consumer behavior (see Chapter 9 in this book), alternative theories or explanations can predict the *same results*. Thus if increased advertising readership occurs for a product just purchased, is this due to an attempt by consumers to overcome dissonance, or because the brand is more likely to be noticed because it is more salient following purchase?

Theoretical positions may also yield conflicting research results. An important need is to examine carefully and contrast alternative theories and to test varying predictions. For example, opposite results can be predicted from dissonance theory versus learning theory (see Cohen and Goldberg, 1970). Dissonance theory predicts that the *less* the inducement to initiate a certain behavior, the greater the dissonance and the greater the resulting attitude change; learning theory, in contrast, predicts that the *more* the inducement, the greater the reinforcement, and, potentially, the greater the attitude change. In order to shift brand preferences, therefore, should switching be encouraged using a 5-cents-off deal or a 25-cents-off deal? Clearly, more integrated research is necessary.

Models: Comprehensive and Limited

A particularly significant development in consumer behavior research has been the emergence of models. It is useful to distinguish between integrative, comprehensive models, such as those of Nicosia (1966), Howard and Sheth (1969), and Engel, Kollat, and Blackwell (1968); and models that are considerably more limited in scope, such as Urban's new product model (1968), Amstutz's work in computer simulation of competing marketing responses (1967), and media planning models (see, for example, Ray and Sawyer, 1971). Although many "limited scope" models do not focus explicitly on consumer behavior, most include assumptions about aspects of consumer behavior.

The introduction of models in consumer behavior research is particularly important, since formal, integrative models hold promise for more adequate empirical analysis of consumer behavior problems usually involving complex, multivariate phenomena. This would resolve a major contemporary problem in consumer research, since, as we have discussed, most previous work was generated from a particular conceptual framework, resulting in a lack of integration of findings.

Models are best understood in terms of their functions. Lachman suggests various related functions (1960). Among them are:

1. Pictorial Representation. The most elementary and didactic function of models is to provide visual representation of theoretical and/or empirical phenomena. Lewin's topological and field theory models (discussed in Chapter 3) provide a case in point.

2. Inferential. Models may provide the rules by which theoretical notions are related to one another (e.g., Hull's learning theory discussed in Chapter 2).

3. Interpretational. Advanced models may also serve to interpret these inferential rules, as in Estes's statistical learning theory (Estes, 1959).

Lachman (1960) argues that models are separate systems from theories. *Theories* consist of principles, postulates, or hypothetical ideas and relations among them, theorems or statements derived from them, and coordinating definitions relating theoretical terms to empirical statements and hypotheses. *Models,* on the other hand, provide representational, inferential, or interpretational functions for theories. Thus models are related to—but not the same as—theories. Lachman argues that it is of highly questionable value to posit representational models in the absence of theory, pointing out that model building of this type has been considered disreputable in physics Nevertheless, in modern physics, such models are now generally recognized as valuable in the *initial* stages of theory construction.

Since there is no single, unified *theory* of consumer behavior, what functions do models serve in consumer behavior research? In psychology several models may function for a theory; for example, various models concerning aspects of classical conditioning theory. In consumer behavior it would seem that several theories function for a single model. The several comprehensive, integrated models now available draw upon many theoretical areas, including, for example, social class, attitudes, and perception. Ehrenberg (1968) criticizes one such model—posed by Nicosia (1966)—as consisting mainly of "long listings of variables that might possibly enter into such a [consumer behavior] model with little, if any, explicit treatment of how they are interrelated" (p. 334). Ehrenberg goes on to take the extreme position that models such as Nicosia's should be derived from empirical knowledge, rather than from a conceptual theoretical foundation.

Such criticism is unduly harsh, since most comprehensive consumer behavior models are characterized by implied relationships. Moreover, concepts and variables that are related may vary in levels of abstraction and measurement, and analysis may be exceedingly difficult. These difficulties were amply demonstrated in Farley and Ring's empirical test of the Howard-Sheth model of buyer behavior (1970). In what was essentially a formalization of the Howard-Sheth model, Farley and Ring posed the following criteria in their empirical evaluation:

1. Consistency of predictions in the direction of individual relationships with those expected from the theory.
2. Goodness of fit of data with the model.
3. Superiority and/or similarity to results from competing models.

Using simultaneous regression equations, the authors tested relationships between 11 endogenous variables and 16 exogenous variables. Their analysis suggested that considerable advances are required in measures before valid assessment of the model can be established. Nonetheless, Farley and Ring's work is important, since it demonstrated that although Howard and Sheth's model does not provide an interpretational function of any single theory, it is more than a simple pictorial representation. The implied relationships in the model provide some rules by which inferences may be derived and relationships subjected to empirical test.

CONTEMPORARY REACTIONS TO CONSUMER BEHAVIOR RESEARCH

To date, the field of consumer behavior has apparently had mixed success. In terms of the objectives of academicians, who do the major research in consumer behavior, advances in understanding have undoubtedly occurred. However, since many different concepts from diverse behavioral-science areas have been applied separately to marketing problems, findings are disjointed and lack consistency and integration in formal, predictive theories and models.

In terms of the objectives of marketers, who are the main users of consumer behavior research, the field has not provided consistent decision rules. In fact, some marketers are almost cavalier in their dismissal of consumer research as "too academic." This reflects the somewhat different interests of professors and businessmen. It may be that both the producers and the consumers of consumer behavior research are not doing a particularly good job of communicating. The lack of communication is to some extent the fault of consumer behavior researchers, who may not adequately define research in terms of problems that are seen by management as relevant, and may do a poor job of articulating findings. However, the problem also rests with managers, who frequently have neither the patience to adequately articulate problems for research, nor the persistence to interpret and extrapolate consumer behavior research results in terms of their decision needs.

The crux of the problem would seem to be that, although consumer behavior research can indeed contribute to effective problem solution, academic researchers may occasionally lose sight of marketing problems in their quest for abstract, general knowledge and theory construction. On the other hand, there is a lack of understanding about the nature and priorities of consumer behavior research among marketers who continually face demands for here-and-now applications of knowledge. As Bauer points out (1963):

The action problems of marketing are engineering problems, not scientific ones. By this I mean marketing action demands a specific rather than a generalized solution of its problems. Thus, while many scientific principles are involved in the design of a bridge, each bridge demands its specific solution to its specific problems (p. 75).

Guetzkow (1959) provides another view concerning barriers to conversion of behavioral-science concepts into practice. He argues that

The process of utilizing . . . theories is very different from the task of generating them. Applied knowledge is used toward particular ends, and the goals determine what information is relevant; theories are not valued of themselves, but only as they are applicable to the achievement of concrete, specific purposes (p. 69).

In Guetzkow's view the fact that the social sciences are still in their infancy explains, in large part, why theories are often inadequate for application to particular situations and problems. However, he also argues that problems in application arise due to inadequate dissemination of basic knowledge among practitioners:

The practical questions of (the practitioner) are disparate with the theoretical schemes. Often the applier merely asks for "more knowledge" instead of inquiring how a particular independent variable or two will exercise their effect upon a given, well-defined dependent variable (p. 72).

It is Guetzkow's position that progress toward effective application of social sciences to practical problems can result from:

1. Reidentification and measurement of basic variables in concrete settings.
2. Construction of relevant models from alternative theories, for application to problems.
3. Accurate assessment of the magnitude of important constants in the selected model, so that specific predictions may be made for each different situation.

Guetzkow also suggests that individuals could be trained as "social engineers" or "social-science technicians" to serve as middlemen between scientists on the one hand and practitioners and ultimate users of knowledge on the other. The suggestion is an intriguing one. In consumer behavior several university-affiliated organizations represent attempts to focus consumer behavior knowledge on specific marketing problems, thus narrowing the gap between consumer research and management needs. Examples include the Institute of Research in the Behavioral, Economic, and Management Sciences at Purdue, the Marketing

Science Institute at Harvard, the Management and Behavioral Science Center at Wharton, and the Berkeley Consumer Behavior Research Project.

APPROACHES TO CONSUMER BEHAVIOR RESEARCH: FORMAL THEORY VERSUS PROBLEM-SOLVING METHODS

By "approaches to research in consumer behavior" we mean how the researcher formulates a problem for study. We are not concerned here with methodological issues, such as sampling or statistical analysis, nor with specific content areas that provide a basis for problem formulation.

The discussion to follow contrasts *formal theory* and *problem-solving approaches* to structuring consumer behavior research problems. Sommers discusses these approaches to research in terms of three research traditions (1971, p. 14):

1. The descriptive or taxonomic tradition (e.g., how much, of what, is sold by whom?).
2. The prescriptive tradition (e.g., what should be the firm's strategy on this brand?).
3. The explanatory tradition (e.g., what makes consumers do what they do?).

Formal-theory approaches reflect the explanatory tradition, whereas problem-solving approaches reflect the descriptive tradition (e.g., a firm's use of market research data) and the prescriptive tradition. Such classification schemes for approaches to research should not, however, necessarily be considered mutually exclusive.

Formal Theory

Examination of the history of science reveals that there are essentially two paths to systematic, cumulative research which serve ultimately to increase our understanding of events, and sometimes even to predict events. One path of scientific inquiry starts from a basis of formal theory from which hypotheses can be deduced and tested. Research results are integrated and accumulated to test, enrich, and expand the theory. For example, such elegant, formal theories characterize economics. Some fairly rigorous formal theories can also be seen in the behavioral sciences, such as Festinger's "theory of social comparison processes" (Festinger, 1954) and Homans's "theory of exchange" (Homans, 1961).

A second path of scientific inquiry essentially involves a problem-solving approach. Empirical research is undertaken in response to the need to solve specific problems. Such an approach is not particularistic or descriptive, however, since researchers construct models or paradigms as research progresses and findings accumulate (Ray, 1969). Such an approach characterizes much inquiry in the history of the physical sciences (see Kuhn, 1970, for an intriguing review).

**Formal Theory Generation in
Consumer Behavior**

If formal definitions of theory are accepted, it is difficult to imagine a theory or theories of consumer behavior, since there are no unique concepts that form the basis for investigation of designated phenomena. Moreover, there is not a unique theoretical or conceptual framework from which propositions and hypotheses can be deduced.[1] Interestingly, in fact, philosopher of science Abraham Kaplan (1964), sees enormous difficulties for formal-theory development in any area of behavioral science. In his view attempts to develop theory in applied fields (such as consumer behavior) are naive and doomed to failure. He argues that the behavioral sciences are not building on what is known, but rather laying out new foundations, or conducting research which is essentially redundant to previous research.

If the requirements for defining theory are relaxed and less formal definitions accepted, it may be possible—or at least fruitful—to seek theoretical and conceptual development in applied fields such as consumer behavior. If the definition of theory is expanded to mean reasonably coherent frameworks for analysis of phenomena, consisting of integrated concepts that may be operationally defined and functionally related in research, then such theoretical development in consumer behavior is indeed possible.[2]

Such broadened definitions of theory are applied to areas of accumulating knowledge in several fields. For example, the growing body of research on reference groups is sometimes characterized as theoretical (Deutsch and Krauss, 1965). The writings of Freud are sometimes cited as theory, presumably because he does advance several concepts (actually, hypothetical constructs), and functional relationships among them are specified. A problem with Freudian concepts, however, is the difficulty in operationally defining and testing them.

Problem-Solving Research

An alternative to the formal deductive theory approach to consumer behavior research is to take a problem-solving point of view, that is, to isolate a particular problem involving consumer behavior and to conceptualize and design research which will appropriately bring empirical data to bear on that problem.

---

[1]For discussions of philosophy of science and definitions of theory, see Cohen and Nagel (1954), Kuhn (1970), Kaplan (1964), and Northrup (1947).

[2]Useful and contrasting views concerning how theoretical development may occur in marketing and consumer behavior are provided by Howard (1965), Mittelstaedt (1971), Tucker (1967), and Halbert (1965).

This approach does not mean that the consumer behavior researcher is relieved of the necessity of conceptualizing his research in terms of a broader theoretical or conceptual framework. The theoretical and problem-solving approaches are not mutually exclusive; in fact, they are closely related. To ignore the necessity for conceptualization is simply to engage in individual case analyses, which, although relevant to immediate problems, tend most often merely to describe the phenomena under investigation and rarely to explain anything. It is essential that problem-solving research be conceptually oriented so that added studies will contribute to a growing, coherent knowledge base and so that results will generalize to other problems. Figure 1 illustrates the steps involved in problem-solving approaches to research in consumer behavior.

FIGURE 1. **Problem-Solving Approach to Consumer Behavior Research**

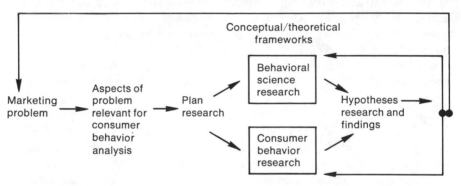

Source: M. E. Shaw and P. R. Costango, *Theories of Social Psychology,* p. 350. Copyright 1970 by McGraw-Hill Book Company. Used with permission of McGraw-Hill Book Company.

In the problem-solving approach, marketing problems provide opportunities for consumer behavior research. The researcher must initially isolate the particular aspects of the problem that relate to consumer behavior. For example, consider the problem of toy marketers. Their products are "consumed" by children, but the purchaser may be parents, siblings, relatives, or others. Relevant consumer behavior research may be conducted on such questions as "What are the processes of intrafamily communication and influence as they relate to toy buying?" or "How do children perceive and evaluate advertising for toys?"

The question of intrafamily communication suggests several potential areas for research, including:

1. How male and female children in various age and social class groups influence their parents.
2. What types of stimuli serve to motivate influence attempts.
3. What characteristics of parents and children are associated with the incidence of types of influence attempts.

These research-oriented issues are only illustrative of what might provide useful data inputs for marketing decision making.

The researcher's next step is probably the most difficult one—he must actually plan the research and specify hypotheses. Such specification permits research to meet at least two criteria for scientific inquiry: (1) it orients the research to predictive objectives, and (2) it orients the research to the goal of seeking causal connections.

Hypothesis formulation requires use of some existing conceptual or theoretical notions, since the researcher is obligated to have some basis for prediction other than his own hunches. Specification of hypotheses derived from previous work permits the researcher to meet another criterion of scientific inquiry—that research be cumulative. Finally, hypotheses provide a commonly accepted basis for research: data will either support or fail to support each hypothesis, and in statistical analysis the researcher will either reject or fail to reject each hypothesis.

After the research has been designed and conducted, the findings of the investigation should feed back to the marketing problem, the conceptual frameworks used in hypothesis derivation, and to the growth of knowledge and conceptual development in the field of consumer behavior itself (see Figure 1). Ideally, that is, the research stimulated by the toy marketer's problem should:

1. Provide the marketer with knowledge useful in designing and executing more efficient marketing programs.

2. Add to the set of cumulative knowledge in the fields that provided the conceptual framework for the study (e.g., communications, sociology, psychology, and anthropology).

3. Contribute to the development of knowledge of types of consumer processes involved in toy buying and similar kinds of activities, and to the development of conceptual notions to explain such processes.

The important point is that in the design and conduct of the research, and in the analysis of findings, the researcher must have in mind both the marketing problems and the conceptual framework. To ignore the former is to do only behavioral research without due regard for applications; but to ignore the latter is to do only company-relevant situation-specific research. Findings should feed back both to the marketing problem and its solution and to the framework that provided the relevant conceptual and theoretical base. Such dual feedback may also foster the development of conceptual frameworks specific to consumer behavior.

There are disadvantages to problem-solving approaches to consumer behavior research. One problem is that findings may not accumulate or "fit together" for purposes of ultimately explaining broader classes of phenomena. For example, in attempting to identify personality types of consumers, many early researchers simply attempted to correlate scores on existing, standardized personality tests with buying behavior. For example, one investigation attempted to relate personality characteristics to the purchasing of one- versus two-ply bathroom tissue (Advertising Research Foundation, 1964)! These types of studies were rather spectacularly unsuccessful, since the kinds of personality measures used were derived for considerably different purposes than market or consumer research. More importantly, these studies did not accumulate, in the sense of adding to our systematic knowledge of specific aspects of consumer behavior. In recent years consumer behavior researchers have continued to investigate the role of personality in buying decisions, but within tighter theoretical frameworks and using measures that are relevant to the consumer problem being investigated (see Chapter 4). Such developments should result in greater cumulative knowledge in this area.

A second problem is that taking a problem-solving approach to consumer behavior research does not necessarily suggest research priorities which may lead to the most adequate definition and development of the field of consumer behavior (Kollat, Engel, and Blackwell, 1970). One can argue, however, that the establishment of priorities for research has been difficult in most fields of inquiry, especially multidisciplinary fields similar to consumer behavior, including, for example, communications. Moreover, the argument can be made that, in a field which focuses on applications of research findings, the development and definition of the field should follow the priorities suggested by problems of marketers and other patrons of consumer behavior research.

MIDDLE-RANGE THEORY

The discussion to this point has not meant to imply that formal theory building and problem-solving approaches to consumer behavior research are mutually exclusive. In fact, they are closely related. Consider, for example, that no existing theories were available to Newton to help him understand and predict the behavior of falling bodies. But his solution to the problem, in which he related the fall of an apple and the maintenance of the moon in its orbit in terms of the concept of gravity, gave great impetus to the development of theory in physical science.

The notion of middle-range theories was expressed by Merton (1957) as an essential need in sociology. He called for "theories intermediate to the minor working hypotheses evolved in abundance during the day-to-day routines of research, and the all-inclusive speculations comprising a master conceptual scheme" (pp. 5-6). Merton's particular concern was that the field of sociology was not ready for the "master" or "grand" theory, and that it was premature to look for it.

Middle-range theories can be distinguished in terms of their scope and the nature of the system of underlying, interrelated concepts. Formal, elegant theories permit the derivation of hypotheses through logical deduction from a system of logically connected concepts that are both theoretically and empirically defined, and linked to the observable world.[3] Derivation of hypotheses from middle-range theories, on the other hand, is often based on plausible inferences rather than logical deductions because of the inexpressed assumptions and implicit meanings involved in many conceptualizations. For example, one could adequately conceptualize and derive hypotheses relating to the marketer's problem of toy promotion discussed earlier; but concepts such as influence, social class, and motivation are not a priori conceptually and empirically defined and connected in a formal system from which hypotheses are logically derived. Hypotheses can be derived, but more on the basis of plausible inference rather than logical deduction.

In a sense, middle-range theories are both deductive and inductive. As Bauer (1967) points out: "Science moves in two directions; toward broad propositions of a higher level of abstraction and of general validity, and toward more detailed propositions which enable us to explain more of the phenomena of the world." Thus, consumer behavior researchers derive hypotheses from conceptualizations relating to problems; findings are brought to bear on problems; and, at the same time, accumulation occurs toward the ultimate goal of explanation and prediction of a range of phenomena and the development of broad theory. Many of the research traditions in consumer behavior during the 1960s discussed previously, such as the work on perceived risk or diffusion of innovations, are examples of middle-range research traditions.

The notion of accumulation of middle-range research studies is expressed by Cox in the introduction to his work, which summarized various studies in the area of consumer risk taking and perceived risk (1967, p. 2):

> After an initial period of "overexpectation" of the utility of direct application of behavior science concepts, researchers have begun to settle down to the difficult job of devising and testing concepts and theoretical models that are becoming more specifically tailored to consumer behavior and marketing problems. Nevertheless, there remains a need for better theoretical development, though not necessarily the development of "a" theory of consumer behavior. Inevitably, a good deal of research in consumer behavior has concentrated on discovering what might be termed "descriptive relationships," i.e., finding relationships between Variable X (self-confidence) and Variable Y (persuasibility). As these descriptive relationships begin to accumulate, so do we begin to accumulate the building blocks for models and theories which will help improve understanding of consumer behavior.
>
> But, in any sound structure, physical or theoretical, the building blocks must be tied together. In the case of theoretical structures, my opinion is that the tying together can be best accomplished in depth if the foundation elements have sprung from a unified approach or theme.

---

[3]For example, Deutsch and Krauss (1965) point out that to define the psychological concept of goal, one must also define other logically connected concepts, such as motive, intention, success, failure, and expectation, and "provide a statement of the procedures involved in the observation of the phenomena that refer to the concept" (p. 8).

Critics say that some consumer behavior research has tended to massage data in search of findings, or to test overly specific hypotheses not related to any broader conceptual scheme. It can be argued that any piece of empirical evidence is a building block toward theoretical development, but this notion is difficult to justify when the mortar is not being placed between the bricks. Empirical data do not in and of themselves ensure accumulation of systematic knowledge, nor construction of theoretical and conceptual frameworks. Data must be interpreted and organized in terms of broader frameworks if the conceptual underpinnings of consumer behavior are to develop.

All the papers in this book are not, precisely speaking, middle-range theoretical formulations. Rather, they are summaries of areas of research—including personality, attitude, interpersonal perception, and communication—that have flourished as a consequence of middle-range theoretical research and have proved useful to researchers interested in consumer behavior. Thus we have taken the position that there is no *theory* of consumer behavior, or any one *theory* in any behavioral-science discipline which even approaches adequate explanation and prediction of the complexities of consumer behavior. Rather, we believe that there are theories—more accurately, middle-range, theoretical schemes—which can be used to advance understanding, explanation, and prediction of human actions in the consumption role.

As with any new, interdisciplinary area of research—particularly one having strong ties to applications-oriented users of the research output—there are myriad problems facing the researcher and few sources to draw upon as models for effective resolution of the problems. A pervasive and fundamental problem concerns the basic approach and orientation of the field of consumer behavior itself. Basic conflicts center around such issues as:

1. Is the field too applications-oriented or not applications-oriented enough?

2. Should researchers approach areas for study from the point of view of problems faced by those who actually must deal with consumers (marketers, policy makers, educators, etc.), or does this only confuse priorities and force researchers to simply address immediate, narrow problems without due regard to accumulation of knowledge useful in the longer run?

3. Should researchers address themselves to the formulation and testing of complete models of consumer behavior, or are such models premature?

Other problems touch at equally fundamental aspects of the field of consumer behavior. These problems concern the advisability of borrowing concepts from the behavioral sciences; the lack of consistency in the use of many variables employed in consumer behavior studies; the issue of how much variance is explained by the characteristics of individuals across consumer situations versus the influence of situation-specific variables; and, finally, concern over methodological approaches in consumer behavior research.

ISSUE OF BORROWING

Wholehearted borrowing from the behavioral sciences has been quite unsettling to some people in the consumer behavior field, and considerable concern has been devoted to the possibility of developing theory specific to the consumption role. This is a legitimate concern in some ways. Nicosia (1966), for example, concludes that "At present, marketing's borrowings from the behavioral sciences seem not to be very successful. This is in part because of the prevalence of the economic frame of reference of marketing students, but also because of the complexity of the behavioral sciences and the variety of their images of man" (p. 40). In Nicosia's view unsystematic borrowing may lead to distortions in applications to consumer behavior research.

This view is underscored by Mittelstaedt, who argues that (1971, p. 10)

> While there have been several attempts at building theories of consumer behavior based on a single point of view or frame of reference, most of the borrowing from other fields has been on an eclectic, even piecemeal basis. In an effort to "integrate and synthesize" behavioral findings many appear to have called forth a newly borrowed concept to explain each new observation. No doubt part of the reason for the attempt to seek eclectic explanations is the undeniable complexity of the behavioral sciences themselves. Most of the disciplines from which borrowing has been done are evolving rapidly and new theories keep crowding upon a scene where many already exist.

The issue of borrowing, and the inherent dangers in doing so, are now being explicitly recognized in regard to applications of personality theory in consumer behavior research. (This is discussed at length in Chapter 4 by Wells and Beard.) A reasonable number of studies have now been conducted by consumer behavior researchers relating personality, as measured by a variety of self-designating, standardized personality inventories, to aspects of consumer decision making, such as brand selection, innovativeness, and product usage level. Conflicting and inconclusive results have generally emerged as a function of

1. Using instruments based on somewhat varying personality theories and containing different variables.

2. Using instruments designed to measure gross personality traits, often of an abnormal nature.

3. Most importantly, using concepts, theories, and measures indiscriminately, that is, simply assuming their relevance to consumer problems without adequate thought as to why such concepts, theories, and measures, developed for completely different and general purposes, should be related to such specific phenomena as consumer behavior.

Kassarjian (1971) takes the position that "if unequivocal results are to emerge, consumer behavior researchers must develop their own definitions and design their own instruments to measure the personality variables that go into the purchase decision rather than using tools designed along a medical model to measure schizophrenia or mental stability" (pp. 415-16). Thus personality traits relevant to behavioral disorders should not necessarily be those that lead to the selection of a particular brand of detergent, or to a desire to purchase new products.

This point of view, however, cannot be carried too far. What is necessary is to recognize the underlying conditions in regard to borrowing. There is a vast efficiency in an infant discipline's borrowing theories, concepts, and methodologies from more developed disciplines of scientific inquiry. It could be suboptimal to devote attention to building consumption-role-specific notions and theories. If excessive and inappropriate borrowing has occurred, what is necessary is the specification of some principles for borrowing.

Principles of Borrowing

An initial consideration in borrowing is that the borrower must be able to provide *justification* for why he has borrowed. Again, in regard to personality theory, an overwhelming criticism is that most consumer behavior research has lacked a rationale for relating personality constructs and measures to specific consumption-related variables under various conditions. Brody and Cunningham (1968) have made the point that personality should be related to consumption only under conditions of high performance risk in the product. Their contention has not been adequately tested, but it is a step toward the specification of the instances in which specific personality variables may be expected to relate meaningfully to consumption variables.

A second criterion in borrowing is that the borrowed constructs and approaches should have *relevance* to consumer behavior. For example, psychological theories of attitude formation and change have been employed in various consumer behavior research applications. However, some attitude theories hold more promise for consumer behavior research than others. Balance-theory approaches to attitude change, for example, have demonstrated considerable relevance to explanations of behavior in the consumption role. Applications include cognitive-dissonance research related to postpurchase behavior phenomena (Venkatesan, 1972). In contrast, the "functional approach" to attitude change (Katz, 1960) has been less relevant to studies of change in consumer behavior, perhaps because it is more relevant to psychoanalytically oriented change strategies.

A third criterion for borrowing is to apply those theories which hold the highest degree of *legitimation* and support. The reason for this is simply because, in an applied field, insufficient efforts are devoted to testing and legitimizing the theory; instead, research is immediately conducted with consumption-related variables. Established legitimation, therefore, is a desirable prior attribute.

A fourth consideration is that borrowing should not be done out of *context.* For example, information theory was originally derived from laws of thermodynamics for use in predicting information-processing capacities. The borrowing of central concepts from information theory (such as entropy and redundancy) and their application to consumer information problems are exceedingly difficult, since the consumer context and the context for which the theory is intended are very different.

A fifth rule for borrowing is to recognize the *complexity* of the behavioral sciences and the available competing theories. Shaw and Costanzo (1970), for example, compare some theories of group behavior and process in terms of a number of criteria. While selecting the "best theory" for consumer behavior research, it is still necessary to recognize alternative, competing theories and the possible incompleteness of any one theory.

Implicit in much of the discussion on borrowing to this point is the question of how situation bound a particular theory happens to be. The final rule for borrowing, therefore, is to recognize the *situational constraints* that are present. For example, Krugman's (1965) "learning without involvement" proposition is based on "nonsense learning" research in psychology, but he has focused its relevance on a specific set of mass communication stimuli—television advertising for consumer products. This specific focus takes advantage of the unique aspects of the television advertising phenomena but, of course, limits the application of Krugman's notions to dissimilar forms of media.

It is probably very fair to state that consumer behavior researchers have tended to ignore most situational constraints. In mass-communication research, for example, we have eagerly accepted Klapper's (1960) view that the mass media generally reinforce predispositions and rarely convert attitudes and opinions. But many have failed to understand the range of phenomena to which Klapper's statements can be applied and to take into account the situations to which the research cited by Klapper could reasonably be expected to apply. That is, we should not expect that findings from attitude-change experiments, conducted for the most part among college student populations and often employing controversial issues as message stimuli, will generalize to all consumer phenomena, or to such matters as attitude formation among children and adolescents.

ACTOR VERSUS SITUATION

Consumer behavior research has emphasized almost exclusively the *characteristics of the actor.* Typical research has investigated issues such as what kinds of people are heavy users of private brands, what are the characteristics of the brand-loyal-prone consumer, and what is the profile of the consumer opinion leader or innovator?

The most common research design to study these questions is to derive a scale of private-brand usage, brand-loyalty proneness, opinion leadership, innovativeness, or whatever, and to run a set of independent variables searching for differences. Sometimes these independent variables are carefully specified and hypotheses are presented, but sometimes a whole series of variables is intuitively used with the idea of "letting the data fall where they may."

The problem is that there may be no such thing as a private-brand-prone consumer, a brand-loyal-prone consumer, an innovator, or an opinion leader—nor do researchers ever provide a rationale as to why there should be. These behavioral tendencies appear to be activated in fairly specific situations. The characteristic of innovativeness rarely is observed across product categories. Research on opinion leadership has been quite discouraging in documenting any consistent set of variables contributing to consumer influence (Robertson, 1971). The predominant conclusion today is that we can only define actor characteristics in less aggregate spheres of activity—perhaps, for example, on a product-category basis.

This may even be overly ambitious in that situational variables may account for considerably more variance than actor-related variables. For example, in regard to opinion leadership is there any prescription for this role in society and do individuals deliberately accept this role? It might be argued that the opinion-leader role has prescriptions attached only for situations deemed important by society. Prescriptions are attached to the medical-opinion-leader role and to the lifeguard role but not to the packaged-food opinion-leadership role. Whereas acceptance of the roles bearing prescriptions may be highly deliberate, acceptance of nonsalient societal roles may be quite random and without commitment. Furthermore, since the role enactment is not important to the society, there may be considerable latitude for acting it out. The problem is compounded therefore: Are there opinion-leader roles for aspects of consumption? Is role enactment prescribed—if not, can our measuring instruments document role performance under such varying enactments? Are actor characteristics implied, or can a consumer adopt the role at will, depending largely on situation-specific variables such as the purchase of a new car?

The situational research approach, then, would study the situation under the assumption that it governs response more than actor characteristics. The contrast between the two approaches can be seen in the context of whether the poor are poor because of inherent actor-related characteristics or because of overriding situational variables. Surprisingly, a majority of the U.S. population blames the poor for their own poverty and ascribes such actor-related characteristics as laziness, lack of thrift, drunkenness, and low morals as the cause of their poverty (Feagin, 1971).

The point of all this is not that either approach is right; in fact, either approach alone is misleading. We have, however, overstated our emphasis on actor characteristics in consumer behavior research and have largely ignored situational variables. Consumer behavior can be most productively viewed as the interaction of the actor and the situation—a viewpoint expressed by Frank and Massy (1971). Yet, as documented by these authors, general actor-related variables, such as personality and demographic characteristics, have had low predictive ability with buying behavior. Their conclusion is that "One of the most fruitful directions for future research . . . *is the study of psychological and sociological characteristics which are idiosyncratic to both the consumer and the product and not to the consumer alone*" (p. 18). Thus to explain consumption of breakfast cereals, the researcher might be advised to consider attitudes toward breakfast as a meal rather than measuring general personality traits.

Nicosia[4] also makes the point that consumer behavior is a function of both internal and external situational variables, and that a specific subclass of external situational variables "may activate only a specific subclass" of internal variables. Finding the links between the internal or individual processes that contribute to consumer action and the external or situational events that influence or activate these processes would seem to be an important general area for consumer research.

METHODOLOGICAL ISSUES IN CONSUMER BEHAVIOR RESEARCH

The development of the consumer behavior research tradition has not been particularly systematic. Kollat, Engel, and Blackwell (1970) make the very salient critique that "The consumer research literature shows that a substantial percentage of research was the result of the availability of data, the convenience of research and mathematical techniques, and/or the appeal of certain behavioral constructs" (p. 328). Although it can be argued that the use of available data strengthens the consumer behavior researcher's ties to "the real world," problems can result in that research is based on opportunism rather than carefully considered priorities for study. Moreover, when available data are proprietary, there is often a problem of replication.

Methodological Advances

Perhaps because the issue of coordination and integration of consumer behavior research is so complex and so far from resolution, some feel that the most significant advances in behavioral science and consumer behavior research will be in method rather than in theory (Ray, 1969). Multidimensional scaling (Green, 1969), for example, has had a major impact within consumer behavior and may be an important generator of future theory.

Advances in methodology and the use of increasingly sophisticated methodological techniques (e.g., multidimensional scaling, canonical analysis,

[4]Private communication to the authors.

and multivariate analysis) may help overcome certain conceptual weaknesses in earlier research. For example, Kollat, Engel, and Blackwell (1970) point out that

> ... although there is evidence that information seeking is a cumulative process involving several sources, most attempts to determine characteristics of information-seeking consumers and the determinants of search utilize unidimensional scales (p. 329).

These authors also point out that many attitude studies fail to predict behavior, possibly because only one dimension of attitude is measured, in spite of the fact that it is generally recognized to be a multidimensional concept.

Lack of Replication

Replication is a rare phenomenon in consumer behavior research. The literature is almost entirely based on single-study results. Research on the diffusion of new products, for example, has seldom, if ever, used the same set of explanatory variables with similar operational measures in equivalent sampling frames. This leads to a lack of definitive evidence and conflicting findings, which may be the result of methodological artifacts.

Cross-Sectional Surveys

Perhaps the predominant methodology in consumer behavior research has been the cross-sectional survey used in a single administration. The limitations of this methodology have tended not to be recognized, and alternative methodologies have been underutilized. Cross-sectional research, especially in single administrations, lacks the ability to study the dynamics of a process. For example, research evidence reveals that college students today are less achievement oriented toward material possessions than a sample of college graduates interviewed 10 years after graduation (Ward, et al., 1971). What, however, does this mean? Is this a phenomenon that will continue when today's college students are the graduates of 10 years ago, or is this result a manifestation of different life situations leading to different long-term values? Clearly, longitudinal research is needed to begin to understand the nature of the phenomenon.

Similarly, in the development of propositions on the diffusion of new products, Zaltman and Stiff (Chapter 11) observe that the adoption process must be studied over time and within a social structure. This necessitates going beyond the single-administration survey; the researcher must consider experimental designs, multiple administrations over time of survey instruments, panel studies, and methods such as Coleman's (1958) relational analysis, or other forms of sociometric analysis that link individuals to their social systems.

Longitudinal research is expensive, difficult to administer, and the research payoff is longer term than for cross-sectional research. Longitudinal research does not, however, necessarily require a lifetime's devotion to a topic. An investigator could examine different groups of people, with follow-up research efforts in each group. For example, one could study the development of consumer skills among children by conducting research among 5-, 8-, and 11-year-olds. Research could then be conducted 2 or 3 years later with the same children, providing data based on a combination of longitudinal and cross-sectional research methods.

Standardized Definitions and Variable Categories

Early in the process of formulating a research problem, the researcher must review previous studies that have dealt with aspects of the same or similar problems. This review is necessary not only to ensure that the research is not "reinventing the wheel"; it is also necessary to establish where the proposed research will fit into the cumulative research tradition relevant to the problem, and to acquaint the researcher with particular assumptions, definitions, and procedures in previous work.

A problem—not peculiar to consumer behavior research—is the variation in definitions of key concepts and variables. The researcher interested in brand loyalty, for example, will find the concept has been defined in terms of brand-choice sequences, proportion of purchases, repeat purchase probabilities, and brand preference over time (Kollat, Engel, and Blackwell, 1970). To the extent that lack of definitional standardization inhibits comparison and integration in consumer behavior research, this is a methodological and conceptual problem for the field. Clearly, more recognized and relatively standard definitions would contribute to more efficient progress in consumer behavior research.

However, the problem of nonstandardized conceptual definitions should not be confused with three circumstances:

1. A concept may be impossible to explicate and define adequately because it is too abstract, vague, and so forth (e.g., influence or credibility).
2. A concept may be adequately defined, conceptually and operationally, but applied in widely varying contexts.
3. It may be possible to explicate adequately a concept for research, but the investigator has not done so.

Vague and general concepts can be measured, but they are unsatisfactory for research because they cannot be adequately defined in conceptualizations. That is, one could construct a scale to measure communicator credibility, but the concept is complex, referring to several source attributes, such as expertise, and relational concepts, such as trust. Thus the general term contributes little to standardized definition and general understanding and to a coherent research framework.

The researcher must also recognize when a concept is adequately defined, but variations in definitions exist due to the different research contexts in which the concept is applied. For example, an investigator may be interested in attitude change as a function of alternative message strategies. The concept of attitude is reasonably well defined, but the investigator should review uses of the concept in studies of various problems in order to provide perspective for his particular area of research interest.

Finally, lack of clear, standardized definitions and variable categories may result from proliferation of concepts that are poorly explicated, although they could be. For example, Tucker observes that (1967, p. 3)

> The frequent use of the notion of cognitive dissonance in discussions of consumer behavior, for instance, demands more than the recognition of cognitive dissonance as a circumstance relating to the simultaneous existence of conflicting notions within the organism. This dissonance is said to be motivating in that it encourages behavior designed to reduce the dissonance. If one fails to realize that this is essentially a homeostatic theory, based on the concept of an "ideal" state (quite comparable to psychological concepts dealing with thirst or hunger, but derived from more basic biological processes) one is ill-equipped to understand its insufficiency or the nature of cases it fails to explain, and may, in fact, overlook powerful notions such as rationalization or even fail to see the relationship between the two.

Validity and Reliability in Consumer Behavior Research

Validity may be defined as the extent to which differences in scores on a measuring instrument (e.g., attitude scale, personality inventory behavioral response code) "reflect true differences among individuals, groups or situations in the characteristic which it seeks to measure, or true differences in the same individual, group or situation from one occasion to another, rather than constant or random errors" (Selltiz, et al., 1964, p. 155). *Reliability,* on the other hand, refers to the extent to which variations in scores are due to inconsistencies in measurement.

There are various methods for validity and reliability assessments. Extended discussion is beyond the scope of this paper, although all the following papers in this volume discuss methodological and conceptual issues that could at least be clarified by validation of key concepts and research to assess the reliability of measures.

As an example, consumer behavior researchers have borrowed the concept of opinion leadership from rural sociologists and communication researchers (see

Chapter 11). The essential notion is that certain individuals in society are looked to as opinion leaders by virtue of their rank, status, or expertise. Opinion leaders are viewed by some as mediators of mass communication influence (e.g., in the formulation of the two-step flow model of communication effects). The validity of the opinion leadership concept has been open to question. Although several measures of self- or other-designated opinion leadership exist, the validity question concerns whether the measures reflect the actual process implied by the term opinion leadership; that is, are there *truly* people who mediate mass media effects and consistently exert influence over the attitudes and behavior of a set of followers?

In addition to the validity controversy, questions have been raised about the reliability of scales used to measure opinion leadership and to identify opinion leaders in various situations (Rogers and Cartano, 1962). Frequently, scales are used that consist of a small number of questions without any established reliability. Kirchner (1969) calls into question much of the reliability in opinion-leadership measurement.

Recently, consumer behavior researchers have shown greater concern with the reliability and validity questions. This is evidenced by studies that employ several independent measures relevant to a problem, such as opinion leadership. Some researchers have employed concepts from Campbell and Fiske's (1959) "multitrait-multimethod matrix" approach to establishing validity and reliability. Ray (1968) observes that the matrix is based on four points:

1. Validation is typically *convergent,* a confirmation by independent measurement procedures. Independence of methods is a common denominator among the major types of validity.

2. For the justification of novel trait measures, for the validation of test interpretation, or for the establishment of construct validity, *discriminant validation* as well as convergent validation is required. Tests can be invalidated by too high correlations with other tests from which they were intended to differ.

3. Each test or task employed for measurement purposes is a *trait-method unit,* a union of a particular trait unit with measurement procedures not specific to that content.

4. To examine discriminant validity, and to estimate the relative contributions of trait and method variance, *more than one trait* as well as *more than one* method must be employed in the validation process . . . a multitrait-multimethod matrix.

In an application of multitrait-multimethod concepts to the opinion-leadership question, Silk (1971) analyzed items on a scale that had been administered twice to the same sample with reference to opinion leadership on two different subjects: furniture purchasing and cooking. According to multitrait-multimethod criteria, Silk observes, the correlations between the different measures of the same trait should be high (evidence of convergent validity). Another criterion employed by Silk was that "a variable should correlate higher with another measure of the same trait than it does with other variables having neither trait nor method in common" (1971, p. 391). This would be evidence of discriminant validity. In general, Silk found that the scale met the criteria for convergent and discriminant validity.

Establishment of validity and reliability is an ongoing process. The questions are crucial ones for any empirical science, perhaps particularly for consumer behavior. Researchers in the field may be in such haste to apply seemingly relevant, borrowed concepts or scales to consumer problems that questions of validity and reliability are not adequately investigated. One hopes that such techniques as the multimethod-multitrait matrix, discussed here, will signal an end to this problem (although many other techniques also exist for reliability and validity assessment).

PAPERS IN THIS VOLUME

The central objective of each of the twelve original papers in this volume is to acquaint the reader with a particular area of research and theory that has been particularly useful in stimulating middle-range research and conceptual development in consumer behavior. Some of the areas covered are more basic than others (e.g., economic models, field theory, personality theory, or learning theory), and one area is concerned largely with methodological contributions (stochastic models of consumer choice behavior). The ultimate objective is to contribute to research in consumer behavior that will be conceptually rooted, cumulative in nature, and useful in the solution of consumer behavior problems.

Basic Theoretical Areas

One of the more basic theoretical areas is learning, discussed by Michael L. Ray in Chapter 2. The point was made earlier in this chapter that a problem in consumer behavior research has been the difficulty in adequate explication and specification of concepts and variables. Ray indicates that this problem is particularly acute in the consumer behavior literature that attempts to deal with the concept of learning. He illustrates the utility of the concept for such problems as brand loyalty, advertising repetition, and other marketing strategy applications. Ray defines the nature of learning-theory research in psychology, traces the history of theory and research, and proposes a framework for understanding social phenomena from learning theories. Finally, he applies the framework to consumer behavior research issues and discusses trends in applications of learning theories in consumer behavior.

Harold H. Kassarjian discusses field theory and its utility for the examination of the consumption role in Chapter 3. Just as field-theory notions have been borrowed by consumer behavior researchers from Gestalt psychologists (field theory in psychology is generally traced to Kurt Lewin), Kassarijian points out that psychologists actually borrowed the term from physicists. Field theory is basic in that it is highly abstract and, as Kassarjian observes, it touches every facet of consumer behavior. Field theory has stimulated areas of research that have been particularly useful in consumer behavior research, such as group dynamics and balance theory.

William D. Wells and Arthur D. Beard (Chapter 4) review concepts of personality—an area of research and theory in psychology that has had a major impact on consumer behavior. The authors trace the bases of modern personality theories to their roots in the early writings of Freud, Jung, and others. They discuss applications to consumer problems in earlier motivational research traditions and in contemporary quantitative research traditions. They also evaluate the promise of personality traits as links between products and media and as predictors of consumer behavior. A useful review of personality traits and significantly related aspects of consumer behavior is provided and the authors discuss recent applications in psychographics or attitude and activity research.

The chapter by Wells and Beard, dealing with personality theories, focuses on what have traditionally been conceptualized as intra individual processes, with relatively direct implications for interpersonal behavior. Similarly, Daniel Wackman (Chapter 5) examines theories of person perception, which, like personality theories, are often based on intra-personal constructs but have direct implications for interpersonal behavior. He discusses two alternative approaches in person perception research: the *accuracy* approach, which focuses on skills in interpersonal perception, and the *process* approach, which focuses on the various ways people perceive and form opinions of others. He concludes with a discussion of new perspectives in person perception research, especially the approaches of Erving Goffman.

In Chapter 6 Lyman Ostlund reviews the considerable research literature in the areas of role theory and group dynamics. Although role theory and group dynamics are reasonable distinct areas of research and theory, the conceptual bases of both areas of research are similar. Ostlund first considers research in the area of role theory, explaining the concept and discussing role selection and expectations, the relationship of role and personality, role demands, enactment, and conflict. Ostlund's discussion of group dynamics begins with consideration of the concept of reference groups. He reviews classic research concerning conformity to group influences as a function of group norms, size of group, personality variables, and cohesiveness, and discusses risk-handling and communication networks. The third part of Ostlund's chapter discusses applications of role-theory and group-dynamics concepts and findings to consumer behavior research. He discusses how the individual consumer's reference groups affect product and brand attitudes, and analyzes the concept of opinion leadership in the context of general interpersonal communication research. He concludes with a discussion of family decision making, a neglected area of consumer research but one that would benefit from analyses based on role-theory and group-dynamics concepts.

George H. Haines, Jr., provides an overall review of economic models of consumer behavior, derived from microeconomic theory, in Chapter 7. Economics is basic to virtually every facet of consumer behavior, although the level of abstraction of microeconomic theory makes direct application of concepts to consumer research difficult. The Haines paper should suggest to consumer researchers some key research areas for which microeconomic concepts are relevant if not directly applicable. Additionally, research in consumer behavior would seem to have the unique potential of making significant return contributions to economics. For example, basic to legislation in the area of monopolistic competition are assumptions, rooted in economic theory, concerning the relationship of product and brand differentiation and advertising expenditure (Chamberlain, 1933, 1950). The essential notion is that product differentiation is a function only of advertising expenditures. Differences perceived by consumers based on other factors are illusory and are not taken into account in legislation (Caves, 1967). Perhaps research in consumer behavior could ultimately demonstrate the existence and nature of consumer perceptions of products and brands as a function of various factors, including advertising, but also product-use patterns, consumer personality, and so forth. Such research could contribute to refined economic models, and, one hopes, to more enlightened legislation.

Focused Theoretical Areas

Unlike the broad theoretical areas discussed in the first six papers, five of the six remaining papers concern relatively focused conceptual or theoretical areas of research. The final paper reviews stochastic models of consumer choice behavior and evaluates the potential of these models to stimulate a new tradition of integration in consumer behavior research.

Theories of attitude structure and change are discussed by George S. Day in Chapter 8. The first part of Day's chapter provides a useful illustration of extensive explication and definition of a concept. As discussed earlier, a major problem in consumer behavior is the lack of such clear explication necessary to ensure both adequate conceptualization for research and general definitional agreement. Day then describes measurement issues in attitude research and the problem of relating attitudes to behavior. The latter part of his paper deals with five major theoretical approaches to attitude-change research.

Some motivational and attitude theories posit that individuals strive to maintain logical consistency. Balance theories of attitude change, for example, are based on such a homeostatic notion. But do people sometimes seek novel, unfamiliar, and even psychologically disquieting states of affairs? These notions of cognitive consistency and novelty seeking are discussed in a paper by M. Venkatesan (Chapter 9). Concern with novelty seeking is relatively recent, and the subject is complex. Venkatesan discusses the relationship of the concept with cognitive-consistency notions and dissonance theory and reviews the two collative and variation-seeking approaches to explaining novelty-seeking behavior. He discussed a related concept in consumer behavior research—the personality factor of venturesomeness—and suggests additional areas for consumer behavior research for which novelty-seeking notions are relevant.

Steven H. Chaffee and Jack M. McLeod base their discussion of consumer decisions and information use (Chapter 10) on major areas of research in the field of communications. They do not take as a point of departure concepts such as selective exposure, or information seeking, preferring instead to address more precise issues concerning how consumers use information relevant to decision making. They present a decision matrix, based on pioneering work by Carter (1965), that permits conceptual analysis of consumer decisions between objects based on interrelationships of attributes, or dimensions of judgment on which two or more objects can be compared, and values associated with each object. Such factors as information availability, information needs, and involvement and discrimination are discussed as they influence consumer decisions in the context of the model, and a discussion of decision stages and intervening information processes is presented. The authors assess several methodological problems attending most communication research problems, and conclude with a discussion of areas for research in information processing and implications for marketing strategies.

Like attitude research, theories of diffusion and innovation have been applied extensively in the field of consumer behavior. Gerald Zaltman and Ronald Stiff review these applications after placing diffusion research in the context of social change (Chapter 11). The authors discuss criteria for a useful diffusion theory in consumer behavior and the research methods required for such theoretical development. They trace the development of diffusion theories in sociology and communications research, and review and evaluate various process models by which innovations are accepted in social structures.

Consumer problems among low-income and minority groups provide a point of departure for Frederick D. Sturdivant's analysis of anthropological and sociological concepts as they relate to consumer problems (Chapter 12). Sturdivant discusses the meaning of the central concept of culture in terms of a number of qualities. He then turns to the topic of subculture, and the extent to which values and influences overlap or differentiate between subgroups within overall cultures. He stresses methodological problems associated with the use of the subculture concept as an analytical device, and presents a framework for structuring analyses of subcultural groups. The elements of the framework are the concepts of acculturation, assimilation, and social class. Studivant also reviews a number of studies concerning low-income and minority-group consumers in the United States, stressing the need for more research that examines values and underlying motivations within and between subcultural groups.

The final paper in this book (Chapter 13) deals with stochastic models of consumer behavior, that is, models in which consumer responses are the outcome of some probabilistic process. Unlike the other papers, which deal with the content of basic or more focused theoretical areas of behavioral research, David B. Montgomery and Adrian B. Ryans examine modeling approaches to consumer behavior analysis that may encourage integration and more efficient use of consumer behavior concepts. This chapter does not pose a complete model of consumer behavior. The intent is rather to discuss the fundamental properties of stochastic choice models and to illustrate applications to types of marketing problems.

CONCLUDING NOTE

The development of the field of consumer behavior depends upon the competence, originality, and perseverance of researchers, and the raw material with which they work. This raw material is comprised of the kinds of concepts and theoretical notions that are represented in this volume. The goal of research is to build toward theories that are adequate to explain and predict phenomena through a system of interrelated concepts. The optimal route to this goal is a controversial matter. It is perhaps more complex and controversial in consumer behavior and other fields of study that borrow concepts from many other fields. Moreover, pathways to theory are made complex by the pressure for immediate applications by the professional community, which comprises a major source of support for consumer behavior research. This is not to suggest that taking real-world problems as points of departure for research and theoretical development are mutually exclusive events. The point is that a master blueprint for integrating problem-oriented research and theoretical development has not yet emerged.

One possible blueprint is to develop the field through middle-range research, as we have suggested here. There are alternatives. We have discussed the alternative view that the best path is through development of relatively complete models of consumer behavior. Others may eschew middle-range research or complete models in favor of what is seen as more immediately practical research.

These controversies may never be fully resolved. In fact, it can be argued that a variety of research philosophies is desirable for a field of study. For example, B. F. Skinner represents an alternative to more prevalent deductive research traditions in psychology and his research provides an opposing viewpoint and a basis for comparison of research.

What is of more immediate and practical importance is the development of viewpoints among consumer behavior researchers. The consumer behavior field needs researchers who know what they are doing and why.

There would seem to be four stages in the maturation of the researcher. In the first stage he *learns* about an area—in this case, about the basic concepts, interests, and propositions in the field of consumer behavior. In the second stage he becomes *aware* of alternative points of view in the area of inquiry. For example, the budding researcher is sometimes harshly reminded of the differences between the practitioner's point of view about consumer behavior problems and the academician's. As other examples, he may become aware that there are several viewpoints about processes of attitude change, or, as we have discussed, that there are various views about the goals of consumer behavior and the means for reaching them.

In the third stage the researcher learns to *integrate* various points of view; that is, he learns that most propositions are complementary rather than competing. For example, under some conditions balance theories of attitude change may correctly explain phenomena; under other conditions, functional notions may be more valid. More importantly, concepts other than attitude may also bear on the phenomena under study. Understanding the nature of these contingent propositions is fundamental to integration of the various concepts and processes that underlie the complexities of consumer behavior.

The fourth stage is *formulation.* If the researcher can understand and integrate various and alternative points of view, he may then be able to formulate new conceptual directions for research. Consider, for example, the depth of understanding and the extent of integration of various theoretical areas in social psychology that preceded and formed the basis for the development of cognitive dissonance theory (Festinger, 1957), or the new directions in communications research that occurred as the transactional model of mass communication effects displaced the traditional direct-effects model (Bauer, 1960).

We hope the papers in this volume will help those interested in the field of consumer behavior to develop their own viewpoints, based on understanding and integration of important areas of research. This does not imply an eclectic field; rather, it implies that the field will grow as original contributions emerge as an ongoing consequence of understanding and integration of research. The problems of consumers, which such research ultimately strives to resolve, would seem to demand no less.

REFERENCES

Advertising Research Foundation, Inc., *Are There Consumer Types?* New York: Advertising Research Foundation, 1964.

Amstutz, A. E., *Computer Simulation of Competitive Market Response.* Cambridge, Mass.: The MIT Press, 1967.

Bauer, R. A., "Consumer Behavior as Risk Taking," in *Proceedings of the American Marketing Association,* ed. S. Hancock. Chicago: American Marketing Association, 1960, 389-98.

Bauer, R. A., "The Role of the Audience in the Communication Process," in *Proceedings of the American Marketing Association,* ed. S. A. Greyser. Chicago: American Marketing Association, 1963, 73-82.

Bauer, R. A., "Games People and Audiences Play." Paper presented at Seminar on Communication in Contemporary Society, University of Texas, 1967.

Bauer, R. A., and A. H. Bauer, "America, Mass Society and Mass Media," *The Journal of Social Issues,* 16 (1960), 3-66.

Bauer, R. A., S. M. Cunningham, and L. H. Wortzel, "The Marketing Dilemma of Negroes," *Journal of Marketing,* 29 (July 1965), 1-6.

Blood, R. O., and D. M. Wolfe, *Husbands and Wives: The Dynamics of Married Living.* New York: The Free Press, 1960.

Bourne, F. S., "Group Influence in Marketing and Public Relations," in *Some Applications of Behavioral Science Research,* ed. Rensis Likert and S. P. Hayes. Paris: UNESCO, 1957, 217-24.

Brody, R. P., and S. M. Cunningham, "Personality Variables and the Consumer Decision Process," *Journal of Marketing Research,* 5 (February 1968), 50-57.

Campbell, D. T. and D. W. Fiske, "Convergent and Discriminant Validation by the Multitrait-Multimethod Matrix," *Psychological Bulletin,* 56 (1959), 81-105.

Carter, R. F., "Communication and Affective Relations," *Journalism Quarterly,* 42 (Fall 1965), 203-12.

Caves, Richard, *American Industry: Structure, Conduct, Performance* (2nd ed.). Englewood Cliffs, N. J.: Prentice-Hall, Inc., 1967.

Chamberlain, E. H., *The Theory of Monopolistic Competition.* Cambridge, Mass.: Harvard University Press, 1933.

Chamberlain, E. H., "Product Heterogeneity and Public Policy," *American Economic Review,* 40 (May 1950), 85-92.

Chapanis, N. P., and Alphonse Chapanis, "Cognitive Dissonance: Five Years Later," *Psychological Bulletin,* 6 (January 1964), 1-22.

Cohen, J. B., and M. E. Goldberg, "The Dissonance Model in Post-Decision Product Evaluation," *Journal of Marketing Research,* 7 (August 1970), 315-21.

Cohen, M. R., and Ernest Nagel, *An Introduction to Logic and Scientific Method.* New York: Harcourt Brace Jovanovich, Inc., 1954.

Coleman, J. S., "Relational Analysis: The Study of Social Organizations with Survey Methods," *Human Organization,* 16 (Winter 1958), 28-36.

Cox, D. F., ed., *Risk Taking and Information Handling in Consumer Behavior.* Boston: Division of Research, Harvard Business School, 1967.

Day, G. S., *Buyer Attitudes and Brand Choice Behavior.* New York: The Free Press, 1969.

Deutsch, Martin, and R. M. Krauss, *Theories in Social Psychology.* New York: Basic Books, Inc., Publishers, 1965.

Ehrenberg, A. S. C., "A Book Review of *Consumer Decision Processes* by Francesco M. Nicosia," *Journal of Marketing Research,* 5 (August 1968), 334.

Engel, J. F., "Are Automobile Purchasers Dissonant Consumers?" *Journal of Marketing,* 27 (April 1963), 55-58.

Engel, J. F., D. T. Kollat, and R. D. Blackwell, *Consumer Behavior*. New York: Holt, Rinehart & Winston, Inc., 1968.

Estes, W. K., "The Statistical Approach to Learning Theory," in *Psychology: A Study of a Science*, S. Koch, ed. Vol. 2. New York: McGraw-Hill Book Company, 1959.

Evans, F. B., "Psychological and Objective Factors in the Prediction of Brand Choice," *Journal of Business*, 32 (October 1959), 340-69.

Farley, J. U., and L. W. Ring, "An Empirical Test of the Howard-Sheth Model of Buyer Behavior," *Journal of Marketing Research*, 7 (November 1970), 427-38.

Feagin, J. R., *American Attitudes Toward Poverty and Antipoverty Programs*. Washington, D.C.: National Institute of Mental Health, 1971.

Festinger, Leon, "A Theory of Social Comparison Process," *Human Relations*, 7 (May 1954), 117-40.

Festinger, Leon, *A Theory of Cognitive Dissonance*. Stanford, Calif.: Stanford University Press, 1957.

Frank, R. E., "Brand Choice as a Probability Process," *Journal of Business*, 32 (January 1962), 43-56.

Frank, R. E., and W. F. Massy, "Noise Reduction in Segmentation Research." Research Paper Series, Research Paper No. 26, Stanford University, August 1971.

Gans, H. J., *The Urban Villagers*. New York: The Free Press, 1962.

Glock, C. Y., and F. M. Nicosia, "Sociology and the Study of Consumers," *Journal of Advertising Research*, 3 (September 1963), 21-27.

Green, P. E., "Multidimensional Scaling: An Introduction and Comparison of Nonmetric Unfolding Techniques," *Journal of Marketing Research*, 6 (August 1969), 330-41.

Guetzkow, Harold, "Conversion Barriers in Using the Social Sciences," *Administrative Science Quarterly*, 4 (June 1959), 68-81.

Halbert, Michael, *The Meaning and Sources of Marketing Theory*. New York: McGraw-Hill Book Company, 1965.

Homans, G. C., *Social Behavior: Its Elementary Forms*. New York: Harcourt Brace Jovanovich, Inc., 1961.

Howard, J. A., *Marketing: Executive and Buyer Behavior*. New York: Columbia University Press, 1963.

Howard, J. A., *Marketing Theory*. Boston: Allyn and Bacon, Inc., 1965.

Howard, J. A., and J. N. Sheth, *The Theory of Buyer Behavior*. New York: John Wiley & Sons, Inc., 1969.

Jones, M. G., "The FTC's Need for Social Science Research," in *Proceedings of the 2nd Annual Conference, Association for Consumer Research*, ed. D. M. Gardner. Chicago: American Marketing Association, 1971, 1-9.

Kaplan, Abraham, *The Conduct of Inquiry: Methodology for Behavioral Science*. San Francisco: Chandler Publishing Company, 1964.

Kassarjian, H. H., "Social Character and Differential Preference for Mass Communication," *Journal of Marketing Research*, 2 (May 1965), 146-53.

Kassarjian, H. H., "Personality and Consumer Behavior: A Review," *Journal of Marketing Research*, 8 (November 1971), 409-19.

Kassarjian, H. H., and J. B. Cohen, "Cognitive Dissonance and Consumer Behavior," *California Management Review,* 8 (Fall 1965), 55-64.

Katona, George, *The Powerful Consumer.* New York: McGraw-Hill Book Company, 1960.

Katz, Daniel, "The Functional Approach to the Study of Attitudes," *Public Opinion Quarterly,* 24 (Summer 1960), 163-204.

Katz, Elihu, and P. F. Lazarsfeld, *Personal Influence.* New York: The Free Press, 1955.

King, C. W., "Fashion Adoption: A Rebuttal to the 'Trickle Down' Theory," in *Proceedings of the American Marketing Association,* ed. S. A. Greyser. Chicago: American Marketing Association, 1963, 108-25.

Kirchner, D. F., *Personal Influence, Purchasing Behavior and Ordinal Position.* Unpublished Ph.D. dissertation, University of California at Los Angeles, 1969.

Klapper, J. T., *The Effects of Mass Communication.* New York: The Free Press, 1960.

Kollat, D. T., J. F. Engel, and R. D. Blackwell, "Current Problems in Consumer Behavior Research," *Journal of Marketing Research,* 7 (August 1970), 327-32.

Kotler, Philip, "A Generic Concept of Marketing," *Journal of Marketing,* 36 (April 1972), 46-54.

Krugman, Herbert, "The Impact of Television Advertising: Learning Without Involvement," *Public Opinion Quarterly,* 29 (Fall 1965), 349-56.

Kuehn, A. E., "Consumer Brand Choice as a Learning Process," *Journal of Advertising Research,* 2 (December 1962), 10-17.

Kuhn, T. S., *The Structure of Scientific Revolutions.* Chicago: University of Chicago Press, 1970.

Lachman, R., "The Model in Theory Construction," *Psychological Review,* 67 (1960), 113-29.

Lazarsfeld, P. F., "Sociological Reflections on Business: Consumers and Managers," in *Social Science Research on Business: Product and Potential,* ed. R. A. Dahl, Mason Haire, and P. F. Lazarsfeld. New York: Columbia University Press, 1959, 99-155.

Levy, S. J. "Social Class and Consumer Behavior," in *On Knowing the Consumer,* ed. J. W. Newman. New York: John Wiley & Sons, Inc., 1966, 146-60.

Levy, S. J., "Symbols for Sale," *Harvard Business Review,* 37 (July-August 1959), 117-24.

Luck, David, "Broadening the Concept of Marketing—Too Far," *Journal of Marketing,* 33 (July 1969), 53-54.

Merton, R. K., *Social Theory and Social Structure.* New York: The Free Press, 1957.

Mittelstaedt, R. A., "Criteria for a Theory of Consumer Behavior," in *Consumer Behavior: Contemporary Research in Action,* ed. J. Holloway, R. A. Mittelstaedt, and M. Venkatesan. Boston: Houghton Mifflin Company, 1971.

Nicosia, F. M., *Consumer Decision Processes.* Englewood Cliffs, N. J.: Prentice-Hall, Inc., 1966.

Nicosia, F. M., "Consumer Research: Problems and Perspectives," *The Journal of Consumer Affairs,* 3 (Summer 1969), 9-25.

Northrup, F. S. C., *The Logic of the Sciences and the Humanities.* New York: The Macmillan Company, 1947.

Oshikawa, Sadaomi, "Can Cognitive Dissonance Theory Explain Consumer Behavior?" *Journal of Marketing,* 33 (October 1969), 44-49.

Ray, Michael, "Neglected Problems (Opportunities) in Research: The Development of Multiple and Unobtrusive Measurement," in *Proceedings of the American Marketing Association Fall Conference,* ed. R. L. King. Chicago: American Marketing Association, 1968, 176-82.

Ray, Michael, "The Present and Potential Linkages between the Microtheoretical Notions of Behavioral Science and the Problems of Advertising." Paper presented at the Symposium on Behavioral and Management Science in Marketing, University of Chicago, 1969.

Ray, Michael, and A. G. Sawyer, "Behavioral Measurement for Marketing Models: Estimating the Effects of Advertising Repetition for Media Planning," *Management Science,* 18 (December 1971), 73-90.

Robertson, T. S., *Innovative Behavior and Communication.* New York: Holt, Rinehart & Winston, Inc., 1971.

Rogers, E. M., and D. G. Cartano, "Methods of Measuring Opinion Leadership," *Public Opinion Quarterly,* 26 (Fall 1962), 435-41.

Scott, W. D., *The Theory of Advertising.* Boston: Small, Maynard & Company, 1903.

Selltiz, Claire, et al., *Research Methods in Social Relations.* New York: Holt, Rinehart & Winston, Inc., 1964.

Shaw, M. E., and P. R. Costanzo, *Theories of Social Psychology.* New York: McGraw-Hill Book Company, 1970.

Silk, A. J., "Response Set and the Measurement of Self-Designated Opinion Leadership," *Public Opinion Quarterly;* 35 (Fall 1971), 383-97.

Sommers, M. S., "Problems and Opportunities in the Development of Consumer Behavior Theory," in *Consumer Behavior: Contemporary Research in Action,* ed. R. J. Holloway, R. A. Mittelstaedt, and M. Venkatesan. Boston: Houghton Mifflin Company, 1971.

Stafford, J. E., "Effects of Group Influence on Consumer Brand Preferences," *Journal of Marketing Research,* 3 (February 1966), 68-75.

Stefflre, V. J., "Market Structure Studies: New Products for Old Markets and New Markets (Foreign) for Old Products," in *Application of the Sciences in Marketing Management,* ed. F. M. Bass, et. al. New York: John Wiley & Sons, Inc., 1968, 251-68.

Sturdivant, F. D., ed., *The Ghetto Marketplace.* New York: The Free Press, 1969.

Tucker, W. T., *Foundations for a Theory of Consumer Behavior.* New York: Holt, Rinehart and Winston, Inc., 1967.

Urban, G. L., "Market Response Models for the Analysis of New Products," in *Proceedings of the American Marketing Association,* ed. R. L. King. Chicago: American Marketing Association, 1968, 105-11.

Veblen, Thorstein, *The Theory of the Leisure Class.* B. W. Huebsch, 1899.

Venkatesan, M., "Cognitive Dissonance," in *Handbook of Marketing Research,* ed. Robert Ferber. New York: McGraw-Hill Book Company, 1972.

Ward, Scott, T. S. Robertson, and William Capitman, "What Will Be Different About Tomorrow's Consumer?" in *Combined Proceedings of the American Marketing Association,* ed. F. C. Allvine. Chicago: American Marketing Association, 1971, 371-74.

Wells, W. D., and George Gubar, "Life Cycle Concept in Marketing Research," *Journal of Marketing Research,* 3 (November 1966), 355-63.

Westley, B. H., "Scientific Method and Communication Research," in *Introduction to Communications Research,* ed. R. O. Nafziger and D. M. White. Baton Rouge: Louisiana State University Press, 1963.

Zaltman, Gerald, *Marketing: Contributions from the Behavioral Sciences.* New York: Harcourt Brace Jovanovich, Inc., 1965.

Basic
Theoretical Areas

2

Psychological Theories and Interpretations of Learning

Michael L. Ray
Stanford University

NATURE OF LEARNING RESEARCH

Two Animal Learning Paradigms. Verbal-Learning Research Tradition. Animal and Verbal Traditions Compared. Example of Research and Theory Development: The Partial-Reinforcement Extinction Effect. Conclusions.

THREE STREAMS OF MIDDLE-RANGE THEORY IN LEARNING

Watson, Behaviorism, and Contiguity Theorists: *S-R*. Thorndike and Reinforcement Theorists: Feedback of *R*. Tolman and Perceptual and Cognitive Theorists: Feedback of *S*. Consolidation of the Three Streams: $S \rightleftharpoons O \rightleftharpoons R$.

LEARNING FRAMEWORK FOR CONSUMER BEHAVIOR ANALYSIS

Comparison with Other Conceptualizations. Pseudoconflicts between Consumer Behavior Notions. How the Framework Should Be Used. Stimulus (*S*): Perceived, Relative, and Generalized. Drive (*D*): Primarily Innate, Multifaceted, Nonmonotonic. Incentive, Expectancy, Valence (*K*): Key Variable in Social Learning. Habit Strength (*H*): Practice and Information without Reward. Response Tendency (*R*): Intervening Variable, A Hierarchy of Measures. Weights and Equation Form: Microtheoretical Notions.

MICROTHEORETICAL NOTIONS ON LEARNING IN CONSUMER BEHAVIOR

Spontaneous Recovery in Consumer Behavior. Order Effect: Primacy and Recency. Rote Learning of Evaluation. Brand Loyalty and Brand Attitude. Source Credibility and the Sleeper Effect. Fear Appeals. Inducing Resistance to Persuasion. Curious Disbelief. Personality and Attitude Change. Learning Relationships to Attitude Change and Behavior. Combinatorial Rules for Perception and Attitude.

PARADIGM FOR CONSUMER RESEARCH ON LEARNING

Research Procedures. Notions and Findings.

PERSPECTIVES FOR THE FUTURE

REFERENCES

Learning is the more or less permanent acquisition of tendencies to behave in particular ways in response to particular situations or stimuli. Because it involves the development of linkages between stimuli (S) and responses (R), the study of learning has been called *S-R psychology*. Because it tends to emphasize the observation of outer responses or behavior as opposed to inner or cognitive concepts, learning psychology has often earned the title of *behaviorism*.

In consumer behavior the *stimuli* can be products, advertisements, services, political candidates, ideas, packages, and prices. The *responses* can be purchasing, voting, noticing, remembering, understanding, evaluation, attitude change, recommending, and steadfast loyalty. The possibilities are almost limitless and are as rich as consumer behavior itself.

The promise of learning theory is simply this. If learning theory indicates how responses are linked to particular stimuli, it can help explain how consumers develop their understanding of the environment and apply it to a variety of consumption acts.

The problem of learning-theory application to consumer behavior can be stated simply also. Existing learning theory is not directly relevant to consumer behavior. It has been developed in the abstract or in regard to animal or rote learning, which does not have the richness of consumer behavior.

The author would like to express his indebtedness to D. T. Campbell, W. F. Hill, B. J. Underwood, and E. J. Webb for early intellectual stimulation; to the AAAA Educational Foundation and the Marketing Science Institute for monetary support; and to his D. M., whose house and life were messy so he could do this thing.

But the promise and the problem of learning-theory application are not unrelated. It is precisely because learning theory has been developed in simplified situations that it holds promise for illuminating the more complicated processes underlying consuming. All that is needed for adequate learning-theory application is an understanding of its basic nature and a framework for applying it to more complex issues. This chapter attempts to provide such a basic understanding and framework.

NATURE OF LEARNING RESEARCH

Learning theories are sets of laws, theorems, postulates, and hypotheses. They cannot be understood or applied adequately unless the research paradigms from which they are derived are understood also.

Although learning research has been done in many fields, this chapter emphasizes psychological research, because it is basic to the study of learning in other areas, including consumer behavior.

Psychologists who study learning typically examine individual rather than interindividual or mass behavior. And they study it primarily in two settings. One tradition of research actually involves animal rather than human learning. The other stream of research involves human behavior, but it is typically verbal behavior of a very simple sort manifested in a relatively sterile laboratory environment.

Two Animal-Learning Paradigms

Although psychological research with animals is relatively more recent in its beginnings than that with humans, much of the learning theory which has relevance for consumer behavior began with animal studies.

The basic paradigm, *classical conditioning,* was introduced by the Russian physiologist Pavlov (1927, 1928) in his studies examining the salivary conditioning of dogs to tones.

In classical conditioning a stimulus, such as food, that naturally evokes a response, such as salivation, is presented following a stimulus, such as a tone, that normally does not result in the response. If the tone-food pairing is presented often enough, the salivating response will become conditioned to the tone, so that the onset of the tone alone will cause salivation.

Many relevant learning variables can be derived from the classical conditioning paradigm. *Reinforcement,* for instance, occurs when the tone and the meat powder are paired. *Extinction* of the conditioned response will occur if there are extended trials without the reinstatement of the reinforcement. The phenomenon of *stimulus generalization* was discovered by Pavlov when he noticed his dogs salivating to accidental sounds like keys or coins jingling. The tone salivating had generalized to stimuli that were similar to the original tone. When experimental subjects can accurately pick out just the right tone or conditioned stimulus from others similar to it, they are said to have made a *stimulus discrimination,* a phenomenon that is obviously related to generalization.

The other type of animal research paradigm is *instrumental conditioning,* first studied by the Russian Bekhterev (1913) and the American psychologist Thorndike (1911). In classical conditioning the relevant stimulus precedes the relevant response. In instrumental conditioning the reverse is true. The response to be conditioned precedes the conditioning stimulus and is "instrumental" in its onset.

This is the kind of conditioning that is often used by animal trainers. The animal's movements or trick become the instrumental response, which is then conditioned by means of a food reinforcer. The leading exponent of instrumental conditioning in the laboratory is B. F. Skinner. Animals, such as rats or pigeons, receive rewards in his "Skinner Box" if they make appropriate movements and then depress levers or peck keys to receive a food reinforcement. Skinner and his many followers have been able to do amazing things with this simple apparatus, including teaching pigeons to play Ping-Pong and to act as the guiding system in a missile!

More important for consumer behavior, however, is the fact that instrumental conditioning is the kind most heavily emphasized by social psychological approaches to human learning, such as those of Bandura (1965, 1971; Bandura and Walters, 1963), Miller (Miller and Dollard, 1941; Dollard and Miller, 1950), Homans (1961), and Campbell (1963, 1965). Skinner's laboratory work with instrumental conditioning has not only contributed to general interpretations of learning but has also led to discussions of human verbal learning (1957), programmed learning and teaching machines (1961; O'Day, 1971), a behavioral science fiction book about a Utopian society (1948), serious suggestions for the design of cultures (1966, 1971), and behavior modification treatments of behavioral disorders (Wolpe, 1969). In marketing, instrumental conditioning has been used as the basis for a laboratory measure of advertising wear-out effect (Lindsley, 1962; Winters and Wallace, 1970).

Verbal-Learning Research Tradition

The beginning of the psychological study of human learning and perception is given as 1875, the year in which psychological laboratories were founded by Wundt in Leipzig, Germany, and by James at Harvard (Watson, 1968). It was in this era that the German, Ebbinghaus (1885, 1902), did his studies of the learning of nonsense syllables. His research, still widely quoted and discussed in psychology today (e.g., Shebilske and Ebenholtz, 1971), forms the basis of the psychological study of verbal learning and has found ample support in consumer behavior studies.

Typical of early psychological research, which used very few subjects and often asked for introspective responses from them, Ebbinghaus's research involved just one subject, himself. He would learn lists of nonsense syllables of various lengths and then test for memory by attempting to relearn the lists at a later time or date.

Two of Ebbinghaus's major and most durable findings are illustrated in Figure 1. Rather than show Ebbinghaus's own data, this figure is taken from an advertising research study that showed almost perfect replications of his findings. Figure 1 is from Zielske (1959), who sent advertisements for a grocery product to housewives under two scheduling conditions, once a week and once a month. The fitted curves in the figure constitute a replication of Ebbinghaus's findings of exponential acquisition and extinction curves for verbal learning. Despite the fact that the materials and the situation are quite different in Zielske's study from those of Ebbinghaus, the results hold quite well. Furthermore, the effect of the two scheduling treatments in the study is supported by verbal-learning research on mass versus distributed practice.

FIGURE 1. Learning and Forgetting Curves of Zielske (1959)

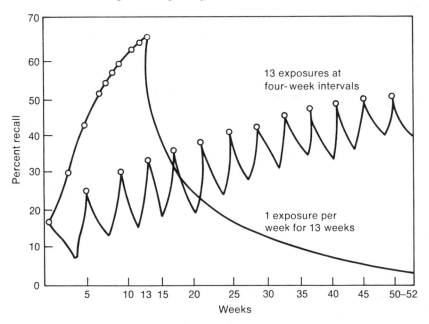

Another venerable Ebbinghaus finding is the serial-position U-curve effect; that is, in learning a list of verbal stimuli, subjects will find those items in the early list positions easiest to learn, those in the last position next easiest, followed by the most difficult middle positions. In consumer behavior both Krugman (1962) and Ray (1969a) obtained the U-curve result often when the measure was the proportion of times advertisements were mentioned first in playback in advertising copy tests. Ray (1969) examined over 70 four-position copy test results and found that the U-curve result occurred over three times more often than would be expected by chance for the first-mentions measure, nearly twice chance expectation for an attitude-change measure, and slightly less than chance expectation for correct recognition. These results are similar to countless replications for the Ebbinghaus findings; the U-curve is consistently found over wide variations in materials (e.g., McCrary and Hunter, 1953; or see review in Ray, 1969), but is somewhat sensitive to extreme decreases in list length and to changes in strength of response required.

The results of the last several paragraphs—exponential acquisition and forgetting curves, mass and distributed practice effects, and the serial-position U-curve effect—are typically all the verbal-learning phenomena that are reported in the consumer behavior literature. This is unfortunate, because the verbal-learning field is probably the fastest growing in psychology. Indeed, Hintzman (1971) and others have called the recent surge of cognitive psychological applications to verbal learning a "renaissance" in comparison to the "dark ages" of strict behavioristic, animal-based learning theory.

There are actually five standard research paradigms—serial learning, paired-associate learning, free recall, recognition, and verbal discrimination—that are at the base of this resurgence in verbal-learning research:

1. *Serial learning* has already been mentioned in connection with Ebbinghaus's work. The subject in a serial-learning study must play back a list of verbal stimuli in the same order they were presented to him.

2. *Paired-associate learning* involves a series of pairs of verbal stimuli. The respondent is shown the stimulus member of each pair and must then provide the response half of the pair on the basis of previous exposure of the pairs. This type of research has been compared to learning a foreign language. It also has a similarity to the process consumers go through when they connect a new brand-name response to a familiar product stimulus or, conversely, a new product response to the familiar stimulus of an established brand name.

3. *Free-recall learning* is like serial learning with the difference that the presentation order of the items varies from trial to trial, which consists of each item being presented for a short period of time and, after presentation of the entire list, respondent recall of the items in any order desired.

4. In *recognition learning* the items are presented in much the same way as in free-recall learning, but the testing is done in terms of a variety of recognition procedures.

5. In *verbal-discrimination learning* the respondent attempts to pick the item in each pair or set of items that has been arbitrarily designated as correct by the experimenter.

The free recall, recognition, and discrimination procedures obviously elicit part of the psychological process responsible for the establishment of what is commonly known in consumer behavior as brand awareness, especially of what Howard and Sheth (1969) have called the "evoked set" of acceptable brands.

In marketing, these verbal-learning research paradigms are similar to those used in advertising copy testing and posttesting. Some advertising readership services (e.g., Starch) use recognition; others have used recall (e.g., Gallup and Robinson). Lucas (1960; Lucas and Britt, 1963) has discussed these differences.

The gross differences between recall, recognition, and other forms of learning are exhibited in the results of a study by Luh (1922) shown in Figure 2.

FIGURE 2. **Comparison of Forgetting As Indicated by Various Verbal Learning Tasks**

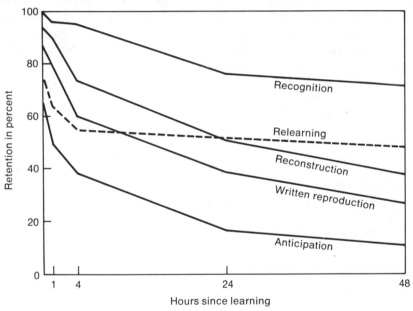

Source: Luh, 1922.

Although there are some cases in which recall is superior to recognition, this is almost never true, and there are some amazing studies (e.g., Shepard, 1967) in which subjects were able to recognize hundreds of items correctly after only one exposure. It certainly seems important for marketers to take the nature of these forms of learning into account when discussing such issues as hierarchy of effects (e.g., Aaker, 1970, and later in this chapter). Also, the ease and simplicity of the recognition task make it of doubtful and limited value in advertising studies (Appel and Blum, 1961; Lucas, 1960; Lucas and Britt, 1963; Wells, 1964).

Animal and Verbal Traditions Compared

Due to differences in subjects and research paradigms, there is a key and obvious difference between verbal-learning microtheories and the theories of the animal-learning area. Since the subjects in the verbal studies can talk, the concepts in this area tend to be more cognitive and less outer-behavior oriented. There is more concrete discussion about images, concept identification and learning, development of molar plans, learning of language, and logical relationships.

Animal-learning theorists tend more to concentrate on the outer indications of the nature of the stimuli and responses and the connections between them over time.

Many verbal, cognitive psychologists seem intent on demonstrating that their ideas are quite distinct and cannot be explained by the concepts of the animal-learning theorists. For instance, Kintsch (1970) cites several studies which he feels demonstrate that reinforcement has very different effects in animal and in human research. The basic difference noted by Kintsch and others (Bem, 1968, 1972; Campbell, 1963, 1965; Eisenberger, 1972; Festinger and Carlsmith, 1959; Kelley, 1967; McGuire, 1969) is that, in human learning, reinforcement is considered as one source of information as opposed to just a direct strengthener of effect.

These differences between verbal and animal notions will be discussed often in this chapter. Since most of the more complete, formal theories have grown out of the animal literature, they will be used to provide a general framework on learning for the consumer-behavior student. The microtheories of verbal learning do deal with important forms of behavior, however, and they will be used to extend the learning framework into consumer response. Furthermore, there is a trend toward full theory in the verbal or cognitive realm (e.g., Kelley, 1967; Kintsch, 1970; Miller, Galanter, and Pribram, 1960). Since these full cognitive theories have been shown to have many elements that are isomorphic to aspects of animal behavioristic theories (see Campbell, 1963, 1965; Kintsch, 1970; Millenson, 1967; Suppes, 1969), this chapter will attempt to anticipate the eventual merging of these two forms of theory in the consumer behavior area.

Example of Research and Theory Development:
The Partial-Reinforcement Extinction Effect

Although the previous sections have indicated the basic forms of learning research, there has not been a demonstration of the way they lead to useful theory. That is the purpose of this section. Here one small but venerable and important finding for consumer behavior—the partial-reinforcement extinction effect—is used as a vehicle to show how and why the theories of learning are developed and may be applied.

First, consider a common problem in marketing. Suppose that a new product development manager is concerned about the way his introductory budget should be spent. In a gross sense his major concern is whether his budget should be concentrated in certain time periods and locations or spread out over the year and the nation. If his product is a new convenience good, this gross consideration becomes a reality in terms of the way that the consumer will be exposed to advertising and public-relations messages about the product, to in-store promotion and product display, to experience with the product itself, and to word-of-mouth information about the product. How can research and theory on learning help?

One way the literature can help is by considering the effect various allocation strategies have on the conditions of learning about the product. Past research and theory might indicate the possible strength of that learning over periods in which the budget will not allow additional inputs. There may be information on the effects of competitive efforts that provide the consumer with contradictory inputs.

To use the learning literature to deal with the manager's problem, it is necessary to make a huge conceptual jump. Specifically, it is necessary to assume that concentrated budgets produce something like total or continuous reinforcement and that spread-out budgets produce something like partial reinforcement. But this is not such a great problem for the use of the learning research information, since there is evidence that different degrees of partial reinforcement produce effects like those from continuous and partial reinforcement. And what the manager is ultimately most interested in here is not the specific effects, but the outside variables that might affect the nature of the outcomes in both the learning laboratory and the marketing environment.

In the learning laboratory the basic finding is that partial reinforcement produces effects which are more resistant to extinction than does continuous reinforcement. This effect has been shown only in instrumental conditioning in animal research, but is demonstrated by the frequent superiority of distributed over mass practice in verbal-learning research. A recent study indicated that the partial-reinforcement effect applies in the attitude-research area (Kerpelman and Himmelfarb, 1971). Figure 1 is actually an example of the effect in a consumer behavior situation.

In fact, there is so much research on the partial-reinforcement extinction effect that there have been literature reviews about every 10 years since 1950 (Jenkins and Stanley, 1950; Lewis, 1960; Robbins, 1971). The literature is so vast that the most recent review had to be restricted to "A Selective Review of the Alleyway Literature Since 1960" and still contained 142 references!

Why this large number of studies and papers on such a well-established finding? Actually, psychologists do the studies because they are theoretically interesting. In both the animal- and verbal-learning fields it is recognized that one way to understand learning is to understand the variables that affect forgetting or extinction. And extinction under partial reinforcement is most theoretically interesting, because it goes against the simple assumption of the early learning theorists that more reinforcement leads to more learning.

The volume of studies on partial reinforcement is also important to consumer behavior research because of their theoretical significance. The theoretical notions deal with the variables that are important to the effect. Thus not only do these notions serve to summarize a large body of data for the researcher, but they also pinpoint types of variables that might be important to consumer behavior.

The partial-reinforcement extinction results have been analyzed in at least seven different ways by learning researchers:

1. *Antitheoretical (Skinner).* Many psychologists prefer to work only within the confines of several research paradigms and avoid what Skinner and his followers call "premature raising of explanatory ghosts." Skinner avoids even the averaging of experimental subjects' responses and typically shows response curves for only one subject at a time.

Two arguments can be made against this approach. In the first place, it does not actually exist in any real sense since even Skinner uses explanatory concepts to apply his laboratory results to human behavior. Second, without theoretical notions it is impossible to summarize the vast and extremely complex findings in the area and apply them to fields like consumer behavior.

2. *Response-unit hypothesis.* One early explanation for the partial-reinforcement finding could be derived from the simple notions of reinforcement mentioned earlier. The response-unit hypothesis was simply that the experimental subjects who receive partial reinforcement during acquisition get used to making more responses before reinforcement. So they can stand more extinction trials than the continuously reinforced subjects. This interpretation has received some experimental support (Mowrer and Jones, 1945), but recently studies have been negative (Robbins, 1971).

3. *Generalization.* Another explanation for the effect takes, in a sense, a more cognitive, perceptual approach than the response-unit hypothesis. Under the generalization notion it is assumed that reinforcement is generalized to the nonreinforced trials during partial reinforcement so that the extinction situation is not perceived as being different from acquisition in partial as it is for continuous reinforcement.

This hypothesis has led to studies in which the interval between training trials is varied to see if the generalization can be eliminated. On balance, these studies have not shown a great deal of support for the notion.

The generalization explanation should not be totally ignored by consumer behavior researchers, however. There are some marketing situations in which reinforced and nonreinforced experiences or exposures related to a product are similar enough for generalization to occur. This might be true, for instance, when competitors are using similar appeals for their brands. Although competitive advertising should be considered a negative or nonreinforced trial for the opposing brand, it may be that the combination of advertising for the two brands may lead to something like the partial-reinforcement extinction effect when advertising for one of the brands is dropped. Perhaps the generalization notion, in combination with some others to follow, can be used to predict such an effect in the consumer behavior situation.

4. *Cognitive dissonance.* Lawrence and Festinger (1962) have applied Festinger's (1957) dissonance theory to the extinction effect. Their explanation is that running a nonreinforced trial stimulates, in effect, a drive of dissonance in the subject. In other words, the partially reinforced subject must find some "extra attractiveness" in the nonreinforced runs to justify the behavior and reduce dissonance.

Those readers familiar with the arguments of dissonance theory (see Brehm and Cohen, 1962; Festinger, 1957, 1964; Festinger and Carlsmith, 1959; and Chapter 9 of this book) will recognize that the Lawrence and Festinger notion and subsequent findings in animal research are typical of those used by the proponents of the theory to show that it is superior to learning theory. In fact, some of the Lawrence and Festinger findings are really just another version of the partial-reinforcement extinction effect, which had been studied by learning theorists for many years before dissonance theory was formulated.

As to the dissonance explanation itself, there are a variety of findings which indicate that it alone is insufficient to explain the partial-reinforcement effect (Robbins, 1971).

Once again, however, although an explanation has met with contradictory findings in animal research, it should not be ignored in marketing. The trend of the learning theorists is toward the use of drive concepts and of some kind of "extra attractiveness" (often known as K or incentive motivation in the theories to be discussed later in this chapter). Dissonance has been a useful concept in explaining the consumer behavior phenomena that occur when products do not come up to expectations (Engel and Light, 1968; Maloney, 1962). It is likely that it will be useful, along with other explanatory variables, to deal with partial-reinforcement situations in marketing.

5. *Competing responses.* This idea explains the effect by assuming that disfunctional or competing responses are eliminated by habituation on nonreinforced trials, thereby enabling partially reinforced subjects to achieve greater acquisition and greater resistance to extinction. There is only limited support for the competing-response postulate, however. It requires a partial-reinforcement acquisition effect, and this often does not occur. Competing responses are discussed later in this chapter in terms of advertising and brand misidentification.

6. *Frustration.* Amsel (1958, 1962) and Spence (1956, 1960) posit a drivelike concept of frustration that is in some ways similar to the dissonance concept discussed earlier. The frustration notion has been one of the most popular used to explain the partial-reinforcement extinction effect. The explanation goes as follows. In acquisition subjects become frustrated during the nonreinforced trials of the partial condition. They develop running responses that are classically conditioned to proprioceptive stimuli in the nonreinforced condition. These running responses which

develop from the frustration of partial reinforcement are then effective in maintaining performance during extinction.

The frustration notion has greatest difficulty in explaining results in which groups given a block of nonreinforced trials before continuous reinforcement are more resistant to extinction than continuous groups without the initial nonreinforcement. It is difficult to see how the former groups could be frustrated in a situation in which they had received no prior reward. The same difficulty is encountered for the frustration notion in those studies finding the partial effect with very few trials.

Although the frustration notion has not survived recent experimental tests, the idea of drives and mediating responses has much value in consumer behavior application of learning notions. For instance, Smith (1972) has suggested that frustration may be an efficient segmenting variable, particularly in minority or ethnic markets.

7. *Sequential hypothesis.* A refined version of what above was called the generalization explanation has been proposed by Capaldi (references in Robbins, 1971). He assumes that nonreinforcement has "stimulus consequences"; that is, nonreinforcement builds up the awareness or importance of certain stimuli perceptually present to the subject on the nonreinforcement trials. These stimulus consequences increase to some asymptotic strength with successive nonreinforcements. They are remembered and conditioned to the running response on the reinforcement trials, and thus are available to promote resistance of extinction in the partial-reinforcement condition. Capaldi's hypothesis is the only one that can account for results such as those which go counter to the frustration idea. Its biggest advantage over the other notions is that it includes perceptual and informational concepts which are so important in explaining human behavior. The stimulus consequences will probably be different in consumer behavior than they are in the animal laboratory, but they will be important just the same. And, even more important, we can ask respondents what the stimulus consequences are. In fact, two concepts discussed later in this chapter—Zajonc's "attitudinal effects of mere exposure" and Krugman's "learning without involvement"—can be derived from the sequential hypothesis of partial-reinforcement extinction effect.

The research and notions on the partial-reinforcement extinction effect demonstrate that the field of learning is a constantly expanding body of cumulative knowledge. Each idea about a dependable phenomenon is tested with precise experimentation.

Moreover, each study gets at a particular variable or variables that may help explain the analogous situation in consumer behavior. For instance, the response unit and generalization hypotheses showed how the environment must be defined from the viewpoint of the consumer. The dissonance and frustration ideas emphasized the importance of various drives in explaining learning. The competing responses and sequential hypotheses showed the importance of intermediate responses in particular situations.

None of the notions about partial reinforcement received 100 percent support from research. *But each was supported in some situations.* This is the core of the value of learning research to consumer behavior. The learning findings give consumer behavior researchers clues as to which variables are significant in each situation.

Partial-reinforcement notions are being applied in consumer behavior in several ways. Some have been mentioned previously. In addition, Strong (1972) is applying these ideas to deal with partial reinforcement or scheduling findings such as those shown in Figure 1. Ray (1967b) applied the drive, intermediate responses, and generalization notions to develop a partial-reinforcement explanation of various forms of inducing resistance to persuasion. This latter application is discussed in greater detail later in this chapter.

Conclusions

This section began with a short statement indicating the importance of understanding the nature of the research upon which learning theory is based. The pages that followed that statement contained a number of general parameters of learning research that should be kept in mind by the consumer behavior researcher:

1. *Emphasis on causal inference and experimentation.* The *S-R* psychology label for learning theory underscores the importance attached to prediction and inference in the field. Research is done to determine which independent variables (stimuli) affect which dependent variables (responses). This area of research has long been known as a hard, scientific discipline as opposed to those areas of psychology which are not based on observable responses to well-defined stimulus conditions in controlled experiments. This emphasis carries over to the kind of research done by *S-R* psychologists, such as Hovland and his coworkers (see discussion of research styles in McGuire, 1969). It also relates to the blossoming of experimental work in marketing (Holloway, 1968; Ray, 1972a; Sawyer, 1972).

2. *Unusual research sites and the need for translation.* Because the inferential goals of psychological research on learning are so demanding, psychologists have pursued them in unusual situations in which superior control and variation of stimulus and response are possible. Thus if marketing and consumer behavior researchers want to use the findings, they must be prepared to develop procedures for translating the laboratory research to the field. This section has indicated that this translation procedure will involve thorough understanding of the variables that operate in the laboratory situation. This must be combined with application and research in consumer behavior settings.

3. *Learning is a hypothetical construct.* As was noted in the section on partial reinforcement, it is often said in the learning literature that learning

can be best understood by examining the nature of forgetting or extinction. This underscores the fact that the responses that are taken to indicate learning are not learning itself. It is entirely possible to change a person's behavior, that is, improve his performance, without altering the amount he has learned. Ebbinghaus and the countless verbal-learning subjects who have followed him all would *seem* to know more on a recognition test than on a relearning test than on a recall test. Yet all are tapping the same degree of learning. The careful experimental procedures mentioned above are used to get measures of learning. But remember that they are only measures. This is especially important when the measure of learning changes from the muscle movements of the animal in a maze to the verbal responses of a human respondent.

4. *Large amount of research.* The field of learning has been said to be synonymous with the science of psychology. And learning research also goes on in sociology, anthropology, economics, and a number of other fields. This is why this chapter has been restricted to just the basic learning research theory that has been done in psychology. Even with this restriction, the literature is huge. This was demonstrated in this section by the large literature just on partial reinforcement.

5. *Need for theory.* Because there has been a tremendous amount of research involving many complex sets of results, there is a great need for organizing theory in psychological learning. Theory is even more important to the student of consumer behavior who needs it in order to make the translation from laboratory results to the field. Fortunately, there is a group of microtheories and general theoretical trends in psychology that can be of great use in organizing approaches to learning in marketing situations.

6. *Trend toward cognitive and motivational components.* There have been strong criticisms of learning research and theory. Most of these criticisms were really against a straw man—a type of learning theory that is based only on muscle twitches and animal behavior. As was illustrated by the explanations of partial-reinforcement effect, however, learning research and theory are very much concerned with cognition, motivation, and perception. Applications in social psychology have had to consider much more molar and sophisticated behavior than learning theory is often given credit for. This is the kind of learning theory that has real meaning for marketing. It will be discussed in the following sections.

THREE STREAMS OF MIDDLE-RANGE THEORY IN LEARNING

Revolving around the almost countless studies and phenomena of animal- and verbal-learning research are scores of notions similar to the seven related to the partial-reinforcement extinction effect. And surrounding these notions are a number of middle-range theories that help to organize the field. Each theory is based on some central idea or concept. Each stems from a particular body of research. And each is useful in a particular type of learning situation.

These learning notions and middle-range theories are really too numerous to fully discuss here. Hill (1971), Hilgard and Bower (1966), and Kintsch (1970) provide such discussions.

It is possible to outline three significant *streams* of research, notions, and theory, however. None can be ignored in the evaluation or understanding of learning theory. All three must be applied to fully examine consumer behavior. The following paragraphs discuss the three streams and their significant theorists, theories, and applications to consumer behavior.

Watson, Behaviorism, and Contiguity Theorists: *S-R*

Although learning research owes much to Ebbinghaus, the roots of learning theory are more closely tied to Pavlov. Its development began around the turn of the century with notions from British associationism. The most important of these notions was contiguity, that all that is necessary for learning to take place is repeated contiguity of stimulus and response.

The idea was popularized by Watson (1924), who used the term *behaviorism* and, because he believed only in classical conditioning of *S-R* bonds, probably was originally responsible for the mechanistic stereotype of learning psychology. Not surprisingly, this popularizer spent the latter part of his career with the J. Walter Thompson advertising agency.

But Watson's was not really a theoretical position. It remained for Guthrie (1952) to state a more complete contiguity position. He based his explanation of learning on one principle: "A combination of stimuli which has accompanied a movement will on its recurrence tend to be followed by that movement" (Guthrie, 1952, p. 23). Thus Guthrie's is an "all-or-none" learning idea. But Guthrie can take account of incremental learning in that different parts of the response and different parts of the stimuli are involved in each learning situation, thus leading to incremental improvements in the response with repeated exposures. And although Guthrie eschewed the concept of reinforcement, he explained it by contiguity on the basis that a reinforcer was the stimulus which occurred when the last response was made in a situation.

Guthrie's ideas force one to very carefully consider the situation in which learning occurs. Because of this, many of his simple suggestions are similar to those that might be made from the more recent attribution (Kelley, 1967) or self-perception (Bem, 1968, 1972) theories. That is, if someone is forced by the situation to do something, he will see this as his own habit or attitude.

Consumer behavior is indebted to the contiguity position in terms of mathematical learning theory, which has been heavily applied to studies of brand loyalty, new product introductions, and brand switching. Probably the most used is the linear-learning model of Bush and Mosteller (1955), which is covered in this book in Chapter 13 on stochastic models of buyer behavior.

Estes's (1959, 1967) statistical learning theory is more nearly a mathematical representation of Guthrie's contiguity position. Estes makes surprising predictions in visual and verbal discrimination tasks and is typically supported by data. Recently (Estes, 1970), he has made applications to the study of education and mental retardation. His attack on these issues has some tinges of the other two streams of theory: the reinforcement and the cognitive.

Thorndike and Reinforcement Theorists: Feedback of *R*

Although the early contiguity theorists based their work on classical conditioning, the reinforcement theorists tended toward instrumental conditioning. The first of these was Thorndike (1898, 1911), who covered the contiguity position through his "law of exercise" but stated a clear reinforcement emphasis in his well-known "law of effect," which was "Of the responses made to a situation, those which satisfy the organism's needs tend to be retained, while those which fail to satisfy these needs tend to be eliminated" (Thorndike, 1911, p. 224).

Skinner has carried this position far beyond Thorndike. Many of his ideas have been reviewed earlier in this chapter. He, like Thorndike, gives a nod to the contiguity-classical conditioning stream. He calls such conditioning *respondent* behavior and relegates it to the learning of involuntary reflexes. More important, says Skinner, is instrumental conditioning, which he calls *operant* behavior.

In their emphasis on reinforcement, both Thorndike and Skinner conclude that positive reinforcers are generally more effective for learning than negative reinforcers, although the latter have advantages in certain situations. A similar point has been made in an argument for the consideration of negative appeals in marketing (Ray and Wilkie, 1970).

Skinner's work on schedules of reinforcement (Ferster and Skinner, 1957) is quite relevant to the marketing and advertising scheduling problem mentioned earlier. Skinner has found that reinforcement given at *fixed* times or rates is not as effective as *variable* reinforcement.

Although there are many current applications of Skinner's notions, they are really not complete enough to deal with much of the variety of consumer behavior. For more complete reinforcement theory it is necessary to move to Hull (1940, 1943, 1952) and expansions of his theory by Spence. Hull attempted to construct a theory on the basis of the hypothetico-deductive approach with a full set of postulates and theorems. These were stated in algebraic form that gave an impression of precision, allowed criticism, and generated a great deal of research. The basic Hullian system is illustrated in Figure 3.

The theory is the first one we have encountered that specifically uses *intervening variables,* although these have been mentioned often in this chapter,

FIGURE 3. A Schematic Representation of Hull's Basic System

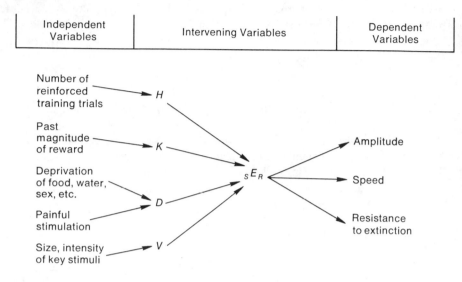

particularly with regard to the explanation of the partial-reinforcement extinction effect. Intervening variables are internal states of the organism that are posited to exist between the stimulus and the response.

Such concepts have enormous usefulness. For instance, in Figure 3 there are essentially four independent variables given as examples of drive producing stimuli. Each of these variables could be related in a specific way to each of the three dependent variables—giving twelve possible relationships. But this can be reduced to only seven by assuming that each independent variable produces a state of drive (D) and that drive, in turn, affects each dependent variable. Thus a theory with intervening variables provides an enormous classifying function for our knowledge about consumer behavior. We should never make the mistake of either reifying these intervening variables or of dismissing them with derogatory terms like "explanatory ghost."

Hull defined his explanatory variables in both literary and operational terms (Underwood, 1957a). In literary terms the intervening variables in Figure 3 are defined as follows:

1. Habit strength, $_SH_R$, is the strength of the connection or bond between stimulus and response that is increased by practice trials. In Hull's first system, $_SH_R$ (pronounced *S-H-R*) was based partially on the size of reinforcement. In the final system the effects of the size of reinforcement, with the exception of some unspecified minimal amount that was said to affect whether a trial was effective or not, are represented in K and V. In a

sense this is some concession to the cognitive theorists, which was even further intensified by Spence.

2. Incentive motivation, K, is the expectation that the organism has of reward in the situation due to past rewards in it. This formulation grew out of Hull's dealing with contradictory "latent learning" experiments developed by Tolman and his followers.

3. Drive, D is the organism's activated state of need.

4. Stimulus intensity dynamism, V indicates that a stronger stimulus will produce a stronger response, all other variables being equal.

5. Reaction potential, $_SE_R$, is the probability of response or the strength of propensity to respond.

Hull's final 1952 system had many problems in terms of inconsistencies and ambiguities. In spite of these problems, Hull did provide a framework that might be used to account for all the variables in learning situations. This is essentially the framework that will be suggested for consumer behavior analysis later in this chapter.

Many of the inconsistencies and ambiguities of Hull's approach were eliminated by the theoretical notions of Spence (1956, 1960) and his followers (Kendler and Spence, 1971). His contributions were, in a way, a reaction to the contiguity and cognitive theorists.

His major theoretical revision had to do with the way reinforcement was expressed. He completely eliminated reinforcement from H. Incentive motivation, K, was his key reinforcement concept. For Spence, K depended on the size of the stimulus and past experience with it. It was an expectation of reward, a more cognitive concept that he used to deal with the unusual outcomes of the cognitive theorists, such as their findings in stimulus generalization and discrimination.

Reinforcement theorists, like Hull and Spence, have been quite flexible in their attempts at completeness. They have, in fact, subsumed many of the concepts of the other two theoretical streams. It is because of this that their form of theory has been used so often by those who attempt to make application to social areas. This is especially true in consumer behavior, where reinforcement theories are at the core of several systematic interpretations (e.g., Amstutz, 1967; Howard, 1965; Howard and Sheth, 1969).

Tolman and Perceptual and Cognitive Theorists: Feedback of S

What are the cognitive learning theories that challenged the reinforcement approach? Essentially, they developed from the perceptual, view-of-the-world, insight-based Gestalt psychology and Lewin's field theory, which are covered most thoroughly in this volume's chapter on field theory. The perceptual approach became more relevant to learning with the growth of neo-Gestalt, phenomenological, or "new look" psychology, because it contained historical variables that could be used to predict behavior (Bruner, 1951; Postman, 1951). But perhaps the earliest and best example of cognitive learning theories is Tolman's (1932) *purposive behaviorism.*

Tolman was concerned about the molar goals of the organism during learning. To take molar purposes into account, it was necessary for him to represent cognitions as intervening variables in his theory. Because he worked only with animal research, he bridged the gap between the human and animal researchers and introduced cognition into behavioristic research. And since cognitions could not be directly observed in his animals, it was necessary for him to introduce the idea of intervening variables into psychology.

This cognitive theory needled the reinforcement theorists in the form of critical experiments that demonstrated learning without reward. *Latent-learning* studies showed the learning effects of previous experience with a situation, even though it had contained no reward. *Place-learning* studies showed that subjects would move in the most efficient path to a goal, even though this meant ignoring previously rewarded paths.

Tolman's intervening variables became popular terminology, not only within psychology but in other fields as well. He used, for instance, the term *cognitive map* to describe the content of learning in the latent- and place-learning studies. His *sign-gestalt-expectation* is abbreviated to *sign-expectancy* in an interesting discussion by Myers and Reynolds (1967) of product, brand, and price perception studies in consumer behavior, although these authors do not cite Tolman.

Consolidation of the Three Streams: $S \rightleftharpoons O \rightleftharpoons R$

Although cognitive theorists still attempt to carve a distinctive position in description of several spheres of human behavior, the trend in the learning area is toward consolidation of the three streams of middle-range theory. Rather than being a mechanistic *S-R*, recent learning theories have begun to consolidate with a consideration of internal states of the organism (*O*) and an $S \rightleftharpoons O \rightleftharpoons R$ relationship.

The consolidation is demonstrated by the contiguity theorist Estes's (1970) use of reinforcement and cognitive notions to deal with issues in mental retardation, by the development in the Hull-Spence theory, and by Campbell's (1963) demonstration of isomorphism between behavioristic and perceptual approaches to social issues.

In consumer behavior research such consolidation is seen in terms of emphasis on internal states like the concept of attitude. Recent conceptualizations of attitude (Boyd, Ray, and Strong, 1972; Campbell, 1963; Kiesler, Collins, and Miller, 1969; Myers, 1968) include both perceptual, image, or *S* components, as well as preference, action, or *R* components. And like relevant learning theories, these attitude concepts reflect the residue of past experience (the arrows into the O in $S \rightleftharpoons O \rightleftharpoons R$) and have the potential of directing or predicting future perceptions or responses (the outward arrows in $S \rightleftharpoons O \rightleftharpoons R$).

The search in learning theory is to discover how people develop tendencies to respond. The contiguity theorists emphasize a familiarity explanation. The reinforcement thinkers say people do what they are rewarded for doing. The cognitive psychologists suggest that people make plans for behavior. Now it appears that all three streams are right, depending on the situation.

LEARNING FRAMEWORK FOR CONSUMER BEHAVIOR ANALYSIS

What sort of conception of learning should be used in the study of consumer behavior? Clearly, it should include all three ideas—contiguity, reinforcement, and cognition. Intervening variables will be necessary since consumer behavior can seldom be observed directly or consistently enough for straight behaviorism in the sterile sense. A middle-range conceptualization is necessary to take account of the variation of phenomena across consumer situations.

Of all the middle-range theories that have been discussed thus far, the only one that meets these criteria is Hull's. Because Hull and Spence were flexible, their theory took all three streams of thought into account. Intervening variables of the sort valuable to consumer behavior predominate in the theory. And the theory is certainly a middle-range one. Although Hull's formulaton is no longer strictly followed by active researchers, his work resulted in an Esperanto or general language of learning theory.

The outlines of this language are presented in Hull's performance equation. One version of this equation was

$$ {}_SE_R = {}_SH_R \times D \times V \times K - ({}_S\bar{H}_R \times I_R \times {}_SI_R). $$

The first five variables were defined in the discussion of Hull and in Figure 3. They indicate that reaction potential $({}_SE_R)$ is equal to the product of habit strength, drive, stimulus intensity dynamism, and overbar incentive motivation. The variables in the parentheses are competing havits $({}_S\bar{H}_R)$ and inhibition $(I_R, {}_SI_R)$, which build up with repetition and are subtracted from reaction potential.

The framework suggested in the following paragraphs is similar to Hull's but is based on a social-psychology approach to learning developed by Campbell (1961, 1963, 1965; Levine and Campbell, 1971). The value of Campbell's approach is that it deals with human social behavior and thus has meaning for students of consumer behavior. This approach has the additional advantage of providing a framework within which many of the theoretical approaches discussed earlier can be understood and related. Rather than get concerned about the differences between theories, Campbell and others (Berlyne, 1968; Kelley, 1967; Morris, 1964; Mowrer, 1960) have emphasized the similarities, and then concentrated on common research areas, processes, variables, and structures.

Campbell points out that there are essentially three types of theorists working in social psychology. The concepts of the behavioral theorists are based primarily on research involving observation of responses. The concepts of perceptual or phenomenological theorists are based on research involving human views of the world. Motivational theorists concentrate almost solely on drive and its symptoms. Thus it is not surprising that the terms used by the different theorists are different, whereas their underlying findings and ideas are quite similar.

Although Campbell feels the perceptual or phenomenological approach is probably most relevant for understanding social behavior, he summarizes the principles of social psychology in terms of this behavioral elicitation equation:

$$R = S \times H \times D \times K.$$

Note that its components are quite similar to Hull-Spence's (with the exceptions that $S^E R$ is converted to R and V to S). The major difference is that terms related to inhibition are not included. Campbell prefers to deal with inhibition and extinction of response in terms of negative drives and negative incentive motivation.

Also note that Campbell's approach is used only as a point of departure here. The interpretation of specific variables and interactions in the following paragraphs sometimes differ from Campbell's.

Comparison with Other Conceptualizations

The generality and usefulness of this equation is quite clear. A comparison with other concepts is shown in Table 1.

Campbell himself (1963) brilliantly compares the propositions of the neo-Gestalt and behavior theorists to show that, when compared on the basis of the behavioral elicitation equation, they are saying essentially the same things with different words. He specifically compares Lewin's theoretical concepts with those in the equation to show the equivalence:

Lewin's structured pathways to the goal region = H
Lewin's valence = K
Lewin's tension system = D

A more obvious comparison is with the social-learning notions of Miller (Dollard and Miller, 1950; Miller and Dollard, 1941), who in his books with

TABLE 1. Comparison of Components of the Campbell Behavior Elicitation Framework with Other Conceptualizations in Learning and Social Psychology

Concepts	R	S	D	K	H
Behavioral elicitation framework ($R = S \times D \times K \times H$)	Response potential	Stimulus	Drive	Incentive motivation	Habit
Hull's performance equation	$_SE_R$ (reaction potential)	V (stimulus intensity dynamism)	D	K	H
Lewin's field theory	-	-	Tension system	Valence	Structured pathways to the goal regions
Miller and Dollard	-	Cue	Drive	Reward	Response
Utility theory $B = f(U) = g(M, I, P)$	B (behavior) U (expected utility)	-	M (motivational disposition)	I (objective value)	P (subjective probability) changes with experience.
Rotter's social learning theory	Behavior potential	-	Reinforcement value	Expectancy	Expectancy

Dollard posited four elements of learning-drive, cue, response, and reward. These are quite close to the Campbell elements of drive, stimulus, habit, and incentive motivation. In the Miller and Dollard reinforcement theory the order of elements is explicitly indicated as the order of elements in a learning response. This is obviously an instrumental conditioning paradigm.

Howard (1965) points out that the variables of the elicitation equation are also represented in utility theory. In the utility theory equation,

$$B = f(U) = g(M, I, P).$$

Behavior (B) and expected utility (U) are both concepts similar to R. Motivational disposition (M) is a D concept. Objective value (I) is similar to K. And P is the subjective probability of the product having certain value. Since it changes with amount of experience, it is an H concept.

Another example of equivalence is Rotter's (1954) social-learning theory. His behavior potential is similar to R, expectancy to H and K, and reinforcement value to D.

Pseudoconflicts between Consumer Behavior Notions

The Campbell learning framework highlights the nature of conflicts between theoretical interpretations that have been heavily applied in consumer behavior. A look at Table 2 will indicate that, to some extent, these have been pseudo-conflicts. Different theories just get at different aspects of a total behavior pattern. Or they call the same things by different names.

The most direct applications of learning theory are in terms of the hierarchy of effects models. These are typically thought of as learning theory in consumer behavior, because they emphasize the necessity of some learning-awareness, comprehension, knowledge (habit and stimulus)—before evaluation or preference change (K—expectancy of reward) and then action (R—response) can take place. In Table 2, three of these hierarchy approaches are shown: McGuire's (1972) information processing approach, the Lavidge and Steiner (1961) hierarchy, and the adoption process of diffusion theory (see Chapter 11).

None of these hierarchy notions contains a drive (D) component, and they have been attacked in consumer behavior by individuals espousing heavily D-loaded interpretations. These are shown in Table 2 in terms of dissonance (Engel and Light, 1968; Festinger, 1957, 1964), curiosity (Berlyne, 1960; see also Chapter 9), and reactance (Brehm, 1966) theories. Each of these approaches attempts to fully examine the implications of a particular type of motivation.

Each drive theory has two shortcomings. They tend to ignore many other relevant drives, and they do not put enough emphasis on components of behavior other than drive.

It should be clear, however, that these single-drive approaches have been

TABLE 2. Notions Used in Consumer Behavior in Light of the Elicitation Equation

Concepts	R	S	D	K	H
McGuire's information processing approach	Yielding-behavior	Presentation-attention	-	Retention	Comprehension
Lavidge-Steiner hierarchy	Intention-action	Awareness	-	Liking-preference	Awareness-knowledge
Adoption process	Trial-adoption	Awareness	-	Interest-evaluation	Awareness
Dissonance theory	-	-	Dissonance	-	-
Curiosity theories	-	Variety, complexity	Curiosity	-	-
Reactance theory	-	-	Reactance	-	-
Self-perception, attribution theories	-	Self-perception, attribution	-	Self-perception attribution	-
Attitude structure components	Conative	Cognitive	Affective	Affective	Cognitive

quite useful in pointing out exceptions to the strict hierarchy formulation in particular situations. Our view of man is much more complete because of them.

The theories in social psychology that are being used to expand beyond the single-drive notions are self-perception (Bem, 1968, 1972) and attribution (Kelley, 1967) theories. These ideas are beginning to filter into consumer behavior. As shown in Table 2, they perform the valuable service of highlighting self-perception (S) and resulting expectancy (K). The theories suggest that individuals perceive their own reactions and use that perception to decide what particular attitude they have. This self-perceived attitude can then affect future behavior.

It is perhaps unfair to place entries for these theories in only the S and K columns. They do touch on other aspects of the behavioral elicitation equation. But, like the single-drive theories, these have value because they have over-emphasized particular components.

The last line in Table 2 classifies a common view of attitude structure, the cognitive, affective, conative one. In social psychology, attitudes have been the main unit of analysis (McGuire, 1969). This is probably true in consumer behavior also, where there has been a tremendous proliferation of books and articles on attitude research (see Chapter 8).

Table 2 shows that the main advantage of attitudes is that they do cover all components of the behavior elicitation framework. They can have both perception and preference aspects of consumer behavior (Boyd, Ray, and Strong, 1972). Their disadvantage is that they are not as specific as they might be. Only three components are used. But recent instrumentality approaches to attitude are much more specific in terms of the five components of the framework (Mitchell and Biglan, 1971).

The plea being made by this chapter, and indeed this book, is that consumer-behavior researchers should analyze all components of behavior in each particular situation. This means that all the conceptualizations shown in Table 2 should be considered. It is disfunctional to get involved in pseudo-conflicts between various theoretical directions when all must be used for a thorough analysis of behavior. The behavioral elicitation equation, derived from learning theory, provides a solid framework for such analysis.

How the Framework Should Be Used

Consumer-behavior researchers should use the framework primarily as a classificatory device or checklist. It forces one to ask a series of questions in each consumer situation:

1. *Response (R).* What is the nature of the possible responses in this situation?
2. *Stimulus (S).* What kind of stimulus dimensions are important?

3. *Drive (D).* What drives are critical and how do they interact?

4. *Incentive motivation (K).* What incentive to respond or expectation of reward do consumers have in the situation?

5. *Habit (H).* What knowledge or practice of the response have consumers had or will they have in the situation?

6. *Weights.* What weights should be put on each of the components of the equation; that is, how important are *S, D, K,* and *H* in this situation?

7. *Form.* What are the mathematical relationships between *S, D, K,* and *H*? Are they multiplicative in this situation? Or are they something else?

Notice that the last two questions on weights and form of the equation make quite clear that this is just a framework which is to be applied differently in each situation. The multiplicative form of the relationship suggested by Campbell or the even bolder equations of Hull are rejected here for a simple functional relationship.

$$R = f(S, D, K, H).$$

In other words, response is equal to *some* function of stimulus, drive, incentive motivation, and habit. The exact function in consumer behavior will depend on applications in specific situations.

The first five questions cannot be answered unless each component of the equation is well understood. It is especially critical to understand the nature of *S, D, K, H,* and *R* in social, human settings and their relation to the laboratory versions. Much research and change have occurred in these concepts. Recent social and consumer behavior versions of them are discussed in the following sections.

Stimulus (S): Perceived, Relative, and Generalized

The meaning of the stimulus component of the behavior elicitation equation can be seen in terms of its position in the elicitation equation itself; specifically, *S* appears as an intervening variable, not an external independent one. This is the work of the social perception, neo-Gestalt, perceptual psychologists. The implication of this positioning is that *S* is considered to be more than a physical entity in human learning. The *S* exists as the person perceives it.

Of course, an *S* that is totally dependent on the nature of the response is a tautology. Ideally, *S* can be measured physically, and the subjective responses would be represented in theory in terms of other intervening variables, such as *H, D,* and *K.* But a long tradition of research in psychophysics has developed means for measuring independent responses to social objects (Fishbein, 1967; Scott, 1968; Stevens, 1968). It is upon such measurement that the following notions are based.

1. The Stronger the Stimulus, the Stronger the Response Tendency. Although this is often found to be true, there have been many findings in social learning which indicate that the variations of the Yerkes-Dodson law (1908; Schönpflug, 1966) apply in the social area. Thus when fear-appeal messages are ranked in terms of the amount of fear they cause, their effectiveness in terms of attitude or response change seems to be a curvilinear one, with moderate levels of fear stimulus being most effective (Janis, 1967). The curvilinear or nonmonotonic notions, which have to do with competing tendencies, can give a good idea of the nature of stimulus-response relationships in complex situations. Suffice it to say at this point that the *S-R* relation seems to be monotonic only within a certain range.

2. Stimulus Relativism. Stimulus Strength is a Function of the Relative (not absolute) Intensity of the Stimulus Object. This notion not only explains some of the occurrence of nonmonotonic functions, but it also is the basis for Sherif's (1936) frame-of-reference concept, Helson's (1964) adaptation level concept, and Sherif's (Sherif and Hovland, 1961; Sherif, Sherif, and Nebergall, 1965; Sherif and Sherif, 1967) social judgment-involvement approach, which is emphasized so heavily in Chapter 8 on attitudes. These approaches get at the issue of how extremely different a stimulus, say, a product claim, has to be before it is seen as different or perhaps lack credibility.

3. Stimulus Generalization or Equivalence. To the Degree that Two Stimuli are Similar, They Tend to Evoke the Same Response to the Same Degree. Generalization has already been mentioned in terms of Pavlov's original findings and in terms of Spence's predictions. In consumer behavior this is a key concern for companies bringing out new products. Thus it is not too surprising that stimulus equivalence is the basis of the new-product or market-structure studies of Stefflre (1968). Stefflre bases his new-product-development work on a variant of the stimulus-equivalent notion; that is, *novel stimuli will tend to elicit the responses of the familiar stimuli to which they are most similar.* Making this assumption, Stefflre gets responses to old products and objects to predict the way that people will react to new products that are in some degree similar to the old.

4. Generalization Gradients are Flatter Early in Learning, Under Conditions of Fatigue or Frustration, for Approach Habits Than for Avoidance, and for Acquisition of Response as Opposed to Inhibition. A generalization gradient is the curve that shows the degree of response strength to stimuli which are progressively more dissimilar from the original one that elicited the response. Figure 4 shows two generalization gradients that illustrate most of the notions on *S* that have been mentioned here. The dashed flatter gradient is for early learning or responses "primitivized" by, say, fatigue. Note that in such conditions the findings have indicated that people are more likely to confuse stimuli than under the opposite conditions indicated by the steeper solid-line gradient.

FIGURE 4. Stimulus Equivalence Gradients for Various Situations

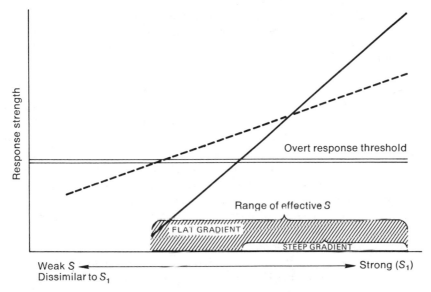

Solid gradient for response strength in late learning, escape or avoidance response, or inhibition. Dashed line for early, primitivized, or approach response.

When the two lines are taken as approach (flatter, dashed) and avoidance (steeper, solid) gradients, the findings of Miller (1944) on the nature of the approach-avoidance conflict are illustrated. Explanation of the resolution of this conflict requires more than S concepts, however. In fact, some critics of dissonance theory implied that dissonance is a drive which is operative when such conflict cannot be resolved in any other way (e.g., Collins, 1961). Such comment was dismissed by the publication of Festinger's (1964) *Conflict, Decision, and Dissonance,* which indicated that dissonance is a phenomenon that occurs only after decision.

Drive (*D*): Primarily Innate, Multifaceted, Nonmonotonic

There has been a great deal of change in the concepts of drive, reinforcement, and reward. This change has been noted by several observers of learning theory. For example,

> In the past two decades it has become more and more apparent that the Hullian and Freudian theories of motivation are not sufficiently congruent with the empirical facts (Howard and Sheth, 1969, p. 100).
> No single impending change in S-R emphasis has been fraught with

so much argument and difficulty as that involving the concept of *drive* (Berger and Lambert, 1968, p. 102).

One of the most critical unsolved problems of psychology concerns the nature of reinforcement. What conditions determine whether something will reinforce a learned response and, if so, how strongly? (Berlyne, 1967, p. 1).

Obviously, Thorndike's "law of effect" has exploded beyond his wildest dreams. The impetus for this change in development of the drive concept has come from several sources. One of these is from physiological psychology, where studies of the reticular activating formation (see review in Berlyne, 1967) have introduced the possibility of a general arousal or activated condition. Another source of the new drive concepts has been within reinforcement theory itself, where studies of drive stimuli (Miller, 1957, 1959) have led to the possibility of very specific drives. Finally, the contributions of the cognitive theorists, which have already been mentioned, have led to a deemphasis of drive and greater emphasis on *S*- and *K*-type concepts.

Where has all this development left us? We still have the notion that there are basically two kinds of drives: those that are innate and basically physical (hunger, thirst, pain, sex) and those that are learned. For instance, Howard and Sheth's (1969) concept of motivation in consumer behavior is based largely on Cofer and Appley (1964), who posit basically an innate-learned classification of drives.

Although this division of drives is still used, it now appears that there are many more innate drives than were formerly thought to exist. Drives thought to be secondary or conditionable in the laboratory have, in fact, not been learned in this way. These are typically nonphysical drives, which have enormous importance for consumer behavior. For instance, a growing number of studies and interpretations indicate a series of drives that might be categorized under the headings curiosity, exploration, or novelty seeking. Both animals and people seem to need variety, and they will seek this variety despite or in addition to the utility of the responses that they make (Berlyne, 1960, 1967; also see Chapter 9). Another kind of drive that in a sense might be opposed to the exploratory drives is that for balance or consonance.

The findings on these drives indicate that they are not learned drives which can be affected by outside influence attempts. Other drives, such as achievement, affiliation, altruism, and power (Berkowitz, 1969), may be learned, but over such a long period of time that marketing efforts cannot affect them. The job for the analyst of consumer behavior is to determine what kinds and mixture of drives will operate in any given marketing situation.

Some help in making this determination has come from research on arousal and the orienting reflex (Duffy, 1962; Maltzman and Raskin, 1965). Originally, it was felt that the individual experiences conditions of general arousal, indicated by a variety of physiological responses. During such conditions, the individual was said to be reinforced by a variety of arousal modifiers. Schachter (1964; Schachter and Singer, 1962), in his research on emotional responses, provided some demonstration that emotional responses are due to a combination of physiological conditions and environmental cues. Individuals having an arousal reaction could identify this in terms of either anger or joy, depending on the cues Schachter provided for them. More recently, there is evidence (Berlyne, 1967) that arousal reactions may be specific to certain kinds of stimuli (see particularly Lacy, 1967).

This has led to the concept of *optimal arousal* (e.g., Fiske and Maddi, 1961), which is the notion that people tend to seek moderate levels of arousal. Under this assumption it is possible to take account of the operation of both consistency- and curiosity-type drives. If the individual is too aroused, a consistency-type drive would explain behavior. If, on the other hand, there is not enough arousal, the exploratory- or activity-type drives seem to be more important. The optimal-arousal idea can also explain many of the inverted U-curve findings in psychology and consumer behavior. Stimuli that are moderate in intensity, complexity, and novelty should be more likely to hit the optimal level. Of course, the problem with this explanation is that the optimal level depends on a variety of definitions of the situation. This problem will be discussed later in regard to the use of fear appeals.

Another approach to determining which drives are operating in any given situation has been developed by Premack (1962). Premack's notion is very simple. He assumes that responses that occur more frequently can reinforce less frequent responses. He does experiments in which, for instance, he first observes whether children, given the choice, prefer more often to eat candy or play a pinball machine. Those children who more often eat candy can be made to play in order to get candy—indicating that the candy was reinforcing the playing. Those children who were prevented from playing the pinball machine could be trained to eat candy in order to be able to play. This is the reverse of the usual food-reinforcement finding, and it illustrates Premack's main point.

The optimal-arousal and the Premack response-reinforcement ideas provide leads to the consumer behavior researcher who needs to deal with drive and reinforcement concepts. As a number of consumer behavior researchers have indicated (Boyd and Massy, 1972; Boyd, Ray, and Strong, 1972; Engel, Kollat, and Blackwell, 1968; Howard and Sheth, 1969), a number of drives at various levels vie for attention in any buying situation. Boyd and Massy talk about this in terms of a "demand hierarchy." Howard and Sheth suggest that there is a means-end chain. In any case, notions like those of Premack indicate that marketing research can determine, on the basis of behavioral responses, the drives that are most likely to be operative in any given situation. Furthermore, the strategists applying these findings should remember the optimal-arousal notion. That is, it is likely that these drives interact in such a way that some moderate level of arousal is most efficacious.

Incentive, Expectancy, Valence (K):
Key Variable in Social Learning

To use learning findings, consumer behavior researchers must somehow take responses at a very simple level and expand them to complex human social behavior. The *K* or expectancy variable is the key to such expansion. It was used by reinforcement theorists to deal with the findings of the cognitive and perceptual movement within psychology.

This variable refers to expectations of the good or bad that (1) will result from a given response, or (2) has become attached to a particular set of stimuli or situations. Note that there can be positive or negative *K;* that is, it is possible for *K* to either promote or inhibit response.

The particular value of *K* in making the translation from, say, animal to consumer behavior can be seen by considering alternative *modes of learning.*

In animal learning there are typically two modes:

1. Blind trial and error.
2. Perception.

The reinforcement theorists were dealing with blind trial and error. They assumed an organism almost without perception and certainly without thought. The perceptual-cognitive theorists like Tolman showed that just seeing a maze, even without a reward, could affect performance. Thus the reinforcement theorists had to posit some expectancy of reward and developed the *K* variable to deal with perceptual-learning phenomena.

But consumers do more than just perceive situations and objects. Researchers must take additional modes of learning into account to explain social behavior. These modes would include

1. Observation of others' responses.
2. Observation of others' rewards and punishments during learning.
3. Verbal instructions about responses.
4. Verbal instructions about rewards and punishments.

The observational modes of learning were employed in the earliest attempt at social applications of reinforcement theory. This was Miller and Dollard's (1941) *Social Learning and Imitation.* They posited a form of learning called *matched dependent behavior.*

An example would be a child learning to shop. If that child observed her mother buying frozen orange juice instead of fresh oranges on one shopping trip, the youngster might run to the freezer and pull out a can of juice on the next shopping trip. The mother might then reward the child with a kind word or an affectionate squeeze. That reward would lead to a buildup of *K*, or an expectancy that buying frozen orange juice would have a reward connected to it.

The matched dependent response could be generalized to other stimuli or could be strengthened by observation of persons similar to the mother. For instance, the youngster might be more likely to buy frozen forms of other juices rather than buying fresh oranges. Or, in the future she might be more likely to imitate persons who seemed similar to her mother.

The key aspect of matched dependent behavior is that the matching or imitation has to be rewarding *to the imitator*. In Miller and Dollard's terms there has to be drive-cue-response-reward. Because it is based on reward for specific patterns of imitated response, however, matched dependent behavior has only minimal application to many of the complex forms of social learning. As evidence, note that this kind of learning is hardly mentioned in Dollard and Miller's (1950) book on personality and psychotherapy.

Other forms of K buildup have more exciting implications for consumer behavior. One is a version of social-observational learning, which Bandura (1962, 1965, 1971; Bandura and Walters, 1963) calls vicarious or no-trial learning. In this type of learning a person can develop K by simply observing behavior of another person (the model), providing the conditions of observation are adequate to inform the observer of the outcome of the model's responses. Reward to the learner is not necessary. One could imagine, for instance, our youngster developing a preference for frozen orange juice on the basis of observing another child enjoying it on television.

Extensions of this basic form of learning can be developed through generalization. One particular model, for instance, can develop the ability to increase K, because he has been seen to be rewarded or punished for his responses in previous situations. Generalization can occur across models also, so that the responses of a particular model will be particularly efficacious in K buildup if that model is similar to previous models that have been observed to be rewarded or punished.

Bandura and his colleagues have applied vicarious learning to child development, personality, and psychotherapeutic problems. In consumer behavior vicarious learning has been related to mass-media effects. Bandura's research, as well as the research of Berkowitz (1962, 1971), demonstrated that it is possible in a short-term laboratory situation to increase the aggressiveness of experimental subjects by showing them films of aggressive behavior. Findings are similar for sexual behavior, although less strong. Contradictory and weaker findings in longer-term field experimentation (Feshbach and Singer, 1971), should warn the reader of the difficulty of translating these laboratory studies to the field, which has so many other variables that might affect response (Berkowitz, 1971; Hovland, 1959).

Campbell (1961), in an application of the elicitation equation to the conformity literature, showed that the phenomenon of generalization across the responses of a particular model or generalization across models is a quite common method used by people to deal with their environment. In other words, people tend to use their knowledge about the successes and failures of particular models or particular types of models in deciding what to do in particular situations. This kind of conformity is really quite basic to the issues in interpersonal perception and in diffusion of innovations, which are discussed in this book in Chapters 5 and 11, respectively.

Imitation-matched-dependent behavior, vicarious and no-trial learning, and generalization of these tendencies can also occur through verbal communication. Simple propositions about verbal communication in the buildup of K would be stated as follows:

1. *Verbally developed matched dependent behavior.* Hearing it said that certain acts or objects will be rewarding to the listener (follower, imitator) leads to positive K for those acts and objects (and hearing that he will be punished leads to negative K).

2. *Generalization across situations for a particular source.* The more that the listener has in the past been rewarded or punished for following the advice of a specific communicator, the more influential that communicator will be.

3. *Generalization across sources.* The more that the listener has in the past been rewarded for following the advice of similar communicators, the more influential a novel but similar communicator will be.

4. *Verbal form of vicarious learning.* Hearing it said that certain acts or objects are rewarding to the communicator (or rewarding in general) creates positive K's for those acts and objects (and in a complementary way, reports of punishment create negative K).

5. *Source prestige.* The more the communicator's own responses have been observed to be in general rewarding to the communicator, the more influential are his communications about positive and negative K. This, in general, is called the "expertness" (Bauer, 1965) of a source.

6. *Source prestige generalization.* The more that similar communicators have been observed in the past to have their own responses rewarded, the more influential will be the communications of a novel communicator.

Readers familiar with the recent literature on source-credibility effects (e.g., Triandis, 1971) will recognize that the K principles on source that are listed give only one part of the source effect, which interacts with the rest of the components of the elicitation equation in quite interesting ways. These will be discussed in the section on microtheoretical notions.

The principles of K are from the psychological or intraindividual perspective, but they have clear implications for consumer behavior that must be looked at on an interindividual basis. This is certainly true for the issues of interpersonal perception and diffusion of innovation that will be covered later in this book. The basis of a learning approach to social psychology is the intraindividual process, even when it is expanded to the situation in which one individual or group of individuals acts as a stimulus that develops K within the individual.

Habit Strength (H): Practice and Information without Reward

Habit strength was, of course, the first intervening variable considered in learning theory. Its definition was once just a contiguity one, then it moved toward a reinforcement conceptualization, and more recently it has moved back to just the contiguity viewpoint. In a social context *habit* refers to a familiarity or *habitualization* of a stimulus-response connection. There is no reinforcement implied in this definition. The reinforcement component is now given to the D and K variables.

It seems, therefore, that Thorndike's law of frequency and exercise is being applied quite directly to social behavior. This is almost the case, but the buildup of H in human learning can be achieved through more than trial-and-error learning; that is, it can be acquired in social behavior by visual search of the environment, observation of another person making a response, verbal instructions, and thinking.

Thus it is possible to have H buildup analogous to the vicarious forms of K development discussed in the previous section. The difference in the vicarious forms of H increase is that they are acquired totally without reward.

The fact that H is acquired without reward makes it a less valuable explanatory tool than the other components of the elicitation equation. True, the recent surge in verbal-learning and cognitive psychology is based on the idea that reward is only effective to the extent that it provides *information*, a synonym for H. But D and K concepts associated with exploratory and consistency behavior have to be invoked to explain which stimuli and what practice will provide information to any given individual. And some phenomena that seem to be based on H actually can only be explained by invoking K, D, and S. This is true, for instance, with Zajonc's (1968) "attitudinal effects of mere exposure" and Krugman's (1965) "learning without awareness," discussed later in this chapter.

What findings and notions are left that are purely H in nature? Some have been stated already. That is, in human social learning H can be generated in several ways in addition to blind trial and error. In addition, the following statements about the nature of H in social learning can be made quite confidently.

1. The Stronger the H the Stronger the R to the S. In other words, the more familiarized a person is, the more he knows about a response in a situation, the more he in fact has done it in the past, the more likely he is to make that response in that situation again, all other things being equal.

2. Early Learning, Primacy Effects, Inertia of Attitudes. There is a solid body of evidence and theory to support the notion that early experience with a response and a situation is more important than late experience. A broad body of literature supports this—from Freud's emphasis on the importance in neurosis and personality development of the first few years of life, to Asch's (1964) findings of primacy effects (first adjectives in a list have greatest effect) in forming interpersonal perception, to Skinner's demonstration of "superstitious" behavior in pigeons.

The effect of first impressions is nothing new in consumer behavior. Many new products have failed because first versions of them were inadequate, out-of-stock conditions produced disappointment, and so forth.

3. Overlearning. Both animal- and verbal-learning studies have had to contend with overlearning; that is, in any experimental group there are some subjects who will learn to a criterion earlier and will be run for several trials beyond this criterion. In some studies subjects actually are run for a large number of practice trials beyond a criterion of, say, perfect recall (Postman, 1962). Since Ebbinghaus (1885), the finding has been that overlearning, or increased numbers of practice trials beyond criterion, produced increased retention or, we might say, increased buildup of H. This kind of "meaningless" practice is behind Krugman's (1965) characterization of television advertising effect as "learning without awareness." It is also behind the assumption that slogans, ID announcements, and billboards work by countless repetitions strengthening H.

On the other hand, as Zajonc (1968) points out, there is the counter assumption of "familiarity breeds contempt." In marketing terms, there is the possibility of wear out or negative effects with increased repetition. In animal and verbal discrimination studies there is the "overlearning reversal effect"; that is, subjects who experience overlearning are quicker to learn new contrary discriminations than those subjects who have not had overlearning.

Once again, a phenomenon like overlearning, which seems based mainly on H or practice buildup, must be understood and further exposed in terms of other components of the elicitation equation. Practice leads to buildup of H, but it also produces negative K due to fatigue and habituation. And this depends on the situation as defined by all the variables and their interactions.

4. Massed Versus Distributed Practice. The initial findings on massed versus distributed practice indicated that massed practice trials are not as effective in producing learning as is distributed practice. The result was roughly illustrated in Figure 1, which showed Zielske's data with advertising schedules of weekly and monthly exposures. Note that although massed (weekly) trials produce a higher recall level immediately after the last exposure, the distributed (monthly) schedule produces a more lasting effect.

Reviews and discussion of the literature (Deese and Hulse, 1967) indicate that distribution of practice has varying effects depending on a variety of factors. The main one is meaningfulness. If the items to be learned are meaningful, if there is high structure in the material, if there is high motivation to learn, massed practice can be as effective or more effective in learning than distributed practice. The other factors (K, S, D) intervene to mediate the effect of H buildup. In consumer behavior an interaction between meaningfulness or involvement and distribution of practice should be assumed. The nature of this interaction will vary somewhat in each consumer behavior situation.

5. Spontaneous Recovery. A number of researchers, starting with Pavlov, have observed that subjects who receive trials to extinction (without reward) will return to a preextinction response rate if they are allowed to rest before being given additional nonreinforced trials. Obviously, the explanation for this phenomenon, called *spontaneous recovery*, must utilize D and K but is partially explained by a buildup of H during nonreinforced trials.

Both spontaneous recovery and overlearning have application in consumer behavior when large numbers of "practice" trials (exposure to product, brand, and advertising) are unreinforced, but later have an effect in a situation in which they become relevant. For instance, advertising research may not find an ad effect on attitude-change measures in the general population, but there will be an effect on just those people who are at the decision point of buying a product in a store.

Response Tendency (R): Intervening Variable, a Hierarchy of Measures

The reader should not make the error of confusing the R of the elicitation equation with some observed response. As pointed out earlier, learning is a hypothetical construct, and R, like Hull's $_sE_R$, is an intervening variable that only represents the potential for making responses.

As such, the developments in thinking about R can be represented in terms of two expansions: (1) multiple measures of R, and (2) multiple R's or competition and interference.

Multiple measures of R are at the heart of what is known as the *hierarchy of effects* hypothesis (Aaker, 1970; Colley, 1961; Palda, 1966). In marketing this notion in the most extreme form is that changes in awareness must precede changes in comprehension, must precede changes in affect, must precede changes in intention, which precede changes in action, and so on. In learning theory all these can be seen as measures that represent an R of a particular strength. In animal-learning theory, such as Hull's, the $_sE_R$ was represented in terms of the amplitude, speed, and resistance to extinction of response. In social forms of learning theory R is represented by measures such as physiological responses, relearning, recognition, answers to knowledge questions, observation of overt response, and so on.

The hierarchy hypothesis here is that these measures vary in strength as

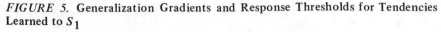

FIGURE 5. Generalization Gradients and Response Thresholds for Tendencies Learned to S_1

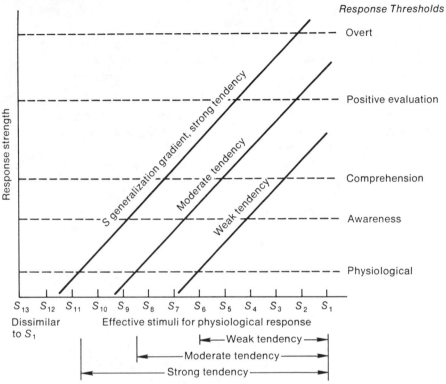

shown in Figure 5, and that stronger R will be manifested in the most difficult measures as well as all the weakest ones. From such a chart, showing the threshold of strength, a variety of stimuli, and R's of various levels, it is possible to derive a number of commonsense principles about R. For instance,

1. The stronger the disposition (R), the more stimuli there are that will elicit a response.
2. The stronger the R, the greater the number of measures it will be manifested in.
3. The stronger the R, the more likely it will be elicited.
4. The stronger the R, the more dissimilar to the original stimulus (S^1 in Figure 5) a stimulus can be and still elicit the observable response.
5. A novel stimulus (such as Rorschach Ink Blot), which is way to the left in Figure 5, will elicit the strongest of many competing R's.
6. An R shown by responses to the least appropriate stimulation (those to the left in Figure 5) will also be shown to situations in general.

7. An R shown to a measure with a high threshold will also be shown to other weaker measures (such as those lower in Figure 5).

8. An R shown for weaker measures, such as autonomic response or awareness, may fail to appear for stronger measures, such as verbalized statements or overt responses.

9. The lower the threshold of a measure, the more frequently it will be elicited, even with inappropriate stimuli. Thus autonomic or physiological responses, such as galvanic skin response (GSR), pupillary dilation, or cardiovascular response, may show a very nonspecific arousal (see Duffy, 1962; Shapiro and Crider, 1969; Ray, 1965) with no positive or negative valence or identity.

Of course, these notions coming from a hierarchy framework are challenged by dissonance and balance notions, which note that action measures or response symptoms occur before the affective or cognitive symptoms. But the conflict between the learning-hierarchy notion of measuring the hypothetical R and the dissonance position should be studied more clearly than it has been in the past.

Some observers, particularly in marketing (e.g., Haskins, 1964), have assumed that the learning position is that learning or recall automatically leads to behavior. Actually, as shown in Figure 5, this is only assumed to be the case when the R is strong enough to elicit overt action as well as the lower-level verbal response. And the verbal response usually identified as "learning" in the marketing literature must be carefully defined in order for it to be linked to a particular overt response syndrome (see Fishbein, 1967; Greenwald, 1968).

Another common misconception about the hierarchy-learning position on measures of R is that it is incompatible with R formation on the basis of behavior occurring before affective or attitudinal changes. This is not true. The hierarchy-learning position as shown in Figure 5 indicates nothing about R formation. It just says that of the R's that are formed, the stronger will be represented in higher threshold measures. If we accept the typical dissonance process of R formation—conflict, decision (action), dissonance, attitude change—wouldn't the expectation in terms of measures be exactly what is shown in Figure 5? That is, wouldn't all the measures be shown for that particular R? For weaker R's, even those formed through dissonance, it may be that autonomic responses and awareness responses will serve as evidence, but higher-level measures may not be exhibited. This is not to say that there is no conflict between learning and dissonance positions on R formation. It is true, however, that there is no conflict between the two theoretical positions in terms of the hierarchy of measures of R.

Before closing this section on R, the long-existing and continuing verbal-learning work on competing R's and R interference must be discussed. In consumer behavior this issue is found in terms of *clutter,* the confusing array of products, brands, and advertisements that face the buyer. There is some suspicion that not only does the bulk of product messages cause fatigue, but it also invokes competing responses and response interference, the technical terms for confusion. The implications are extensive both for marketing effectiveness and for the societal effects of marketing (anonymous, 1971; Maneloveg, 1971; Webb, 1971).

In verbal learning, competition and interference have been used to explain a number of phenomena, such as forgetting, the serial-position U-curve, spontaneous recovery, distribution-of-practice effects, and paired-associate learning. Interference theory has become a major issue in the field (Kintsch, 1970), although it is really a developing microtheory or set of notions about particular phenomena, rather than a theory.

Many of the verbal-learning notions relate to the earlier discussions of forms of verbal-learning tasks. That is, the extent to which there is apparent R interference depends on whether the measurement is in terms of recall, recognition, and so forth.

One important point for the consumer situation has to do with the notions of retroactive and proactive inhibition. Originally, forgetting was explained by retroactive inhibition; that is, experience after learning interfered with or inhibited the learned response. But Underwood (1957b) showed that in verbal-learning studies proactive inhibition from previous similar learning caused much

FIGURE 6. **Recall As a Function of Number of Previous Lists Learned from a Number of Studies**

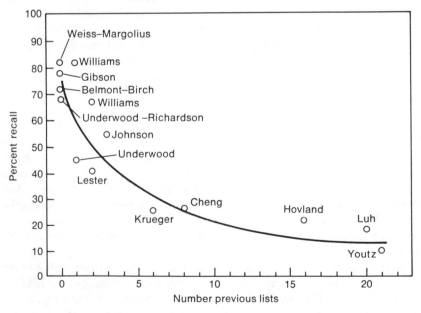

Source: Underwood, 1957b

of the apparent decrement in recall. As shown in Figure 6, if the number of previously learned lists is used as the independent variable, the recall curve produced is very much like the typical negatively accelerated forgetting curve.

The implications for consumer behavior are twofold. First, researchers should carefully consider consumer segments in terms of their past experience with the product class, advertisement brand, and so on. Second, it is clear that a certain amount of misindexing and misinformation will occur in advertising no matter how lucid it is. This misindexing must be considered carefully in light of proactive and retroactive inhibition existing in most consumer situations.

Weights and Equation Form: Microtheoretical Notions

Once the consumer behavior researcher knows the nature of the stimuli, drives, expectancies, habits, and response tendencies in any situation, he can begin to learn the weights attached to each element of behavior and the form of the relationship among the elements.

The learning framework provides a point of view or research style within which specific problem areas or situations can be examined. Berger and Lambert (1968), in discussing application of *S-R* psychology to social phenomena, call the trend toward such situational application "the study of processes." Miniature models, interaction principles, or hypotheses are developed to explain the findings in each problem, process, or situation area. A perfect example of such research and theory application was our previous discussion of the partial-reinforcement extinction effect.

When consumer behavior researchers apply the learning framework to specific problem areas, they construct what are really *microtheoretical notions* (Ray, 1973). Technically, microtheoretical notions would be exemplified by the behavioral elicitation equation completely filled out with regard to specific situations. In a more general sense, they are interaction predictions, indicating which variables are important and how they relate to each other. They are microtheoretical in the sense that they apply to a small area of human phenomena but always relate to a larger, middle-range theory, such as the learning framework. They are notions in that they are stated in a somewhat informal sense, stimulated on the basis of a problem or empirical finding, ready for additional testing and development.

Each of the preceding sections on the components of the elicitation equation contained a number of interaction predictions that may have relevance to consumer behavior situations, when expanded to microtheoretical notions on the basis of the full learning equation. For instance, the approach-avoidance conflict situation was said to be due to the interaction of two *S*-generalization gradients. The optimal arousal concept of *D* is based on interaction between several drives. Conformity was seen to be due to a weighting of intra- and interpersonal sources of *K,* or reward expectancy. Spontaneous recovery was implied to be the result of interaction of acquisition and extinction *H* buildup.

And measurements of R were seen to be due to an interaction between competing R's and the eliciting stimuli.

A wise man once said that a science cannot be built on all possible interaction predictions. Scientists seek parsimonious main effects. But in a field like consumer behavior, especially in its applications to marketing, interactions are valued because they identify the conditions in which a variable or technique will work or not. And interactions occur in nature. It is for these reasons that microtheoretical notions are so important.

It should be clear that microtheoretical notions can be developed on the basis of a variety of middle-range theories. For instance, Lawrence and Festinger developed a partial-reinforcement notion on the basis of dissonance theory. Kassarjian develops some in Chapter 3 on the basis of field theory. They appear in almost every chapter of this book.

The learning framework has distinct advantages over other middle-range theories, however, because it contains a wider range of components that have been specifically considered in research on behavior. Microtheoretical notions in consumer behavior research are thus more likely to be complete if they are based on the learning framework.

MICROTHEORETICAL NOTIONS ON LEARNING IN CONSUMER BEHAVIOR

In many ways consumer behavior is ripe for the application of the learning framework because of the wide variety of clearly defined consumer situations. In addition, consumer researchers have employed not only laboratory techniques but also field-experimental and computer-analysis techniques that are necessary to expand the laboratory-learning findings to specific real-life situations.

What are the critical situations or problem areas that make up the study of consumer behavior? Many are defined in the introductory chapter of this book. Models of consumer behavior perform the valuable function of classifying these key situations into the steps of the process of purchase decision making (e.g., develop need, search, purchase, and postpurchase response).

Communication models relevant to consumer behavior suggest that the key situations can be classified by the questions *Who* said *what* to *whom* through which *channels* with what *effect*? Other communication approaches highlight the relationship between the *source* of a *message*, transmitting it to a *destination* or audience which then provides a *feedback* message.

In marketing the key situations can be classified into the steps of strategy development (e.g., market analysis, product development, campaigns, control, and evaluation).

The following paragraphs review a number of research directions for consumer behavior. Each constitutes a particular consumer situation and the microtheoretical notions that have or could be developed out of the learning framework to deal with the situation. These range from simple learning notions of spontaneous recovery and order effects to more complex situations involving communication and attitude.

The reader should be cautious in use of this review. There is an attempt here to state the nature of present findings and notions so that consumer behavior researchers can consider the application of the learning framework. But each situation represents an area of research comparable to the partial-reinforcement one. And only a sampling of situations is considered here. So the reader should certainly use this review as only an incomplete catalog that allows a choice among a number of research areas and microtheories, which must be more completely investigated.

Spontaneous Recovery in Consumer Behavior

One frequent phenomenon in the market place is the short-term consumer "romance" with some new product or idea followed by a return to an established and familiar old product. Or advertising copy testers are surprised when an ad for a new product that tested well in a short-term one-shot copy test fails to convert to purchasing responses in the long term.

Both of these situations can be understood by the simple learning notion of spontaneous recovery, that is, the apparent recovery of a response tendency after a rest following extinction trials. Previously, it was described and explained in terms of the buildup of $_IH$ or nonreinforced habit strength on extinction trials.

A more complete consumer-related description and explanation is shown in Figure 7. Here the original learning trials (advertising and so forth) for the established product are shown in terms of a negatively accelerated learning curve. A period of extinction occurs while the established brand employs maintenance promotion and a new brand is catapulted up by a strong introductory budget. When this extinction period is over, the established brand is subject to a less steep portion of the forgetting curve than is the new brand. Once again the old brand has the stronger response tendency and spontaneously recovers.

The same spontaneous-recovery explanation can be given for the copy testing situation. A copy test is like the extinction period in Figure 7. An ad for a new brand does especially well during the test (the white area in Figure 7 actually moves above the shaded, old-brand response strength during the test period), but the respondents forget it after the test and favor the established brand in purchasing.

This spontaneous-recovery explanation is called a simple learning notion, because it is based on the simple contiguity, H-related learning notions of early verbal-learning researchers. Figure 7, for instance, uses Ebbinghaus's elementary, negatively accelerated learning and forgetting curves. A similar simple learning notion was Jost's (1897) second law: Of two habits of equal strength at

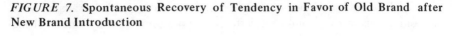

FIGURE 7. Spontaneous Recovery of Tendency in Favor of Old Brand after New Brand Introduction

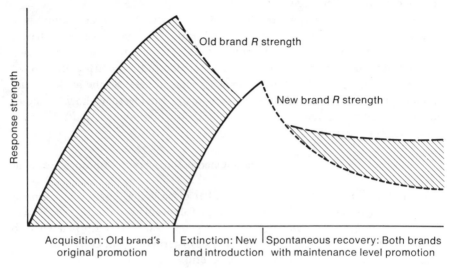

a given time, the older one will be stronger with a passage of time. A careful examination of Figure 7 will show that Jost's law both can be derived from the negatively accelerated forgetting curve and can be used to explain the spontaneous-recovery phenomenon.

The job for consumer behavior researchers is to develop appropriate micro-theoretical explanation beyond the simple learning notion. In consumer situations all components of the elicitation equation will interact. Both learning and forgetting curves are likely to be of different shapes. In the copy testing situations, for example, it may be that the new brand ad would produce so much expectancy of reward (K) from the new brand that no forgetting and no spontaneous recovery would occur. The simple learning ideas provide the basis for development of more complex microtheoretical notions.

Order Effect: Primacy and Recency

Another simple learning notion can be used as the basis for microtheoretical explanation of order effect in consumer behavior. The issue in this situation is whether primacy or recency holds. Primacy is the condition in which the first or early items in a series—in consumer behavior these would be products, ads, packages, claims, and so on—are more effective than later items, solely because of an early position in the list. Recency is the opposite condition, that is, greater effectiveness because of being second in a pair or last in a series.

A large literature (Hovland, et al., 1957; Lana, 1964; Ray, 1969a) has examined the question of the effect of position on learning effectiveness. Lund (1925) claimed there is a "law of primacy" in persuasion. But Hovland and

Mandell (1957) pointed out that Lund's procedures were biased toward primacy and that many variables can affect the order-effect results. Later investigators have shown that it is possible to get either primacy or recency, depending on the familiarity of the topics involved (Lana, 1965) and the "spread of effect" of reinforcements placed either before or after two communications (Rosnow, 1968).

But primacy-recency refers to effects of position alone. What is the simple learning basis for these phenomena? Miller and Campbell (1959) claim that it is the operation of forgetting curves and proactive and retroactive inhibition on a combination of response tendencies. The Miller-Campbell model is shown in Figure 8. The effect of each communication is shown to decrease over time in a negatively accelerated forgetting curve. The nature of order effect is dependent solely on the length of time between messages and the time from the end of the second message to measurement. The situation (condition 1) with equal-strength adjacent messages and immediate measurement would produce a slight recency effect. When measurement is delayed (condition 2), no order effect is predicted. When there is an interval between the messages and immediate measurement (condition 3), a strong recency effect is predicted. When there is both an interval between message and a delay in measurement (condition 4), a lesser recency effect is predicted. Miller and Campbell found essentially the predicted results shown in Figure 8 for recall of facts from a speech.

FIGURE 8. **Hypothetical Forgetting Curves for a First and a Second Competing Persuasive Communication When Both Are Presented During a Single Session (Curves A and B) or When the Two Are Presented 1 Week Apart (Curves A and B')**

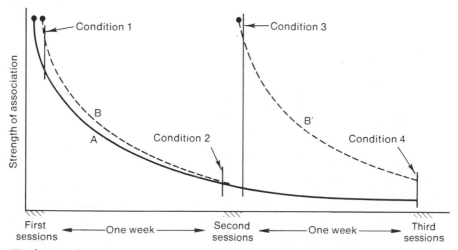

The four conditions, appearing as vertical slicings, represent the timing of measurements. (Similar results were obtained by Miller and Campbell, 1959, for memory of facts in speech.)

Once again, however, the consumer behavior situation is likely to involve more than simple forgetting curves. For one thing, because stimulus (S), drive (D), and expectancy (K) variables interact in consumer situations, positions could be invested with particular efficacy beyond that indicated by forgetting curves.

As an example, it is possible to predict primacy effects within the Miller-Campbell model by assuming an S and K effect of the first position, giving it a higher starting position. Perceptual theorists dealing with order effects (e.g., Luchins, 1957) assume that primacy will occur, because the first message will distort perception of the second message (an S effect). Also, Hovland and Mandell (1957), in explaining Lund's primacy findings, argue that they may have occurred because Lund himself presented the communications, and his students may have felt that whatever he presented first was his favored message. This would be a D and K effect and probably occurs in many communication situations in consumer behavior where source effects might be present.

Miller and Campbell would explain such primacy effects on the basis that the first message would start at a higher level before the forgetting curve began. In fact, they obtained the results that would be predicted by a higher starting level for the first message, when attitude (favorable evaluations in a mock court case) was the dependent variable. Thus Figure 8 probably holds best for H-type measures. When evaluation is the measure, then D, K, and S variables come into play, as they most certainly do in consuming. Applications of the Miller-Campbell model in the marketplace should be interesting, especially if they are based on the full complement of variables in the learning framework.

Rote Learning of Evaluation

Another simple learning notion has to do with a truly pervasive question in consumer research. The question is, to what extent does repeated exposure alone, similar to that in the verbal-learning studies with nonsense syllables, lead to changes in the liking or evaluation of the repeated object?

In advertising the question translates into the common issue of whether the gross size of the budget and the resulting number of impressions alone determine the success of a campaign. An even stronger statement would indicate that even though consumers may dislike certain advertisements, such as those in the headache remedy field, they are affected by them to buy the product, just by the ads' sheer persistence.

When consumer research considers the social effects of the mass media, the question comes up again. The media issue is whether societal attitudes—particularly those of children—are molded just by tremendous exposure to nonevaluative media treatments of sex, violence, materialism, and so on. In politics the question is whether the candidate with the largest budget to spend in the mass media, no matter what his qualifications, will be the one elected to office.

In a general sense many mathematical models of consumer behavior, particularly those involving repeated purchase sequences, make the assumption that strings of product exposures alone will lead to a greater likelihood of future purchase.

The simple learning notion that underlies these questions and assertions would be a straight application of verbal-learning findings. We would assume, all other things being equal, that evaluation would increase as an exponential learning curve with repetition. Then after a certain point additional repetitions might produce stimulus satiation and a turn down of evaluation. That is, overly increased familiarity breeds contempt.

Consumer studies by Krugman (1943; Krugman and Hartley, 1960) have indicated that the rote-learning model holds for only a minority of situations. Learning to like products sometimes is dependent on sheer repetitive exposure to them, but this holds only for particular situations. The definition of these situations depends on microtheoretical notions offered by Krugman and new ones that may be offered by consumer researchers on the basis of the learning framework.

In related research the social psychologist Zajonc (1968) posits that mere repetitive exposure to social stimuli enhances the affective or attitudinal feeling toward them. He supports this assertion with (1) data indicating that positively valenced words are used more often in printed English, (2) positive effects of experimental manipulation of word, nonsense syllable, and symbol frequency, and (3) positive correlation between word frequency and attitude toward the word's referents.

Like Krugman's earlier consumer research, Zajonc's provides only partial support for the rote-learning idea. But in doing so it indicates the behavior elicitation variables that may be important in rote consumer learning.

Zajonc himself points out that the correlational evidence (between word frequency and valence) is weak. It may be, for instance, that it is due to the fact that there are fewer positively valenced words in English, so that they each have to be used more.

The experimental evidence is questioned on the basis that Zajonc's design includes "demand characteristics" (Orne, 1962). In other words, it is argued that there are aspects of the experiment (instructions, experimenter bias, clues to the experimental hypothesis) that lead subjects to more positively rate the foreign words or characters that are repeated more often in the studies. In a sense the idea is that experimental subjects have guessed the experimental hypothesis. Evidence of this has been reported in studies by Suedfield, et al. (1971) and Zajonc, et al. (1971). Sawyer (1972) has replicated the Zajonc (1968) results by simply describing to subjects the typical experimental procedure and then asking them to report the way they think they would respond. Nearly 20 percent of Sawyer's subjects correctly guessed the experimental hypothesis. These "aware" subjects accounted for most of the positive evaluation advantage for those stimuli that were repeated more often.

Despite these contradictory results, there is still substantial evidence that there is some attitudinal effect of mere exposure. By gathering evidence from a wide variety of sources, Zajonc and his associates provide substantial confirmation for some effect. And Zajonc and Rejecki (1969) have obtained positive but weaker results in a less demand-prone field experiment. What is most likely is that there are attitudinal effects of repeated exposure, but those effects, as most marketing and advertising people assume, are due to more than just "mere" exposure. There is more than just the operation of H buildup going on.

To explain rote learning of evaluation in a consumer situation, it will be useful to reconsider the partial-reinforcement extinction effect discussed earlier in this chapter. One explanation for the effect was Capaldi's sequential hypotheses. This notion was that stimulus consequences were built up on unreinforced trials, and they carry over to mitigate extinction. This same kind of notion can be used to deal with Zajonc's phenomenon. Obviously, repetition of any stimulus will increase H and even S strength. If a subject has no other basis for choosing a response in an experiment, he will choose the most practiced one. But in the field it is quite likely that words, symbols, brand names, and so on, repeated more often will be more likely to be exposed under reinforcement as well as nonreinforcement conditions. Reinforcement will build up positive K that will interact in a positive way with the H buildup of nonreinforced exposures. In this way the total R is increased without the habituation or stimulus satiation that might occur under total reinforcement or total nonreinforcement.

Brand Loyalty and Brand Attitude

In a sense the movement of the brand-loyalty concept toward a more complete brand-attitude idea is representative of one development of the rote-learning notion into a microtheory for consumer behavior.

The initial studies of brand loyalty (Brown, 1952, 1953) examined data from consumer panels to determine whether consumers were consistently purchasing one brand over another. When a brand constituted a large proportion of total purchases in a product class, it was assumed that the consumer was loyal to that brand. More recently, there has been an explosion of studies applying this simple learning idea in stochastic and linear-learning models of brand-purchasing sequences. This type of study is reported most thoroughly in Chapter 13.

These purchase-sequence approaches omit a specific consideration of the learning dynamics behind brand loyalty. The dynamics are better considered in research involving brand attitude. This research has as its base that brand loyalty is due to preferences (R) which are based on perceptions (S, D, K, H) about the brands in question. It may be possible for a consumer to show brand loyalty by a purchasing sequence but not have a very high brand attitude level. This may be due to aspects of the environment—such as product distribution, shelving, and continued deals for that brand—that are irrelevant to the brand attitude in question.

Researchers like Day (1969) and particularly Jacoby (1971a, b) are attempting to determine the product attributes that lead to high brand attitude and thus to high brand loyalty. Jacoby's multibrand model of brand loyalty takes into account the Howard and Sheth (1969) notion of evoked set and the Sherif idea of latitudes of acceptance and rejection (Sherif, 1967).

This development of the brand-loyalty and brand-attitude concepts is similar to the development of learning theory from contiguity to cognitive positions. The original brand-loyalty studies were based on not much more than H concepts; that is, they dealt with brand purchases as practice trials. The current notions of brand attitude and its link to brand loyalty are adopting all the components of the behavioral elicitation equation and indicating what the meaning of those practice trials might be. The key for management is to learn which perceptions ($H, D, S,$ and K) lead to which preferences (R), that is, the relation between brand attitude and brand loyalty. One possible research technique is to study the formulation of loyalty and attitudes among foreign visitors (Sheth, 1968) or new residents (Andreason and Durkson, 1968).

Source Credibility and the Sleeper Effect

This is the first of several communication content issues considered here. It also involves a simple rote-learning notion (negatively accelerated forgetting curves) that is being expanded in a microtheoretical direction in consumer behavior. The key issue is whether, and in what way, the credibility of the source of a message, product, and so on, affects response tendency.

One of the most venerable findings in the source-credibility area was a surprising one when first discovered. This is the source-credibility sleeper effect (Hovland and Weiss, 1951; Kelman and Hovland, 1953). When measured immediately after exposure, those groups receiving a message associated with a high-credibility source exhibited greater opinion change than those groups receiving messages associated with a low-credibility source. But when measurement was delayed for 4 weeks, the high-credibility message seemed to lose effectiveness. Thus there was a *sleeper effect* which seemed to develop over time.

The sleeper effect can be explained as a simple learning notion in several ways. The most parsimonious explanation would be that the forgetting curve for the source is steeper than the forgetting curve for the content of the messages. This is reasonable to assume, since the message content has a great deal more redundancy in it, which would provide a built-in repetition or buildup effect.

Most of the negative effect of the source is dropped away for the low-credibility group, creating the seemingly positive sleeper effect. Support for this simple learning interpretation is found in the study by Kelman and Hovland (1953) in which opinion change levels close to those found in the immediate-measurement condition were achieved when respondents were reminded of the message source at the delayed-measurement point.

These initial studies on source effect considered credibility as a unitary concept. If a source was "credible," this led to a positive increase in the perception of the stimulus (S) message. More recent research (Giffin, 1967) has considered all components of the elicitation equation by analyzing source in terms of such variables as expertise, liability, intentions, activeness, personal attractiveness, and the majority opinion of the listener's associates.

Bauer (1965) analyzes source effect on the basis of whether the audience is playing the "problem-solving game" (possibly a tendency toward H and S build-up) or the "psychosocial game" (an emphasis on D and K effect). McGuire (1969) suggests three components of the power of a source. As Triandis (1971) points out, there are interactions between the components of source credibility. If the audience is in a problem-solving mood, source expertness is important, but attractiveness might be detrimental. Zimbardo et al. (1965) indeed did find interactions of the type suggested by Triandis. The components of the elicitation equation can be used to analyze such interactions.

Some research relevant to source is on audience D or involvement. Proponents of the social judgment involvement approach (Sherif, Sherif, and Nebergall, 1965; see also Chapter 8 in this book) and of dissonance theory make different predictions partially due to the differential assumptions of the interaction of D and S.

Fear Appeals

The research on fear-appeal effects has moved beyond simple learning notions and toward a microtheoretical notion that can be used to deal with consumer behavior.

The initial study by Janis and Feshbach (1953) indicated that low-fear messages were more effective than high-fear messages in producing behavior change. Subsequent studies (see Ray and Wilkie, 1970) have shown the opposite relationship, with high fear most effective. The resolution of these findings has usually been made by positing a nonmonotonic relationship between level of fear and desired response.

McGuire (1963, 1969) explains this nonmonotonic, inverted U-curve relationship on the basis of the interaction of two components of the behavioral elicitation equation. In general, McGuire suggests that a yielding or D-K function goes up with increased fear, whereas an understanding or S-H function goes down. The interaction of the two produces the inverted U-curve with moderate levels of fear most effective.

Ray and Wilkie (1970), following the lead of Janis (1969), point out that fear can have a variety of facilitating and inhibiting effects. These interact as competing R's to produce the U-curve shown in Figure 9. Ray and Wilkie show how this basic tendency can be used with market segmentation to predict consumer behavior as a result of exposure to fear-appeal messages. The basic idea is that different segments, such as those with different past exposure on the subject, have different fear-effect curves and different optimum points. Wheatley (1971) provided some confirmation for one of the Ray and Wilkie segment hypotheses in a separate study. Consumer researchers should also pay close attention to the careful theoretical analysis of Leventhal (1970).

Inducing Resistance to Persuasion

Another fully developed microtheoretical notion about messages has to do with the situation of heavy competition in marketing. This recurring problem is handled by a quantitative, operations research or management approach in terms of competitive parity forms of budgeting (MacNiven, 1969; Peckham, 1966; Weinberg, 1960). A more micro, behavioral approach is to consider the types of appeals that might be used to "induce resistance to persuasion."

FIGURE 9. **Facilitating and Inhibiting Effects Leading to Nonmonotonic Curve**

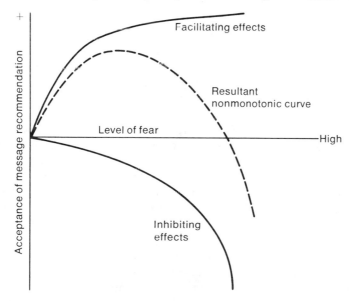

Source: Ray and Wilkie, 1970

Narrowed even further, the question becomes one of whether competition or its appeals should be mentioned in advertising and packaging. The social-psychological research in this area has compared one-sided or supportive messages (which present only arguments in favor of the brand) with two-sided or refutational messages (which briefly present arguments competitive to the brand and then refute them in a positive appeal).

To some extent the social-psychological research has been an extension or translation of the animal-learning findings on partial reinforcement. The one-sided supportive approach can be compared to continuous reinforcement. The two-sided refutational approach can be compared to partial reinforcement. The animal-learning results would lead us to predict that there may not be much difference between the two types of messages in acquisition, but that the two-sided refutational message would stand up best in extinction in the face of competition.

The animal-learning notion has in fact been supported by social-psychological research. When presented alone, the supportive, one-sided message does better in affecting beliefs than does the refutational one. But when the types of messages are followed by competitive messages, the refutational type of message does a better job of inducing resistance to persuasion. That is, the competitive message is less effective following the refutational appeal than when it follows the supportive.

This finding—slightly greater effectiveness of the supportive message in a noncompetitive acquisition environment and greater effectiveness of the refutational in a competitive extinction environment—has been found over and over again in communication and persuasion studies. McGuire (1964), who has done most of this research, has obtained the result so often that he has called it the "paper-tiger" effect, the paper tiger being the supportive message that looks so good without competition, but falls apart under the pressure of it.

Most of the research in the area has not been to demonstrate the finding but rather to explain it. This is fortunate for consumer researchers, because the explanations give some indication of whether these message types would work in consumer situations. McGuire (1964) in his *inoculation theory* explains the effect on the basis of a medical analogy. The refutational message is like an inoculation of a reduced form of disease bacilli. It stimulates the audience to prepare defenses for their belief. In addition, it provides information for that defense. McGuire shows the nature of the stimulation and information components of the message in a series of studies that selectively eliminate each of the components.

Tannenbaum (1967) explained the extra refutational message effect on the basis of the *congruity principle* (Osgood and Tannenbaum, 1955). He developed several additional forms of message to demonstrate that it was not the stimulating character of the refutational message that made it more effective, but rather its ability to change the audience's perception of the subsequent attack messages. Much of the more recent work in this area (e.g., Rodgers and Thistlewaite, 1969) involves pitting these two explanations, stimulation motivation to defend and reduced credibility of attacks, against each other.

Put together, these studies show the entire operation of the refutational effect in terms of a microtheoretical notion using the four components of the behavioral elicitation equation (Ray, 1968). McGuire's stimulation motivation to defend is obviously a D concept. His information-for-defense component is really equivalent to a buildup of H. Tannenbaum's reduced credibility of attacks is an S concept. Another way of stating it is to say that the refutational messages change the audience's perception of the stimuli of competitive attacks. In addition, part of the refutational effectiveness is due to the audience's satisfaction in the defense of their beliefs. This increases the K associated with the message.

The value of this four-component explanation is that now the nature of these components can be examined in consumer behavior situations. Predictions can be made as to the operation of the components in realistic situations. In addition, it will be possible to use the learning literature information on each of the components. For instance, McGuire (1964) was able to make such an application in accurately predicting the effectiveness, over time, of messages having different amounts of the D and H components. Ray (1967a) used the components to make predictions of the effectiveness of the various forms of message under conditions of selectivity, controversy, and choice. Sawyer (1971) used them to make predictions about the effectiveness of the messages with repetitive exposure to consumer groups with differential purchasing history.

Curious Disbelief

Some microtheoretical notions about messages are generated from other than the learning framework but can be understood more fully by applying the total elicitation equation. Tannenbaum's congruity-principle application to the refutational effect was one example. Another example is provided by Maloney (1962, 1963) who pointed out that messages which generated *curious disbelief* could be more effective in generating attitude and intention change than messages that generated either total belief or total disbelief. He developed his analysis on the basis of a balance-theory approach. But the extra effectiveness of the curious-disbelief message could also be explained on the basis of the behavioral elicitation equation. Totally believed messages affect H and perhaps K. Completely noncredible messages will probably produce negative K. But a curious-disbelief message has a potential of generating not only H and K but also the curiosity D that can move audiences to attitude change or reaction.

Personality and Attitude Change

Can segmentation on the basis of personality types provide groups that are differentially susceptible to communication messages? Initial studies on personality and persuasibility (Hovland and Janis, 1959) sought a linear relationship between a series of personality variables and the extent to which a person was persuasable. These studies indicated that there was little support for a general trait of persuasability.

More recent research looks for the relationship between the degree a person has any particular personality characteristic and the extent to which their opinions or attitudes can be changed by communication messages. McGuire (1969, 1973) has proposed a general microtheoretical notion to explain the results of these studies. He calls this notion the *compensation principle*. His idea is that any independent variable that affects one component of the behavioral elicitation equation (although he does not use this term) in a positive way will have a negative effect on other variables of the equation.

Take the personality variable of self-esteem, for example. Increases in self-esteem should increase the H and S components that are developed from a communication message, because high self-esteem people should work harder to learn a message and will probably have extra ability, which allows them to understand the message. At the same time, this intelligence and confidence that allow content learning, or H and S buildup, would have negative effects on K and D components, thus decreasing the extent to which the message is accepted. The interaction of these two effects—reception and acceptance—leads to an inverted U-curve prediction for the relationship between self-esteem and opinion change. The same kind of inverted-U predictions, due to the interaction effects across two sets of variables in an elicitation equation, can be predicted for the effect of personality variables such as intelligence and chronic anxiety. The typical linear relationship would still be posited for some personality variables, such as conservatism, dogmatism, achievement orientation, and closemindedness.

Learning Relationships to Attitude Change and Behavior

Consumer behavior researchers often find little relationship between the mere retention of brand names, product characteristics, or advertising appeals and the supposedly resulting attitude change or behavior (Haskins, 1964).

The typical reaction to such low recall-attitude-behavior relationships is puzzlement and an implicit rejection of learning theory as adequate for describing consumer behavior. But some researchers have moved beyond this simple rote-learning idea toward microtheoretical notions that explain the nature of the recall-attitude-behavior relationships.

The social psychologist Greenwald (1968), for instance, concentrates on issues in measurement of the learned-response tendency. He contrasts two forms of measurement, which he calls *cognitive learning and cognitive response.*

Cognitive learning is the straight rote recall of message content. Cognitive response exists when subjects report that the message caused them to think about something in addition to its content.

Not surprisingly, Greenwald finds a greater relationship between cognitive response and attitude change than he does between mere cognitive learning and attitude change. In terms of the previous discussion on measures of *R,* it is obvious that cognitive response is a more precise measure of a response tendency from the learning individual's viewpoint than is cognitive learning. Therefore, the cognitive response is a more adequate representation of the attitude-change measure, which is a summary statement of each individual's response tendency.

When seeking a theoretical framework to explain his results, Greenwald depends on cognitive theories, such as the social-judgment approach, reactance theory (Brehm 1967), commodity analysis (Brock, 1968), and functional analysis of attitude change (Katz, 1960). The behavioral elicitation equation can also take the cognitive response-attitude change relationship into account. First, there is the extra effect on *H* and *D* of thinking, which is involved to a greater extent in the cognitive-response situation. Second, there is the extra effect on *D* that is involved in a respondent-generated response. Third, there is the possibility that respondent-developed cognitions are more likely to fit with past rewards than is the content of the communication itself. Thus an extra boost to *K* buildup is achieved by cognitive response as opposed to cognitive learning.

In consumer behavior research there has also been use of cognitive-response types of learning measures. Leavitt's (1968) approach to response protocols is called *structural analysis,* and he bases it on an extension of Gestalt principles of visual organization. Krugman's (1965, 1967) *connections* measure indicates respondent involvement with and from a communication, such as an advertisement. He attempts to determine the extent to which consumers connect the advertising content to relevant issues in their lives. Both Leavitt and Krugman report good relationships between their learning measures and other measures of response tendency, such as day-after recall, attitude change, and behavior.

FIGURE 10. **Krugman's Learning without Involvement Notion**

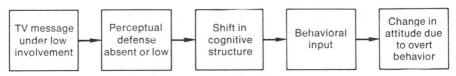

Source: David Aaker and John Myers, *Advertising Management,* Englewood Cliffs, N.J.: Prentice-Hall, Inc., forthcoming.

Krugman's approach deserves additional study, because it is based on a microtheoretical notion relevant to an understanding of the learning-attitude-behavior relationship in particular situations. His notion was originally developed to explain the effects of television advertising, which he calls "learning without awareness." Figure 10 provides an outline of the process of effect that he posits.

He assumes that the viewing of television advertising is a low-involvement situation. Because television viewers are not involved with the television message, their defense against the message is low, and on the basis of repeated repetition there is a shift in their cognitive structure. It is important to see the first three steps—exposure under low involvement, low perceptual defense, and shift in the cognitive structure—as essentially a learning process. In terms of the behavioral elicitation equation, Krugman is talking about changes in S and H. His conceptualization differs from the strict hierarchy-learning viewpoint in the next two steps in the figure. He believes that a cognitive shift is not represented in attitude change until there is first a behavior, say, a purchase and use of a product, which then leads to a change in attitude.

This conception has several implications for communication learning and communication research. First, when there is low involvement (or low D), it is probably most effective to emphasize the repetition of very simple noninvolving messages. Different strategies would be appropriate for high-involvement situations. Also, it is important to realize that measurement of just attitude change (in terms of product evaluations) may not be very effective in the assessment of television advertising.

To use Krugman's ideas, it will always be critical to determine the amount of involvement in the product and in the advertising situation. This should be done before planning communications or measuring their effects.

It should also be clear that Krugman's viewpoint is supported by the behavior elicitation equation, with D having an effect in involvement, H and S in terms of cognitive structure change, and K being the change in attitude due to behavior experience. The notion is enormously valuable, because it shows how the components of the equation are developed in two specific situations: (1) in a straight hierarchy form for high-involvement situations, and (2) in a learning (H, S)-to-behavior-to-attitude (D, K) form for low-involvement situations.

This then leads to a variety of research hypotheses for even more specific situations. For instance, Rothschild (1972) posits that in political voting consumers fall into two segments. Zero-order-involved voters vote just because it is their duty. They are *affected* by broadcast media advertising as Krugman describes. Higher-order-involved voters actually *use* the media, primarily print, to make their voting decision. They react negatively to relatively superficial broadcast messages.

Combinatorial Rules for Perception and Attitude

An extension of the cognitive-response-measure idea has been made in order to improve predictions of behavior. This extension involves a precise series of questions to determine the exact nature and form of the elicitation equation for each behavior and situation.

Such situation-specific equations have been called *instrumentality theories* in psychology (Mitchell and Biglan, 1971). These combinatorial rules have been developed for verbal learning (Dulaney, 1968), industrial psychology (Vroom, 1964), and opinion and attitude change (Anderson, 1968; Fishbein, 1967; Rosenberg, 1956). The Fishbein (1972) approach has received special attention in consumer behavior and is discussed in Chapter 8 on attitudes.

The instrumentality approaches, which are often thought of as cognitive in orientation, actually have concepts similar to those of the learning-framework elicitation equation. For instance, Dulaney (1968) proposes a theory of propositional control for verbal conditioning. His central equation is

$$B \approx BI = [(RHd)\ (RSv)]\ w0 + [(BH)\ (MC)]\ w1$$

Here B is observed behavior and BI (behavioral intention) is equivalent to R. RHd (hypothesis of the distribution of reinforcement) and RSv (subjective value of the reinforcement) are related to K, MC (motivation to comply) to I, and BH (behavioral hypothesis) to H. The w's are weights to be determined experimentally.

In a way, the combinatorial rules or instrumentality theories constitute an approach for developing microtheoretical notions similar to those suggested in this section. The researcher should be careful, however, that these experimentally determined equations not become a tautology. Thus they may work just for the particular instance of a situation from which the coefficients were determined. Microtheoretical notions should have greater generality. Otherwise the intervening variables serve no purpose.

PARADIGM FOR CONSUMER RESEARCH ON LEARNING

Learning theory's value to consumer research is primarily in terms of the focus it places on particular variables and processes critical to consumer behavior. This value cannot be realized, however, unless research is developed that examines marketplace responses specifically in terms of the repetition and forgetting situations, which are both necessary to fully examine the learning process.

An example of consumer research examining both repetition and forgetting is that done by Ray and others (Heeler, 1972; Ray, 1969b, 1971, 1972a, b, 1973; Ray and Heeler, 1971; Ray and Sawyer, 1971a, b; Ray, Sawyer, and Strong, 1971; Ray and Wilkie, 1970; Reed, 1972; Webb, 1972). These researchers have developed techniques for generating and measuring learning and forgetting curves for a variety of learning measures, both in the laboratory and in the field.

Research Procedures

The laboratory procedure is similar to the free-recall learning paradigm of verbal learning. The difference is that instead of nonsense syllables the stimuli are advertisements, which can each embody a different form of communications. Scheduling treatments within the laboratory, therefore, can be made analogous to the competitive situations in the real world. And measurements can be made of not just recall, but also of other manifestations of learning in a consumer situation, such as physiological response, evaluation, intention, and action.

The field validation procedures employed involve techniques that are used often in consumer research and have advantage for application of learning findings. Before field testing, the laboratory results are first put into a computer simulation, which utilizes past research findings on the nature of each consumer situation (e.g., typical consumer exposure patterns and effects of competitive response). The simulations seem improved with the use of empirically derived repetition and forgetting curves (Heeler, 1972; Ray and Sawyer, 1971b; Strong, 1972). Once the simulation is done there is a clear prediction, based on a variety of findings, as to how the particular stimuli ought to affect learning in the field. These predictions are then ready for testing in field experimentation (Ray, 1972b; Strong, 1972a).

Notions and Findings

Ideas from a variety of theoretical frameworks might be tested in such a laboratory-model-field approach. But, not surprisingly, the repetition research that has been done with it thus far has emanated out of the learning framework.

The multiple measures of repetition effect are used as representations of the components of the elicitation equation including response tendencies of various strengths. The basic notion underlying the repetition research is that repetition will have its greatest effect on the measures which indicate simpler learning variables or which are weaker indications of response tendency.

This basic hierarchy-of-measures notion has received a great deal of support in the repetition findings, both from the laboratory and the field. A sample set of findings is shown in Figure 11, which depicts the repetition functions obtained from exposures of well-known and not-well-known advertisements. Note that the repetition functions are steeper for the weaker recall measures than they are for the stronger, more difficult purchase-intention one. Note also that the recall curve for not-well-known brand advertisements almost perfectly mirrors the rote-learning curves found for nonsense syllables. This finding provides support for the validity of the laboratory procedure.

The other curves in the figure show how repetition works for more complex variables and stimuli. For the well-known brand ads the recall curve is higher but drops off in a more pronounced way. The purchase-intention measure shows no effect of repetition for the not-well-known ads and a slight delayed increase followed by a drop-off for well-known ads. It is data like these, showing the learning curves for consumer situations beyond rote learning, that are necessary to utilize microtheoretical notions in consumer behavior.

FIGURE 11. A Repetition Result for Well Known and Lesser Known Brands (168 and 84 Responses, Respectively, per Condition)

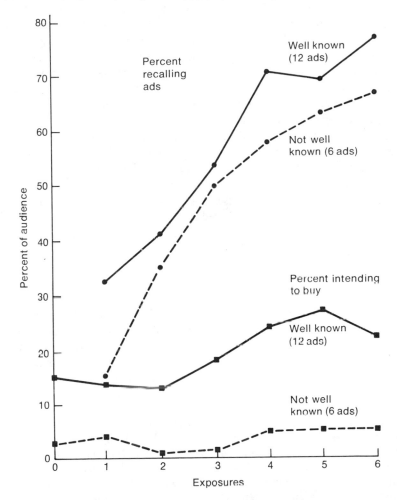

In fact, another notion underlying the repetition project is that the form of the learning curve will differ, depending on the situation. This notion has received a great deal of support in the project. Learning curves have differed significantly in level, shape, and slope, depending on the measure of response, market segment, product type, brand advertisement format, advertising illustration, advertisement color, media scheduling, media, ad appeal, and competitive situation.

The repetition research has provided data on several of the microtheoretical notions that were discussed in the previous section. McGuire's (1973) compensation principle, that communication strategies affecting one level of the hierarchy will have opposite effects on other levels, has been demonstrated repeatedly in terms of opposite sloping learning curves (e.g., Ray and Sawyer, 1971a, pp. 27-28). Refutational and supportive messages were shown to have predictably different functions for product users and nonusers (Ray and Sawyer, 1971b). The difference between cognitive learning and cognitive response was shown in one study in which color versions of ads were found to be superior to black and white in cognitive learning. Just the reverse was true in terms of a measure closer to Greenwald's cognitive response. For that measure, black and white ads produced a steeper repetition function than did the color ads (Ray, Sawyer, and Strong, 1971).

The message here for consumer behavior researchers seems clear. If the ideas on learning expressed in this chapter are to be applied to consumer situations, it will be necessary to use research procedures that allow learning to be demonstrated. This requires some laboratory research with repetition and opportunity for forgetting and extinction. It also requires computer simulation and applications to the field. With such procedures it will be possible to get at the contiguity, reinforcement, and cognitive notions that are all surely present in consumer behavior.

PERSPECTIVES FOR THE FUTURE

It is no accident that this chapter is one of the longest in this book. Learning, as mentioned at the outset, is a basic not only to consumer behavior but to all human and animal behavior. Even restriction to the psychological and social-psychological approaches to learning does not carve a very small territory. It is with this vastness in mind that the following four key points from this chapter are listed:

1. Psychological research in learning is done in settings that are very different from those found in consumer behavior. By understanding that there is a vast literature from animal- and verbal-learning laboratories, the consumer behavior researcher and student should begin to realize the importance of accomplishing translation from the laboratory to the application area he is interested in. He can accomplish this only if he understands that learning is a hypothetical construct which may be applied to a variety of situations.

2. An overview of learning-theory development indicated that in this century the explanation of learning has moved from an *S-R* to an *S-O-R* perspective. Another way of stating this is that we have moved from congruity explanations of learning to reinforcement explanations to cognitive explanations. Now all three theoretical streams are represented in social-learning ideas such as the concept of attitude.

3. Learning theory provides a flexible framework for understanding consumer behavior. This framework is Campbell's *behavioral elicitation*

equation, which stems from the learning theory developed by Hull. It was possible in this chapter to review recent social-psychological approaches to learning under the headings of each of the components of the equation [R = f(S, D, K, H)]. Also reviewed were some microtheoretical notions, which are interaction predictions using components of the equation in specific situations. The suggestion of this chapter is that the behavioral elicitation equation can provide a framework or classificatory device within which microtheoretical notions in specific consumer behavior problem areas can be developed.

4. Applications of the learning framework to consumer behavior issues require research procedures that allow observation of consumer learning in a controlled situation. Also necessary are techniques for applying controlled laboratory findings to realistic field settings.

What is on the horizon in terms of the development of learning ideas and their applications? First, it is clear that in social psychology and also in consumer behavior there will be a continual trend toward translation and application of learning ideas in more molar or complex behavior situations. McGuire's (1972) information-processing approach is one example of this trend, as is Bem's (1968, 1972) self-perception approach and Kelley's (1967) attribution-theory analysis. Such molar applications seem to have more promise than direct applications of learning theory and research to laboratory situations such as those by Staats (1965, 1968) and Weiss (1968). Research on social learning is another manifestation of this molar-application trend, as is the sociological research on diffusion, which is reported in other parts of this book.

A second trend that is bound to accelerate in the coming years is a tendency toward an expansion of cognitive intervening variables in learning. This is seen in attitude research in terms of a structuralism and specification of the components of attitude (see Chapter 8). In consumer research this has led to the use of introspective questions asking respondents to report what they were thinking as they viewed advertising or other stimuli. The research of Greenwald (1968), Krugman (1966), and Leavitt (1968), which asks consumers for indication of response rather than a playback of messages, is also representative of this trend. The use of physiological response as one measure in a battery of tests also is an attempt to get at another component of the intervening variables. The recent article entitled "Psychology in the Year 2,000: Going Structural?" by Foa and Turner (1970) underlines the importance and long-run nature of this trend.

A third trend is the increasing rapprochement among *S-R* learning theorists and cognitive approaches to behavior. Although there are still disputes, even in psychology, there are also significant trends toward bringing the areas together. This is seen in consumer behavior in terms of models such as the one developed by Howard and Sheth and in this book's chapters on attitude and on cognitive consistency and novelty seeking. The most likely area for the *S-R* and cognitive ideas to merge in is that of the cyberno-behavioristic models (Maloney, 1968;

Miller, Galanter, and Pribram, 1961; Solley and Murphy, 1960). These models are based on cybernetics and general systems theory and lead toward specifying the links between the components of the behavioral elicitation equation. Another cognitive *S-R* combination is in the instrumentality theories or models that emphasize specific combinations of elements for behavioral prediction. For instance, attitude approaches such as those of Fishbein and Rosenberg come partially out of the cognitive orientation, but are stated in a behavioristic form that is not unlike the components of the behavioral elicitation equation. Again, the advantage of this bringing together of theoretical perspectives is in terms of the possibility of a specific statement of the functional relationships in the elicitation equation.

A fourth trend in the learning area is in terms of mathematical applications. It is no longer appropriate to separate quantitative and behavioral researchers in consumer behavior. A good behavioral researcher must be quantitative. This is illustrated in this book by the strong chapters on stochastic models and economic approaches to consumer behavior. In basic learning research it is represented by the heavy emphasis on mathematics in verbal-learning research. Computer simulation is also a part of this trend, and it is in strong evidence in marketing in the form of consumer behavior models such as that of Amstutz (1967) and Nicosia (1966, 1968).

A final trend that has pervaded this chapter and is critical for the application of learning is the trend toward a process-oriented middle-theory approach. There is less of a tendency today than there was in the past for critical experiments which attempt to differentiate between global theoretical perspectives. As has been mentioned at several points in this chapter, the "theories" that are often listed in psychology are really only a collection of middle-range notions. In consumer behavior this is quite important, because these notions can be applied to specific situations. Indeed, the result of such application of these middle-range notions may be the development of comprehensive theories based on solid empirical evidence. This, of course, is the ultimate trend in any scientific discipline.

REFERENCES

Aaker, D.A., "Setting Advertising Objectives," Working Paper Number 58, Institute of Business and Economic Research, University of California, Berkeley, March, 1970.

Aaker, D.A., and J. Myers, *Advertising Management*. Englewood Cliffs, N. J.: Prentice-Hall, Inc., forthcoming.

Amsel, A., "The Role of Frustrative Nonreward in Continuous Reward Situations," *Psychological Bulletin,* 55 (1958), 102-19.

Amsel, A., "Frustrating Nonreward in Partial Reinforcement and Discrimination Learning," *Psychological Review,* 69 (1962), 306-28.

Amstutz, A. E., *Computer Simulation of Competitive Market Response.* Cambridge, Mass.: MIT Press, 1967.

Anderson, N. H., "Integration Theory and Attitude Change," *Psychological Review,* 78 (1971), 171-206.

Andreasen, A. A., and P.G. Durkson, "Market Learning of New Residents," *Journal of Marketing Research,* 5 (1968), 166-76.

Anonymous, "The Clutter Crisis," *Media Decisions* (December 1971), 42ff.

Appel V., and M.L. Blum, "Ad Recognition and Response Set," *Journal of Advertising Research,* 1 (June 1961), 13-21.

Asch, S. E., "Forming Impressions of Personality," *Journal of Abnormal and Social Psychology,* 41 (1946), 258-90.

Bandura, A., "Social Learning through Imitation," in *Nebraska Symposium on Motivation: 1962, Vol. X,* ed. M. R. Jones. Lincoln, Neb. Univ. of Nebraska Press, 1962, 211-69.

Bandura, A., "Vicarious Processes: A Case of No-Trial Learning," in *Advances in Experimental Social Psychology, Vol. II,* ed. L. Berkowitz. New York: Academic Press 1965, 534-36.

Bandura, A. (ed.), *Psychological Modeling.* Chicago: Aldine Publishing, 1971.

Bandura, A., and R. II. Walters, *Social Learning and Personality Development.* New York: Holt, Rinehart, and Winston, 1963.

Bauer, R. A., "A Revised Model of Source Effects," paper presented at the annual meeting of the American Psychological Association, Chicago, Sept. 1965.

Bekhterev, V. M., "Objective Psychologie oder Psychoreflexologie," *Die Lehre von den Assoziations Reflexen.* Leipzig: Teubner, 1913.

Bem, D. J., "Attitudes as Self Descriptions: Another Look at the Attitude-Behavior Link," in *Psychological Foundations of Attitudes,* eds. A. G. Greenwald, T. C. Brock, and T. M. Ostrom. New York: Academic Press, 1968.

Bem, D. J., "Self-Perception Theory," in *Advances In Experimental Social Psychology; Vol. 6.* ed. L. Berkowitz. New York: Academic Press, 1972, 2-62.

Berger, S.M., and W. W. Lambert, "Stimulus-Response Theory in Contemporary Social Psychology," in *The Handbook of Social Psychology, Vol. I* (2nd ed.) eds. G. Lindzey and E. Aronson. Reading, Mass.: Addison-Wesley, 1968, 81-178.

Berkowitz, L., *Aggression: A Social Psychological Analysis.* New York: McGraw-Hill, 1962.

Berkowitz, L., "Social Motivation," in *The Handbook of Social Psychology, Vol. III* (2nd ed.), eds. G. Lindzey and E. Aronson. Reading, Mass.: Addison-Wesley, 1969, 50-135.

Berkowitz, L., "Sex and Violence: We Can't Have It Both Ways," *Psychology Today,* 5 (December 1971), 14-23.

Berlyne, D. E., *Conflict, Arousal, and Curiosity.* New York: McGraw-Hill, 1960.

Berlyne, D. E., "Arousal and Reinforcement," in *Nebraska Symposium on Motivation, 1967; Vol. XV,* ed. D. Levine. Lincoln, Neb.: University of Nebraska Press, 1967, 1-110.

Berlyne, D. E., "Behavior Theory as Personality Theory," in *Handbook of*

Personality Theory and Research, eds. B. Borgatta and W. W. Lambert. Chicago: Rand-McNally, 1968.

Boyd, H. W., Jr., and W. F. Massy, *Marketing Management.* New York: Harcourt-Brace-Jovanovich, 1972.

Boyd, H. W., Jr., M. L. Ray, and E. C. Strong, "An Attitudinal Framework for Advertising Strategy," *Journal of Marketing,* 36 (1972), 27-33.

Brehm, J. W., *A Theory of Psychological Reactance.* New York: Academic Press, 1966.

Brehm, J. W., and A. R. Cohen, *Explorations in Cognitive Dissonance.* New York: John Wiley, 1962.

Brock, T. C., "Implications of Commodity Theory for Value Change," in *Psychological Foundations of Attitudes,* eds. A. G. Greenwald, T. C. Brock, and T. M. Ostrom. New York: Academic Press, 1968, 243-76.

Brown, G., "Brand Loyalty—Fact or Fiction?" *Advertising Age,* 23 (June 19, June 30, July 14, July 28, August 11, September 1, October 6, December 1, 1952).

Brown, G., "Brand Loyalty—Fact or Fiction?" *Advertising Age,* 24 (January 26, 1953).

Bruner, J.S., "Personality Dynamics and the Process of Perceiving," in *Perception, An Approach to Personality,* eds. R. S. Blake and G. V. Ramsey. New York: Ronald Press, 1951, 121-49.

Bush, R. R., and F. Mosteller, *Stochastic Models for Learning.* New York: Wiley, 1955.

Campbell, D. T., "Conformity in Psychology's Theories of Acquired Behavioral Dispositions." in *Conformity and Deviation,* eds. I.A. Berg and B.M. Bass. New York: Harper, 1961, 94-172.

Campbell, D. T., "Social Attitudes and Other Acquired Behavioral Dispositions," in *Psychology: A Study of a Science, Vol. 6,* ed. S. Koch. New York: McGraw-Hill, 1963, 94-172.

Campbell, D. T., "Lectures in Social Psychology," mimeo. Evanston, Ill.: Northwestern University, 1965.

Cofer, C. N., and M.H. Appley, *Motivation: Theory and Research.* New York: Wiley, 1964.

Colley, R., *Defining Advertising Goals for Measured Advertising Results.* New York: Association of National Advertisers, 1961.

Collins, B.E., "A Learning Theory Interpretation of Conflict-Dissonance," unpublished paper, Northwestern University, 1961.

Day, G.S., "A Two-Dimensional Concept of Brand Loyalty," *Journal of Advertising Research,* 9 (September 1969), 29-36.

Deese, J.E., and S.H. Hulse, *The Psychology of Learning* (3rd ed.). New York: McGraw-Hill, 1967.

Dollard, J., and N.E. Miller, *Personality and Psychotherapy.* New York: McGraw-Hill, 1950.

Duffy, E., *Activation and Behavior.* New York: Wiley, 1962.

Dulaney, D.E., "Awareness Rules and Propositional Control: A Confrontation With S-R Behavior Theory." in *Verbal Behavior And General Behavior*

Theory, eds. D. Horton and T. Dixon. Englewood Cliffs, N. J.: Prentice-Hall, Inc., 1968.

Ebbinghaus, H., *Über das Gedachtnis.* Leipzig: Dunker, 1885. Translation by H. Ruyer and C. E. Bussenius, *Memory.* New York: Teachers College, Columbia University, 1913.

Ebbinghaus, H., *Gründzuge der Psychologie.* Leipzig: Veit & Co., 1902.

Eisenberger, R., "Explanation of Rewards That Do Not Reduce Tissue Needs," *Psychological Bulletin,* 77 (1972), 319-39.

Engel, J.F., D.T. Kollat, and R.D. Blackwell, *Consumer Behavior.* New York: Holt, Rinehart and Winston, 1968.

Engel, J. F. and M. L. Light, "The Role of Psychological Commitment in Consumer Behavior: An Evaluation of the Theory of Cognitive Dissonance," in *Applications of the Sciences in Marketing Management,* eds. F.M. Bass, C.W. King, and E.A. Pessemier. New York: John Wiley, 1968, 179-206.

Estes, W. K., "The Statistical Approach to Learning Theory," in *Psychology: A Study of a Science, Vol. II.* ed. S. Koch. McGraw-Hill, 1959, 380-491.

Estes, W. K., "Reinforcement in Human Learning," Technical Report No. 125, Institute for Mathematical Studies in the Social Sciences, Stanford, Calif., 1967.

Estes, W. K., *Learning Theory and Mental Development.* New York: Academic, 1970.

Ferster, C.S., and B.F. Skinner, *Schedules of Reinforcement.* New York: Appleton-Century-Crofts, 1957.

Feshbach, S., and R.D. Singer, *Television and Aggression.* San Francisco: Jossey-Bass, 1971.

Festinger, L., *A Theory of Cognitive Dissonance.* Evanston, Ill.: Row-Peterson, 1957.

Festinger, L., "Behavioral Support for Opinion Change," *Public Opinion Quarterly,* 28 (1964), 404-17.

Festinger, L., and J.M. Carlsmith, "Cognitive Consequences of Forced Compliance," *Journal of Abnormal and Social Psychology,* 58 (1959), 203-11.

Fishbein, M., *Readings in Attitude Theory and Measurement.* New York: John Wiley, 1967.

Fishbein, M., "The Search for Attitudinal-Behavioral Consistency," in *Behavioral Science Foundations of Consumer Behavior,* ed. J. B. Cohen. New York: The Free Press, 1972, 245-52.

Fiske, D. W., and S. R. Maddi, *Functions of Varied Experience.* Homewood, Ill.: Dorsey, 1961.

Foa, U. G., and J.L. Turner, "Psychology in the Year 2000: Going Structural?" *American Psychologist, 25 (1970),* 244-47.

Griffin, K., "The Contributions of Studies of Source Credibility to a Theory of Interpersonal Trust in the Communication Process," *Psychological Bulletin,* 68 (1967), 104-20.

Greenwald, A.G., "Cognitive Learning, Cognitive Response to Persuasion, and Attitude Change," in *Psychological Foundations of Attitudes.* eds. A.G. Greenwald, T.C. Brock, and T.M. Ostrom. New York: Academic Press, 1968, 147-70.

Guthrie, E.R., *The Psychology of Learning* (rev. ed.). New York: Harper & Row, 1952.

Haskins, J. B., "Factual Recall as a Measure of Advertising Effectiveness," *Journal of Advertising Research,* 4 (March 1964), 2-8.

Heeler, R. M., "A Laboratory Investigation of Inter-related Effects of Mixed Media, Multiple Copy and Multiple Insertions in Advertising Campaigns," unpublished doctoral dissertation, Stanford University, 1972.

Helson, H., *Adaptation-Level Theory.* New York: Harper & Row, 1964.

Hilgard, E. R. and G. H. Bower, *Theories of Learning* (3rd ed.). New York: Appleton-Century-Crofts, 1966.

Hill, W. F., *Learning: A Survey of Psychological Interpretations* (rev. ed.). Scranton, Pa.: Chandler, 1971.

Hintzman, D. L., "Markov Excellence," *Contemporary Psychology,* 16 (1971), 337-39. A review of *Learning, Memory, and Conceptual Processes* by Walter Kintsch (New York: John Wiley, 1970).

Holloway, R. J., "Experimental Work in Marketing: Current Research and New Developments," in *Applications of the Sciences in Marketing Management,* eds. F. M. Bass, C. W. King, and E. A. Pessemier. New York: John Wiley, 1968, 383-431.

Homans, G. C., *Social Behavior: Its Elementary Forms.* New York: Harcourt Brace and World, 1961.

Hovland, C.I., "Reconciling Conflicting Results Derived from Experimental and Survey Studies of Attitude Change," *American Psychologist,* 14 (1959), 8-17.

Hovland, C.I., and I. Janis, (eds.), *Personality and Persuasibility.* New Haven, Conn.: Yale University Press, 1959.

Hovland, C. I., W. Mandell, E.H. Campbell, T. Brock, A.S. Luchins, A. R. Cohen, W. J. McGuire, I. L. Janis, R. L. Feierabend, and N. H. Anderson, *The Order of Presentation in Persuasion.* New Haven, Conn.: Yale University Press, 1957.

Hovland, C. I., and W. Weiss, "The Influence of Source Credibility on Communication Effectiveness," *Public Opinion Quarterly,* 15 (1951), 635-50.

Howard, J. A., *Marketing Theory.* Boston: Allyn and Bacon, 1965.

Howard, J. A., and J. N. Sheth, *The Theory of Buyer Behavior.* New York: John Wiley, 1969.

Hull, C. L., *Principles of Behavior.* New York: Appleton-Century-Crofts, 1943.

Hull, C. L., *A Behavior System: An Introduction to Behavior Theory Concerning the Individual Organism.* New Haven, Conn.: Yale University Press, 1952.

Hull, C. L., C. I. Hovland, R. T. Ross, M. Hall, D. T. Perkins, and F. G. Fitch, *Mathematico-Deductive Theory of Rote Learning.* New Haven, Conn.: Yale University Press, 1940.

Jacoby, J., "A Model of Multi-Brand Loyalty," *Journal of Advertising Research,* 11 (1971a), 25-31.

Jacoby, J., "Brand Loyalty: A Conceptual Definition," *Proceedings,* 79th Annual Convention of the Americal Psychological Association, 1971b, 655-56.

Janis, I. L., "Effects of Fear Arousal on Attitude Change: Recent Developments in Theory and Experimental Research," in *Advances in Experimental Social Psychology; Vol. 3* ed. L. Berkowitz, New York: Academic Press, 1967, 167-224.

Janis, I. L., and S. Feshbach, "Effects of Fear-Arousing Communications," *Journal of Abnormal and Social Psychology,* 48 (1953), 78-92.

Jenkins, W. O., and J. C. Stanley, Jr., "Partial Reinforcement: A Review and Critique," *Psychological Bulletin,* 47 (1950), 193-234.

Jost, A., "Die Assoziationsfestigkeit im ihrer Abhangigkeit von der Verteilung der Wiederholungen," *Zeitsheift für Psychologie,* 14 (1897), 436-72.

Katz, D., "The Functional Approach to the Study of Attitudes," *Public Opinion Quarterly,* 24 (1960), 163-204.

Kelley, H. H., "Attribution Theory in Social Psychology," in *Nebraska Symposium on Motivation, 1967; Vol. 15* ed. D. Levine, Lincoln, Neb.: University of Nebraska Press, 1967.

Kelman, H. C., and C. I. Hovland, "Reinstatement of the Communicator in Delayed Measurement of Opinion Change," *Journal of Abnormal and Social Psychology,* 48 (1953), 327-35.

Kendler, H. H., and J. T. Spence (eds.), *Essays in Neobehaviorism.* New York: Appleton-Century-Crofts, 1971.

Kerpelman, J. P. and S. Himmelfarb, "Partial Reinforcement Effects in Attitude Acquisition and Counterconditioning," *Journal of Personality and Social Psychology,* 19 (1971), 301-5.

Kiesler, C. A., B. E. Collins, and N. Miller, *Attitude Change.* New York: John Wiley, 1969.

Kintsch, W., *Learning, Memory, and Conceptual Processes.* New York: John Wiley, 1970.

Krugman, H. E., "Affective Response to Music as a Function of Familiarity," *Journal of Abnormal and Social Psychology,* 3 (1943), 388-92.

Krugman, H. E., "An Application of Learning Theory to TV Copy Testing," *Public Opinion Quarterly,* 26 (1962), 626-34.

Krugman, H. E., "The Impact of Television Advertising: Learning without Involvement," *Public Opinion Quarterly,* 29 (1965), 349-56.

Krugman, H. E., "The Measurement of Advertising Involvement," *Public Opinion Quarterly,* 30 (1967), 583-96.

Krugman, H. E., and E. L. Hartley, "The Learning of Tastes," *Public Opinion Quarterly,* 24 (1960), 621-31.

Lacey, J. I., "Somatic Response Patterning and Stress: Some Revisions of Activation Theory," in *Psychological Stress.* eds. M. H. Appley and R. Trumbull. New York: Appleton-Century Crofts, 1967, 14-42.

Lana, R. E., "Existing Familiarity and Order of Presentation of Persuasive Communications," *Psychological Reports,* 15 (1964), 607-10.

Lavidge, R., and G. A. Steiner, "A Model for Predictive Measurements of Advertising Effectiveness," *Journal of Marketing,* 25 (1961), 59-62.

Lawrence, D. H., and L. Festinger, *Deterrents and Reinforcement: The Psychology of Insufficient Reward.* Stanford, Calif.: Stanford University Press, 1962.

Leavitt, C., "Response Structure: A Determinant of Recall," *Journal of Advertising Research,* 8 (September 1968), 3-8.

Levine, R. A., and D. T. Campbell, *Ethnocentrism: Theories of Conflict, Ethnic Attitudes, and Group Behavior.* New York: John Wiley, 1971.

Lewis, D. J., "Partial Reinforcement: A Selective Review of the Literature since 1950," *Psychological Bulletin,* 57 (1960), 1-28.

Lindsley, O., "A Behavioral Measure of Television Viewing," *Journal of Advertising Research,* 2 (September 1962), 2-12.

Lucas, D. B., "The ABC's of ARF's PARM," *Journal of Marketing,* 25 (1960), 9-20.

Lucas, D. B., and S. H. Britt, *Measuring Advertising Effectiveness.* New York: McGraw-Hill, 1963.

Luchins, A. S., "Experimental Attempts to Minimize the Impact of First Impressions," in C. I. Hovland *et al., The Order of Presentation in Persuasion.* New Haven, Conn.: Yale University Press, 1957.

Luh, C. W., "The Conditions of Retention," *Psychological Monographs,* 142, (1922).

Lund, F. H., "The Psychology of Belief: IV. The Law of Primacy in Persuasion," *Journal of Abnormal and Social Psychology,* 20 (1925), 183-91.

Maloney, J. C., "Curiosity Versus Disbelief in Advertising," *Journal of Advertising Research,* 2 (June 1962), 2-8.

Maloney, J. C., "Is Advertising Believability Really Important?" *Journal of Marketing,* 27 (1963), 1-8.

Maloney, J. C., "Man as an Economic Subsystem," unpublished paper, Medill School of Journalism, Evanston, Ill., 1968.

Maltzman, I., and D. S. Raskin, "Effects of Individual Differences in the Orienting Reflex on Conditioning and Complex Responses," *Journal of Experimental Research in Personality,* 1 (1965), 1-16.

Maneloveg, H. D., "Television Isn't Alone in Commercial Clutter—Magazines, Newspapers Have It, Too," *Advertising Age,* 42 (October 11, 1971), 47.

McCrary, J. W., Jr., and W. S. Hunter, "Serial Position Curves in Verbal Learning," *Science,* 117 (1953), 131-34.

McGuire, W. J., *Effectiveness of Fear Appeals in Advertising.* New York: Advertising Research Foundation, 1963.

McGuire, W. J., "Inducing Resistance to Persuasion: Some Contemporary Approaches," in *Advances in Experimental Social Psychology, Vol. 1,* ed. L. Berkowitz. New York: Academic Press, 1964, 191-229.

McGuire, W. J., "Personality and Attitude Change: An Information-Processing Theory," in *Psychological Foundations of Attitudes,* eds. A. G. Greenwald, T. C. Brock and T. M. Ostrom. New York: Academic Press, 1968, 171-96.

McGuire, W. J., "The Nature of Attitudes and Attitude Change," in *The Handbook of Social Psychology, Vol. 3* (2nd ed.), eds. G. Lindzey and E. Aronson. Reading, Mass.: Addison-Wesley, 1969.

McGuire, W. J., "An Information Processing Model of Advertising Effectiveness," in *The Behavioral and Management Sciences in Marketing,* eds. H. Davis and A. J. Silk. New York: The Ronald Press, 1973.

McNiven, M. A., (ed.), *How Much to Spend for Advertising? Methods for Determining Advertising Expenditure Levels.* New York: Association of National Advertisers, 1969.

Millenson, J. R., "An Isomorphism between Stimulus-Response Notation and Information-Processing Flow Diagrams," *Psychological Record,* 17 (1967), 305-19.

Miller, G. A., E. Galanter, and K. H. Pribram, *Plans and the Structure of Behavior.* New York: Holt, Rinehart, and Winston, 1960.

Miller, N. and D. T. Campbell, "Recency and Primacy in Persuasion as a Function of the Timing of Speeches and Measurements," *Journal of Abnormal and Social Psychology,* 59 (1959), 1-9.

Miller, N. E., "Experimental Studies in Conflict," in *Personality and the Behavior Disorders,* ed. J. McV. Hunt. New York: Ronald Press, 1944, 431-65.

Miller, N. E., "Experiments on Motivation: Studies Combining Psychological, Physiological, and Pharmacological Techniques," *Science,* 126 (1957), 1271-78.

Miller, N. E., "Extensions of Liberalized S-R Theory," in *Psychology: A Study of a Science; Vol. 2,* ed. S. Koch. New York: McGraw-Hill, 1969, 196-292.

Miller, N. E., and J. Dollard, *Social Learning and Imitation.* New Haven, Conn.: Yale University Press, 1941.

Mitchell, T. R., and A. Biglan, "Instrumentality Theories: Current Uses in Psychology," *Psychological Bulletin,* 76 (1971), 432-53.

Morris, C. W., *Signification and Significance.* Cambridge, Mass.: MIT Press, 1964.

Mowrer, O. H., *Learning Theory and Behavior.* New York: John Wiley, 1960.

Mowrer, O. H., and H. M. Jones, "Habit Strength as a Function of Pattern of Reinforcement," *Journal of Experimental Psychology,* 35 (1945), 293-311.

Myers, J. G., *Consumer Image and Attitude.* Berkeley, Calif.: Institute of Business and Economic Research, University of California, 1968.

Myers, J. H., and W. H. Reynolds, *Consumer Behavior and Marketing Management.* Boston: Houghton-Mifflin, 1967.

Nicosia, F. M., *Consumer Decision Processes: Marketing and Advertising Implications.* Englewood Cliffs, N. J.: Prentice-Hall, Inc., 1966.

Nicosia, F. M., "Advertising Management, Consumer Behavior, and Simulation," *Journal of Advertising Research,* 8 (March 1968), 29-38.

O'Day, E. F., *Programmed Instruction: Techniques and Trends.* New York: Appleton-Century-Crofts, 1971.

Orne, M., "On the Social Psychology of the Psychological Experiment: With Particular Reference to Demand Characteristics and Their Implications," *American Psychologist,* 17 (1962), 776-83.

Osgood, C. E., and P. H. Tannenbaum, "The Principle of Congruity in the Prediction of Attitude Change," *Psychological Review,* 62 (1955), 42-55.

Palda, K. S., "The Hypothesis of a Hierarchy of Effects: A Partial Evaluation," *Journal of Marketing Research,* 3 (1966), 13-24.

Pavlov, I. P., *Conditioned Reflexes.* London: Oxford University Press, 1927.

Pavlov, I. P., trans. W. H. Gantt *Lectures on Conditioned Reflexes.* New York: International, 1928.

Peckham, J. O. "Can We Relate Advertising Dollars to Market Share Objectives?" *Proceedings of the 12th Annual Conference of the Advertising Research Foundation.* New York: ARF, 1966, 53-58.

Postman, L., "Toward a General Theory of Cognition," in *Social Psychology at the Crossroads,* eds. J. H. Rohrer and M. Sherif. New York: Harper and Row, 1951, 242-72.

Postman, L., "Repetition and Paired-Associate Learning," *American Journal of Psychology,* 75 (1962), 372-89.

Premack, D., "Reversibility of the Reinforcement Relation." *Science,* 136 (1962), 255-57.

Ray, M. L., "Pupil Dilation and Other Physiological Measures of Advertising Effect," *Report 5502-B-65-8,* Chicago: Foote, Cone and Belding, 1965.

Ray, M. L., *The Effect of Choice, Controversy and Selectivity on the Effectiveness of Various Defenses to Persuasion,* unpublished doctoral dissertation, Northwestern University, 1967.

Ray, M. L., "The Refutational Approach to Advertising," mimeo, Advertising Division, Association for Education in Journalism Meetings, 1967.

Ray, M. L., "Biases in Selection of Messages Designed to Induce Resistance to Persuasion," *Journal of Personality and Social Psychology,* 9 (1968), 335-39.

Ray, M. L., "Can Order Effect in Copy Tests Be Used as an Indicator of Long Term Advertising Effect?" *Journal of Advertising Research,* 9 (March 1969a), 45-52.

Ray, M. L., "Predicting Repetitive Effects of Advertising on the Basis of Laboratory Results," paper presented to the Institute for Management Sciences Tenth American Meeting, October 1969b.

Ray, M. L., "A Behavioral-Laboratory-Model-Field Study of Alternate Message Strategies in Competitive Advertising Situations," *Research Paper No. 83,* Graduate School of Business, Stanford University, 1972a.

Ray, M. L., "Prospects for Management-Behavioral Science Interaction in Media Modeling." in *Evaluating Current Developments in Advertising.* ed. S. A. Greyser. Champaign, Ill.: University of Illinois Press, 1972b.

Ray, M. L., "The Present and Potential Linkages between the Microtheoretical Notions of Behavioral Science and the Problems of Advertising," in *The Behavioral and Management Sciences in Marketing,* ed. H. Davis and A. Silk. New York: Ronald Press, 1973.

Ray, M. L., and R. H. Heeler, "The Use of the Multitrait-Multimethod Matrix for the Trait Development: Cluster Analysis and Nonmetric Scaling Alternatives," *Research Paper No. 10,* Graduate School of Business, Stanford University, 1971.

Ray, M. L., and A. G. Sawyer, "Repetition in Media Models: A Laboratory Technique," *Journal of Marketing Research,* 8 (February 1971a), 20-30.

Ray, M. L., and A. G. Sawyer, "Behavioral Measurement for Marketing Models," *Management Science,* Part II, 18 (December 1971b), 73-89.

Ray, M. L., A. G. Sawyer, and E. C. Strong, "Frequency Effects Revisited," *Journal of Advertising Research,* 11 (February 1971), 14-20.

Ray M. L., and W. L. Wilkie, "Fear: The Potential of an Appeal Neglected by Marketing," *Journal of Marketing,* 34 (January 1970), 54-62.

Reed, J. B., "Physiological Measures of Recall of Advertising," unpublished paper, Graduate School of Business, Stanford University, 1972.

Robbins, D., "Partial Reinforcement: A Selective Review of the Alleyway Literature since 1960," *Psychological Bulletin,* 76 (1971), 415-31.

Rodgers, R. W., and D. L. Thistlethwaite, "An Analysis of Active and Passive Defenses in Inducing Resistance to Persuasion," *Journal of Personality and Social Psychology,* 11 (1969), 301-8.

Rosenberg, M. J., "Cognitive Structure and Attitudinal Affect," *Journal of Abnormal and Social Psychology,* 3 (1956), 367-72.

Rosnow, R. L., "A 'Spread of Effect' in Attitude Formation," in *Psychological Foundations of Attitudes,* New York: Academic Press, 1968, 89-107.

Rothschild, M. L., "Two Types of Involvement: A Microtheoretical Notion," unpublished paper, Graduate School of Business, Stanford University, 1972.

Sawyer A. G., "A Laboratory Experimental Investigation of the Effects of Repetition of Advertising," unpublished doctoral dissertation, Stanford University, 1971.

Sawyer, A. G., "Laboratory Experiments about the Effect of Repetition: A Critical Review and Some New Findings," unpublished paper presented to the ACR-AMA Workshop on Consumer Information Processing, University of Chicago, November 2, 1972.

Schachter, S., "The Interaction of Cognitive and Physiological Determinants of Emotional State," in *Advances in Experimental Social Psychology; Vol. I,* ed. L. Berkowitz. New York: Academic Press, 1964, 49-81.

Schachter, S. and J. Singer, "Cognitive, Social, and Physiological Determinants of Emotional State," *Psychological Review,* 69 (1962), 379-99.

Schonpflug, W. P., "Behaltensdauer and Aftivierung," *Psychologie Forschung,* 29 (1966), 132-48.

Scott, W. A., "Attitude Measures," in *The Handbook of Social Psychology, Vol. II* (2nd ed.), eds. G. Lindzey and E. Aronson. Cambridge, Mass.: Addison-Wesley, 1968.

Shapiro, D., and A. Crider, "Psychophysiological Approaches in Social Psychology," in *The Handbook of Social Psychology, Vol. III* (2nd ed.), eds. G. Lindzey and E. Aronson. Reading, Mass.: Addison-Wesley, 1969, 1-49.

Shebilske, W., and S. M. Ebenholtz, "Ebbinghaus' Derived-List Experiments Reconsidered," *Psychological Review,* 78 (1971), 553-55.

Shepard, R. N., "Recognition Memory for Words, Sentences, and Pictures," *Journal of Verbal Learning and Verbal Behavior,* 6 (1967), 156-63.

Sherif, C. W., M. Sherif, and R. E. Nebergall, *Attitude and Attitude Change: The Social Judgment-Involvement Approach.* Philadelphia: Saunders, 1965.

Sherif, M., *The Psychology of Social Norms.* New York: Harper and Row, 1936.

Sherif, M., *Social Interaction, Process and Products: Selected Essays.* Chicago: Aldine Publishing, 1967.

Sherif, M., and C. I. Hovland, *Social Judgment: Assimilation and Contrast Effects in Communication and Attitude Change.* New Haven, Conn.: Yale University Press, 1961.

Sherif, M., and C. W. Sherif, "Attitude as the Individual's Own Categories: The Social Judgment-Involvement Approach to Attitude and Attitude Change," in *Attitude, Ego-Involvement and Change,* eds. C. W. Sherif and M. Sherif. New York: John Wiley, 1967, 105-39.

Sheth, J. N., "How Adults Learn Brand Preference," *Journal of Advertising Research,* 8 (September 1968), 25-36.

Skinner, B. F., *Walden Two.* New York: Macmillan, 1948.

Skinner, B. F., "Teaching Machines," *Scientific American,* 205 (1961), 90-102.

Skinner, B. F., "Contingencies of Reinforcement in the Design of a Culture," *Behavioral Science,* (1966), 159-66.

Skinner, B. F., *Beyond Freedom and Dignity.* New York: Alfred A. Knopf, 1971.

Smith, C., "Frustration as a Surrogate to Segment the Black Market," unpublished paper, Graduate School of Business, Stanford University, 1972.

Solley, C. M., and G. Murphy, *Development of the Perceptual World.* New York: Basic Books, 1960.

Spence, K. W., *Behavior Theory and Conditioning.* New Haven, Conn.: Yale University Press, 1956.

Spence, K. W., *Behavior Theory and Learning: Selected Papers.* Englewood Cliffs, N.J.: Prentice-Hall, Inc., 1960.

Staats, A. W., "A Case in and a Strategy for the Extension of Learning Principles to the Problems of Human Behavior," in *Research in Behavior Modification,* eds. L. Krasner and L. P. Ullman. New York: Holt, 1965, 121-44.

Staats, A. W., "Social Behaviorism and Human Motivation: Principles of the Attitude-Reinforcer-Discriminative System," in *Psychological Foundations of Attitudes,* eds. A. C. Greenwald, T. C. Brock, and T. M. Ostrom. New York: Academic Press, 1968, 33-66.

Stefflre, V. J., "Market Structure Studies: New Products for Old Markets and New Markets (Foreign) for Old Products," in *Application of the Sciences in Marketing Management,* eds. F. M. Bass, C. W. King, and E. A. Pessemeir. New York: John Wiley, 1968.

Stevens, S. S., "Measurement, Statistics, and the Schemapiric View," *Science,* 161 (1968), 849-56.

Strong, E. C., "The Effects of Repetition in Advertising: A Field Experiment," unpublished doctoral dissertation, Stanford University, 1972.

Suedfeld, P., Y. M. Epstein, E. Buchanan, and P. B. Landon, "Effects of Set on the 'Effects of Mere Exposure'" *Journal of Personality and Social Psychology,* 17 (1971), 121-23.

Suppes, P., "Stimulus-Response Theory of Finite Automata," *Journal of Mathematical Psychology,* 6 (1969), 327-55.

Tannenbaum, P. H., "The Congruity Principle Revisited: Studies in the Reduction, Induction, and Generalization of Persuasion." in *Advances in Experimental Social Psychology; Vol. 3,* ed. L. Berkowitz. New York: Academic Press, 1967.

Thorndike, E. L., "Animal Intelligence: An Experimental Study of the Associative Process in Animals," *Psychological Review,* monograph supplement, 2 (1898).

Thorndike, E. L., *Animal Intelligence.* New York: Macmillan, 1911.

Tolman, E. C., *Purposive Behavior in Animals and Men.* New York: Appleton-Century-Crofts, 1932.

Triandis, H. C., *Attitude and Attitude Change.* New York: John Wiley, 1971.

Underwood, B. J., *Psychological Research.* New York: Appleton-Century-Crofts, 1957a.

Underwood, B. J., "Interference and Forgetting," *Psychological Review,* 64 (1957b), 49-60.

Vroom, V. H., *Work and Motivation.* New York: John Wiley, 1964.

Watson, J. B., "The Unverbalized in Human Behavior," *Psychological Review,* 31 (1924), 273-80.

Watson, R. I., *The Great Psychologists from Aristotle to Freud* (2nd ed.). Philadelphia: Lippincott, 1968.

Webb, P., "Mis-identification of Brand Names from Advertising," unpublished paper, Graduate School of Business, Stanford University, 1971.

Webb, P., "Advertising Mis-identification and Evoked Set," unpublished paper, Graduate School of Business, Stanford University, 1972.

Weinberg, R. S., "Sales and Advertising of Cigarettes," *Report of the Third Meeting of the Operations Research Discussion Group.* New York: Advertising Research Foundation, 1960.

Weiss, R. F., "An Extension of Hullian Learning Theory to Persuasive Communication," in *Psychological Foundations of Attitudes,* eds. A. G. Greenwald, T. C. Brock, and T. M. Ostrom. New York: Academic Press, 1968, 109-45.

Wells, W. D., "Recognition, Recall and Rating Scales," *Journal of Advertising Research,* 4 (September 1964), 2-8.

Winters, L. C., and W. H. Wallace, "On Operant Conditioning Techniques," *Journal of Advertising Research,* 10 (October 1970), 39-45.

Wolpe, J., *The Practice of Behavior Therapy.* New York: Pergamon Press, 1969.

Yerkes, R. M., and J.D. Dodson, "The Relation of Strength of Stimulus to Habit Formation," *Journal of Comparative Psychology,* 18 (1908), 459-82.

Zajonc, R. B., "Attitudinal Effects of Mere Exposure," *Journal of Personality and Social Psychology,* monograph supplement, 9 (1968).

Zajonc, R. B., and D. W. Rejecki, "Exposure and Affect: A Field Experiment," *Psychonomic Science,* 17 (1969), 216-17.

Zajonc, R. B., W. C. Swap, A. A. Harrison, and P. Roberts, "Limiting Conditions of Exposure Effect: Satiation and Relativity," *Journal of Personality and Social Psychology,* 18 (1971), 384-91.

Zielski, H. A., "The Remembering and Forgetting of Advertising," *Journal of Marketing,* 23 (1959), 239-43.

Zimbardo, P. G., M. Weisenberg, I. Firestone, and B. Levy, "Communicator Effectiveness in Producing Public Conformity and Private Attitude Change," *Journal of Personality,* 33 (1965), 233-56.

3

Field Theory in
Consumer Behavior

Harold H. Kassarjian
University of California, Los Angeles

FIELD THEORETICAL APPROACH
   Constructive Method. Ahistorical Approach.
CONSTRUCTS
   Life Space. Differentiation of the Environment. Differentiation of the Person.
DYNAMIC CONCEPTS
   Tension. Energy. Valence. Force.
SUMMARY
CONCLUSIONS
REFERENCES

The field of consumer behavior, since its emergence from the amorphous mass of social science, economics, mathematics, and marketing, has been searching for theories adaptable to its unique subset of human behavior. We have turned from the simple elegance of utility theory in economics to psychoanalytic theory, from experimental psychology to cultural anthropology, from deterministic points of view to stochastic models. This chapter discusses Lewinian field theory from a consumer behavior perspective. The first part sets the historical stage for the emergence of field theory and later parts describe the foundations and constructs of the formulations.

Just as the past two decades have been exciting times in the field of consumer behavior with new experiments, new data, and new hypotheses and models being developed, so too the later part of the nineteenth century was a particularly exciting time in physics. New ideas were being introduced into the physical sciences, which altered the prevailing scientific conceptions and served as a model for new conceptions in the biological and social sciences, and, years later, were to significantly influence thought in marketing and consumer behavior.

As Deutsch has pointed out, the systematic relationships of these ideas—contributions of such men as Faraday, Maxwell, and Hertz—became known as *field theory.* "Newtonian mechanics had asserted that it was possible to explain physical phenomena by assuming that simple forces acted between unalterable particles. Here if one knew the mass, the velocity, the direction, the location, and so forth, of material particles, one could accurately predict what would occur when a number of them interacted." Brilliant theorizing and ingenious experimenting by these field theorists demonstrated that it is useful to think not of simple forces acting on particles in empty space, but of regions or fields through which electromagnetic forces are spread, and to assume that these forces exist when there are no material particles present to which the forces are applied. It was concluded that a knowledge of the properties of the electromagnetic field is sufficient to explain electromagnetic phenomena, and that, given this information, knowledge about the source of the electromagnetic field is unnecessary. In other words, the field has a reality independent of the individual particles (Deutsch (1968), p. 412-13).

This work,[1] culminating in Einstein's theory of gravitation and powerful theory of relativity in the early twentieth century, had an important impact on psychological thought, leading to the Gestalt movement initiated by Wertheimer, Kohler, and Koffka. "The chief tenet of Gestalt psychology was that the way in which an object is perceived is determined by the total context or configuration [or field] in which [the] object is embedded. Relationships among components of a perceptual field rather than the fixed characteristics of the individual components determine perception" (Hall and Lindzey, 1957, p. 206). In other words, parts or elements do not exist in isolation but are perceptually organized into units or wholes. When we look at an automobile, we do not see glass and steel and plastic and bolts and paint. We see instead an organized whole—an automobile. And perhaps not even just an automobile but also comfortable transportation, prestige, status, and a symbolic sense of achievement. This is the familiar Gestalt dictum: the whole is different from, if not greater than, the sum of the isolated parts. The integration of the parts is determined by various principles of organization such that the best Gestalt or figure is perceived under the given conditions (Shaw and Costanzo, 1970).

Associated with the Gestalt psychologists in Berlin at the time of World War I was a theoretician and researcher—Kurt Lewin—who was later to be acknowledged as perhaps the most brilliant figure in recent psychological history and thought. It would be rather difficult to overestimate Lewin's contributions to social psychology and, through psychology, his impact on consumer behavior.[2] His influence permeates consumer behavior, ranging from studies on group

---

[1] A brief history of field theory in physics can be found in Williams (1966).

[2] Perhaps a sampling of his doctoral students and colleagues on whom his trademark appears will give a flavoring of his impact: Fritz Heider, Bluma Zeigarnik, Chris Argyris, Alex Bavalas, Warren Bennis, Dorwin Cartwright, Mason Haire, John R. P. French, Harold H. Kelley, Morton Deutsch, Leon Festinger, Alvin F. Zander, Robert R. Sears, Eric Trist, John W. Thibaut, Rensis Likert, Ronald Lippitt, Donald W. MacKinnon, David Krech, Alfred H. Marrow, Kenneth Benne, Claire Selltiz, and Stanley Schacter, among others (Marrow, 1969).

dynamics to attitudes, from cognitive organization to balance theories, from racial prejudice to food-eating habits.[3]

The basic characteristics of Lewin's field theory are as follows:

1. Behavior is a function of the field that exists at the time the behavior occurs.

2. The field is defined as the totality of coexisting facts, including both the person and his psychological environment, all of which are mutually inter-dependent. Every specific instance of behavior (say, a change of attitude about a product or the purchase of a refrigerator) must be viewed as the result of the interaction and integration of a variety of influences or forces impinging upon the person. The description of behavior cannot concentrate exclusively on one or another of the variables involved. In other words, such variables as advertising, influence of the salesman, learning, personality, social influence, politics, or economics cannot be studied independently from each other, without great peril, if one is attempting to describe consumer behavior.

3. Analysis must begin with the situation as a whole from which the component parts can be differentiated. Instead of beginning with a study of the isolated elements, say, in a purchase decision, one must first begin with a description of the situation as a whole. Only then is it possible to examine the specific elements and the interactions among the elements.

FIELD THEORETICAL APPROACH

Constructive Method

Before proceeding with the theory, several basic foundations must be discussed. Field theory is constructive in logic rather than classificatory. The classificatory approach, rampant in marketing and consumer behavior, has as a basic assumption that somehow by collecting data on the aggregate we shall understand the consumer and his actions. From aggregated data we distill valueless concepts, such as the "typical Mustang buyer," "normal person," "average child," and "middle-class TV viewer." Generalizations from individual consumers lead to concepts about, say, housewives in a given socioeconomic class and to female consumers in general. However, using such an approach there is no logical way back from the concept "lower-class female consumer" to the

---

[3]In the marketing literature Lewin was perhaps first introduced by Clawson (1950) and W. F. Brown (1950). Bilkey (1951, 1953, 1955, 1957) has been the first marketer that has attempted to provide research data. Howard and Sheth (1969) have incorporated some field theoretical principles in their approach to consumer behavior, and several other authors have made a passing reference to Lewin's work.

individual (Lewin, 1951). Hence one resorts to statistics and probability. Perhaps it was fortunate for the development of the physical sciences that modern statistics were not available to Galileo and Newton. Seldom do the physical sciences resort to statistics, since it is generally not the purpose of laws to summarize the distribution of observed events (Deutsch, 1954). Laws cannot be developed by generalizing from molecular data. In other words, in studying some event or act, say, purchase behavior, one cannot study the isolated parts such as price, personality, reference groups, frequency of purchase, or political conditions, separately in the expectation that it will eventually be possible to reconstruct the whole by adding together the parts (Jacques, 1948). To understand the entire event one must study the whole problem, then by continuous experimentation and logical manipulation the parts of the whole can be differentiated and placed in correct relationship with each other.

If one studies the effect on early American style furniture of price, the influence of the retail outlet, pressures exerted by children in a family decision, and the personal influence of neighbors, and hence develops abstractions and generalizations, these individual parts cannot be put together to describe or predict why any individual person made the purchase he did. What is lost is the interrelationship of the parts, the interactions and confounding of one influence with the other. Hence, a field theoretical approach represents a level of analysis that attempts to transform the language of data into a language of constructs or genotypes; a mode of analysis that starts with the entire behavior pattern and attempts to extract the relevant relationships, rather than first studying the individual parts and from them futilely attempting to reconstruct the purchase act. Laws cannot be developed by classification and aggregation based on phenotypic characteristics—the observable properties. With a constructive logic, laws are not based on phenotypic characteristics, such as hair color or social class, but rather on the underlying genotypic properties.

For example, the same genotypic physical laws govern the course of the stars, the falling of stones, and the flight of supersonic jets. Physics does not require a separate law for falling rocks, pebbles, apples, and lower-class female consumers. The law of falling bodies, $s = \frac{1}{2}gt^2$, applies to stars, baseballs, and dead butterflies, irrespective of their observable phenotypic differences. Furthermore, behavior is not explained or understood by resorting to statistical or historical analysis. The law does not state that the relationship holds regularly or frequently, 60 percent of the time, or even at the 0.05 level of statistical confidence. And, in fact, outside of theory, the relationship can never be observed on earth and can only be approximated under the most carefully constructed and artificially controlled conditions. The law is not determined historically by historical actuary, or by counting and empirically measuring falling apples to see what percentage behave according to hypothesis and what percentage do not. In short, the falling of all bodies is determined by genotypic relationships—the fortuitousness of the individual case is not undertermined, random, chance, or an exception to the data to be ignored.[4]

Ahistorical Approach

A second basic foundation of a field theoretical orientation to consumer behavior is its emphasis on an ahistorical approach. Only the facts that exist in the present can directly affect present events. Since consumer behavior depends upon the forces and influences acting upon the individual at a given moment in time, the moment the behavior itself occurs, past events and future events that do not exist in the present cannot affect his behavior. The relationship of the past to the present is so indirect that its explanatory value is slight (Hilgard, 1956). This is not to completely deny the effect of previous experiences in the behavior of the consumer, but rather to keep it in perspective. Only the directly relevant facts from previous behavior that exert an influence on the present are to be considered, rather than childhood experiences and frustrations as used by the motivation researcher, the personality development of the neo-Freudian, or number of previous trials for the learning theorist or Markov analyst. Furthermore, future events, aspirations, and expectations, as they are relevant and represented in the present, are accounted for by field theory, concepts difficult to deal with in many of the other theoretical approaches to consumer behavior. Thus consumer behavior must be explained in terms of the properties that exist at the time the event occurs.

In short, behavior must be analyzed in terms of the field at the time the behavior occurs. The approach must be systematic rather than historical in nature. This is one of the major distinctions between theories based upon the Gestalt orientation and those derived from learning theory or the psychoanalytic viewpoint. Field theory asserts that it does not matter how the situation came to be the way it is at the present time; it has the same effect on behavior regardless of its historical antecedents (Shaw and Costanzo, 1970).[5]

[4]In the opinion of the author this is the core of what Tucker is trying to tell us in his insightful, and perhaps most misunderstood book, *Foundations for a Theory of Consumer Behavior* (1967). A theory of consumer behavior must be able to explain in similar terms the purchase of furniture by one family, the purchase of a swimming pool by another, a shirt by a peasant, or the acquisition of a peach-faced parrot or new Volkswagen. One must not ask if the purchasing behavior of a specific family is common to all families or 60 percent of the families, or what proportion of the previous purchases of children's bedroom furniture consisted of early American maple from a particular retail outlet? One must not claim that these are random events, single instances that need not concern the consumer behavior theorist, any more than one may claim that the rate of fall of a fortuitous meteor is not related to the laws of astronomy.

[5]As a final foundation of field theory, it should be pointed out that Lewin emphasized the need to mathematize the theoretical structure in order to quantify the theory. The first attempt was to apply topological geometry modified somewhat by vector and scalar

CONSTRUCTS

Life Space

The most important of the Lewinian hypothetical constructs is that of the *life space* or psychological field. All behavior—consuming, purchasing, thinking, laughing, crying—is a function of the life space, which in turn consists of the total manifold of "facts" (all the influences) that psychologically exist for an individual at a given moment in time. The life space is the totality of the individual's world as he himself perceives it; it is the individual's perception of reality, the totality of possible events (Lewin, 1936).

The life space includes all things that have existence and excludes those things which do not have existence. For Lewin, a thing exists if it has demonstrable effects. It is the task of the consumer researcher to devise methods for determining specifically what things exist for any given individual, and hence represent the life space, and to finally develop genotypic laws concerning the properties of the life space. For example, a person's needs, aspirations, goals, a nagging roommate, and a pair of ripped trousers may exist in the life space. Just as clearly the wholesale price of sugarcane in the Philippines, of which he is unaware and unconcerned, may not exist in his life space, and hence cannot influence his behavior. The latter "fact" is in the *foreign hull* outside the boundaries of his life space. It may be, however, that the price of sugarcane is in fact so seriously depressed in the Philippines that it may financially pressure a Filipino girl friend to return home. Once made aware of the price of sugarcane and its relevance to him, that "fact" has now entered his life space and hence can be most influential for his behavior—say, by finding a new partner or even traveling across the Pacific himself.

The individual himself, of course, is represented in the life space (see Figure 1). The person is one of the differentiated regions in a dynamic interrelationship with the environment or remainder of the life space. The environment, in turn, does not refer to the objective world or physical stimuli, but rather is the psychological world as it exists for the individual under study. It contains only those facts which exist for him at a given point in time, somewhat analogous to a phenomenological field, although unconscious determinants of behavior are not excluded (Cartwright, 1959). In turn, behavior is a function of the properties within the life space. For behavior to occur, some change within the life space must occur. A change in the geographic world or "objective" environment, such as a change in package design, color of label, price, or physical characteristics of a consumer product, that is not represented by a change in the psychological field of the consumer cannot lead to a behavior change.

---

mathematics (Lewin, 1938). The contributions of J. F. Brown (1936a, 1936b) and the introduction of graph theory by Harary and Norman (1953) indicate the potential for the use of mathematics in a field theoretical approach both on a theoretical and applied plane.

FIGURE 1. **Life Space**

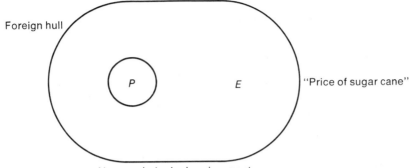

P (person) $+$ E (environment) $=$ l S (life space)
B (behavior) $=$ f (LS)

Differentiation of the Environment

An undifferentiated environment would be one in which all the facts are equally influential and there are no barriers to impede movement. Obviously, such a state of affairs does not represent reality. The environment must be subdivided into regions. The life space of the newborn child may be described as a field that has relatively few and only vaguely distinguishable areas, perhaps only greater or lesser comfort. No definite representations of objects or persons exist, future events or aspirations do not exist, nor even an area that can be called "my own body." The child is ruled by the situation immediately at hand; he has no conception of past experiences or future expectations. As he grows, there is an increased differentiation within this life space. Areas such as his own body, his mother, edible food, and nonedible objects can be distinguished.[6] Included also is a differentiation of the time dimension as plans extend farther into the future and activities of increasingly longer duration are cognitively organized as one unit. A mature adult can differentiate between brands of products, two models of an automobile, or two candidates within the same political party.

The various differentiated regions, however, are not equally accessible to the person. The boundaries of the region may from time to time become more or less permeable and may act as a barrier to locomotion into the region. To the child the region representing his mother may be easily accessible at all times, roller skating with much older children may be a less permeable region, and purchasing a bottle of Scotch may represent an impermeable area.

For example, let us consider in Figure 2 the conceivable life space of a mother and child in a supermarket. The psychological environment of the child consists of his mother, a cart, a Coca-Cola vending machine of which he is

---

[6]Kurt Lewin, "Behavior as a Function of the Total Situation," in Lewin (1951).

FIGURE 2.   Life Space (Shopping in a Supermarket)

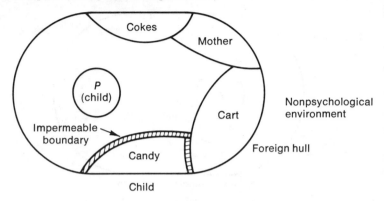

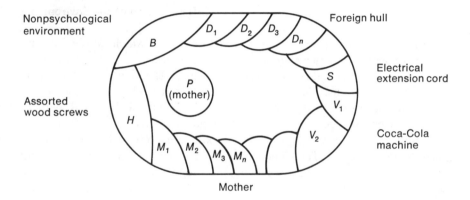

$D_{1,2,3,\ldots,n}$	= brands of soft drinks
$V_{1,2}$	= vegetables
$M_{1,2,3,\ldots,n}$	= cuts of meat
H	= husband's preferences
B	= beliefs about what would impress guests Saturday night
S	= brand of detergent

particularly fond, and perhaps some candy. Candy, however, is represented by an impermeable boundary. He knows he cannot have any. The life space of his mother is far more differentiated. It consists of various brands of bottled soft drinks, varieties of fresh and frozen vegetables, cuts of meats, paper goods, cereals, and a variety of other products with which she is involved. Perhaps a point-of-purchase display has introduced into her life space a brand of detergent. Also relevant in her psychological world are her husband's particular brand preferences or idiosyncratic dislikes, and beliefs about what would impress her guests Saturday night. However, other items exist within the nonpsychological foreign hull that are not represented in her life space—small packages of assorted wood screws, several types of electrical extension cords, and a Coca-Cola vending machine. Things not in the life space, such as the available assortment of wood screws, the price of sugarcane in the Philippines, or an unknown neighbor's dislike of canned meat, cannot influence her behavior.

Not only are regions within the life space more or less permeable, but the boundaries of the life space itself may from time to time become more or less permeable. An impermeable life-space boundary indicates that the person is living entirely within his psychological environment and "facts" from the geographic world or foreign hull have little influence on him. He is completely unaware of the advertising for a new type of frozen dessert; the product does not exist for him; he does not "see" it on the supermarket shelf and continues to buy his usual dessert.

A permeable boundary would indicate a close communication with the physical world, and slight changes in the foreign hull are immediately reflected in the life space. The young working girl who is immediately aware of slight changes in fashions and reorganizes her overtime working hours in order to be able to locomote into the region of a high-fashion pair of shoes is an example.

The life space can also include a time perspective and a *reality-irreality* dimension. Fantasy and imagination are more irreal than the "objective" aspects of the life space. Regions toward the irreal end of this dimension are more permeable and fluid, and boundaries less rigid. A man can easily locomote into the region of owning a Mercedes-Benz sports car with an attractive blond on his arm. On the reality end of the continuum, these boundaries may be far less permeable. If the life space includes or extends into the past or future, the real-irreal dimension collapses (see Figure 3), locomotion becomes confused with expectations, and memories of what happened become confused with what he wished had happened. Thus the behavior of the consumer, either in a super-market selecting among products or in the living room semiconsciously planning the purchase of a dishwasher or of a new home, can be represented as a function of the psychological field or cognitive structure of the individual.

There is nothing fixed or static about the life space. All regions are in dynamic interrelationship with each other and are constantly changing or being cognitively reorganized. Impermeable boundaries, such as the purchase of an expensive cut of meat the day before payday, suddenly become permeable as new paths to the goal are cognitively organized. For example, in Figure 4 the person appreciates that he can locomote to the goal region by first going to a friendly liquor store and cashing a check. As the psychological reality changes from moment to moment or hour to hour, the life space representations also change. There are few if any constants over a short period of time, and un-doubtedly none with a longer time perspective. Habits, rigid belief systems, values, loyalties, and personality variables all change.

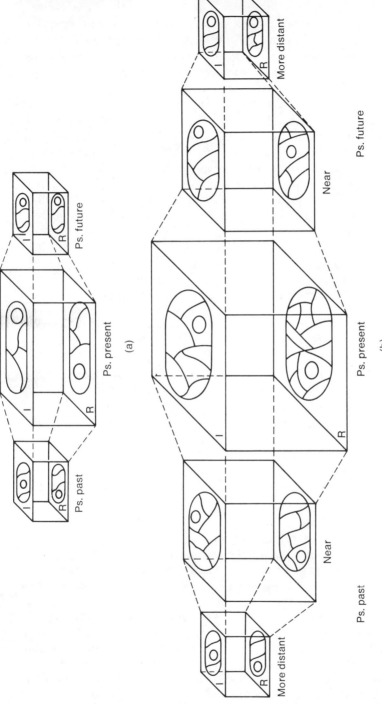

FIGURE 3. Life Space at Two Developmental Stages

(a)

(b)

The upper drawing represents the life space of a younger child. The lower diagram represents the higher degree of differentiation of the life space of the older child in regard to the present situation, the reality-irreality dimension, and the time perspective. (R = level of reality; I = level of irreality; Ps past = psychological past; Ps present = psychological present; Ps future = psychological future.) (Reprinted with permission from K. Lewin, *Field Theory in Social Science.* New York: Harper & Row, Inc., 1951.)

The Gate. As can be seen in Figure 4, the path to the goal region of buying meat often requires locomoting through other regions. A child who prefers a particular brand of cereal may realize that the most efficient path to his goal requires getting dressed; walking with mother to the store, helping mother with the shopping cart, nicely asking at the proper moment for his cereal brand, having a temper tantrum, getting spanked, and finally acquiring the sought after goal.

FIGURE 4. **Path to the Goal**

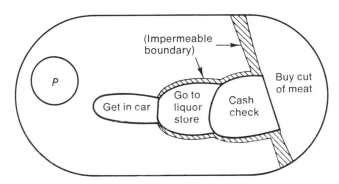

However, certain regions within the path may function as a gate. The passing or not passing (locomoting) of an item through the whole series of regions or channels depends on what happens at the gate. Lewin (1958) suggests that a good example of a gate region might be found in a university. It may be very difficult to get admitted to graduate studies, but once the student passes the gate, every effort is made to keep him until he receives his degree. That is, the pressures or forces before and after the gate region are different. Entering through the gate is difficult, but, once a student has entered, passing out through the gate is also difficult. Failing a student is a difficult and distasteful experience to be avoided by all concerned if at all possible.

The Gatekeeper. In the event a channel has a gate, of critical importance is the gatekeeper. In the home it is the housewife that chooses products and brands. Her life space is naturally influenced by the likes and tastes of her family, her guests, and perhaps her neighbors, but nevertheless the control of the gate is in her hands. The gatekeeper becomes particularly important to industrial salesmen when, perhaps, the decision to purchase millions of dollars of computer equipment lies not in the hands of the board of directors but rather with a lowly paid computer programmer.

Berey and Pollay (1968) have studied the influence of the gatekeeper in the selection of cereals within a family and particularly the role of the child in brand decision making. Their data indicate that the purchase behavior by the mother of a child's preferred packaged cereals was related to the child's assertiveness and the mother's child centeredness. More assertive children were more likely to have their favorite brand of cereal purchased. Interestingly, however, the more child centered the mother, the less likely the child is of getting his favorite cereal. It could be that the mother who is more child centered has a greater tendency to purchase cereals following her own view of what is right and healthful and will do the child the most good. The authors conclude that awareness of the strength of this gatekeeper effect has strong implications for marketing. Given that the mother is not only a purchasing agent for the child but also an agent who superimposes her preferences over those of the child, it is clear that a lot of advertising would be well directed at the mother, even if the mother is not a consumer of the product. Without such advertising, the child's influence attempts may be largely ignored if the mother thinks the brand desired is an inferior good.

Differentiation of the Person

As the environment is differentiated, so is the person. The structure representing the person is subdivided into separate interdependent parts. The outside is the perceptual-motor region, and imbedded within it is an inner-personal region (see Figure 5). Once again the boundaries are more or less permeable. Any communication of the inner person with the environment must pass through the perceptual-motor region. The tensions (needs, values, demands) of the person on the other hand originate within the inner-personal region and are communicated to the life space again through the perceptual-motor region. These concepts may become clearer as we discuss the dynamic concepts of the theory.

FIGURE 5.   **Differentiation of the Person**

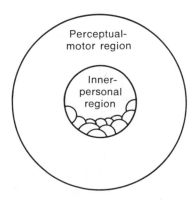

DYNAMIC CONCEPTS

The life space, as a topological representation of the cognitive organization of the individual, is not sufficient in and of itself to account for behavior. To fully explain the behavior of the consumer—why one purchased Coca-Cola rather than Pepsi-Cola or rather than a package of cigarettes—requires several dynamic concepts.

Tension

The first of these concepts is that of tension, a state of the person within the life space. A tension is a state of the inner-personal region of the person relative to other inner-personal regions. Tensions, in turn, demand reduction or return to a state of equilibrium. Any process such as thinking, purchasing, remembering, behaving, or perceiving may reduce the tension. The need to impress guests for the Saturday evening dinner can be conceptualized as a tension. Planning the menu, purchasing an expensive beef cut, cooking, polishing the silverware, and even daydreaming of hiring a butler are processes by which this tension is reduced. The source of all behavior is the need to reduce tensions and achieve equilibrium within the system. Depending upon the particular cognitive organization of an individual at any given slice of time, the attempt at tension reduction within the total system may, however, require increased tension within a subsystem. For example, the housewife may decide that the desired route to reduce her tensions or needs related to impressing her guests is to prepare the beef by using an exotic recipe available only in an unavailable gourmet cookbook. Now a new tension has developed as she runs to libraries and bookstores to acquire the cookbook. During the cooking process, fears of failure and concerns over making an error may in fact increase her tensions to highly uncomfortable levels. To achieve equilibrium, to reduce the need to impress guests, may at times require paths that in some subregions severely increase tensions, although the overall process of behavior is guided by tension reduction.

Perhaps the concept of tension can replace vague and unparsimonious generalizations such as needs, wants, motives, drives, and urges. Physiological conditions, such as hunger or sex, and social demands, such as high-fashion clothing, a new hat, a Corvette, or a candy bar, are best conceptualized as tension or pressure against the boundaries of some region within the inner-personal system (Argyris, 1952). A need, motive, or drive can be defined as a concept trying to explain a syndrome of behavior by taking into account the tension within a person to achieve some goal. As soon as the goal is reached, the region is no longer in tension; that is, the system achieves equilibrium.

A state of tension in a particular region will tend to equalize itself with the amount of tension in the surrounding regions. Hence a need for sexual gratification may lead to a need for sports cars, cosmetics, high-fashion clothing, and an expensive apartment, or vice versa. The tension can be equalized by any process such as thinking, remembering, purchasing, consuming, or even daydreaming to achieve equilibrium.

Energy

Furthermore, the person can be seen as a complex energy system. This physical energy is released as the person attempts to return to equilibrium after he has been thrown into a state of disequilibrium by the arousal of a tension in one part of the system (Hall and Lindzey, 1957).

Valence

The third dynamic property of a field theoretical approach is that of valence, a conceptual property of a region of the psychological environment representing its value to the individual, its attractiveness or repulsiveness. A valence is obviously coordinated with a tension; that is, whether a particular region of the environment has a positive or negative value depends directly upon a system in a state of tension. To a hungry person food will have a positive valence; to a satiated individual even the odor of food can be quite repelling or negative. Although food in general may well have a positive valence, a particular product that is sold by a disliked retailer or manufactured by a producer responsible for obnoxious advertising may well take on a negative valence. Hence even to a hungry person a particular food may be repelling. The strength of the tension in combination with other prevailing factors determines the strength of the valence (Hall and Lindzey, 1957).

Force

A valence plus energy creates a force—a property of the psychological environment rather than the person. A force is defined as that which causes change. Its properties are direction and strength. Thus for any given point in the life space, the construct force represents the direction of and tendency to change. A number of these forces can act on the same point at a given time. The mathematical combination or resolution of these forces is the net resultant force (Shaw and Costanzo, 1970). The strength and direction of the forces can be represented as a vector acting upon the person (Lewin, 1938), causing locomotion or, in our terminology, behavior. That is, there is either locomotion in the direction of that force or there is a reorganization of the cognitive structures that is equivalent to locomotion.

Naturally, at any given moment conflicting vectors are likely to exist—the decision between two brands of gasoline both of which have a positive valence, the choice between being drafted or branded a coward, both with negative valences, or the purchase of a dishwasher with a positive valence related to its function and a negative vector created by its cost. In such cases the direction of locomotion, away or toward entering the purchase region, will be the resultant of the various vectors. The net valence, if above threshold, will determine whether or not the dishwasher is purchased. Presuming the two choices are perceived to be exactly identical within the life space of the individual, vascillation, indecision, greater tension, and higher nonpecuniary cost of consumption might result.

Vascillation or indecision is not an effective route to tension reduction. Perhaps loyalty to a brand or particular service station and the seeking of very fine discriminations among brands and manufacturers, when in fact the physical products are "known" to be identical, are tension-reducing mechanisms aimed at lowering this nonpecuniary cost of consumption.[7] Carrying a credit card and the "belief" that in fact Standard Oil products are superior can be a very useful behavior pattern. For example, while driving on the highway as the fuel needle approachs empty, the decision to stop at the next Standard station is a lower-cost decision perhaps than wondering where to stop, how many miles more should I go, should I stop here, and so on? Again the simple decision rule to purchase the lowest-priced brand of canned peaches at the supermarket or loyalty to the Del Monte brand may not be a price-quality type of economic decision, not a learned behavior pattern based on number of previous purchases, but rather a cognitive attempt to resolve the conflict between two equal forces operating in opposite directions. A simple decision rule, such as brand loyalty, preferences for a particular outlet, or "blacklisting" products of disliked advertisements, immediately changes the strength of the force or vector in conflict situations. And conflict between brands in these days of standardized products and well-educated consumers may be the rule rather than the exception.

Perceived Risk. In fact, much of the work on risk taking indicates the perceived risk is little more than unresolved tension due to opposing vectors or forces. Risk emerges from any of the following factors (Cox, 1967):

1. Uncertainty as to buying goals.
2. Which of several purchases (product, brand, model, etc.) best matches the buying goals.
3. Possible adverse consequences if the purchase is made (or not made).

---

[7]Brand loyalty is a tension-reducing mechanism only if all brands are available. If the preferred brand is unavailable, the net result should be much greater tension.

In short, risk is a function of two elements, uncertainty and consequences (Cox, 1967). Hence risk, or tension, can be reduced by either reducing the possible consequences or increasing the certainty of the possible outcomes. Changes in the psychological field can be accomplished by reading *Consumer Reports,* examining the product, turning to opinion leaders, purchasing nationally advertised products for assurance of quality, or turning to private labels to reduce the financial risk, or by expecting less and less from the product and lowering the level of aspiration, thus protecting oneself from perceived failure in the purchase decision. Arndt (1968), for example, has found that high-risk perceivers were more brand loyal, tended to avoid being among the first persons to try new products, switched brands less often, were more likely to seek information, and were more likely to respond to the information they had sought.[8]

Opposing Forces. Obviously, the behavior of the consumer is a function of many often opposing forces, with the individual seeking to achieve equilibrium. Lewin emphasized the two alternatives facing a change agent. Either the forces can be added in the desired direction, or the opposing forces can be diminished. The seller's role is either to enhance the positive values of a product, say, a new suit of clothes in terms of its color, fit, style, and approval of others, or to reduce its negative forces, such as cost, fitting time, or the value of purchasing a new suit over, say a pair of shoes or fishing tackle. Bilkey (1953, 1955) attempted to measure the influence of the net resultant of such forces on the purchase of consumer durables, such as a car, washing machine, rug, and sewing machine, in addition to food consumption.

In a sense, Bilkey asked subjects to indicate their net resultant of forces toward the purchase of the item and the resultant force opposing the purchase over a period of several months by asking subjects to rate each on a 0 to 100 scale. The analysis of the data from a single respondent in the purchase of a rug is quite interesting. In the month of February the subject stated her desire for a rug was 75, while the negative force was 0, with a net valence of +75. However, the net valence for a new stove was +100. In March she purchased a new stove. In May the positive force for the purchase of a rug was rated at 25 and negative force at 0. The subject commented that she had been shopping for clothes a few days before the interview and that she was so satisfied with her stove that she no longer had much desire for a new rug. In the month of June the interviewee had priced rugs and discovered the cost to be about twice what she expected to pay. That month she set her positive valences at 25 and the negative valence at 100, with a resultant of -75. In September her positive force climbed to 90 and the negative force to 50, with a net of +40. In October she purchased the rug and commented she now wants a new refrigerator.

---

[8] However, later studies are not as clear on these points.

Although Bilkey was measuring the stated resistances and desires for consumer goods and in many ways (with a post hoc critique) appears somewhat simplistic, Bilkey's work has been one of the first attempts in consumer behavior to apply Lewinian theory directly. He concluded on the basis of his entire study that there is a quantitative relationship between people's stated psychic tensions regarding the purchase of particular items and their expenditures for those items.

Food consumption has been rather extensively studied by Lewin and his colleagues (Lewin, 1951). The purpose of the projects was basically to change the eating habits of Americans such that there would be greater acceptability of certain food items, such as undesirable cuts of meat. Obviously, physical availability is not sufficient to lead to consumption. Grasshoppers, snails, and pigs ears are not acceptable items in some cultures while delicacies in others. Food comes to the table through various channels. It can be purchased in a supermarket, home baked or canned, gardened, or purchased ready to eat. Once purchased it must be stored, prepared, and brought to the table. Food moves step by step through the channels but not by its own impetus. Entering or not entering a distribution channel and moving from one channel to another is effected by a gatekeeper, ultimately the housewife. Each section of the channels offers a certain amount of resistance to movement. If food is expensive, two forces of opposite direction act on the gatekeeper. The housewife is in conflict. One force corresponding to the attractiveness of the food tends to bring it into the channel and the other force away from spending too much money keeps the food away from the channel. Food is bought if the total force toward buying becomes greater than the opposing forces until the food basket is filled.

Behavior in Groups. Still other examples of opposing forces may be found in group behavior. An individual may differ in his personal level of conduct from the level that represents group standards only by a certain amount. The degree of permitted differences varies from group to group and from culture to culture. If the individual diverges too much, pressures such as ridicule, laughter, and expulsion are brought to bear to keep him in line. Lewin (1951) described such behavior as a quasi-stationary equilibrium. For example, piecework production in a factory is kept at employee group set standards or levels. The forces to make more money and hence produce more are in equilibrium with an opposing force—the group fear that management will change the rate if production is too great.

The equilibrium preventing change can be attacked by a three-step process: *unfreezing* the present level, *moving* to a new level, and freezing the group at the new level. Since the level is determined by a force field, permanency implies that the new force field is made relatively secure against change. The unfreezing involves quite different approaches in different situations. Lewin and his followers have felt that the most effective method of unfreezing, moving, and freezing behavior is through group decision. The equilibrium of forces established by the group is sufficiently powerful to demand conformity from the individual. The greater the social value of the group standard, the greater is the resistance of the individual group member to move away from this level.[9]

A study by B. L. Wellerman (Lewin, 1951, p. 233) attempted to change eating habits of students from white bread to whole wheat bread. When the change was individually requested, the degree of eagerness to eat white bread varied greatly with the degree of personal preference for the food item. In the condition when the decision to change was made by the group, eagerness to consume whole wheat seemed to be relatively free of personal preference. The individual acted as a group member.

Other experiments produce similar results. In the attempt to increase the consumption of beef hearts, sweetbreads, and kidneys one set of groups was given attractive lectures relating to the nutritional economic value of these cuts and recipes in their preparation. Other groups discussed the advantages and disadvantages of serving viscera. Follow-up studies indicated that 3 percent of the lecture group and 32 percent of the discussion group members began to prepare and serve these meats to their family (Lewin, 1958). Similar results have been found in increasing the consumption of fresh milk, orange juice, cod-liver oil, and evaporated milk (Lewin, 1947). Also, these increases and the discrepancy between individual and group decision were not short term, but follow-up studies indicated that the changes appeared to be permanent.

SUMMARY

With the topological structure of the life space and the dynamic properties of tension, need, valence, and forces or vectors, let us consider an example. On a midweek afternoon a housewife considers going downtown to see a motion picture. The need to "do something" and the desirability or positive valence of the goal—the motion picture—create a vector or force in the direction of the goal within her life space. Her life space is structured to contain two paths to the goal: (1) walk to the corner, take the bus, buy a ticket, and enter the goal region; and (2) get the car keys, walk to garage, drive car, park car, buy ticket, and enter goal region. Suddenly remembering that the garage is locked and her husband walked off with the key, the region of the life space encompassing "drive car" is inaccessible; the boundaries of her life space are impermeable. To overcome the barrier to her psychological movement requires a circuitous route. She decides to walk, and in preparation for the trip passes by the refrigerator. A new stimulus has now entered her life space for the foreign hull as she remembers that she has no vegetables for dinner that evening and that she must go to the supermarket. Suddenly plans for the theater are discarded, and her life

[9] See, for example, Coch and French (1948) and Lewin (1947).

space is restructured around her grocery shopping. The new regions of her life space consist of walking to the market, selecting the produce, paying for it, and entering the positive goal region to reduce the tension. Other possible paths or methods of obtaining vegetables, such as planting seeds and raising carrots, do not occur to her and are not part of her life space. Having selected the carrots at the market, her life space again is restructured as she contemplates a new path for entering the goal region (see Figure 6). Rather than pay for the vegetables she can shoplift; however, the negative consequences of this behavior and the concomitant negative vector induce her to pass through the check-out stand to reach the goal, reduce the tension, and restore equilibrium.

FIGURE 6.   **Acquiring Vegetables at the Market**

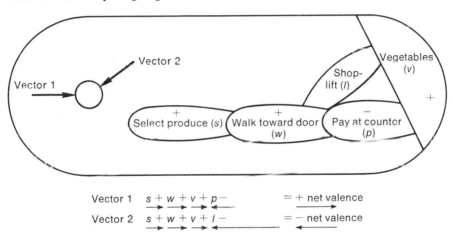

| Vector 1 | $s + w + v + p -$ | $= +$ net valence |
| Vector 2 | $s + w + v + l -$ | $= -$ net valence |

The net valence of shoplifting path to the goal (vector 2) acts as a force away from illegal behavior. Consumer pays for the vegetables (vector 1) to reach the goal, reduce tension, and move towards equilibrium.

In summary, it is maintained that human behavior and its subset, consumer behavior, can and should be conceptualized from a field theoretical perspective. Analysis of the consumer's actions should begin with the entire situation as a whole from which the relevant parts can be differentiated. The behavior of the consumer is a function of the psychological field or life space of the individual that exists at the time the behavior occurs. In turn, the life space consists of the person and environment interacting in a mutually interdependent relationship. Locomotion or behavior is a function of all the dynamic interrelated forces acting simultaneously within the field. Causality is the resultant of the coexisting forces that can be rigorously conceptualized and measured and is not probabilistic. And finally, the field perhaps can be represented mathematically by the use of topology, non-Euclidean geometry, and vector theory.

CONCLUSIONS

Lewin once stated, "There is nothing so practical as a good theory." It had been the major goal of Lewin and his students to make field theory operational, useful, and practical. The various attempts at mathematization of the concepts are examples in this direction, as are the studies conducted in the attempt to create individual and social change. Field theory is an all-encompassing point of view of why people behave as they do and how one might go about changing their behavior.

The following chapters in this book are concerned not with the all-encompassing theories but rather with middle-range theories—points of view that do not attempt to explain all behavior but rather merely a subset of them. Hence cognitive dissonance is concerned only with post-decision anxiety, novelty seeking only with its defined set of activities, and so on. Field theory on the other hand is an attempt to explain all human behavior. The key question, then, is how much research has the theory generated and stimulated?

In social psychology field theory has led to hundreds of experimental studies testing facets of the theory as applied to individual and group behavior as well as human relations. The great masses of research that have been generated from the Group Dynamics Research Center at the University of Michigan are but one example. Turning to consumer behavior, the theory in a direct sense has had very small impact. Outside of a few studies by Lewin and his students and the work of Bilkey and Brown, direct references are difficult to find. Interestingly, however, field theory has touched almost every facet of consumer behavior through the influence of the middle-range theories. Perceived risk, cognitive dissonance, much of the work in attitudes and perception, the work in group dyanmics and group influence, adoption of innovations, and studies in factories and organizations all have been influenced by the work of Lewin and his colleagues and students.

The level of abstraction is such that on one hand it can touch every facet of consumer behavior, and on the other, because the theory is all encompassing, direct and simple research ideas are not always immediately evident. However, as one reads the rest of this book the enormous impact of Lewinian theory can be seen woven throughout the theories and experiments that will be discussed. Lewin's impact in the social sciences cannot be overestimated, and his impact in consumer behavior has been woefully underestimated.

REFERENCES

Argyris, Chris, *An Introduction to Field Theory and Interaction Theory.* New Haven, Conn.: Labor and Management Center, Yale University, 1952.

Arndt, Johan, "Word of Mouth Advertising and Perceived Risk," in *Perspectives in Consumer Behavior,* ed. H. H. Kassarjian and T. S. Robertson. Glenview, Ill.: Scott, Foresman and Company, 1968, 330-36.

Berey, L. A., and R. W. Pollay, "The Influencing Role of the Child in Family Decision Making," *Journal of Marketing Research,* 5 (February 1968), 70-72.

Bilkey, W. J., "The Vector Hypothesis of Consumer Behavior," *Journal of Marketing,* 16 (October 1951), 137-51

Bilkey, W. J., "A Psychological Approach to Consumer Behavior Analysis," *Journal of Marketing,* 18 (July 1953), 18-25.

Bilkey, W. J., "Psychic Tensions and Purchasing Behavior," *Journal of Social Psychology,* 41 (1955), 247-57.

Bilkey, W. J., "Consistency Test of Psychic Tension Ratings Involved in Consumer Purchase Behavior," *Journal of Social Psychology,* 45 (1957), 81-91.

Brown, J. F., *Psychology and the Social Order.* New York: McGraw-Hill Book Company, 1936a.

Brown, J. F., "On the Use of Mathematics in Psychological Theory," *Psychometrika,* 1 (1936b), 77-90.

Brown, W. F., "The Determination of Factors Determining Brand Choice," *Journal of Marketing,* 14 (April 1950), 699-706.

Cartwright, Dorwin, "Lewinian Theory as a Contemporary Systematic Framework," in *Psychology: A Study of a Science,* ed. Sigmund Koch, Vol. 2, *General Systematic Formulations, Learning and Special Processes.* New York: McGraw-Hill Book Company, 1959.

Clawson, Joseph, "Lewin's Psychology and Motives in Marketing," in *Theory in Marketing,* ed. Reavis Cox and Wroe Alderson. Homewood, Ill.: Richard D. Irwin, Inc., 1950.

Coch, Lester, and J. R. P. French, "Resolving Social Conflicts," *Human Relations, I* (1948), 512-32.

Cox, D.F., ed., *Risk Taking and Information Handling in Consumer Behavior.* Boston: Division of Research, Graduate School of Business Administration, Harvard University, 1967.

Deutsch, Morton, "Field Theory in Social Psychology," in *Handbook of Social Psychology,* Vol. 1., ed. Gardner Lindzey, Reading, Mass.: Addison-Wesley Publishing Company, Inc., 1954, 181-222.

Deutsch, Morton, "Field Theory in Social Psychology," in *Handbook of Social Psychology* (2nd ed.), ed. Gardner Lindzey and Elliot Aronson. Reading, Mass.: Addison-Wesley Publishing Company, Inc., 1968, 412-87.

Hall, C. S., and Gardner Lindzey, *Theories of Personality.* New York: John Wiley & Sons, Inc., 1957 (2nd. ed., 1970).

Harary, F., and R. Z. Norman, *Graph Theory as a Mathematical Model in the Social Sciences.* Ann Arbor, Mich.: Institute for Social Research, 1953.

Hilgard, E. R., *Theories of Learning* (3rd ed.). New York: Appleton-Century-Crofts, 1956.

Howard, J. A., and J. N. Sheth, *The Theory of Buyer Behavior.* New York: John Wiley & Sons, Inc., 1969.

Jacques, Elliott, "Field Theory and Industrial Psychology," *Occupational Psychology,* 22 (July 1948), 126-33. As quoted in Argyris (1952).

Leeper, R. W., *Lewin's Topological and Vector Psychology: A Digest and a Critique.* Eugene, Oreg.: University of Oregon Press, 1943.

Lewin, Kurt, *A Dynamic Theory of Personality.* New York: McGraw-Hill Book Company, 1935.

Lewin, Kurt, *Principles of Topological Psychology.* New York: McGraw-Hill Book Company, 1936.

Lewin, Kurt, *The Conceptual Representation and the Measurement of Psychological Forces;* Monograph series: *Contributions to Psychological Theory,* Vol. 1, No. 4, Serial No. 4. Durham, N. C.: Duke University Press, 1938.

Lewin, Kurt, *Resolving Social Conflicts: Selected Papers on Group Dynamics.* New York: Harper & Row, Inc., 1943.

Lewin, Kurt, "Frontiers in Group Dynamics," *Human Relations,* 1 (1947), 5-41.

Lewin, Kurt, *Field Theory in Social Science: Selected Theoretical Papers.* New York: Harper & Row, Inc., 1951.

Lewin, Kurt, "Forces Behind Food Habits and Methods of Change," *The Problem of Changing Food Habits,* report of the Committee on Food Habits, 1941-43; *Bulletin of the National Research Council,* 108 (October 1943). Results of the studies are summarized in Lewin, Kurt, "Group Decision and Social Change," in *Readings in Social Psychology* (3rd ed.),ed. E. E. Maccoby, T. M. Newcomb, and E. L. Hartley. New York: Holt, Rinehart and Winston, Inc., 1958, 197-211.

Lewin, Kurt, T. Dembo, L. Festinger, and P. S. Sears, "Level of Aspiration," in *Personality and the Behavior Discorders,* ed. J. M. Hunt. New York: The Ronald Press Company, 1944, 333-78.

Marrow, A. J., *The Practical Theorist: The Life and Work of Kurt Lewin.* New York: Basic Books, Inc., Publishers, 1969.

Shaw, M. E., and P. R. Costanzo, *Theories of Social Psychology.* New York: McGraw-Hill Book Company, 1970.

Tucker, W. T., *Foundations for a Theory of Consumer Behavior.* New York: Holt, Rinehart and Winston, Inc., 1967.

Williams, L. P., *The Origins of Field Theory.* New York: Random House, Inc., 1966.

4

Personality and Consumer Behavior

William D. Wells and Arthur D. Beard
University of Chicago

PERSONALITY THEORIES

Freud's Psychoanalytic Theory. Jung's Analytical Psychology.
Adler's Individual Psychology. Karen Horney. Riesman's Social
Typology. Harry Stack Sullivan's Interpersonal Theory. Erik
Erikson. Henry Murray. Maslow's Hierarchy of Needs. William
H. Sheldon's Constitutional Psychology. Factor Analysis.

SYNDROME MEASUREMENT

Authoritarian Personality. Manifest Anxiety.

SUMMING UP

USES OF PERSONALITY THEORIES IN MARKETING

Qualitative Period: Motivation Research. Quantitative Period:
1959 to the Present.

PERSONALITY TESTS AS LINKS BETWEEN PRODUCTS AND
MEDIA

Use of Personality Tests to "Predict" Consumer Behavior. Intensive Study of Groups of Traits. The Factor Analysis of Consumer Behavior. Start from Scratch.

IN CONCLUSION

REFERENCES

PERSONALITY THEORIES

In a magazine article about executives looking for jobs, a "top-level head hunter" is quoted as saying, "Sometimes they make almost unbelievable mistakes—like wearing white socks to an interview."

Now why should an executive recruiter be concerned about the color of a man's socks? Evidently, this recruiter has a theory (which may or may not be correct) that wearing white socks to an employment interview has something to do with behavior in other areas. He is assuming that there is some underlying unity, some general link—such as "good social judgment" or "awareness of what others are apt to think," perhaps—that allows him to infer future executive performance from this seemingly trivial observation.

Stated another way, the recruiter is assuming that the applicant's behavior is an integrated system, and that the parts of the system are interconnected by broad, general underlying dispositions that explain and control its separate parts. This system, the system that unites, integrates, and in some sense produces an individual's behavior, is the domain of the personality theorist.

Marketers have been extremely interested in personality theory because they have been led to believe that it will help them understand purchasing behavior. They assume that if they really understand the way a consumer's psyche is put together, they can understand why he makes the purchasing decisions he makes and perhaps do something to influence those decisions.

Exactly what are the broad, general underlying dispositions that govern behavior in all of its many forms? Where do they come from? How do they work? How can they be detected? There are as many answers to these questions as there are personality theorists—more, because several theorists, like Freud, had the courage to revise their theories and recant when they discovered they were wrong.

The first sections of this chapter will describe the major personality theories, beginning with Freud's, and will point out some of the special contributions of each.

The theories differ in many ways, but there are some common threads. These threads are important because they have had a major impact upon our understanding of what makes people behave the way they do. They are especially important to the student of consumer behavior, because they have had a strong influence upon the activities of those involved in advertising, marketing, and other forms of communication.

The order in which the theories are reviewed approximates the birth order of the theorists, as shown in Figure 1. After the theorists and their theories have been reviewed, the later sections of the chapter will describe and discuss attempts to apply these images of man to the much more specific problem of understanding why consumers behave the way they do.

FIGURE 1. **Life Spans of the Personality Theorists**

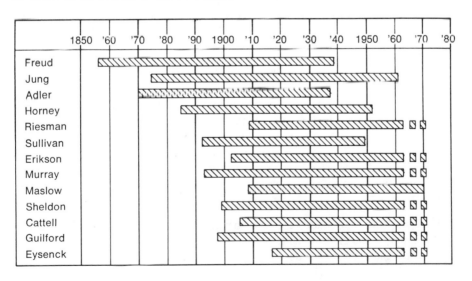

Freud's Psychoanalytic Theory

In the early 1880s, Sigmund Freud began treating patients who had disease symptoms but no apparent organic malfunction. His treatment method was to have patients lie on the famous couch and talk about their symptoms and anything else that came to mind. The rule for the talk was that the patient must relax not only physically (the reason for the couch) but mentally as well. He must "let go" and not follow the inhibiting rules of logic, courtesy, and self-defense that circumscribe ordinary conversation.

Freud would sit out of the patient's line of sight, taking mental notes that he would record after the patient had left. Occasionally, when he thought it would help, he would interpret the hidden, latent, or symbolic meaning of the patient's free associations, or he would interpret the hidden meaning of an apparently senseless dream.

Freud would listen to the same patient periodically for extended periods of time, sometimes for years. As the treatment progressed, the patient would begin to remember early childhood experiences, often of a sexual nature. Once a key experience had been recovered and relived by the patient under the guidance of the analyst, the symptom of illness would sometimes disappear.

In his personality theory Freud attempted to explain the content of his patient's monologues, and to detail the underlying dispositions that might link the disappearance of a symptom to a patient's conscious analysis of seemingly unrelated and long-forgotten events.

Freud's experience as a listener, and his interpretation of the literature, art, and mythology of his own and other cultures, led him to the conclusion that man's behavior is generated by internal energy under the control of three separate entities within the mind. These entities are functional, not physical. They cannot be mapped on the anatomy of the brain or revealed by an autopsy. The three entities are:

The Id. It converts power generated by the body into psychic energy. It is the energy input to the personality and can be thought of as the personality's biological component. The id is the residence of everything psychological that is inherited at birth. It includes the instincts, which attempt to push the individual into certain behaviors, especially sexual and aggressive behaviors that interfere with the smooth and orderly functioning of society. If the id were in complete control of everyone's behavior, society could not exist. Uncontrolled behavior that directly satisfies the instincts is therefore, in Freud's view, inherently "bad."

The Ego. The ego acts as a broker between the demands of the id and the constraints of the environment. It has "control" of the perceptual and thinking processes and uses these to set priorities and strategies for satisfying the instincts. The id transfers operating energy to the ego because the ego's abilities to satisfy the demands of the id are superior to the id's abilities to satisfy those demands unaided.

The Superego. This entity censors the strategies and priorities established by the ego, using rules transmitted by society to the individual through his parents.

Behaviors that have been punished are incorporated into the conscience, and when one of these behaviors is committed, or contemplated, the person feels guilt. Behaviors associated with reward are incorporated into the *ego-ideal.* When one of these behaviors is enacted, the actor feels proud. The id allocates energy to the superego because the superego embodies the reward and punishment structure of society, and is therefore instrumental in satisfying the instincts with a minimum of pain or guilt and a maximum of pride.

The id is entirely unconscious; the ego and superego are partially unconscious and partically conscious. The conscious functioning of the ego and the superego gives the false impression that man is in conscious control of his own behavior, but in fact it is the unconscious interactions of the id, ego, and superego that determine what people do.

The sexual instincts of the id play a critical role in the development of the personality. Freud conceived of personality development as progressing through a series of stages, each labeled by the area of the body on which the sexual instincts focus at the time.

For the first 5 years of life, the person centers his sexual interest on himself. The first year involves the pleasure of stimulation received from the mouth, and is therefore called the oral stage. A crisis develops near the end of this stage as the infant is weaned away from his mother's breast or its surrogate. During the second year, the primary source of pleasure involves the process of elimination, and this period is therefore called the anal stage. The end of the anal stage is marked by another crisis involving toilet training.

The next crisis occurs during the phallic stage—the third, fourth, and fifth years, when the sex organs are the center of self-oriented sexual pleasure. This crisis centers around the child's sexual feelings toward the parent of the opposite sex, and the manner in which it is resolved affects later relationships with persons of the opposite sex and with authority figures of all types, including teachers, political leaders, and superiors in business firms.

Freud believed that after the fifth year the sexual instincts were quiescent, emerging again with the beginning of adolescence. The crisis of adolescence requires that these self-centered sexual urges be fused into a desire for reproductive activities with persons of the opposite sex. If the crisis is adequately resolved, the individual's personality enters into what Freud called the genital stage.

In his entertaining but serious book, *Games People Play*, the psychiatrist-author Eric Berne (1964) finds roots in the Freudian stages for the strategies people develop in their relationships with each other. In one of these games, "Schlemiel," the individual "accidently" inflicts minor damage to another person's property—spilling a drink on his dinner host's new rug, for instance. The spiller expresses his regret and ultimately receives forgiveness, which is the objective of the game. The host takes pride in his own maturity and self-control in this situation, and is a willing player. The root of this game, according to

Berne, is the child's mess-making while being toilet trained. The two players are the irresponsible but lovable child and the forgiving and therefore also lovable parent.

Each of the crisis situations described causes successive surges of tension, which Freud called traumas. If the traumatic experience is associated with the individual's passage from one stage of personality development to the next, his personality can become partially or completely arrested or *fixated* at the current stage. If an individual becomes partially or completely fixated in the anal stage, for example, he cannot progress completely to the phallic stage, and his adult personality will show signs of this fixation in traits such as stinginess, obstinacy, excessive need for neatness, and problems in relating to other prople. If the individual becomes fixated at the earlier oral stage, he might as an adult be overly dependent upon others, as a tiny infant is upon its mother. Freud noted that the symptom of a fixated personality is an unevenness of personality development, not an across-the-board retention of childish characteristics. The fixation is not necessarily permanent; it may merely represent a period of time during which the expected development does not occur.

If the ego cannot handle a crisis, it may resort to one or more *mechanisms of defense,* so called because they are self-defense strategies adopted by the ego to help reduce tensions that would otherwise be unbearable. The mechanisms are all unconscious, but they are employed by everyone in everyday behavior. Closely allied to fixation is the defense mechanism called *regression.* A traumatic experience may cause the person to retreat to an earlier stage of development, usually one at which the personality had fixated earlier in the individual's life. Mature behavior is replaced by immature behavior. *Projection* is the name given to the defense mechanism by which feelings that stem from a person's own id or superego are ascribed to another person or group of persons. For instance, a man's desire to inflict severe punishment upon homosexuals may be a symptom of his fear and hatred of his own unconscious homosexual impulses. Prejudices of all sorts are believed to have this source; we hate in others what we hate in ourselves.

Unconscious feelings toward others may be converted into their opposites in consciousness through *reaction formation.* Thus a wife who unconsciously desires to overspend her husband's salary so as to deprive him of his masculine provider role may consciously be a pinchpenny, or a mother who unconsciously hates her child may feel the hatred consciously as love. Freud noted that a feeling derived from reaction formation is apt to be characterized by excessiveness, by exaggeration. The mother who is covering unconscious hate with conscious love will be more lavish in the expression of her love than the mother whose love has a different motivational base.

The most basic defense mechanism is called *repression.* Subjected to more stimulation—either from internal or external sources—than it is capable of handling, the ego will select out certain stimuli to overlook or to forget. The individual will miss certain details that are in plain sight, or not be able to remember certain painful or threatening experiences. The unconscious will retain such experiences and the memories of repressed stimuli. Psychic energy will be continuously expended to prevent them from intruding into conscious awareness. Repression is considered the most basic of the defense mechanisms because a certain amount of repression is necessary for the effective operation of any of the others. Since all the defense mechanisms are self-deceptive, they cannot be maintained while reality is looked full in the face.

A defense mechanism is analogous to a military retreat; in this case, a retreat from reality. The ego also employs a mechanism that is analogous to a political agreement. This mechanism, called *displacement,* is a compromise between a desire of the id and a contrary restraint from the superego. The id may focus a man's sexual desire on his neighbor's wife. Because the superego forbids an attempt to consummate this desire, the desire is displaced to a socially acceptable behavior, such as offering to repair a broken kitchen appliance. The object of the id's desire may be displaced even farther from its original focus. The individual might begin painting portraits of beautiful women or even beautiful landscapes, or engaging in some other creative activity that is linked in the unconscious with the original object. If an instinctual desire is translated into a socially acceptable achievement, the process is a special type of displacement called *sublimation.* Freud believed that virtually all an adult's interests, preferences, tastes, habits, and attitudes represent displacements of energy from original instinctual object choices.

Another mechanism that plays a role in the personality's development is called *identification.* This is a process by which the individual unconsciously imitates another person who appears to have dealt successfully with the anxieties the individual currently feels. It is the basis of the appeal of drama and novels, and it is the core of certain advertising campaigns. Consider the following familiar plot: A young man applies the sponsor's brand of after-shave lotion to his face, and in the next scene he successfully takes the first step toward seducing a beautiful girl. The advertiser assumes that men of all ages will identify with the hero of this minidrama and that a significant number of them will imitate at least the first act.

The id, ego, and superego, together with the ego's mechanisms for dealing with conflicts, can be viewed as a tension-reducing system operating on energy supplied by the id. The tension is the anxiety generated by events in the world outside the mind or by the demands of the instincts. The ego uses energy in attempting to reduce the tension within the constraints imposed by the superego. If the ego cannot engineer a reduction within those constraints, it utilizes defense mechanisms to do so.

A well-adjusted person requires few defense mechanisms, and uses them sparingly. A neurotic depends on one or more of the defense mechanisms to maintain a semblance of stability, and this overdependence on defense mechanisms draws off energy that would otherwise be available for useful and productive mental work. It is the deterioration of mental life caused by this energy drain that alerts the neurotic and sends him to the psychiatrist's office.

One must ask what the perfectly adjusted individual would be like. Adjustment depends on the society in which the individual lives. In Freud's view, the goals of the instincts and of society are in opposition to one another, creating a series of conflicts throughout the life span. By the operation of displacement the well-adjusted individual displaces the original objectives of the instincts to objectives that are in accord with the strictures of society. But with each displacement the reservoir of undischarged tension is enlarged, creating a force that drives the individual to search for new and more satisfying outlets for the tension. New displacements are established, and new contributions to culture are made through sublimation. Freud believed that the search for new objects on which to displace the instincts accounts for the variety of human behavior.

It might seem that to accept Freud's tension-reduction model in the light of our observation of the world around us—a world of bustling commerce, creativity, and conflict—we must also accept his view that man's instincts are in conflict with society, and that neither side will ever attain a clear-cut victory. But it is not necessary to assume that it is society that is good and the instincts that are bad. Freud's model would work equally well if the reverse were true—all that is necessary is that there be a built-in conflict that creates the propellant for man's activity. Other personality theorists disagree with Freud on the basic qualities of society and man, saying that man is inherently good, but can be perverted by his society.

Freud's ideas have had a major influence on the study of consumer behavior. As a brilliantly original and controversial theorist, he broke the nineteenth century faith in the basic rationality of man. His work and the work of his followers has left little doubt that much behavior, including much consumer behavior, is influenced and perhaps even determined by illogical forces of which the individual is at most only partially aware. Second, by pointing out the far-reaching implications of sexual motives, he drew attention to an extremely important set of forces that until his time had not been much discussed. Designers of products, writers of books, plays, and motion picture scripts, and creators of advertising campaigns have all seized eagerly upon the sexual implications of Freud's work. Third, as the first psychoanalyst, Freud was the intellectual father of a line of thinkers who have had a profound influence on our current understanding of the nature of man. And finally, as later sections of this chapter will show, his methods and his findings have been applied directly in developing methods of studying consumer behavior and in interpreting research results.

When Freud set down his theory of personality in all its rich detail, he did so with the conviction of a man who had seen a holy vision. He spoke and wrote with great confidence and skill. He attracted many disciples and he tolerated little disagreement.

Two of his most famous followers, Jung and Adler, were both presidents of organizations created to propagate Freud's work, and both publicly resigned when, their differences of opinion with Freud became intolerable. When Jung or Adler broke with Freud, the break was not due to a mere difference of opinion. It was the casting out of a disbeliever.

Jung's Analytical Psychology

Like Freud, Carl Gustav Jung was a physician who built a theory to explain his observations of mental patients. He was younger than Freud, but was his contemporary, and was strongly influenced by Freud's theories. Jung disagreed with Freud's belief in the pervasiveness of the sexual instincts. He saw a baby's craving for his mother's nipple as a sign of a need for nutriment as much as a need for sex. He viewed the structure of personality differently than Freud, particularly in regard to the individual's psychological inheritance, and theorized a *pulling* force in the development of man's personality, as well as the pushing force of the Freudian instincts.

Jung, like Freud, pictured the personality as being composed of functional entities between which psychic energy is transferred in the course of the personality's development. These entities are:

The Ego. The ego is the conscious mind. It is made up of the individual's conscious perceptions, memories, thoughts and feelings, and is responsible for his feelings of identity. Unlike the ego conceived by Freud, the ego conceived by Jung is entirely conscious. It is the center of the personality in the first half of man's life.

The Personal Unconscious. The personal unconscious is made up of once conscious experiences that have been repressed, forgotten, selectively ignored, or are not strong enough to be consciously perceived. It includes *complexes* —groups of feelings, thoughts, perceptions or memories that seem to "go together." Referring to a patient who brings home stray cats and injured birds and devotes hours to their grooming and recuperation, Jung would say, "She's got a mother complex." Sometimes a complex may control behavior like an autonomous personality, and can be considered a separate entity in and of itself. In his patients Jung found all possible varieties of complexes, from small collections of unconscious representations to full-fledged multiple personalities. The personal unconscious gathers the material for building its complexes from three sources: the ego, the world outside the mind, and the collective unconscious.

The Collective Unconscious. The collective unconscious is the entity with which the individual is born. It includes the instincts, plus psychological and behavioral "programming" that is the product of man's evolutionary development. Jung regarded it as a source of wisdom whose signals, seen in dreams and as symptoms, should be heeded. Included in the collective unconscious is a legion of ideas, called *archetypes,* shared by men the world over. The archetypes create images or visions, may be models for behavior, and have the power to drive men to seek a correspondence with them in the real world. According to Jung, Freud's Oedipus complex—sexual attachment to the parent of the opposite sex—is merely one of many archetypes. One aim of Jung's psychotherapy is to facilitate the emergence of various archetypes into the patient's conscious awareness. The collective unconscious is the most powerful of the personality's components. In pathological cases it overwhelms both the ego and the personal unconscious. Although the collective unconscious is Jung's most dramatic contribution to personality theory, its mystical quality has made it unacceptable to many other theorists.

The Self. The self is an archetype that assumes particular significance when the individual is in his thirties or early forties, when it develops out of the boundaries of the collective unconscious and becomes the nucleus around which all the entities of the personality become clustered. It is able to utilize the perceptions and processes of both the conscious and unconscious, to retain a firm grip on the realities of both the external and internal worlds. The self holds the entities of the personality together in a balanced and stable relationship to one another. Its development is associated with a lessening of instinctual "push," giving more emphasis to the natural "pull" of man's innate goal to develop himself to his full potential. The satisfaction of this goal is *self-actualization.* It often takes place within the boundaries of organized religion. The concept of self-actualization assumes a key role in other later theories.

Among the many archetypes of the collective unconscious, one of special interest to marketers is the *persona.* The persona originates out of the history of man's social interactions and can be thought of, in part, as social psychological programming inherited from one's forebears. Upon this base is built a behavioral and attitudinal mask developed in response to the demands of social convention, tradition, and the individual's reference groups. The persona is a sort of personal packaging or image, and many image-enhancing commercial products owe their sales largely if not entirely to the individual's desire to protect and embellish his public face.

The impulses, thoughts, feelings, and actions that are inconsistent with the demands that created the persona are incorporated into the *shadow,* where they are kept outside the range of the individual's awareness. Although hidden to the individual, his shadow may be perfectly obvious to those around him. A father may perceive himself as kind and loving, but his children may fear him as an unfeeling tyrant. The shadow can also be projected—the individual will see his own undesired thoughts and feelings reflected in another person whom he may choose as a scapegoat. At times, under the influence of alcohol or drugs, the shadow can temporarily dominate a person, who later may be quite surprised at his behavior.

Jung classified people into psychological types along two dimensions: *attitudes* and *functions*. The attitude categories are perhaps Jung's best-known and most widely accepted contribution to personality theory. They refer to the basic orientation of the personality. The attitude of *extroversion* orients the individual toward the external objective world; the attitude of *introversion* orients him toward the inner subjective world. The extreme form of extroversion is hysteria; the extreme form of introversion is schizophrenia. Both attitudes are thought to be present in each individual in varying degrees, and may alternate in dominating his view of life.

The functions are the four basic psychological processes: *thinking, feeling, sensing,* and *intuiting.* Thinking is ideational and intellectual; it supplies meaning. Feeling gives man his subjective experiences of pleasure and pain, anger, fear, joy, and love. Sensing yields facts about the world. Intuition is unconscious perception that gives an additional, if mystical, dimension of data to an experience. One function is usually developed more than the others and is called the *superior function.* The eight combinations of attitude and superior functions are shown in Table 1.

Jung is also well known for another effort that goes hand in hand with classification: that of objective measurement. He gained early repute for his use of the word-association test in conjunction with measurements of pulse and breathing rate. He theorized that changes in these measurements associated with certain words were clues to the existence and makeup of the complexes described earlier. Similar clues were given by a patient's inability to associate a word with one read to him, or a delay in responding. Today this technique of taking measurements during a dialogue has evolved into the use of the polygraph, or lie detector, in work with criminal suspects and prospective corporation and government employees. The word-association test was used by market researchers to help American Telephone & Telegraph name its automatic long-distance phone service. The name chosen: Direct Distance Dialing (Stryker, 1956).

As did Freud, Jung believed that personality develops through the conflict of elements within the personality. The ego opposes the shadow, the persona, and the other components of the collective unconscious; the persona battles other archetypes; introversion competes with extroversion; masculinity fights feminity; thinking contests with feeling, and sensation with intuition. Whereas Freud saw resolution of conflict between the instincts and the individual's culture or environment as the critical process of development, Jung saw the

TABLE 1. Jung's Psychological Types[a]

Attitude / Function	Extroverted	Introverted
Rational—based on judgment, abstraction and generalization		
Thinking	Directs his life and that of his dependents according to fixed rules; his thinking is positive, synthetic, dogmatic.	A man who lacks practical sense, he isolates himself after unpleasant experiences with his fellowmen. He desires to get to the bottom of things, and shows great boldness in his ideas but is often hindered by hesitations and scruples.
Feeling	Keeps to the values he has been taught, respects social conventions, does what is proper and is very emotional.	Unassuming, quiet, oversensitive individual difficult to understand by his fellowmen; in the case of women, she exerts a mysterious power over extroverted men.
Not rational—based on perception		
Sensing	Pleasure loving, sociable, adjusts himself easily to people and circumstances.	A quiet person who looks upon the world with a mixture of benevolence and amusement, and is particularly sensitive to the esthetic quality of things.
Intuiting	Shows insight in life situations, detects and is attracted by new possibilities, is talented for business, speculation, and politics.	A daydreamer who ascribes the utmost value to his inner trend of thought; easily considered odd or eccentric by others.

[a]Source: Ellenberger, 1970. Chapter 9, "Carl Gustav Jung and Analytical Psychology," pp. 701-2.

polar elements as checks and balances. He describes the healthy personality as one in which the psychic energy is evenly distributed among the elements. Even development of all the elements of personality produces harmony, relaxation, and contentment, and frees more psychic energy for productive and cultural pursuits.

Jung also agreed with Freud in conceptualizing personality as the product of successive developmental stages, but, unlike Freud, Jung theorized that development takes place over the individual's entire life span. The infant begins life with a nondifferentiated collective unconscious. A conscious ego slowly emerges, along with a personal unconscious. Before age 5, sexual values begin to appear, and reach their height during adolescence. In his youth and early adult years, the individual's basic life instincts and vital processes predominate: he is energetic, impulsive, passionate, and still dependent on others. But with middle age these early values do not attract the discharge of psychic energy as they once did. If the individual does not find cultural or spiritual pursuits to absorb this energy, the energy is not discharged and is free to upset the equilibrium of the personality. The shift from the fires of youth to a more mature, spiritual orientation in the middle of life is both normal and desirable. In Jung's view, the pseudo-youth of aging people in Western countries is self-defeating, and stands in vivid contrast to the dignity of the elders of other cultures. Because he felt that the personality's development is a continuing process, Jung saw the roots of neurosis in the patient's present situation, not in remote childhood. He defined neurosis as a "sick system of social relationships." Jung thought that Freud's emphasis on the early years of life as the source of current problems was like attributing the political difficulties of nineteenth century Germany to the ancient Roman conquests.

Adler's Individual Psychology

Like Jung, Alfred Adler was a younger contemporary of Freud who broke with the master over the importance of the sexual instincts in the development of personality. But unlike Jung (and Freud), Adler was not so much interested in cataloging the functional elements of the psyche as he was in working out practical methods for effecting cures. He used the theoretical methodology of present-day price theorists who contend that people behave "as if" such and such hypotheses were true. In contrast to the dogmatic Freud, Adler did not believe it necessary that his hypotheses be literally correct as long as they lead to improved mental health.

More than either Jung or Freud, Adler took the Enlightenment view that man is essentially rational and in control of his own destiny. His "as ifs" in support of this view are as follows:

1. The mind and the body are one and work in harmony.

2. Life is movement toward goals: the individual is pulled by his unconscious goals, not pushed by his unconscious instincts. (Freud's theory is a "push" theory; Jung's is a "push-pull" theory; Adler's is a "pull" theory.) Although Adler did not envision discrete stages of development, he felt that the individual's life goals were set in early childhood and could rarely be changed thereafter except with therapeutic help. One child may be seen to be pursuing the goal of athletic excellence early in his life, whereas another will be observed concentrating on his intellectual development. The ultimate goal for man is a striving for completion or perfection of himself as a unique individual; it is not a pursuit of pleasure.

3. Sensations, perceptions, images, memories, fantasies, and dreams converge toward the line of direction the individual is taking toward his

goal. As the individual matures, this pattern becomes adjusted to the standards of the community. Alder called it the *style of life*.

4. Man naturally perceives the principles that rule the relationships of men to each other and spontaneously agrees to live by these principles. A social interest is inborn, but intelligence and creativity are required for its development; stifle either and an antisocial individual may be the result. The specific relationships between individuals are determined by society and must be learned.

5. An individual is never in an isolated and static situation. An action in the social environment will create a reaction to which the individual must adjust.

6. There is a norm that consists of an optimal balance between two opposing forces: the requirements of the individual and those of the community. The degree of deviation from this norm is a measure of the severity of the individual's disturbance, ranging from unhappiness to outright criminality.

Adler's social orientation reflects the findings of anthropologists of his time that the human personality can be molded in many ways, and has caused his theory to be thought of by some as the first in a family of social-psychological personality theories that have assumed great importance in the United States today. He believed that the individual adult must fulfill responsibilities in three social areas: to love and family, to profession, and to the community. The indication of a successful therapy is the patient's ability to meet all three of these tasks.

Early in his explorations Adler conceived the notion for which he is most famous, the *inferiority complex*. An individual may come to believe that he has an inferiority of some kind; the inferiority may be real or imagined. A healthy person will work to overcome his feelings of inferiority, to *compensate* for them, within the principles of his community. If an individual exaggerates the extent of his inferiority, he is said to have an inferiority complex and may *overcompensate* for the inferiority in socially unacceptable ways. An example is the sick child who later becomes a bully or a political tyrant. If the individual fails to compensate successfully, he may develop a neurosis and limit his social participation.

Adler pointed out that our public and private institutions rest upon the prejudice of the superiority of the male, and that it is nurtured in boys as well as girls by education and subtle and often unconscious suggestion. This led him to propose that women in general may try to compensate for their consequent feelings of inferiority through what he called the *masculine protest*.

The goal of Adler's therapy was the same as Freud's, to free the patient from his symptoms and to help him live a happy, productive life. But his treatment technique was considerably more direct. Whereas Freud sat silently out of sight as his patient reclined on a couch, Adler sat facing his patient, conversing actively. Whereas Freud sought to have his patients relive agonizing experiences dredged up from the depths of the unconscious, Adler sought to free his patients from the complexes and false goals that impeded natural progression toward realistic goals. Adler was fundamentally optimistic about the nature of man and the possibility of achieving both happiness and success. It is perhaps for this reason that his ideas have received considerable attention in the United States. They are compatible with the Horatio Alger tradition, the tenets of "pro-gressive" education, and the assumption that all men have an inalienable right to life, liberty, and the pursuit of happiness.

Karen Horney

Freud, Jung, and Adler were Europeans, and remained in Europe most of their lives. Karen Horney was born and educated in Germany, but practiced psychoanalysis in both Europe and the United States. The differences between her European and American patients helped influence her to emphasize the importance of social factors, especially the shaping role played by parents, in the development of personality.

Horney believed that Freud overemphasized sex because he generalized the characteristics of his early twentieth-century Viennese patients to all of mankind. She believed that it is not enough to assume that sex is involved in every repressed desire, but rather that sexual desires represent only one of many desires that an individual might hide, and that it is part of the analyst's task to determine the nature of the disturbing subterranean feelings.

Horney's work led her to believe that the key determinant of behavior is *neurotic anxiety* generated by the child's feeling of being "isolated and helpless in a potentially hostile world" (Horney, 1945). To cope with this anxiety, the child develops a set of dispositions that fall into three primary groups:

1. The need to move *toward* people—the need for love, affection, and approval.
2. The need to move *away from* people—the need for self-sufficiency, independence, and unassailability.
3. The need to move *against* people—the need for power and exploitation of others.

These needs are neurotic when overexpression of one need prevents balanced expression of the others, and when overexpression of any one need (in response to an oversupply of basic anxiety) provokes a hostile reaction from the environment and thus increases basic anxiety even more.

In Horney's scheme the parents' actions play the major role. Through the amount of security they provide, they determine the amount of basic anxiety that will develop. By rewarding some of the child's tactics and punishing others, the parents (and later other important people) determine the strategy the child will adopt to cope with the anxiety he feels. The strategy itself—the relative amount of moving *toward* others, moving *away from* others and moving *against* others—forms the basic structure of adult behavior.

In her later writings Horney came to agree with Adler that the striving toward self-realization is the main drive in man. She felt this drive is impeded by the inflated self-picture a man might form to compensate for his anxiety; attempts to live according to this fictitious self-image are manifested as neurotic behavior.

Horney's work has had considerable impact upon American psychologists and psychoanalysts, and through them on contemporary American thought. In particular, her emphasis on the parents' roles in the development of personality and her break with the Freudian notion that the basic structures of personality are "built into" the organism have found a receptive audience in the United States. Horney's system is also of interest to students of consumer behavior, because the concepts of moving toward, moving against, and moving away from are the basis for one of the few attempts to develop a personality questionnaire to link a well-known personality theory to the behavior of consumers. The results of this work by Cohen (1967) will be noted later in this chapter.

Reisman's Social Typology

In his analysis of trends in the political and social history of Europe and the United States, the sociologist David Riesman has made a case for three distinct themes in the direction of behavior (Riesman, Denney, and Glazer, 1950). Through the Middle Ages and on into fairly recent times, Riesman noted, much of the behavior of most men was *tradition directed:* a rigid set of rules, usually backed by powerful religious beliefs, prescribed what should be done under what circumstances, and why. But as the hold of religion weakened in the eighteenth and nineteenth centuries, and as greater value began to be placed on the rights and achievements of the individual, more of the behavior of more men became *inner directed:* each man had to decide for himself, in view of his own enlightened self-interest, the proper course to take in a world that was becoming increasingly complex.

In the United States today, Riesman asserted, the tradition-directed man is almost gone, existing only in a few small custom-bound communities that have managed to remain isolated from the cultural mainstream. Even the inner-directed man, the nineteenth century American ideal, is now, according to Riesman, being replaced by the *other-directed* man—the man who directs his behavior so as to secure the esteem and approval of his immediate peers. Thus the definition of what is right is for many present-day Americans "that which is most popular." Note the similarity of inner-directed behavior to Jung's concept of introversion, and of other-directed behavior to extroversion.

Riesman said that the shift from tradition directedness to inner directedness to other directedness has had a profound impact on the behavior of consumers. In tradition-directed societies people wear, eat, and drink that which tradition says they should wear, eat, and drink, and little else, for even minor deviations are punished. In inner-directed societies consumption of products and of services, like religious instruction and education, is determined by the contribution this consumption makes to the long-term benefit of the individual. But in other-directed societies, consumption is determined by the contribution consumption makes to status and popularity.

Since the United States is in the process of shifting (slowly) from inner directedness to other directedness, the U.S. population contains, and will continue to contain for some time to come, substantial numbers of consumers who follow one or the other of these two incompatible life styles. It is therefore inevitable that consumer choices by the other-directed segment of the population will be determined largely by motives that the inner-directed segment regards as frivolous, superficial, and ethically wrong.

In addition to setting forth an intriguing hypothesis about an on-going shift in American national character and proposing some reasons for the current controversy over the "proper" motivations for consumer behavior, Riesman's work suggests still another general dimension system along which consumers may be segmented. As will be seen later in this chapter, this system has been among the many so employed.

Harry Stack Sullivan's Interpersonal Theory

More than the theories discussed so far, Sullivan's interpersonal theory specifically emphasizes the social context in which men live. Although he recognized that heredity and maturation affect the development of personality, Sullivan believed that learning through social interaction contributes that which is uniquely human. He felt that personality could be defined only in terms of the individual's overt or covert reactions to the other people in life's recurring interpersonal situations. An individual, even when alone, is influenced by his prior experiences with others, and by his expectations of their opinions of him in the future. The other people need not be real or alive. An individual may be influenced by the teachings of a long-dead philosopher, the television image of a fictional character, or a vision of his descendents. The individual's dreams revolve around other people: he dreams of successes that will impress others.

Sullivan called the smallest unit of recurring reactions a *dynamism.* He used this term to describe certain patterns of feelings and behaviors—fear and aggression are examples—and also to describe the entities or mechanisms that are the components of personality. Sullivan felt that the term *mechanism* was too static and that it did not indicate the personality's ever-present potential for change. Dynamisms are relatively enduring and accumulate throughout life. The well-adjusted person possesses an inventory of dynamisms, none of which receive a particular emphasis in his life. A mentally disturbed person is characterized by an extraordinary dependence on one particular dynamism.

Perhaps the most important of the dynamisms is the self-system, a complex of dynamisms built around the energizing force of anxiety. Anxiety begets tension, and tension is painful. The aim of the self-system is to reduce tension by making the individual feel competent to deal with other people without becoming aware of the many threats to his self-esteem that are implicit in almost any social situation. The self-system develops as a result of anxiety that is first transmitted empathetically from a mother to her baby, and is developed further by anxiety-producing interpersonal experiences throughout the individual's life. With increasing anxiety the self-system becomes more highly developed and isolated from the rest of the personality. Selective inattention and self-delusion develop hand in hand with the self-system, making it increasingly difficult for the individual to appraise himself or his environment objectively, thereby interfering with his constructive interaction with others. A highly developed self-system—akin to a collection of well-practiced defense mechanisms—stands in the way of personality changes. In a schizophrenic the self-system and the real self exist as independent entities, or dual personalities, within the same individual.

Like Freud, Sullivan viewed the personality as a tension-reduction system. He defined two sources of tension: (1) needs, the physiochemical requirements of life, and (2) anxiety. The individual's interpersonal relations—first, dependent relations with older and more powerful people, later with peers—determine the array from which he will select the behaviors that will come to characterize his personality. The less anxiety he experiences in these interpersonal situations, the more "secure" he is and the more appropriate will be his selection.

Associated with tension reduction is the development of *personifications*, clusters of feelings, attitudes, and conceptions concerning oneself or another individual that have their roots in early experiences and are therefore based on the distortions of primitive cognitive processes. Any person resembling the original personified concept gains the reputation, good or bad, of the original personification. Personifications are maintained because they reduce the tension inherent in the individual's encounters with new people. If the same personification is found among many people, it is called a *stereotype*. A brand image might be considered the product analog of a personification on an individual level and of a stereotype on a group level.

Sullivan proposed six stages for the individual's social maturation, each stage marked not by a crisis, but rather by a qualitative change in the social learning process. Successively, the individual begins the development of his self-system;

learns the discipline of language; develops the conception of gender and begins to fear those around him; discovers the existence of ingroups, outgroups, and ostracism; becomes open and trusting with a peer of the same sex; develops a pattern of heterosexual activity; and ultimately enters adulthood between the ages of 20 and 30, having learned the rituals and behaviors that will work best for him in his society. If the individual does not learn the lessons associated with each stage, his adult personality will reflect the deficit. For instance, if he does not learn to deal with the early fear of those around him, the fear will emerge as paranoia, causing the individual to suspect the intentions of all those people with whom he must interact. If he does not learn a pattern of heterosexual activity, the individual's preadolescent needs for a chum of the same sex may become homosexual erotic impulses.

Freud felt that the basic structure and pattern of personality were fixed at an early age. Sullivan did not believe this to be true: he felt personality could change at any time as new interpersonal situations arise. Sullivan's major theoretical contribution was to loosen the fetters of early events on the later behavior of the individual, at the same time rooting that behavior more in the social context of the developing individual's life.

Sullivan saw the opposition of man's biological needs to the rules of society as a major source of anxiety and mental illness, as did Freud, but he did not believe that man was inherently bad and society inherently good. He felt that anxiety was produced by the irrational aspects of society.

In many ways Sullivan marks a transition from an individual instinct-oriented conception of personality that was characteristic of the early psychoanalysts to a more society-oriented conception of personality that is more characteristic of psychoanalysts today. Of the society-oriented psychoanalysts, the outstanding contemporary figure is undoubtedly Erik Erikson.

Erik Erikson

Erikson, like Sullivan, does not believe the individual's personality is set in early childhood. He pictures personality changing over a full lifetime in response to crises that are ordered and spaced by one's culture.

The first is the crisis of *trust versus mistrust.* As Horney and Sullivan emphasized, it is to be expected that a young child will feel helpless and alone in an unpredictable and hostile world. A young child *is* helpless: he cannot care for his own needs and the world *is* full of dangers. This helplessness can be ameliorated somewhat by parents (or their substitutes) who are consistently attentive, warm, and responsive; and it can be made much more acute when parents are inconsistent, rejecting, harsh, or cold.

In Erikson's view, the actions of the parents during the child's first year set the tone of the child's basic stance toward life. The optimal outcome is a general disposition to trust others. The negative outcome is a general attitude of hostility or a disposition to withdraw. Here, the correspondence between Erikson's view and Horney's is quite close.

The second crisis, which occurs in the second and third years, is the crisis of *autonomy versus doubt.* During these years the child develops the ability to manipulate the physical world and to propel himself around it, and in doing so he is bound to cause a certain amount of inconvenience to those who must see that he does not injure himself too seriously, throw valuable objects down the toilet, or do irreversible damage to the cat. If the child's attempts to manipulate and explore the world are supervised with an unusual degree of patience, the outcome is a general disposition to be one's own man—to try things and see how they will work. The corresponding negative disposition is a general trait of hesitancy and doubt.

In Erikson's view the third crisis is *initiative versus guilt.* In the first 3 years of life the child's activities tend mostly to be initiated by others, either by direct suggestions and commands or by the less obvious process of serving as models. In the fourth and fifth years, however, the child begins to initiate more and more activities on his own and to be held responsible for what he has done. If his attempts to learn and explore physically and his attempts to produce intellectually are valued and encouraged by those around him, the outcome is a general disposition toward initiative. If, on the other hand, his less than perfect performances are ridiculed or punished, the outcome is a general feeling of self-blame that Erikson calls *guilt.*

Crisis number four occurs during the 6- to 11-year stage when the influence of the immediate family is supplemented by the influence of the school. During these years the child is given opportunities to achieve in sports and games, in school work, and in extracurricular social activities. Success in these activities, defined by positive reactions from important people in the child's life, enhances the general disposition to persevere when things do not go right the first time. Repeated failures—repeated put-downs by important people—generate an overall feeling of worthlessness, a feeling that the game is not worth the effort because there is so little chance to win. *Industry versus inferiority* is the crisis name.

The adolescent years bring on the *identity crisis (identity versus role confusion)*, a term so acutely appropriate that it is hard to see how observers of adolescence ever got along before it appeared. Adolescents are smart enough to realize that they will shortly be required to be something and somebody quite different from what they have been or now are, that the world at best is far from perfect, and that decisions about what they are going to be are largely up to them. If previous crises have been resolved in trust, autonomy, initiative, and industry, the adolescent has the foundation from which to build a strong and effective identity. If not, adolescence and early adulthood will be a period of severe conflict over "who am I, and who will I be?"

The sixth crisis, *intimacy versus isolation,* is the crisis of young adulthood. Intimacy refers not only to the free giving of oneself to a sexual partner, but also to affectional relations with many others, including especially family and close friends.

Generativity versus self-absorption is the long crisis of middle life. By generativity Erikson means not only the re-creation of one's self in one's own biological children, but also an active concern about the world in which succeeding generations will live. The opposite extreme is exclusive or near exclusive concern with self, a concern that is certain to be self-defeating because of the inevitable isolation it brings.

Finally, as life nears its close and the individual looks back on what he has accomplished and what might have been, the last crisis occurs, the crisis of *integrity versus despair.* If there is a sense of accomplishment and fulfillment, the resolution is what Erikson calls a sense of integrity. If life appears at this point to have been a long series of mistakes, the outcome is despair, because it is now too late. These last two stages are similar in nature to the period Jung specified as being devoted to self-actualization.

Erikson's work is important to students of consumer behavior for several reasons. First, as one of the most highly regarded spokesmen for the modern psychoanalytic movement, Erikson represents the culmination of a line of study that has had an immense impact on contemporary views of human nature. Literature, theater, movies, television, advertising—virtually all contemporary popular culture—bear the imprint of the psychoanalysts' emphasis on symbolism and unconscious motivation. Advice to parents, dispensed through school courses, women's magazines and "how to" books by pediatricians, all emphasize the vital role of childhood experience in molding the adult personality.

At the same time that Erikson has retained many of the basic features of orthodox psychoanalytic theory, he has shifted away from exclusive focus on the early years of life, and, following Sullivan's lead, he has devoted much more attention than earlier analysts to the continuing development and redevelopment of personality through the life span. Since adults are the primary consumers of a great many goods and services and the bulk of the audience of many of the mass media, Erikson's work has at least as much relevance to marketing problems as has the work of Freud. In many ways Erikson's work is a valuable companion piece to the sociologists' analysis of the family life cycle (Lansing and Kish, 1957; Wells and Gubar, 1966).

Henry Murray

Henry Murray is unlike the earlier theoreticians in two special ways. He felt very strongly that a theory of personality based only on the observation of disturbed subjects was bound to be limited in its applicability. And he felt that detailed description was a necessary prelude to theory building. In line with these beliefs, Murray and his colleagues (Murray, 1938) conducted a series of studies of young adults that resulted in an influential list of environmental forces, called *presses,* and internal *needs* that interact with the presses to produce behavior. According to this view, everyone has the same basic set of needs, but persons differ greatly in the priority by which each will be satisfied. In Murray's theory the strongest unsatisfied needs of the moment, interacting with presses exerted by the present environment, cause people to act.

What are the basic psychosocial needs? The list developed by Murray and his followers (Murray, 1938) includes the following (Edwards, 1957):

1. *Achievement:* to do one's best, to accomplish something of great significance.

2. *Deference:* to find out what others think, to accept the leadership of others.

3. *Exhibition:* to say witty and clever things, to talk about personal achievements.

4. *Autonomy:* to be able to come and go as desired, to say what one thinks about things.

5. *Affiliation:* to be loyal to friends, to make as many friends as possible.

6. *Intraception:* to analyze one's motives and feelings, and to analyze the feelings of others.

7. *Dominance:* to be a leader in the groups to which one belongs, to tell others how to do their jobs.

8. *Abasement:* to feel guilty when one does something wrong, to feel inferior to others in most respects.

9. *Change:* to do new and different things, to participate in new fads and fashions.

10. *Aggression:* to attack contrary points of view, to get revenge for insults.

11. *Heterosexuality:* to become sexually excited, to be in love with someone of the opposite sex.

This list of needs has been important in some studies of consumer behavior because it formed the basis of the Edwards Personal Preference Schedule, one of the paper-and-pencil personality questionnaires that students of consumer behavior have employed in attempts to relate personality characteristics to purchasing decisions and brand choice. The outcomes of these attempts will be described later.

Another product of Murray's work was the Thematic Apperception Test, or TAT. The TAT is a standard set of pictures, most of which resemble magazine story illustrations, that depict a wide variety of persons (and some animals) engaged in various activities—talking, thinking, daydreaming, running, fighting, and so on. The person taking the test is asked to look at each picture and make up a story about it, including what happened in the past leading up to the events shown in the picture, what the characters in the story are feeling and thinking, and what will happen in the future. These stories are examined for evidence of needs and presses, on the assumption that the story teller has projected himself into them, and that recurring needs and presses in the story are therefore apt to be important needs and presses in the storyteller's own life.

Modifications of the TAT have been used in projective studies of consumer behavior. Pictures of a product-related event—such as a man and a woman trying to decide whether or not to stop at a particular company's gas station, or a man informing his wife that he has decided to start smoking cigars—are shown to respondents, and the resulting stories are analyzed so as to illuminate consumers' attitudes toward the product or the company involved (Smith, 1954).

Maslow's Hierarchy of Needs

The point of view expressed by Murray and his followers contained explicit recognition of the notion that any one individual's needs form a hierarchy, but that the priority assigned to various needs may vary from one individual to another. The psychologist A. H. Maslow (Maslow, 1954) carried this thinking forward by positing a general universal hierarchy that is the same for all people. This notion has influenced thinking about human behavior, including consumer behavior, from almost the moment it appeared.

Maslow pointed out that the *physiological drives*, such as hunger, thirst, and the need for sleep, are at once very important and very unimportant in determining day-to-day activities. They are important because when they are chronically unsatisfied they become dominant—one's "whole philosophy of the future" changes, to use Maslow's apt phrase. But most of the time, for most Americans, the basic physiological needs are satisfied regularly and easily, and under these circumstances other "higher" needs emerge.

At the level immediately above the basic needs for body maintenance are the needs for *safety*. These needs are earliest seen in the infant's spontaneous startled reaction to loud noises, bright lights, or sudden loss of support. Later they are seen in the child's need for repetition and routine, and in his flight to his mother at the appearance of anything uncontrollable, new, or strange. In the adult they are seen in panic reactions to unexpected emergencies.

When the safety needs are not met, they also dominate the "whole philosophy of the future." But when they are met, as they are for most Americans most of the time, the next "higher" level of needs—the *love* needs—become prepotent. These are the needs for strong affectional bonds with other people, especially with children and husband or wife. According to Maslow, the thwarting of love needs is, in contemporary American society, "the most commonly found core in cases of maladjustment and more severe psychopathology."

Once the individual is secure in his affectional relations with family and friends he will still seek the recognition and approval of others. He strives to satisfy his *esteem* needs.

Finally, even with easy and regular satisfaction of the physiological, safety, love, and esteem needs, the individual will still be driven by the "desire to become more and more what one is, to become everything one is capable of becoming." Maslow based this concept on the ideas of Jung and Adler, and, like Jung, he labeled it *self-actualization*. The need for self-actualization represents the top of the need hierarchy, depending as it does upon continuous and repeated satisfaction of all the needs below it.

This way of thinking about motivation is important to students of consumer behavior for several reasons. First, it is a neat way of reconciling some common observations that otherwise are hard to fit together. For instance, it is obvious that the physiological body maintenance motives are in some sense basic to all human behavior, yet these motives seem to have little to do with the direction of what most Americans do most of the day. Maslow's answer is that these motives (and each successive "higher" motive group) become prepotent only when they are chronically unsatisfied. Similarly, Maslow's formulation predicts that the satisfaction of one set of strivings will not lead to quiescence, as a naive drive-reduction explanation of behavior would predict, but rather to further strivings for satisfactions at the next level. Maslow's scheme restates a well-known fact: people do not quit striving when they get what they think they want. In fact, it posits that people will not quit striving *especially* when they get what they think they want.

Maslow's theory also summarizes and puts in place a variety of other topics often studied separately. For instance, status-seeking behavior (see Chapter 8 of this book) can be seen as response to esteem needs. The level of aspiration studies that grew out of field theory (see Chapter 2) can be seen as an instance of moving from one level of a motive hierarchy to another. In the consumer field, a great many of the activities of the homemaker are directly related to the maintenance and enhancement of affectional relationships within the family. Savings programs, life insurance, and medical-care plans can be seen as responses to the safety needs, and so on.

Incidentally, Maslow's formulation suggests the interesting hypothesis that consumer products designed to satsify self-actualization and esteem needs should flourish best in times of peace and security, whereas times of danger and unrest should produce more consumer behavior directed toward the familiar, the regular, the secure, the tried and true.

William H. Sheldon's Constitutional Psychology

American psychology has been strongly environmental, downplaying the importance of a genetic inheritance that might lend direction to, and set limits on, an individual's psychological development. In a departure from this general trend, William H. Sheldon's constitutional theory links certain broad classes of behavior to an individual's observable and genetically determined physical characteristics.

Observers of human nature have long noted that there is some congruence between body build and behavior. Shakespeare had Caesar say, "Let me have men about me that are fat; sleek-headed men, and such as sleep o'nights. Yon Cassius has a lean and hungry look; he thinks too much; such men are dangerous." Kretschmer, one of the most important figures in the development of psychiatry, noted that in mental hospital populations the schizophrenics tend to be tall and thin, while the manic-depressives tend to be short and fat. Novelists invariably give physical descriptions of their central characters, as though a person's physical description helps forecast how he will behave.

By far the most systematic and rigorous examination of the relationships between behavior and body build is to be found in the work of William H. Sheldon, an American physician and psychologist who has spent most of his professional life at Harvard and Columbia, working first with experimental psychologists and then with physicians.

Sheldon developed a rigorous technique for estimating from standardized front-, back-, and side-view photographs of adults, the relative contribution of each of three types of body tissue to the total body structure. Thus a "skinny" person (in Sheldon's terminology, an *ectomorph*) would have, relative to the norm, more of his body made up of tissue that arose from the outer, ectodermal layer of the embryo. A professional football linebacker would have a greater than average amount of mesodermal tissue (muscle and bone) in his physique. And Santa Claus—at least as he is portrayed in most illustrations of *'Twas the Night Before Christmas*—would have more of his body made up of tissue growing out of the endoderm (inner) layer of embryo cells that develop into the digestive system.

Sheldon developed this way of measuring physique because he was trying to link physical dimensions to behavior. For the description of behavior, he chose *traits*. Consider the following list of words:

absentminded	energetic	reasonable
ambitious	feminine	restless
anxious	frank	selfish
calm	friendly	sentimental
cautious	honest	strong
clean	idealistic	stingy
confident	impulsive	stubborn
cruel	lazy	timid
dependent	obstinate	trustworthy
dull	orderly	weak

These words are names of traits—adjectives that describe general dispositions to behave in designated ways. They are common words that people use to describe themselves and each other; and their use always implies something about probable future behavior in situations as yet unforeseen.

If we simply count the number of trait names in a standard dictionary, the number of traits appears to be exceedingly large—around 18,000 in a count made by Allport and Odbert in 1936. But many trait names are near synonyms (selfish, self-seeking, self-indulgent, self-interested, self-centered; virtuous, meritorious, deserving, worthy, righteous, praiseworthy, noble); and even when traits are not synonyms, some seem to go together much better than others. Ambitious, energetic, impulsive, and restless sound as though they describe a person; absentminded, calm, cruel, and dull do not.

The fact that certain traits seem to go together even when they denote somewhat different kinds of behavior suggests that there may be certain underlying somethings that cause the traits that "go together" to go together. Maybe ambitious, energetic, impulsive, and restless go together because they are all outward manifestations of some more basic entity; whereas absentminded, ambitious, calm, cruel, and dull do not mesh because they signify entities that do not usually occur in the same person. Sheldon's goal was to identify a set of basic trait clusters, and then to relate these dimensions of personality to dimensions of physique.

From an original inventory of 650 traits culled from the personality literature, Sheldon and his colleagues selected 50 that seemed representative of the larger group. By the method of personal observation and interview they rated subjects on each of the 50 traits over a year's time, using a seven-point scale for each trait. The resulting scores were intercorrelated and three clusters—traits that seemed to go together—were found. The three clusters, conceived as dimensions of temperament, were called *viscerotonia, somatotonia,* and *cerebrotonia.* A high viscerotonia score denotes relaxation in movement and posture, love of physical comfort, love of eating, amiability, and strong need for affection and approval. A high score on somatotonia denotes assertiveness of posture and movement, love of physical adventure, need for exercise, need for dominance and power, willingness to take risks, boldness, and directness of manner. And a high cerebrotonia score denotes restraint in movement, love of privacy, mental over-intensity, secretiveness of feeling, and emotional restraint (Sheldon, 1942).

Sheldon and his collaborators then proceeded to correlate scores on the three temperament dimensions to scores representing the relative dominance of each of the three types of body tissue. Viscerotonic individuals were found to have a strong tendency to be endomorphs; somatotonic individuals were found to have a strong tendency to be mesomorphs; and cerebrotonic individuals were found to be ectomorphs. The correlations were surprisingly strong, in fact so strong that many critics insisted they were too good to be true. Although independent investigations of these relationships have not confirmed Sheldon's findings exactly—especially with respect to the strength of the relationships—enough independent evidence has been forthcoming to indicate that body-personality relationships do indeed exist, and that the strength of the relationships is greater than many personality theorists had thought.

One major question associated with Sheldon's work is the question of cause and effect. Is the aggressive mesomorph aggressive because the genes that make for large shares of bone and muscle also make for an aggressive temperament? Or is the mesomorph aggressive because, having been bigger and stronger than his age mates most of his life, a strategy of aggressiveness worked pretty well most of the time? Sheldon himself is not clear on this point.

Sheldon's scheme for classifying personality traits into three basic behavioral dimensions, derived originally through an empirical clustering of trait ratings, bears a marked resemblance to Horney's three-dimensional personality scheme. The comfort-loving, affectionate, approval-seeking viscerotonic moves *toward* other people. The dominant, assertive, power-oriented somatotonic moves *against* others. And the secretive, sensitive, restrained cerebrotonic moves *away from* them. When similar findings come from independent investigators in different fields, confidence in them is increased.

There are also remarkable resemblances between the body build-behavior relationships found by Sheldon and the observations of human behavior recorded by novelists and dramatists. The bold hero is invariably a mesomorph. The sneaky crook (as distinguished from the violent crook) and the thinking detective (as distinguished from the fighting detective) are always ectomorphs. And affectionate, generous, jolly characters are usually endomorphs. Thus Sheldon's work is relevant to the type casting of actors in movies and television programs, and to the selections of appropriate models for image-building advertising. It would never do to use an ectomorph to portray the Marlboro Man.

The Factor Analysts

Cattell (1965) divided the systematization of knowledge about personality into three historical phases. The first is the literary and philosophical phase in which personal insight and traditional beliefs are paramount. Observations about the nature of man that are to be found in the Bible, in writings of the moral philosophers, and in the works of essayists, novelists, and playwrights represent this first level of development. The second phase—represented by Freud, Jung, Adler, and their followers—is one of organized observation and theorizing that grew up through the attempts of medicine to cope with abnormal behavior. Cattell noted that this phase "finished in a kind of intellectual shouting match." The third phase is the quantitative and experimental phase. Murray and his colleagues were early representatives of this phase. Sheldon also laid great emphasis on measurement and quantification. And the most elaborate development of this phase can be seen in the plans and activities of the factor analysts.

Without going into detail, let it be said that factor analysis is a mathematical technique requiring numerical input that is designed to reduce large numbers of interrelationships into a smaller set of more basic *dimensions* or *factors*. Sheldon's clustering of traits into three basic personality dimensions was a crude sort of factor analysis, as was Murray's classification of a wide variety of psychosocial motives into a limited but comprehensive list of needs.

Although almost any kind of numerical input can be factor analyzed, the most common application of factor analysis in the study of personality has been the analysis of responses to personality inventories and other types of paper-and-pencil, self-report questionnaires.

Personality inventories originated during World War I, when the U.S. Army tried to screen emotionally unfit men out of units being sent overseas. At first the screening was done by psychiatric interviewers, but as the expeditionary force grew large, army authorities soon found that they did not have enough interviewers to handle the job. They therefore decided to have the men screen themselves by filling out a "Personal Data Sheet" (Woodworth, 1918) that asked questions like

Did you have a happy childhood?
Have you ever had a vision?
Did you ever have a strong desire to commit suicide?

Each acknowledged problem added to a neurotic-tendency score, and men with high scores were called in for detailed psychiatric interviews.

Following this comparatively humble beginning as a rough screening device, the personality inventory grew and prospered in a variety of different settings. Most importantly, new "dimensions" were added at a prodigious rate, so that soon questionnaires in print allegedly measured not only neurotic tendency but also extraversion, sociability, dominance, emotional maturity, masculinity, creativity, friendliness, honesty, tolerance, and almost any other trait that one could name.

It was obvious that these dimensions were not independent—that many of the personality scales with different names actually were measuring much the same thing. The problem was how could this large and diverse array of scales with different names be analyzed and organized in such a way as to reveal the true basic underlying dispositions or dimensions that accounted for the inter-relationships among them. Furthermore, how could the basic dimensions that account for the results of personality questionnaires be related to and integrated with the basic dimensions that account for the relationships among other ways of measuring personality, such as objective physiological tests and ratings made by observers of the individual's behavior?

Factor analysis seemed ideally suited for this job. The hope of many factor analysts was that repeated factorings of personality-trait scores obtained by different measurement methods in different segments of the population would show the same group of basic dimensions (factors) emerging over and over again, so that one could say, "Here is the basic framework; here is the skeleton of human nature, at least in America at this time."

Unfortunately, the problem has turned out to be more complex than that. The dimensions that have emerged have differed, depending on the type of person measured, the particular technique of factor analysis used to extract the factors, and the type of measurement employed. Dimensions obtained in studies of college sophomores have differed from dimensions obtained in studies of executives, and both have differed from dimensions produced by studies of military personnel. Some varieties of factor analysis have extracted many "basic dimensions"; others have extracted only a few—even when differing techniques were used to analyze the same set of data. Self-inventories, ratings by others, and measurements obtained from objective tests have produced different "basic dimensions."

Although the factor analyst's hope of discovering the fundamental dimensions of personality has not yet been fulfilled, the results are worth some study. When a territory has not been thoroughly explored, a chart is useful even if parts of it are missing or wrong.

One of the most dedicated, ambitious, and prolific factor analysts of the personality domain is Raymond B. Cattell. A series of investigations extending over more than 20 years has produced a set of seven dimensions that he regards as basic, at least as far as paper-and-pencil inventories are concerned. The dimension list of another prominent factor analyst, J. P. Guilford, includes ten; the English psychologist H. J. Eysenck lists only two. These lists are shown in Table 2.

Although these three dimension systems differ from each other in many respects, they have enough in common to indicate that there is something there—that different investigators using different measurement techniques on different sets of persons tend to find somewhat the same sort of terrain. Dimensions 1 through 7 in the Cattell list are at least roughly analogous to dimensions 1 through 7 in the Guilford list, and both lists contain groups of dimensions that can be summarized as ego strength versus neuroticism, and extraversion versus introversion, the two "attitudes" earlier proposed by Jung. Later in this chapter there will be examples of how these maps have been used in consumer research.

SYNDROME MEASUREMENT

Another important quantitative strategy in the study of personality has been to select some limited, related, and significant group of traits, and to study the origin and functioning of that group of traits in great detail. Instead of attempting to develop a comprehensive framework of personality dimensions, as

TABLE 2. Dimensions of Personality: Findings of Three Factor Analysts

Cattell (1965)	Guilford (1959)	Eysenck (1960)
1. Adventurous, likes meeting people vs. shy, timid, withdrawn	1. Sociable vs. shy	
2. Self-assertive, confident, boastful vs. submissive, unsure, modest	2. Ascendent vs. submissive, retiring	Extraversion vs. introversion
3. Cheerful, joyous, sociable, responsive vs. depressed, pessimistic, seclusive, retiring	3. Action-oriented vs. thoughtful and reflective	
4. Good-natured, easy-going, cooperative vs. critical, grasping, obstinate	4. Friendly vs. hostile	
5. Mature, steady, persistent vs. changeable, unable to tolerate frustration	5. Emotionally stable vs. worrying, nervous	Ego-strength vs. neuroticism
6. Emotionally mature, independent-minded vs. demanding, impatient, dependent	6. Thick-skinned vs. sensitive	
7. Persevering, determined, responsible vs. quitting, frivolous, fickle	7. Serious-minded vs. carefree and impulsive	
	8. Speedy, lively, productive vs. slow and deliberate	
	9. Tolerant vs. suspicious	
	10. Masculine vs. feminine	

the factor analysts did, the investigators who adopted this strategy focused attention on a narrower portion of the field—getting a close-up, so to speak, instead of a panoramic view. This strategy has usually employed paper-and-pencil self-report instruments, although investigators who have adopted it have frequently employed other techniques as well. Two of the most important examples of this approach are the investigations of the authoritarian personality, and a long and elaborate set of studies by many different investigators who were interested in manifest anxiety.

Authoritarian Personality

Shortly after the close of World War II, a group of social scientists at the University of California set out to examine prejudice, especially anti-Semitism. With the Nazi concentration camps fresh in mind, they sought to find out what causes prejudice, with the hope that its growth could be prevented, or at least contained.

In a series of investigations that employed intensive clinical interviews, projective tests, and, finally, paper-and-pencil personality and attitude questionnaires, they came to the conclusion that anti-Semitism is but one trait in a larger constellation they called *ethnocentrism*—the generalized belief that anyone outside the ingroup is despicable—and that ethnocentrism itself is part of an *authoritarian syndrome* that has its origins in early childhood. Harsh, inconsistent, overly demanding parents, the California group concluded, produce offspring who as adults cope with their feelings of inadequacy by believing outgroups are inferior. Self-doubt and (unconscious) hatred of parents are projected outward onto the most available scapegoat, usually some racial minority (Adorno, et al., 1950).

This investigation provided a challenging view of the nature and origins of prejudice. It also produced a measuring instrument (the F-Scale) that itself had an important impact on social psychology. Because the F-Scale was brief, easy to understand, and easy to administer, because the dimension it measured— profascist tendencies—was (and is) of immense social significance, and because the research that produced it was linked both to general social psychology and to psychoanalysis, the F-Scale precipitated something of a research fad. In the decade following its publication, literally hundreds of studies employing it appeared, relating F-Scale scores to other personality dimensions, to a wide variety of attitudes and opinions, and to almost every conceivable kind of social behavior

Little of this work has a direct bearing on the study of consumers, except in the rather limited sense that purchases of hate literature, boycotts of outgroup merchants, and financial support of "fascist" (or "antifascist") politicians are all instances of consumer behavior. The most significant aspect of this work in the present context is the strategy it employed: the development of a relatively simple instrument to measure a limited, interrelated, and highly significant group of attitudes and traits, and the repeated and widespread use of this instrument to explore its many relationships with other traits and attitudes and with behavior. In the study of consumer behavior it is conceivable that the development of instruments to measure syndromes like opinion leadership or innovativeness might play such a role.

Manifest Anxiety

A second example of this same general approach is the work that has focused on the concept of *manifest anxiety*. As in the work on authoritarian personality, a measuring instrument emerged that had the virtues of being simple, interesting, and easy to use, and these qualities, along with the importance of the theory network in which the instrument was embedded, promptly produced a research fad.

Virtually all factor analytic studies of personality traits indicate the presence of a dimension (or dimensions) characterized by general mental health and emotional stability at one end and various neurotic symptoms at the other. In Cattell's work this contrast can be seen in several dimensions, including "mature, steady, persistent versus changeable, unable to tolerate frustration." In Guilford's scheme it shows up as "emotionally stable versus worrying, nervous," and in Eysenck's work it emerges as the single dimension of "ego-strength versus neuroticism."

A dimension much like this also permeates the work of the psychoanalysts. Indeed, in most cases the psychoanalysts' patients propel themselves into the consulting room mainly because they seek relief from neurotic symptoms.

In a series of steps that employed both the judgments of clinical psychologists and the objective techniques of psychometric scale construction, Janet Taylor Spence developed a paper-and-pencil measure of manifest anxiety. The *Manifest Anxiety Scale* asks in various ways whether and how often the respondent feels worried, upset, nervous, and tense (Taylor, 1953).

By itself this scale would have created little interest, because scales of this kind had often been developed before. But its author was able to show that relatively anxious people, as defined by scores on the scale, tend to acquire conditioned reflexes faster than less anxious people. Thus the scale formed a link between the clinical concept of anxiety on one hand and the vast structure of learning theory on the other.

Again, as was the case with the authoritarian personality studies, the availability of a simple and interesting measuring instrument produced an outpouring of research, all aimed at further understanding of the dimension the instrument measured. And, as with the authoritarian personality, interest was partly a result of the real-world significance of the dimension, and partly the result of the fact that the scale could be shown to fit into an important body of theory.

The research on manifest anxiety has somewhat more direct relevance to marketing problems than has the research on the authoritarian personality. Many commercial products, such as headache remedies, sedatives, and tonics, are advertised as relievers of the symptoms of anxiety. There is good reason to suppose that various forms of insurance are purchased at least in part in response to anxiety motivation. But, like the research on authoritarian personality, the most significant application to marketing of this work is the strategy it employed: construction of a simple instrument to measure an important dimension, and articulation of this dimension with an important body of theory.

SUMMING UP

We have now seen a variety of approaches to the question of the origin and nature of the basic dispositions that unite and precipitate behavior. The clinical studies of the psychoanalysts convinced them that the structure of adult personality is cast in the earliest years of development, if not in the history of the race. Later analysts, especially Erik Erikson, drew attention to the significance of episodes later in life, though even Erikson's view concedes that the possibilities for later evolution are constrained by the outcome of crises that occur in the early formative years. Adler, Horney, and Sullivan deemphasized the biological determinants of man's behavior and placed him in the context of his social environment.

To this picture of human nature, the work of Sheldon adds another dimension—the significance of physique. And the work of Riesman calls attention to the impact on behavior, especially consumer behavior, of shifts in social norms.

The factor analysts attempted to become the organizers of the field. Using a variety of measurement techniques, but depending most especially upon paper-and-pencil personality inventories, they attempted to lay bare the basic structure, the skeleton, of personality by uncovering its basic dimensions and determining how these dimensions were related to each other and to behavior.

Finally, the studies of the authoritarian personality and of manifest anxiety illustrate still another quantitative approach to the analysis of traits. Instead of attempting to encompass the entire range of behavior, this approach concentrates on a limited but significant trait group, and attempts to discover its origin and its role in the economy of the person.

Readers who are interested in learning more about the personality theorists and their theories are referred to *Theories of Personality* by C. S. Hall and Gardner Lindzey (1970). This book is the standard reference in the field, and it covers most of the theories described above in considerably more detail. Readers with particular interest in Freud, Jung, and Adler are referred to *The Discovery of the Unconscious* by H. F. Ellenberger (1970).

USES OF PERSONALITY THEORIES IN MARKETING

In one sense marketers cannot help using the concepts developed by personality theorists; they permeate the atmosphere around them. The results of Freud's work on symbolism and unconscious motivation can be seen at every turn in the mass media that carry advertising, and in the style and content of advertising itself. The psychoanalysts' emphasis on early childhood has echoed and reechoed through both informal and formal education, including the writings of Dr. Spock, and has influenced the purchase of books, toys, games, foods, and many other products and services. Concepts like other-directedness, self-actualization, extraversion-introversion, and identity crisis flow into the stream of comment on contemporary American life and then take their places in the frame of reference from which marketing decisions are made. Even though a marketer may never read the work of a personality theorist, the authors he reads read personality theorists. Thus basic research on personality plays a role in determining the marketer's view of the world.

Direct and explicit use in marketing of the concepts and methods of the personality theorists roughly parallels the development of personality theory itself. It began with a period of qualitative applications of the basic psychoanalytic ideas. Gradually, greater emphasis was put on objectivity, quantification, and more rigorous research designs. Presently, in both personality study and in the study of consumer behavior, there is an upswing in the use of the computer to exploit the advantages of multivariate statistical techniques.

Qualitative Period: Motivation Research

The impulse to contribute to charity is not an effort to assuage guilt feelings as is often supposed, but is an expression of a sense of power first experienced when a child finds he can please or displease his mother by obliging or refusing to oblige in his toilet functions. This Freudian interpretation of the motivation for giving to charity is credited to Ernest Dichter, who has long been known as the leading exponent and practitioner of *motivation research.* Dichter received his Ph.D. degree in psychology from the University of Vienna in 1934. Like his elderly neighbor, Sigmund Freud, Dichter practiced psychoanalysis in Vienna until driven out by the Nazis at the start of World War II.

When the war ended, American industry resumed the full production of consumer goods, and American advertising and marketing were both very much in the mood for a fresh start, for something new. That something new was supplied by Dichter and motivation research.

In place of the often rather dreary economic and demographic analysis that had been common in marketing studies, Dichter, his colleagues, and (almost immediately) his imitators offered engaging, sexy, and always surprising explanations of why consumers behave the way they do. With a minimum of hard evidence and a maximum of insight, wit, and skill at presentation, they expounded the "real" reasons a man buys a convertible (as a substitute for a mistress), likes corn flakes (reminiscent of crunching an enemy's bones), and does not like air travel (he anticipates leaving his wife a widow and suffers "posthumous guilt"). See Dichter (1964) and Packard (1957) for more on this.

Motivation research was an immediate hit. Even the most staid advertisers and advertising agencies jumped on the bandwagon. In 1953 the Advertising Research Foundation published a directory of 82 commercial organizations offering motivation-research services.

In addition to Freudian theory with its emphasis on unconscious motivation, hedonism, and guilt, the motivation researchers borrowed many research techniques from the psychoanalysts and clinical psychologists.

Among the most important of these techniques are the *depth interview,* an extended, probing, unstructured interview designed to reveal in great detail the respondent's thoughts, feelings, ideas, and attitudes about a product, a service, or a brand; the previously mentioned thematic apperception test; and the word-association test—"I'm going to give you a series of words, and for each word I want you to tell me the first thing that comes into your mind." Often discussed, but less often used in marketing studies, are the Rorschach inkblots, the sentence-completion technique ("I think prunes are———"), and the Szondi Test, a collection of grainy pictures of psychotics. When motivation research was in full bloom, the more exotic the technique, the better.

Motivation research eventually declined in popularity, partly because marketers got tired of hearing about the unconscious, and partly because there are major differences between the problems that arise in the clinical study of personality and the problems that arise in marketing. In the study of personality, for example, the ideal is a complete understanding of the individual. In marketing, since no consumer product can be marketed to one person at a time, this much information about the individual cannot be used, even if it can be obtained. In the clinical study of personality, questions of the representativeness of the persons being studied are usually ignored. In marketing, questions about the representativeness of the sample must be answered. In the clinical study of personality it is customary to invest substantial resources in the collection and analysis of data about each case. In marketing studies, where the time and cost constraints are usually very real, the time and cost of detailed case-by-case analysis is generally higher than the marketer can afford. Finally, users of motivation research soon found that translating the results of a motivation-research study into advertising or marketing practice is much more difficult than it first had seemed. The motivation researchers argued convincingly that consumers are complex, devious, difficult to understand, and driven by mighty forces of which they are unaware. How then could one predict with confidence consumers' reactions to any product or any ad? Motivation researchers insisted they could do it, but marketers began to demand at least a modicum of proof that they could. This modicum of proof was often very hard to find.

Quantitative Period: 1959 to the Present

As motivation research passed its peak of popularity, a period began that was (and is) characterized by the use of paper-and-pencil instruments to provide numerical representations of personality traits for multivariate statistical analysis. Instead of borrowing the individual-oriented person-to-person unstructured techniques from the psychoanalyst and clinical psychologist, researchers of this persuasion borrowed, or built upon, the instruments and techniques of the psychometrician.

This period was ushered in by a landmark study by Evans (1959). Evans sought to test the assertion, often made by motivation researchers, that choice of an automobile is a reflection of the buyer's personality. In a well-designed and carefully executed study, he selected matched groups of Ford owners and Chevrolet owners, administered the Edwards Personal Preference Schedule to them, and attempted by means of discriminant analysis to find personality dimensions that distinguished the owners of Chevrolets from the owners of Fords. Although he found a few variables that discriminated between Ford owners and Chevrolet owners to a degree that was statistically significant, and although reanalysis of Evans's data by other methods produced a few more statistically significant findings, the differences between Ford owners and Chevrolet owners were far from impressive and much smaller than the claims of the motivation researchers would have led one to expect.

Of course the Evans study was challenged by those whose beliefs it threatened. Some said that the Edwards Personal Preference Schedule, designed to measure 11 of Murray's "needs," was the wrong instrument. Some said that Ford and Chevrolet were the worst possible pair of car makes between which to look for owner personality differences. Some said the statistical analysis was wrong. And some said that the sample of respondents was inappropriate. Nevertheless, Evans's major findings still stand, and his study remains among the most important in the field—both because it was one of the first, and because it stimulated so much controversy and follow-up research.

Among the standardized personality inventories employed in the search for relationships between consumer personality and consumer behavior the Edwards Personal Preference Schedule, used by Evans, has been the most popular. The Thurstone Temperament Schedule, a questionnaire designed to measure the dimensions he found by factor analysis has also been employed (Westfall, 1962), as has a questionnaire by Cattell to measure the major dimensions in his factor scheme (Myers, 1967). Elements from the California Psychological Inventory have been used in studies by Robertson and Myers (1969), Boone (1970), and Fry (1971). Other personality tests employed in this search are a set of scales developed by Cohen to measure Horney's concepts of moving toward, moving away from, and moving against others (Cohen, 1967); a questionnaire to measure Riesman's dimension of inner directedness versus other directedness (Kassarjian, 1965); and a questionnaire developed by Eysenck to measure ego-strength-neuroticism and extraversion-introversion (Eysenck, et al., 1960). These standardized questionnaires have been used in two somewhat different ways: (1) in attempts to establish psychological links between use of certain products and exposure to certain advertising media, and (2) in attempts to "predict" the purchase of products or services from measurements of the buyer's personality.

PERSONALITY TESTS AS LINKS BETWEEN PRODUCTS AND MEDIA

It has been suggested that personality traits might be used as links between products and advertising media. Advertisers want their messages to go to the right people. For consumer or industrial advertising this usually means prospective purchasers or persons who influence prospective purchasers. For "institutional" advertising this means the citizen who is apt to have a strong voice in relevant decisions.

Since different advertising media reach somewhat different segments of the population, advertisers have always attempted to employ those media that appear to be the best buy in terms of reaching the right audience at the lowest possible cost.

Traditionally, selection of media has been guided by broad demographic trends. Products purchased by women are advertised in women's magazines. Products sold only in one geographic region are not advertised in another if the waste circulation can be avoided. Extremely expensive products are not advertised in media that reach mainly low- and middle-income families, and so on.

For the most part, advertisers use demographics to select media in a most straightforward way: they either collect or imagine data on the *demographic profile* of their best prospects. The media collect demographic data on their audiences. And advertisers attempt to match media to products by some combination of calculation and intuition.

It has seemed possible that personality traits might prove a useful adjunct to demographic data in the media-selection process. Perhaps the best prospect for a cleaning product is not just a middle-aged middle-class housewife, but a middle-aged middle-class housewife with a compulsive need for cleanliness. Perhaps the best prospect for an expensive set of books is not just a well-educated male, but a well-educated male who is substantially above average on achievement motivation. If media, for whatever reasons, draw disproportionate numbers of compulsive housewives or achievement-oriented males, personality characteristics might improve the product-media match.

In addition to reducing waste circulation, the availability of personality profiles of media audiences would seem to offer the opportunity for *message segmentation*. If an advertiser knows which medium he is going to use and if he knows the personality characteristics of its readers, listeners, or viewers, he can tailor his messages to people with whom he hopes to communicate.

In spite of these possibilities, progress in this area has been very slow. Other than a report by Kassarjian (1965) that inner-directed subjects prefer inner-directed print ads, there is no evidence on what kind of appeals are the most appropriate for what personality types.

Nor is there much evidence dealing with media choice and personality. Boone (1970) found that innovative people are likely to subscribe to Cable Antenna TV service ahead of non-innovators. Koponen (1960) found a low but significant association between men's preference for an unspecified magazine and the needs for heterosexuality, nurturance, order, and succorance. Other than these two scraps, evidence of significant relationships between media use and scores on standardized personality tests has not reached the published literature, if indeed such evidence exists.

USE OF PERSONALITY TESTS TO "PREDICT" CONSUMER BEHAVIOR

A second use of standardized personality questionnaires has been the attempt to "predict" an individual's consumption of products or services. Almost invariably, these studies have asked whether there is some significant correlation between questionnaire response and product use at one point in time, rather than between questionnaire response now and behavior sometime in the future. In this context, then, the term "prediction" is not to be taken literally.

For several reasons one would expect the relationships obtained in these studies to be quite low. First, the size of the relationship that can be obtained depends in part on the reliability of the measuring instrument, and reliability in turn depends in part upon the number of items the instrument contains. (Reliability is used here in the technical sense of the word—the degree to which the instrument is a consistent measurer of whatever it measures.) The exigencies of marketing research bias the choice of instruments toward short, easily administered, and thus less reliable scales.

A second reason one would expect low correlations between personality test scores and consumer behavior is that the maximum obtainable correlation also depends to an important degree upon the reliability with which the behavior to be "predicted" is measured. Here again brief measures with questionable reliability have been the norm.

Third, in studies that have attempted to "predict" specific events, such as an individual's purchase of a specific brand, adoption of a specific new product, or purchase of a specific car, there is the problem of the reliability of the behavior itself. To the degree that changing circumstances change specific behaviors while general dispositions remain the same, it is unreasonable to expect strong predictions of specific events from measures of general dispositions alone.

Finally, quite apart from weakness in "prediction" to be expected from the various measurement problems noted above, personality theory itself would predict that valid relationships between generalized personality traits and specific bits of consumer behavior would be further attenuated in the following ways:

1. The same personality trait can be made manifest in very different ways, depending on local and temporary conditions and circumstances. The need for esteem, for instance, can lead to the purchase of an expensive car. But, if everyone on the block knows that Mr. Jones can afford an expensive car, and if all his friends own expensive cars, the need for esteem may lead to the purchase of a secondhand Ford.

2. The same behavior can be the product of very different traits. Consumption of religious services, for instance, can be the product of a deep need for contact with God. It can also be the product of a need to establish oneself as a "fine, upstanding" citizen in the community, or a need to meet an appropriate member of the opposite sex.

3. Through the process Freud called *reaction formation* a personality trait can be expressed by opposite behavior. A mother who feels deep hostility toward her child may shove him out of her life. On the other hand, she may overprotect him, showering him with attention, presents, and care.

4. Behavior is most often the product of a mixture of needs. A homemaker who bakes frequently, for example, may be expressing her affection for her family. She may also be expressing a need for approval from the neighbors and a need to save money. Any one of these needs, alone, may be insufficient to produce the behavior. The Brody and Cunningham (1968) study described later is an important illustration of this point.

5. Depending on the actor's role, the same underlying trait can lead to opposite forms of consumer behavior. Achievement motivation—the drive to produce work of excellent quality—may lead the artist or the scholar to ignore such irrelevancies as personal appearance; but, since personal appearance is one of the tools of a business executive's trade, strong achievement motivation may lead an executive to focus considerable attention on grooming and clothes.

6. As Riesman and others have noted, there are constant shifts in cultural norms. So a strong basic need for conformity may produce one kind of behavior in one subculture, and quite the opposite behavior in another. In the United States today differences of this kind can be seen in attitudes toward advertising, in use of liquor and drugs, in costume and length of hair.

Considering all the factors that operate against obtaining high correlations between personality-questionnaire responses and specific bits of behavior, it is something of an accomplishment to get any correlation at all. It is rare indeed, even in "basic" research on personality, to find that a personality trait predicts specific behavioral events with great accuracy.

Since 1959, many studies relating scores on various standardized personality tests to various kinds of consumer behavior have appeared. Types of behavior represented include brand loyalty (Carman, 1970; Massy, Frank, and Lodahl, 1968), innovativeness (Robertson and Myers, 1969), private-brand proneness (Myers, 1967), saving (Claycamp, 1965), use of specific products (Cohen, 1967; Eysenck, et al., 1960; Koponen, 1960; Tucker and Painter, 1961), reactions to advertising (Kassarjian, 1965), and selection of specific brands (Evans, 1959; Westfall, 1962).

Table 3 gives an overview of the personality traits and the behaviors they were used to "predict." The finding in every one of the studies listed in Table 3 has been statistically significant but with very small correlations between scores

TABLE 3. Personality Traits and Significantly Related Consumer Behavior

Personality Trait	Instrument[a]	Consumer Behavior	Investigator
Need for abasement (self-depreciation)	EPPS	Cigarette smoker more likely to prefer an unfiltered type[b]	Koponen (1960)
		Greater proportion of one-ply toilet tissue purchased is colored; lower number of total units of two-ply toilet tissue purchased	Advertising Research Foundation (1964)
		Fewer consecutive purchases of beer in favorite store	Massy, et al. (1968)
		Wife: More loyal to favorite brand of two-ply toilet tissue	Advertising Research Foundation (1964)
		Higher average number of beer units purchased per shopping trip; fewer shopping trips to purchase coffee	Massey, et al. (1968)
Need for achievement	EPPS	Cigarette smoker more likely to prefer an unfiltered type; men smoke more cigarettes per day and prefer one unspecified magazine to another	Koponen (1960)
		Husband: Lower proportion of two-ply toilet tissue purchased is colored	Advertising Research Foundation (1964)
		Wife: More loyal to favorite brand of two-ply toilet tissue	
		Prefer to hold thrift deposits in savings and loan associations rather than commercial banks	Claycamp (1965)
Achievement via independence	CPI	Early adoption of CATV	Boone (1970)
Active	TTS	Preference for convertible over standard or compact car	Westfall (1962)
		Early adoption of push-button telephone service	Robertson (1967)

Personality variable	Instrument	Findings	Source
Need for affiliation (association)	EPPS	Preference for Chevrolet over Ford	Evans (1959)
		Husband: More loyal to favorite brand of one-ply toilet tissue; fewer total units of one-ply toilet tissue purchased; lower proportion of two-ply toilet tissue purchased is colored	Advertising Research Foundation (1964)
		Fewer consecutive purchases of the same brand of coffee at the same store; higher proportion of coffee and tea units purchased on a deal; less loyal to second- and third-choice brands of coffee; fewer coffee units purchased; fewer shopping trips to purchase coffee; more total tea units purchased; more shopping trips to purchase tea	Massy, et al. (1968)
		Wife: Lower average number of beer units purchased per shopping trip	
		Prefer to hold thrift deposits in savings and loan associations rather than commercial banks	Claycamp (1965)
		If need for affiliation greater than need for dominance, preference for Chevrolet over Ford; if need for dominance greater than need for affiliation, preference for Ford over Chevrolet	Marcus (1965)
Need for aggression	EPPS	Cigarette smoker more likely to prefer an unfiltered type; men smoke more cigarettes per day	Koponen (1960)
		Husband: Fewer consecutive purchases of coffee in a given store; more total tea units purchased	Massy, et al. (1968)
		Wife: Less store loyalty for beer purchases	

Personality Trait	Instrument[a]	Consumer Behavior	Investigator
Aggressiveness		Men prefer a brand of dress shirt whose advertising emphasizes masculinity, a manual razor over electric razor, and a brand of beer associated with taverns that cater to "an outspokenly masculine group of students"; use more cologne and after-shave lotion	Cohen (1967)
Ascendency	GPP	Low use of headache remedies and vitamins, acceptance of new fashions	Tucker and Painter (1961)
Need for autonomy	EPPS	Preference for Chevrolet over Ford	Evans (1959)
		Cigarette smoker more likely to prefer an unfiltered type	Koponen (1960)
		Husband: Greater proportion of coffee units purchased on a deal; greater store loyalty for coffee purchases; more total tea units purchased; higher average number of tea units purchased per shopping trip	Massy, et al. (1968)
		Wife: More loyal to favorite brand of one-ply toilet tissue	Advertising Research Foundation (1964)
		More loyal to first-, second-, and third-choice brands of coffee; higher average number of coffee units purchased per shopping trip	Massy, et al. (1968)
		Prefer to hold thrift deposits in savings and loan associations rather than commercial banks	Claycamp (1965)
Capacity for status	CPI	Early adoption of CATV	Boone (1970)
Need for change	EPPS	Cigarette smoker more likely to prefer a nonfilter type	Koponen (1960)
		Husband: Greater proportion of one-ply toilet tissue purchased is colored	Advertising Research Foundation (1964)

		Less loyal to first-choice brand of tea; more loyal to second- and third-choice brands of tea; higher average number of beer units purchased per shopping trip	Massy, et al. (1968)
		Wife: Greater proportion of coffee units purchased on deals; more consecutive purchases of first-choice brand of beer at the same store; less loyal to store for coffee purchases	
Communality	CPI	Housewife more innovative in appliance purchases	Robertson and Myers (1969)
Need for compliance (deference)	EPPS	Men smoke more cigarettes per day	Koponen (1960)
		Husband: Less loyal to first-choice brand of coffee; higher proportion of coffee units purchased on deals; fewer consecutive purchases of first-choice brand of tea at the same store; less loyal to the second- and third-choice brands of beer; lower proportion of tea units purchased on deals; fewer consecutive purchases of first-choice brand of beer in a given store; fewer total coffee units purchased; fewer shopping trips to purchase coffee; fewer beer units purchased; fewer shopping trips to purchase beer; lower average number of beer units purchased per shopping trip	Massy, et al. (1968)
		Wife: More loyal to first-choice brand of coffee; more consecutive purchases of the same brand of coffee at the same store; lower proportion of coffee units purchased on a deal; more shopping trips to purchase tea	
Compliance		Men more likely to use a mouthwash and to prefer a given brand of deodorant—contrasted with men high on aggressiveness and detachment, who prefer a different brand; prefer a highly advertised brand of soap; more likely to have brand preference for toilet or bath soap	Cohen (1967)
Compulsiveness		Antacid-analgesic use	Gottlieb (1959)

Personality Trait	Instrument[a]	Consumer Behavior	Investigator
Conservatism (cautiousness)		More favorable attitude toward buying a small car	Jacobson and Kossoff (1963)
Detachment		Low interest in brands; men less likely to have brand preferences for toilet or bath soap; consume more tea	Cohen (1967)
Dogmatism		Unmarried coeds less likely to buy a new brand, a new fashion innovation, a new form of an existing product, or to use an existing product in a new way	Jacoby (1970)
Dominance	CPI	Early adoption of CATV	Boone (1970)
	TTS	Early adoption of push-button telephone service	Robertson (1967)
Need for dominance	EPPS	Preference for Ford over Chevrolet	Evans (1959)
		Cigarette smoker more likely to prefer a filter type; men prefer one unspecified magazine to another	Koponen (1960)
		Husband: Smaller proportion of one-ply toilet tissue purchased is colored	Advertising Research Foundation (1964)
		Wife: Greater proportion of one-ply toilet tissue purchased is colored	
		If need for dominance is less than need for affiliation, preference for Chevrolet over Ford; if need for dominance is greater than need for affiliation, preference for Ford over Chevrolet	Marcus (1965)
Emotional stability	GPP	Low use of headache remedies and vitamins; high use of chewing gum	Tucker and Painter (1961)
Need for endurance	EPPS	Husband: Less loyal to favorite brand of two-ply toilet tissue; more total units of two-ply toilet tissue purchased	Advertising Research Foundation (1964)

184

Trait	Instrument	Findings	Source
		More loyal to first-choice brand of tea and beer; more loyal to store for purchases of coffee and tea; more tea units purchased; more shopping trips to purchase tea	Massy, et al. (1968)
		Wife: More consecutive purchases of first-choice brand of coffee at the same store; more loyal to second- and third-choice brands of coffee; less loyal to second- and third-choice brands of tea; more consecutive purchases of first-choice brand of coffee at a given store; more coffee and beer units purchased, more trips to purchase coffee and beer; higher average number of coffee units purchased per trip	
Enthusiasm	SPFQ	Housewives and working women more likely to have a favorable attitude toward private brands of grocery store products	Myers (1967)
Need for exhibition	EPPS	Husband: Fewer consecutive purchases of beer in a given store; more shopping trips to purchase beer; higher average number of beer units purchased per shopping trip	Massy, et al. (1968)
		Wife: Greater proportion of two-ply toilet tissue purchased is colored	Advertising Research Foundation (1964)
		More loyal to second- and third-choice brands of tea; more consecutive purchases of tea in a given store	Massy, et al. (1968)
Extraversion		More cigarettes smoked each day	Eysenck, et al. (1960)
Need for heterosexuality	EPPS	Men smoke more cigarettes per day and prefer one unspecified magazine to another	Koponen (1960)
		Preference for holding thrift deposits in savings and loan associations rather than commercial banks	Claycamp (1965)
Hypochondria		Antacid-analgesic use.	Gottlieb (1959)

185

Personality Trait	Instrument[a]	Consumer Behavior	Investigator
Impulsive	TTS	Preference for convertible over standard or compact car	Westfall (1962)
		Early adoption of push-button telephone service	Robertson (1967)
Inner directed		Preference for inner-directed over other-directed printed advertisements	Kassarjian (1965)
		More likely to try new grocery store products (pre-soak rinse, canned pudding, freeze-dried fruit cereals)	Donnelley (1970)
Intellectual efficiency	CPI	Early adoption of CATV	Boone (1970)
Interest in people	Derived from SVIB	Preference for common stocks over savings accounts, convertibles over sedans	Pennington and Peterson (1969)
Need for intraception (analysis)	EPPS	Husband: More total units of one-ply and two-ply toilet tissue are purchased	Advertising Research Foundation (1964)
		More loyal to second- and third-choice brands of coffee; less loyal to store for beer purchases; more coffee units purchased; more shopping trips to purchase coffee	Massy, et al. (1968)
		Wife: Lower proportions of one-ply and two-ply toilet tissue are purchased; greatest loyalty to favorite brand of two-ply toilet tissue when need for intraception is average	Advertising Research Foundation (1964)
		Higher average number of beer units purchased per shopping trip	Massy, et al. (1968)
Masculinity	CPI	Regular brand of cigarette perceived as more masculine	Vitz and Johnston (1965)
		Less masculine men prefer cigarettes perceived as feminine	Fry (1971)

Need for nurturance (assistance)	EPPS	Men prefer one unspecified magazine to another	Koponen (1960)
		Husband: Fewer consecutive purchases of the same brand of coffee at the same store; more consecutive purchases of tea in favorite store; more trips to purchase tea Wife: More loyal to second- and third-choice brands of beer; higher average number of units purchased per trip	Massy, et al. (1968)
Need for order	EPPS	Men smoke more cigarettes per day; men prefer one unspecified magazine to another	Koponen (1960)
		Husband: More loyal to favorite brand of one-ply and two-ply toilet tissue	Advertising Research Foundation (1964)
		Less loyal to first-choice brand of tea; less loyal to second- and third-choice brands of beer; fewer coffee units purchased Wife: More loyal to first-choice brand of tea; more loyal to second- and third-choice brands of tea; fewer consecutive purchases of the same brand of beer at the same store; less loyal to store for tea purchases; more consecutive purchases of tea in a given store; more shopping trips to purchase tea; higher average number of beer units purchased per shopping trip	Massy, et al. (1968)
Other-directed		Preference for other-directed over inner-directed printed advertisements	Kassarjian (1965)
		Less likely to try new grocery market products (prescak rinse, canned pudding, canned cake frosting)	Donnelley (1970)
Punitiveness		Antacid-analgesic use	Gottlieb (1959)
Responsibility	GPP	Low use of vitamins, mouthwash, and alcoholic drinks; higher use of chewing gum; preference for standard over sporty automobiles	Tucker and Painter (1961)

187

Personality Trait	Instrument[a]	Consumer Behavior	Investigator
Rigidity		Fewer cigarettes smoked per day	Eysenck, et al. (1960)
Self-acceptance	CPI	Housewives more innovative in appliance purchases	Robertson and Myers (1969)
		Early adoption of CATV	Boone (1970)
Self-confidence, self-esteem		More difficult to persuade male college students	Janis (1954)
		The higher or lower, the more difficult to persuade; the more moderate, the easier to persuade –generalized self-confidence –self-confidence specific to car-buying ability	Cox and Bauer (1964) Bell (1967b)
		New car buyers high or low in generalized self-confidence, but low in self-confidence specific to buying a car, take friends to the showroom to help them in the purchase	Bell (1967a)
Sense of well-being	CPI	Early adoption of CATV	Boone (1970)
Shopping proneness		Less store loyal; less brand loyal to coffee, canned fruit, and frozen orange juice	Carman (1970)
Sociability	GPP	Low use of vitamins, acceptance of new fashions	Tucker and Painter (1961)
	CPI	Early adoption of CATV	Boone (1970)
Socialization	CPI	Housewives less innovative in appliance purchases	Robertson and Myers (1969)
Social presence	CPI	Early adoption of CATV	Boone (1970)

Trait	Instrument[a]	Findings	Reference
Need for succorance (dependence)	EPPS	Men prefer one unspecified magazine title to another	Koponen (1960)
		Husband: More total units of two-ply toilet tissue are purchased	Advertising Research Foundation (1964)
		More loyal to second- and third-choice brands of coffee; higher average number of coffee units purchased per shopping trip; more tea units purchased	Massy, et al. (1968)
		Wife: More loyal to first-choice brand of coffee; more consecutive purchases of the same brand of beer at the same store; more loyal to store for coffee purchases; more beer units purchased; more shopping trips to purchase beer	
Tolerance	CPI	Early adoption of CATV	Boone (1970)
Venturesomeness		Early adoption of an unspecified small home appliance innovation	Robertson and Kennedy (1962)

[a]Key to instrument identification:

CPI California Psychological Inventory
EPPS Edwards Personal Preference Schedule
GPP Gordon Personal Profile
MMPI Minnesota Multiphasic Personality Inventory
SPFQ Sixteen Personality Factor Questionnaire
SVIB Strong Vocational Interest Blank
TTS Thurston Temperament Schedule

If instrument column is blank, a nonstandard instrument was used.

[b]Read, "The higher his need for abasement, the more likely it is that a cigarette smoker will prefer an unfiltered type."

on personality questionnaires and scores on one or another index of consumer behavior. This result has been widely regarded as disappointing. Accustomed to the high correlations commonly found in time series predictions based on aggregate data, some investigators have come to the conclusion that personality traits are useless as predictors of consumer behavior.

In one sense, this conclusion is surely correct. If high correlations are required, presently available instruments fall far short of doing the job, and there is little prospect that suitable instruments will ever be developed in the future. Given the many reasons for low relationships between personality traits and overt behavior, and given the added handicaps imposed by the limitations of market-research interviewing, low correlations seem inevitable.

On the other hand, there are good uses in marketing for relationships that are too weak for accurate prediction of individual behavior. Marketing decisions are made about groups of consumers, not about individuals, and information about group characteristics can be helpful (Bass, Tigert, and Lonsdale, 1968). Knowledge that the purchasers of a given product tend to be above average in income can be helpful in making pricing decisions, even though the correlation between income and purchasing is far from perfect. Knowledge that a given brand is used disproportionately by young people can be useful in setting the tone and tempo of the advertising, even when brand choice has only a low relationship with age. Knowledge that women tend to be more (or less) price conscious, or innovative, or communicative than men can be useful in marketing women's products.

Furthermore, there is some evidence, in an insightful study by Brody and Cunningham (1968), that sizable relationships between personality traits and consumer behavior can be found if some attempt is made to account for and make use of the principle that behavior is often the product of a mixture of traits. Using the Edwards Personal Preference Schedule to "predict" choice of coffee brand, Brody and Cunningham found, as usual, that the overall correlations between personality traits and brand choices were very low. But when they isolated a specific group of consumers—consumers who had high self-confidence in their ability to judge coffee *and* who were more interested than others in how coffee tastes—they found that the relationships between EPPS test scores and brand choice had substantially increased. As Brody and Cunningham put it, "the discouraging results in previous studies may have been caused by the way the data were analyzed, not by the variables' inherent deficiencies."

Two uses of personality have been described thus far. The first was to use personality traits as links between products and media. On the basis of present evidence, this use appears to be a forlorn hope. The second was to use personality questionnaires to "predict" behavior. This use appears to be more apt to be productive, provided that it is group rather than individual behavior that is to be "predicted," and providing that the analyst is realistic about the strength of the relationships that are obtained.

INTENSIVE STUDY OF GROUPS OF TRAITS

As noted in the discussion of authoritarian personality and manifest anxiety, one fruitful approach to the study of personality has been to select some limited, related, and significant group of traits, and to study the origin and functioning of that trait group in great detail. For both authoritarian personality and manifest anxiety, the creation of a simple and interesting measuring instrument that was anchored in a recognized body of theory produced a surge of research interest and some important results.

In the field of consumer behavior several dimensions appear to be good candidates for development of this kind. Certainly, venturesomeness with respect to product innovations (Greene, 1959; Robertson and Myers, 1969) would appear to be an important dimension, as would private-brand proneness (Myers, 1967) and mobility (Opinion Research Corporation, 1959).

The experience of psychologists with this approach suggests that the researcher who employs it should take the elementary precaution of finding out whether the traits in the "limited, related, and significant" group are in fact related. Research on dishonesty provides a good illustration of what can go wrong. It seems reasonable to suppose that the tendency to lie, the tendency to cheat, and the tendency to steal are all related aspects of a generalized dimension, dishonesty. Yet tests of behavior in which school children were subjected to temptation in each of these ways showed little overlap. Children who tended to lie about their athletic abilities did not have a strong tendency to cheat on school exams or to steal small amounts of money. Children who tended to cheat did not show strong tendencies to lie or steal, and so on.

One obvious parallel in marketing is the dimension of brand loyalty. It would seem logical that consumers who are highly loyal to a single brand in one product category would also tend to be loyal to a single brand in other product categories—"Once I find a brand I like I stick with it," as some consumers sometimes say. Yet empirical investigations of actual purchasing behavior have repeatedly demonstrated that brand loyalty in one product is not predictive of brand loyalty in another. As a consequence, attempts to discover the causes are bound to produce conflicting and inconclusive results.

The same general problem occurs in the studies of opinion leadership described in the chapter on diffusion and innovation. Most of these studies show that an individual who tends to be an opinion leader with respect to one type of product also tends to be an opinion leader with respect to similar products, but the overlap is far from perfect, and often is quite small (King and Summers, 1970). As a consequence, attempts to find the causes and correlates of a generalized trait of opinion leadership are certain to find different answers, depending upon the specific activities with which opinion leadership is defined.

The same problem occurs with risk proneness. Risk taking on the stock market may be a very different attribute from risk taking on the highway or risk taking with respect to new brands. And research on persuasibility is bound to produce conflicting findings, unless researchers first specify persuasibility about what and by whom.

The lesson here is clear. Although systematic examination of some limited, related, and significant group of traits can be a highly productive approach in research on consumer behavior, it is prudent to be sure that the traits are in fact related before the examination goes very far.

FACTOR ANALYSIS OF CONSUMER BEHAVIOR

In the personality domain the objective of the factor analyst is to find some underlying set of basic dimensions that account for the observed togetherness of surface traits. The analyst's purpose is to find a useful frame of reference from which to view the complexities of behavior, and to stimulate research on the question of why the traits that go together do go together.

In consumer marketing the behaviors of most interest are the purchase of products and services and the use of mass media. Here too it makes sense to use factor analysis to reduce the great variety and complexity of behavior in the hope of finding dimensions that will both form a useful frame of reference and stimulate additional research.

Factor analytic studies of the purchases of grocery and drugstore products have indicated the presence of one dimension of consumer behavior defined by heavy use of such products as toilet soap, toothpaste, laundry detergent, cold cereal, peanut butter, canned soup, and frankfurters—all products that are purchased in large quantities by middle-class mothers with relatively large families (Banks, Wells, and Tigert, 1967; Assael, 1970). This dimension is of interest in its own right, since it represents a substantial proportion of grocery and drugstore purchases. It is also of interest in any consideration of the relationships between consumer personality and consumer behavior. It suggests that for this one important group of products, at least, purchase is much more dependent on the purchaser's stage in the family life cycle than on the purchaser's personality.

Other dimensions that emerge from factor analysis of product purchases seem to be less related to stage in the life cycle than to familiar personality traits. A factor defined by heavy use of furniture polish, floor wax, window cleaner, and oven cleaner seems to be related to the compulsive neatness syndrome of Freudian theory. A self-medication factor defined by heavy use of pain relief tablets, upset stomach tablets, and headache remedies is suggestive of high manifest anxiety.

Still other product-use factors are related to a complex combination of a particular stage in life, the possession of above-average disposable income, and a specific set of activities and values. For instance, a grooming dimension for women is defined by above-average use of eye makeup, lipstick, hairspray, perfume, and nail polish. A wide-horizons dimension for men is defined as above average use of airline trips, long-distance telephone calls, and overseas vacations.

Like factor analysis of personality traits, factor analysis of purchasing behavior suggests the presence of a number of dimensions. Some of these dimensions seem to be related to traditional concepts of personality, but others seem to be more closely tied to broad sociological dimensions like stage in the life cycle and social class.

Another use of factor analysis in the study of consumer behavior is the search for patterns in the public's use of mass media. Factor analytic studies of magazine readership show that magazines fall into types determined by the interests of their audiences (Bass, Pessemier, and Tigert, 1969). On television, westerns define one factor, family situation comedies define another, news programs define another, and so on through many types of offerings (Wells, 1969). Like the product classes that emerge from factor analysis of purchasing behavior, classes of media both provide helpful frames of reference in a complex and confusing world, and raise questions to be answered by additional research.

START FROM SCRATCH

In making use of personality, the student of consumer behavior may wish to start from scratch—to focus on the nature of the problem and to develop concepts and methods that seem apt to solve it, even if they have not been sanctioned by previous use.

One problem the marketer of consumer products always faces is that of obtaining a good description of his customer. From the time a product is just a concept the marketer must ask himself, "What sort of person will buy it?" When the product exists and is ready for introduction, this question becomes even more pressing. It must be answered one way or another before anyone can decide how to package the product, how to price it, where to advertise it, or what stance the advertising should take. After the product has been introduced and on through the rest of its life, the question becomes, "What sort of person is buying it, and what sort of person is more attracted to competing products?" These questions must be answered—through research, through guesswork, or (as is usually the case) through some combination of both. If no one answers these questions explicitly, they will be answered implicitly. The marketer demonstrates through his decisions what he thinks his customer is like.

The commonest way of answering these questions is through the use of broad demographic categories: "This is a product for young mothers," "This is a product for adolescent boys," "This is a product for middle-aged middle-class men." Such roughhewn descriptions are quite helpful in classifying consumers, for no product is used equally in every corner of the demographic map, and there is a wide general understanding among marketers as to what demographic categories mean.

But the need for description is so acute that demographics will not suffice. To envision their customers, marketers need information on tastes, problems, values, ideals, worries, aspirations, daily activities—even, as Sheldon's work would lead one to expect—on physique.

The need for description that goes beyond demographics helped stimulate the "prediction" studies employing personality questionnaires. For the most part, these studies were never actually intended to predict consumer behavior in any literal sense, but rather to describe the consumers of a product or brand in a new and useful way that would facilitate the creation of appeals and the selection of media.

Unfortunately, the standardized personality test is particularly ill suited to this task. Marketing-relevant variables such as price consciousness, opinion leadership, and innovativeness are never included in questionnaires developed in the context of personality research, and the variables that are included are not easy to use. For instance, the marketing manager has great difficulty in deciding what to do with the finding that "respondents classified as private brand acceptors showed some tendency to be more enthusiastic, sensitive and submissive" (Myers, 1967), or the finding that choice of a Ford over a Chevrolet is related to "dominance minus affiliation" (Kuehn, 1963).

Pessemier and Tigert (1966), Wells and Tigert (1971), Wilson (1966), and others have handled this problem by assembling a large number of questions on activities, attitudes, interests, values, opinions, specific activities, and media preferences, as well as personality traits—and determined what mixture of these items was related to the behavior being studied. Since this methodology's focus is on the specific practical problem of describing the consumer in easily understandable terms, it employs bits and pieces from every source that might be of help. Work that has been done with this approach—such as the study that produced the "profiles" in Table 4—suggests that in some cases it may produce richer and more useful findings than reliance on personality alone.

IN CONCLUSION

The study of personality can enrich our understanding of consumer behavior in five ways. First, most basic and most important, the results of research on personality flow into the mainstream of contemporary thought and thereby help shape the frame of reference from which decisions are made. One cannot escape using the work of personality theorists; it fills the air. Second, concepts and techniques derived from psychoanalysis and clinical psychology have been and still are used in investigating consumer behavior and interpreting it in unusual, creative, and engaging ways. Motivation research is alive and well and living on Madison Avenue. Third, questionnaires and other techniques developed in research on personality can sometimes be applied with profit, especially when expectations about what they can and cannot do are realistic.

TABLE 4. Life Styles of the Heavy User of Eye Makeup and the Heavy User of Shortening

Heavy User of Eye Makeup	Heavy User of Shortening
Demographic Characteristics	
Young, well-educated, lives in metropolitan areas	Middle-aged, medium to large family, lives outside metropolitan areas
Product Use	
Also a heavy user of liquid face makeup, lipstick, hair spray, perfume, cigarettes, gasoline	Also a heavy user of flour, sugar, canned lunch meat, cooked pudding, catsup
Media Preferences	
Fashion magazines, *Life, Look,* Tonight Show, adventure program	*Readers Digest,* daytime TV serials, family situation TV comedies
Activities, Interests, and Opinions	
Agrees more than average with	
I often try the latest hairdo styles when they change	I love to bake and frequently do
I usually have one or more outfits that are of the very latest style	I save recipes from newspapers and magazines
An important part of my life and activities is dressing smartly	The kitchen is my favorite room
I enjoy looking through fashion magazines	I love to eat
I like to feel attractive to all men	I enjoy most forms of housework
I want to look a little different from others	Usually I have regular days for washing, cleaning, etc., around the house
Looking attractive is important in keeping your husband	I am uncomfortable when my house is not completely clean
I like what I see when I look in the mirror	I often make my own or my children's clothes
I comb my hair and put on my lipstick first thing in the morning	I like to sew and frequently do
I take good care of my skin	I try to arrange my home for my children's convenience
Sloppy people feel terrible	Our family is a close-knit group
I would like to take a trip around the world	There is a lot of love in our family
I would like to spend a year in London or Paris	I spend a lot of time with my children talking about their activities, friends, and problems
I like ballet	Everyone should take walks, bicycle, garden, or otherwise exercise several times a week
I like parties where there is lots of music and talk	Clothes should be dried in the fresh air and out-of-doors
I like things that are bright, gay, and exciting	It is very important for people to wash their hands before eating every meal
I do more things socially than do most of my friends	You should have a medical checkup at least once a year
I would like to have a maid to do the housework	I would rather spend a quiet evening at home than go out to a party
I like to serve unusual dinners	I would rather go to a sporting event than a dance
I am interested in spices and seasonings	
If I had to choose, I would rather have a color television set than a new refrigerator	
I like bright, splashy colors	
I really do believe that blondes have more fun	

TABLE 4 (cont.)

Disagrees more than average with	
I am a homebody	I would like to have a maid to do the house-
I like grocery shopping	work
I enjoy most forms of housework	My idea of housekeeping is "once over
I furnish my home for comfort, not for	lightly"
style	Classical music is more interesting than
I try to arrange my home for my children's	popular music
convenience	I like ballet
It is more important to have good appli-	I'd like to spend a year in London or Paris
ances in the home than good furniture	
Women should not smoke in public	
There is too much emphasis on sex today	
Spiritual values are more important than	
material things	
If it was good enough for my mother, it's	
good enough for me	

Fourth, research strategies developed in the study of personality can be useful in research on consumers whenever the basic problems are the same. And finally, concepts from the study of personality can sometimes be used in conjunction with concepts from other fields to create new approaches and new methods designed specifically to handle certain problems that are specific to, or at least uniquely important in, studies of product, brand, or media choice.

REFERENCES

Adler, A., *Understanding Human Nature.* New York: Greenberg, 1927.

Adorno, T.W., Else Frenkel-Brunswick, D. J. Levinson, and R. N. Sanford, *The Authoritarian Personality.* New York: Harper & Row, Inc. 1950.

Advertising Research Foundation, Inc., *Are There Consumer Types?* New York: Advertising Research Foundation, Inc. 1964.

Allport, G. W., *Personality, a Psychological Interpretation.* New York: Holt, Rinehart and Winston, Inc., 1937.

Allport, G. W., and H. S. Odbert, "Trait-names: a psycholexical study," *Psychological Monographs, 47,* 211 (1936), 1-171.

Assael, H., *Media Exposure Patterns and Purchase Behavior,* paper delivered at the Annual Meeting of the Association for Consumer Research, Amherst, Mass., 1970.

Bales, R. F., *Personality and Interpersonal Behavior.* New York: Holt, Rinehart and Winston, Inc., 1969.

Banks, S., W. D. Wells, and D. J. Tigert, "Order in the Data," in *Changing Marketing Systems,* ed. R. Moyer. Chicago: American Marketing Association, 1967.

Bass, F. M., D. J. Tigert, and R. T. Lonsdale, "Market Segmentation: Group Versus Individual Behavior," *Journal of Marketing Research,* 5 (August 1968), 264-70.

Bass, F. M., E. A. Pessemier, and D. J. Tigert, "A Taxonomy of Magazine

Readership Applied to Problems in Marketing Strategy and Media Selection," *Journal of Business* (July 1969), 337-63.

Bell, G. D., "Self-Confidence, Persuasibility and Cognitive Dissonance among Automobile Buyers," in *Risk Taking and Information-Handling in Consumer Behavior,* ed. D. F. Cox. Boston: Division of Research Graduate School of Business Administration, Harvard University, 1967a.

Bell, G. D., Self-Confidence and Persuasion in Car Buying," *Journal of Marketing Research,* 4 (February 1967b), 46-52.

Berne, E., *Games People Play.* New York: Grove Press, Inc., 1964.

Boone, L. E., "The Search for the Consumer Innovator," *Journal of Business,* 43 (April 1970), 135-40.

Brody, R. P., and S. M. Cunningham, "Personality Variables and the Consumer Decision Process," *Journal of Marketing Research,* 5 (1968).

Bruce, G. D., and R. E. Witt, "Personality Correlates of Innovative Buying Behavior," *Journal of Marketing Research,* 7 (May 1970).

Carman, J. M., "Correlates of Brand Loyalty: Some Positive Results," *Journal of Marketing Research,* 7 (February 1970).

Cattell, R. B., *The Scientific Analysis of Personality.* Baltimore: Penguin Books, Inc., 1965.

Claycamp, H. J., "Characteristics of Owners of Thrift Deposits in Commercial Banks and Savings and Loan Associations," *Journal of Marketing Research,* 2 (May 1965).

Cohen, J. B., "An Interpersonal Orientation to the Study of Consumer Behavior," *Journal of Marketing Research,* 4 (August 1967), 270-78.

Cox, D. F., and R. A. Bauer, "Self-Confidence and Persuasibility in Women," *Public Opinion Quarterly,* 28 (Fall 1964), 453-66.

Dichter, E., *Handbook of Consumer Motivations.* New York: McGraw-Hill Book Company, 1964.

Donnelley, J. H., Jr., "Social Character and Acceptance of New Products," *Journal of Marketing Research,* 7 (February 1970), 111-13.

Edwards, A. L., *Edwards Personal Preference Schedule* (Manual). New York: Psychological Corporation, 1957.

Ellenberger, H. F., *The Discovery of the Unconscious.* New York: Basic Books, Inc., Publishers; and London: Allen Lane The Penquin Pres. ©1970 by Henri F. Ellenberger.

Erikson, E. H., *Childhood and Society* (2nd ed.). New York: W. W. Norton & Company, Inc., 1963.

Evans, F. B., "Psychological and Objective Factors in the Prediction of Brand Choice," *Journal of Business,* 32 (October 1959).

Eysenck, H. J., *The Structure of Human Personality.* London: Methuen & Company Ltd., 1960.

Eysenck, H. J., M. Tarrant, M. Woolf, and L. England, "Smoking and Personality," *British Medical Journal* (May 1960).

Frank, R. E., W. L. Massy, and T. M. Lodahl, "Purchasing Behavior and Personal Attributes," *Journal of Advertising Research,* 9 (December 1969), 15-24.

Fry, J. N., "Personality Variables and Cigarette Brand Choice," *Journal of Marketing Research,* 8 (August 1971), 298-304.

Gottlieb, M. J., "Segmentation by Personality Types," in *Proceedings of the American Marketing Association,* ed. L. H. Stockman. Chicago: American Marketing Association, 1959.

Greene, J., "Some Psychological Traits of Media and Markets," *Media/Scope,* 3 (November 1959), 68-71.

Guilford, J. P., *Personality.* New York: McGraw-Hill Book Company, 1959.

Hall, C. S., and G. Lindzey, *Theories of Personality* (2nd ed.). New York: John Wiley & Sons, Inc., 1970.

Hamm, B. C., and E. W. Cundiff, "Self-Actualization and Product Perception," *Journal of Marketing Research,* 6 (November 1969).

Horney, Karen, *Our Inner Conflicts.* New York: W. W. Norton & Company, Inc., 1945.

Jacobson, E., and J. Kossoff, "Self-Percept and Consumer Attitudes Toward Small Cars," *Journal of Applied Psychology,* 47 (August 1963), 242-45.

Jacoby, J., "A Multiple Indicant Approach for Studying Innovators," *Purdue Papers in Consumer Psychology,* No. 108, Purdue University, 1970.

Janis, I. L., "Personality Correlates of Susceptibility to Persuasion," *Journal of Personality,* 22 (1954), 504-18.

Kassarjian, H. H., "Social Character and Differential Preference for Mass Communications," *Journal of Marketing Research,* 2 (May 1965), 146-53.

Kassarjian, H. H., "Personality and Consumer Behavior: A Review," *Journal of Marketing Research,* 8 (November 1971), 409-18.

King, C. W., and J. O. Summers, "Overlap of Opinion Leadership Across Consumer Product Categories," *Journal of Marketing Research,* 7 (February 1970), 43-50.

Koponen, A., "Personality Characteristics of Purchasers," *Journal of Advertising Research,* 1 (September 1960), 6-12.

Kuehn, A. A., "Demonstration of a Relationship between Psychological Factors and Brand Choice," *Journal of Business,* 36 (April 1963), 237-41.

Lansing, J. B., and L. Kish, "Family Life Cycle As An Independent Variable," *American Sociological Review,* 22 (October 1957), 512-19.

Marcus, A. S., "Obtaining Group Measures from Personality Test Scores: Auto Brand Choice Predicted from the Edwards Personality Preference Schedule," *Psychological Reports,* 17 (October 1965), 523-31.

Maslow, A. H., *Motivation and Personality.* New York: Harper & Row, 1954.

Massy, W. F., R. E. Frank, and T. M. Lodahl, *Purchasing Behavior and Personal Attributes.* Philadelphia: University of Pennsylvania Press, 1968.

Murray, H. A. (and collaborators), *Explorations in Personality.* New York: Oxford University Press, Inc., 1938.

Myers, J. G., "Determinants of Private Brand Attitudes," *Journal of Marketing Research,* 4 (February 1967), 73-81.

Opinion Research Corporation, *America's Tastemakers.* Princeton, N.J.: Opinion Research Corporation, 1959.

Packard, Vance, *The Hidden Persuaders.* New York: David McKay Company, Inc., 1957

Pennington, A. A., and R. A. Peterson, "Interest Patterns and Product Preferences: An Exploratory Analysis," *Journal of Marketing Research,* 6 (August 1969), 284-90.

Pessemier, E. A., and D. J. Tigert, "Personality, Activity and Attitude Predictors of Consumer Behavior," in *New Ideas for Successful Marketing*, ed. J. S. Wright and J. L. Goldstucker. Chicago: American Marketing Association, 1966.

Riesman, D. M., R. Denney, and N. Glazer, *The Lonely Crowd*. New Haven, Conn.: Yale University Press, 1950.

Robertson, T. S., "Determinants of Innovative Behavior," in *Proceedings of the American Marketing Association*, ed. R. Moyer. Chicago: American Marketing Association, 1967, 328-32.

Robertson, T. S., and J. H. Myers, "Personality Correlates of Opinion Leadership and Innovative Buying Behavior," *Journal of Marketing Research*, 6 (May 1969), 164-68.

Robertson, T. S., and J. N. Kennedy, "Prediction of Consumer Innovators: Application of Multiple Discriminant Analysis," *Journal of Marketing Research*, 5 (February 1968), 64-69.

Sheldon, W. H. (with the collaboration of S. S. Stevens), *The Varieties of Temperament: A Psychology of Constitutional Differences*. New York: Harper & Row, Inc., 1942.

Smith, G. H., *Motivation Research in Advertising and Marketing*. New York: McGraw-Hill Book Company, 1954.

Stryker, P., "Motivation Research," *Fortune*, 53 (June 1956), 144-47.

Sullivan, H. S., *The Interpersonal Theory of Psychiatry*. New York: W. W. Norton & Company, Inc., 1953.

Taylor, J. A., "A Personality Scale of Manifest Anxiety," *Journal of Abnormal and Social Psychology*, 48 (1953), 285-90.

Tucker, W. T., and J. J. Painter, "Personality and Product Use," *Journal of Applied Psychology*, 45 (1961), 325-29.

Vitz, P. C., and D. Johnston, "Masculinity of Smokers and the Masculinity of Cigarette Images," *Journal of Applied Psychology*, 49 (June 1965), 155-59.

Wells, W. D., "The Rise and Fall of Television Program Types," *Journal of Advertising Research*, 9, No. 3 (1969), 21-27.

Wells, W. D., and G. Gubar, "The Life Cycle Concept in Marketing Research," *Journal of Marketing Research*, 3 (November 1966), 355-63.

Wells, W. D., and D. J. Tigert, "Activities, Interests and Opinions," *Journal of Advertising Research*, 11 (August 1971), 27-35.

Westfall, R., "Psychological Factors Predicting Product Choice," *Journal of Marketing*, 26 (April 1962), 34-40.

Wilson, C. C., "Homemaker Living Patterns and Marketplace Behavior—A Psychometric Approach," in *New Ideas for Successful Marketing*, ed. J. J. Wright and J. L. Goldstucker. Chicago: American Marketing Association, 1966.

Woodworth, R. S., *Personal Data Sheet*. Chicago: Stoelting, 1918.

5

Theories of
Interpersonal Perception

Daniel B. Wackman
University of Minnesota

BASIC APPROACHES IN PERSON-PERCEPTION THEORY AND
RESEARCH

Alternative Perspectives. Person-Perception-Process Approach.
Implications for Marketing Research.

RECENT THEORETICAL DEVELOPMENTS RELATED TO PERSON-
PERCEPTION THEORY AND RESEARCH

Alternative Explanations of Marketing Research Findings Suggested by the New Theoretical Perspective. Implications of the
New Theoretical Perspective for Marketing Research.

GENERAL CONCLUSIONS REGARDING THE IMPLICATIONS OF
PERSON-PERCEPTION THEORY AND RESEARCH FOR MARKETING
RESEARCH

REFERENCES

Advertisers sometimes create advertisements aimed at persuading consumers to purchase products in order to become a "new person" or to enjoy a satisfying emotional state. For example, "Use product X and you will become more confident and sure of yourself," "Buy auto Y and you will be a ladies' man," and "Product Z means happiness and good times." Advertisements of this type are related to the topic of this chapter, person-perception theory. The focus of the chapter is on the research questions suggested by person-perception theory and research.

At the outset a distinction should be made between two terms that are often confused. *Person-perception* theory and research focuses upon processes involved in forming judgments of and making predictions about another person's personality and behavior. *Social-perception* theory and research focuses on the social factors, such as group pressures, cultural factors, and so forth, that influence a person's perceptions of objects and events. This chapter will concentrate upon person-perception theory and research, since social-perception theory is discussed in Chapter 6.

The chapter contains two large sections. The first section discusses two alternative perspectives, or approaches, in person perception. First is the accuracy approach, which emphasizes questions regarding how accurate one person is in assessing what another person is "really" like. Second is the process approach, which emphasizes questions regarding the processes by which one person forms impressions and judgments of another person. The second approach is generally more useful for marketing research; consequently, this section will continue with an elaboration of the process approach. Finally, the section concludes with a discussion of implications for marketing research of theory and research generated by the process perspective.

The second major section of the chapter discusses a relatively new perspective in person-perception theory and research. The new perspective, based largely on Erving Goffman's work, will be contrasted with the process approach discussed in the first section. Finally, the chapter will conclude with a discussion of implications of this new perspective for marketing research.

BASIC APPROACHES IN PERSON-PERCEPTION THEORY AND RESEARCH

Alternative Perspectives

The accuracy perspective in person-perception theory and research focuses upon the analysis of one person's accuracy in judging another person's behavior and personality. Researchers utilizing this approach have asked basically two questions: (1) To what extent are people accurate in understanding the meaning of cues communicated by others?, and (2) To what extent are people accurate in forming impressions of what others' personality characteristics are?

Research related to the first question has typically focused upon recognition of emotions communicated nonverbally. For example, experimental subjects are shown a picture of a person's face and asked to indicate whether the stimulus person is expressing anger, fear, surprise, hatred, love, and so on. In other research, subjects listen to a person reading a neutral passage and try to determine what emotion the speaker is trying to portray through vocal characteristics.

Research related to the second question generally has focused on a subject's ability to "understand" another person, that is, to form an accurate impression of the other's personality, or to make accurate predictions regarding the other's behavior. Much of this research has tested whether some subjects have a general trait of empathy, that is, a general ability to accurately judge many other persons' personalities and behaviors. Results indicate little evidence of a general empathic ability (see Bronfenbrenner, Harding, and Gallway, 1958; Cline, 1964; Smith, 1966; Wackman, 1969).

Research based upon the accuracy perspective has become less prominent in the past 10 years for three basic reasons. First, a series of papers during the 1950s indicated the extreme difficulty of measuring accuracy (Cronbach, 1955, 1958; Crow and Hammond, 1957; Gage and Cronbach, 1955). For the most part, problems in measurement have not been overcome. Second, results of research regarding the generality of an "empathy" trait were discouraging. Third, research emphasis shifted in the mid- and late 1950s to the process approach under the urging of a number of social psychologists, in particular Taguiri and Petrullo (1958).

This alternative process approach has focused on psychological and social-psychological processes involved in forming impressions and making evaluations of others. A number of basic questions guided this research. For example, what cues do people use in forming impressions of others, and how do they select these cues? How do people process the information they receive in forming impressions? What effect does the context in which information is received have on the ways people select and process information about others? What effects do current emotional states of perceivers have on the ways they select and process information about others? What personality characteristics influence information selection and processing, and what specific effects do these personality characteristics have?

Although some researchers have suggested that these two research approaches are mutually exclusive (Taguiri, 1958), in fact they have not been. Rather, research with each approach has been useful in suggesting new research utilizing the other approach (Warr and Knapper, 1968). This complementarity will certainly continue in the future.

In general, research based on the process approach is more relevant for marketing research because of the kinds of questions marketing researchers ask. Typically, marketing researchers are not particularly interested in whether a person in an advertisement (the stimulus person) is accurately perceived, that is, his personality is "really" understood by the receiver. Rather, the marketing researcher is more interested in *what* impressions are formed about the stimulus person, *what* cues are selected in developing this impression, and *how* these cues are processed in forming impressions. These questions are the central questions guiding process-approach research.

Marketing researchers are interested in whether an advertisement is effectively communicating what is intended, that is, is being received accurately. Thus accuracy of communication is an important concern in copy testing research. However, the research question of interest is not simply the question of accuracy or inaccuracy. Rather, more significant are such questions as what elements of the stimulus (the advertisement) cause impressions to be formed, and what combinations of these elements result in different impressions—whether these impressions are the ones the advertiser wanted to create or not. Asking these kinds of research questions will enable the marketing researcher not only to evaluate whether an advertisement communicated what it was supposed to communicate, but also *why* it communicated what it did. Answers to the why questions may even provide guidelines for reconstructing the advertisement to achieve communication objectives.

Person-Perception-Process Approach

The remainder of this section will concentrate on theory and research based on the process approach, with some mention of relevant material from the accuracy approach. Also it will focus upon factors in person-perception processes over which marketers have some control. Thus we shall discuss processes people use in making judgments about others and the impact of variations in stimulus inputs on these processes, since marketers exert a great deal of control over stimuli presented in advertisements. We shall not discuss other factors affecting these processes, such as the social context in which stimuli are received, current emotional states of the perceiver, personality characteristics of the perceiver, and so forth, since marketers exert almost no control over these factors. Excellent reviews of these factors are presented in Taguiri (1968) and Warr and Knapper (1968).

A general conceptual model of person perception is presented in Figure 1. This model is a modification of a more elaborate model developed by Warr and Knapper (1968).

FIGURE 1. **Model of Person Perception**

The stimulus is the information presented to the perceiver about the stimulus person. It may be a direct stimulus (i.e., a person with whom the perceiver interacts) or an indirect stimulus (i.e., a person presented to the perceiver through some mediated process, such as a film, a still photograph, a written description, or a list of traits). Most research has used an indirect stimulus.

The *input selector* and the *processing center* are two psychological processes occurring within the perceiver. Although they are conceptually separated, they are not assumed to be independent; rather, it is likely that they occur almost simultaneously. Two separate processes are conceptualized simply for ease of analysis.

The *input selector* is the process in which a perceiver selects cues from the stimulus and assigns meaning to the cues. For example, suppose that a picture of a pretty, smiling blonde is presented to the perceiver. The input selector attends to certain cues—smile, blonde hair, and so forth—and avoids other cues—eye color, lipstick color, and so forth—and draws an inference about the cues (assigns a meaning to the cues): smile means happiness, blonde hair means popular, and so forth.

The *processing center* is the process in which a perceiver combines the meanings of the cues he has attended to and forms a total impression: "Blondes must have fun, maybe even more fun than brunettes or redheads."

The *response* is an internal nonbehavioral response. Warr and Knapper point out three possible kinds of internal responses:

1. Attribution responses, that is, attributions of certain personality characteristics or emotional states to a stimulus person.

2. Expectancy responses, that is, expectancies regarding behaviors of a person with certain characteristics or emotional states.

3. Affective responses, that is, emotional responses to the stimulus person, including attraction, liking, sympathy, fear, and so on.

Another distinction between two types of attribution responses has also been made. *Episodic* attributions are responses regarding the present state of a stimulus person, such as tension, happiness, anger, and so forth. Dispositional attributions are responses regarding more lasting personality traits of the stimulus person (e.g., aggressiveness, generosity, honesty, etc.).

For the most part, person-perception research has focused upon assessing dispositional attributions. However, research in nonverbal communication has generally focused upon episodic attribution responses to facial expressions and vocal characteristics. This research will be discussed where appropriate.

Warr and Knapper include a number of other factors in their model of person perception, including the social context of the perceiver, emotional states of perceivers, personality characteristics of perceivers, and so forth. We shall not discuss these factors, but rather shall focus on the basic model, because, as indicated above, the marketer has little or no control over these factors.

Person-perception research using the process approach can be divided into three categories in terms of the basic model—research concerning the input selector, research concerning the processing center, and research concerning stimulus patterns.

Input-Selector Research. Research on the input selector examines processes of cue selection and of assigning meaning to the cues. Actually, it is probably useful to separate two research questions: (1) What cues does a perceiver attend to, and what cues does he avoid?, and (2) What meaning does the perceiver assign to the cues he actually receives? Little research in person perception has addressed either question.

Engel (1956) conducted research relevant to the first question. He presented two different faces simultaneously to an experimental subject, using a stereoscopic vision device. He found that sometimes one facial input was dominant, so that the other face was effectively invisible to the subject, but in other instances subjects were able to combine the two inputs successfully. In later research Engel (1958) found that combined judgments were often aesthetically preferable to single judgments. The research did not analyze what cues the subjects selected from the facial photographs presented to the subjects.

Later research by Moore (1966) simultaneously presented two photographs, varying in violence of content. Results indicated that the amount of violence perceived increases as the child subjects grow older. Again, the research did not analyze what cues the subjects selected from the photographs.

Research regarding the second question (i.e., the meanings assigned to various cues) is almost nonexistent in the person-perception literature. Some research has indicated that clothing influences perceptions of the status of a stimulus person (Douty, 1962; Hoult, 1951; Thibaut and Riecken, 1955). For the most part, however, little research has examined the dispositional attributions created by stimulus cues.

A large body of research has examined the communication of emotional meanings (i.e., episodic attributions) via nonverbal modes such as facial expressions and vocal characteristics. Both kinds of research use essentially the same experimental design. A subject is presented with a stimulus and asked to determine the emotion a stimulus person is portraying.

The subject is given a list of six to eight emotions from which to choose. In facial-expression research, still photos are typically used as the stimulus; vocal-expression research generally uses a short tape recording of the stimulus person reading a neutral passage, such as the alphabet. This research, much of it based on the accuracy approach, indicated that subjects are generally more accurate than chance in recognizing the emotions a stimulus person attempts to communicate. The research also indicated, however, that not all emotions are equally easy to recognize. For example, anger, sadness, and pride were easy to recognize, but love, nervousness, and jealousy were difficult to recognize (Davitz, 1964, Chapter 11).

Early facial-expression research attempted to isolate central cues, those which were fundamental in conveying emotional meaning. Ruckmick (1921) suggested that the lower half of the face communicated emotional meanings, but Buzby (1924) said the eyes and brow communciated meaning. Dunlap (1927) disagreed with both, claiming that the dominant part of the face depended on the emotion being expressed. Similarly, in vocal-expression research early work attempted to discover fundamental vocal cues. Skinner (1935) found that vocal pitch differentiated expressions of happiness and sadness, but Fairbanks and Hoaglin (1941) reported that speech rate and length of pauses, as well as pitch, were related to the emotional meanings being expressed. Thus early research in both areas suggested that different cues were central in expressing emotions.

Subsequent research has indicated that isolated facial or vocal cues are not central in communicating emotions (Davitz, 1964, Chapter 8; Krause, 1961; Ruesch and Prestwood, 1949; Schlosberg, 1954). Rather total configurations of facial and vocal cues communicate emotions, (i.e., combinations of cues). Furthermore, modern research in nonverbal communication is drawing an analogy from linguistic analysis. In linguistics isolated sounds (phonemes) are not associated with meanings, but combinations of sounds into words (morphemes) are associated with meanings. Similarly, in facial-expression research, isolated cues, such as the height and angle of the eyebrow, curvature of the mouth, and so on, are not associated with meanings. Rather, configurations of facial cues—total facial expressions—are associated with meanings (Sebeok, Hayes, and Bateson, 1964). Research in vocal expression is also using the linguistic analogy (Sebeok, Hayes, and Bateson, 1964). This research is beginning to identify a "vocabulary" of meanings communicated by facial expressions and vocal expressions, especially emotional meanings.

At present there is no equivalent research strategy in person-perception research. Thus little is known regarding the meanings assigned to the configurations of cues that a stimulus person presents. For example, if a stimulus person wears a white coat and glasses, does the perceiver think the person is a medical expert? Does the combination of middle-age woman and a Scandinavian accent mean that the stimulus person is an expert on the subject of coffee? In short, there is presently no "vocabulary" for identifying the meanings communicated by combinations of cues in terms of such traits as expertise, aggressiveness, trustworthiness, and so on.

In summary, little person-perception research has examined the cues people attend to and avoid when forming judgments of others.[1] Furthermore, no person-perception research has studied the meanings assigned to cues—or combinations of cues—in terms of the personality characteristics attributed to persons exhibiting various combinations of cues. The scarcity of research on the input selector has a number of implications for marketing research; these implications will be discussed later in this section.

Processing Center Research. Whereas research on the input selector is scarce, research examining the processing center is plentiful. Generally, this research studies dispositional attribution responses (i.e., attributions of personality characteristics to a stimulus person). The research can be divided into two categories: (1) research examining trait implication, (i.e., the personality traits implied by a specific trait); and (2) research examining the combination rules perceivers use in forming total impressions.

Trait-implication research. Trait-implication research involves determining the traits that are implied by, or go together with, a single stimulus trait. For example, if we tell a subject that a stimulus person is aggressive, what other traits will the subject attribute to the stimulus person? Essentially, what the subject is asked to do is form an impression of the stimulus person on the basis of a small amount of information. The classic experiment in trait implication was conducted by Asch (1946).

Asch's procedure was very simple. He read a set of seven personality

[1]There is an abundance of research concerning general perception processes and attention to different aspects of physical stimuli, such as geometric forms, designs, and the like. Review of this research is not within the scope of the present chapter. General literature reviews of perception research are Hochberg (1964) and Ittelson (1960). Marketing-related research on general perception processes in exposure to advertisements can be found in *The Journal of Advertising Research* and *The Journal of Marketing Research.*

characteristics to subjects and asked them to indicate their impression of the stimulus person in two ways: (1) they wrote a brief character sketch of the person, and (2) they responded to a check list of 18 polar items, selecting the term for each pair that best described the stimulus person. Asch found that subjects made rather broad inferences from very limited cues. Also, he found that subjects tended to use rather specific inferential rules in drawing inferences.

For example, subjects in one treatment group were read the following lists of traits: intelligent, skillful, industrious, warm, determined, practical, and cautious. Subjects in a second group were read the same list, except cold was substituted for warm. Varying only the single trait of warm-cold produced very different impressions of the person's generosity, shrewdness, happiness, irritability, humor, sociability, popularity, ruthlessness, imaginativeness, and self-centeredness. Asch used the technique of varying one characteristic in a list to identify a number of specific processes involved in the formation and change of impressions.

Asch argued that his results showed several general processes occurring in impression information:

1. Certain traits were more central than others in the impressions people form of others (e.g., the warm-cold dimension was more important in influencing impressions than the blunt-polite dimension).

2. Inferences from one cue trait are made to many other traits, but not all (e.g., changing warm to cold did not affect judgment's of the other's honesty, reliability, or persistence, but did influence judgments of his generosity, happiness, etc.).

3. Inferences about a person from a trait are partly dependent upon other attributes of the person (e.g., effects of varying the warm-cold dimension were partly dependent upon the other traits on the list.

Later experiments using Asch's design have attempted to extend the generality of his findings and learn more about specific inference rules people use in forming impressions of others.

Subsequent research has attacked the notion of the inherent centrality of a trait. For example, Wishner (1960) showed that the centrality of a trait in impression formation was dependent upon whether the trait was highly correlated with other traits included on the stimulus list and the impression checklist. For example, if the manipulated trait, such as the warm-cold dimension, is highly correlated with the items included in an impression checklist, the trait will appear to be a central one; however, if the manipulated trait is relatively uncorrelated with items on the list, the trait will not appear to be a central one.

Wishner's analysis and research suggested that the concept of a central trait was essentially a methodological artifact. This artifact could be overcome by a more complete sampling of items for the impression-formation checklist. Research with larger item samples, carried out by Wishner and by Warr and

Knapper (1968, pp. 126-32), indicated that no single trait is *the* central, dominant one, and no small set of traits is the central set in impression formation. Some traits do appear to be more important than others in determining the impressions subjects form of a stimulus person. However, not enough research has been done to determine which traits are the important ones and how much more important these traits are.

Other researchers used a different methodology to investigate trait implication. Rather than presenting lists of traits to subjects that varied one dimension, as Asch had done, subjects were presented with a *single* cue trait. Subjects were then asked to determine what other characteristics went along with this trait.

For example, Bruner, Shapiro, and Taguiri (1958) asked subjects how likely it was that an "intelligent person" was active, aggressive, enterprising, independent, reliable, and so forth. Subjects estimated probabilities of co-occurrence of these traits. Variations of this method were developed by Hays (1958) and Warr and Sims (1965). The latter authors proposed the notion of *cojudgment* as a general principle of trait implication. Cojudgment is a process by which attributes are clustered in relation to their affective tone. Cojudgment occurs when the possession of a desirable trait is assumed to imply the possession of other desirable traits, or when the possession of an undesirable trait is assumed to imply the possession of other undesirable attributes.

The extent to which cojudgment occurs from specific traits was investigated in two studies (Warr and Knapper, 1968, pp. 146-52; Warr and Sims, 1965). All cue traits exceeded chance, confirming the general notion of cojudgment. The level of cojudgment seemed to depend on the valence of the cue trait (i.e., on how highly valued the trait was). For example, "practical" was highly valued by the subjects and had a very high cojudgment score, but "forceful" had a low valence and low cojudgment score.

The general conclusion from this research is that positive traits imply other positive traits, and negative traits imply other negative traits, though the implicatory relation between traits is not perfect. Furthermore, the strength of the implicatory relation depends upon the valence of the trait. These results are highly similar to the results of research on the centrality of traits; in fact, cojudgment and centrality appear to be pretty much the same phenomenon.

Combination rules—relationships among combinations of traits. Other research investigated the combination rules people use in forming impressions of others from a *set* of traits. This research is probably more important than the research concerning inference rules from a single trait, because people typically receive more than one item of information about another person when forming an impression of him. Two basic kinds of combination rules have been discussed in the literature.

First is the linear model. According to this model, a total impression depends on some linear combination of judgments implied by single traits. Two subtypes of linear models have been studied. *Additive* models assume that the total impression is an additive combination of inferences from single traits; therefore, the combination of cue traits AB would imply X more strongly than cue trait A or B alone. Averaging models assume that the total impression is an average of inferences from single traits; for example, if A implied X strongly and B implied X slightly, AB would imply X to a moderate degree.

Anderson (1965) compared additive and averaging models and found results clearly inconsistent with the additive model. On the other hand, the results only partially supported the averaging model. Apparently, an additive model is likely to be inappropriate, but an averaging model is likely to be useful only in certain circumstances.

The second major set of models is *configural* models. Configural models differ from linear models in that they explicitly deny that a total impression is simply a linear combination of single inputs. Whereas linear models assume that the single-stimulus inputs remain valid and unchanged when placed in the context of other inputs, configural models assume that combined inputs have very different implications than two conponents received separately.

Rokeach and Rothman (1965) demonstrated empirically that clear predictions about total impressions from combinations of inputs can be derived from configural models. Furthermore, they showed that their configural model predicted better than a linear model. Dustin and Baldwin (1966) have studied redundancy in pairs of stimulus inputs, redundancy being defined as the extent to which members of a pair imply each other (i.e., extent of cojudgment). For example, "polite" and "considerate" have high redundancy, but "practical" and "cynical" have low redundancy. Results indicated that combination rules are likely to be more extreme than trait-implication rules such as cojudgment, especially when the pair of cue traits has low redundancy. Other successful configural models have been developed by Hammond and Summers (1965) and Hoffman (1960).

A major problem with configural models, however, is that as soon as inputs are considered in groups of more than two or three, the possible number of combinations increases immensely. Also, the large number of interactions and higher-order interactions that is possible when five or six cue traits are combined makes interpretation of results extremely difficult. The research task would seem to be immense.

Only one of these studies showed a clear superiority of a configural model over a linear model. Moreover, in a related context, Meehl (1960) has shown that, although clinicians appear to use configural models in judging the extent of a patient's psychosis, the amount of departure from a linear, additive model does not appear to be very great.

The most reasonable conclusion from the data seems to be that sometimes linear-combination rules and sometimes more complex configural rules are used in forming impressions of others. However, even when configural rules are used, they often do not markedly depart from linear rules.

To summarize research on the processing center, we can conclude that people generally assume that positive traits go together with positive traits, and negative traits with negative traits, when they form impressions of others. Total impressions, however, typically are not simply the sum of the traits attributed to another; rather, combinations of traits result in unique total impressions, though sometimes these configurations are pretty much like an average of the attributed traits. Implications for marketing research will be discussed later in this section.

Stimulus Patterns. Some research in person perception and in nonverbal communication has looked at variations in the presentation of stimuli. Warr and Knapper (1968, pp. 127-32) showed that increasing the complexity of stimulus material reduced the potency of single manipulated cues. They compared impressions formed from two stories in which the same seven traits were embedded. The second story was approximately twice as long as the first story and included more details regarding the stimulus person's career and background. The average difference on rating scales between the two versions of the story was reduced, indicating that increasing the information presented about a stimulus person decreased the impact or *centrality* of a single trait.

A series of studies examined order-of-presentation effects in impression formation (Anderson and Barrios, 1961; Anderson and Hubert, 1963; Luchins, 1957; Richey, McLelland and Shimkunas, 1967; Warr and Knapper, 1968, pp. 269-88). In these studies the general research strategy involves presenting two lists of traits, sometimes embedded in narrative accounts. Both lists contain the same traits, but the order of presentation is varied such that in one list positive traits precede negative traits, and in the other list negative traits precede positive ones. A *primacy* effect (i.e., early stimulus cues are more important than later ones) would result in a positive total impression from the first list and a negative impression from the second list. A *recency* effect would result in the opposite pattern. Results indicated no general primacy or recency effect.

The great majority of studies of impression formation have used only a single channel for communicating information about the stimulus person, typically a list of traits or a narrative story including a set of traits. This is highly unrealistic, since in forming impressions of others people normally receive information through a variety of sense modalities. In advertising, of course, several sense modalities and several channels are typically involved. A few studies did examine impression formation when information about the stimulus person is received through two senses. In several experiments Warr and Knapper (1968, pp. 296-318) studied impressions formed after exposing a subject to both verbal and photographic information about a stimulus person. In these studies subjects read a newspaper story about a person. In one experimental condition subjects also saw a photograph of the stimulus person, but in another condition no photograph was presented. The researchers concluded that generally supplementary photographic information about the stimulus person does change the impression formed.

In one of these experiments Warr and Knapper pitted verbal and visual material against each other directly, using a complete research design (i.e., verbal information only, visual information only, and both verbal and visual information). Utilizing multiple-regressions techniques, the authors determined that the verbal information (a newspaper story) was more important in determining total impressions than the visual information (a supplementary photograph). However, the greater impact of verbal information in this study is probably a function of the context (i.e., newspaper format) and of the length of the story as compared to a single photograph. In other contexts, such as newspaper or magazine advertising, visual material is likely to have a greater impact on the impression formed than verbal material.

Similarly, research on the communication of emotional meaning has typically used only one nonverbal mode to present the stimulus information. Usually either a still photograph or a brief tape recording is presented as the stimulus. However, a study by Levitt (1964) did compare the emotional meaning communicated by facial expressions and vocal expressions.

In this study stimulus persons read a neutral statement six times, attempting to portray six different emotions—joy, surprise, fear, disgust, anger, and contempt. These responses were recorded on sound motion pictures. Judges were asked to identify the emotion being expressed after seeing facial expressions only (a soundless version of the film), hearing the voice only (a tape from the film), or both seeing the facial expression and hearing the voice (a sound version of the film). Results generally indicated that communication of emotional meaning via both facial expression and vocal expression was *not* superior to communication through only one mode. Furthermore, facial expressions generally communicated emotional meaning better than vocal expressions, although accuracy in recognition depended partly on the emotion being expressed.

Communication of impressions or of emotional meaning by other multiple-channel combinations has not been studied. One combination of obvious relevance to advertisers would utilize a sound film with music in the background, that is, a combination of facial, verbal, vocal, and musical expressions of emotional meaning or impressions. That this research has not been done is probably due to (1) a lack of knowledge in the fields of person perception and nonverbal communication regarding the communication of impressions and emotions with a single mode of communication, and (2) the elaborate experimental designs required in this kind of research.

Clearly, research on various stimulus patterns and channel combinations has not progressed very far. Furthermore, research to the present has done little to

clarify the effects of different stimulus patterns and different channel combinations.

Implications for Marketing Research

Of what relevance is theory and research in person perception for marketing
research and marketers? A general conclusion is that the research and findings in
this area are of almost no relevance, but the research questions suggested by
person-perception theory and the research strategies employed are indeed
relevant.

Before elaborating this conclusion, let us make explicit some assumptions
about advertisers' possible intentions regarding the potential effects of advertisements.

When advertisers create ads aimed at trying to persuade consumers to
purchase products in order to become "new people" or to enjoy a satisfying
emotional state, they make several assumptions directly related to person-
perception processes. First, these advertisements present certain cues about the
stimulus person to the consumer—an assumption of the advertiser is that the
consumer will actually attend to these cues, such as blonde hair, a smiling face,
and so forth. Presumably, in designing the advertisement the advertiser expects
(hopes) to arrange stimulus cues and choose channels that will catch the
attention of the consumer. A second assumption is that the consumer will assign
certain meanings and combine them to form a total impression (e.g., "blondes
have more fun than other women" or "men who drive X autos are ladies' men").

These assumptions are assumptions about processes carried out by the input
selector and by the processing center, and about the impact of various stimulus
patterns and channel combinations on the entire person-perception process.
Thus person-perception theory and research should be a central concern of
marketing researchers. Up to the present, however, person-perception research is
not highly relevant to marketing researchers for a number of reasons.

First, research on the input selector has not provided information regarding
either the cues that people actually attend to and avoid or the meanings people
assign to these cues. Little person-perception research has addressed these
questions directly, and research in nonverbal communication is only beginning
to address them. Yet, for marketers, the cues consumers select and the meanings
they assign to these cues are of central concern.

Second, although considerable research has examined the processing center,
findings are not very relevant. The kinds of information provided experimental
subjects have not been very realistic. Typically, subjects have been given a list of
traits and asked to form total impressions of a stimulus person, but seldom do
people receive information of this nature. Rather, in most instances, especially in
advertising, people form impressions on the basis of less direct cues, such as
behaviors, physical appearances, and so forth; these cues require inferences

about the traits the cues represent. Furthermore, even when less direct cues have been used, as in facial-expression research, the mode of presentation has often been somewhat unrealistic (e.g., still photographs rather than more realistic motion pictures). Finally, the traits studied in processing-center research are probably of little interest to marketers (e.g., cynical, forceful, practical, precise, reflective).

Third, stimulus pattern research is not very relevant either. For example, stimulus combinations in order-of-presentation research have typically involved both positive and negative traits. Few advertisers include negative cues in advertisements, however. Also little research has looked at multiple modalities of communication, especially combinations that would be of interest to marketers, such as music, verbal, vocal, and facial.

Although person-perception research findings are not very relevant to marketing researchers, person-perception theory and research are highly relevant in several ways. First, the conceptualization we have used—stimulus, input selector, processing center, response—suggests a number of significant questions the marketing researcher might ask to guide his research:

1. What cues in the stimulus does the consumer attend to, and what cues does he avoid?
2. What meanings does the consumer assign to these cues?
3. What total impressions are formed from various combinations of cues?

Second, certain concepts developed in person-perception research are likely to be relevant in conceptualizing research (e.g., cojudgment, centrality of traits, and configural models). The conceptual distinction between episodic and dispositional attributions might be of considerable relevance in helping the marketing researcher conceptualize his research problem. For example, he might use this distinction to clarify the kind of impression an advertiser tries to create; conceptual clarification would aid him in designing research to test the advertisement's effectiveness in creating this impression. Indeed, elaboration of this conceptual distinction might serve as a basis for replacing Woods's (1960) simplistic classification of the "symbolic characteristics" of products—prestige, maturity, status, anxiety, hedonic, and functional.

Third, methodologies and the general research strategy employed in person-perception research are likely to be highly relevant. Before elaborating this point, however, a classic example of marketing research from a person-perception perspective will be discussed to clarify the use of this perspective in marketing research.

Haire (1950) studied reactions to instant coffee from the person-perception perspective, using Asch's (1946) research procedures. In Haire's study, housewife subjects read a seven-item shopping list and were asked to give their impressions of the personality and characteristics of a woman who bought these groceries.

Two groups of 50 subjects were tested. One group read a list that included Nescafe instant coffee as the fifth item; the other group read a list in which Maxwell House coffee was substituted for the instant coffee. The impressions of the stimulus person formed by subjects in the two groups differed considerably. Half the subjects who read the Nescafe list characterized the stimulus person as "lazy" and a "slipshod planner." But only a few of the subjects who read the Maxwell House list characterized her in these ways.

Haire concluded that Nescafe meant laziness and slipshod planning because impressions were based on shopping lists differing in only one respect: Nescafe or Maxwell House coffee. Haire suggested that Nescafe was (in Asch's terms) a *central cue* in the impressions formed. Remember, however, research discussed previously indicates that (1) the centrality of a cue or trait depends to some extent on other items in the stimulus list, and (2) combination rules are often not simply linear combinations of single traits. Yet the inference Haire drew assumes a linear combination model.

Additional research conducted by Haire and reported in the same paper indicates his conclusion may not have been valid. The second study included four groups. Two groups replicated the original study, reading the two seven-item lists that manipulated type of coffee. Two additional groups read lists that included an eighth item, Blueberry Fill pie-mix, an additional prepared food. Haire concluded that the addition of another prepared food item showed that prepared foods in general, not Nescafe in particular, caused the formation of poor impressions. However, his data do not really support this conclusion, but rather indicate both his original *and* modified conclusions may be invalid.

On several personality traits, Haire's data indicated that the two additional groups were closer to the Maxwell-House-only group than to the Nescafe-only group. But, if prepared foods in general caused the bad impression, the Maxwell-House-only group should have been much lower than the other three groups on negative traits; also, the other three groups should not have differed.

The conclusions Haire drew were essentially backward inferences from the total impression formed (e.g., lazy, slipshod housekeeper) to the meaning of a single stimulus cue. Research indicates that we should be cautious in making this inference, however, since the total impression formed from a stimulus list depends on *all* the items in the list. Adding one other prepared food item to the original list changed the "meaning" of Nescafe substantially. No longer was a "Nescafe housewife" seen as lazy or slipshod in housekeeping; in fact, she was seen as essentially the same as a housewife who used Maxwell House.

A more direct test of the "symbolic meaning" of Nescafe is a study by Westfall, Boyd, and Campbell (1957). They presented housewife subjects with a list of 18 brief descriptions of housewives, such as "a lazy housewife," "the best cook you know," "a thrifty housewife," and so forth. Subjects were then asked to determine whether each type of housewife used "regular or instant coffee." Over three fourths of the subjects perceived the "lazy housewife" and the "housewife who dislikes cooking" as instant-coffee users. These results clearly support Haire's original conclusion that Nescafe connotes laziness.

However, even with the cross validation of these two studies, we should be careful in the conclusion we draw, because people do not see cues or traits in isolation. Rather, they see cues in combination with other cues that may modify the impressions formed, as was the case in Haire's second study. In short, the process of inferring the kind of impressions created by the use of a product is likely to be rather complicated.

Although the research process might be complicated, nevertheless, the impressions or moods created by the use of a product—what is sometimes called the *symbolic meaning* of a product—can be determined if a multiple research strategy is adopted. The first stage of research might attempt to determine what traits are implied by a single product cue. Instead of supplying a checklist of traits, however, the researcher should probably leave the responses open ended. For example, he might ask subjects to describe the "kind of person who uses Product X." Open-ended responses enable the researcher to capitalize on the richness of unstructured response data. This technique has been used in motivation-research studies discussed in Newman (1957).

The second stage might involve attempts to validate the findings of the first stage regarding the traits implied by a single product. Westfall's technique could be used with a structured list of types of people who use a product. Research could use either a forced-choice technique like Westfall's (e.g., does a "lazy housewife" use instant or regular coffee?), or it could use a technique more similar to Bruner's (e.g., how likely is it that a housewife who uses product X is lazy, reliable, etc.?) (Bruner, Shapiro, and Taguiri, 1958). Research in this second stage is likely to provide more reliable data regarding the impressions that single products create.

Finally, the third stage might provide subjects with lists of products used by a stimulus person, as in Haire's study. Subjects would be asked to describe the person and/or to rate the person on a number of traits. Several lists with varying items and varying sequences of presentation should be used. The researcher could then determine whether the impressions created by a product in the first two research stages were relatively stable, or whether impressions created were highly dependent upon the context in which a product was presented. If impressions varied by context (stimulus list), it might be difficult to interpret what symbolic meaning is connoted by the product.

Copy testing might also make use of some of the controlled experimental and measurement techniques used in person-perception research. Researchers might test whether certain honored advertising cues are creating the impression marketers want them to communicate. For example, does dressing an actor in the "scientist's" white coat really create the impression that he is intelligent, objective, an expert on the subject, and so forth?

Research might also help determine how best to display a product to create a favorable symbolic meaning for the product. For example, Hamm and Cundiff (1969) asked housewives to rank 50 products as being most to least like their real self and their ideal self. They found a high consensus among their subjects. The authors suggested that one useful advertising technique for lower-ranked products would be to link these products with highly ranked products (i.e., use the cojudgment principle). For example, fur coats were ranked low. Hamm and Cundiff suggested that a good advertisement for fur coats might be to show a woman wearing a beautiful dress in a beautiful home, putting on a fur coat. Copy testing with various impression-formation measures could be used to determine if such an advertisement were actually creating the favorable impression or symbolic meaning the marketer intended.

RECENT THEORETICAL DEVELOPMENTS RELATED TO PERSON-PERCEPTION THEORY AND RESEARCH

In the second section of the chapter we discuss some recent theoretical and empirical developments in both person-perception research and in marketing research that may be helpful in further specifying the relevance of work in person perception to marketing research. The person-perception research we have discussed so far seems to be based on an implicit model of man with the following characteristics:

1. Man is seen as relatively passive. That is, person-perception research assumes that people are presented information about others, process this information, and form impressions of others without actively seeking additional information to clarify or elaborate their impressions.

2. Man's major purpose in forming impressions of others is to have a *true* understanding of the others' personality and behavior for the purpose of being able to better predict how the other person will behave. Accurate prediction will then prevent the perceiver from being hurt by the behavior of others.

3. To attain true understanding of the other, man pays most attention to those cues which are least under the control of the other person. This assumption implies that some characteristics are easily controlled by a person (e.g., his verbalizations), but others are much less under his control (e.g., facial expressions and vocal patterns).[2]

[2] These appear to be the major assumptions about man implicit in most of the literature on person perception, although there are some exceptions. For example, Jones and Thibaut (1958) suggested that men may have a variety of possible goals in interaction, not simply the goal of achieving true understanding of the other. These alternative goals will influence the judgments made about others.

Warr and Knapper (1968, pp. 227-31) conducted an experiment to test the effects of different interaction goals on impressions formed. One group of subjects was given the goal of understanding the background and experiences of a stimulus person. Another group was

The person-perception model of man bears a strong resemblance to the model of man implicit in much of marketing research, as described by Kover (1967). Kover suggested the marketing model of man assumed that man had these characteristics:

1. He is passive.
2. He is isolated.
3. He is mainly concerned with publicly acceptable needs and appearances.
4. He is basically a life style (i.e., demographic and other characteristics).
5. His needs are mainly satisfied through products and services.
6. He knows what he believes about products.
7. He does *not* know how these beliefs about products affect his behavior.

Kover pointed out that several of these assumptions are contradictory; for example, the assumption that man is isolated and that he is mainly concerned with publicly acceptable needs and appearances; the assumption that man is isolated and that he is basically a member of a social class, an economic class, an age group, and so forth. More important, however, Kover suggested that these assumptions are likely to be wrong much of the time. Research seems to bear him out.

Cox's (1963) analysis of the audience suggests that consumers are neither isolated nor passive. His results show that consumers receive much of their information about products—especially evaluative information—from other people. Furthermore much of the initiative in the consumer-information process involves active information seeking from others, not passive reception of messages from the media or opinion leaders. Ward and Wackman's (1971) research on adolescent consumers suggests that the product purchase process for adolescent consumers is definitely a social process, involving overt communication with parents and peers. It is not an individual decision-making process made by a passive, isolated person.

Both the person-perception model of man and the marketing model of man seem to be derived, in part, from Mead's (1934) symbolic interaction theory. This theory proposed that man develops a conception of self, enabling him to view himself as an object. According to Mead, the self-concept is created mainly through interaction with others. The specific form the self-concept takes is largely a function of others' reactions to the person's behavior. Thus the self-concept that a person develops is largely under the control of others. In short, according to Mead, man is basically passive, since his self-concept results from his acceptance of others' definition of the kind of person he is.

---

given the goal of determining how to behave toward the stimulus person. Each group read a narrative account about the person, then rated him on a set of traits. Subjects in the two groups differed in their ratings on over half the traits measured in the experiment.

In a series of publications, Goffman challenged Mead's assumptions (Goffman, 1957, 1959, 1963, 1967). Goffman asserted that man is not basically passive, but rather is very active in shaping his self-concept by consciously *presenting* an image of himself that he wants others to accept. Goffman agreed with Mead that the self-concept which a person develops is a function of how others react to his behavior. Where he disagreed with Mead was in asserting that man often attempts to present an image of self for others to validate. Thus the specific self-concept a person develops is very much under his control. Goffman also asserted that a person is able to achieve the self-concept he wants because others consciously try to validate his presentation of self (see especially Goffman, 1957).

Goffman's challenge to Mead's assumptions also serves as a basis for challenges to the models of men assumed in the person-perception and marketing research. For example, in arguing that products are also symbols, Levy (1963) suggests that people use products to paint a life style which defines their self-concepts. And in discussing the relation between self-concept and consumer behavior, Grubb and Grathwohl (1967) emphasize the active role the person plays in shaping his self-concept, citing Goffman in support of their ideas. Similarly, in person-perception research, Taguiri (1968) discussed the importance of Goffman's work as a challenge to the traditional assumptions and methodologies used in the area. In his review of the literature, however, Taguiri indicates that little research has been done to pick up on Goffman's suggestions.

Goffman emphasizes the person's active role in attempting to present a self-concept by such means as exhibiting certain behaviors and displaying himself in certain contexts. This emphasis is clearly an alternative to the person-perception and marketing models of man. The question arises, however, is this alternative conception relevant for marketing research? The answer is "yes" in two senses: first, certain findings in the marketing research literature can be explained in terms of this alternative conception; second, the conception suggests several different research questions.

Alternative Explanations of Marketing Research Findings Suggested by the New Theoretical Perspective

This alternative conception can provide several explanations for the *lack* of relationships generally found between measures of personality and product or brand usage. Personality research is discussed in Chapter 4. However, here we shall note a few studies in which relatively negative findings were obtained, and offer several explanations for these findings, based on this alternative conception of man.

Koponen (1960) and Frank, Massy, and Lodahl (1969) analyzed data collected in the J. Walter Thompson consumer panel. In this panel, personality data were gathered as well as various measures of demographic characteristics and consumer behaviors. Several statistically significant relationships were obtained between various personality traits and smoking behavior and product usage of coffee, tea, and beer. However, the personality measures explained only about 1 percent of the variance. Interestingly, demographic variables did not predict very well either, accounting for only 2 to 4 percent of the variance. Findings regarding the prediction of type and brand of automobile owned show essentially the same results (Evans, 1959; Evans and Roberts, 1963; Westfall, 1962).

Woodside (1968) used Kassarjian's measure of inner- and other-directed social character, which had been shown to be related to preferences for different kinds of advertising appeals (Kassarjian, 1965). College subjects differing substantially on the inner-/outer-directed personality scale did not differ in their use of five consumer products (e.g., cigarettes, mouthwash, headache remedies, magazines, and television).

Cohen (1967) argued that personality characteristics ought to be viewed as types of interpersonal orientations, rather than as intrapersonal traits. He developed a measure of three types of people, based on Horney's conceptualization of moving toward, against, and away from people. Results indicated support for several specific hypotheses, but no consistent support for the general hypothesis.

In general, then, personality measures did not predict either product usage or brand choice very well. Three alternative explanations can be advanced for the lack of findings.

First, the personality measures used may be either unreliable, invalid, or poorly chosen. Most of the personality measures administered in this research have relatively high reliability and some validity. In some instances, however, the personality traits measured may have been inappropriate. Frank, Massy, and Lodahl (1969) have suggested that the personality traits measured by the Edwards Personal Preference Schedule used in their study may not be conceptually related to specific consumer behaviors. However, several personality measures were selected or developed specifically to predict product and brand choices. For example, Cohen developed his measure of type of interpersonal orientation to predict the use of products and choice of brands that were especially relevant socially (e.g., mouthwash, deodorant, and beer). Nevertheless, results indicated that this personality measure did not account for much of the variance in consumer behavior, either product usage or brand choice.

Two other possible explanations for the lack of relationship between personality measures and consumer behavior are suggested by Goffman's alternative conception of man. First, Goffman assumes that people consciously attempt to present a certain image of self to others. This is counter to the assumption upon which most personality measures are based—that the personality traits measured are unconscious psychological attributes of people. These unconscious psychological attributes are seen as affecting a person's behavior without his being aware of their influence. (This assumption is very similar to the seventh assumption of the marketing model of man—that man does not know how his beliefs and attitudes about products affect his behavior.)

If we accept Goffman's assumption that men are indeed aware of the self-concept they present, the second explanation for the lack of relationship between personality traits and consumer behavior becomes the following: people do *not* want to present certain self-images; therefore, measures of unconscious traits that people have no interest in presenting will not predict their behavior.

For example, Vitz and Johnston (1965) measured the masculinity and femininity of their subjects, traits which presumably are unconscious. They found a very low relationship between these measures and the masculinity or femininity of subjects' cigarette brand. It may be that most people are not really very interested in portraying themselves as either highly masculine or highly feminine, even though our cultural stereotypes would suggest that this is a very important social and psychological dimension.

This explanation assumes that there is a public consensus regarding the masculinity and femininity of various brands of cigarettes. And it also assumes that a person is highly aware of public consensus regarding the various brands' symbolic meaning. But the explanation also assumes that a person is not interested in presenting his self-concept in terms of the masculine-feminine dimension. Vitz and Johnston's research indicated a high degree of consensus among subjects concerning the masculinity-femininity of different cigarette brands. Their research did not, however, examine subjects' interest in presenting masculine or feminine self-concepts.

This interpretation suggests that it might be useful for marketing researchers to try to determine the self-concepts that people want to display. If indeed people do consciously attempt to present certain self-concepts, it would seem to be important for marketers to attempt to determine the kinds of self-images people are interested in displaying.

Hamm and Cundiff's (1969) research is relevant to this point of view. In their study housewife subjects ranked 50 products in terms of how much the products were like their (1) real selves, and (2) ideal selves. The authors made a number of suggestions concerning how marketers could use data about high-ranking and low-ranking products. For example, enhancing the image of a low-ranked product by linking it with high-ranked products (cojudgment), or attempting to present high-ranked products as those which a "successful wife" uses. Their data could be used also to measure the extent to which housewives see particular products as related to their self-concepts. This kind of research is a start at determining the kinds of self-images people want to present. However, more basic research is needed to examine the kinds of *general* self-concepts people want to present (ideal self), not simply product-defined ideal selves.

A third possible explanation of the lack of relationship between personality traits and consumer behaviors is also based on Goffman's conception of man. If we assume a person consciously tries to present an image of self, we would expect that the person would exhibit behaviors and display products which he felt did express his self-concept. However, not all aspects of a person's behavior or all the products he displays are relevant to his presentation of self, since he may have a variety of goals in his interaction with others, not only the goal of validating his desired self-concept.[3] Thus we would expect that a person would use some products or brands to express a particular self-concept. However, other products may simply be irrelevant to the expression of self-concept, because the person may believe other prople do *not* judge him on the basis of the use or nonuse of these products and brands. Levy (1963) made this point when he suggested that highly visible products are more relevant for portraying a life style than less visible products.

For example, consider Vitz and Johnston's research on cigarette brand preference. It may be that people *do* want to express masculine or feminine self-concepts. However, these people may not believe that others use the brand of cigarettes they smoke as a basis for evaluating their masculinity and femininity. Data from Hamm and Cundiff's study suggest that indeed this may be the case. Cigarettes were among the products housewife subjects sorted to describe real and ideal self. Cigarettes were ranked very low as an expression of both real self and ideal self by almost all subjects. Apparently, housewives simply do not regard cigarettes as important products for expressing their self-concepts; they probably also do not think others use cigarettes to form impressions about them.

A study by Ward and Gibson (1969) presents more direct evidence regarding the use people make of products in evaluating others. The authors asked housewife subjects if they ever formed impressions of others on the basis of certain products, and if the subjects believed others formed impressions of them on the basis of certain products. The questions were asked regarding three products varying in product visibility. The high-visibility product was magazines, medium-visibility was stockings, and coffee was the low-visibility product. Over 70 percent of the women said that they had formed impressions of other women at one time or another on the basis of magazines subscribed to by the other women. However, less than one fourth said that they had ever formed impressions of other women on the basis of the coffee bought by the other women—the low-visibility product. Differences were also substantial on the question of whether the subjects thought other women formed impressions of them on the basis of these products.

Clearly, some products are seen by women as more useful than other products in forming impressions of people. Specifically, highly visible products are seen as more useful in forming impressions than less visible products.

[3]See Jones and Thibaut (1958) for a discussion of various goals in interaction.

Implications of the New Theoretical Perspective
for Marketing Research

Goffman's theoretical perspective and data from the Ward-Gibson and Hamm-Cundiff studies suggest several areas for additional research. First, research should examine the kinds of self-concepts people actually want to present. Research examining definitions of self-concepts both in terms of general psychological and social characteristics and in terms of product and brands preferences would be useful.

Second, additional research is needed to determine which products are seen as being relevant to the expression of self-concepts. More research is needed to identify products people think *others* use in evaluating them, as in the Ward-Gibson study. And more research should investigate which products people feel do express their self-concepts. The sorting technique used in Hamm and Cundiff's study is one useful method for this research, but other methods involving direct questioning should be developed.

Finally, research regarding the *kinds* of self-concepts expressed by the use of different products and brands is needed. This is the kind of research we discussed at the end of the first section (i.e., research regarding the symbolic meanings of products and brands).

These types of research will generate three kinds of information:

1. Information about the types of self-concepts people want to present.
2. Information about the products relevant to the expression of self-concepts (probably high-visibility products).
3. Information about the specific self-concepts being expressed by the use of specific products and brands.

These three kinds of information are interrelated. Unless all three kinds are collected, research based on the new person-perception conception is not likely to be very useful to marketing researchers because interpretations of the data will not be clear. An illustration of the difficulties in interpretation caused by a failure to collect all three kinds of information is a marketing research study by Jacobson and Kossoff (1963). This study was based on a self-concept approach.

In the study, measures of one dimension of self-concept were taken—risk taking or innovativeness –and subjects were divided into three types. "Cautious conservatives" saw themselves as unwilling to take chances, preferring safety, and so forth. "Confident explorers" saw themselves as ready to challenge the unknown, confident in their own ability to handle situations, and so forth. "Middle-of-the-roaders" represented the middle third of respondents on the scale. Subjects' attitudes toward the purchase of a new style of automobile, the compact car of the early 1960s, were also measured.

The authors predicted that "confident explorers" would have the most favorable attitude toward purchasing a compact car. However, contrary to the hypothesis, data indicated that they had the *least* favorable attitude toward the purchase of compact cars. Jacobson and Kossoff appeared to make a number of assumptions about the relation between self-concepts and product purchases as expressions of self-concepts. Their mistake was in failing to collect data to test the assumptions.

First, they assumed that the dimension of self-concept measured in the study—self-perceptions of risk taking and innovativeness—was a *real* dimension to the subjects. It may be, however, that this dimension is not a real one to people in the sense that most people simply do not think of themselves in terms of innovativeness. Thus people generally may not be interested in presenting either "innovative" or "cautious" self-images. The authors did not collect data to evaluate whether this dimension of self-concept was a real and important one for their subjects, or whether it was essentially an irrelevant dimension.

Second, since automobiles are relatively high visibility products, the authors assumed that autos were relevant for expressing self-concepts. However, they did not collect data to evaluate whether an automobile was viewed by subjects as relevant to an expression of their self-concept. Research discussed by Newman (1957) and Grubb and Hupp (1968) suggests that people do view automobiles as expressions of life styles and self-concepts. Thus Jacobson and Kossoff cannot be faulted too greatly for this failure to collect relevant data.

Third, the authors assumed that the purchase of new compact cars expressed certain specific self-images, such as "ability to handle new situations," "readiness to meet challenges," "innovativeness," and so forth. Again, however, they did not collect data to determine whether people thought the purchase of compact cars carried these symbolic meanings. It is likely that these cars did not express these aspects of self-concept; in fact, there was probably no public consensus regarding the symbolic meaning of this new product at all. But the least that the authors could have done is to attempt to determine the symbolic meanings compact cars had, if any.

The relationship Jacobson and Kossoff found, which was the opposite of their hypothesis, probably is a function of a mistake in their assumption regarding the symbolic meaning of compact cars. If the dimension of self-concept measured in the study was irrelevant to the subjects, no differences should have occurred between groups of subjects in attitudes toward purchasing the compact cars. Similarly, no differences between the groups should have occurred if automobiles were not relevant to the expression of self-concepts. However, if the self-concept dimension was relevant to the subjects and if the product class was relevant to the expression of this self-concept, groups should differ in terms of their attitudes toward purchase of the product. Data indicated the groups did differ in their attitudes, but in the direction opposite of that predicted. Thus it is likely that Jacobson and Kossoff's assumption regarding the self-concept expressed by the purchase of a compact car was incorrect. Unfortunately, we cannot determine why the relationship found in the data was the opposite of the prediction, since the data needed to test various alternative explanations were not collected.

This rather extended example was presented for several reasons. First, to indicate that research using the general notion of self-concept has been done in marketing; second, to show that unless data regarding all three kinds of information discussed above are collected, it is difficult to draw clear inferences about the relationship between self-concept and product preference or use. To repeat, these three kinds of information are (1) information about the dimensions and kinds of self-concepts that people want to present, (2) information about the relevance of particular products and product categories for expressing self-concepts, and (3) information about the dimensions and kinds of self-concepts expressed by the use of particular products and brands.

GENERAL CONCLUSIONS REGARDING THE IMPLICATIONS OF PERSON-PERCEPTION THEORY AND RESEARCH FOR MARKETING RESEARCH

The present chapter has indicated that person-perception theory and research are relevant for marketing research in certain specific ways. To recapitulate: First, few of the findings from person-perception research are directly relevant to marketers or marketing researchers. Second, a number of the research approaches and techniques used in person-perception are likely to be highly useful to marketing researchers. Third, person-perception theory is likely to be useful in suggesting new ways to conceptualize the symbolic meaning of products and brands, that is, in terms of the personal impressions created by the use of specific products and brands. Fourth, marketing research related to the person-perception approach suggests that research regarding the symbolic meaning of products and brands should probably be restricted to a subclass of products, that is, those with high social visibility, which people see as relevant to the expressions of self-concepts. Finally, the present chapter suggests a number of specific research questions that marketing researchers might ask:

1. What cues do people attend to in advertisements?
2. What meanings do people assign to these cues, and what total impressions do they form from combinations of cues?
3. What kinds of self-concepts do people want to express?
4. What products and brands are actually relevant for the expression of self-concepts?
5. If a product is relevant for self-concept expression, what specific kinds of self-concepts are expressed by the use of different brands of the product, or different products from a class of substitutable products?

Furthermore, these research questions seem to suggest a research sequence that looks first at the self-concepts people want to express, second at the relevance of products for expressing self-concepts, third at the specific kinds of self-concepts expressed by product or brand usage, and fourth at the relationship of advertising to the creation or reinforcement of these symbolic meanings.

The initial marketing research question should not be "Do people believe that blondes have more fun?" Rather, the initial research question should be "Is that question even relevant?" Clearly, information regarding the relevance of a product for the expression of self-concepts is needed before information about the product's symbolic meaning is gathered.

REFERENCES

Anderson, N. H. "Averaging Versus Adding as a Stimulus-Combination Rule in Impression Formation," *Journal of Experimental Psychology,* 70 (1965), 394-400.

Anderson, N. H., and A. A. Barrios, "Primacy Effects in Personality Impression Formation," *Journal of Abnormal and Social Psychology,* 63 (1961), 346-50.

Anderson, N. H., and S. Hubert, "Effects of Concomitant Recall on Order Effects in Personality Impression Formation," *Journal of Verbal Learning and Verbal Behavior,* 2 (1963), 379-91.

Asch, S. E., "Forming Impressions of Personality," *Journal of Abnormal and Social Psychology,* 41 (1946), 258-90.

Bronfenbrenner, U., J. Harding, and M. Gallwey, "The Measurement of Skill in Social Perception," in *Talent and Society,* ed. D. C. McClelland, A. L. Baldwin, U. Bronfenbrenner and F. L. Strodtbeck. New York: Van Nostrand Reinhold Company, 1958.

Bruner, J. S., D. Shapiro, and R. Taguiri, "The Meaning of Traits in Isolation and in Combination," in *Person Perception and Interpersonal Behavior,* ed. R. Taguiri and L. Petrullo. Stanford, Calif.: Stanford University Press, 1958.

Buzby, D. E., "The Interpretation of Facial Expression," *American Journal of Psychology,* 35 (1924), 602-4.

Cline, V. B., "Interpersonal Perception," in *Progress in Experimental Personality Research,* ed. B. A. Maher. Vol. I. New York: Academic Press, Inc., 1964.

Cohen, J. B., "An Interpersonal Orientation to the Study of Consumer Behavior," *Journal of Marketing Research,* 4 (1967), 270-78.

Cox, D. F., "The Audience as Communicators," *Proceedings of the American Marketing Association,* December 1963, 58-72.

Cronbach, L. J., "Processes Affecting Scores on 'Understanding Others' and 'Assumed Similarity,' " *Psychological Bulletin,* 52 (1955), 177-93.

Cronbach, L. J., "Proposals Leading to Analytic Treatment of Social Perception Scores," in *Person Perception and Interpersonal Behavior,* eds. R. Taguiri and L. Petrullo. Stanford Calif.: Stanford University Press, 1958.

Crow, W. J., and R. K. Hammond, "The Generality of Accuracy and Response Sets in Interpersonal Perception," *Journal of Abnormal and Social Psychology,* 54 (1957), 384-90.

Davitz, J. R., ed., *The Communication of Emotional Meaning.* New York: McGraw-Hill Book Company, 1964.

Douty, H. I. "The Influence of Clothing on Perceptions of Persons in Single Contact Situations." Unpublished Ph.D. dissertation, Florida State University, 1962.

Dunlap, K. "The Role of Eye-Muscles and Mouth-Muscles in the Expression of the Emotions," *Genetic Psychology Monographs,* 2 (1927), 197-233.

Dustin, D. S., and P. M. Baldwin, "Redundancy in Impression Formation," *Journal of Personality and Social Psychology,* 3 (1966), 500-506.

Engel, E., "The Role of Content in Binocular Resolution," *American Journal of Psychology,* 69 (1956), 87-91.

Engel, E., "Binocular Fusion of Dissimilar Figures," *Journal of Psychology,* 46 (1958), 53-57.

Evans, F. B., "Psychological and Objective Factors in the Prediction of Brand Choice: Ford vs. Chevrolet," *Journal of Business,* 32 (1959), 340 69.

Evans, F. B., and H. V. Roberts, "Fords, Chevrolets, and the Problem of Discrimination," *Journal of Business,* 36 (1963), 242-49.

Fairbanks, G., and L. Hoaglin, "An Experimental Study of the Durational Characteristics of the Voice During Expression of Emotion," *Speech Monographs,* 8 (1941), 85-90.

Frank, R. E., W. F. Massy, and T. M. Lodahl, "Purchasing Behavior and Personal Attributes," *Journal of Advertising Research,* 9, No. 4 (1969), 15-24.

Gage, N. L., and L. J. Cronbach, "Conceptual and Methodological Problems in Interpersonal Perception," *Psychological Review,* 62 (1955), 411-22.

Goffman, E., "Alienation from Interaction," *Human Relations,* 10 (1957), 47-59.

Goffman, E., *The Presentation of Self in Everyday Life.* Garden City, N.Y.: Doubleday & Company, Inc., 1959.

Goffman, E., *Behavior in Public Places.* New York: The Free Press, 1963.

Goffman, E., *Interaction Ritual.* Garden City, N.Y.: Doubleday & Company, Inc., 1967.

Grubb, E. L., and H. L. Grathwohl, "Consumer Self-concept, Symbolism and Market Behavior: A Theoretical Approach," *Journal of Marketing,* 31 (1967). 22-27.

Grubb, E. L., and G. Hupp, "Perception of Self, Generalized Stereotypes, and Brand Selection," *Journal of Marketing Research,* 5 (1968), 53-58.

Haire, M., "Projective Techniques in Marketing Research," *Journal of Marketing,* 14 (1950), 649-56.

Hamm, B. C., and E. W. Cundiff, "Self-actualization and Product Perception," *Journal of Marketing Research,* 6 (1969), 470-72.

Hammond, K. R., and D. A. Summers, "Cognitive Dependence on Linear and Non-linear Cues," *Psychological Review,* 72 (1965), 215-24.

Hays, W. L., "An Approach to the Study of Trait Implication and Trait Similarity," in *Person Perception and Interpersonal Behavior,* eds. R. Taguiri and L. Petrullo. Stanford, Calif.: Stanford University Press, 1958.

Hochberg, J. E., *Perception.* Englewood Cliffs, N.J.: Prentice-Hall, Inc., 1964.

Hoffman, P. J., "The Paramorphic Representation of Clinical Judgment," *Psychological Bulletin,* 57 (1960), 116-31.

Hoult, T. E., "Clothing as a Factor in the Social Status Rating of Men." Unpublished Ph.D dissertation, University of Southern California, 1951.

Ittelson, W. H., *Visual Space Perception.* New York: Springer-Verlag New York, Inc., 1960.

Jacobson, E., and J. Kossoff, "Self-percept and Consumer Attitudes Toward Small Cars," *Journal of Applied Psychology,* 47 (1963), 242-45.

Jones, E. E., and J. W. Thibaut, "Interaction Goals as Bases of Inference in Person Perception," in *Person Perception and Interpersonal Behavior,* eds. R. Taguiri and L. Petrullo. Stanford, Calif.: Stanford University Press, 1958.

Kassarjian, H. H., "Social Character and Differential Preference for Mass Communication," *Journal of Marketing Research,* 2 (1965), 146-53.

Koponen, A., "Personality Characteristics of Purchasers," *Journal of Advertising Research,* 1 (September 1960), 6-12.

Kover, A. J. "Models of Man as Defined by Marketing Research," *Journal of Marketing Research,* 4 (1967), 129-32.

Krause, M. S., "Anxiety in Verbal Behavior: an Intercorrelational Study," *Journal of Consulting Psychology,* 25 (1961), 272.

Kuehn, A. A., "Demonstration of a Relationship Between Psychological Factors and Brand Choice," *Journal of Business,* 36 (1963), 237-41.

Levitt, E. A., "The Relationship Between Abilities to Express Emotional Meanings Vocally and Facially," in *The Communication of Emotional Meaning,* ed. J. R. Davitz. New York: McGraw-Hill Book Company, 1964.

Levy, S. J., "Symbolism and Life Style," *Proceedings of the American Marketing Association* (December 1963), 140-50.

Luchins, A. S., Chapters 4 and 5 in *The Order of Presentation in Persuasion,* ed. C. I. Hovland. New Haven, Conn.: Yale University Press, 1957.

Mead, G. H., *Mind, Self and Society.* Chicago: University of Chicago Press, 1934.

Meehl, P. E., "The Cognitive Activity of the Clinician," *American Psychologist,* 15 (1960), 19-27.

Moore, M. "Aggression Themes in Binocular Rivalry Situations," *Journal of Personality and Social Psychology,* 3 (1966), 685-88.

Newman, J. W., *Motivation Research and Marketing Management.* Division of Research, Graduate School of Business Administration, Harvard University, 1957.

Richey, M. H., L. McLelland, and A. M. Shimkunas, "Relative Influence of Positive and Negative Information in Impression Formation and Persistence," *Journal of Personality and Social Psychology,* 6 (1967), 322-27.

Rokeach, M., and G. Rothman, "The Principle of Belief Congruence and the Congruity Principle as Models of Cognitive Interaction," *Psychological Review,* 72 (1965), 128-42.

Ruckmick, C. A., "A Preliminary Study of the Emotions," *Psychological Monographs,* 30, No. 3 (1921), 30-35.

Ruesch, J., and A. R. Prestwood, "Anxiety: Its Initiation, Communication, and Interpersonal Management," *A.M.A. Archives of Neurology and Psychiatry,* 62 (1949), 527-50.

Schlosberg, H. "Three Dimensions of Emotion," *Psychological Review,* 61 (1954), 81-88.

Sebeok, T. A., A. S. Hayes, and M. C. Bateson, eds. *Approaches to Semiotics.* The Hague: Mouton & Company, 1964.

Skinner, E. R., "A Calibrated Recording and Analysis of the Pitch, Force, and Quality of Vocal Tones Expressing Happiness and Sadness," *Speech Monographs,* 3 (1935), 81-137.

Smith, H. C., *Sensitivity to People.* New York: McGraw-Hill Book Company.

Taguiri, R., "Introduction" to *Person Perception and Interpersonal Behavior,* eds. R. Taguiri and L. Petrullo. Stanford, Calif.: Stanford University Press, 1958.

Taguiri, R., "Person Perception," in *Handbook of Social Psychology, Vol. III* (2nd ed.), eds. G. Lindzey and E. Aronson. Reading, Mass.: Addison-Wesley Publishing Company, Inc., 1968.

Taguiri, R. and L. Petrullo, eds. *Person Perception and Interpersonal Behavior.* Stanford, Calif.: Stanford University Press, 1958.

Thibaut, J. W., and H. W. Riecken, "Some Determinants and Consequences of the Perception of Social Causality," *Journal of Personality,* 24 (1955), 113-23.

Vitz, P. D., and D. Johnston, "Masculinity of Smokers and the Masculinity of Cigarette Images," *Journal of Applied Psychology,* 49 (1965), 155-59.

Wackman, D. B., "A Proposal for a New Measure of Coorientational Accuracy or Empathy." Paper presented at the Convention of the Association for Education in Journalism, Berkeley, Calif., 1969.

Ward, S., and D. G. Gibson, "Social Influence and Consumer Communication Behavior." Paper presented at the Convention of the Association for Education in Journalism, Berkeley, Calif., 1969.

Ward, S., and D. B. Wackman, "Family and Media Influences on Adolescent Consumer Learning," *American Behavioral Scientist,* 14 (1971), 415-27.

Warr, P. B., and C. Knapper, *The Perception of People and Events.* New York: John Wiley & Sons, Inc., 1968.

Warr, P. B., and A. Sims, "A Study of Cojudgment Processes," *Journal of Personality,* 33 (1965), 598-604.

Westfall, R., "Psychological Factors in Predicting Product Choice," *Journal of Marketing,* 26 (1962), 34-40.

Westfall, R., H. W. Boyd, Jr., and D. T. Campbell, "The Use of Structured Techniques in Motivation Research, *Journal of Marketing,* 22 (1957), 134-39.

Wishner, J., "Reanalysis of 'Impressions of Personality,'" *Psychological Review,* 67 (1960), 96-112.

Woods, W. A., "Psychological Dimensions of Consumer Behavior," *Journal of Marketing,* 24 (1960), 15-19.

Woodside, A. G., Jr., "Social Character, Product Use, and Advertising Appeals," *Journal of Advertising Research,* 8, No. 4 (1968), 31-35.

6

Role Theory and
Group Dynamics

Lyman E. Ostlund
Columbia University

INTRODUCTION

Multiplicity of Roles. Roles within Groups. Relevance to Consumer Behavior.

RESEARCH CONCERNING ROLE THEORY

Role Selection. Role Expectations. Feedback of Role and Personality. Role Demands. Role Enactment—The Audience. Role Conflict.

GROUP DYNAMICS

Reference Groups. Conformity to Group Influence. Conformity as a Function of Personality Variables. Conformity as a Function of Cohesiveness. Risk Handling by Groups. Communication Flows. Conclusions.

APPLICATION OF ROLE THEORY AND GROUP DYNAMICS TO MARKETING

Reference Groups Affecting Product Category and Brand Attitudes. Impact of Interpersonal Communications. Why is Personal Influence So Potent? Opinion Leadership. Family Decision Making.

CONCLUSIONS

REFERENCES

INTRODUCTION

We are all familiar with the term role when used in the context of the theater or movies. While watching a play that we have read or seen in the past, we have certain preconceptions as to what should happen on stage. Although we fully expect that the actor will be showing us something of himself, we do expect that he will adhere to a certain characterization conceived by the playwright. That is, we allow—in fact desire—the actor to take a certain amount of latitude in interpreting what he finds in a given role, but if his interpretation falls outside the limits we have in mind as appropriate for doing it justice, we feel that actor has exceeded his license.

Role, as defined in social psychology, is really not much different from its meaning in a theatrical context. In fact, its use in the theater precedes by several thousands of years its use in psychology and sociology. Although many definitions have been set forth in the literature as to what the term should stand for in a research sense, it is generally sufficient to define the term *as a set of norms* (regularities in learned behavior) *that apply to categories of persons.* However, a social category, such as pedestrian or smoker, for which only a few norms apply is not considered a role (Brown, 1965, pp. 154-55).

Multiplicity of Roles

All of us in our day-to-day activities are thrust into a variety of roles where we are expected to perform in certain ways, perhaps say certain things, or say them in a certain tone of voice, and even have in mind a certain set of attitudes. A male of age 27 might be fulfilling his role as a father and husband at home, an executive trainee by day, "one of the boys" at the end of the day, an automobile driver as he commutes home, and a little-league coach later that evening. Beyond the course of one day, the number of roles he is expected to enact multiplies not only with the mere passage of time, but as he ascends the socioeconomic ladder, and attempts to perform an ever widening scope of tasks or activities. The norms of a given role may be quite strict and predefined, as in the case of laws and rules of the road applying to the driver, or very open to personal definition, as in the role of father or husband. In all cases, however, enactment of the role reflects in part the personality of the actor, but more importantly the expectations or norms that the audience attaches to the role.

Our reaction to a person who is not adequately fulfilling a role might vary from amusement to extreme frustration or even anger. When we watch "super skier" standing before us in the lift line outfitted in his downhill racer gear and talking a pretty good story about the last run, we are delighted if later we find upon reaching the peak that his downhill performance is a farce. Our reaction may be quite different, however, if instead we are watching the President of the United States behaving like a clod before television cameras.

Roles within Groups

Since the enactment of roles depends critically upon situational variables, the most important of which is the audience or witnesses to the performance, our examination of role theory leads us into a discussion of group dynamics. A critical distinction between man and most other forms of life is his need for social interaction. As society becomes ever more complex, the variety of groups with which we normally interact tends to impose on us an increasing variety of roles. During group interaction, the roles of individuals may alter as the task or reason for meeting alters, as information and influence flow within the group, and as the goals of individual participants change along with their strategies for attaining those goals. The term *group* refers to two or more individuals who share a set of norms, values, or beliefs and have certain implicitly or explicitly defined relationships to one another such that their behavior is interdependent. The definition of role given earlier is thus closely related to the definition of a group. The study of *group dynamics* amounts to investigating the changes that occur over time with respect to the flows of information and influence of the group upon the personalities of individual members.

Relevance to Consumer Behavior

Because of the considerable time that man spends interacting with his fellow humans, and the roles that he undertakes, it would certainly be expected that this would have an effect on his behavior while buying and consuming goods and services. With rising affluence the consumer has at his disposal the means to undertake a widening assortment of roles and act upon the influence of groups with which he interacts. There is no limit to the number of examples that can be cited as to the influence of role norms and group interaction upon the consumer. The influence is naturally greatest in those buying situations in which we are ego involved or for any reason very much concerned about the opinions of others concerning our decisions. Product categories such as clothing styles, home furnishings, automobiles, cosmetics, and certain types of recreational equipment would commonly fit this description for most people. Certainly, the minimum requirement for being an automobile driver, by way of consumption, is to provide oneself with an automobile. But next there are the decisions the buyer must make regarding models and brands of automobiles. We do not normally expect a 28-year-old bachelor to prefer a utilitarian four-door sedan or station wagon over a two-door convertible or hardtop coupe. The brand of automobile may also have a good deal to do with the role being enacted. The characterizations people give of Cadillac owners, for example, differ markedly from those given for Ford owners and not merely regarding income (Wells, Goi, and Seader, 1958). In a more recent study of how the image people hold of themselves relates to the images they hold of products, Volkswagen 1200-1300 series owners were contrasted with Pontiac GTO owners. As expected, the image Volkswagen owners gave of themselves agreed closely with the image of Volkswagen owners in general: thrifty, sensible, creative, individualistic, conservative, practical, economical, and quality conscious. Correspondingly, Pontiac GTO owners described themselves similarly as Pontiac GTO owners in general were described: status conscious, flashy, adventurous, fashionable, style conscious, interested in the opposite sex, and hedonistic (Grubb and Hubb, 1968).

The influence of groups upon consumer behavior can take many forms. A common form is the kind of influence one receives when friends give advice about which brands are best. A more subtle form of influence arises when a woman decides to try a new fashion after noticing that the "right" people are beginning to wear it. Group influence can, however, be present although falling short of affecting actual behavior. A woman's attitudes toward birth control pills may be altered due to group influence from trusted friends, while still falling short of causing a change in behavior because of other inhibiting factors, such as her level of interest in or ability to have children, past religious teachings, or her husband's influence.

Before examining what is known about the impact of role theory and group dynamics upon consumer behavior, attention will be focused on the theory and research that underlie the concepts.

RESEARCH CONCERNING ROLE THEORY

Role theory can be said to stand at the junction of sociology and psychology. Emphasis on studying the person enacting the role places one within the realm of psychology. Placing emphasis on studying the interaction between the individual enacting the role (the actor) and his audience instead draws one into the realm of sociology.

Because contributions to role theory have developed from diverse sources, there is a certain lack of conceptual consistency, or, at best, divergent uses of the term role. At least three different conceptualizations of the term have been suggested (Rommetveit, 1955):

1. A role consists of a set of expectations existing in the social situation surrounding the actor. These expectations govern his behavior toward people assuming other prescribed roles.

2. A role consists of specific expectations the actor perceives as relevant to his behavior when interacting with people assuming other subjective roles.

3. A role consists of specific overt behaviors by the actor when he interacts with people assuming other enacted roles.

Although these three conceptualizations take differing perspectives, they are far less distinctive in an empirical sense. In most social situations people have a fairly accurate perception of what norms or expectations affect their behavior; thus their actual behavior coincides closely with those norms. The prescriptive, subjective, and enacted roles tend to coincide.

It is important to remember that the study of a lone individual, per se, has no place in role theory. The stimulus-response model (see Chapter 2), long popular in psychology, does not help much in the study of the social-psychological behavior involved with role theory. Instead, the questions asked in the study of role theory are of the following sort:

1. Given the situation or environment in which the actor finds himself, has he selected the most appropriate role?

2. Is his enactment of that role proper? In short, how well does he pull it off?

3. Is the enactment of the role convincing or commanding enough to demonstrate that the actor should legitimately occupy the social position involved with that role?

Many roles exist within settings where organizational structure or at least cohesive social structure imposes formal restrictions on appropriate behavior. In such settings, positions will tend to be arranged by some form of status or authority hierarchy. It is important, however, to recognize that social structure alone does not determine the role. Rather, it determines the outer limitations encompassing perhaps several alternative roles for a given social position that could be perceived as legitimate if properly enacted.

Role Selection

As was pointed out earlier, in the course of only a day each of us occupies several roles considered relevant to the given social setting. Our audience may be the people directly around us or it may be an imaginary audience (one's image of how a particular group would react if witnessing certain behavior), contemporary to our behavior or remote. We entered this world without a repertory of roles. A major part of our development consists of learning how to enact an ever-widening number of roles (Baughman and Welsh, 1962).

Because of the number and variety of roles, several attempts have been made at the taxonomy of roles. The best known classification scheme is that by Linton (1945). Roles are divided into *ascribed* roles, that is, those roles that a person is born with or has thrust upon him, such as age, sex, and kinship roles, and roles that a person assumes by way of his efforts or achievements, *achieved* roles, include those concerning one's occupation, marriage, public service, and avocational interests. The ascribed-achieved distinction should be viewed as a continuum, not a dichotomy. That is, many roles result partly from achievement and partly from situational circumstances. A more elaborate attempt at the taxonomy of roles has been suggested by Spiegel (1964). His classification consists of six types of roles, moving from the general to the specific:

1. Biological—age, sex, and body-management roles.
2. Semibiological—ethnic, kinship, and class roles.
3. Institutional—occupational, religious, political, and recreational roles.
4. Transitional—those roles used to get from one state or situation to another, such as "the guest" role.
5. Character—those roles that are assumed with no special effort or approval from others, sometimes for special effect, such as "hero," "villain," "fool."
6. Fantasy—roles attained by simply assuming them, before an audience or in private, for diversion or as an escape mechanism from reality.

Selecting the appropriate role is an important part of being perceived by one's audience as sincere and worthy of being heard. Based upon the Linton ascribed-achieved dimension, one might conclude that role selection is concerned only with roles that are achieved. This, however, is frequently not the case, as is clear from the practice of *role casting* or *alter casting* (Weinstein and Deutchberger, 1963). Role casting occurs when the actor attempts to make clear to his audience the role he is currently assuming in order that they appropriately construe his remarks. For example, a lawyer when advising his brother on a legal matter might say, "As your lawyer...," indicating that he is about to convey professional advice. A moment later he may say, "However, as your brother...," indicating that now his advice comes from a kinship role, and that he no longer addresses him as a client.

Since role selection depends heavily upon the current audience, the interaction of roles must be taken into account. Merton (1957a) refers to the totality of complementary roles related to a given role as a *role set*. Conflict between roles, to be discussed later, results when the roles being enacted in a given social context come into disharmony or disequilibrium with one another.

Role Expectations

The conceptual link between social structure and role behavior is role expectation. The rights and obligations going with any given position within a social structure define the limits within which role behavior is judged as to its appropriateness. Thus role expectations connected with any particular position depend critically upon the other roles in the role set. Role expectations can vary in the extent to which they are general or specific, as well as in their scope of applicability or the proportion of a person's life or daily behavior to which they apply. The regulations and discipline which surround military life exemplify a set of role expectations that are highly specific and all encompassing. Role expectations can also vary in the extent to which they are clearly or only vaguely defined, and the degree to which there is consensus or agreement among people as to the expectations.

To the extent definition or general agreement on the nature of a role is vague, the actor is allowed greater freedom in portraying that role before his behavior becomes inappropriate or in conflict with other roles within his role set (Cottrell, 1942). Roles that take place in an informal social setting generally are less prescribed than those that occur in a formal setting. Whereas the behavior of a club president might be quite rigidly prescribed while an official function is being performed, his actions will more closely reflect his own personality when he is speaking informally to his fellow members.

The study of role theory depends importantly upon obtaining knowledge about the expectations the actor and his audience have regarding a particular role. For this reason considerable effort has been devoted to the measurement of role expectations using techniques commonly used in measuring perceptions and attitudes, such as questionnaires, interviews, or inferences from overt behavior (Sarbin and Allen, 1968). A comparison of the role expectations held by the audience with those held by the actor (role conceptions) can suggest an explanation for the extent to which the audience regards the actor as having met the conditions of his role. It can also happen that such comparisons will disclose that different members of the audience have different expectations for the actor, such that their final evaluation of how well he performed will be a mere reflection of these differing expectations (Block, 1952). A sentence-completion test was used by Thomas, Polansky, and Kounin (1955) to evaluate what people expected in terms of qualifications and mannerisms from a person in a social-service role.

The measurement of role expectations can also shed light on cases in which little agreement appears to exist among members of a group as to how their appointed chairman or leader should function. In positions where the group has only infrequent or distant contact with the leader or administrator, such as would be the case for school board officials, little consensus is commonly found as to the specific requirements of the role under consideration (Gross, Mason, and McEachern, 1958). Agreement of role expectations among committee members has also been found to relate directly with the satisfaction or level of effectiveness at which the committee operated (Bible and Brown, 1963). Because consensus of role expectations appears to be so important in the functioning of groups, it is not surprising that both higher levels of satisfaction and higher levels of consensus among role expectations are found among members of smaller groups than among larger groups (Thomas, 1959).

It has been found that role expectations for that of the husband and wife vary considerably by social class. A lower-class housewife will emphasize the household chores and domestic duties that she considers dominant in her role as wife, whereas the upper-middle-class housewife tends to emphasize being a good companion for her husband (Slater, 1960). Parents also have different role expectations for their sons compared to their daughters, and these expectations vary as well by social class. It is particularly interesting to note that certain of these role expectations cause the parent to exert considerable influence on the child, affecting the tastes and activities that the child exhibits during his development. For example, boys are commonly expected to have greater ability with mathematics than girls, based upon the broad scale measurement of role expectations. In fact, looking at scholastic aptitude test scores, boys usually do score higher on the mathematics portion of the exam, whereas girls score somewhat higher on the verbal portion. In a study by Kuchenberg (1963) it was found that when fathers were separated from their families during the war years of 1941 to 1945, their sons' mathematical aptitude scores relative to verbal scores were lower than in families where the father was present. When the father was present, the boys were getting more encouragement from their father toward improving their proficiency with mathematics. When the father was not present, the lack of similar encouragement caused the usual differential between mathematics aptitude scores and verbal aptitude scores to be absent.

Feedback of Role and Personality

In the theater actors frequently speak about becoming so involved with a role that they feel they are living it. This naturally is a temporary sensation and only rarely does it extend to producing a change in personality. The influence can likewise flow in the opposite direction; the actor selects his role based on what he considers to be his personality. Both directions of influence have been found to be present beyond the stage in a social setting. Merton (1957b) found in his study of bureaucratic social structures that because the worker must be methodical, prudent, and disciplined, these requirements of the job begin to be reflected in the personality characteristics of bureaucrats as valued traits. A particular role can, however, make certain demands that the individual will regard as incompatible with his own personality, thus there develops what might be termed an internal role conflict.

The audience can also be influenced in their perception of appropriate role behavior by what they regard to be the personality of the individual performing the role. Abravanel (1962) found that subjects overhearing a simulated conversation characterized each conversationalist differently as to his personality, depending upon the role label that was attached.

Role Demands

Another set of constraints may be present during a specific role enactment. That is, in addition to a set of role expectations generally attached to a given role, the appropriateness of behavior may be further constrained by role demands that affect a *singular* performance of that role. Role demands are *situation-specific* conditions further limiting the scope of behavior within a role such that it is still perceived as appropriate to that enactment of the role.

A study conducted by Kroger (1967) demonstrated that the test scores from ROTC students taking the Strong Vocational Interest Blank and the Barron-Welsh Figure Preference Test are influenced by the test setting and what is said about the test by the test administrator. Tests were administered to samples of ROTC students in two different settings having different role demands. The first was a military setting, where the test administrator was a military man and the facilities were within the military science department. With the second group of students the tests were administered by a psychologist in a room that contained art posters and magazines. The resulting test scores were decidedly different, thus indicating that the setting and other role demands had placed additional constraints on what the ROTC students regarded as appropriate role expectations for themselves.

Role demands are particularly relevant to the methodological issues surrounding consumer research. It has been demonstrated frequently that panels of students, housewives, or whoever will perform in their role as test subjects differently depending upon what they regard to be an appropriate set of values in the eyes of the test administrator. For example, if subjects involved in a test of conformity are naive as to the true nature of the test, and if the test is administered in such a manner as to give them no additional clues regarding appropriate behavior, a significant level of conformity can generally be induced. It has been found, however, that if subjects are allowed to learn the nature of the test in which they will take part, or if the administrator gives them an indication that values such as independence of opinion, autonomy, or honesty are highly valued, then the subjects will be less prone to exhibit the customary forms of conformity (Bragg, 1966). "It is therefore important to recognize that any situation of real life or laboratory experimentation which departs from the conventional, predictable and the familiar is likely to activate role demands which in turn will seriously influence behavior" (Sarbin and Allen, 1968, p. 513).

Role Enactment—The Audience

Thus far we have spoken primarily about the actor or the individual in a given role. We have acknowledged that his actions are affected by the expectations of his audience and his continuing influence toward them will likewise be determined in large measure by the audience. The term audience has not, however, been carefully considered. Naturally, the size of the group can vary from a dyad (2 people) to a large group. Occasionally, social psychologists will prefer to restrict the term only to large groups where the relationships between the actor or individual in the role and the audience are relatively passive. The use of the term here, however, is not restricted in this manner; thus the audience can be considered as consisting of any of three possible classifications: a large group, a small group (roughly 3 to 15 people), or a dyad. In most cases the influence of role expectations by the audience will become more specific and perhaps even punitive against group deviates as the size of the audience decreases.

Long before the discussion of hallucinatory drugs and their use became so widespread, a study by Becker (1953) that centered on the influence of an audience on marijuana smoking uncovered curious findings. Becker observed that the occasional marijuana smoker did not (at least at that time in history) become a regular smoker until he was convinced that he could behave appropriately and not betray himself as a user before an audience whenever he was high. A consumption parallel may exist among consumers making a radical shift in clothing styles (e.g., from Ivy League to Edwardian, overnight).

Coe (1966) found that the performance of subjects attempting hypnosis was influenced when the subjects were told that they had an audience of five clinical psychology students observing them behind a one-way mirror. Under these circumstances, hypnosis was evidently restricted by the reluctance of subjects to let themselves go in the hypnotic procedure. A less passive form of audience influence has been observed by Scott (1957) in the case of fraternity initiation. Initiates when "razzed" by fraternity members were found to be far less successful in performing a set of physical exercises than when given friendly encouragement, a not unexpected result. Studies involving conformity to group influence (to be discussed in a later section) furnish ample evidence as to how role performance can be influenced by one or more confederates in a laboratory setting.

It was demonstrated in a study by Zimmerman and Bauer (1956) that people can also be influenced by a perspective or imaginary audience, in fact one they may or may not ever meet. Subjects listened to an article read aloud concerning teachers' salaries and were told they would be asked to give a speech before an audience a week later. This article concerned positive and negative points concerning raising teachers' salaries. One half of the sample was told that they would be giving their speech before the "National Council of Teachers"; the other half of the sample was told their speech would be given before the "National Taxpayers Economy League." Measurement immediately after hearing the article read aloud indicated that the retention of material, whether positive or negative regarding teachers' salaries, did not differ between the two sub-samples. However, when this was remeasured a week later significant differences were found in terms of the amount of material recalled. As was expected, the material that was congruent with the perspective audience for the speech was remembered while the incongruent material tended to be forgotten.

Role Conflict

As was discussed in the opening of this chapter, with the multiplicity of roles that one can occupy over a period of time or even simultaneously under certain circumstances, there frequently develop cases when roles come in conflict. Attempting to cope with the conflicting demands of multiple roles can take the form of avoiding or reducing role obligations through delegating certain roles or withdrawing from others. But there are clearly cases when the individual must live with conflicting role obligations and allocate his time, efforts, and loyalties in a manner which appears to him will minimize his strain. The way in which the person goes about this will reflect his commitment to each of the conflicting role norms, his assessment of how his audience will react to his decision, and what he regards as the immediate and eventual rewards or punishments by others in his role set (Sarbin and Allen, 1968). Whatever the form of role conflict, the resulting cognitive strain may cause the individual to undertake efforts toward resolving the conflict. This might take one of the following approaches:

1. Attempt to alter situational events or their timing so as to prevent or at least reduce the conflict among roles. One approach is to attempt a segregation of conflicting roles either in terms of time or in their location. Since the way one behaves before the family might be in conflict with the way one wants to behave before close friends, the actor may attempt to separate these two audiences in time or space.

2. Another approach at conflict resolution might be in terms of settling

upon or contriving a suitable priority of relative role importance such that the apparent role conflict dissolves.

3. If it is possible to merge the two conflicting roles into a single new hybrid role, this might be attempted (Turner, 1962).

If these efforts fail, the individual may follow other strategies:

1. He may withdraw himself either socially or physically from the situation.

2. Rather than attempt to manipulate circumstances or events that contribute to role conflict, the individual may instead, through selective attention, choose to ignore the circumstances or events that contribute to the conflict, and perhaps pay more attention to those events that imply no conflict.

3. Again, without attempting to alter the events or circumstances contributing to conflict resolution, the individual may choose instead through selective perception to alter their relative importance in a cognitive sense. This could also include a change in beliefs or values, temporary or long term, so as to "live with" conflicting roles.

4. In addition to tranquilizers and other chemicals, food or sleep can be taken in overdose proportions to avoid facing conflict. For other people, an attempt to reduce the tension associated with role conflict may take the form of strenuous exercise or physical competition. It should be recognized, however, that all the efforts involving tranquilizers or releasers are attempts to reduce the tension or strain associated with role conflict, not the role conflict itself (Sarbin and Allen, 1968).

GROUP DYNAMICS

The essence of a group is not the similarity or dissimilarity of its members but their interdependence. A group can be characterized as a "dynamic whole"; this means that a change in the state of any sub part changes the state of any other sub part. The degree of interdependence of the sub parts of the members of the group varies all the way from a "loose" mass to a compact unit—*Kurt Lewin* (1948, p. 54).

Attention thus far has been centered on the individual as he assumes one or more roles before an audience of some size. The role set within the audience, in the manner by which it influences role expectations and the appropriateness of behavior based upon these expectations, has been emphasized. In this section we shall go on to examine in greater detail the nature of this influence by the audience or group. It will be shown that group influence can affect behavior and communication flows in many ways.

Both social groups and reference groups will be considered. A rather demanding definition of *social group* has been given by Merton (1957b, p. 299). He states that a social group must be thought of in terms of three criteria: first, that it consists of a group of individuals who interact with each other on the bases of established patterns of behavior; second, that the persons define themselves as group members; and third, these people are defined by others, whether members or nonmembers, as members of the group. The concept of reference group is more inclusive, and will be defined later.

Group dynamics, as considered in this section, will not include behavior in large organizations, where an established hierarchy and regulations governing formality exist, such as in industrial firms or bureaucracies. Although we are not primarily concerned with examining groups as they exist in large, hierarchically structured organizations, much of what will be discussed does apply to the operation of committees within such large organizations, particularly those committees which meet frequently. The reason for this is that such small groups tend to develop an informal social structure which exerts as much or more influence on the operation and achievements of the group as do the formalities of the encompassing organizational environment.

The overlap between role theory and group dynamics should be clear from the fact that groups, whether informal or formal, exist for a purpose; thus people within these groups attempt to perform and be favorably evaluated in given roles.

Reference Groups

The concept of reference groups furnishes a convenient intersection between role theory and group dynamics. Some social psychologists will consider reference groups under the heading of role theory (Sarbin and Allen, 1968); others consider it under group dynamics (Collins and Raven, 1969); still others question whether any body of theory underlies the concept (Deutsch and Krauss, 1965). It has been recognized, however, since the work by Mead (1934) that during maturation an individual learns about the generalized attitudes of the social system in which he lives. This social community or group helps give the individual his sense of self and functions, in Mead's terms, as "the generalized other," in effect, an expansive imaginary audience. This generalized other is then said to influence, through the social system, the behavior of individuals involved with it. Thus groups with which the individual belongs tend to furnish a perspective from which the individual formulates aspects of his self-image and accepts influence over some of his actions.

A reference group can refer to a membership or a nonmembership group, consisting of one or more people, or it may even be a nonexistent or ill-defined group of people such as the "young generation." Thus a reference group is defined more broadly than a social group. Reference groups have been classified into two functional types, the normative and the comparative (Kelley, 1952). In the normative type, standards of behavior are set for the individual and values are provided for assimilation by him. The comparative type of reference group merely acts as a yardstick against which the individual can evaluate his position relative to others.

It is also important to recognize that regardless of whether the reference group functions as a normative or a comparative type, a comparison drawn by the individual between himself and the group may be either positive or negative in orientation. A comparison of positive orientation would be one in which the individual attempts to model his behavior or opinions after those of the reference group, whereas a comparison of negative orientation would be one in which the individual, through his behavior or opinions, attempts to set himself apart from or disassociate himself from a given reference group. Recalling the earlier mention of research by Grubb and Hubb, a young man, perceiving himself as a "swinger" and wanting his swinger friends to perceive him likewise, may be drawn to the purchase of a Pontiac GTO. A second young man might totally reject a good price on a GTO because he "wouldn't be caught dead in one."

An important aspect of reference-group theory consists of considering whether an individual will select a given reference group, and what criteria determine the one he will select among those relevant. Merton (1957b) has suggested that the degree of reference group influence an individual will accept is determined in the following manner:

1. Selecting either a membership or a nonmembership group based upon whether he feels that group will confer prestige on him.

2. The less involved the individual may be in his membership groups, the more likely he will turn toward a nonmembership group as a frame of reference.

3. Within social systems having relatively high rates of social mobility (upward movement in status levels), individuals tend to turn toward nonmembership groups for reference.

4. One might expect that the personality of the individual would in part determine his choice among reference groups.

Research to date, however, has failed to establish any clear patterns.

Very little is known as to the basis on which an individual will select *specific* reference groups. For that matter, there does not exist a set of measurable dimensions with which researchers have had success in obtaining perceptual comparisons by individuals between groups considered for selection. Work by Eisenstadt (1954) and Rosen (1955) suggests that the selection among reference groups tends to be specific rather than general to any decision contemplated. Eisenstadt found, for example, that among a sample of immigrants to Israel the degree to which specific groups could confer prestige on the individual, relative to his specific aspirations, determined his selection of reference groups. Compatibility between the values of the individual and those of a particular reference group appear to be very important as well, as demonstrated by the work of Hartley (1960) and by Becker and Carper (1956).

Conformity to Group Influence

It was observed by Lewin (1947) that the status quo of social life is a dynamic process, not static; thus attention has been directed by several researchers toward the notion of a group striving to maintain some form of equilibrium. This in turn suggests that actions will be undertaken by group members to dampen the effects of deviant opinions so as to increase the chances for both greater productivity and group solidarity or cohesiveness.

Beyond the relatively indirect influence of reference groups upon behavior and attitudes, many studies have been conducted on group influence toward conformity. A large proportion of the experiments conducted on conformity to group influence have taken place in laboratory settings where the size of the group has been relatively small. An early example of such an experiment, and frequently referred to in the study of group dynamics, is one by Sherif (1958). Subjects brought into a dark room were asked to judge the movement of a light as to its direction and distance. In fact, the movement was only apparent, not real, due to the autokinetic effect.[1] With some discussion, participants in the experiment tended to arrive at a common judgment such that when the group left the experiment their individual assessments of the direction and distance of movement tended to align with a judgment reached earlier by the group.

Several of the experiments concerning group influence, whether done with students or consumers, have involved the use of one or more confederates in the laboratory setting in order to induce responses that are counter to common sense or no more correct than one of several other possible responses. An early example of one such experiment was conducted by Asch (1958). In a small-group setting, subjects were asked to select from three lines on one card that line which equaled in length a line on a second card. When the subjects were allowed to make these judgments on their own, virtually no errors were made. However, when confederates were in the group setting and deliberately gave the wrong answers, subjects were prone to agree with these wrong answers, evidently under the pressure of not wanting to be left alone with their opinion.

Conformity under group influence has been studied as a function of several factors, one of which is group size. In the series of experiments by Asch it was found that the pressure toward conformity on an individual increased as the number of confederates increased, but only up to a majority of three. Beyond that point, increasing the size of the majority group of confederates produces no greater influence toward conformity. Experiments similar to those by Asch have been conducted with consumers, and will be discussed later.

---

[1]Autokinetic effect: the apparent drift of a fixed point of light in an otherwise dark room, or the apparent drift of a single star in a night sky.

Conformity As a Function of Personality Variables

Most, if not all, of human behavior can be thought of as consisting of motivated acts. Based upon this, one could conclude that conformity would likewise be a motivated act and be determined by certain personality variables. Although this may be true, patterned behavior, whether it concerns that within a group setting or not, appears to be better predicted by variables describing the social situation than by personality variables. It should be understood that whereas certain studies have found personality differences among people conforming to group influence, the practical import of these findings may not always be large. Second, the discussion of personality differences between any two or more subsamples under study, even though fascinating, may not reflect how conformity would relate to personality characteristics in a real-world setting, because either a nonrepresentative sample of individuals was employed in a given study or the laboratory conditions in which the study was conducted were overly contrived.

Nevertheless, it is worth noting that in several studies conducted in non-coercive, nonreward situations certain personality differences were found to exist between subjects exhibiting differing levels of conformity. An extensive review of this area has been conducted by Steiner (1966). With the cautions given earlier in mind, only a few studies and their findings will be mentioned here.

Studies have been found which indicate that conformity is positively related with the following personality factors: low intelligence (Carment and Miles, 1965; Crutchfield, 1955; Tuddenham, 1959); extroversion (Carment and Miles, 1965); ethnocentrism[2] (Malof and Lott, 1962); weak ego, poor leadership capability, and authoritarianism (Crutchfield, 1955); need for affiliation (Becker and Carroll, 1962); being an only child or firstborn (Becker, Lerner, and Carroll, 1964, 1966; Becker and Carroll, 1962). Strong conformity has also been found to associate with feelings of personal inferiority or inadequacy, an altogether reasonable finding (Krech, Crutchfield, and Ballachey, 1962). Certain of these findings have been rather strong in magnitude and consistent across a variety of task situations, thus suggesting that explanations for conformity based upon balance theories (see Chapter 9) cannot be taken as entirely adequate.

In the highly regimented environment of the military, personality differences have been found to exist between conforming and nonconforming behavior among military officers. Crutchfield (1955) found that the military officer prone to conformity tended to be submissive, compliant, highly respectful of authority, easily confused or disorganized, suggestible, inhibited, with a relatively narrow range of interest, and somewhat insensitive to his own behavior or motives. The officer tending to be nonconforming was a more

---

[2]Ethnocentrism: belief in the superiority of one's race, culture, or nation.

effective leader, persuasive among his peers, looked toward for advice, efficient, active, expressive, and aesthetic in his interests.

Conformity As a Function of Cohesiveness

As was mentioned before, conformity appears to be strongly related to situational variables, one of which is the cohesiveness of the group. Cohesiveness can be defined as "the resultant of all the forces acting on all the members to remain in a group" (Cartwright and Zander, 1960, p. 74). Questions regarding what brings on group cohesiveness are at least as interesting as those regarding what brings on conformity. Thinking in terms of an individual within a group, cohesiveness can usually be thought of as resulting from those forces that cause the person to value highly his membership in a group. This in turn amounts to his assessment of what gains he can obtain through membership relative to what he would obtain belonging to some alternative group (Thibaut and Kelley, 1959). Generally, with high group cohesiveness goes increased influence on group members and a tendency for the group to be less tolerant of opinions of behavior that run counter to those adopted or favored by the group. It should be understood, of course, that the extent of conformity depends on the nature of the task. It has been demonstrated that when a group is asked to arrive at a single answer to a question, pressures are far greater for conformity of opinion than when the group is merely asked to discuss a possible decision (Pennington, Harary, and Bass, 1958).

Although high group cohesiveness generally is present when members regard their group membership as bestowing considerable prestige or other value upon them, cohesiveness can also develop from process sources. That is, a group whose members particularly enjoy each others' company will attach considerable importance to the maintenance of group rapport. Under these circumstances, any member who sets himself apart from group opinion on a major or minor issue may be eased back into the fold not on merits concerning the issue but rather on pleas for group spirit. Because group cohesiveness can depend importantly upon the interaction process, there tend to develop certain role specialties within the group, such as the "task specialist" (Bales, 1958) and "maintenance specialist" (Thibaut and Kelley, 1959). As the term suggests, the task specialist concerns himself mainly with giving opinions and orientation, or asking for them, so as to make sure that the issues being discussed are adequately understood through clarification and repetition. The maintenance specialist concerns himself more with aiding the group by way of showing solidarity or reducing tension as it develops, and serves the instrumental function of reducing antagonism that can develop among struggles to establish points of argument or leadership within the group. It is thus likely to be the maintenance specialist who will make appeals for unity of opinion when he feels that this might be necessary to assure group cohesiveness. An extensive review of studies concerning group cohesiveness can be found in Lott and Lott (1965).

Risk Handling by Groups

The committee, as a decision-making body, has come into considerable prominence in large business organizations. An important example of committee decision making is found in the case of buying committees, either established to make a single decision, such as the purchase of a computer, or to meet periodically and make many decisions, such as in the case of the buying committee for a supermarket chain. It is therefore of interest to consider whether decisions made by groups tend to be riskier or more conservative than would be decisions made by group members considering the issue as individuals.

An earlier study by Stoner (reported in Brown, 1965) found an interesting set of results concerning group handling of risk, using a sample of male graduate students of industrial management. These students were first asked to make private decisions about the amount of risk they would accept in handling 12 hypothetical "life-dilemma" problems. The problems concerned topics such as (1) a choice between positions at a critical point in the career of Mr. A, (2) a football coach considering which play to use in order to win a game, (3) a chess player attempting to beat a champion, and (4) a college senior, wanting to do graduate work in chemistry, attempting to decide whether he should enter a distinguished university where he would be less likely to succeed, or enter a university of lesser standing wherein success would be virtually assured.

Stoner found that among small groups of students, once these life dilemmas had been discussed, each group would arrive at a position far riskier than that which had been considered acceptable to the typical member before the discussion began. Thinking that these results might be caused by the likelihood of industrial management students feeling obligated within a group setting to exhibit a high tolerance for risk, Wallach, Kogan, and Bem (1962) replicated the experiment, this time using liberal arts undergraduates, with one half of the sample male and the other half female. Essentially the same results were found. In several later studies a movement by groups toward riskier decision positions has been found, even when the negative consequences of taking a particular risk have been emphasized in the experiment (Bem, Wallach, and Kogan, 1965).

Before we give up on the groups as being habitually risk happy, we can take comfort in a series of studies reported by Brown (1965, pp. 702-6). If it were not for these findings, we might conclude that risk-prone members of groups tend to be more influential and always guide group opinion toward a riskier ultimate position. The series of studies reported by Brown, however, indicates that it is possible to formulate life-dilemma problems of the sort used by Stoner such that the group will arrive at more conservative positions than would be done by the typical group member before group discussion. Brown draws the conclusion that, depending upon the issue presented, a group will tend to move toward whichever value—risk or caution—is engaged by the particular facts used to formulate the issue or life dilemma.

Research concerning risk-handling behavior by buying committees in an industrial context has apparently not been conducted. Such research would have value both for the industrial marketer and the organizational planner.

Communication Flows

It is important to recognize that a circular relationship can exist between the pattern and flow of communication and factors such as group cohesiveness. Researchers such as Bavelas (1948) and Leavitt (1951) have contributed several concepts for the investigation of how communication patterns or networks existing between members of a group affect group productivity, emergence of leadership, personal satisfaction of group members, and the degree to which the group will demand conformity. Examples of different communication networks investigated are given in Figure 1. The results of research regarding the impact of communication networks on aspects of productivity, leadership, group satisfaction, and demands for conformity have primary application in studying organizational behavior. Where industrial buying is concerned, the manner in which purchasing decisions are made and the outcomes of considering proposals of varying riskiness may well be critically affected by the prevailing communication network.

The flow of communication among group members, as it affects consumer decision making, is more frequently characterized by serial transmission of product information from friend to friend. This informal flow of communication is usually described as word of mouth and will be discussed in a later section concerning its impact on consumer decision making, particularly with regard to new products.

It has been suggested by Cunningham (1963) that although there has been little overlap between studies concerning rumor transmission and those concerning word-of-mouth communication, they both relate to the same phenomenon. The transmission of a rumor is analogous to what goes on when consumers transmit data to one another concerning a product with which they have had experience. With both rumor and word-of-mouth communication, one can expect a certain amount of distortion of the message as it moves along. The patterns of message change (the *embedding process*) by which content is altered have classified by Allport and Postman (1947) as:

1. Leveling—"as rumor travels it tends to grow shorter, more concise, more easily grasped and whole" (p. 75). Details are dropped.
2. Sharpening—as a result of leveling, the central details of the story become the dominant theme (p. 86).
3. Assimilation—the distortion due to prejudice, expectations, linguistic habits, or special interests (pp. 99-115).

DeFleur (1962) points out that the typical research design used in labora-

FIGURE 1.　Communication Networks Used in Experimental Investigations

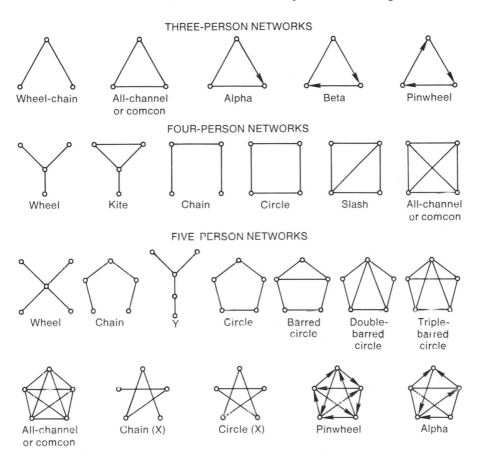

THREE-PERSON NETWORKS

Wheel-chain　All-channel　Alpha　Beta　Pinwheel
or comcon

FOUR-PERSON NETWORKS

Wheel　Kite　Chain　Circle　Slash　All-channel
or comcon

FIVE-PERSON NETWORKS

Wheel　Chain　Y　Circle　Barred　Double-　Triple-
circle　barred　barred
circle　circle

All-channel　Chain (X)　Circle (X)　Pinwheel　Alpha
or comcon

Dots represent positions, lines represent communication channels, and arrows indicate one-way channels. From Shaw (1964).

tory rumor studies (consisting of strict serial retelling of a story from person to person) may not be representative of a normally functioning social system in the real world. Nevertheless, he reports a field study of word of mouth (84 percent diffusion in 3 days) that involved an advertising slogan as the message, and 90 networks or groups within which the message was retold with as many as six stages of retelling of the message. The level of distortion followed the leveling-sharpening-assimilation pattern closely, and the level of distortion was relatively high.

Changes in message content, however, are clearly reduced when the message is relatively simple, as has been demonstrated by Festinger, et al. (1948). It is likewise true that when the message has high interest appeal, it will be transmitted rapidly, even in the absence of established communication channels such as exist between friends or group members.

Another important aspect of the relationship between communication flow and group processes has been identified in the research concerning mass communications effects. A voting study by Lazarsfeld, Berelson, and Gaudet (1948) suggested that information concerning the election did not have the same impact on all people potentially exposed to it. Rather, there seemed to be certain people within the population who were, for some reason, more exposed to the mass media and operated as the filters and transmitters of the information on to the remaining members of the voting public. Given the results, the authors have set forth what has come to be known as the "two-step flow of communication hypothesis," which suggests that the flow of mass communications is not transmitted directly to the audience according to the atomistic model (see Chapter 12), but is filtered through opinion leaders and then on to the remaining public. It is worth noting that this two-step flow hypothesis "is probably the one that has least well been documented by empirical data" (Katz, 1957). Nevertheless, the enthusiasm for this notion and its "democratic society" overtones stimulated other researchers to test the hypothesis more directly.

In a later voting study having essentially the same design, Berelson, Lazarsfeld, and McPhee (1954) found substantiation for the existence of opinion leaders and, consequently, the two-step flow of communications. In addition, however, it was noted that opinion leaders were found to exist in similar proportions in all socioeconomic levels, with conversations being mainly between people of similar age, occupation, and political opinion. Opinion leaders tended to belong to more organizations and reflect a higher level of gregariousness. Most importantly, voters appeared to be more influenced by the opinions of their friends than the mass media, and tended to alter their voting intentions to align with friends or family, members of their own religion, or that of their occupational class.

In a careful attempt to measure the nature and extent of influence by the mass media and by friends during the Kennedy-Nixon debates, Deutschmann (1962) found that the mass media advocated political change while conversations among friends and colleagues were more likely to force maintenance of status quo opinions. Thirty-four percent of those exposed to the debates, but who did not discuss them with friends, changed their candidate preference, whereas only 19 percent of those exposed to the debates, who did later discuss them, changed their preference. Klapper's (1960) survey of mass communication literature tends to add support to this conclusion (pp. 26-37).

Given the importance of mass media to advertising, and advertising to marketing, the findings concerning opinion leadership and the two-step flow hypothesis from voter studies naturally triggered several studies regarding these phenomena as they concern advertising effects. These studies will be taken up in a later section.

Conclusions

The impact of group opinions upon individuals can range from very subtle, as in the case of certain reference-group influences, to highly directional and severe, as in the case of rebuke or even dismissal of an individual from an ongoing small group. Because we all come under the influence of many groups, whether through membership affiliation or not, our behavior and social inter-action are guided in ways we do not always stop to think about or acknowledge. Although personality differences do appear to exist among people concerning the extent to which they will conform to group influence, by and large the similarities among people appear to vastly outweigh these relatively minor differences. In the case of unique environments, such as during military service, extreme pressures toward conformity are more likely to bring out distinctiveness between subjects with regard to psychological factors. By and large, we are all subject to certain levels of conformity that vary primarily with the social setting in which the pressures exist and what we as individuals consider to be at stake in weighing the value of our group affiliation relative to our probable preference to steer an independent course. The communication flow by which influence is exerted has been discussed in terms of how it is affected by communication patterns and how these in turn influence the well-being of the group and its members; the possible distortions in message content when the message must undergo serial transmission; and the apparent existence of opinion leadership and the two-step flow involved with mass communications effects.

APPLICATION OF ROLE THEORY AND GROUP DYNAMICS TO MARKETING

Thus far we have dealt exclusively with role theory and group dynamics studied in nonmarketing situations. Now we turn our focus to work that has substantiated most of these same phenomena as also existing in buyer behavior. Many of the studies to be discussed are essentially replications of studies done earlier in nonmarketing environments. Many concepts discussed in buyer behavior have in fact been borrowed in this manner from other disciplines where they were originally tested.

As we discuss the effects of groups upon individual behavior in a marketing context, it is important to remember what was stated earlier with regard to role theory as it relates to group phenomena. Within any group, regardless of its description or purpose, roles can be defined, expectations measured, and conflicts between roles within a role set observed. It should therefore be remembered that a group cannot be regarded as a single entity viewed in a static mode; rather, we are talking about an interaction process wherein influence flows in terms of the task or purpose (even if primarily social) of the group, the communication network, and the degree of group cohesiveness. We shall begin this section by returning to the consideration of reference-group influences.

Reference Groups Affecting Product Category and Brand Attitudes

Although the influence of reference groups in certain buying situations can be strong, it should be emphasized that there are a great many other buying situations in which the decision process is highly individualistic. The extent to which reference-group influence may be present is largely determined by the nature of the product itself. Most importantly, the product must be conspicuous in terms of two aspects. First, it must be easily seen and identified by others, and, second, it must be conspicuous in terms of uniqueness of ownership; that is, it must be a product that relatively few people own. As the ownership of a kind of product becomes commonplace, there will clearly be little distinctiveness attached to its ownership, and its purchase will tend to be an individualistic act, based largely upon the absolute characteristics of the product itself (Bourne, 1957).

A classification of product categories in terms of how purchase behavior is influenced by reference groups was set forth several years ago by Bourne (1957). This classification, shown in Table 1, has been frequently discussed in marketing

TABLE 1. **Products and Brands of Consumer Goods May Be Classified by Extent to Which Reference Groups Influence Their Purchase**

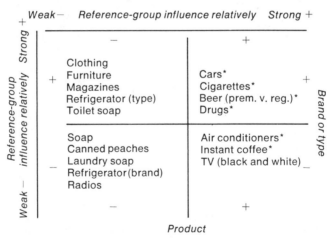

The classification of all products marked with an asterisk is based on actual experimental evidence. Other products in this table are classified speculatively on the basis of generalizations derived from the sum of research in this area and confirmed by the judgment of seminar participants. *Source:* Bureau of Applied Social Research, Columbia University (Glock, unpublished).

literature. The table suggests that for certain product categories reference-group influence will be positive or negative with regard to a product category. In other product categories reference-group influence tends to center instead on the brand of product chosen rather than simply ownership of a product from a particular product category. Although the table may well have been an accurate representation of reference-group influence at the time it was published in 1957, it is very unlikely to be so today. For example, with the market penetration of black and white TV sets nearly 100 percent in the United States and with multiple household ownership frequent, it is unlikely that reference-group influence would be a significant positive factor toward its ownership. It might be more accurate instead to substitute color TV sets. The same is likely to be true for instant coffee. These specific objections, however, are minor since the table could easily be updated, and in any case its principal value is in terms of highlighting how reference-group influence in one situation can center on ownership of a particular brand and/or ownership of any brand in a product category.

As a person changes roles, a change in reference group may frequently be involved. The selection of that reference group will depend partly upon the self-image the person holds. That is, a person will not pattern his actions and attitudes in a manner which is counter to his own best interests and advancement (Lieberman, 1956). Moreover, one's self-image undergoes continual reformulation as successive evaluations are made through comparisons with reference groups. In this sense, the reference group becomes "the frame of reference in the organization of his perceptual field" (Shibutani, 1967).

Although it is not always possible to assess the degree to which a reference group influences particular behavior, there are several studies that have substantiated the fact that consumers do tend to have images in mind of people who regularly buy or currently own particular brands (e.g., Volkswagen owners versus Pontiac GTO owners). Based upon this, the image attached to a particular brand is usually found to reflect the self-image held by the individual. Thus Grubb (1965) found that consumers favoring a particular brand tend to perceive themselves differently from consumers favoring a second brand of the same product category, in this case beer. Congruency between self-concept and the images of automobile brands has also been found (Birdwell, 1964). A study by Dolich (1969) found that favorite brands were consistent with self-image assessments for the product categories studied: beer, cigarettes, bar soap, and toothpaste.

For reference-group influence to be of pragmatic importance to the marketer, it would appear that certain conditions would need to be satisfied. First, it is not always sufficient that one be able to merely identify the reference group that has influence on a given target market. If the stimulus set from the reference group is relatively ambiguous and subject to a variety of interpretations, or if the consequences of the stimuli cannot be predicted, appeals based upon reference-group affiliations may have little importance. Moreover, if the value attached to affiliation with a particular reference group is relatively weak, or if the influence of pressures toward conformity is easily avoided and the sanctions for avoiding conformity are ineffective, marketing efforts directed at employing group influences will be correspondingly ineffective (Kelley, 1952).

Impact of Interpersonal Communications

Reference-group influence is generally rather indirect and avoidable if the individual chooses. In the study by Asch (1958) discussed earlier, confederates in a small-group setting were able to cause naive subjects to express agreement with a judgment regarding the length of a line that was clearly false. A study of Venkatesan (1965), modeled after the Asch experiment, concerned students evaluating the best suit from a set of three identical suits. When the students were allowed to inspect the suits alone and indicate which suit they thought was best, their answers were distributed among the three suits in about equal proportions. But under the influence of a group situation, judgment by individuals as to the best suit tended to conform with group opinion.

Stafford (1966) conducted a study similar to that of Venkatesan (1965) except that his subjects were housewives who already were members of informal groups. He thus had a sample of housewives who were unaware that the study concerned intragroup influences. The product selected for study was bread wrapped in plain wrappers with no trade symbols. With the identical loaves identified only by letters of the alphabet, the housewives were asked to indicate their preferences each week over the course of an 8-week period. Stafford found that the informal groups did in fact exert influence toward conformity as to brand preference (as indicated by a letter of the alphabet); however, group cohesiveness did not appear to be a significant determinant of brand conformity. Moreover, where a group leader emerged, the higher the degree of brand loyalty by the group leader, the more likely the other members of the group were to exhibit the same brand preference, and also become brand loyal.

Group influence can also bring about conformity with regard to purchase behavior, as is illustrated in an earlier study by Lewin (1947). During World War II it was deemed in the national interest for housewives to buy the more plentiful cuts of meat such as kidneys and sweetbread. Lewin found that if housewives were given a lecture on the benefits of such foods, only about 3 percent of the individuals would use the unfamiliar cuts later. But when the housewives also participated in a discussion concerning the meats, 32 percent used them later.

Several studies have concerned situations in which the interpersonal communication process has been largely a matter of supplying information and judgments without any demonstrable efforts directed at demanding conformity to those judgments. Among a study of new residents to a community, subjects were found to turn to a friend, a neighbor, or a recent acquaintance of the same socioeconomic class for advice in the selection of a physician (Feldman and Spencer, 1965). Similarly, in considering the purchases of small electrical appliances, discussions with friends, relatives, and neighbors were given by housewives as "more useful or helpful" than any form of advertising or consumer testing magazines. Only past experience with other appliances of the same brand was judged to be more useful than interpersonal communications (Udell, 1966).

It is not surprising that consumers would turn to their friends and neighbors for judgment when considering the purchase of a complex or costly product. However, even when the product is relatively simple or inexpensive, seeking and/or accepting the advice of others is usually present when the products are new to the market. Several examples of this were found in a study that concerned two new brands of toothpaste, a new liquid detergent, and a new soap (Haines, 1966). The impact of personal contacts was said to be greater than that from magazine or television advertising or store display. The only greater source of influence was product sampling.

Similar to the findings of Udell (1966) are those by Bell (1963) in which early buyers, or innovators, of appliances and home entertainment equipment were found to judge the personal influence of friends as more important informational sources than the mass media. It should be noted, however, that three-fourths of these early adopters said they consulted no persons outside the home for such purchase decisions, which must imply that the term "friend" largely refers to family member, particularly one's spouse.

Why Is Personal Influence So Potent?

The concept of *perceived risk* has been given as one possible explanation for why consumers turn to interpersonal communications when considering certain products. Arndt (1967) found that housewives who perceived relatively high risk in deciding among brands of coffee tended to be more brand loyal and less likely to buy private-label brands. When presented with a new brand of coffee, these high-risk perceivers were less likely to buy it. Moreover, the high risk perceivers made more effort to obtain information through interpersonal communications with those who apparently saw less risk in the new brand. This conclusion that high perceived risk associated with a particular purchase decision tends to mean greater importance attached to interpersonal communications was also supported in a study by Perry and Hamm (1969). Levels of risk associated with 25 different types of purchase decisions (e.g., color TV, ball-point pen, automobile battery) were related to interpersonal communications. Analysis indicated, however, that the relationship between the socioeconomic risk and interpersonal influence was significant for only 10 of the 25 purchase decisions. Where the correlation was significant, social risk was found more important than economic risk.

The finding by Coleman, Katz, and Menzel (1966) that the influence of interpersonal communication increases as uncertainty, or risk, concerning the adoption of a particular drug rises has been supported in work by Bauer and Wortzel (1966). In considering drugs of increasing riskiness, doctors turned increasingly toward other physicians rather than following the advice of commercial drug-information sources. A study by Cunningham (1966) examined the relationship between the volume and nature of interpersonal communication relative to the amount of risk perceived in headache remedies, fabric softeners, and dry spaghetti. No significant differences were found for either the number of people talked to or the frequency of talking when related to the level of perceived risk associated with each product category. As for recency of talking, there was found to be a substantial difference only for fabric softeners; that is, those high in perceived risk for fabric softeners had talked more recently about brands in that category. However, this conclusion is open to question in that during the test period "a substantial amount of promotional activity for fabric softener in the survey locale [was going on] which was, undoubtedly, partially responsible for the greater percentage of talkers among fabric softener users" (p. 705). It is only reasonable to assume that it also influenced recency of talk as well.

There have been alternative explanations set forth, in addition to perceived risk, as to why people engage in word-of-mouth or interpersonal communication regarding products. Although based upon a sketchy description of empirical support, Dichter (1966) has set forth an intuitively appealing list of possible motivations:

1. Other involvement; the need to help or share benefits.
2. Having inside information.
3. Self-involvement and self-confirmation, as in gaining attention, showing connoisseurship, "feeling like a pioneer," suggesting status, "spreading the gospel," or asserting superiority.
4. Product involvement; to reduce postpurchase tension.
5. Message involvement; reacting to an ad as an entertainment medium and playfully quoting ad slogans or discussing ads in word of mouth.

Notice, however, that Dichter's list concerns only motivations for the talker, not the listener. Very little research has been done on the characteristics or motivations of a listener in the process of interpersonal communication. It has been suggested that a considerable volume of interpersonal communication goes on which is listener initiated. For example, Cunningham (1966) found that approximately one half of conversations were initiated by the listener seeking information, and the other half initiated by the leader or talker volunteering it. Robertson (1971, Chapter 4) has stated, "the fallacy of viewing all personal influence as one-way is tied in with the assumption that personal influence is most often deliberate. It is not. The proportion of cases in which communication is initiated with the objective of effecting change is probably very small." As Robertson points out, when respondents are asked to describe the conditions under which conversation developed regarding a product, it becomes clear that none of the participants to the conversation—talkers or listeners—had an axe to grind, or, more formally, that persuasion was not the primary objective in bringing up the topic. If Robertson is correct, and it seems likely that he is, opinion leadership (to be discussed in the next section) should be looked upon as a very weak form of leadership, indeed, not deserving of the term.

Given this conclusion, it is important to consider what factors make a listener listen. Granbois (1963) has suggested a set of possible reasons based upon the assumption that consumers seek information when confronted with a situation of uncertainty or risk. It should be noted that this list treats interpersonal communication as consisting of both verbal and visual stimuli.

1. Entering a new phase in one's life cycle (e.g., marriage), or modifying one's life style, or considering a new product creates a lack of information since past experience is not relevant.

2. For certain purchases the item is socially very visible; thus the opinions of others constitute very important information.

3. The products under consideration each have advantages and disadvantages that make the choice difficult.

4. Past experience with a product in the same category may have been unpleasant.

5. Deliberation over which product to buy might prompt disagreement among family members so that the family or decision maker turns to outsiders for guidance.

As suggested by Granbois, interpersonal communication must be considered in both its oral and visual modes. It goes without saying that what we do by way of gestures, actions, or merely facial gestures can tell as much about our opinions or moods as any number of words. Studies concerning interpersonal communications have occasionally overemphasized oral communications relative to visual communications, sometimes totally ignoring the latter. A study (King, 1963) in which this appears to have happened concluded that, in womens' fashion, style influence does not flow downward in terms of socioeconomic levels. The basis for drawing this conclusion was that "influentials," women who claimed to have influence over their friends with regard to fashion, were found to exist in the same proportion among early and late buyers of new fashion styles. The housewives in the study were asked to self-designate themselves as influential if they tended to give advice to friends concerning new fashions. Beyond any criticism directed at the use of this self-designating technique, the emphasis on oral communication sidesteps the well-known fact that fashion is a highly conspicuous topic. Thus although women of higher socioeconomic levels may not draw their friends and acquaintances into conversation so as to influence them on the topic of fashion, they are clearly in a position to provide considerable visual display through wearing new fashions because of having more money and more involvement with activities that require a good wardrobe. The study by King has not therefore demonstrated a "rebuttal to the trickle down theory." It is, however, true that many fashion trends are originating from sources other than the top designers; but this is largely due to the fashion revolution that started with Carnaby Street, not any radical change in interpersonal communication patterns.

Opinion Leadership

Operational Definitions and Measurements. Interest in identifying opinion leaders stemmed from the findings of Lazarsfeld, Berelson, and Gaudet (1948) concerning the "two-step flow of communications hypothesis." To review, it was found that certain members of the social system are more exposed to the mass media and tend to operate as filters and transmitters of information for the remaining members of the social system. Since differential knowledge can also imply differential influence, the notion has developed that opinion leadership consists of leaders doing something to followers. In terms of marketing practice, the opinion-leader concept, on its surface, has some of the seductive aspects of the earlier hypodermic-effect notion (Klapper, 1960, p. 5), only with more finesse. Rather than "sink the needle" in all consumers alike, one can visualize a selective process in which the opinion leaders are given the germ of an idea, and then left to spread the "disease."

But the world is not that simple. Cox (1963, pp. 62-63) states flatly that "As a practical matter, it is virtually impossible to identify all of the specific opinion leaders for most consumer products . . . As a consequence, direct communication between the marketer and the opinion leader is not possible. The marketer, if he wished to communicate at all with opinion leaders, would be forced to use the mass media."

Notwithstanding these operational difficulties, the opinion-leadership concept is important. Some of the confusion that surrounds the concept is in part a result of the inconsistencies that have developed with respect to its definition and measurement. A good many studies have treated opinion leadership as a dichotomous variable, dividing the research sample into leaders and followers. More recent research has suggested that the concept should be considered a continuous variable, something everyone has in varying amounts for varying topics before varying audiences. Without assuming this expanded view of the concept, a detailed examination of opinion-leadership studies over the years would generate some hopeless conclusions.

The measurement of opinion leadership in a consumer context has generally been in terms of a battery of questions by which respondents designate themselves as "leaders" or "followers." The battery of questions commonly administered, in some form or other, is that developed by Rogers and Cartano (1962). The questions, which appear to contain considerable redundancy, ask the respondent to indicate whether she usually gives or seeks information or advice with respect to a particular topic or product category. A second approach in measuring opinion leadership involves the use of "key informants." With this method the researcher selects one or more members of a particular social system or group who in turn are asked to name which person or persons the members of that group or social system generally turn toward for advice. A third approach for assessing opinion leadership involves a sociometric technique by which respondents are asked to whom they go for advice or information concerning a type of issue or decision. The research then traces out the communication network within a group and designates the leader in terms of flow concentration.

Katz and Lazarsfeld (1955) first used a single question to obtain self-designated opinion leaders and then attempted to verify whether or not this assessment was valid by interviewing people who the self-designated leaders claimed were under their influence. The researchers gave up, however, because too many gaps and entanglements existed in the social system. Rogers and Cartano (1962), in a study concerning farmers, obtained respectable correlation coefficients between the classifications generated by the three measurement approaches. Given the heavy reliance upon the more convenient self-designating technique, it would be comforting if a substantiating study existed, comparable to that by Rogers and Cartano, which had been conducted in a consumer context.

Characteristics of Opinion Leaders. Considerable work has centered on identifying the consumer opinion leader and his or her characteristics in terms of demographic, socioeconomic, psychological, product usage, brand loyalty, or new-product purchase variables. It should be recognized, however, that opinion leadership, as merely one form of leadership, is a role designation. Certainly, personality and other descriptive characteristics can occasionally be found that will discriminate between the leader and the follower. However, situational variables appear to have as much or more importance in determining who will occupy the role of leader and the style of leadership that will be exercised.

The Katz and Lazarsfeld (1955) study considered opinion leadership in four areas of interest: food shopping, public affairs, fashion, and movies. Respondents designated as opinion leaders regarding food shopping tended to be married women with large families and gregarious. They tended to influence women of the same social status level, and were as likely to be found on one status level as another. The public-affairs leader tended to be of higher social status, exercising her influence downward to a lower status level. She was also characterized by moderately high gregariousness. The fashion leader tended to be of higher status, high in gregariousness, but relatively young. The movie goer was not distinguished by status or gregariousness but tended to be young and single.

A study by King (1963) of fashion adoption also found that opinion leaders were generally of the same social status as their followers. The opinion leader among physicians with regard to new drug adoption was found in a study by Coleman, Katz, and Menzel (1966) to have high professional credentials, pay greater attention to medical meetings and professional journals, and be more profession oriented than patient oriented.

In a far different context, the opinion leaders for auto insurance, surprisingly enough, were often found to have no more knowledge on the subject than those they influenced (Nicosia, 1964). Thus it may be possible that for topics for which technical knowledge is not vital (or hard to obtain without special study) gregariousness plus some degree of product experience are primary determinants of opinion leadership.

In examining studies primarily from rural sociology Rogers (1962) has concluded that three characteristics of the opinion leader stand out: social status, social participation or integration, and cosmopolitanism, meaning an orientation beyond one's local social system. Cosmopolitanism is evidenced among farmers at least in terms of having relatively more friends beyond the local community and more time devoted to out-of-town meetings. Again, concerning farmers for the most part, studies have found close association between the early adoption of new products or methods (innovative behavior) and opinion leadership, although it is not clear which comes first. Robertson (1966) concluded that innovators toward a new-model telephone were more likely than noninnovators to exert opinion leadership or influence although their self-perceptions regarding leadership did not seem to differ. Personality dimensions were found by Robertson and Myers (1969) to make little improvement over chance in predicting opinion leadership.

A large study recently reported by Summers (1970) concerning fashion opinion leaders claims to have found opinion leaders to be younger, to have more education and higher incomes, to be of a higher occupational status, higher in geographic mobility, involved with both organizational and informal social activities, significantly distinguishable on certain personality and attitudinal dimensions, naturally more involved in fashion as an interest area, but to have no unique media exposure profile. These differences, although of interest, are partially the result of the large sample size (1000) and the use of chi-square as a test of significance. Summers does not go on to report how these differences would translate into explained variance using multivariate statistics. The proportion of his sample self-designated as opinion leaders amounted to 28.3 percent, at least indicating that although significant differences may exist, if one of three people have these differences, the ratio of leader to follower does not reduce by much the size of the target audience, even if a fashion marketer were to conclude that he should aim at fashion opinion leaders within a particular population.

A review of opinion-leader characteristics by Robertson (1971) concludes that little uniqueness has been identified thus far.

Summarizing these opinion leader traits would suggest a tentative profile of the opinion leader: age varies by product category; social status is most often the same as that of advisees; a high degree of gregariousness is uniformly the case; cosmopolitanism, or orientation beyond the local community, is generally cited but has not been explicitly tested for consumer goods; knowledge is generally greater; no distinguishing personality features exist; norm-adherence is greater; and greater innovativeness is found.

Overlap of Opinion Leadership. With Katz and Lazarsfeld (1955) having found differing profiles for leaders in each of the four topic areas in their study, additional analysis indicated to them that overlap of opinion leadership for any one interest area with that for any second interest area was virtually nonexistent. Similarly, Rogers and Cartano (1962) concluded that little overlap existed among different types of opinion leaders. However, they tempered this position with the observation that in social systems with more traditional norms, overlap was likely. In such social systems, less specialization of roles might contribute to greater overlap.

Marcus and Bauer (1964), however, undertook a reanalysis of the Katz and Lazarsfeld (1955) data, disagreeing on theoretical grounds with the basis on which Katz and Lazarsfeld had concluded that no overlap existed. Katz and Lazarsfeld had analyzed the data in terms of, for example, overlap in any two but only two interest areas. Marcus and Bauer observed that it would make more sense to add in opinion leaders for three and four areas as well. Using this approach in calculating overlap, and applying it to the Katz and Lazarsfeld data, Marcus and Bauer found significant opinion-leader overlap for fashion and public affairs, food shopping and public affairs, and fashion and food shopping. However, the magnitude of overlap was still relatively small.

Using the Marcus and Bauer approach for calculating overlap, Silk (1966), in a study concerning products and services related to dental hygiene, found no significant overlap. Myers and Robertson (1969), also studying closely related product categories, did find significant overlaps in opinion leadership, but again not of great magnitude. King and Summers (1970) claim, however, that opinion-leader overlap does exist and is greatest between "common interest" product categories. Product categories represented in their study were packaged food products, women's clothing fashions, household cleansers and detergents, cosmetics and personal grooming aids, and large and small appliances. For each product category, the proportion of respondents self-designated as opinion leaders varied from 24 to 30 percent. It is worth noting, however, that even with these relatively generous cutoff points, the actual percentage of overlap among any two or more areas of opinion leadership varied from a maximum of 15 percent for the overlap between packaged food products and household cleansers and detergents to a minimum of 2.2 percent for overlap across all six opinion-leader areas. Thus although the actual percentages of overlap in all cases exceeded those which might be expected exclusively on the basis of chance, it is only fair to conclude that all the studies examined, including that by King and Summers, have not found levels of opinion-leader overlap which are inspiring to the marketer.

The observation made by King and Summers (1969) that overlap should be greatest among product categories having "common interest dimensions" has been tested in a study by Silk and Montgomery (1969). The categories of purchasing activity were automobiles, household work, buying food, preparing food, clothes, health, and furnishing a home. For each area of purchasing activity, the following question was used to assess interest in the activity: "Compared with most other women you know, how *actively* interested would you say you are in this topic?" For assessing opinion leadership, one of the questions from the Rogers-Cartano (1962) opinion-leadership battery was used: "Compared with most other women you know, how likely are you to be asked for your ideas or your advice on this topic?" The patterns of purchase-activity overlap, with respect to interest and with respect to opinion leadership, were found to be closely similar. However, as the authors acknowledge, this result may merely reflect the parallel wording of the two questions combined with the fact that the questions were repeated for each of the seven purchase-activity categories.

Opinion-Leader Exposure to Mass Media. Since the work by Lazarsfeld, Berelson, and Gaudet (1948), the notion has developed that opinion leaders have greater exposure to the mass media and rely more heavily on it than nonleaders. The work by Coleman, Katz, and Menzel (1966), discussed earlier, indicated that opinion leaders among physicians are more likely to read professional journals than nonleaders. It has likewise been stated by Rogers (1962) that opinion leaders in farm communities have more contact with professional sources of farming information than do other farmers.

Nevertheless, the findings by Nicosia (1964) that opinion leaders with respect to automobile insurance were no better informed than nonleaders and no more exposed to the mass media suggest that once again a characteristic of opinion leadership is tied closely to the nature of the product category considered. In fashion studies by both Summers (1970) and King (1965), and by Robertson and Rossiter (1968), greater exposure to fashion magazines was found among opinion leaders.

It is perhaps safest to conclude that, like opinion leadership, exposure to mass media is simply a reflection of interest areas. That is, the opinion leader for a given product category will naturally pay attention to any mass medium or other informational source that contributes to satisfying his interest in a given product category.

Family Decision Making

Perhaps the most important source of group influence on all of us arises as a part of family decision making. It is, nevertheless, surprising that relatively little research has been done on the influence flow within the family. For that matter, some of the conclusions drawn by researchers sound amusingly obvious. As an example, Katz and Lazarsfeld (1955) make the observation that in the purchase of food items family members have greater impact on what is purchased than people outside the family (p. 214). Again, containing no surprises, Robertson (1966) found that in the decision to have a new-model telephone, family members had the greatest impact on the decision.

Role specialization within the family can affect both the interaction process and decisions. It should first be noted that the degree of dominance by the husband or wife role can vary with cultural factors. Strodtbeck (1951) examined three cultural groupings: white Protestants, Mormons, and Navajo Indians. The husband's dominance during family arguments was slightly different between the groupings, with greatest dominance exhibited in Mormon couples and least dominance exhibited in white Protestant couples. Blood and Wolfe (1960) have reported that husband dominance appears to be more likely when the husband is successful in his occupation or profession and has higher income. The wife's dominance increases if she is employed, and in any event increases with age. Marital satisfaction seems to be lowest in those families in which the wife is dominant. In a replicating study, Centers, Raven, and Rodrigues (1968) found general agreement with these findings. However, the pattern of dominance that emerged in a family situation was found to depend critically upon the particular decision area.

The communications pattern can also predict patterns of family role dominance. Strodtbeck (1954) has reported a study where whichever spouse talked first and the most generally won the argument. A study by Kenkel (1961) of 50 married couples in which the husband was a college student substantiated these findings. Moreover, when the husband did more talking than his wife, purchase plans tended to be directed toward items for the children or the husband rather than for the wife or the household. In 60 percent of the couples more ideas and suggestions as to how to spend a hypothetical sum of $300 were contributed by the husband. In 72 percent of the cases, wives tended to play the social-emotional role by making remarks to raise the status of the husband, showing affection or consideration, or trying to reduce tension. In those remaining families in which the husband played the social-emotional role, the proportion of personal items for the wife was higher.

Earlier research by Kenkel and Hoffman (1956) indicated that, when interviewing families shopping for major appliances, the husband is usually credited with providing the judgment on mechanical aspects of the equipment, even though additional probing frequently indicates little basis for this. Credit given to the husband for mechanical judgment appeared often to be only an expressed view by the respondent of the proper masculine role. This bias in terms of respondent perception regarding appropriate role behavior implies that studies relying upon interviews of the husband and wife in order to expose decision-making patterns must be approached with caution.

An example of a study that relied upon reported decision-making patterns is one by Wolgast (1958). The husband was claimed to exert dominance in deciding when to buy a new car; the wife was said to be dominant concerning the management of money and bills. Both partners shared equally the questions of when to buy household goods and furniture and how much to save.

A recent study by Davis (1970) investigated possible dimensions of role specialization in family decision making, at least as it concerns automobiles and furniture. Concerning the last automobile purchased, husbands and wives were asked to indicate who decided (1) when to purchase, (2) how much money to spend, (3) make, (4) model, (5) color, and (6) where to purchase. For furniture the questions were (1) how much money to spend, (2) when to buy, (3) what furniture to buy, (4) where to buy, (5) what style to buy, and (6) what color and fabric to select. As was expected, husband-wife dominance varied considerably as to the particular question being settled. Moreover, spouses, when questioned individually, were found to be in general agreement as to which partner tended to dominate each of these 12 purchase decisions. Agreement varied from 59 percent (what furniture to buy) to 75 percent (what color and fabric to select), except for the question when to buy the furniture, where it fell to 48 percent.

The financial and mechanical aspects of auto purchase evidently cause the husband to exert dominance over all but perhaps issues of model and color (Table 2). For furniture, however, the influence of husband and wife appear more equal. It should be noted, however, that the Davis study was based upon a convenience sample of only 97 couples, drawn from three church groups and a grade school PTA in suburban Chicago. Serious biases may therefore exist in the data.

Superimposed on these differences with regard to role specialization based upon the task under consideration is a set of differences based upon economic well-being of the household. In families of low or high economic standing, deliberation with regard to purchase decisions tends to be the least. Low-income families are not in a position to consider purchases much beyond necessities. Moreover, the wife commonly exerts greatest dominance. In families of high economic status, discussions over the appropriate expenditure of money are relegated to a position of less importance since rationing of resources generally is not necessary. With middle-income families, particularly those at the upper end of the middle-income range, purchase decisions tend to be made with a good deal of planning and involve more equally both husband and wife (Komarovsky, 1961).

TABLE 2. Marital Roles in Selected Automobile and Furniture Purchase Decisions

(N = 97)

Patterns of Influence (%)

Who Decided	As Perceived by Husbands			As Perceived by Wives		
	Husband Has More Influence Than Wife	Husband and Wife Have Equal Influence	Wife Has More Influence Than Husband	Husband Has More Influence Than Wife	Husband and Wife Have Equal Influence	Wife Has More Influence Than Husband
Automobiles						
When to buy?	68	29	3	68	30	2
Where to buy?	62	35	3	59	39	2
How much to spend?	62	37	1	62	34	4
What make (brand)?	60	32	8	50	50	-
What model?	41	50	9	47	52	1
What color?	25	50	25	25	63	12
Furniture						
When to buy?	16	45	39	18	52	30
Where to buy?	7	53	40	6	61	33
How much to spend?	22	47	31	17	63	20
What pieces to buy?	3	33	64	4	52	44
What style?	2	26	72	2	45	53
What color and fabric?	2	16	82	2	24	74

Source: Adapted from Tables 1 and 2, Davis (1970).

The kinds of decisions and the decision-making process confronted by a family vary decidedly over different phases of the adult or life cycle. The life cycle can be considered as consisting of four phases; young adulthood or family formation, the middle years, toward retirement, and retirement (Meyer, 1957). During early adulthood, the husband is concerned with getting his career under way, expenditures on housing and home furnishings are heavy, and children are born and enter school. Moving on to the middle years, the family has developed a defined set of friendships, church and club affiliations, and generally enjoys both good physical and financial health. The cycle termed toward retirement witnesses the start of greater leisure time for the husband and wife. The children are no longer living at home and may even have families of their own. Mother and father are left with ample time and financial resources on their hands. Finally, the retirement phase is reached and many changes must be made, which are reflected in new living and consumption patterns, such as retirement homes.

Although relatively little is known about the interaction process involved in family decision making, an appealing model has been set forth by Pollay (1968), as yet untested. The model starts out with the assumption that two or more members of the family are involved in a particular set of purchase decisions. Each possesses different preference structures and is motivated to maximize his own utility while still maintaining *distributive justice*. Distributive justice refers to the players, "long term interests in seeing to it that rewards or utility are distributed among the players, or family members, on some agreed upon mutually satisfactory basis." Within a given family, priorities are assumed to exist as to which members of the family, for a given decision, tend to receive preference in the order by which utility is distributed.

A bargaining process develops centered on altering priority structures and attempting to cope with utility debts that are incurred between family members. Phase I bargaining involves attempts by one or more bargaining parties to persuade remaining members that their interests are better served by accepting his product preferences. If this is accomplished, other family members can be expected to accept his favored decision alternative. Failing in this process, a decision may still be made, although the priority structure of who receives utility first is still to be negotiated in Phase II bargaining. Following this, the utility debt can be mutually agreed upon. An example of the husband attempting to assert his priority for product utility might be a statement such as, "I earn all the money around here, so what I say is important." The wife might respond by attempting to get her way through reminding him of a utility debt he incurred in the past by a remark such as, "We always decide things your way." To the extent clarity exists with respect to role definition, bargaining over priority structures will be limited.

After the decision has been made and the consequences are at least partially known, an update takes place through Phase III bargaining regarding the postdecision utility debt—the "net residual from the family's prior history of decisions and behavior."

This model by Pollay, although untested, has great appeal for it centers on the interaction process involved in family decision making, and it might facilitate the orderly discussion of how that process differs among families of varying role sets, differing stages in a life cycle, or in different social classes.

In spite of the sizeable proportion of consumer decisions that are really family decisions, models of consumer behavior such as those by Howard and Sheth (1969), Nicosia (1966), and Amstutz (1967) have been formulated in terms of individual cognition and behavior. Family decisions are thus assumed to merely reflect the resultant of some interaction process among family members. Except for the embryonic model by Pollay, little attention has been devoted to developing family decision-making models built upon the interaction process and role specialization that takes place.

CONCLUSIONS

This chapter has discussed the importance of roles, how they relate to group behavior, and the influence that both roles and groups have on buyer behavior. That our behavior should be influenced by roles we occupy and the groups with which we associate is an entirely normal aspect of the human experience. In fact, it is quite inappropriate to label conformity to role expectations as being necessarily indicative of a character weakness or abnormal behavior. Being concerned about others' opinions of us as humans and our decisions is not irrational either. The most rational behavior in given situations might, in fact, require a great sensitivity to other people's opinions.

Given the powerful impact of role behavior and group dynamics upon human behavior, it is not surprising that marketers and researchers alike have gone out of their way to claim that these phenomena can be manipulated in one way or another to achieve marketing success. It should be recognized, however, that particularly group dynamics are very much a product of situational variables, usually beyond the reach of the marketer. Moreover, informal social relationships among friends are a private matter, somewhat fragile, and cannot be expected to remain natural under the incursion of promotional efforts or obtrusive measurement of the interactive process.

Because of this, the closing sections of research studies often contain suggestions on how the marketer can utilize group-dynamics findings that are impossible to correctly implement. One example of this has been the suggestion offered by several researchers that interpersonal communications be monitored by the marketer and the information used to plan and evaluate marketing efforts (e.g., Cox, 1963, p. 71; Bell, 1963, p. 94; Robertson, 1970, p. 236). However, no adequate and operational monitoring scheme has been presented. The few ideas that have been set forth for monitoring schemes would rely upon obtaining recall from respondents regarding recent product-related conversations with friends. Obviously, such a method would obtain little of the actual message content that was exchanged and certainly would not expose the interaction process. This author's own attempt at developing a satisfactory monitoring scheme has convinced him that to obtain useful information without considerable bias is an impossibility (Ostlund, 1968).

Given the sloppiness with respect to the definition and measurement of opinion leadership in studies that have related it to consumer behavior, the concept also appears to be removed from direct usefulness by the marketer. Influence does, indeed, flow among people regarding products, but any suggestion that the marketer can identify and reach selectively, and with considerable efficiency, opinion leaders and wait for those leaders to influence their followers or nonleaders ignores important research conclusions: (1) opinion leadership involves a low ratio of followers or nonleaders to leaders; (2) opinion leaders cannot be reached selectively with methods or media different from those that would be applied to reach the total target market; (3) conversations between leaders and nonleaders appear to be often initiated by the nonleader; as Dichter (1966) has observed, people, including opinion leaders, talk about products for a variety of reasons and undoubtedly would not characterize themselves as megaphones available for use by the marketer.

With the family unit representing the most important source of group influence, it is indeed unfortunate that more attention has not been devoted to the development of models concerning this interaction process. It is doubtful whether the microlevel models developed by Howard and Sheth (1969), Nicosia (1966), and Amstutz (1967) sufficiently allow for the bargaining process that can go on within the family, particularly concerning major expenditures.

An important question concerning group influence remains unanswered: what personality and situational variables determine the group toward which an individual is likely to look for influence or at least from which accept influence? A predictive scheme of this nature would do much to better structure the knowledge concerning role and group theory, and lead the way for applications of the theory to marketing.

REFERENCES

Abravanel, E. A., "A Psychological Analysis of the Concept of Role." Unpublished master's thesis, Swarthmore College, 1962.

Allport, G. W., and Leo Postman, *The Psychology of Rumor.* New York: Holt, Rinehart and Winston, Inc., 1947.

Amstutz, A. E., *Computer Simulation of Competitive Market Response.* Cambridge, Mass.: The MIT Press, 1967.

Arndt, Johan, "Role of Product-Related Conversations in the Diffusion of a New Product," *Journal of Marketing Research,* 4 (August 1967), 291-95.

Asch, S. E., "Effects of Group Pressure upon the Modification and Distortion of Judgments," in *Readings in Social Psychology* (3rd ed.), ed. E. E. Maccoby, T. M. Newcomb, and E. L. Hartley. New York: Holt, Rinehart and Winston, Inc. (1958), 174-83.

Bales, R. F. "Task Roles and Social Roles in Problem-Solving Groups," in *Readings in Social Psychology* (3rd ed.), ed. E. E. Maccoby, T. M. Newcomb, and E. L. Hartley. New York: Holt, Rinehart and Winston, Inc. 1958.

Bauer, R. A., and L. H. Wortzel, "Doctors: The Physician and His Sources of Information About Drugs," *Journal of Marketing Research,* 3 (February 1966), 40-47.

Baughman, E. E., and G. S. Welsh, *Personality: A Behavioral Science.* Englewood Cliffs, N.J.: Prentice-Hall, Inc., 1962.

Bavelas, A., "A Mathematical Model for Group Structures," *Applied Anthropology,* 7 (1948), 16-30.

Becker, H. S., "Becoming a Marihuana User," *American Journal of Sociology,* 59 (1953), 235-42.

Becker, H. S., and J. W. Carper, "The Development of Identification with an Occupation," *American Journal of Sociology,* 61 (1956), 289-98.

Becker, S. W., and Jean Carroll, "Ordinal Position and Conformity," *Journal of Abnormal and Social Psychology,* 65 (1962), 129-31.

Becker, S. W., M. J. Lerner, and Jean Carroll, "Conformity as a Function of Birth Order Payoff, and Type of Group Pressure," *Journal of Abnormal and Social Psychology,* 69 (1964), 318-23.

Becker, S. W., M. J. Lerner, and Jean Carroll, "Conformity as a Function of Birth Order and Type of Group Pressure," *Journal of Personality and Social Psychology,* 3 (1966), 242-44.

Bell, W. E., "Consumer Innovators: A Unique Market for Newness," in *Proceedings of the American Marketing Association,* ed. S. A. Greyser, Chicago: American Marketing Association, 1963, 85-95.

Bem, D. J., M. A. Wallach, and N. Kogan, "Group Decision Making Under Risk of Adverse Consequences," *Journal of Personality and Social Psychology,* 1 (1965), 453-60.

Berelson, B. R., P. F. Lazarsfeld, and W. N. McPhee, *Voting: A Study of Opinion Formation in a Presidential Campaign.* Chicago: The University of Chicago Press, 1954.

Bible, B. L., and E. J. Brown, "Role Consensus and Satisfaction of Extension Advisory Committee Members," *Rural Sociology,* 28 (1963), 81-90.

Birdwell, A. E., "A Study of the Influence of Image Congruency on Consumer Choice." Unpublished Ph. D. dissertation, University of Texas, 1964.

Block, J., "The Assessment of Communication Role Variations as a Function of Interactional Context," *Journal of Personality,* 21 (1952), 272-86.

Blood, R. O., Jr., and D. M. Wolfe, *Husbands and Wives.* New York: The Free Press, 1960.

Bourne, F. S., "Group Influence in Marketing and Public Relations," in *Some Applications of Behavioral Research,* ed. Rensis Likert and S. P. Hayes. Paris: UNESCO, 1957, 208-24.

Bragg, B. W., "Effects of Knowledge of Deception on Reaction to Group Pressure." Unpublished Master's thesis, University of Wisconsin, 1966.

Brown, Roger, *Social Psychology.* New York: The Free Press, 1965.

Carment, D. W., and C. G. Miles, "Persuasiveness and Persuasibility as Related to Intelligence and Extraversion," *British Journal of Clinical Psychology,* 4 (1965), 1-7.

Cartwright, Dorwin, and A. F. Zanders, eds., *Group Dynamics: Research & Theory.* Evanston, Ill.: Harper & Row, Inc., 1953.

Cartwright, Dorwin, and A. F. Zander, *Group Dynamics* (2nd ed.). New York: Harper & Row, Inc., 1960.

Centers , R. B., H. Raven, and A. Rodrigues, "Cultural and Social Class Factors in Power Structure: Decision Patterns in the Family," U.C.L.A. Technical Report No. 23, Contract Nonr. 233, 1968.

Coe, W. C., "Hypnosis as Role Enactment: The Role Demand Variable," *American Journal of Clinical Hypnosis,* 8 (1966), 189-91.

Coleman, J. S., Elihu Katz, and Herbert Menzel, *Medical Innovation: A Diffusion Study.* Indianapolis: The Bobbs-Merrill Company, Inc., 1966.

Collins, B. E., and B. H. Raven, "Group Structure: Attraction, Coalitions, Communications, Power," in *The Handbook of Social Psychology,* ed. G. Lindzey and E. Aronson, Vol. 4. Reading, Mass.: Addison-Wesley Publishing Company, Inc., 1969.

Cottrell, L. S., Jr., "The Adjustment of the Individual to His Age and Sex Roles," *American Sociological Review,* 7 (1942), 617-20.

Cox, D. F., "The Audience as Communicators," in *Proceedings of the American Marketing Association,* ed. S. A. Greyser. Chicago: American Marketing Association, Winter 1963, 58-72.

Cox, D. F., ed., *Risk Taking and Information Handling in Consumer Behavior.* Graduate School of Business Administration, Harvard University, Boston, 1967.

Crutchfield, Richard, "Conformity and Character," *American Psychologist,* 10 (1955), 191-98.

Cunningham, S. M., "Some Comments on the Relationship Between Rumor and Informal Communications." Unpublished paper, January 3, 1963.

Cunningham, S. M., "Some Comments on the Relationship between Rumor and Information," in *Proceedings of the American Marketing Association,* ed. R. M. Haas. Chicago: American Marketing Association, 1966, 698-721.

Davis, H. L., "Dimensions of Marital Roles in Consumer Decision Making," *Journal of Marketing Research,* 7 (May 1970), 168-77.

DeFleur, M. L., "Mass Communication and the Study of Rumor," *Sociological Inquiry,* 22, No. 1 (Winter 1962), 51-69.

Deutsch, Morton, and R. M. Krauss, *Theories in Social Psychology.* New York: Basic Books, Inc., Publishers, 1965.

Deutschmann, P. J., "Viewing, Conversation, and Voting Intentions," in *The Great Debates,* ed. S. Krauss, Bloomington, Ind.: Indiana University Press, 1962, 232-52.

Dichter, Ernest, "How Word-of-Mouth Advertising Works," *Harvard Business Review,* 44 (November-December 1966), 147-66.

Dolich, I. J., "Congruency Relationships Between Self-Images and Product Brands," *Journal of Marketing Research,* 6 (February 1969), 80-84.

Eisenstadt, S. N., "Studies in Reference Group Behavior: I. Reference Norms and the Social Structure," *Human Relations,* 7 (1954), 191-216.

Feldman, Sidney, and M. C. Spencer, "The Effect of Personal Influence in the Selection of Consumer Services," in *Proceedings of the American Marketing Association,* ed. P. D. Bennett. Chicago: American Marketing Association, 1965, 440-52.

Festinger, Leon, et al., "A Study of a Rumor: Its Origin and Spread," *Human Relations,* I (1948), 464-86.

Granbois, D. H., "The Role of Communication in the Family Decision-Making Process," in *Proceedings of the American Marketing Association,* ed. S. A. Greyser. Chicago: American Marketing Association, 1963, 44-57.

Gross, N. W., L. Mason, and A. W. McEachern, *Explorations in Role Analysis.* New York: John Wiley & Sons, Inc., 1958.

Grubb, E. L., "Consumer Perception of 'Self-Concept' and its Relation to Brand Choice of Selected Product Types," in *Proceedings of the American Marketing Association,* ed. P. D. Bennett. Chicago: American Marketing Association, Fall 1965, 419-22.

Grubb, E. L., and Gregg Hubb, "Perception of Self, Generalized Stereotypes, and Brand Selection," *Journal of Marketing Research,* 5 (February 1968), 58-63.

Haines, G. H., "A Study of Why People Purchase New Products," in *Proceedings of the American Marketing Association,* ed. R. M. Haas. Chicago: American Marketing Association, Fall 1966, 685-97.

Hartley, R. E., "Relationship between Perceived Values and Acceptance of a New Reference Group," *Journal of Social Psychology,* 51 (1960), 181-90.

Howard, J. A., and J. N. Sheth, *The Theory of Buyer Behavior.* New York: John Wiley & Sons, Inc., 1969.

Katz, Elihu, "The Two-Step Flow of Communication: An Up-to-Date Report on an Hypothesis," *Public Opinion Quarterly,* 21 (Spring 1957), 61-78.

Katz, Elihu, and Paul Lazarsfeld, *Personal Influence.* New York: The Free Press, 1955.

Kelley, H. H., "Two Functions of Reference Groups," in *Readings in Social Psychology* (rev. ed.), ed. G. E. Swanson, T. M. Newcomb, and E. L. Hartley. New York: Holt, Rinehart and Winston, Inc. 1952.

Kenkel, W. F., "Decision-Making and the Life Cycle: Husband-Wife Interaction in Decision Making and Decision Choices," *Journal of Social Psychology,* 54 (August 1961), 255-62.

Kenkel, W. F., and D. K. Hoffman, "Real and Conceived Roles in Family Decision Making," *Marriage and the Family,* 17, No. 4 (November 1956) 311-16.

King, C. W., "Fashion Adoption: A Rebuttal to the 'Trickle Down' Theory," in *Proceedings of the American Marketing Association,* ed. S. A. Greyser. Chicago: American Marketing Association, 1963, pp. 108-25.

King, C. W., "Communicating with the Innovator in the Fashion Adoption Process," in *Proceedings of the Educators' Conference,* ed. P. D. Bennett. Chicago: American Marketing Association, Fall 1965, pp. 425-39.

King, C. W., and J. O. Summers, "Overlap of Opinion Leadership across Consumer Product Categories." Working paper, Krannert Graduate School of Industrial Administration, Purdue University, 1968.

King, C. W., and J. O. Summers, "Generalized Opinion Leadership in Consumer Products: Some Preliminary Findings." Working Paper No. 224, Institute for Research in the Behavioral, Economic and Management Science, Purdue University, January, 1969.

King, C. W., and J. O. Summers, "Overlap of Opinion Leadership Across Consumer Product Categories," *Journal of Marketing Research,* 7 (February 1970) 43-50.

Klapper, J. T., *The Effects of Mass Communication.* New York: The Free Press, 1960.

Komarovsky, Mirra, "Class Differences in Family Decision-Making," in *Household Decision-Making,* ed. N. N. Foote, New York: University Press, 1961, pp. 255-65.

Krech, David, Richard Crutchfield, and Egerton Ballachey, *Individual in Society.* New York: McGraw-Hill Book Company, 1962.

Kroger, R. O., "The Effects of Role Demands and Test-Cue Properties upon Personality Test Performance," *Journal of Consulting Psychology,* 31 (1967), 304-12.

Kuchenberg, K. G., "Effect of Early Father Absence on Scholastic Aptitude." Unpublished Ph. D. dissertation, Harvard University, 1963.

Lazarsfeld, P. F., Bernard Berelson, and Hazel Gaudet, *The People's Choice* (2nd ed.). New York: Columbia University Press, 1948.

Leavitt, H. J., "Some Effects of Certain Communications Patterns on Group Performance," *Journal of Abnormal and Social Psychology,* 46 (1951), 38-50.

Lewin, Kurt, "Group Decision and Social Change," in *Readings in Social Psychology,* ed. T. M. Newcomb and E. L. Hartley. New York: Holt, Rinehart and Winston, Inc., 1947, 330-44.

Lewin, Kurt, *Resolving Social Conflicts.* New York: Harper & Row, Inc., 1948.

Lieberman, Seymour, "The Effects of Changes in Roles on the Attitudes of Role Occupants," *Human Relations,* 9, No. 4 (November 1956), 399.

Linton, Ralph, *The Cultural Background of Personality.* New York: Appleton-Century-Crofts, 1945.

Lott, A. J., and B. E. Lott, "Group Cohesiveness as Interpersonal Attraction: A Review of Relationships with Antecedent and Consequent Variables," *Psychological Bulletin,* 64 (1965), 259-309.

Malof, M., and A. J. Lott, "Ethnocentrism and the Acceptance of Negro Support in a Group Pressure Situation," *Journal of Abnormal and Social Psychology,* 65 (1962), 254-58.

Marcus, A. S., and R. A. Bauer, "Yes: There Are Generalized Opinion Leaders," *Public Opinion Quarterly,* 28 (Winter 1964), 628-32.

Mead, G. H., *Mind, Self and Society,* ed. C. W. Morris. Chicago: University of Chicago Press, 1934.

Merton, R. K., "The Role Set," *British Journal of Sociology,* 8 (1957a), 106-20.

Merton, R. K., *Social Theory and Social Structure* (rev. ed.). New York: The Free Press, 1957b.

Meyer, H. D., "The Adult Cycle," *The Annals of the American Academy of Political and Social Science,* 313 (September 1957), 58-67.

Myers, J. H., and T. S. Robertson, "Dimensions of Opinion Leadership." Working paper, Graduate School of Business, University of Southern California, 1969.

Nicosia, F. M., "Opinion Leadership and the Flow of Communication: Some Problems and Prospects," in *Proceedings of the American Marketing Association,* ed. L. George Smith. Chicago: American Marketing Association, 1964, pp. 340-58.

Nicosia, F. M., *Consumer Decision Processes.* Englewood Cliffs, N.J.: Prentice-Hall, Inc., 1966.

Ostlund, L. E., "Word of Mouth Communications." Unpublished paper, Harvard Graduate School of Business, 1968.

Pennington, D. F., F. Harary, and B. M. Bass, "Some Effects of Decision and Discussion on Coalescence, Change, and Effectiveness," *Journal of Applied Psychology,* 42 (1958), 404-8.

Perry, Michael, and B. C. Hamm, "Canonical Analysis of Relations Between Socioeconomic Risk and Personal Influence in Purchase Decisions," *Journal of Marketing Research,* 6 (August 1969), 351-54.

Pollay, R. W., "A Model of Family Decision Making," *British Journal of Marketing,* August 1968.

Robertson, T. S., *An Analysis of Innovative Behavior and Its Determinants.* Unpublished Ph.D. dissertation, Northwestern University, 1966.

Robertson, T. S., *Consumer Behavior.* Glenview, Ill.: Scott, Foresman and Company, 1970.

Robertson, T. S., *New Product Diffusion.* New York: Holt, Rinehart and Winston, Inc., 1971.

Robertson, T. S., and J. H. Myers, "Personality Correlates of Opinion Leadership and Innovative Buying Behavior," *Journal of Marketing Research,* 7 (May 1969), 164-68.

Robertson, T. S., and J. R. Rossiter, "Fashion Diffusion: The Interplay of Innovator and Opinion Leader Roles in College Social Systems." Working paper, Graduate School of Business, University of California at Los Angeles, 1968.

Rogers, E. M., *Diffusion of Innovations.* New York: The Free Press, 1962.

Rogers, E. M., and D. G. Cartano, "Methods of Measuring Opinion Leadership," *Public Opinion Quarterly,* 26 (Fall 1962), 435-41.

Rommetveit, Ragnar, *Social Norms and Roles: Explorations in the Psychology of Enduring Social Pressures.* Minneapolis: University of Minnesota Press, 1955.

Rosen, B. C., "The Reference Group Approach to the Parental Factor in Attitude and Behavior Formulation," *Social Forces*, 34 (1955), 137-44.

Sarbin, T. R., and V. L. Allen, "Role Theory," in *Handbook of Social Psychology*, ed. G. Lindzey and E. Aronson, Vol. 1. Reading, Mass.: Addison-Wesley Publishing Company, Inc., 1968.

Scott, W. A., "Attitude Change Through Reward of Verbal Behavior," *Journal of Abnormal and Social Psychology*, 55 (1957), 72-75.

Shaw, M. E., "Communication Networks," in *Advances in Experimental Social Psychology*, ed. L. Berkowitz, Vol. 1. New York: Academic Press, Inc., 1964, 111-47.

Sherif, Muzafer, "Group Influences Upon the Formation of Norms and Attitudes," *Readings in Social Psychology*, ed. E. E. Maccoby, T. M. Newcomb, and E. L. Hartley. New York: Holt, Rinehart and Winston, Inc., 1958, pp. 219-32.

Shibutani, Tamotsu, "Reference Groups as Perspectives," in *Marketing and the Behavioral Sciences* (2nd ed.), ed. Perry Bliss. Boston: Allyn and Bacon, Inc., 1967, 255-97.

Silk, A. J., "Overlap Among Self-Designated Opinion Leaders: A Study of Selected Dental Products and Services," *Journal of Marketing Research*, 3 (August 1966), 255-59.

Silk, A. J., and D. B. Montgomery, "Patterns of Overlap in Opinion Leadership and Interest for Selected Categories of Purchasing Activity," in *Proceedings of the Educators' Conference*, P. R. McDonald, ed. Chicago: American Marketing Association 1969, 377-86.

Slater, Carol, "Class Differences in Definition of Role and Membership in Voluntary Associations among Urban Married Women," *American Journal of Sociology*, 65 (1960), 616-19.

Spiegel, J. P., "Interpersonal Influences within the Family," in *Interpersonal Dynamics*, ed. W. Bennis et al. Homewood, Ill.: Dorsey Press, Inc., 1964.

Stafford, J. E., "Effects of Group Influences on Consumer Brand Preferences," *Journal of Marketing Research*, 3 (February 1966), 68-75.

Steiner, I. D., "Personality and the Resolution of Interpersonal Disagreements," in *Progress in Experimental Personality Research*, ed. B. A. Maher, Vol. 3. New York: Academic Press, Inc., 1966, 195-240.

Strodtbeck, F. L., "Husband and Wife Interaction Over Revealed Differences," *American Sociological Review*, 16 (1951), 468-73.

Strodtbeck, F. L., "The Family as a Three-Person Group," *American Sociological Review*, 19 (1954), 23-29.

Summers, J. O., "The Identity of Women's Clothing Fashion Opinion Leaders," *Journal of Marketing Research*, 7 (May 1970), 178-85.

Thibaut, J. W., and H. H. Kelley, *The Social Psychology of Groups*. New York: John Wiley & Sons, Inc., 1959.

Thomas, E. J., "Role Conceptions and Organizational Size," *American Sociological Review*, 24 (1959), 30-37.

Thomas, E. J., N. Polansky, and J. Kounin, "The Expected Behavior of a Potentially Helpful Person," *Human Relations*, 8 (1955), 165-74.

Tuddenham, R. D., "Correlates of Yielding to a Distorted Group Norm," *Journal of Personality*, 27 (1959), 272-84.

Turner, R. H., "Role-Taking: Process Versus Conformity," in *Human Behavior and Social Process,* ed. A. M. Rose. Boston: Houghton Mifflin Company, 1962, 20-40.

Udell, J. G., "Prepurchase Behavior of Buyers of Small Electrical Appliances," *Journal of Marketing,* October 1966, 50-52.

Venkatesan, M., "An Experimental Investigation in the Conditions Producing Conformity to and Independence of Group Norms in Consumer Behavior," in *Proceedings of the American Marketing Association,* ed. P. D. Bennett. Chicago: American Marketing Association, 1965, 461-62.

Wallach, M. A., N. Kogan, and D. J. Bem, "Group Influence on Individual Risk Taking," *Journal of Abnormal and Social Psychology,* 65 (1962), 75-86.

Weinstein, E. A., and P. D. Deutchberger, "Some Dimensions of Altercasting," *Sociometry,* 26 (1963), 454-66.

Wells, W. D., F. J. Goi, and S. Seader, "A Change in a Product Image," *Journal of Applied Psychology,* 42 (1958) 120-21.

Wolgast, E. H., "Do Husbands or Wives Make the Purchasing Decisions?" *Journal of Marketing,* 22 (October 1958), 151-58.

Zimmerman, Claire, and R. A. Bauer, "The Effect of an Audience upon What Is Remembered," *Public Opinion Quarterly,* 20 (1956), 238-48.

7

Overview of Economic Models of Consumer Behavior

George H. Haines, Jr.
University of Rochester

INTRODUCTION

BASIC CONCEPTS

GRAPHICAL EXPOSITION

REVEALED PREFERENCE

AXIOMATIC ANALYSIS

ADDITIONAL DEVELOPMENTS WITHIN THE CLASSICAL FRAMEWORK

Social Interaction. Changes in Tastes. The Household. Prices in
the Utility Function. Empirical Testing.

CONCLUDING COMMENTS

APPENDIX: MATHEMATICAL EXPOSITION OF THE ELEMENTARY
THEORY

REFERENCES

INTRODUCTION

The following represents an effort to present an overview of economic models of consumer behavior. The usual disclaimers are in order here with a vengeance. Much relevant material may have escaped my attention, and, in any case, what is important has a subjective element. The aim of this presentation is simply to introduce a reader to the theory and the literature. There is no attempt to include everything ever written, and the reference list contains only material referenced in the exposition. The interested reader may turn to longer and more extensive discussions, such as Wu and Pontney (1967). The focus is generally upon the individual consumer with less attention paid to aggregate theory. Finally, it must be stressed that nothing in this overview is very new; that is not the purpose of it.

The presentation itself starts with a statement of assumptions, then a verbal development of the traditional theory, with a mathematical development of the traditional theory presented in the Appendix. Then some additional developments within the classical framework are discussed, including a few comments on aggregation and intersection, and some concluding remarks. The theory takes as its central focus the explanation of product purchases by the individual consumer. It is postulated that all that is necessary to explain the product purchase patterns of the individual consumer is knowledge of the consumer preferences, his or her income, and the prices faced in the market for alternative products: this is the simplest form of the theory. However, as will be seen, the theory also predicts relations between consumption and price, and consumption and income, which may be studied empirically without knowledge of individual consumer preferences. Finally, it should be noted that the theory is static. Time is neither a dependent nor an independent variable.

BASIC CONCEPTS

This section provides an elementary exposition of the standard economic theory of consumer behavior. The purpose of this theory is to describe the behavior of individual people in their roles as consumers.

Certain basic concepts underlie this theory. First of these is that there is a fixed number of different commodities, including services, each of which is assumed to have a well-defined unit of measure. The prices of unit measure of each commodity exist and are positive. A budget alternative is composed of specified quantities of each of the commodities; these quantities are nonnegative. The budget alternatives, which cover a fixed period of time, refer to a particular individual, called the consumer. The consumer has a positive sum of income at his disposal for purchases during the budget period. The basic question is what budget alternative will the consumer choose? Equally important is the question of what happens when a price alters, or when the consumer's income changes. There are other important behavioral questions, but discussion of these will be deferred until later.

Answers to these questions require certain behavioral postulates. The first postulate is that a consumer has a definite order of preferences for budget alternatives (i.e., bundles of goods); this order is stable and transitive. The order of comparison has the following meaning. Suppose that there exist two different bundles of commodities. Three alternatives are possible: the first bundle will be preferred to the second bundle, or the second bundle of goods will be preferred to the first, or the consumer will be indifferent between them. This means the consumer is able to compare the two different bundles. Transitivity means that the order of preferences is logically consistent in a particular way. Suppose that there are three bundles of goods. If the consumer prefers the first to the second, and prefers the second to the third, then he will prefer the first to the third. This relation also holds if the phrase "is indifferent between" is substituted for the word "prefers" in the above sentence.

Finally, there is the axiom of choice. The consumer chooses a budget such that the one chosen is preferred to any other budget he can obtain, provided, of course, that such a budget exists.

One line of research in this area also imposes a set of regularity assumptions that enables one to use elementary mathematical analysis on the problem. Fundamentally, the regularity assumptions imply that the loci of indifference, which express the consumers preferences, form a system of $(n-1)$-dimensional surfaces that fill the entire budget space, and that these surfaces will be twice differentiable.

One form of these regularity assumptions has been given by Wold (1953); the necessary assumptions can be stated as follows:

1. A larger budget is always preferred to a smaller one. Comment: Not only is this an assumption of nonsatiety; it also implies that all loci of indifference reduce to $(n - 1)$-dimensional surfaces, and, therefore, that through every point q of the budget space there passes one, and only one, indifference surface.

2. Let $q^{(1)}, q^{(2)}$, and $q^{(3)}$ be any budgets such that $q^{(1)}$ is preferred to $q^{(2)}$, and $q^{(2)}$ to $q^{(3)}$. Let L be the line in the budget space that connects $q^{(1)}$ with $q^{(3)}$. Then L passes through a budget q that is equivalent to $q^{(2)}$. Comment: This is an assumption of continuity; it assumes the loci of indifference will never take the form of surface fragments.

Given these two assumptions, one can define a function $f(q_1, \ldots, q_n) = c$, where c is a constant. This function forms a well-defined point set in the budget space. Wold (1953) calls the system of such loci obtained for different values of c the "level map" of f. He then proves the following theorem:

Any indifference map allows the representation of a level map, say,

$$U(q_1, \ldots, q_n) = c \quad \text{or (briefly)} \quad U(q) = c, \qquad (1)$$

where c ranges continuously from 0 to ∞, and U is a well-defined function that is continuous and increasing in each variable q_i.

A final comment is the following. Consider an arbitrary indifference map and the corresponding representation (1); let $\psi(x)$ be any increasing function. Then

$$\psi(U(q_1, \ldots, q_n)) = U^*(q_1, \ldots, q_n); \qquad (2)$$

the same map allows the representation

$$U^*(q_1, \ldots, q_n) = c.$$

A function $U^*(q_1, \ldots, q_n)$ of type (2), of which (1) is a special case, is called a preference index function of the consumer, or briefly, a preference function.

3. The preference function $U(q)$ as defined by (1) has continuous derivatives of first and second order.

GRAPHICAL EXPOSITION

If the above conditions are met, it is possible to construct an ordinal "utility" function that describes the individual consumer's preference structure. Furthermore, from such a function indifference curves may be readily derived.

Indifference curves can be used to present a graphic picture of consumer tastes and preferences in the case of two goods. Such presentation is hardly new; the reader will find it developed in many places, including Leftwich (1956) and Stigler (1954).

A single indifference curve shows the different combinations of the two goods Q_1 and Q_2 that yield equal "satisfaction" to the consumer, or between which the consumer is indifferent. Figure 1 shows two examples, labeled I_1 and I_2, of indifference curves. The goods may be any good, but very often Q_1 is taken as a numeraire commodity and Q_2 as some specific commodity, such as rye (in pints). Each quantity is also measured per unit of time, often taken to be a year or a quarter in empirical work. Thus Q_1 and Q_2 are measured in units of the commodity consumed per unit time. Notice also that innumerable indifference curves can be drawn on the diagram depicting all degrees of satisfaction. All combinations on one indifference curve are of equal satisfaction to the consumer. All combinations on "higher" (i.e., farther from the origin) indifference curves are preferable to those lying on "lower" indifference curves. Thus, for example, in Figure 1 any combination on I_2 is preferred to any

FIGURE 1. **Indifference Curves**

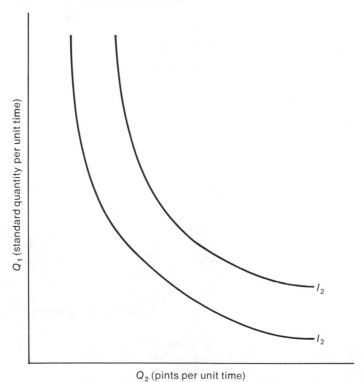

Q_2 (pints per unit time)

combination on I_1, whereas, of course, the consumer is indifferent between any two different combinations that both lie on I_2 (or I_1).

The assumptions that have been made in constructing this theory reflect themselves in three characteristics of indifference curves:

1. They slope downward to the right.
2. They are convex toward the origin of the indifference-curve diagram.
3. They are nonintersecting.

Consider the things that lie behind these characteristics:

1. The usual case will be that if the consumer's satisfaction is to remain constant when he gives up units of one commodity, the loss must be compensated for by additional units of another commodity. The result, shown graphically in Figure 1, is an indifference curve sloping downward to the right.

2. To understand what lies behind convexity it is first necessary to introduce a definition of the marginal rate of substitution of Q_2 to Q_1. The marginal rate of substitution of Q_2 for Q_1 (denoted $MRS_{Q_2Q_1}$) is defined as the amount of Q_1 the consumer is just willing to give up to get an additional unit of Q_2. Now let us consider the convexity characteristic. First, the more Q_1 and the less Q_2 the consumer has, the more important a unit of Q_2 is to him as compared with a unit of Q_1. Now as the quantity of Q_2 increases, the amount of Q_1 the consumer is willing to surrender to get more Q_2 decreases: that is, $MRS_{Q_2Q_1}$ decreases (from top to bottom). Therefore, an indifference curve is convex toward the origin. However, as we shall see, this kind of argument is considerably more complex if one moves away from considering only two products to considering many.

3. The nonintersecting characteristic follows naturally from each indifference curve representing different levels of satisfaction.

Now let us consider complementarity and substitutability relationships in an economic sense. The first thing to observe is that complementarity and substitutability of commodities in an economic sense are reflected in the curvature of the indifference curves. Indifference curves for goods that are substitutes, although not perfect substitutes, have some degree of convexity to the origin. The poorer substitutes (in an economic sense) the two products are for each other, the greater the degree of convexity. The better substitutes the two products are, the flatter or less convex the indifference curves will be.

It must be noted that the economic concepts of substitution and complementarity are not synonymous with technical or functional substitutability or complementarity. It may be, and often is, the case that the two concepts correspond, but it is not necessary that this be so.

Now, given the consumer's attitudes toward available products, what does the consumer do? The basic behavioral postulate is that the consumer tries to maximize his satisfaction within the limits of his resources.

The consumers' set of indifference curves shows what he is willing to do with respect to different combinations of Q_1 and Q_2.

What the consumer is able to do depends upon the respective prices of Q_1 and Q_2 and the consumer's income. This income is ordinarily expressed in units of the numeraire commodity Q_1. These opportunity factors—prices and income—are summed up in the consumer's *line of attainable combinations;* one example of such a line is shown in Figure 2. Notice that the consumer takes as given the opportunity factors: his income, the price of a unit of Q_1, and the price of a unit of Q_2.

FIGURE 2.   **Line of Attainable Combinations**

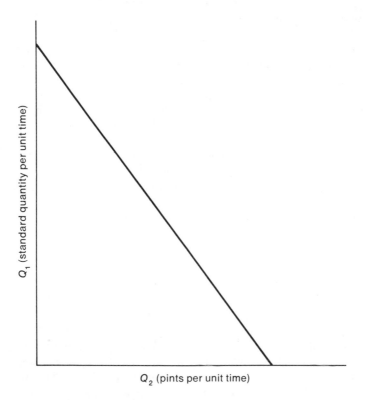

Q_2 (pints per unit time)

The line of attainable combinations and the indifference map, taken together, will show the combination of Q_1 and Q_2 that will maximize his satisfaction. Notice that the slope of the line of attainable combinations depends on the prices of Q_1 and Q_2 (let these be denoted P_1 and P_2, respectively), since

$$\frac{\text{income}}{p_1} = \text{total number units of } Q_1 \text{ the consumer could purchase if he bought no } Q_2,$$

$$\text{and} \quad \frac{\text{income}}{p_2} = \text{total number units of } Q_2 \text{ the consumer could purchase if he bought no } Q_1,$$

$$\text{and} \quad \text{slope} = \frac{\text{rise}}{\text{run}} = \frac{\text{income}/p_1}{\text{income}/p_2}$$

$$= \frac{p_2}{p_1}.$$

The indifference curve to which the line of attainable combinations is tangent is the highest one the consumer can reach. At this point,

$$\text{MRS}_{Q_2 Q_1} = \frac{p_2}{p_1}$$

To see that this is so, recall that

1. The slope of an indifference curve at any point represents the amount of Q_1 the consumer is willing to give up to get an additional unit of Q_2, maintaining the same level of satisfaction.

2. The slope of the line of attainable combinations at any point represents the amount of Q_1 the consumer would have to give in the market to get an additional unit of Q_2 at that point.

Figure 3 shows how one can combine Figures 1 and 2 to obtain a consumption point. Figure 3 displays the line of attainable combinations denoted by LAC, and the indifference curve, I, to which it is tangent. The point of tangency determines particular values for Q_1 and Q_2.

Now it is possible to show how this theory can be used to derive some additional implications: Engel curves and demand curves for individual consumers.

An Engel curve shows the different quantities of a particular good that the consumer will take at various levels of income, other things being equal. This relation may be readily derived from the information already given in Figure 3. Figure 4 illustrates the derivation. LAC_1 denotes the line of attainable combinations when the consumer has income M_1; at the tangency of LAC_1 and I_1 it can be seen that the consumer consumes q_1 pints per unit time of Q_2 (say, rye). At a higher income with everything else constant, the line of attainable combinations shifts up (i.e., away from the origin). Since only the consumer's income has altered, the new line of attainable combinations, LAC_2, is parallel to LAC_1. At the tangency of LAC_2 and I_2 it can be seen that the consumer consumes q_2 pints of rye per unit time.

This information may be plotted on a graph showing the relation between

FIGURE 3.   **Derivation of Consumption Point**

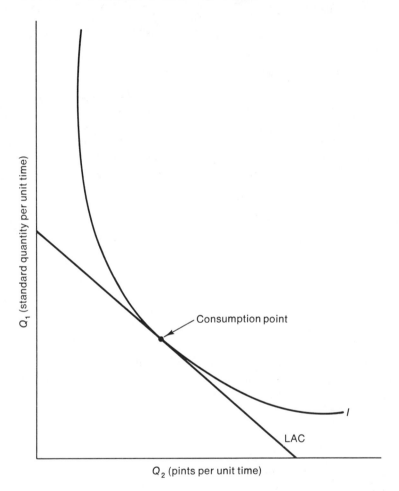

Q_2 (pints per unit time)

M, income per unit time, and the quantity of the good consumed per unit time. Such a plot is shown in the upper-right-hand corner of Figure 4. The resulting relation is called an Engel curve. It shows the different quantities of a particular good that the consumer will consume at various levels of income, other things being equal.

A second implication of this theory is the concept of a demand curve. However, there is no such thing as "a demand curve." An economic problem that calls for the use of a demand curve will in general contain the information necessary for deciding which species of demand curve is relevant to it (Usher, 1965).

The standard textbook demand curve shows the different quantities of a

FIGURE 4. **Derivation of an Engel Curve**

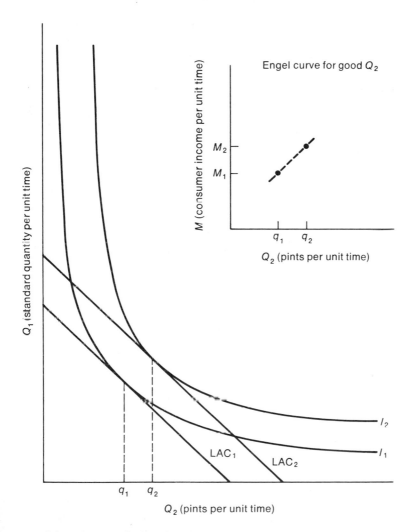

good (per unit time) that the consumer will consume at various possible prices of the good, other things being equal. In practical applications of demand theory this is not always the best definition; but it is reasonable to defer a brief discussion of alternatives to show how this standard demand curve can be derived.

Figure 5 displays graphically the derivation of a standard textbook demand curve for the good Q_2 (rye). When the price of Q_2 is p_1, the consumer will consume q_1 units of good Q_2 per unit time. This reflects itself in the tangency of LAC_1 with I_1. A represents the quantity of Q_1 the consumer is able to purchase if the consumer buys only Q_1; B the quantity of Q_2 the consumer is able to purchase if the consumer buys only Q_2. A lower price for Q_2 would mean the consumer could purchase more Q_2 if the consumer bought Q_2. LAC_2 represents such a circumstance, and C the amount of Q_2 the consumer could buy if the consumer bought only Q_2. q_2 represents the amount of Q_2 the consumer will purchase after taking his or her preferences into account. Notice that the point A is the same for both LAC_1 and LAC_2. The only thing that has altered is the price of Q_2, and p_1, the price of Q_2 associated with LAC_1, is higher than p_2, the price of Q_2 associated with LAC_2. As before, this relationship may be plotted, and it is in the diagram in the upper-right-hand corner of

FIGURE 5.   Derivation of a Demand Curve

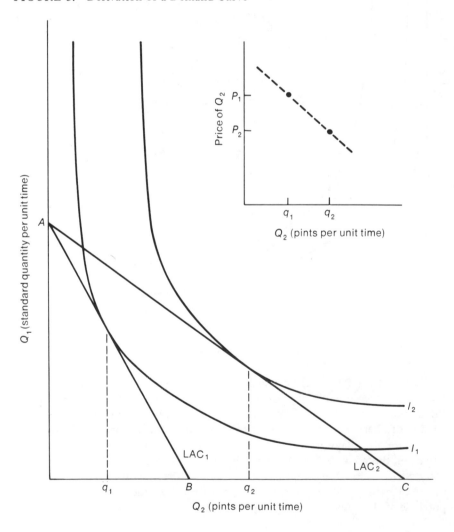

Figure 5. The resulting relation between the price of Q_2 and the quantity of Q_2 consumed by the consumer is the standard textbook demand-curve good for the good Q_2. It is usually argued that these individual demand curves can be aggregated to yield a market demand curve; quite often it is assumed that the relevant market is the nation as a whole. If this is true, the income applicable to the market demand curve is the national income.

This version of the demand curve is usually attributed to Marshall (1948); a much more detailed examination of it is given in Hicks (1939). However, as Usher (1965) points out, other definitions of demand curves are important in practical and theoretical studies of consumer behavior. These may be briefly reviewed. Walras (1884) and Wicksell (1934) used the concept of a demand curve applicable to a person who, in a two-commodity world, goes to market with a given stock of the two goods and may purchase more of either, depending upon the going relative market price of the two goods. The exact derivation of this curve from indifference curves has been worked out by Boulding (1945). Pigou (1910), followed by Bailey (1954), used a definition assuming not income but conditions of supply of all other commodities to be fixed during movements along the demand curve. Friedman (1966) has argued that a demand curve on which all points represent conditions of equal utility is useful for certain purposes. Finally, Usher (1965) and Pearce (1953) have argued for a variable-income demand curve, pointing out that in most applications of demand theory whatever is causing a joint movement of quantity and price along the demand curve may quite likely affect national income as well. The essential point is that there is no need to use only one interpretation of the demand-curve concept; rather, the specific concept used should properly address the specific problem.

There is another way of looking at the effect of a change in the price of a good. That is to show that the effects of a change in the price of a good on the amount consumed of it can be divided into substitution and income effects. Suppose that the price of good Q_2 falls. The consumer may wish to substitute Q_2 for Q_1 for two reasons: (1) Q_2 has become cheaper relative to Q_1, and (2) the fall in the price of Q_2 is equivalent to an increase in the consumer's income. How much of the increased consumption of Q_2 can be attributed to each of these causes?

The substitution effect describes the reallocation that will take place among consumer purchases if a price change is compensated by a simultaneous income change that forces the consumer to remain on the same indifference curve. The discrepancy between this point and the final point of equilibrium is accounted for by the income effect. This analysis is illustrated in Figure 6.

AB is the original line of attainable combinations (LAC_1), with R being the corresponding point of equilibrium. After the change in the price of good Q_2, AC is the new line of attainable combinations (LAC_2), and the new consumption point is at T. The movement from R to T can be decomposed into two steps: (1) R to S, and (2) S to T. How is the point S determined? The point S is

FIGURE 6. **Income and Substitution Effects**

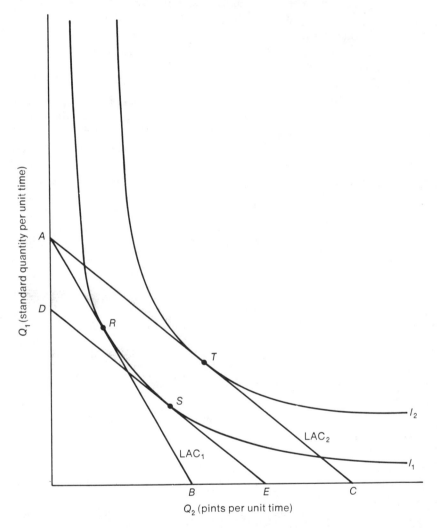

the tangency point between the original indifference curve I_1 and a line of attainable combinations *DE*, which is parallel to the line of attainable combinations *AC*. That is, after the price change the consumer's income alters so that the consumer remains on the same indifference curve. The tangency point alters, however, because the relative prices have altered. Thus it is said that the movement from *R* to *S* is accounted for by a substitution effect, and the movement from *S* to *T* by an income effect.

A mathematical exposition of this elementary theory is given in the Appendix.

This theory can be extended in several other ways; some of these extensions will be discussed in the succeeding material. First, however, it is useful to review an alternative approach to the basic problem.

REVEALED PREFERENCE

Samuelson (1938) proposed basing the study of consumer behavior only on consideration of individual price-quantity situations rather then in terms of derivatives of demand functions. By the latter restriction he hoped to make the theory more immediately verifiable; however, it was not until the work of Koo (1963) that actual empirical results were reported.

Samuelson proposed to look at price-quantity relations in terms of value sums instead of in terms of price-quantity relations such as those discussed previously. Value sums are sums of quantities each multiplied by its relevant price.

Consider an individual who buys the quantities $q_1^1, q_2^1, \ldots, q_n^1$ when the market prices are $p_1^1, p_2^1, \ldots, p_n^1$. His total expenditure is consequently

$$\sum_{i=1}^{n} p_i^1 q_i^1.$$

Consider a second bundle of commodities $q_1^2, q_2^2, \ldots, q_n^2$ whose cost

$$\sum_{i=1}^{n} p_i^1 q_i^2$$

is no more, at the prevailing market prices, than the cost of the bundle that he actually bought. Consequently, the consumer could have bought the second bundle when he actually bought the first. By choosing the first bundle rather than the second, he revealed a preference for the first. Therefore, it is possible to say that the first bundle is revealed preferred to the second, or in symbols $q^1 R q^2$.

Suppose that there exists a set of prices $p_1^2, p_2^2, \ldots, p_n^2$ at which the second bundle q^2 is actually bought. What can be said about the cost of the first bundle at the second set of prices? It has already been shown that the first bundle is revealed to be preferred to the second, and so the second bundle ought not to be revealed preferred to the first if the consumer's preferences have not altered. It follows then that

$$\sum_i p_i^2 q_i^1 > \sum_i p_i^2 q_i^2.$$

Consistency of preferences requires that if the second bundle can be bought at the first set of prices, then the first bundle cannot be bought at the second set of prices. This implication, of course, goes only one way. If the second bundle is too expensive at the first set of prices, nothing follows about the cost of the first bundle at the second set of prices.

This is simply a generalization of the law of demand (Cournot, 1838) to arbitrary price changes. To see the relation to the ordinary law of demand it is only necessary to set

$$\sum_i p_i^1 q_i^2 = \sum_i p_i^1 q_i^1$$

and to assume that the vectors p^1 and p^2 are identical except for one, let it be the first, price. It follows that if

$$\sum p_i^1 q_i^2 = \sum p_i^1 q_i^1 \quad \text{then} \quad \sum (p_1^1 - p_1^2)(q_1^1 - q_1^2) < 0.$$

If a price changes in such a way that in the new situation the consumer can buy what he bought in the old, then the price change and the quantity change are necessarily of opposite signs. If p^1 and p^2 differ in more than one component, the implication becomes (for $\sum_i p_i^1 q_i^2 = \sum_i p_i^1 q_i^1$)

$$\sum (p^1 - p^2)(q^1 - q^2) < 0.$$

This illustrates the fact (Hicks, 1939) that complementarity is on balance weaker than substitution, so that on the whole the relation between price changes and quantity changes is still negative.

AXIOMATIC ANALYSIS

At this point it was an open question whether revealed preference had really exhausted the implications of the older analysis model. This question touched off a series of research papers and studies. These are carefully reviewed in Houthakker (1961). The culmination of the resulting research was the formulation of two sets of axioms, one referring to preferences and the other to demand functions, which are logically equivalent to each other, by Uzawa (1960). Essentially, Uzawa showed that two such axiom systems are equivalent to one another. This settled the issue concerning the relation between the classical approach to consumer's choice and the revealed-preference approach. It is fair to comment, however, that the revealed-preference approach led to two considerable results. First, it was certainly successful in achieving much theoretical clarification. Second, it reinforced the emphasis on observable implications and made possible, at least in theory, much empirical research. Finally, it added the terminology and tools of symbolic logic to the study of the foundations of consumer choice; this in itself had much to do with the theoretical clarification achieved.

ADDITIONAL DEVELOPMENTS WITHIN THE CLASSICAL FRAMEWORK

This section discusses certain developments in the theory of individual consumer choice. The focus continues on the classical framework, that is, the static theory for a single consumer in which only small changes around an equilibrium point are studied. The attempt of this section will be to review briefly those extensions which bear on attempts to study phenomena discussed in the earlier chapters so that the reader can compare how they are handled within the classical economic framework with the earlier discussions.

Social Interaction

The formation of preferences is to some extent a social process in which the influences of others are important elements. These consequences were explored by Duesenberry (1949), who focused upon differences between savings functions estimated from cross-sectional and time-series data. Prais and Houthakker (1955) argued that when the budget constraint is properly taken into account the consequences of social interaction are not as straightforward as they seem at first sight.

The basic conception in this literature was to introduce a shift parameter into the individual's utility function, and then ask how the decisions of the consumer alter with changes in the shift parameter.

This parameter may be interpreted as a summary parameter representing the effect of the consumption of others upon the individual in question. It is well known that economic decisions of individuals may be dependent at least in part upon learning from other individuals. This phenomenon is usually called *personal influence* and is quite well documented, especially with respect to the increase in use of innovations (Rogers and Shoemaker, 1971). The model extended with a shift parameter therefore views the process of preference change through the phenomenon of interpersonal interaction. The model represents a comparative static analysis of the diffusion phenomenon from the viewpoint of individual consumer decision making.

Changes in Tastes

The attempts to study social interaction effects made clear the usefulness of being able to study changes in tastes in general. In a series of important papers Ichimura (1951), Tintner (1952), and Basmann (1954, 1955, 1956) developed from the framework of introducing a shift parameter into the utility function one existing theory of consumer behavior with variable preferences. This theory was based upon Ichimura's definition of an "isolated change in wants" as a change in preferences by which the marginal rate of substitution of a given commodity for all other commodities is multiplied by some fixed factor. The marginal rates of substitution among all other commodities are constant. The effect of such an isolated change on the demand for any other commodity is proportional to the cross-substitution effect in the Slutsky equation. Thus, for example, the effect of an isolated change in taste for guns on the demand for butter is inversely proportional to the effect on butter of a compensated change in the price of guns.

The theory was developed in the hope that the analysis would provide a theoretical explanation of the way a consumer, who always maximizes his utility function, would reallocate a fixed total expenditure on purchases when his or her preference structure was not altered. The notion was that in this way preference-altering phenomena, such as advertising and interpersonal interaction, could be incorporated into the traditional economic-analysis model. However, as the earlier chapters have pointed out, these phenomena are quite complex. In the end, this theoretical development led to a proof that if it were assumed that a change in preferences increased the marginal utility of one product, leaving unaffected the marginal utilities of the other products, then this change would increase demand for the product under examination. However, nothing can lead one to suppose that the effects of advertising and/or interpersonal interaction are so simple.

The more general case, studied by Massy (1960) and Haines (1969), allows for shifts to occur in the substitution terms. If this does occur, the theory breaks down internally in the sense that one cannot deduce even the signs of changes in substitution effects. This means, in applied terms, that if one knew the individual consumer's original demand curve for guns, and that a general shift in preferences occurred so that the consumer desired more butter, it would be impossible to state what the consumer's demand for guns would now be.

The result is not too surprising if it is considered carefully. The theory it derives from rests on the assumption of stable tastes. This assumption is then relaxed, being replaced by the added assumption that tastes change and the direction of their change is known. It really would be surprising if a great deal could be said about consumer behavior in such situations with such minimal information requirements.

This result has been, in part, one of the forces that has pushed economic analysis of consumer behavior in different directions recently. Baumol's (1967) abstract product notion, Lancaster's (1966, 1971) recent work, and that of Haines (1969) are all examples of alternative approaches that attempt to introduce more specific assumptions and more information into the analysis of consumer behavior.

The Household

It is customary in economic analysis to consider the family to be the basic decision-making unit. Samuelson (1956) showed that this custom is theoretically valid under certain specified conditions. Thus the problem of aggregation over individuals is solved by showing that the family can be analyzed as a single individual. The important point is that for this to be correct requires a social-welfare function which describes the relation of the utility levels of the individual members to the utility level of the household as a whole. Consistency for the household as a whole only requires that income be redistributed in accordance with one such function. It follows that empirical research on household budgets, such as that of Barten (1965), has paid much attention to the influence of household composition.

An entirely different focus has recently arisen on the part of economists concerned with household behavior, which consists of developments entirely outside the classical framework. A careful review of this literature has been given by Ferber (1962); the interested reader should consult this review as this literature lies outside the bounds of this paper.

Prices in the Utility Function

A long-standing problem in the literature on the economic theory of consumer behavior was solved by Kalman's (1968) article. Kalman extended the theory to cover situations in which prices enter the consumer's utility function. He derived the necessary conditions for consumer equilibrium in this case, a generalized Slutsky equation that differs from the traditional Slutsky equation. He also derived a set of qualitative restrictions on demand functions, of which a subset is identical to the traditional restrictions.

These results bear directly upon the issue of whether consumers judge quality by price. However, they have been up to now ignored in recent literature on price-quality relations. To understand the nature of the test required, a discussion of empirical testing of the theory is needed.

Empirical Testing

Kalman's theory contains as its empirical content the statement that consumers maximize their utility. By differentiating the maximization conditions with respect to prices and income, restrictions on the demand functions necessary for maximization of utility are derived. The empirical issue is whether these restrictions hold. If they do not hold, utility is not maximized. Court (1967) derived a statistical test of restrictions and then applied it to the demand for New Zealand meats. The test is only asymptotic, and there are possible complications arising from the necessity for aggregation, so there is more to be done yet in this area. The asymptotic tests, corrected by degrees of freedom, yield a test statistic that cannot be rejected at a type I error of 5 percent. This would tend to indicate that the null hypothesis of utility maximization cannot be rejected. However, the matter is not really that simple, and much work remains to be done.

One possible extension would be to repeat the above test with the extended constraints provided by Kalman's analysis. Another extension would be to repeat the analysis with other products. At the present time, however, one can conclude that empirical verification of a modest sort for the classic economic model of consumer behavior has been found.

CONCLUDING COMMENTS

This completes a brief overview of classical consumption theory. This is a thoroughly developed branch of economic theory. The bulk of the remaining work to be done must lie outside this framework, that is, by relaxing the assumptions of the theory described. The preceding theory assumes the consumer has definite preferences for varying quantities of a well-defined number of commodities and that the consumer chooses the best combination available to him subject to a given total expenditure. There is no explicit reference to time, and there is, in general, no way of knowing whether the maximizing quantities are positive or negative. The quantities themselves are assumed to be infinitely divisible.

It need hardly be said that these assumptions are for the most part unrealistic. Yet Court's work has shown it is not obvious either that the theory is empirically incorrect. Still, it seems fair to say, as does Houthakker (1961), that the future usefulness of consumption theory will depend largely on the extent to which it will be possible to derive meaningful conclusions from more widely applicable assumptions. In a very real sense the discussion in the earlier chapters of this book must present a review of part of the current effort to create such useful extensions.

APPENDIX: MATHEMATICAL EXPOSITION OF THE ELEMENTARY THEORY

Suppose that there are n commodities labeled $1, 2, \ldots, n$, and a given consumer. A commodity bundle is a vector q whose ith coordinate represents an amount of the ith commodity. Suppose also that prices of each of the n commodities are given. Let p be the price vector. Given a commodity bundle q, it is assumed that the consumer derives a certain satisfaction $U(q)$, where, as before, U is a real-valued twice-differentiable function. Let us, for the moment, assume also that $U(q)$ is a strictly convex function, although the theory can be readily developed considering a more general class of functions. As has already been discussed, for economic-analysis purposes U could be equally well replaced by a monotonic increasing transformation of itself. However, the description of the consumer's behavior should be independent of the particular transformation applied to U. Finally, suppose that the consumer has a given amount of income, M.

Subject to the budgetary constraint

$$p^1 q = M \qquad \text{(superscript 1 denotes transpose)}, \qquad (3)$$

the consumer tries to maximize his satisfaction $U(q)$.

Let

$$L = U(q) - \sigma(p^1q - M). \tag{4}$$

Then, to maximize $U(q)$, one differentiates (4):

$$\frac{\partial L}{q} = \frac{\partial(Uq)}{\partial q}, \tag{5}$$

$$\frac{\partial L}{\partial \sigma} = p^1q - M.$$

The first-order condition for a maxima sets these partial derivatives equal to zero:

$$\frac{\partial L}{\partial q} = \frac{\partial U(q)}{\partial q} - \sigma p = 0, \tag{6}$$

$$\frac{\partial L}{\partial \sigma} = p^1q - M = 0.$$

Notice that the function L is differentiated with respect to the decision variables q and σ, the Lagrangian multiplier. σ is usually interpreted as the marginal utility of income. The solution (6) will exist if the assumptions that underlie the analysis are correct. The solution to (6) gives specific values for the elements q; these are the quantities of the n commodities the consumer will consume.

Now, if M and/or p alter, what are the corresponding changes in q and σ that must occur for (6) to remain satisfied? To see the answer to this, first some notation must be defined. Let

$$S = \frac{\partial^2 U(q)}{\partial q_i \partial q_i}, \qquad i, j = 1, 2, \ldots, n, \tag{7}$$

recalling that for the ith good, by equation (6)

$$\frac{\partial^2}{\partial q_i} = \frac{\partial U(q)}{\partial q_i} - \sigma p_i = 0.$$

For a maximum, $0 > h^1 \, Sh$ for all h such that $p'h = 0$. Notice that $p'h$ is an orthogonality constraint, and does not yet directly enter the calculations. The problem is for given dp and dM, what dq and $d\sigma$ follow so that equation (6) remains in effect? Let us find a linear approximation of dU/dq. To do this, one can use Taylor's series:

$$\frac{dU}{\partial q_i} = \sum_{j=1}^{n} \frac{\partial}{\partial q_j} \frac{\partial U}{\partial q_i} dq_j, \tag{8}$$

evaluated at the previous equilibrium position. The matrix that (8) generates is the Hessian S, and thus

$$S \, dq - d\sigma(p) - \sigma(dp) = 0. \tag{9a}$$

$\delta L / \sigma q$ is thus an implicit function in q, σ, and p. Deriving the tangent-plane equation at the original solution, one can find out how the solution changes with a parameter change. Here we seek how the relations $q_i = f_i \, (p, M)$ alter among each other. To do this, equation (9a), a linear approximation, has been derived. For the second part of (6) the linear approximation is

$$p' \, dq - dM + q' \, dp = 0. \tag{9b}$$

Now there are $n + 1$ equations in $2n + 1$ unknowns. We seek a parametric solution of dq in terms of prices and incomes. Recalling that dp and dM are parameters, and dq and $d\sigma$ are unknowns, one equation may be derived:

$$\begin{pmatrix} S & P \\ p' & 0 \end{pmatrix} \begin{pmatrix} dq \\ -d\sigma \end{pmatrix} = \begin{pmatrix} \sigma \, dp \\ dM - q' \, dp \end{pmatrix}, \tag{10}$$

which may be rewritten (Herstein, 1953) as

$$\begin{pmatrix} \dfrac{1}{\sigma} S & p \\ p' & 0 \end{pmatrix} \begin{pmatrix} dq \\ \dfrac{-d\sigma}{\sigma} \end{pmatrix} = \begin{pmatrix} \sigma \, dp \\ dM - q^1 \, dp \end{pmatrix}. \tag{11}$$

Now, assume symmetry, and then define the subpieces of the inverse matrix:

$$\begin{pmatrix} X & \gamma \\ \gamma^1 & C \end{pmatrix} \begin{pmatrix} \dfrac{1}{\sigma} S & p \\ p^1 & 0 \end{pmatrix} = \begin{pmatrix} I & 0 \\ n \times n & n \times 1 \\ 0 & 1 \\ 1 \times n & 1 \times 1 \end{pmatrix}. \tag{12}$$

Notice that strict convexity means S is negative definite and that the inverse of S exists. This is stronger than the usual assumption; it implies also that the marginal utility of money is concave to the M axis.

Defining the subpieces of the inverse as in (12) can be rephrased as saying that the determinant does not vanish as this is the last bordered determinant. Hence the inverse does exist. Therefore,

$$\begin{pmatrix} dq \\ \dfrac{-d\sigma}{\sigma} \end{pmatrix} = \begin{pmatrix} X & \gamma \\ \gamma' & C \end{pmatrix} \begin{pmatrix} dp \\ dM - q^1 \, dp \end{pmatrix}$$

and it follows that

$$\frac{dq}{(n \times 1)} = (X - \gamma q^1)\, dp + \gamma\, dM. \qquad (13)$$

Therefore, $q = f\,(p,\, M)$. Taking a linear approximation,

$$dq_i = \sum_{j=1}^{n} \frac{\partial f_i}{\partial p_j}\, dP_j + \frac{\partial f_j}{\partial M}\, dM. \qquad (14)$$

Therefore, we identify γ with the slope of the Engel curve. The income effect is where γ is multiplied by dp. The matrix X represents the substitution effects; these describe consumer behavior when satisfaction is assumed to be held constant.

Let us consider two special cases of changes in the parameters.

(a) $\qquad\qquad\qquad dp = p\, d\alpha,\qquad$ where $d\alpha =$ scalar,

and so there is a proportional change in all prices. Substituting into (14), with $dM - O$,

$$dq = (x - \gamma q^1)p\, d\alpha.$$

$Xp = 0$ and $q^1 p = M$ from the matrix definition, and therefore

$$dq = -\gamma M\, d\alpha.$$

The change in total quantities that occurs is proportional to γ because $M d\alpha$ is scalar. Hence such a change in prices acts just like a change in income. Therefore, if

$$dM = M\, d\alpha,\qquad \text{then } dq = -\gamma M\, d\alpha + \gamma\, dM = 0.$$

(b) Another thing customarily examined is compensated price variations. Let

$$dU = \left(\frac{dU}{dq}\right)^1 dq$$

be a linear approximation of the utility function. Then

$$dU = \sigma p^1\, dq.$$

Using (9b), one obtains

$$dU = \sigma(dM - q^1\, dp).$$

Therefore, a compensated price change implies that

$$dM = q^1\, dp,$$
$$dq = (X - \gamma q^1)\, dp + \gamma q^1\, dp = X\, dp.$$

It is also known, from the matrix equations (11) and (12), that

$$\frac{1}{\sigma} XS + \gamma p^1 = I$$

$$\gamma^1 p = 1. \tag{15}$$

From (15) we observe X must be symmetric. Notice that

$$\gamma p^1 = \begin{pmatrix} \gamma_1 \\ \vdots \\ \gamma_n \end{pmatrix} (p_1 \ldots p_n).$$

The Slutsky equation (Slutsky, 1915) comes from the symmetry property:

$$\gamma_i = \frac{\partial q_i}{\partial M}, \quad \text{and} \quad \frac{\partial q_i}{\partial p_j} = X_{ij} - \gamma_i q_j$$

$$= X_{ij} - \frac{\partial q_i}{\partial M} q_j.$$

Since $X_{ij} = X_{ji}$,

$$\frac{\partial q_i}{\partial p_j} + \frac{\partial X_i}{\partial M} q_j = \frac{\partial q_j}{\partial p_i} + \frac{\partial X_j}{\partial M} q_i, \tag{16}$$

which is the Slutsky equation.

Two final comments relate to possible extensions of this model. First, if the constraining relation is nonlinear, the nonlinear relation can be rephrased as an eigenvalue problem. Further discussion of this may be found in Samuelson (1947). Similarly, if there are several constraining relations, the theory can be readily extended to take these into account.

REFERENCES

Bailey, M. J., "The Marshallian Demand Curve," *Journal of Political Economy,* 62 (1954), 255-66.

Barten, A. P., "Family Composition, Prices and Expenditure Patterns," *Colston Papers,* 16 (1965), 277-92.

Basmann, R. L., "A Note on an Invariant Property of Shifts in Demand," *Metroeconomica,* 2 (1954), 27-32.

Basmann, R. L., "Application of Several Econometric Techniques to a Theory of Demand with Variable Tastes." Unpublished Ph.D. thesis, Iowa State College, 1955.

Basmann, R. L., "A Theory of Demand with Consumer's Preferences Variable," *Econometrica,* 24 (1956), 47-58.

Baumol, W. J., "Calculation of Optimal Product and Retailer Characteristics: The Abstract Product Approach," *Journal of Political Economy,* 75 (1967), 674-85.

Boulding, K., "The Concept of Economic Surplus," *American Economic Review,* 35 (1945), 851-69.

Cournot, A., *Researches into the Mathematical Principles of the Theory of Wealth,* 1838. Reprinted by Augusus M. Kelley, 1960.

Court, R. H., "Utility Maximization and the Demand For New Zealand Meats," *Econometrica,* 35 (1967), 424-46.

Duesenberry, J. S., *Income, Saving and the Theory of Consumer Behavior.* Cambridge, Mass.: Harvard University Press, 1949.

Ferber, P., "Research on Household Behavior," *American Economic Review,* LII (1962), 19-63.

Friedman, M., *Lectures in Price Theory.* Chicago: Aldine-Atherton, Inc., 1966.

Haines, G. H., Jr., *Consumer Behavior: Learning Models of Purchasing.* New York: The Free Press, 1969.

Herstein, I. N., "Some Mathematical Methods and Techniques in Economics," *Quarterly of Applied Mathematics,* 11 (1953), 249-62.

Hicks, J. R., *Value and Capital.* New York: Oxford University Press, 1939.

Hicks, J. R., *A Revision of Demand Theory.* New York: Oxford University Press, 1956.

Houthakker, H. S., "The Present State of Consumption Theory," *Econometrica,* 29 (1961), 704-40.

Ichimura, S., "A Critical Note on the Definition of Related Goods," *Review of Economic Studies,* 18 (1951), 179-83.

Kalman, P. F., "Theory of Consumer Behavior When Prices Enter the Utility Function," *Econometrica,* 36 (1968), 497-510.

Koo, A. Y. C., "An Empirical Test of Revealed Preference Theory," *Econometrica,* 31 (1963), 646-64.

Lancaster, K. J., "A New Approach to Consumer Theory," *Journal of Political Economy,* 74 (1966), 132-57.

Lancaster, K. J., *Consumer Demand: A New Approach.* New York: Columbia University Press, 1971.

Leftwich, R. H., *The Price System and Research Allocation.* New York: Holt, Rinehart and Winston, Inc., 1956.

Marshall, A., *Principles of Economics* (8th ed.). New York: The Macmillan Company, 1948.

Massy, W. F., *Innovation and Market Penetration.* Unpublished Ph.D. dissertation, Massachusetts Institute of Technology, 1960.

Pearce, I. F., "Total Demand Curves and General Equilibrium," *Review of Economic Studies,* 20 (1953), 216-27.

Pigou, A. C., "A Method of Determining Numerical Values of Elasticities of Demand," *Economic Journal,* 20 (1910), 636-40.

Prais, S. J., and H. S. Houthakker, *The Analysis of Family Budgets.* New York: Cambridge University Press, 1955.

Rogers, E. M., and F. F. Shoemaker, *Communication of Innovations: A Cross Cultural Approach.* New York: The Free Press, 1971.

Samuelson, P. A., "A Note on the Pure Theory of Consumer's Behavior," *Economica,* 5 (1938), 61-71, 353-54.

Samuelson, P. A., *Foundations of Economic Analysis.* Cambridge, Mass.: Harvard University Press, 1947.

Samuelson, P. A., "Social Indifference Curves," *Quarterly Journal of Economics,* 70 (1956), 1-22.

Slutsky, E., "Sulla Teoria del Bilancio del Consomatore," *Giornale degli Economisti,* 51 (1915), 1-26.

Stigler, G. J., *Theory of Price.* New York: The Macmillan Company, 1954.

Tintner, G., "Complementarity and Shifts in Demand," *Metroeconomica,* 1 (1952), 1-4.

Usher, Dan, "The Derivation of Demand Curves from Indifference Curves," *Oxford Economic Papers,* 17 (1965), 24-46.

Uzawa, H., "Preference and Rational Choice in the Theory of Consumption," in *Proceedings of a Symposium on Mathematical Methods in the Social Sciences.* Stanford, Calif.: Stanford University Press, 1960.

Walhas, L., *Elements d'economie politique pure.* Lausanne, 1884.

Wicksell, K., *Lectures on Political Economy.* New York: Macmillan, 1934.

Wold, H., with L. Jureen, *Demand Analysis.* New York: John Wiley & Sons, Inc., 1953.

Wu, Shih-Yen, and J. A. Pontney, *An Introduction to Modern Demand Theory.* New York: Random House, Inc., 1967.

Focused
Theoretical Areas

8

Theories of
Attitude Structure and Change

George S. Day
Stanford University

INTRODUCTION

NATURE OF ATTITUDES

How Do Attitudes Work? Attitude Structure: Cognitive-Affec-tive-Conative Analysis. Attitude Structure: Models Based on Cognitive Consistency Theory. Attitude Specificity. Stability of Attitude Structures. Criteria for Evaluating Models of Atti-tude Structure. Preference and Perceptual Mapping Models. Re-lationship of Attitudes and Behavior.

ATTITUDE-CHANGE THEORIES

Information-Processing Approach. Role of Learning Theory. Process Models of Behavior. Cognitive-Consistency Theories. Social Judgment Theory. Functional Theories.

SUMMARY

REFERENCES

The study of attitudes is well entrenched in marketing theory and practice. The acceptance by theorists is evident in the pivotal role that the concept of attitude plays in the major descriptive models of consumer behavior (Engel, Kollat, and Blackwell, 1968; Howard and Sheth, 1969; Nicosia, 1966). Practitioners have tended to take a more limited view of attitude as a readily observable construct that they can use to understand their market, and perhaps to evaluate the effect of a persuasive communication. In reality, these practitioners are inveterate theorists, constantly invoking experiential theories of attitude change to predict changes in purchasing or usage behavior as a consequence of alternative strategies for changing attitudes. For example, consider the following problems: (1) A farm equipment manufacturer in a developing country wants prospective distributors to adopt a new scheme for financing inventories. First he has to change their presently negative attitudes; but how? (2) The makers of low pollution emittant and low-lead gasolines wish to associate pollution abatement with their product in a positive manner. What appeals should they use? (3) Birth control pill manufacturers need to predict the long-run responses of users of the pill to negative information from high-credibility sources, such as a Senate subcommittee. (4) Consumers have a strong aversion to "reprocessed" forms of materials such as textiles and plastics. Can these attitudes be changed before we run out of raw materials? In these and literally thousands of other situations each year in the public and private sector predictions and decisions are made on the basis of implicit or explicit theories of the conditions that lead to attitude change.

The basic premise of this chapter is that there are explicit theories of attitude change which can illuminate the problems of the decision maker. This light will often seem dim and diffuse, for most social psychologists who study attitude change are less interested in changing attitudes than in studying basic psychological processes (for interesting exceptions see Zimbardo, 1969). We shall start with a definition of attitude and the relevant measures, so it will be clear what is being formed and changed. Since we are talking about consumer behavior, the emphasis will be on attitudes in choice situations where competing alternatives must be considered. This leads us naturally to the ageless question of the relationship of attitudes and behavior. The middle of the paper will describe and evaluate a number of complementary (although sometimes competing) theories of attitude change. Because of space constraints, little attention will be given to the many provocative minitheories, such as those dealing with fear appeals, source credibility, order effects in persuasive presentations, and the relationship of personality and persuasibility. We conclude by using the theories to compare the strategies of confirming existing attitudes, changing existing attitudes, or forming new attitudes.

NATURE OF ATTITUDES[1]

Fifty years[2] of active theoretical development centering on the concept of attitude have contributed more confusion than consensus as to the meaning of attitude. Consequently, it is still mandatory that a chapter such as this begin with a careful statement of terms. Indeed, there is still room for papers that are entirely about definitions (Rokeach, 1967). We shall distinguish between the formal theories of *how attitudes work,* and the pragmatic, measurement-oriented definitions of *what they are.* The emphasis on measurement is important, for we are dealing with an underlying construct that can be only imperfectly observed. It is easy to make subtle theoretical distinctions that overtax both the measures and the respondents.

How Do Attitudes Work?

A commonsense answer is that attitudes structure the way the consumer perceives his environment, and guide the ways in which he responds to it (Lunn, 1970). A more precise definition, that effectively touches most of the interesting

[1] Much of the material in this section comes from Day (1972).

[2] An early, influential work was that of Thomas and Znaniecki (1918), which explicitly equated social psychology with the study of attitudes. For a history of attitude theory from that date, see Ostrom (1968).

theoretical issues, was proposed by Allport (1935) and is still widely accepted. An attitude is (1) a mental and neural state of readiness to respond, (2) organized (3) through experience (4) exerting a directive and/or dynamic influence on behavior. Following McGuire (1969), we shall describe the current thinking related to each of the four definite characteristics.

Mental and Neural State of Readiness to Respond. An attitude is viewed as a mediating (or intervening) construct that has two links with observable reality. One link is with the *antecedent* conditions that lead into it; these might be the stimulus of an advertisement, a move into a new house, and so forth. The second link is with the *consequents* that follow from the attitude, including search and purchasing behavior. There is nothing in this definition that says we can directly observe the mediating construct, so researchers who adopt this definition generally feel anxious about the ability of their instruments to accurately infer the presence of an attitude. Because of the ultimately unobservable nature of the mediating construct, some theorists (DeFleur and Westie, 1963) view an attitude as a collection of consistent responses to a stimulus (and not as a readiness to respond). This is roughly equivalent to saying that attitudes are what attitude scales measure. This is not a very useful theoretical statement and presents problems whenever inferences must be drawn about the relationship of verbal and overt (i.e., buying) behavior.

The mental and neural distinction suggests that measures can be either verbal reports of introspection (of which we shall say more later) or physiological measures of change in the person's autonomic activation level when he sees the object of the attitude. Early enthusiasm for such physiological indices as galvanic skin response (Cook and Selltiz, 1964) and pupil dilation (Hess, 1965) seems to have waned recently as evidence accumulates that these indices can say little about the direction of favorableness of the attitude.

Organized. In the next section, on the structure of attitudes, we shall discuss the extent to which a single attitude is made up of separate components.

Through Experience. There is widespread agreement with this contention, although little longitudinal research has been done (some is reviewed by Smith, 1968), and a person can rarely explain how any of his attitudes were acquired. Among the various processes by which attitudes are thought to be formed are

1. Integrating a number of similar experiences; whether direct experience through usage, observation of the outcomes of others' explorations, information about performance, and so forth. Campbell (1963) argues that attitudes based on these means of acquiring information through experience are psychologically equivalent; that is, they all work the same way, although the different means may vary considerably in their efficiency.

2. Differentiating from general to specific situations. Most narrow, highly focused attitudes are partly derived from broad attitudes already held. This

is the basis of consistency theory, which would, for example, predict that attitudes toward women drivers will be consistent with the basic underlying attitude toward the general competency of women. Attitudes are also important components of personality (Smith, 1968) because they help to establish identity. As such, some specific attitudes will be accepted because they are more compatible with a person's personality than others. Adorno et al. (1950) used this approach to view the formation of prejudicial attitudes as a means of bolstering self-esteem. Regrettably, personality traits have been ineffective indicators of either buyer behavior, including choice of automobile brands (Evans, 1959) or commercial banks versus savings and loan associations (Claycamp, 1965), or buyer attitudes such as toward private brands (Myers, 1967).

3. Identification. Attitudes are often initially formed by imitating the attitudes of admired individuals. An effective individual in this sense is probably also an effective source in a persuasive communication. If this is so, the three components of source valence, credibility, attractiveness, and power, are useful predictors of the degree of identification (these concepts are most fully developed by Kelman, 1961). *Credibility* is the extent to which a source is perceived as knowing the right answer and being willing to communicate it. *Attractiveness* is determined by the receiver's similarity to, familiarity with, or liking of the source. Similarity of economic backgrounds, physical characteristics, and political and other attitudes are important determinants of a successful relationship between a salesman and a customer (Evans, 1963). The last component, *power*, depends on the ability of the source to apply positive and negative sanctions to the recipient and stay around to observe whether a desired attitude or behavior is achieved.

As we shall see later, the above processes by which attitudes are formed by experience are similar to the ways attitudes are changed:

Exerting a Directive and/or Dynamic Influence on Behavior. There is wide agreement that attitudes have at least a directive or preferential influence; they determine the choice of one among a set of alternatives. According to McGuire (1969), it appears that an attitude imposes this preferential influence by determining the *perception* of the various alternatives, rather than by determining which possible *response* will dominate the others. This distinction may not appear too meaningful in abstract, but it is at the heart of the differences between response-oriented (learning) and perceptual theories of attitude change, as we shall see shortly.

There is less agreement among psychologists as to whether attitudes also have a dynamic influence. This would mean that they affect the absolute level of energy as well as determine the channel of expression. There seems to be no easy answer to this matter, although it is relevant to many issues, including whether the increased favorableness toward some products as objects of consumption will influence the overall need to consume.

Summary. So far we have established that an attitude is a readiness to respond in a preferential manner. In a marketing context this usually means the consumer's preference for, and readiness to buy, a brand or product, rather than the available alternatives (Maloney, 1966, p. 3). But these attitudes are not simple likes or dislikes. They are the complex outcome of many separate judgments about the various attributes of the object, such as styling, convenience, economic value, and so forth. Much of the diagnostic value of attitudes comes from the information about these attributes. In the next section we shall look closely at one approach to dividing attitudes into component parts.

Attitude Structure: Cognitive-Affective-Conative Analysis

The notion that the intervening state between stimulus and behavior is richer than affect (or liking) is widely supported, and for good reason. First, by having three components to explain and interrelate we have a richer and more flexible construct. This has been a great boon to theorists, especially the cognitive-consistency group. Second, there is impressive empirical support from the measurement of meaning tradition (Osgood, Suci, and Tannenbaum, 1957) for the validity of this view. Finally, as McGuire (1969) notes, there have historically been three existential stances man can take with respect to the human condition: knowing, feeling, and acting. We shall review each in turn.

The cognitive or perceptual component represents a person's information about an object. Each piece of information can be broadly classified as either beliefs *in* the existence of the object or evaluative beliefs *about* the object (Fishbein and Raven, 1962). The former category of beliefs includes familiar awareness measures, such as aided and unaided recall of brand names and advertising copy claims. We could also include awareness of services offered; in the case of a retailer does the consumer know that the store delivers, provides credit, makes free alterations, and so forth?

Evaluative beliefs are more interesting, for they provide information about the judgments the consumer makes. In marketing these are usually comparative judgments of one brand or product versus the alternatives. These may be (1) *attribute judgments:* which one is bigger? which one tastes better? which one is more durable? and so forth,[3] or (2) *similarity judgments,* which ask the individual whether he perceives the objects as being similar or different; that is, are Pinto and Mustang more alike than Mustang and Lincoln? Similarity judgments are highly generalized, and respondents are not usually given any basis for the comparison of objects.

The affective or feeling component deals with the person's overall feelings of like or dislike for a situation, object, person, policy, idea, and so forth. It is

---

[3]We assume that the reader is familiar with the semantic-differential and Likert rating, which are usually employed to measure these judgments. If not, see Green and Tull (1970) and Upshaw (1968).

usually measured on a unidimensional scale; this was the rationale for the classical scaling procedures (Guttman, 1950). Most theorists regard affect as the core of the attitude concept and derived from the more specific cognitive components. However, there is some controversy over the nature of the cognitive-affective relationship, hinging largely on the distinction between affect (like-dislike) and evaluation (the object is good-bad, disagreeable-agreeable, harmful-beneficial, and so forth).

One group, with a wide following in marketing, treats affect and evaluation as synonymous. The overall attitude is measured by a scale (or scales) involving general evaluative criteria (such as good-bad; see Osgood, Suci, and Tannenbaum, 1957). Usually these scales will incorporate an explicit comparative judgment, where scale positions read none better—one of the best—a lot better—a little better—about average—below average. These scales recognize competitive reality and consequently are more sensitive to brand and product differences (Abrams, 1969). The major implication of the affective-evaluative congruity notion is that overall attitude judgments are entirely based on the various evaluative beliefs. We shall examine several models of attitude structure based on cognitive consistency theory that make use of this notion.

A competing view holds that the affective component is only partially determined by the evaluative-belief components. For example, Bem (1970, p. 15) offers the following "nonsyllogism":

> Cigarettes taste terrible, cause cancer, make me cough, and offend others (evaluative beliefs). I dislike terrible tastes, cancer, coughing, and offending others. But I still like cigarettes.

There are probably other evaluative beliefs about cigarettes appearing in other syllogisms that help account for this result—if we could find them! Bem argues, even beyond this, that "emotional, behavioral and social influences can also play important roles, and cognitive 'reasoning' of the type represented in the syllogism may be absent altogether." Scaling theorists, in and out of marketing, have reached a similar conclusion. Greenberg (1968) contrasts attribute judgments, which reflect *information* about products (and on which there may be substantial agreement), and preference judgments, which reflect information about both the products and the people's ideal points. The former judgment is which is sweeter? or bigger? The latter asks, which sweetness do you prefer? which is the better size? In many instances one prefers that which is highly evaluated, but evaluation and affect are not necessarily synonymous.

The conative or intentions component refers to the person's gross behavioral expectations regarding the object; is he "very, somewhat, or not at all likely" to buy a refrigerator, a foreign car if he buys any kind of car, or vacation on the Galapagos Islands? Usually intentions are limited to a finite time period that depends on the prospective buyer's repurchase cycle or planning horizon. There is a widespread feeling within marketing that intentions differ from attitudes (as measures of affect) by "combining a consumer's regard for the item with an assessment of its purchase probability" (Wells, 1961, p. 82). A more appropriate position is that intentions are correlated or congruent with attitudes under certain conditions (Fishbein, 1966). The trick is, of course, to be able to specify the conditions. Current evidence in marketing (Day, 1970a) is that there is a high degree of congruency of attitudes and intentions (1) among *buyers* of the product class—obviously a nonbuyer has no buying intention regardless of his attitude, (2) when the alternatives are reasonably close substitutes, as when auto market boundaries are defined by a class of cars (compacts, intermediate station wagons or Grand Prix touring cars), but not by all cars, and (3) when the market is in equilibrium with respect to the number of brands. It appears that attitudes are less sensitive in the short run than intentions to the perturbation of demand created by a new entry into an established market (Day, 1970b).

Attitude Structure:
Models Based on Cognitive Consistency Theory

Those advocates of a consistency theory approach define attitude toward an object as a composite of the perceived instrumentality of that object as a means of attaining certain goals, weighted by the relative importance or saliency of those goals. If, instead of "goals," one reads "values and beliefs" in the sentence above, it is clear that attitude is a weighted function of all the evaluative beliefs associated with that object. Various weights and functional forms have been proposed for this model.

Saliency Weights.   Saliency has been defined as "the strength of the belief about the object," that is, the probability that the object is related to the concept, attribute, or other object (Fishbein, 1967). Thus a salient attribute is one that is actually used to evaluate the attitude object. Such attributes can be identified by elicitation from the person of judgments using true-false, probable-improbable, or likely-unlikely scales (Sampson and Harris, 1970).

Importance or Desirability Weights.   Marketing researchers tend to assume saliency has been achieved by considering only attributes that have been elicited from consumers. Their hypothesis is that some of these salient attributes will be more *important* than others in discriminating between brands or more *desirable* or essential for the product to have. In other words, it is possible to have salient but unimportant attributes, as in one study where it was possible to elicit between 40 attributes (for women's hosiery) and 130 attributes (for general merchandise stores) (Achenbaum, 1966). Although many of these attributes may be intercorrelated, the evidence from studies of statistical vs. clinical prediction suggest that the average person cannot take all possible factors into account. Thus important or desirability judgments are often used to prune a lengthy list of salient attributes. However, there are several problems associated with this type of attitude judgment.

First, individuals differ in the relative importance they attach to each salient attribute. In fact, segments can be described according to systematic between-group differences in the configuration of attributes, or product benefits sought (i.e., regarded as important). Haley (1968) argues that "benefit" segmentation is the most fundamental system of segmentation, because it deals with causal rather than descriptive (demographic and geographic) factors.

Second, an attribute that is rated as important may not be *determinant*, because it does not differentiate one brand or product from another (Myers and Alpert, 1968; Foote, 1961). This occurs when the attribute is taken for granted by consumers, which is frequently the case with basic performance functions or values such as safety.

Third, it is implicitly assumed that the respondent *knows* why he buys or prefers one product to another. In fact, many consumers do not understand their reasons and "are making choices in terms of quickly reconstructed general impressions" (Maloney, 1966, p. 13). These consumers may still give answers to detailed judgment questions because they are unwilling to appear thoughtless or irrational.

Fourth, Greenberg (1969) argues that even when the consumer knows his reasons he cannot be depended upon to "truthfully" indicate the salient dimensions. Instead, "there is a strong tendency for people to give socially acceptable or function-oriented responses in an attempt to appear highly rational.[4] [Thus] the toothpaste purchaser says she is looking primarily for decay prevention, whitening and brightening, not flavor."

Finally, as Semon (1969) notes, attribute labels have different *meanings* at various stages in the purchase-decision process. The price of a refrigerator is first a factor in deciding whether a brand should even be considered; then there is the issue of the value of additional features, and the final question is which retailer will give a better price on the desired model. The relative importance of price versus other product attributes may change markedly from one stage to another.

Weighting Models. *Averaging* or cognitive balancing theorists (Anderson, 1965; Osgood, Suci, and Tannenbaum, 1957) predict that overall attitude is a function of the mean of the weighted evaluative belief scores. *Additive* theorists postulate that attitude is given by the algebraic sum of the belief scores (Fishbein and Hunter, 1964). The burden of evidence seems to be slightly in favor of the additive model, mainly because set size is important. Thus when an individual is attributed with more traits with the same valence as those with which he was previously attributed, the overall evaluation does increase (for a comparative study see Anderson and Fishbein, 1965).

---

[4]This is an interesting observation in view of the prevailing opinion within the consumer movement that manufacturers are too responsive to nonmaterial and nonfunctional benefits (such as status, taste, texture) that consumers say they want in products. For an expression of this view, see Turner (1970).

The usual form of the additive model as adapted to marketing problems is:

$$A_b = \sum_{j=1}^{n} W_j P_{bj}$$

where:

A_b = a consumer's attitude toward an object such as a brand

W_j = the importance weight attached to the jth attribute of the set of objects

P_{bj} = the extent to which a consumer believes the brand possesses the jth product attribute

n = the number of salient attributes.

The additive model has received considerable attention from British marketing researchers. Their results have been mixed, with Sampson and Harris (1970) reporting r^2's between A_b and $\Sigma\ W_j P_j$ in the range of 0.05 and 0.31 for topics such as ordering by mail. Chapman (1970), however, reported frequent correlations of 0.6 (r^2 = .36) and above, and attributed the poor results of Sampson and Harris to using nonsalient belief items, phrasing the belief items incorrectly, or using insensitive measuring instruments. Unfortunately, Chapman did not discuss his techniques, particularly how he measures saliency. Sheth and Talarzyk (1972) also tested the additive model with even poorer results: the r^2's across 30 different brands were uniformly low, with only 3 exceeding 0.11. In fact, eliminating the importance variable from the additive model resulted in an improvement in the correlations. The "suppressing" effect of importance may have been an artifact of the particular measure used or may reflect substantial consensus on importance judgments among respondents. To the extent that these problems narrow the variance of the importance scores, the correlations will be reduced.

Improving Consistency Theory Models. The indecisive performance of the simple additive or averaging models has prompted a number of suggestions for improvement. First, measures of importance or attribute evaluation invariably require absolute judgments rather than comparative judgments, which are more appropriate for choice situations. Scales (such as the semantic differential) that require an absolute judgment lead to badly skewed distributions and a lack of variance, and they tend to confound level of importance and strength of evaluation. A more appropriate measure is the constant-sum scale, which requires the respondent to distribute some portion of a fixed set of weighting or evaluation "points" to each alternative attribute or object.

Second, the interrelated arguments that evaluative judgments and affect are not necessarily synonymous, and that choices of brands (or other objects) depend on how well they satisfy the qualities desired by the consumer, have led some researchers to incorporate information about the ideal object into their models. This approach was used by Lehmann (1971) to predict television show preference with the following model:

$$A_s = \sum_{j=1}^{n} W_j \, |P_{sj} - I_j|^k$$

where:

A_s = overall preference for television show s measured as the distance to the ideal point

W_j = importance weight attached to show j

P_{sj} = the show's belief score on attribute j (in this study the predetermined attributes were action, suspense, humor, personal involvement, quality of production and topical or educational value)

I_j = ideal position on attribute j

n = number of attributes

k = integer defining the distance measure.

This model was tested in a disaggregated form in which the weighted attribute discrepancies were introduced in a regression as separate elements, rather than summed into a single score. This procedure retains all the information and avoids possible cancelling effects; for this reason or because of the use of ideal point information, the R^2's averaged .49 over the 20 shows studied. One surprising result was that an arbitrary ideal show located at the extreme end of each attribute scale worked better than a question designed to identify the ideal show. This result seems contrary to the nature of television viewing, where the ideal may depend on context, mood, and other situational variables, and ignores possible contradictions between attributes such as suspense and humor. There is also a basic question as to whether respondents can meaningfully conceptualize their ideal program.

Despite the measurement and conceptual problems associated with the ideal point concept, an increasing number of models are incorporating this feature. Einhorn and Gonedes (1971) recently tested a theoretically attractive model in which attitude decreases at an exponentially declining rate as the discrepancy increases between the object's position and the ideal. The rate of decrease of attitude, associated with a given attribute discrepancy, also depends on the importance of that attribute.

Third, perhaps the most crucial question is whether the additive (and primarily linear) models reviewed here can accurately capture the complexities of choice behavior. For example, no consideration is given to possible interactions between attributes. Yet there is evidence from clinical judgment studies (Sawyer, 1966) that subjects will utilize interactions when the attitude objects are simple but will revert to "main effect" additive models to cope with more complex situations.

The additive models may not be appropriate when a sequential decision process initially narrows the range of alternatives to a "consideration" class satisfying some minimum standards. In this situation, one unacceptable attribute judgment, such as too high a price, would lead to outright rejection and make the rest of the attributes irrelevant. Once a brand or object is within the consideration class the information on all the attributes would be processed in an additive model in order to make the final choice. In some situations, all the objects in the consideration class are chosen, accounting for multibrand usage in convenience food categories, for example. For this reason, Montgomery (1971) found that this type of gate-keeping or *minimum evaluation* model was sufficient to accurately describe the behavior of a supermarket buying committee. New grocery products were authorized for stock if they were rated as average or better in quality, company reputation, sales presentation, and category volume, and were less than 110% of the cost of the closest substitute. Failure to meet any one of these requirements meant the product was not considered further.

Other possible attribute combination models are more difficult to relate to buying behavior, but deserve exploration. There is evidence that a *maximum evaluation* model applies when special conditions are sought. Here the object is judged on the best attribute, regardless of the others (just as a football player on a specialty team is chosen for his kicking or run-back skills). More speculative is the *lexicographic* model, in which the attributes are first ordered in importance and a decision is made on the basis of the most important attribute before proceeding to the next ordered variable. However, subsequent attributes are only considered when there is equivalence among attributes on the preceding ordered attribute.

The variety of combination models offers many possibilities to researchers, especially since different segments might use different models, or individuals might use portions of several models.

Attitude Specificity

The discussion to this point has presumed that the attitudes are toward specific attributes, objects, or issues. These attitudes do not exist independently, but are linked in complex ways to a hierarchy of increasingly fundamental beliefs and attitudes.

Most fundamental are *values* which are attitudes toward end-states of existence (such as equality and self-fulfillment) or modes of conduct (like honesty and friendship) (Rokeach, 1968a). Values are ends, and one controversial view holds that marketing deals with the means of achieving these ends (Bauer and Greyser, 1967). Motivation researchers have traditionally taken the point of view that this is the most productive level in the hierarchy to obtain insights into buying and consumption behavior. Unfortunately these deep-seated values and attitudes are often unconsciously held, and thus are difficult to unambiguously identify with the usual projective and related clinical techniques.

Their remoteness from the specific attitudes and behaviors of interest to marketers has further reduced their usefulness for diagnostic purposes.

The relative failure of motivation research has focused research attention on middle-level beliefs and attitudes about buying, consumption patterns, and product requirements. The goal of this research (frequently called *psychographics*) is to find descriptive classifications, such as bargain seeking, economic orientation, experimentalism, style consciousness, home centeredness, and traditionalism (Lunn, 1966; Heller 1968), that provide more insights and more clearly delineated market segments than those based on demographic variables. Although this area of research holds a great deal of promise for marketing, the realization of the promise will hinge on (a) improvements in the measuring instruments that will reduce the present cumbersome batteries of questions, (b) more effective utilization of data-reduction techniques, and (c) a more precise specification of the scope of the research. This latter step will help reduce the confusion resulting from including explorations at the very general level of life cycle and life style with the very specific and product-related search for benefit segments within the same classification.

Stability of Attitude Structures

Information about the *polarity* of an attitude (the degree of liking or disliking) or the number of salient beliefs does not give a complete picture of the quality of attitude structure and, in particular, the strength of the motives relevant to behavior toward that object. Two additional structural properties, which are often considered, are *involvement* with the attitude object and *confidence* in the various evaluative and affective judgments. These two structural properties jointly determine the stability of the observed attitudes and, in turn, the ease with which an attitude can be changed (Sherif, Sherif, and Nebergall, 1965).

Involvement. This describes the general level of interest in the attitude object, or the centrality of the object to the person's ego (Day, 1970a). The specific roles of involvement (or the equivalent concept of commitment) have been well summarized by Engel and Light (1968):

1. Attitudes are easier to change when the existing mass of stored information is small. In this connection, involvement is related to the concept of cognitive complexity, "the richness of the ideational content or the number of ideas the person has about the subject" (Scott, 1968).

2. Attitudes having centrality are the most resistant to change. "This is a function of the extent to which the object is intimately related to the self-concept, important values or motives" (Engel and Light, 1968)

3. "Attitudes that are highly interconnected with others resist change" (Engel and Light, 1968).

Studies of involvement in the marketing context have focused on differences between products. For instance, Bogart (1967) has found that involvement depends on the frequency of decision making and the amount of economic risk incurred in the purchase. In general, the greater the involvement, the more active and purposeful the search for information. However, interest or involvement in the product will not necessarily lead to strong interest in the differences between brands. This is likely to be the case when the buyer is interested in the benefits that can be delivered by the product, but does not perceive that there are significant differences between brands.

Confidence. The degree of confidence depends on the amount of uncertainty about the correctness of the brand judgment or ambiguity as to the meaning of the attitude object. Both these factors depend, in turn, on the amount of information the buyer has about the brand. A lack of information may result when (1) the buyer seeks information but cannot obtain a satisfactory amount with a reasonable search cost; low confidence or high anxiety (Lipstein, 1968) might result when brands make widely different claims about quality or performance, and the consumer has limited ability from usage with which to judge the validity of the claims; (2) the buyer may not be interested in obtaining information. This suggests that there is likely to be a significant relationship between involvement and confidence. In the section on the predictive value of attitudes we shall examine this relationship more closely, and show how much information about attitude structure can be gained from knowledge of their joint effects.

Criteria for Evaluating Models of Attitude Structure

The complexities and perversities of the human mind can easily overwhelm simple representations of attitude structures. Recent developments in multidimensional preference and perceptual mapping have been hailed as more promising ways of capturing this complexity. The test will be whether they are able to satisfy most of the criteria utilized in the evaluation of the cognitive consistency model:

1. Maintain a distinction between cognitive judgments (both perceptual and evaluative) and affective or preferential judgments through consideration of the buyers' ideal point.
2. Recognize that a respondent may be unable or unwilling to identify the attributes which are the primary determinants of their choice decisions.
3. Incorporate individual differences in the saliency of attributes.
4. Allow for a variety of decision rules for combining attribute judgments into an overall preferential judgment.

5. Utilize comparative judgments of the attitude object relative to other objects in the choice situation.

6. Represent differences in the stability of the attitude structure.

7. Account for changes in the role of determinant attributes as the context of the choice situation changes.

8. Finally, it would be desirable if the data received from the respondent could be treated as nonmetric, in view of the uncertainty regarding the ability of respondents to make interval-scale comparative judgments.

These criteria have been expressed in very specific and operational terms. We should not lose sight of the broader requirements for construct and predictive *validity* and *managerial usefulness.* The latter requirement is also a warning against excessive complexity that would interfere with interpretation. These are the ends, while our operational criteria are merely the means to those ends.

Preference and Perceptual Mapping Models

We shall see from a brief description of preference and perceptual mapping, and a representative application, that many of the specific criteria can be better satisfied. However, it is important to keep in mind that these models were given birth through advances in computer algorithms and are presently rather atheoretical. In this section we are making explicit some of the implicit behavioral notions held by the psychometricians who have done most of the development work. To allay the impression that these models are a panacea, we conclude by describing some new problems posed by these techniques.

Perceptual Spaces. The raw material for such a space is a matrix containing the similarity judgments between each pair of objects that compose an attitude domain. Recent research has seen attitude domains defined by automobile and computer models (Green and Carmone, 1969), common stocks (Green and Maheswari, 1969), nations (Wish, Deutsch, and Rogers, 1969), snacks, cold remedies, and overseas trips (Stefflre, 1969), and brands of laundry detergents (Greenberg, 1969).[5] A perceptual space (or more accurately a multidimensional scaling representation) is obtained when the objects are positioned in a geometric space that at best has no more than two or three dimensions. Experience shows that perceptual structures of more than three dimensions cannot be comprehended by the analyst (Shepard, 1969) and are unrealistic in view of the limited number of dimensions consumers typically use to evaluate products (Klahr, 1968).

Scaling programs (e.g., Kruskal, 1968; Young and Torgerson, 1967)

---

[5]For a comprehensive review of applications, algorithms, and future possibilities see Green and Carmone (1970a).

generally strive to construct spaces in which the rank order of distances in the reduced space maximally corresponds with the rankings of the pairwise similarity judgments. The distances in the space are metric, whereas the input similarities data are nonmetric.

In terms of the criteria established earlier, perceptual spaces require only *cognitive* judgments, generally use pairwise direct comparisons of similarity, and do not require any *prior specification* of the attributes along which the judge is to compare the objects. The most important attributes should be revealed by the structure obtained from the analysis. This usually occurs in simulation experiments using known geometric patterns of colors, for example. However, in practice, the dimensions of the reduced space are frequently difficult to identify. To avoid this problem, it is usually advisable to include standard attribute judgment questions in mapping studies that can be correlated with derived dimensions, to aid identification. In some situations identification can be facilitated by incorporating reference stimuli whose characteristics are well-known or asking respondents to specify the criteria they used in arriving at a specific preference or perceptual judgment.

Similarity measures may also be derived by comparing the profiles of each pair of objects on their objective characteristics, or judgments of each object regarding suitable use occasions or location on pre-specified attributes. However, if the data on attribute judgments can be assumed to be interval scaled, more direct procedures for constructing perceptual spaces do a better job of conserving information. One approach uses multiple discriminant analysis to find dimensions that are weighted combinations of attributes that maximize the F-ratio of between-object to within-object variance (Johnson, 1971). As with the models described earlier, there are problems in ensuring that all salient attributes are included. Also, there is presently no means to introduce explicit information on the relative importance of each attribute.

Joint Spaces That Include Preferences.   A logical next step is to include *people* locations, based on preference judgments, within the space that represents the locations of the various stimulus *objects.* Such joint spaces usually summarize the preference information in the form of an ideal point, which Greenberg (1969, p. 12) defines as "that combination of stimulus attributes which would be maximally desirable to the individual (who is) represented by the point . . . It is usually assumed that an individual's preferences for products will be inversely proportional to their distances from his ideal point." The data in a joint space are highly complementary: the ideal point gives evidence of the most preferred brand, for example, while the relative positions of the objects in the space describe the patterns of substitution and competition once a brand has been chosen. Stefflre (1968, 1969) has reported correlations as high as 0.85 (with median of 0.70) between similarity judgments and brand-switching data from consumer panels. This is persuasive evidence of the *validity* of the perceptual mapping procedure. No comparable evidence exists to evaluate the validity of the joint-space model.

Actual applications of ideal-point models have been very limited because of the newness of the techniques. In theory, however, joint-space models can be used to identify new product opportunities in the regions containing clusters of ideal points and few if any products. The problems of using joint spaces for these and other diagnostic purposes are critically evaluated in terms of a recent application (Homayounfar, 1970) to an industrial marketing problem.[6]

An Application of Joint-Space Analysis. In the course of a study of the economic feasibility of converting gold-mine tailings into calcium silicate brick it was necessary to estimate the potential California demand for such bricks compared to common clay, adobe, and artificial sandstone bricks. Only the single-family home market was considered since this absorbed most of the demand in the state. The analysis was based on a joint-space model of 12 bricks, which covered the range of available prices, colors, textures, and materials. The sample consisted of 44 architects, designers, and builders who had varying influence on the decision to use bricks. In general, larger firms were over-represented. The respondents were shown the actual bricks, suitably labeled with name, price, and manufacturer, rather than descriptions, before they made their judgments.

Identifying the ideal point. Preference data can be mapped into a common perceptual space by an explicit ideal point, or some representation of the rank order of preferences for the various objects. The explicit ideal point is the simplest to implement, since it involves inserting an additional *ideal* object into the perceptual space itself. That is, the respondent is asked to imagine his ideal brand, service, or company, and to judge the similarity of the ideal to the actual objects. This approach has not been widely used, despite its ease of implementation. It is not known whether respondents can directly conceptualize so abstract a notion as an ideal. Another problem is whether subjects retain the same frame of reference when they move from a similarities to a preference context (Green and Carmone, 1970a). Most researchers (in particular, Carroll and Chang, 1967) have preferred to infer the location of each individual's ideal point from the rank order of preferences. The rank order of the psychological distances of each object from the ideal point in the perceptual space is the same as the individual's rank order of preferences.

The average explicit and implicit ideal points are illustrated and compared in Figure 1. They are embedded in a two-dimensional perceptual space that fits the data very closely. The labels were easy to infer in this case; for example, the horizontal price axis represented the fact that bricks C and Q cost between $60

---

[6]I am indebted to F. N. Homayounfar for the opportunity to describe his work in detail.

FIGURE 1.   **Joint-Space Ideal-Point Representation**

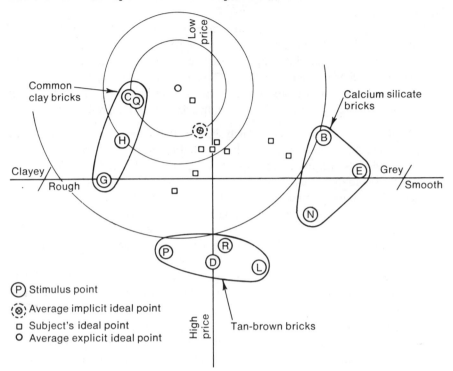

and $90 per unit, whereas bricks P, D, L, and R all cost between $110 and $140. Both ideal points agree on the ideal quadrant, although they are not congruent. However, when circles centered on each ideal point were used to reclaim the rank order of preferences of bricks, the two resulting rank orders were almost perfectly correlated. Thus both ideal points gave essentially the same results. It should be noted that these results apply only in specific situations where bricks are being considered as decoration in medium-priced homes. Different use contexts will yield different results.

Issue of homogeneity of perceptions. Joint-space models frequently assume a common perceptual structure, with heterogeneity only in preferences. The durability of the homogeneity of perception assumption is apparently a consequence of studies showing high correlations of average similarity scores between different *groups* (Stefflre, 1968). However, there is much recent evidence (surveyed by Green and Carmone, 1970b) that there are individual differences in perceptions within these groups. Sometimes there is a single predominant point of view, coupled with unsystematic individual variation; in other cases (e.g., Neidell, 1968) several obviously different groups have been found. Identification of groups or segments with systematic differences in perceptions can be achieved either by (a) analyzing the matrix of between-subject similarities (the Tucker-Messick, 1963, points-of-view analysis), or (b) assuming that all subjects in the group share a common space but differ in the weights or salience they assign to the dimensions of this space (Carroll and Chang, 1969). These techniques deserve exploration for they can be coupled with preference judgments to reveal the decision rules used to combine attribute judgments into an overall preference—and in theory satisfy one of our earlier criteria. Furthermore, to the extent that these techniques isolate segments that can be identified from other respondent characteristics, they will facilitate segmentation strategies.

Unresolved Limitations of Joint-Space Models. The joint-space models based on multidimensional scaling appear to be an improvement on the more structured models based on consistency theory because they demand less complex and fragmented data from respondents. However, as shown in the discussion of the problems of interpreting the dimensions of the space, one is not getting something for nothing. These models introduce a whole new set of problems, many of which revolve around the necessity for at least eight objects in the stimulus set before meaningful solutions can be obtained (Klahr, 1968). With fewer than eight objects there is a high probability of obtaining spuriously good fits in a few dimensions even when the data are randomly generated.

Consider a perceptual space representation of 8 objects that requires a subject to make at least 28 separate similarity judgments. The first assumption is that he is aware of all 8 objects (brands, companies, or services), and indeed that there are at least 8 definable objects in the domain. The problem of the respondent who is virtually ignorant of most of the objects in the attitude domain has not been satisfactorily resolved. In the course of plodding through 28 or more judgments one is at the mercy of respondents: (1) who are un-involved in the topic of the study, and thus are careless or confused; (2) who may have only the vaguest knowledge of some of the objects being judged; (3) who change their frame of reference and decision rules during the course of the judging; and (4) who may confound similarities and preference judgments. Such data are highly unstable, which means that the preference judgments will certainly lack predictive validity. There will also be intransitivities in both the preference and perceptual judgments that reduce the quality of the fit between the data and the model. Methods are needed which incorporate information on the respondent's confidence in his ability to make discriminating similarity judgments. This might require separate treatment of respondents with low confidence or limited knowledge about the entire stimulus set, and exclusion of the specific objects about which the respondent lacks adequate knowledge or awareness. This would reduce the variability in the quality of the input judgments. However, the cost of this improvement would be high if the stimulus set became too small for the joint-space algorithms to be used. The resolution of this trade-off will have a large bearing on the usefulness of joint-space models in marketing.

Joint-space models may oversimplify the nature of attitude structures. Stefflre argued from a linguistics perspective that the dimensions of perceptual spaces are not simple bipolar constructs. Instead, these spaces consist of discontinuous labeled regions, in which one end of the space means something different from the other end. This problem is illustrated with the horizontal axis in Figure 1, which subsumes variations in both color and texture, and it is never clear which one dominates. However, this problem appears to be more a matter of interpretation than a basic shortcoming.

Finally, little is known about the effect of major changes in the stimulus set on the relative positions and distances between objects in the space. Green, et al. (1969), have obtained encouraging results regarding configuration invariance. They argue for more work on stimulus domains that appear to form nested sets, such as cola drinks, soft drinks, and all beverages. It is very unlikely in such situations that the same dimensions or configurations will be evoked as the stimulus domain is broadened.

Summary. The quest for models that provide better descriptions and understanding of multifaceted attitude structures has been proceeding along two distinct tracks. One has its roots in consistency theory and requires highly structured judgments about specific attributes. The other, which incorporates preference judgments into a perceptual space, is based on multidimensional scaling techniques, which make fewer demands of respondents. In some senses the research tracks are converging as hybrid methods that borrow strong points from each approach are developed (Johnson, 1971). These efforts need to be encouraged, for neither approach fully satisfies the criteria for evaluating models of attitude structures that were developed in this chapter. The potential for convergence is, of course, limited since the approaches are basically different and competing. Thus there is a great need for the kind of comparative study recently reported by Talarzyk and Moinpour (1970). Validation work, such as that reported by Stefflre (1969), between similarities and brand-switching data is also highly desirable. Basically, we still know relatively little about predictive validity or the sensitivity of these models to changes in attitude. For this reason, the chapter bifurcates at this point, as we revert to the unidimensional measures of attitude that are almost exclusively used to study theories of attitude change and the predictive value of attitudes.

Relationship of Attitude and Behavior

There is probably more controversy over the *predictive* relationship than any other aspect of attitude research and theory. At the risk of oversimplifying the issues we can broadly delineate the positions of believers and skeptics.

Believers draw solace from numerous studies showing sizable differences between the attitudes of users and nonusers, when both measures are obtained during the same survey (Lunn, 1970). The position of the believers has recently been reinforced by findings that aggregate measures of brand attitude are highly correlated with objective measures of market share for single time periods (Maloney, 1966), and predict changes in market share in time series equations (Assael and Day, 1969).

The *skeptics* base their position on various revelations of contrary evidence. One argument is that attitudes do not predict usage, "because they are measuring a relatively simple function of the same underlying variable." Fothergill (1968, p. 889) drew this conclusion from a reanalysis of three-wave panel data reported by Achenbaum (1967) and Dubois (1967). These conclusions appear most pertinent to stationary markets in which purchasing decisions are both repetitive and routine. There may be confounding methodological artifacts since the usage and attitude information came from the same survey, and respondents tend to eliminate inconsistencies in answers to contiguous questions. This raises a question about the nature of the "underlying variable" postulated by Fothergill.

The predictive relationship is also weakened to the extent that attitudes serve the additional role of giving meaning to behavior. This is a prediction of several formal attitude-change theories, and in particular of Krugman's theory (1967) of the effect of low involvement on communication effects. In this theory a brand advertisement may change the "perceptual structure" by a process of incidental learning, such as is characteristic of the learning of nonsense syllables, without a corresponding shift in affect. A "behavioral opportunity" such as in-store shopping may later trigger supportive and consistent attitudes. Thus "if the brand is purchased the new way of seeing it may for the first time be expressed in words."

The bulk of the contrary evidence on the attitude-behavior relationship has come from studies of attitudes toward jobs, members of minority groups, cheating, public housing, and similar highly involving issues. A recent review of 32 such studies concluded "that it is considerably more likely that attitudes will be unrelated or only slightly related to overt behaviors than that attitudes will be closely related to actions" (Wicker, 1969, p. 65). Most researchers do not conclude from such results that attitudes have nothing to do with behavior, but rather that other factors than attitude also contribute to overt behavior. Most of the emphasis has been on situational factors, on the assumption that the more similar the situations in which verbal and overt behavior are obtained, the stronger will be the attitude-behavior relationship. For example, Rokeach (1967) would specify an "attitude-toward-situation" within which the attitude-object is encountered, facilitating or inhibiting the expression of the "attitude-toward-object." If an individual is induced to buy a product because of a coupon deal, this represents a situational change and a changed attitude toward the situation.

Some of the dimensions along which situation influences occur are

1. Extent to which an anonymous interview situation is free of the coercive forces of everyday life, in which the respondent may have to justify his actions or be influenced by group pressures (Hyman, 1949).
2. Differences in roles assumed by respondents when verbal and behavioral responses are elicited (Fendrich, 1967).
3. Availability of alternative behaviors. Insko and Schopler (1967) note that an inconsistent behavior may occur because there is no alternative.
4. Differences in the specificity of the attitude object, or the nature of the context, between the verbal and overt behavioral situations. The former tends to be very general; the latter is usually very specific.
5. Finally, there is a strong likelihood that unforseen circumstances may intervene between the attitude measurement and the actual behavior.

Very little research has been reported on the relative influence of these situational factors; in fact, there has only been one attempt to combine several factors into a systematic formulation. This theory is an extension of Fishbein's means-ends analysis, utilizing Dulany's (1968) propositional control theory. According to Fishbein (1967a, p. 490), "Rather than viewing attitude toward a stimulus object as a major determinant of behavior with respect to that object, the theory identifies three kinds of variables that function as the basic determinants of behavior: (1) attitudes towards the behavior; (2) normative beliefs (both personal and social); and (3) motivation to comply with the norms." The first component reflects the individual's "beliefs about the consequences of performing a particular behavior (in a given situation)," and his evaluation of these consequences.

This theory is of greatest value when social and group norms are important. It is doubtful whether it can be extended to marketing contexts, because there is no explicit consideration of choice decisions or individual differences, and norms of behavior are relatively less important. A theory tailored to brand-choice decisions has been developed by Day (1970a). The components of the model used to test the theory are brand attitudes, A_i, treated as unidimensional measures of affect, and probability of purchasing the brand $P[B]_i$ (conditional on purchase of the product class). These variables are related as follows:

$$P[B]_i = \alpha - \beta A_i + U_i, \qquad i = 1, \ldots, N \text{ brands.}$$

The β or slope parameter varies according to the inhibiting or facilitating effects of the environment, including the attraction of competing brands, preferences of family and friends, changes in advertising and promotion, price changes, out of stocks, and so forth. The error term, U_i, reflects individual differences in response to similar environment influences due primarily to differences in attitude stability and buying style (including impulsiveness, innovativeness, and economy consciousness). In effect, the individual differences interact with the environmental or situational factors to determine the predictive value of brand attitudes. In one test the relationship was weak for a total sample of 220 buyers of a convenience food product. The average slope was flat, and only 24 percent of the variability in purchase probability was accounted for by the attitude measure, as measured by R^2 of 0.24 (this was not improved by introducing intentions and specific attribute judgments into the equation). Thus, overall, the environmental influences dominated the directive influence of attitude. However, when the sample was split into six groups on the basis of attitude stability and the relationship reestimated, the results were startling. The most stable group had a steep slope parameter and an R^2 of 0.54; the least stable group had a flat slope parameter and an R^2 of 0.04. Within the unstable group brand-choice decisions are almost completely determined by the environment at the time of purchase, and interbrand differences are virtually meaningless. Clearly, information about attitude stability is crucial to a full understanding of attitude structures.

ATTITUDE-CHANGE THEORIES

The focus of the remainder of this chapter is toward the questions of *how* people's attitudes are changed, *who* changes, and *why* they change.

These questions pervade all programs that have the goal of modifying attitudes in a desired direction. Characteristically, the relevant theories have emphasized the *why* question, because the theorists are mainly interested in psychological processes and because it is logically prior. In this review we shall give extra emphasis to the more operational question of specifying the circumstances under which attitude change is most likely to occur.

The study of attitude change was launched into a mature stage of synthesis and reconciliation in the mid 1960s.[7] Out of this work has come a consensus that there are four basic theoretical approaches which are more complementary than competitive. The information-processing approach is the most general and the most widely adopted in marketing. It differs from the consistency, social-judgment, and functional approaches by assuming a rational decision maker who tries to process and deal with new information as logically as possible. The emphasis is almost exclusively on the stimulus characteristics of the communication situation (i.e., order of arguments, source credibility, and characteristics of the audience). The other approaches "tend to view the person as

---

[7]The outcome of this process of synthesis was a series of comprehensive and valuable reviews of research published between 1967 and 1969 (Insko, 1967; Smith, 1968; Abelson, et al., 1969; Kiesler, Collins, and Miller, 1969; and McGuire, 1969). These have been extensively employed in the preparation of this chapter. The guiding and clarifying role of these reviews at each point in the discussion may not always be appropriately acknowledged, but was substantial indeed.

more contentious or self-centered, depicting his behavior in a persuasive communication situation as attempting actively to resist it or to utilize it for needs of his own that have very little to do with the context of the communication" (McGuire, 1971).

Information-Processing Approach

This approach explains the response to a persuasive communication in terms of

1. The receiver's initial position.
2. A series of behavior steps through which he must proceed (see Figure 2).
3. His motivation for accepting the proposed position.

FIGURE 2. **Steps in the Response to a Communication**

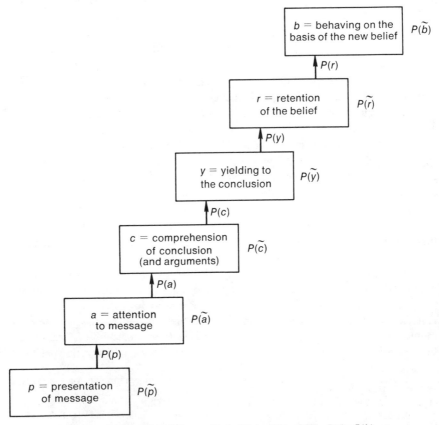

Probability of desired behavior $= P(p) \cdot P(a) \cdot P(c) \cdot P(y) \cdot P(r) \cdot P(b)$

These three elements act together so that a person's probability of proceeding from one step to another depends on both initial position and acceptance motivation.

Before an individual can be persuaded by a communication he must first have the message *presented* to him via informal or formal media; then the message must get and hold his attention. Attention-getting properties, such as novelty, opening rhetoric, and nature of competing stimuli, will not necessarily hold attention. The ability of a message to hold attention depends on whether the receiver can *comprehend* the arguments and conclusions. This is influenced by the complexity and clarity of the message relative to the level of the receivers. Comprehension also depends on "the receiver's intelligence, relevant experience, openmindedness, and 'cognitive tuning set' (readiness to pass the information on, to be entertained, etc.)" (Zimbardo and Ebbesen, 1969, p. 21).

The likelihood of acceptance or *yielding* to the comprehended message is theorized to depend on the extent of incentives. The incentives in the message may be in the form of arguments or reasons why the advocated point of view should be accepted in favor of the old attitude, or the arousal of expectations that have reinforcing value. An important expectation, which is enhanced by a highly credible source, is of being right or wrong. Suspicion of someone's manipulative intent is another expectation that will nullify the prospects of acceptance, because it is seen as a threat to one's freedom to decide for oneself (see Brehm, 1966). Finally, a communication can lead to the expectation of social approval or disapproval. Social approval is seen as rewarding; thus anything in the communication that credibly indicates that acceptance will be socially acceptable will increase acceptability.

If the recipient has taken the fourth step of *yielding* or accepting the message, there is the additional question of whether he will *retain* the new position until he has an opportunity to *behave* accordingly. As a rule the retention of an opinion over time depends on the informational content of the message and the incentives for acceptance.

Each step in the chain is taken with only a certain probability, and its occurrence depends on the probabilities associated with the earlier steps in the chain. The model suggests that the probabilities are multiplicative; so if there were a probability of a 0.5 at each step there would be a less than 0.02 probability that purchase behavior would be influenced by the persuasive message. If this were the true situation, it would go far toward explaining the ineffectiveness of most advertising campaigns. However, this analysis is largely speculative, in absence of knowledge about the various probabilities and uncertainty as to whether a step such as attention is a prerequisite for subsequent yielding. Perhaps, as Krugman suggests, some attitudes are acquired by a process of incidental learning without the aid of explicit attention.

Role of Learning Theory

The information-processing approach, as it has been articulated by Hovland, Janis, and Kelley (1953), is apparently derived from learning and related behavioristic (*S-R*) theories. Thus they follow the Hullian distinctions between skill (*H*) and incentive motivation (*K*) by suggesting that yielding requires (1) learning the new response through practice or mental rehearsal, and (2) the creation of incentives to make the new response. However, Kiesler, Collins, and Miller (1969) suggest that learning theory serves primarily as a linguistic system to guide the empirical research. In fact, the orientation of the Hovland group was strongly toward problems, and not theory.[8]

The essence of empirical work using the information-processing approach is to (1) treat the various steps leading to attitude change as the dependent variable and the components of the communication as independent variables, then (2) predict the relationship of a given independent variable and attitude change (3) in terms of the known or conjectured relationship of that independent variable to learning (McGuire, 1969).

A rich array of independent variables is available for study. A representative list, derived from the Lasswell (1948) paradigm of *who* said *what*, via which *media*, to *whom*, aimed at what kind of *behavior*, is shown in Table 1. Details on recent research relevant to each of these variables can be found in McGuire (1969).

These variables have been most extensively studied by the group associated with Carl Hovland at Yale University in the Attitude Change and the Communication Research Projects. Although the research style of the influential group was very eclectic, there was a tendency to study independent variables where hypotheses derived from learning theory could be employed with some confidence. (For a discussion of some of these possibilities see the chapter on learning theory in this volume.)

The research in this tradition has generally evolved away from this early orientation toward specific contingent theories that deal with a specific independent variable. This has made the broad theoretical utility of this approach suspect (Brown, 1965), although not diminishing the heuristic usefulness. One example of this evolution is the research on fear appeals.

Process Models of Behavior

The information-processing approach shares a number of characteristics with other process models of buying behavior. The most familiar of these related models are the *"hierarchy of communication effects"* (Lavidge and Steiner,

---

[8]There have been more formal attempts to apply behavioristic (including learning) theories more directly to attitude change (Staats, 1967; Weiss, 1962). These efforts have been limited in scope and have stimulated relatively little research.

TABLE 1.   **Five Components of a Persuasive Communication (McGuire, 1971)**

I. *Source Variables*

   A. Credibility (expertise, trustworthiness)

   B. Attractiveness (similarity, familiarity, liking)

   C. Power (control over means and ends, follow-up on compliance)

II. *Message variables*

   A. Type of appeal (style, positive versus negative or fear appeals, reinforcements)

   B. Inclusions and omissions (implicit versus explicit conclusions, refutational appeals, repetition)

   C. Order of presentation (with respect to conclusions, climax, and refutational and supporting arguments)

   D. Discrepancy from receiver's initial position (selective exposure, perceptual distortion)

III. *Channel variables*

   A. Direct experience with object versus a communication about it

   B. Modality (eye versus ear)

   C. Personal versus impersonal media

IV. *Receiver variables*

   A. Active versus passive role

   B. Generality of susceptibility

   C. Demographic variables

   D. Ability factors

   E. Personality factors

V. *Destination variables*

   A. Effects beyond specific issue

   B. Immediate versus delayed impact

   C. Direct impact versus immunization against counterarguments

   D. Verbal attitude change versus behavior change

1961) and the adoption process model borrowed from rural sociology (for a review of the latter see the chapter on diffusion and innovation). From the comparison in Table 2 it can be seen that all models postulate a series of stages beginning with lack of awareness and culminating in some form of behavior.

All these models share a view that consumers follow a rational problem-solving approach and base their decisions on the persuasive information provided. Furthermore, as Robertson (1971) notes, these models also share the same shortcomings: (1) the consumer may make decisions in a "nonrational" manner. That is, he may not secure, process, or carefully evaluate all the available information; "he may make adoption decisions on impulse or to ingratiate himself with other people"; he may be playing a psychosocial game

TABLE 2. Process Models of Behavior

Information-Processing Model	Hierarchy of Communication Effects	Adoption Process Model
Presentation of message		
Attention to message	Awareness	Awareness
Comprehension of conclusion	Knowledge	Interest
Yielding to conclusion	Liking	
	Preference	Evaluation
Retention of the belief		
	Conviction	Trial
Behaving on the basis of the new belief	Purchase	Adoption

(Bauer, 1964) rather than solving a problem; (2) "There is not a specified *sequence* of stages which must occur. Any such model must make allowances for consumers to "skip" stages, and (3) must also provide *feedback* loops, since such a process will not necessarily be linear and unidimensional." The earlier discussion of the attitude-behavior relationship is pertinent here, inasmuch as the strongest criticisms of the hierarchy have focused on the ambiguous empirical support for a one-way causal relationship (Palda, 1966; Haskins, 1964).

Cognitive-Consistency Theories[9]

Consistency theories share the basic assumption that an individual strives to achieve consistency within his cognitive system and between his cognitive system and overt behavior. These theories usually make the additional assumption that inconsistency produces a *psychological tension,* which is uncomfortable or disturbing. The resulting tension is the motive force for the efforts to modify or change the cognitive system. The amount of tension can be considerable. Consider the awkward position of a conservationalist when Nader attacks Muskie on his efforts to control pollution; and if he is an avowed anticommunist, how did he feel when Nixon visited Communist China? Appreciable tension is also a consequence of everyday problems, such as when a favorite brand is out of stock and only a previously disdained private brand is available,

---

[9]For a more detailed evaluation and application of these theories, see the chapter in this volume, "Cognitive Consistency and Novelty Seeking."

or the performance of a new appliance or toy does not match the high expectations formed by advertising. The specific mode of resolution of these latter inconsistencies is obviously of concern to the manufacturer and retailers involved. A number of similar theories deal with the sources and resolution of inconsistency. We shall emphasize here the common features of these theories and only briefly describe three of the most significant theories. In conclusion we shall discuss how a behaviorist would explain the same phenomena.

Origins of Inconsistency. McGuire (1966) has noted the paradox of positing "a strong tendency towards consistency and yet always managing to find sufficient inconsistency within the system to allow predictions to be made and tested." He has listed a number of ways in which inconsistency can be created within an individual. Much inconsistency is a result of a person simultaneously occupying two or more conflicting social roles. Careful shopping, with considerable time devoted to the collection of information and comparison of alternatives, may complement one's social role as a well-informed individual and careful decision maker. However, these time demands are increasingly conflicting with the need to spend more time on the job, at leisure, and attending to the social needs of the family. Linder (1970) predicts that the process of allocating decreasing personal time will lead to increasing tension in society. Second, McGuire suggests that a person's environment may change, leaving him "encumbered with a conceptual baggage that no longer accords with reality." Third, a person may be pressured into behaving in ways inconsistent with his attitudes. These *forced-compliance* situations have been extensively studied by dissonance theorists. Fourth, a person may be persuaded to change his attitude via new information, interpersonal interactions, or direct experience, only to find that the cognitions associated with this attitude are inconsistent with other cognitions. Fifth, there are human logical shortcomings that may produce logical fallacies, although inconsistency theory is usually based on "psycho-logic" rather than formal logic (Abelson and Rosenberg, 1958). Finally, there is the possibility that the individual seeks inconsistency, either because of a desire for change or novelty (Fiske and Maddi, 1961; Fowler, 1965), or to mask more deep-seated conflicts that cannot be resolved through action (Pepitone, 1966).

The various theories based on the consistency principle generally emphasize different sources of inconsistency. The most notable differences occur between the balance and dissonance theories described next.

Balance Theories. This theory is credited with initiating the reorientation of social psychology toward consistency theory. The seminal paper by Heider (1946) dealt with the seemingly narrow problem of identifying states of balance and imbalance in the cognitive structure of a perceiver, *P*, who has specified relationships with another person, *O*, and with some object, *X*. Two types of relations exist between each pair in the triad: liking or disliking and a unit relation involved in perceiving persons or objects as belonging together or being associated. The relations in the *P-O-X* triad are balanced when all three relations are positive, or when two are negative and one is positive. Otherwise, imbalance occurs. The key implication is that balanced states are stable and resist change; unbalanced states should change so that balance is attained.

At present this theory is most interesting because of its limitations, which have been the starting points for many of the newer theories.[10] First, the liking relation is ambiguous and lacks specificity. As Zajonc (1960) notes, "no matter how much . . . (a child) . . . likes Popeye you can't make him like spinach, although according to balance theory he should." Second, there is no provision for degrees of balance or imbalance, or intensity of the relations. Third, the model cannot cope with complex situations involving multiple relations within a triad, or the inclusions of other persons and objects. Last, the theory contains no basis for predicting the route by which balance will be attained. This is a problem of great practical importance that confronts all consistency theories.

Abelson and Rosenberg's *cognitive balancing model* (1958; Rosenberg and Abelson, 1960) is an extensive modification of the original balance model with greater utility. They posit a single affective relationship between psychological objects, which may be positive, negative, or null. They also recognize that there are a number of alternative ways of restoring balance, and hypothesize that the probability of using a particular method is inversely proportional to the amount of psychological effort required by that method. The least effortful method is operationally defined as requiring the fewest sign changes before balance is restored. Thus a persuasive communication will be accepted only to the extent that it helps resolve cognitive imbalances with a minimum of effort.

The early empirical work on this model lead Abelson and Rosenberg to hypothesize a preference for solutions that maximize hedonic gain which operates independent of the striving for consistency. That is, an individual will try to maximize potential gain and minimize potential loss. A balanced outcome is only achieved when the tendencies toward hedonic gain and consistency operate in the same direction. Although this model is certainly an improvement on the basic balance model, the empirical support is decidedly unimpressive. Not the least of the problems is how to measure the notion of hedonic gain. This question is of considerable interest in economic-choice situations, which usually involve functional risk (will it work?) and psychosocial risk (will it enhance one's well-being or self-concept?). Indeed there may be some advantages to incorporating the well-developed concept of perceived risk (Bauer, 1960; Cox, 1967) into the general balance theory.

Osgood's *congruity model* (Osgood, Suci, and Tannenbaum, 1957; Osgood, 1960; Tannenbaum, 1967) is a variant of balance theory that deals with the problem of communication effects. In this special case there is a person (*P*) who

---

[10]These limitations are discussed in greater detail in Kiesler, Collins, and Miller (1969), pp. 166-68.

receives pro or con information from a source (S) about an object, issue, or other person (O) about which P has an attitude. The effect of the communication depends upon how much P likes or dislikes S and O, as well as the nature of the message. The attitudes are measured with reasonable precision by the semantic differential scale. The model yields quite precise predictions (after heuristic corrections for directional shift and the likelihood of incredulity). One prediction is that when incongruity exists (i.e., P likes both S and O, whereupon S says something derogatory about O), P's attitudes toward both O and S will change. The change will be in the direction of increased congruity. Furthermore, the amount of attitude change will be in inverse proportion to the initial intensity of the attitude. That is, Osgood asserts that extreme attitudes will exhibit the least amount of change. The theory has performed quite well within its limited domain, which should give pause to anyone considering giving or accepting an endorsement of a product. If the product is disliked, the endorsing celebrity will suffer a loss in esteem, and of course the opposite holds in that a celebrity with an unsavory reputation will "contaminate" the product.

Cognitive-Dissonance Theory. This theory has had a particular fascination for both marketers and social psychologists. The latter have been motivated by both theoretical fertility and controversy to produce over 300 studies in 10 years (Zimbardo and Ebbesen, 1969). Marketers are attracted by the unique insights the theory offers into postdecision behavior.

According to the theory (Festinger, 1957; Brehm and Cohen, 1962; Aronson, 1968) any two cognitive elements—beliefs or bits of knowledge—may be consonant, dissonant, or irrelevant to one another. As in the discussion of attitude structure, it is frequently difficult to specify which beliefs or attributes are relevant. But assuming they are, dissonance or inconsistency occurs when one cognitive element follows psychologically from the contrary of the other. Thus a buyer finds himself in a dissonant state by agreeing to a series of large credit payments on a new appliance despite an overextended personal budget that leaves no room for such expenditures. We emphasize that dissonance is a postdecision state of mind; when the buyer is in the process of making a choice decision he is in a state of conflict.

The amount of the dissonance created depends on the situation. In purchase decision-making situations, for example, dissonance is likely to be high when

1. The decision is important in terms of the financial outlays or the psychological significance to the individual. Furthermore, by making the commitment in public, the decision maker has lost his flexibility in adjusting to new dissonant cognitions; for example, *Consumer Reports* issues a critical evaluation of the newly purchased brand (Brehm and Cohen, 1962).
2. A number of desirable alternatives are available (Brehm and Cohen, 1959; Anderson, Taylor, and Holloway, 1966).

3. The alternatives are dissimilar; there is little "cognitive overlap" or sharing of features. Thus a choice between a car and boat creates more dissonance than a choice between a Volkswagen and a Ford Pinto.
4. The choice decision is the result of free will with little or no outside applied pressure. If pressure is applied, the individual complies without letting his cognitions be challenged (Festinger and Carlsmith, 1959).

Of course, dissonance is aroused in many other circumstances than those following a decision. The theory has also been applied to the topics of selective avoidance of information, defensive projection, and discrepancy between the positions of the source and the receiver.

Modes of Resolving Inconsistency. It is worthwhile to pay special attention to this issue because of the valuable insights into the sometimes paradoxical feedback effects of choice behavior on attitudes. At least seven different modes have been identified. However, it should be understood that these are more likely to be complementary rather than mutually exclusive. First, one can attempt to *revoke the decision*. Retail stores with liberal return policies encourage this mode. They assume that the other modes may reduce future patronage. A second basic mode involves a *change in the attitude* toward the product or situation, by increasing cognitive overlap (searching for or misperceiving aspects of functional equivalence) or seeking out consonant elements. The latter mode does not remove the inconsistency, but submerges it among a larger body of beliefs that are consistent with the conflicting one (Abelson, 1959). A related attitude-change mode for postdecision dissonance is to increase the attractiveness of the chosen alternative and/or decrease the attractiveness of the unchosen alternative. The net effect is that attitude change *follows* and gives meaning to a prior behavior change. This is the basis for the frequent suggestion that a forced change in behavior is one of the most effective ways of changing behavior.

A third basic mode of resolution is *downrating* the importance of the area in which the inconsistency occurs. An implicit decision is made against investing emotional resources on the grounds that the issue is petty. This perhaps accounts for consumers' apparent tolerance of petty abuses or unconfirmed expectations about low-cost consumer products. However, we should note that there are considerable individual differences in tolerance of inconsistency, which seem to depend on both personality and situational variables (Glass, 1967). Thus another mode is to simply *accept* the inconsistency, which is relatively easy for some people.

McGuire (1966, p. 11) suggests that inconsistency may also be reduced by changing the perception of the object, rather than the attitude toward the object. Thus a college student will increase the status of "politician" after being told his peers ranked the profession much higher than he by reinterpreting "politicians" as statesmen rather than wardheelers (Asch, 1948).

One specific implication of the various modes of inconsistency resolution, and of cognitive-dissonance theory in particular, is that a buyer experiencing dissonance will *seek* information that confirms his choice and *avoid* discrepant information. The former postulate has been consistently supported in field and experimental studies, whereas evidence for a selective-avoidance tendency is equivocal at best (Freedman and Sears, 1965). In response dissonance theorists have posited an interaction effect, wherein the selective-avoidance tendency is accentuated as the person's confidence in his choice weakens (Canon, 1964). So long as the buyer is confident of his decision or of his original belief, he perceives himself to be capable of utilizing relevant information from any source. He may also have a "set" to notice any information that is pertinent regardless of source. This would explain why those who have recently purchased new cars tend to notice advertisements about all brands. In general, the selective-avoidance hypothesis has been a poor predictor, because people have many needs for information that outweigh the adverse consequences of discrepancy. Thus there is a novelty value to hearing something new, and if the choice has to be publicly defended, there is a definite advantage to knowing the arguments against the choice. Finally, Maloney (1962) argues that the typical immediate reaction to a persuasive mass communication is dissonant or curious nonbelief, rather than categorical disbelief. Thus "a consumer's criticism that an advertisement is 'hard to believe' may simply betray her heightened curiosity about the advertisement's claims ... This dissonant non-belief is itself conducive to attitude change because it typically stimulates a search for additional message-relevant experience or information." To the extent that curiosity rather than disbelief is aroused, selective avoidance will not be evident.

Behavioristic Alternative to Dissonance Theory. Considerable controversy has recently been stirred by Bem's (1967, 1968) development of *self-perception theory* as an alternative interpretation of cognitive-dissonance phenomena. He argues that "an individual's attitudes and the attitudes that an outside observer would attribute to him may be functionally similar in that both are partial 'inferences' from the same evidence: the public behaviors and accompanying cues upon which the socializing community has relied in training him to make such self-descriptive statements in the first place" (1968, pp. 201-2). That is, an individual infers his own attitude by observing his own overt behavior.

This seemingly simple concept has been employed to explain consistency phenomena as learning of the appropriate responses to inconsistency, with the motivational basis for the learning residing in the needs satisfied by the rewards originally used to reinforce the responses. This is quite different from dissonance theory, which postulates that inconsistency has a distinct motivating property, and the rewards come from the reduction of the inconsistency. These two competing formulations usually make the same predictions, which has made it difficult to devise comparative tests. One approach is to put people in the role of observers of a subject in a dissonance experiment and ask them to infer the subject's attitude. The justification is that observers will take account of the behavior of the subject as well as the circumstances surrounding the behavior. As an illustration (Bem, 1970), we attribute the enthusiasm of a celebrity for a product he is endorsing to cash rather than conviction. Bem observes that in the face of such skepticism, advertisers have moved to "candid camera" interviews with "homey folks." The advertisers hope, because the endorsers are not paid, that viewers will infer that they really must prefer the product when they say so. In a similar fashion, observers have been able to successfully estimate the attitudes of subjects in a number of well-known forced-compliance and free-choice dissonance experiments. However, Jones, et al. (1968) have argued that Bem's observers ignore the fact that the act is dissonant and use the reasons that subjects comply with discrepant requests to infer the attitude. This promises to be a fertile controversy of special interest to marketers interested in post-decision behavior.

Social Judgment Theory

Although this theory has long been overshadowed by cognitive dissonance theory, it may in the long run prove more relevant to the marketing context. Its virtues are explicit hypotheses about the joint effects of discrepant communications and differential ego involvement on the extent of changes in comparative judgments of objects or concepts. The theory itself is based on empirical generalizations about judgment processes that are largely derived from the psychophysical literature (see Sherif and Hovland, 1961, and Sherif, Sherif, and Nebergall, 1965, for a summary of these generalizations).

Attitude Organization. In this theory an individual's attitude toward an object or a social issue is treated as a range of acceptable positions (an acceptance region) rather than a single point. Operationally, this region is usually defined by the Thurstone-type statements that are considered acceptable or tolerable, including the single most acceptable statement. The rest of the attitude dimension is divided into a rejection region and a noncommitment region. The latter category is generally the residue after the acceptable and objectionable positions have been determined. For people with moderate positions on an issue there may be two rejection regions—one at each extreme. This accommodates those who cannot tolerate the far left or the far right wing of the political spectrum, for example.

This view of attitude structure resembles the familiar brand attitude scale, which identifies a *consideration class,* a *buying class,* and a *nonconsideration class* of brands (Smith, 1965; Day, 1970a). The consideration or acceptable class is also akin to the theoretical notion of an *evoked set* (Howard and Sheth, 1969) of brands that are within the buyer's reach and are adequate for his needs. Jacoby and Olson (1970) have also used this notion for their model of brand loyalty, because it incorporates the widely observed phenomena of multibrand or dual-brand loyalty. The key point is that the regions or classes are derived from a judgment process that combines an evaluation and *comparison* of all the objects in the stimulus set (Sherif and Sherif, 1967). As we noted before, an effective attitude scale for choice situations requires explicit comparative judgments.

Contrast and Assimilation. Attitude change in response to a persuasive communication is seen as a two-step process. First, the recipient makes a judgment that positions the message on a subjective scale of favorability with respect to the issue or object. The amount of attitude change then depends on the judged discrepancy between the message and the recipient's own position. When the message falls within the recipient's acceptance or neutral region, it will be seen as more similar to the recipient's position than it actually is (*assimilation* effect). A persuasive message will be maximally effective when the position advocated by the message falls close to the boundary of the rejection region. However, if the message advocates a position that is *within* the rejection region, a *contrast* effect will occur. Then the judged discrepancy is likely to be exaggerated, the communication will be unfavorably evaluated, and the recipient will resist persuasion. Worse, a very discrepant message is likely to reinforce the recipient's initial attitude and perhaps produce a boomerang effect.

This simple judgment-displacement process is highly subject to distortion from the following sources:[11]

1. Ambiguity as to the position of the communication (Sherif and Sherif, 1967).

2. Limited past experience.

3. Situational factors that do not require the respondent to discriminate between attitude positions.

4. Deep involvement in one's position on an issue (Kiesler, Collins, and Miller, 1969, p. 246).

Most of the research however has focused on the effect of involvement.

Role of Involvement. This variable was earlier described as a major determinant of the ease with which an attitude may be changed. In terms of social-judgment theory the attitude of a person highly involved in his position will be hard to change, because that position is strongly anchored within the total belief system. The consequence of increasing involvement is that discrepant communications pose greater threats to one's position and are more likely to fall in the rejection

---

[11]There is also a complicating methodological problem: displacement effects occur with the method of equal-appearing intervals, but not with the method of paired comparisons. Ager and Dawes (1965) raise the possibility that an individual's attitude may only affect his use of category boundaries.

region. This is the reason that involvement is defined operationally by the size of the rejection region. In the early formulations of the theory it was hypothesized that increasing involvement would lead to a shrinking of the range of acceptable positions. However, the empirical findings have been ambiguous on this matter (Sherif, Sherif, and Nebergall, 1965), and it is now assumed that the acceptance region remains constant for a given stimulus situation.

The involvement level also influences the degree of perceptual distortion of a discrepant message, as well as whether an assimilation or contrast effect will occur. For a communication within the acceptance region the involved respondent will assimilate the message much more than an uninvolved respondent, and consequently will perceive the message as advocating less change. Analogously, when the message is in the rejection region, the involved respondent will displace it farther from his own position and find it less credible and less persuasive. Thus, regardless of the level of discrepancy, an involved subject will always be more difficult to persuade. These predictions are summarized in Figure 3.

FIGURE 3. **Effect of Involvement on (1) Distortions in Judged Position of a Communication, and (2) Changes in Lattitude of Rejection**

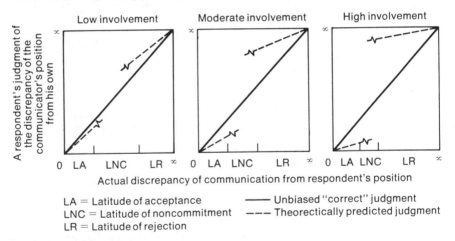

LA = Latitude of acceptance   —— Unbiased "correct" judgment
LNC = Latitude of noncommitment   ––– Theoretically predicted judgment
LR = Latitude of rejection

Source: Kiesler, Collins, and Miller, 1969, p. 247.

Figure 3 takes the position that the magnitude of assimilation (contrast) varies as a function of discrepancy, rather than being a constant amount. This implies that the greatest assimilation and the greatest contrast occur when the message falls within the noncommitment region. However, the theory is vague on this matter, and it is also possible that the contrast *increases* within the latitude of rejection (Kiesler, Collins, and Miller, 1969, p. 260), rather than decreases as shown in Figure 3.

Once again we see how essential it is to determine the degree of involvement of potential buyers in the product class or in differences between brands. When involvement is low, which could be the case when a number of brands are considered acceptable substitutes, or brand differences are of little interest, buyers are very prone to switch and are open to persuasion. In these circumstances an advertiser can develop a message that is quite different from the average position of the target segment and expect it to be effective in changing attitudes. Conversely, if buyers are strongly committed to a particular brand, we would expect that competitive communications would fall into the rejection region and be discredited or screened out. Perhaps only messages from the preferred brand would be attended to, which would reinforce the present position.

Despite the apparent relevance of social-judgment theory, there are virtually no reported applications to marketing problems. One could speculate that this is due to lack of familiarity with the theory or, failing that, to uncertainty over the appropriate methodology for measuring involvement and communication discrepancy within consumer segments. There is also the problem that social judgment appears to dispute the better known cognitive-dissonance theory. This is particularly so with predictions about involvement and discrepancy as determinants of attitude change.

Involvement-Discrepancy Controversy. When two theories make competing predictions about important phenomena, the ensuing attempts at explanation or reconciliation can effectively illuminate the strengths and weaknesses of the theories. In this controversy we find that social-judgment theory predicts a curvilinear relationship between discrepancy and attitude change, and decreased persuasion as involvement with a stand becomes more intense. In opposition is cognitive-dissonance theory. Greater discrepancy is predicted to generate more dissonance, which would lead to increasing attitude change, if this were the mode of reducing dissonance. Dissonance theory also predicts that the more important the initial attitude becomes, the more dissonance is created by a discrepant communication and the greater the pressure to reduce dissonance (and change the initial attitude). As might be expected, considerable ingenuity has been expended to specify alternative modes of resolution of the discomfort occasioned by these seemingly incompatible predictions.

The preferred resolution of the *discrepancy* controversy has been to introduce the communicator credibility characteristics into the analysis. This is a recognition that there are other differences between a communicator and his audience than simply a discrepancy in the positions advocated. First, it has been noted that a nonmonotonic relationship is more likely to occur with low-credibility sources (Aronson, Turner, and Carlsmith, 1963) when the issues are unambiguous (Insko, Murashima, and Saiyadain, 1966). This is a convenient finding for dissonance theory, for it suggests that as communicator credibility decreases derogation replaces attitude change as the mode of dissonance reduction when discrepancy is great. This phenomena is largely ignored by social-judgment theory. However, Kiesler, Collins, and Miller (1969, p. 295) suggest that as the communicator becomes more credible the respondent's latitude of acceptance broadens. "This simply implies that the inflection point in the function relating attitude change to discrepancy is shifted to higher levels of discrepancy as positive attributes of the source are increased." With one exception (Freedman, 1964) the relevant research supports these hypotheses about the interactive effect of credibility. To the extent that advertisers are seen as low in credibility, the implication is clearly that discrepant messages will be counterproductive.

The controversy over the role of *involvement* has been confused by difficulties in defining and measuring involvement. Both dissonance and social-judgment theory define involvement in terms of the original position. That is, will mention of the issue itself be sufficient to generate concern and interest? However, most experiments which find that involvement increases attitude change have looked only at involvement in the response (Zimbardo, 1960; Freedman, 1964). This concerns the importance of the results of a new response to the individual. In effect, he is given an incentive to change toward the new position, such as a friend's approval or the opportunity to appear intelligent. Naturally, he will change toward this new position. If only studies dealing with issue involvement are considered, the attitude-change results are generally consistent with social-judgment theory. Once again, inconsistent results do not disconfirm dissonance theory, for attitude change is only one avenue for dissonance reduction. Apparently, as involvement increases attitude change becomes a less preferred mode, and the probability of disparaging the source or distorting the position of the source is increased (Eagly and Manis, 1966).

The answer to what initially seemed to be a serious controversy over the effects of involvement and discrepancy has been seen to lie with the numerous modes of resolution of discrepancy available to a respondent. McGuire's comment (1969, p. 224) is more appropriate here:

> It is useful to conceive of the recipient of a persuasive message as an "honest broker" beseiged by conflicting claims and needs, who is trying for a "least-squares solution" to the various pulls being exerted on him. When confronted with a large discrepancy it seems likely that he will respond with a little attitude change, a little source derogation, a little perceptual distortion, etc., stressing on any given occasion the use of one or another of these modes as his own proclivities and the situational conditions allow.

Functional Theories

The theoretical approaches we have just considered put their stress on the relationship of a person's attitude toward an object and his information about, perception of, and behavior toward that object. Little attention is given to the motivational underpinnings of this attitude. The crux of the various functional approaches to attitudes (Smith, Bruner, and White, 1958; Katz and Stotland, 1959; Katz, 1960)[12] is that the same attitude may be held by different persons for different reasons. To the extent that the motivational bases for attitudes differ, the techniques for changing the attitudes must also differ. We shall study these techniques in terms of the various functions presumed to be held by an attitude: the utilitarian (adaptive) function, the knowledge function, the value-expressive (self-realizing) function, and the ego-defensive function.

Utilitarian (Adaptive) Functions. Positive attitudes are developed toward objects or paths that have been instrumental in achieving desirable goals or avoiding undesirable goals. Similarly, negative attitudes are developed toward objects that thwart desirable goals. These are learned responses that depend on one's past reinforcing experiences with the object (Katz, 1960). Hence this function strongly resembles the behavioristic information-processing approach.

Because utilitarian attitudes toward objects are formed through experience, they are posited to be fairly difficult to change through direct verbal appeals. Also, "the area of freedom for changing utilitarian attitudes is of course much greater in dealing with methods of satisfying needs than with the needs themselves. Needs change more slowly than the means for gratifying them, even though one role of the advertiser is to create new needs" (Katz, 1960, p. 178). By a process of exclusion, the most effective means for changing such attitudes are changing the buyer's perception of the ability of the product or brand to satisfy the needs, or emphasizing need and better ways of need satisfaction.

Knowledge Functions. Attitudes also function to help the individual cope with a complex world that cannot be grasped in its entirety. Accordingly, people seek stereotypes and broad frames of reference or categories that will provide "a simplified and practical manual of appropriate behavior toward specific objects" (McGuire, 1969, p. 158).

We saw in the discussion of attitude structure that people use relatively few categories and rules to judge their environment. Once a new object is placed in an existing category, it becomes the focus of the existing repertory of behaviors which are appropriate to that overall category. This spares the individual the time-consuming and sometimes painful effort of deciding how to relate to the new object. New-product marketers are acutely conscious of this fact and generally avoid positioning a new product where it defies easy categorization. A better strategy is to demonstrate that the new product fits into several existing categories at the same time and thus delivers additional benefits. A good example is the success of refrigerators that provide crushed or cubed ice through

[12]We shall not discuss the related approach to the study of the process of attitude change by Kelman (1958) because it shares many characteristics of the functional theories.

an outside spigot. This additional benefit is easy to categorize because buyers have experienced similar devices in other contexts. A more challenging problem is the new product that is so innovative that the existing attitudes are rendered inadequate. In this situation "the individual's need for cognitive structure is such that he will either modify his beliefs to impose structure or accept some new formula presented by others" (Katz, 1960, pp. 190-91). This loose prediction by Katz is all the functional theories tell us about the probable responses to new and changing situations. For more explicit predictions it may be necessary to revert to consistency theories on the grounds that people will attempt to structure all the new information they receive in a consistent fashion.

Expressive (Self-realizing) Functions. Attitudes also function as part of the total belief system to give positive expression to the individual's central values and his self-concept. As such they reflect and confirm his notion of the kind of person he is. But, conversely, the expression of an attitude can also help the individual define his self-concept. This self-realization function appears to be very similar to the dissonance notion that a person adopts attitudes to bolster or justify his behavior—especially in the face of a difficult decision.

According to Katz (1960, p. 189), "people are much less likely to find their values uncongenial than they are to find some of the attitudes inappropriate to their values." Thus one way to change a specific value-expressive attitude is to show that it is inconsistent with a more basic value. Marketers are more likely to take advantage of existing attitudes by portraying their brand as a means of expressing the values and self-concepts of particular market segments. This is particularly true in hard-to-evaluate products such as cosmetics and cigarettes. However, the available research on self-concept as a determinant of brand or product choice has not been particularly successful either because of poor implementation of the strategy, inadequate methodology, or an inapplicable theory. The worth of this approach is still open to question.

Ego-Defensive (Externalization) Function. Some attitudes toward objects or social situations serve primarily to help an individual deal with his inner conflicts and have only the most limited relationship to that object. They may protect him from internal anxieties or from facing up to potential danger through building defense mechanisms or rationalizing the problem. Of greater interest is the tendency noted by Smith, Bruner, and White (1958) for people to see events or objects in terms of their own concerns, "covert strivings," or "preferred adjustive strategies." Thus internal problems, which may be unconscious, may well color or bias a person's perception of a social problem. Thus a person who has suffered from a series of problems with product quality or service is especially sensitive to revelations that others are suffering from the same problems. Furthermore, such a person is likely to propose solutions that resemble a successful strategy for dealing with a personal problem. Because ego-defensive attitudes are often irrelevant to the object and may be unconscious, they are probably impervious to conventional informational approaches. Indeed knowledge of such attitudes may only be useful to marketers insofar as it is possible to avoid communications that elicit them.

Overview. So little research has been devoted to functional theories that their ultimate usefulness cannot be appraised. Although their scope is appealing, it appears that many aspects have been subject to more detailed interpretation within the other theories reviewed in this chapter. The major contribution, and the greatest value for marketing, should come from insights into individual differences. Other theories (such as social-judgment theory) also incorporate individual differences, but predict the main effects of persuasive messages. With functional theories no such prediction can be made without knowing the function the attitude serves for the individual. At present this cannot be determined, for there is virtually no technology for assessing the function of attitudes. Such a development would be very useful for the design and evaluation of marketing communications.

SUMMARY

The research on attitude change we have reviewed is provocative; it speaks directly to the immediate problems of communicators. But at the same time it is difficult to utilize directly for developing promotional strategy. For example, it is characteristic of laboratory experiments to obtain large changes in attitude, whereas the direct attitudinal effects of mass media are sometimes indiscernable in the field. Too few field studies of attitude exist for one to be confident of the generality of the many specific findings from the laboratory that we have reviewed in this chapter. One area where there is increasing agreement (see Hovland, 1959; Klapper, 1960; Bauer, 1964) is that an audience exerts considerable initiative in interpreting and using the incoming persuasive messages for its own purposes. This initiative may be so large outside the laboratory as to suppress the desired effects, unless other environmental conditions are supportive (DeFleur, 1970). It is more probable that the environment of competing brands will have an overall canceling effect.

Another limitation of the existing research is a cavalier disregard of the subtleties of attitude structure (Smith, 1968) or the interaction of mass media and word-of-mouth communications (Katz and Lazarsfeld, 1955). There is growing evidence (summarized in Day, 1971) that marketing communications can better achieve other objectives than attitude change, including

1. Increasing awareness.
2. Forming attitudes.
3. Triggering favorable word of mouth (Arndt, 1967).
4. Changing the perception of product category membership.

5. Changing the saliency of individual product attributes.
6. Denigrating the competition.
7. Reinforcing existing attitudes.

In fact, a recent review of the related voting literature (Weiss, 1969) concluded that "the preponderance of total media effects is contributed by the reinforcement or substantiation of vote decisions brought about by other factors, such as habitual patterns of voting or social and personal influences." What is clearly needed is more research on the effects of persuasive communications on all aspects of attitude structures to tease out these subtle but important effects. This is not an unreasonable hope in view of recent improvements in our understanding of attitude structures.

REFERENCES

Abelson, R. P., "Modes of Resolution of Belief Dilemmas," *Journal of Conflict Resolution,* 3 (1959), 343-52.

Abelson, R. P., E. Aronson, W. J. McGuire, T. N. Newcomb, M. J. Rosenberg, and P. Tannenbaum, eds., *Theories of Cognitive Consistency: A Sourcebook.* Skokie, Ill.: Rand McNally & Company, 1969.

Abelson, R. P., and M. J. Rosenberg, "Symbolic Psycho-Logic: A Model of Attitudinal Cognition," *Behavioral Science,* 3 (1958), 1-13.

Abrams, Jack, "Reducing the Risk of New Product Marketing Strategies," *Journal of Marketing Research,* 6 (May 1969), 216-20.

Achenbaum, A. A., "Knowledge is a Thing Called Measurement," in *Attitude Research on the Rocks,* ed. Lee Adler and Irving Crespi. Chicago: American Marketing Association, 1966.

Achenbaum, A. A., "Relevant Measures of Consumer Attitude." Paper presented to the June 1967 Conference of the American Marketing Association, Toronto, Canada.

Adorno, T. W., Else Frenkel-Brunswick, D. J. Levinson, and R. N. Sanford, *The Authoritarian Personality.* New York: Harper & Row, Inc., 1950.

Ager, J. W. and R. M. Dawes, "The Effects of Judges' Attitudes on Judgments," *Journal of Personality and Social Psychology,* 1 (1965), 533-48.

Allport, G. W., "Attitudes," in *Handbook of Social Psychology,* ed. C. Murchison. Worchester, Mass.: Clark University Press, 1935, 798-884.

Anderson, L. K., J. R. Taylor, and R. J. Holloway, "The Consumer and His Alternatives: An Experimental Approach," *Journal of Marketing Research,* 3 (February 1966), 62-67.

Anderson, L. R., and Martin Fishbein, "Prediction of Attitude from the Number, Strength and Evaluative Aspect of Beliefs about the Attitude Object: A Comparison of Summation and Congruity Theories," *Journal of Personality and Social Psychology,* 3 (1965), 437-43.

Anderson, N. H., "Averaging Versus Adding as a Stimulus-Combination Rule in Impression Formation," *Journal of Experiment Psychology,* 70 (1965), 394-400.

Arndt, Johan, *Word of Mouth Advertising.* New York: Advertising Research Foundation, 1967.

Aronson, Eliot, "Dissonance Theory: Progress and Problems," in *Theories of Cognitive Consistency: A Sourcebook,* ed. R. P. Abelson, E. Aronson, W. J. McGuire, P. M. Newcomb, M. J. Rosenberg, and P. H. Tannenbaum. Skokie, Ill.: Rand McNally & Company, Inc., 1968.

Aronson, Eliot, J. A. Turner, and J. M. Carlsmith, "Communicator Credibility and Communicator Discrepancy as Determinants of Opinion Change," *Journal of Abnormal and Social Psychology,* 67 (1963), 31-37.

Asch, S. E., "The Doctrine of Suggestion, Prestige, and Imitation in Social Psychology," *Psychological Review,* 55 (1948), 250-76.

Assael, Henry, and G. S. Day, "Attitudes and Awareness as Predictors of Market Share," *Journal of Advertising Research,* 8 (December 1969), 3-10.

Bauer, R. A., "Consumer Behavior as Risk-Taking," in *Dynamic Marketing for a Changing World,* ed. R. S. Hancock. Chicago: American Marketing Association, 1960, 389-98.

Bauer, R. A., "The Obstinate Audience: The Influence Process from the Point of View of Social Communication," *American Psychologist,* 19 (1964), 319-28.

Bauer, R. A., and S. A. Greyser, "The Dialogue that Never Happens," *Harvard Business Review,* 45 (November-December 1967).

Bem, D. J., "Self-Perception: An Alternative Interpretation of Cognitive Dissonance Phenomena," *Psychological Review,* 74 (1967), 183-200.

Bem, D. J., "Attitudes as Self-Descriptions: Another Look at the Attitude-Behavior Link," in *Psychological Foundations of Attitudes,* ed. A. G. Greenwald, T. C. Brock, and T. M. Ostrom. New York: Academic Press, Inc., 1968, 197-215.

Bem, D. J., *Beliefs, Attitudes and Human Affairs.* Belmont, Calif.: Wadsworth Publishing Company, Inc., 1970.

Bogart, Leo, *Strategy in Advertising.* New York: Harcourt Brace Jovanovich, Inc., 1967.

Brehm, J. W., *A Theory of Psychological Reactance.* New York: Academic Press, Inc., 1966.

Brehm, J. W., and A. R. Cohen, "Re-evaluation of Choice Alternatives as a Function of Their Number and Qualitative Similarity," *Journal of Abnormal and Social Psychology,* 58 (1959), 373-78.

Brehm, J. W., and A. R. Cohen, *Explorations in Cognitive Dissonance.* New York: John Wiley & Sons, Inc., 1962.

Brown, Roger, *Social Psychology.* New York: The Free Press, 1965.

Campbell, D. T., "Social Attitudes and Other Acquired Behavioral Dispositions," in *Psychology: A Study of a Science,* ed. S. Koch, Vol. 6. New York: McGraw-Hill Book Company, 1963.

Canon, L. K., "Self-Confidence and Selective Exposure to Information," in *Conflict, Decision and Dissonance,* L. Festinger. Stanford, Calif.: Stanford University Press, 1964, 83-95.

Carroll, J. D., and J. J. Chang, "Relating Preference Data to Multidimentional Scaling Solutions via a Generalization of Coomb's Unfolding Model." Mimeographed report, Bell Telephone Laboratories, 1967.

Carroll, J. D., and J. J. Chang, "A New Method for Dealing with Individual Differences in Multidimensional Scaling." Mimeographed report, Bell Telephone Laboratories, 1969.

Chapman, W. S., "Some Observations on 'A User's Guide to Fishbein,'" *Journal of the Market Research Society,* 12 (July 1970), 189-91.

Claycamp, H. J., "Characteristics of Owners of Thrift Deposits in Commercial Banks and Savings and Loan Associations," *Journal of Marketing Research,* 2 (1965), 163-70.

Claycamp, H. J., and L. E. Liddy, "Prediction of New Product Performance: An Analytical Approach," *Journal of Marketing Research,* 6 (November 1969), 414-20.

Cook, S. W., and Claire Selltiz, "A Multiple-Indicator Approach to Attitude Measurement," *Psychological Bulletin,* 62 (1964), 36-55.

Coombs, C. H., *A Theory of Data.* New York: John Wiley & Sons, Inc., 1964.

Cox, D. F., ed., *Risk Taking and Information Handling in Consumer Behavior.* Cambridge, Mass.: Division of Research, Graduate School of Business Administration, Harvard University, 1967.

Day, G. S., *Buyer Attitudes and Brand Choice Behavior.* New York: The Free Press, 1970a.

Day, G. S., "Using Attitude Change Measures to Evaluate New Product Introductions," *Journal of Marketing Research,* 7 (November 1970b).

Day, G. S., "Attitude Change and the Relative Influence of Media and Word of Mouth Sources," *Journal of Advertising Research,* (December 1971).

Day, G. S., "Evaluating Models of Attitude Structure," *Journal of Marketing Research,* 9 (August 1972).

DeFleur, Melvin, *Theories of Mass Communication* (2nd ed.). New York: David McKay Company, Inc., 1970.

DeFleur, M. L., and F. R. Westie, "Attitude as a Scientific Concept," *Social Forces,* 42 (1963), 17-31.

Dubois, Cornelius, "Twelve Brands on a See-Saw," *Proceedings of the Advertising Research Foundation,* Annual Conference, November 1967.

Dulaney, D. E., "Awareness, Rules and Propositional Control: A Confrontation with S-R Behavior Theory," in *Verbal Behavior and General Behavior Therapy,* ed. T. R. Dixon and D. L. Horton. Englewood Cliffs, N.J.: Prentice-Hall, Inc., 1968.

Eagly, A. H., and M. Manis, "Evaluation of Message and Communication as a Function of Involvement," *Journal of Personality and Social Psychology,* 3 (1966), 483-85.

Einhorn, Hillel J., and Nicholas J. Gonedes, "An Exponential Discrepancy Model for Attitude Evaluation," *Behavioral Science,* 16 (March 1971), 152-57.

Engel, J. F., D. T. Kollat, and R. D. Blackwell, *Consumer Behavior.* New York: Holt, Rinehart and Winston, Inc., 1968.

Engel, J. F., and M. L. Light, "The Role of Psychological Commitment in Consumer Behavior: An Evaluation of the Role of Cognitive Dissonance," in *Applications of the Sciences in Marketing Management,* ed. F. M. Bass, C. W. King, and E. A. Pessemier. New York: John Wiley & Sons, Inc., 1968.

Evans, F. B., "Psychological and Objective Factors in the Prediction of Brand Choice: Ford versus Chevrolet," *Journal of Business,* 32 (1959), 340-69.

Evans, F. B., "Selling as a Dyadic Relationship—A New Approach," *American Behavioral Scientist,* 6 (May 1963), 76-79.

Fendrich, J. M., "A Study of the Association Among Verbal Attitudes, Commitment and Overt Behavior in Different Experimental Situations," *Social Forces,* 45 (1967), 347-55.

Festinger, Leon, *A Theory of Cognitive Dissonance.* Stanford, Calif.: Stanford University Press, 1957.

Festinger, Leon, and J. M. Carlsmith, "Cognitive Consequences of Forced Compliance," *Journal of Abnormal and Social Psychology,* 58 (1959), 203-10.

Fishbein, Martin, "The Relationships between Beliefs, Attitudes and Behavior," in *Cognitive Consistency: Motivational Antecedents and Behavioral Consequents,* ed. S. Feldman. New York: Academic Press, Inc., 1966.

Fishbein, Martin, "Attitude and the Prediction of Behavior," in *Readings in Attitude Theory and Measurement,* ed. M. Fishbein. New York: John Wiley & Sons, Inc., 1967a

Fishbein, Martin, "A Behavior Theory Approach to the Relations between Beliefs about an Object and the Attitude toward the Object," in *Readings in Attitude Theory and Measurement,* ed. M. Fishbein. New York: John Wiley & Sons, Inc., 1967b

Fishbein, Martin, and Ronda Hunter, "Summation versus Balance in Attitude Organization and Change," *Journal of Abnormal and Social Psychology,* 69 (1964), 505-10.

Fishbein, Martin, and B. H. Raven, "The A-B-Scales: An Operational Definition of Belief and Attitude," *Human Relations,* 15 (1962), 35-44.

Fiske, D. W., and S. R. Maddi, *Functions of Varied Experience.* Homewood, Ill.: Dorsey Press, Inc., 1961.

Foote, N. N., *Consumer Behavior: Household Decision-Making.* New York: New York University Press, 1961.

Fothergill, Jack, "Do Attitudes Change Before Behavior?" in *Papers: Esomar Congress 1968,* Opatigo, September 1968, 875-900.

Fowler, H., *Curiosity and Exploratory Behavior.* New York: The Macmillan Company, 1965.

Freedman, J. L., "Involvement, Discrepancy and Change," *Journal of Abnormal and Social Psychology,* 69 (1964), 290-95.

Freedman, J., and D. Sears, "Selective Exposure," in *Advances in Experimental Social Psychology, Vol. 2,* ed. L. Berkowitz. New York: Academic Press, Inc., 1965, 57-97.

Glass, D., "Theories of Consistency and the Study of Personality," in *Handbook of Personality Theory and Research,* ed. E. F. Borgatta and W. W. Lambert. Skokie, Ill.: Rand McNally & Company, 1967.

Green, P. E., and F. J. Carmone, "Multidimensional Scaling: An Introduction and Comparison of Nonmetric Unfolding Techniques," *Journal of Marketing Research,* 6 (1969), 330-41.

Green, P. E., and F. J. Carmone, *Multidimensional Scaling and Related Techniques.* Boston: Allyn and Bacon, Inc., 1970a.

Green, P. E., and F. J. Carmone, "Stimulus, Context and Task Effects on Individuals Similarity Judgments." Unpublished working paper, University of Pennsylvania, January 1970b.

Green, P. E., and Arun Maheswari, "Common Stock Perception and Preference: An Application of Multidimensional Scaling," *Journal of Business,* 42 (1969), 439-57.

Green, P. E., Arun Maheswari, and V. R. Rao, "Dimensional Interpretation and Configuration Invariance in Multidimensional Scaling: An Empirical Study," *Multivariate Behavioral Research,* 6 (April 1969), 159-80.

Green, P. E., and D. S. Tull, *Research for Marketing Decisions* (2nd ed.). Englewood Cliffs, N.J.: Prentice-Hall, Inc., 1970.

Greenberg, M. G. "The Analysis of Preference and Attribute Judgment Data." Unpublished working paper, November 1968.

Greenberg, M. G., "Multidimensional Scaling" in *Handbook of Marketing Research,* ed. Robert Ferber. New York: McGraw-Hill Book Company; forthcoming (chapter manuscript dated 1969).

Guttman, Louis, "The Problem of Attitude and Opinion Measurement," in *Measurement and Prediction,* ed. S. A. Stouffer. Princeton, N.J.: Princeton University Press, 1950.

Haley, R. I., "Benefit Segmentation: A Decision-Oriented Research Tool," *Journal of Marketing,* 32 (July 1968), 30-35.

Haskins, J. B., "Factual Recall as a Measure of Advertising Effectiveness," *Journal of Advertising Research,* 4 (March 1964), 2-8.

Heider, F., "Attitudes and Cognitive Organization," *Journal of Psychology,* 21 (1946), 107-12.

Heller, H. E., "Defining Target Markets by their Attitude Profiles," in *Attitude Research on the Rocks,* ed. Lee Adler and Irving Crespi. Chicago: American Marketing Association, 1968.

Hess, E. H., "Attitude and Pupil Size," *Scientific American,* 212 (1965), 46-54.

Homayounfar, F., *Production of High Pressure Steam-Cured Calcium Silicate Building Materials from Mining Industry Waste Products: A Market Study.* Technical Report No. 138, Department of Civil Engineering, Stanford University, September 1970.

Hovland, C. I., "Reconciling Conflicting Results Derived from Experimental and Survey Studies of Attitude Change," *American Psychologist,* 14 (1959), 8-17.

Hovland, C. I., I. L. Janis, and H. H. Kelley, *Communication and Persuasion.* New Haven, Conn.: Yale University Press, 1953.

Howard, J. A., and J. N. Sheth, *The Theory of Buyer Behavior.* New York: John Wiley & Sons, Inc., 1969.

Hustad, Thomas P., and Edgar A. Pessemier, "Segmenting Consumer Markets with Activity and Attitude Measures," unpublished working paper, Purdue University, March 1971.

Insko, C. A., *Theories of Attitude Change.* New York: Appleton-Century-Crofts, 1967.

Insko, C. A., F. Murashima, and M. Saiyadain, "Communicator Discrepancy, Stimulus Ambiguity and Influence," *Journal of Personality,* 34 (1966), 262-74.

Insko, C. A., and J. Schopler, "Triadic Consistency: A Statement of Affective-Cognitive-Conative Consistency," *Psychological Review,* 74 (1967), 361-76.

Jacoby, Jacob, and J. C. Olson, "An Attitudinal Model of Brand Loyalty: Conceptual Underpinnings and Instrumentation Research." Paper presented at the University of Illinois Conference on Attitude Research and Consumer Behavior, Urbana, Illinois, December 1970.

Johnson, Richard M., "Market Segmentation: A Strategic Management Tool," *Journal of Marketing Research,* 8 (February 1971), 13-9.

Jones, R. A., D. E. Linder, C. A. Kiesler, M. Zanna, and J. W. Brehm, "Internal States or External Stimuli—Observers' Attitude Judgments and the Dissonance Theory—Self-Persuasion Controversy," *Journal of Experimental Social Psychology,* 4 (1968), 247-69.

Katz, Daniel, "The Functional Approach to the Study of Attitudes," *Public Opinion Quarterly,* 24 (1960), 163-204.

Katz, Daniel, and E. Stotland, "A Preliminary Statement to a Theory of Attitude Structure and Change," in *Psychology: A Study of a Science,* ed. S. Koch, Vol. 3. New York: McGraw-Hill Book Company, 1959, 423-75.

Katz, Elihu, and P. F. Lazarsfeld, *Personal Influence.* New York: The Free Press, 1955.

Kelman, II. C., "Compliance, Identification and Internalization: Three Processes of Attitude Change," *Journal of Conflict Resolution,* 2 (1958), 51-60.

Kelman, H. C., "Processes of Opinion Change," *Public Opinion Quarterly,* 25 (1961), 57-78.

Kiesler, C. A., B. E. Collins, and Norman Miller, *Attitude Change: A Critical Analysis of Theoretical Approaches.* New York: John Wiley & Sons, Inc., 1969.

Klapper, J. T., *Effects of Mass Communication.* New York: The Free Press, 1960.

Klahr, David, "A Monte Carlo Investigation of the Statistical Significance of Kruskal's Nonmetric Scaling Procedure," paper presented at the Congress of the International Federation of Information Processing, Edinburgh, Scotland, 1968.

Krugman, H. E., "The Impact of Television Advertising: Learning without Involvement," *Public Opinion Quarterly,* 30 (1966-67), 583-96.

Kruskal, J. B., "How to Use MDSCAL: A Program to Do Multidimensional Scaling and Multidimensional Unfolding," (Version 4 and 4M). Bell Telephone Laboratories, March 1968.

Lasswell, H. D., "The Structure and Function of Communication in Society," in *Communication of Ideas,* ed. L. Bryson. New York: Harper & Row, Inc., 1948.

Lavidge, R. C., and G. A. Steiner, "A Model for Predictive Measurements of Advertising Effectiveness," *Journal of Marketing,* 25 (October 1961), 59-62.

Lehmann, Donald R., "Television Show Preference: Application of a Choice Model," *Journal of Marketing Research,* 8 (February 1971), 47-55.

Linder, S. B., *The Harried Leisure Class.* New York: Columbia University Press, 1970.

Lipstein, Benjamin, "Anxiety, Risk and Uncertainty in Advertising Effectiveness Measurements," in *Attitude Research on the Rocks,* ed. Lee Adler and Irving Crespi. Chicago: American Marketing Association, 1968.

Lunn, J. A., "Psychological Classification," *Commentary* (now *Journal of the Market Research Society*), 8 (1966), 3.

Lunn, J. A., "Attitudes and Behavior in Consumer Research–A Reappraisal" unpublished working paper. London: Research Bureau Limited, 1970.

Maloney, J. C., "Curiosity Versus Disbelief in Advertising," *Journal of Advertising Research*, 2 (June 1962), 2-8.

Maloney, J. C., "Attitude Measurement and Prediction." Paper presented at the Test Market Design and Measurement Workshop, American Marketing Association, Chicago, Ill., April 1966.

McGuire, W. J., "The Current Status of Cognitive Consistency Theories," in *Cognitive Consistency: Motivational Antecedents and Behavioral Consequents*, ed. S. Feldman. New York: Academic Press, Inc., 1966.

McGuire, W. J., "The Nature of Attitudes and Attitude Change," in *Handbook of Social Psychology, Vol. III* (2nd ed.), ed. G. Lindzey and E. Aronson. Reading, Mass.: Addison-Wesley Publishing Company, Inc., 1969, 136-314.

McGuire, W. J., "An Information-Processing Model of Advertising Effectiveness," in *Behavioral and Management Science in Marketing*, ed. H. Davis and A. Silk. New York: The Ronald Press Company, 1973.

Miller, G. A., "The Magical Number Seven, Plus or Minus Two: Some Limits in our Capacity for Processing Information," *Psychological Review*, 62 (1956), 81-97.

Montgomery, D. M., "A Gate-Keeping Model of Supermarket Buying Committee Decisions." Unpublished working paper, Stanford University, Graduate School of Business, 1971.

Myers, J. G., "Determinants of Private Brand Attitude," *Journal of Marketing Research*, 4 (1967), 73-81.

Myers, J. H., and M. I. Alpert, "Determinant Buying Attitudes: Meaning and Measurement," *Journal of Marketing*, 32 (October 1968), 13-20.

Neidell, L. A., "Physicians' Perception and Evaluations of Selected Ethical Drugs: An Application of Nonmetric Multidimensional Scaling to Pharmaceutical Marketing." Unpublished Ph.D. thesis, University of Pennsylvania, December 1968.

Nicosia, F. M. *Consumer Decision Processes: Marketing and Advertising Implications*. Englewood Cliffs, N.J.: Prentice-Hall, Inc., 1966.

Osgood, C. E., "Cognitive Dynamics in the Conduct of Human Affairs," *Public Opinion Quarterly*, 24 (1960), 341-65.

Osgood, C. E., G. I. Suci, and P. H. Tannenbaum, *The Measurement of Meaning*. Urbana, Ill.: University of Illinois Press, 1957.

Ostrom, T. M., "The Emergency of Attitude Theory: 1930 to 1950" in *Psychological Foundations of Attitudes*, ed. A. G. Greenwald, T. C. Brock, and T. M. Ostrom. New York: Academic Press, Inc., 1968.

Palda, K. S., "The Hypothesis of a Hierarchy of Effects: A Partial Evaluation," *Journal of Marketing Research*, 3 (February 1966), 13-24.

Pepitone, Albert, "Some Conceptual and Empirical Problems of Consistency Models," in *Cognitive Consistency: Motivational Antecedents and Behavioral Consequents*, ed. S. Feldman. New York: Academic Press, Inc., 1966.

Ray, M. L., and W. L. Wilkie, "Fear: the Potential of an Appeal Neglected by Marketing," *Journal of Marketing,* 34 (January 1970), 54-62.

Robertson, T. S., *Innovation and the Consumer.* New York: Holt, Rinehart and Winston, Inc., 1971.

Rokeach, Milton, "Attitude Change and Behavior Change," *Public Opinion Quarterly,* 30 (Winter 1966-67), 529-50.

Rokeach, Milton, *Beliefs, Attitudes and Values.* San Francisco: Jossey-Bass, Inc., Publishers, 1968.

Rokeach, Milton, "The Nature of Attitudes," in *Encyclopedia of the Social Sciences, Vol. I,* ed. D. L. Sills. New York: Crowell Collier and Macmillan, Inc., 1968b, 449-57.

Rosenberg, M. J., "Cognitive Structure and Attitudinal Affect," *Journal of Abnormal and Social Psychology,* 53 (1956), 367-72.

Rosenberg, M. J., and R. P. Abelson, "An Analysis of Cognitive Balancing," in *Attitude Organization and Change,* ed. M. J. Rosenberg, et al. New Haven, Conn.: Yale University Press, 1960, 112-63.

Sampson, Peter, and Paul Harris, "A User's Guide to Fishbein," *Journal of the Market Research Society,* 12 (July 1970), 145-89.

Sawyer, J., "Measurement and Prediction: Clinical and Statistical," *Psychological Bulletin,* 66 (1966), 178-200.

Scott, W. A., "Attitude Measurement," in *Handbook of Social Psychology,* ed. G. Lindzey and E. Aronson. Reading, Mass.: Addison-Wesley Publishing Company, Inc., 1968.

Semon, T. T, "On the Perception of Appliance Attributes," *Journal of Marketing Research,* 6 (February 1969), 101.

Shepard, R. N., "Some Principles and Prospects for the Spatial Representation of Behavioral Science Data." Paper presented at the Mathematical Social Science Board Advanced Research Seminar on Scaling and Measurement, Balboa Bay Club, June 13-16, 1969.

Sherif, C. W., Muzafer Sherif, and R. E. Nebergall, *Attitude and Attitude Change: The Social Judgment-Involvement Approach.* Philadelphia: W. B. Saunders Company, 1965.

Sherif, Muzafer, and C. W. Sherif, "Attitude as the Individual's Own Categories: The Social Judgment-Involvement Approach to Attitude and Attitude Change," in *Attitude, Ego-Involvement and Change,* ed. C. W. Sherif and M. Sherif. New York: John Wiley & Sons, Inc., 1967., 105-39.

Sherif, Muzafer, and C. I. Hovland, *Social Judgment: Assimilation and Contrast Effects in Communication and Attitude Change.* New Haven, Conn.: Yale University Press, 1961.

Sheth, Jagdish N., and W. Wayne Talarzyk, "Perceived Instrumentality and Value Importance," *Journal of Marketing Research,* 9 (February 1972), 6-9.

Smith, Gail, "How GM Measures Ad Effectiveness," *Printer's Ink* (May 14, 1965).

Smith, M. B., "Attitude Change," in *Encyclopedia of the Social Sciences, Vol. I,* ed. D. L. Sills. New York: Crowell Collier and Macmillan, Inc., 1968, 458-67.

Smith, M. B., J. S. Bruner, and R. W. White, *Opinions and Personality.* New York: John Wiley & Sons, Inc., 1958.

Staats, A. W., "An Outline of an Integrated Learning Theory of Attitude Formation and Function," in *Readings in Attitude Theory and Measurement,* ed. M. Fishbein. New York: John Wiley and Sons, Inc., 1967.

Stefflre, V. J., "Marketing Structure Studies: New Products for Old Markets and New Markets (Foreign) for Old Products," in *Application of the Sciences in Marketing Management,* ed. F. M. Bass, C. W. King, and E. A. Pessemier. New York: John Wiley & Sons, Inc., 1968.

Stefflre, V. J., "Some Applications of Multidimensional Scaling to Social Science Questions." Paper presented at the Mathematical Social Science Board Advanced Research Seminar on Scaling and Measurement, Balboa Bay Club, June 13-16, 1969.

Talarzyk, W. Wayne, and Reza Moinpour, "Comparison of an Attitude Model and Coombsian Unfolding Analysis for the Prediction of Individual Brand Choice," paper presented at the Workshop on Attitude Research and Consumer Behavior, University of Illinois, 1970.

Tannenbaum, P. H., "The Congruity Principle Revisited: Studies in the Reduction, Induction and Generalization of Persuasion," in *Advances in Experimental Social Psychology,* ed. L. Berkowitz. New York: Academic Press, Inc., 1967.

Thomas W. I., and F. Znaniecki, *The Polish Peasant in Europe and America.* Boston: Badger, 1918.

Tucker, L. R., and S. Messick, "An Individual Differences Model for Multidimensional Scaling," *Psychometrika,* 28 (1963), 333-67.

Turner, J. S., *The Chemical Feast.* New York: Grossman Publishers, 1970.

Upshaw, H. S., "Attitude Measurement," in *Methodology in Social Research,* ed. H. M. Blalock and A. B. Blalock. New York: McGraw-Hill Book Company, 1968.

Weiss, R. F., "Persuasion and Acquisition of Attitudes: Models from Conditioning and Selective Learning," *Psychological Reports,* 11 (1962), 709-32.

Weiss, Walter, "Effects of the Mass Media of Communication," in *Handbook of Social Psychology,* ed. G. Lindzey and E. Aronson, (2nd ed.) Vol. 5. Reading, Mass.: Addison-Wesley Publishing Company, Inc., 1969, 77-195.

Wells, W. D., "Measuring Readiness to Buy," *Harvard Business Review,* 39 (July-August 1961), 81-87.

Wicker, A. W., "Attitudes versus Actions: The Relationship of Verbal and Overt Behavioral Responses to Attitude Objects," *The Journal of Social Issues,* 25 (Autumn 1969), 41-78.

Wish, Myron, Morton Deutsch, and L. B. Rogers, "Individual Differences in Nation Perception." Bell Telephone Laboratories, Murray Hill, N.J., June 1969.

Young, F. W., and W. S. Torgerson, "TORSCA: A FORTRAN IV Program for Shepard-Kruskal Multidimensional Scaling Analysis," *Behavioral Science,* 12 (1967), 498.

Zajonc, R. B., "The Concepts of Balance, Congruity and Dissonance," *Public Opinion Quarterly,* 24 (1960), 280-96.

Zimbardo, P. G., "Involvement and Communication Discrepancy as Determinants of Opinion Conformity," *Journal of Abnormal and Social Psychology*, 60 (1960), 86-94.

Zimbardo, P. G., and E. B. Ebbesen, *Influencing Attitudes and Changing Behavior.* Reading, Mass.: Addison-Wesley Publishing Company, Inc., 1969.

9

Cognitive Consistency and Novelty Seeking

M. Venkatesan
University of Iowa

INTRODUCTION

COGNITIVE CONSISTENCY

   Balance Theory. Congruity Principle. Cognitive Dissonance.

COMPLEXITY THEORIES AND NOVELTY SEEKING

   Collative Approach. Variation-Seeking Approach. Individual
   Differences in Novelty Seeking.

ALTERNATIVE EXPLANATIONS

   Incongruity Theory. General Incongruity Adaptation Level Hypothesis. Reprise.

NOVELTY SEEKING IN CONSUMER BEHAVIOR

   Theoretical Perspective. Empirical Evidence. Some Directions
   for Research.

CONCLUSIONS

REFERENCES

In general, we come to love what is familiar and the unfamiliar is always discomforting, be it a new form of art, a new recipe, or new architecture and other such new things. However, it is common knowledge that what is unfamiliar at one time becomes familiar sooner or later.

This chapter is concerned with the novelty-seeking behavior of consumers. This area is currently devoid of theoretical perspectives, and this is not surprising, for the psychologists whose basic concern is in explaining behavior have only recently started (from the 1950s) systematic investigations of curiosity behavior. Much remains to be done in researching curiosity among humans.

The organization of this chapter follows a logical sequence. First, cognitive-consistency theories relevant to consumer behavior are reviewed with a view to understanding their relevance to novelty-seeking behavior. Then alternative formulations, which go under the name of *complexity theories,* are considered. Following this a choice is made for a theoretical perspective, which is explained in detail, and then available empirical evidence for the novelty-seeking behavior of consumers is presented. The chapter closes with some directions for research efforts in novelty seeking.

COGNITIVE CONSISTENCY

As human beings, we have information or knowledge about objects and we hold beliefs or evaluations about them. Such knowledge, opinions, and beliefs

I am grateful to Jagdish Sheth, Alvin Silk, and Jim Bettman for their interesting discussions on this subject and some helpful ideas. I also want to thank Thomas Copley for providing materials on his study before they became formally available.

about objects, about oneself, about one's actions, and about the environment constitute the cognitions of an individual. In the booming, buzzing confusion surrounding his world, the individual, it is held by some psychological theories, strives to maintain logical ("psycho-logical") consistency. That is, these psychological theories known as consistency theories point out that individuals seek and maintain cognitive consistency, as any cognitive inconsistency is viewed as psychologically uncomfortable. Any inconsistency arouses psychological tension in the individual (motivational state) in much the same way as any other drive state, such as thirst, and the organism is expected to engage in drive-reduction activities. The inconsistency involved is mostly psychological in character and it is among an individual's cognitions. There are three major formulations of cognitive-consistency theories and some modifications. These formulations find their philosophical and theoretical basis in many of the aspects of the field-theory framework of Lewin (Deutsch, 1968) and are mainly based on the field theoretic concepts. While the balance theorists refer to the state of imbalance and the seeking of balanced relations among cognitions, congruity theory is concerned with incongruity and striving for consistency among attitudes. The dissonance school is preoccupied with dissonant cognitions and reduction of dissonance (consonance). Although the terms used are different, the fundamental assumption of all these theories is that there is a tendency towards consistency; most of them spell out the antecedent conditions, and some of them indicate modes of inconsistency reduction. In this section a brief review is provided of Heider's balance theory (1958), Osgood and Tannenbaum's congruity theory (1955), and Festinger's dissonance theory (1957).

Balance Theory

Heider (1958) was concerned with the structural property of cognitive elements. The cognitive elements have to do with a person, P, an object, X, and some other person, O. P has simultaneous cognitions about O and X, and he is interested in O's cognitions about X. Relations among the cognitive elements can be positive or negative. For example, P likes or dislikes object X (or O), or O likes or dislikes X, and so on. Relations among the elements in this cognitive set can be balanced; if not, the relations may instigate action to modify the cognitive elements—to bring them in balance relationships. Newcomb (1968) identifies three psychological states: balance, imbalance, and nonbalance. In the balance state, the set of cognitive elements is accepted as it is; in the second state, modification will be attempted; and in the third state, indifference between acceptance and modification may prevail. The balanced relationship among the triad is obtained if the algebraic product of the three signs is positive, and the relationship is considered imbalanced if the product is negative.

The balance theory asserts that balanced states will be preferred over imbalanced states, and imbalanced states will lead to activities to change them to balanced states. The theory is not concerned with the modes of obtaining balanced states. It makes intuitive sense to view this theory as applicable to practical problems of consumers; virtually no empirical evidence is available. Even empirical studies in social psychology have not progressed beyond demonstrating the validity of the basic definition (Zajonc, 1968).

Newcomb's (1953) *A-B-X* system and his strain toward symmetry formulation is a special case of balance, and his theory is mainly concerned with interpersonal relations. Cartwright and Harary (1956) refined and formalized Heider's concept of cognitive balance and extended the concept to cover more than triadic relationships. As Zajonc (1968) aptly observed, the mathematical treatment of Cartwright and Harary (1956) did not lead to any profound effects on empirical work in testing the balance theory.

The balance theory recognizes implicitly the need for turning to persons one is accustomed to trust. This may seem to be the important factor in considering the cognitive set relevant to seeking new products and other such novelty. One study (Jacoby, 1970) was concerned with the nonobvious advertising strategy suggested by the balance-theory model for generating consumer preference, especially for new or unknown products. In this study subjects were told that a disliked source (by them) had made statements indicating dislike for a set of products. The subjects were then asked to indicate how they felt about that particular product and, given such a situation, were they likely to buy the product. Results of this study indicated that negatively valenced sources stating their dislike for novel consumer items will generate increased preferences and intent to buy for that item.

Although the hypothesis and the results obtained are interesting, the balance-theory formulation cannot be of much use in explaining novelty seeking. According to this theory, interest in relationships among cognitions arises after *P* has formulated simultaneous cognitions about object *X* and some other person *O*. Our interest is in *how* this cognition about *X*, the new product, is formulated or *how one seeks novelty;* for this purpose, the concepts of balance theory do not appear helpful.

Congruity Principle

The second major consistency formulation to be considered here is the congruity principle. This theory is concerned with an identifiable source making an assertion for or against a particular object or concept. The individual, generally, maintains any type of attitude toward any number of concepts and sources. Any assertion by the source relates the source and the concept held by the individual. If the individual was favorably disposed toward the source and the concept prior to the assertion by the source, and the assertion is favorable, then there is no incongruity. If the same conditions obtain with the exception that now the assertion by the source is not favorable toward the concept, then *incongruity* is said to prevail. The state of incongruity generates a pressure for change in the attitudes held toward the source and/or the concept, and the changed attitudes are expected to lead to a congruous situation. Thus the congruity principle attempts to specify precisely the direction of change and to indicate whether the change will be with respect to the source or with regard to the concept or object, since assertion is already made and it can only be positive or negative. Although the model would seem to apply only in situations where a source has made some assertion and the pressure is to change only the existing attitude toward either the source or the concept (object), Tannenbaum (1968) considers that there is a considerable range of generality for this theory. However, as he points out, "testing is still restricted to particular types of communications situations, and that generalization beyond those situations is a rather tenuous procedure" (Tannenbaum, 1968, p. 71).

Considerable amounts of empirical support are available in the social-psychological literature for the congruity principle. However, while implications of these theoretical formulations for consumer behavior have gained wide currency in the literature, very limited empirical work can be found to test the theory's general implication, and none found for novelty seeking. It seems reasonable to assert that the congruity principle will be more relevant in the case of new products. Thus the following illustration provided by Robertson (1970) is reflective of the type of application that could be envisaged:

> For example, assume a consumer has a balanced set of attitudes regarding food products. Let us further assume that this consumer has favorable attitudes toward General Foods and its coffee brands (+) and an unfavorable attitude toward new coffee products, which she perceives as inferior substitutes (-). General Foods then introduces Maxim Freeze-dried coffee, stressing its superiority (+). Under these conditions, attitudinal imbalance is obvious and change is likely to occur (Robertson, 1970, p. 59).

The more usual situation obtained may be something like the following: the buyer's attitude is favorable toward the source (brand). The source (manufacturer) will most likely make positive or favorable assertions about its new product. The consumer has already a set of dispositions toward the source and the concept, in this case the product class. If a new product of the same brand is introduced, and if his attitude toward the new product is positive, no incongruity is aroused; if his attitude toward the new product category is negative, it will change in the positive direction in the face of positive assertion by the source and he might then seek the new product. If his attitude toward the source was negative, even if his attitude toward the product category is positive, the change will be in the negative direction; the novelty under such circumstances will not be sought.

The congruency formulation relates to a very limited and restricted set of circumstances with respect to novelty seeking. Many situations may not involve attitude changes such that they will lead to novelty seeking. Thus the principle of congruity is not amenable for a full explanation of novelty seeking.

Cognitive Dissonance

Whereas the balance theory is concerned with interpersonal perception, and the congruity principle deals with attitude changes as a result of association(s) from a source(s) regarding a concept(s), the theory of cognitive dissonance, proposed by Festinger (1957), seems to have wider applications than the others. The formulations of this theory are flexible, and there is ample empirical evidence supporting its major formulations.

According to the theory, relations exist between the relevant cognitions of an individual. If there is a satisfactory relationship between two relevant cognitions, they may be said to exist in "fitting" or consonant relationship. However, for one reason or another if they do not "fit," the relationship is characterized by a dissonant relationship. Dissonant relations between cognitions are psychologically uncomfortable, and therefore the organism is aroused to find ways to reduce dissonance. Thus these all-encompassing formulations have broader applications. Since "fitting" or "nonfitting" relations between any two cognitions have to do with the individual who has these cognitions, many areas of individual decision making, attitudes, behavior, and other factors from the environment, past experience, and the like, are likely to provide situations giving rise to dissonance.

There are a number of ways in which dissonance experienced can be reduced: Changing one's cognitions or adding new consonant cognitions is one way of reducing dissonance. He can change his behavior; he can decrease the importance of relevant cognitions; he can revoke his decision. Since there are a multitude of ways of reducing dissonance, it is not possible to specify in advance a particular mode of dissonance reduction. An illustration will make this point clear. Kassarjian and Cohen (1965) examined the oft-quoted but classic case of the cigarette smoker and the surgeon-general's finding linking cigarette smoking with lung cancer. Awareness of this finding by the cigarette smoker should produce dissonance among his cognitions and a need to reduce dissonance. Their study found that confirmed smokers, who were aware of the surgeon-general's findings, justified the continuance of smoking by the use of one or more of the following dissonance-reducing mechanisms: (1) by dissociating their responsibility over their decisions; (2) by denying, distorting, misperceiving, or minimizing the degree of health hazard involved; and (3) by selectively drawing out new cognitions and new information that would reduce the inconsistency of their behavior.

Festinger (1964) clearly indicates that dissonance arousal and its reduction take place *only* after a decision is made involving firm commitments, so that consequences are expected to flow from the decision. Due to its simplicity and obvious applications to problems of buyer behavior, a number of studies have appeared in the consumer-behavior literature. Most of the studies are concerned with dissonance arousal and reduction in choice-making situations (see, for example, Anderson, 1966; Bell, 1967; Holloway, 1967; LoSciuto and Perloff, 1967; Mittelstaedt, 1969; Sheth, 1968, 1970). Some have been concerned with information seeking (see Cohen and Goldberg, 1970; Engel, 1963; Hunt, 1970; Kassarjian and Cohen, 1965). A single study (Cardozo, 1965) deals with disconfirmation of expectation. There are a few other studies that relate peripherally to buyer behavior (see Venkatesan, in press).

Dissonance Theory and Novelty Seeking. Festinger (1964) has provided empirical evidence that impartial collection and evaluation of information take place as part of the cognitive process *before* a decision is made, and once a decision is made the psychological situation changes decisively. The process is characterized now by less objectivity and more partiality and bias. Thus from a dissonance-theory framework, since a state of dissonance does not exist when new cognitions relevant to impending or future action are acquired, novelty seeking is similar to voluntary exposure to cognize any relevant information or element. Impartial collection and evaluation are part of the cognitive process in the predecision stage, and since dissonance is a postdecision phenomenon, there is nothing special about novelty seeking—it is acquiring cognitions about all aspects and alternatives relevant to future action. By the time dissonance is aroused, a decision is already made and all the alternatives are presumably evaluated. What was "novel" at the impartial collection stage is no longer novel at the postdecision stage. It is more than likely that what was novel before the decision has now become familiar, as its pros and cons have already been evaluated. In such a framework, novelty-seeking behavior is not explained with any antecedents, but is subsumed as part of the predecision evaluation process.

From the foregoing it would appear that seeking of novelty should be viewed as occurring after a decision is made, so as to relate this behavior to dissonance framework. That is, the novel stimulus must be sought in some way, as accidental exposure to new information and/or novelty might result in increase in dissonance, and forced exposure to any new cognition is not always expected to produce dissonance (Festinger, 1957, pp. 132-33). How, then, can the theory of cognitive dissonance be viewed with respect to the problem of novelty seeking? It would seem that novelty seeking can be viewed in the framework of the individual actively seeking out new information as a result of having experienced dissonance. The dissonance formulation tended to emphasize that the selective information seeking or stimulus seeking would be for consonant information or stimuli, and dissonance producing stimuli would be avoided. However, Festinger (1964) found that while new consonant information was sought, there was no evidence for the avoidance of dissonance-producing information. Both the Jecker (1964) and the Cannon (1964) experiments indicated that individuals do not avoid dissonance-producing information if the person is confident that he can cope with the dissonant information and if it is perceived that that information will be *useful*. Thus, in order to seek novelty, already the individual must be experiencing dissonance. The novel item or information in such a circumstance must be perceived to be useful, need not be consonant information, and may even increase the magnitude of dissonance that already exists. Generally, the recent findings (McGuire, 1968) in the area of seeking consonant information and avoiding dissonant information are equivocal. Although the empirical evidence is nonconfirming in this area, knowing that individuals may expose themselves to dissonant information that is new or novel does not reflect in any heuristic power resting with such an explanation for understanding novelty-seeking behavior.

Festinger (1964) has recognized many other antecedent conditions apart from the existence of dissonance that will produce active seeking out of new information. He points out that "active curiosity and the sheer pleasure of acquiring information for its own sake cannot be ignored in any discussion of voluntary seeking out of new information" (1964, p. 124). He points out that such seeking out of new information is relevant to the individual's possible future behavior, and therefore considerable motivation exists to acquire cognitive elements.

It would appear that neither the dissonance formulations relative to seeking out supportive material or the modified view of not avoiding discrepant material provide adequate or satisfactory explanations of novelty-seeking behavior. Modifications to the dissonance formulations or casting these formulations in a different framework might, perhaps, provide insightful explanations for novelty-seeking behavior. After an extended review of the evidence on selective exposure, McGuire (1968) concluded that complexity theories which predict a tendency quite the opposite to selective avoidance should receive greater attention and that we should "discontinue the current excessive preoccupation with this one possible tactic of defensive avoidance" (p. 800).

COMPLEXITY THEORIES AND NOVELTY SEEKING

The consistency framework, in general, does not appear to provide adequate and satisfactory explanations for the becoming aware of and seeking of novelty. While the cognitive-consistency theorists have been striving to be consistent about all areas of human behavior, a group of theories categorized for want of a better or more appropriate name as *complexity theories* has been concerned with finding explanations for novelty (complexity) seeking. McGuire (1966) saw this as "inevitable correction" setting in for the swing of the pendulum towards consistency-seeking research. Only Berlyne's (1960) seminal formulations receive major attention here because of their rich conceptual system and because of the convergence of theoretical ideas that they represent. A brief review of Maddi's (Fiske and Maddi, 1961) variety-seeking formulations is presented as a complementary way of looking at novelty seeking.

Collative Approach

Berlyne's (1960, 1963, 1968) collative approach is based mainly on the drive-reduction approach. In essence, the drive or arousal and its reduction lead to exploration of novelty. Berlyne's approach is conceptually rich and here only the essentials are presented for the sake of keeping the formulations simple.

This approach starts out with the now well-known proposition that many types of external stimuli can be motivating. For novelty-seeking behavior to take place, the organism has to be aroused; that is, it should be "awakened" or "alerted." Since our concern is not with any stimulus, but with novel stimuli, Berlyne identifies some of the important and outstanding attributes of the stimulus pattern. These properties, called *collative properties,* are novelty, surprisingness, change, ambiguity, incongruity, blurredness, and power to induce uncertainty (Berlyne, 1963, p. 290). These are called collative properties as they depend on collation or comparison with others, present and past. These properties are not mutually exclusive; in fact, they are highly interdependent. The suggestion is that these collative properties give the external stimulus the power to induce and increase arousal. Exploratory behavior accompanies arousal. This is the response to the stimulus. But exploratory behavior can be divided into three varieties:

1. Orienting responses.
2. Locomotor exploration.
3. Investigatory responses.

In the case of a novel object, the novelty itself is a collative property. This property of the stimulus induces arousal of the organism. Since the stimulus is novel, only a small amount of information is received from the stimulus by the individual, leading to considerable uncertainty. This uncertainty is viewed as a form of conflict, which can be resolved by exploration. Thus the motivational effects of the collative variables depend on and work through *conflict.* Berlyne classified this state of drive produced by the collative property of the novel object as *perceptual curiosity.* Since the novel object is responsible for the arousal, it can help to relieve it. Generally, all three or any one of the forms of exploratory behavior can be brought in the service of reduction of tension created by the arousal. Exploration of the novel object may secure access to information from aspects of the object, may prolong stimulation so that the conflict is resolved by habituation,[1] or may provide time to work out a response such that the effects of novelty are mitigated (Berlyne, 1963, p. 303).

Exploration activities, so far, are related to curiosity arousal by the novel object, and curiosity reduction in this context involves specific exploration. "Specific exploration has the function of providing stimulation from a definite source. No other source will do instead. It is the kind of behavior that we perform when we are said to be 'looking for' or 'taking a closer look' at 'something in particular' " (Berlyne, 1963, pp. 289-90). Many times we come into contact with unexpected and unlooked for stimuli. Berlyne's explanation for such encounters is that the unexpected stimulus first raises and then reduces drive, the processes taking place in close succession. In such occasions *diversive exploration* is involved. A person seeking entertainment, relief from boredom, or new experiences will be satisfied with stimuli from any of a wide range of sources, provided only that their collative properties are just right. This is called diversive exploration by Berlyne (1960). In Berlyne's view boredom also creates an aversive drive state, as the situation is characterized by the familiar stimuli, monotony, and is devoid of stimulation. Diversive exploratory behavior is likely to be very strong in these circumstances.

Although the above description indicates that human beings reduce their perceptual curiosity by exposure to the novel stimulus, most often the exploratory responses of human beings take the form of epistemic responses. That is, on the other side of the coin there is that brand of arousal that motivates the acquiring of knowledge, and such arousal is relieved when knowledge or information is procured. Berlyne (1960) terms it *epistemic curiosity*. The stored information gives rise to internal symbolic responses, which can guide behavior in the future. The motivational effects of epistemic behavior depend here on *conceptual conflict*, which refers to incompatibilities between symbolic response tendencies, such as beliefs, attitudes, conceptions, and the like. Conceptual conflict is also related to subjective uncertainty and to the collative properties of novelty, surprise, and incongruity. Conceptual conflict is relieved by information acquisition. Such an action tends to strengthen one of the competing beliefs and weaken the alternatives. Other modes are to seek information selectively and to rearrange the symbolic structures. In general, several modes of relieving conceptual conflict are available and which will be used is dependent on the nature of the response tendencies in conflict, stimulus context, and learned proclivities within the subject.

Berlyne assumes that the individual will be interested in maintaining an optimal or intermediate level of stimulus impact. That is, arousal varies with

---

[1] By *habituation* is meant that the novel property loses its collative effects having once occurred, and especially when having occurred repeatedly (Berlyne, 1960, p. 19). Hunt (1963, p. 83) used the term *recognition* to indicate the repeated encounters one has had with various patterns of stimuli.

collative and other properties of the stimulus variables. This is called arousal potential. The relationship between arousal and arousal potential is viewed, by Berlyne, as likely to be curvilinear. The reasoning is as follows: at any given moment the organism is capable of a minimum arousal. External and internal conditions affect the location of the minimum. In his view, not only very novel or unfamiliar stimulus conditions but very familiar or monotonous stimuli will lead to high arousal. Thus arousal is a U-shaped function of arousal potential. So only a moderate degree of arousal potential will be most attractive.

> When arousal stands above its possible minimum, we assume that there will be an aversive state and that anything that serves to bring it down toward its possible minimum will have a reward value. Maintaining the level of arousal near its possible minimum will mean seeking just the right intermediate influx of arousal potential and escaping from environments where arousal potential is too high or too low (Berlyne, 1963, p. 317).

The specific collative property of interest to us, novelty, and its arousal potential can be seen as related to arousal as shown in Figure 1.

Berlyne's collative approach has a good amount of empirical support. The implications of this theory are wide ranging, and certainly its applications to novelty seeking by consumers are obvious. In a later section these applications are outlined.

FIGURE 1.   **Relation between Arousal and Arousal Potential**

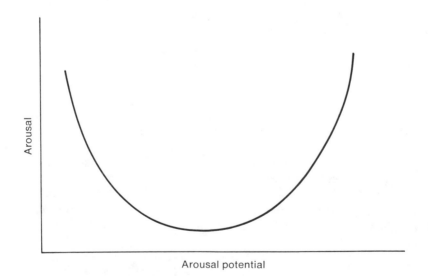

After Berlyne (1963), p. 319.

Variation-Seeking Approach

Maddi (Fiske and Maddi, 1961; Maddi, 1968) is concerned with a component contrary to consistency. That is, there is a force in the organism which on occasion seeks variety, although at other times it might be concerned with seeking consistency—personality and situational factors determine which behavior will be elicited. Although Maddi opposes Berlyne's (1960) position that novelty seeking is subservient to tension reduction, Maddi's approach has much in common with the collative approach.

The variation-seeking approach starts with the proposition that novelty or varied experience is sought out for the inherent satisfaction, that is, for its own sake. Maddi contends that this position makes sense, as human life is complex and it cannot be understood properly with easy consistency explanations alone. The basic similarity of this approach lies in its agreement that exploratory behavior is motivated: *novel,* complex, incongruous, or surprising stimuli elicit exploratory behavior. Three types of exploratory behavior are distinguished:

1. Orienting response, such as visual fixation.
2. Investigatory response, which involves the physical relationship between the individual and his environment.
3. Play.[2]

Evidence is presented by Maddi to indicate novel stimulus is an important determinant of visual fixation in the human being. In an experiment, Maddi (Fiske and Maddi, 1961) varied the level of novelty among toys. Five levels of novelty were created: 0, 25, 50, 75, and 100 percent. The findings indicated that intermediate degrees of novelty (25 to 75 percent) were very effective in eliciting choice or investigatory responses. Thus novelty, as a stimulus variable, is seen to elicit both orienting and investigatory responses.

The theory posits that *variation* is important and basic to the arousal of exploratory behavior or novelty seeking. Variation here refers to the variation in stimulation, and thus novelty and surprisingness constitute variation. For Maddi the motivational significance of novelty seeking lies in the *need for variation.* The organism's need for variation results in exploratory responses. The degree of novelty seems also to be associated with the extent of exploratory responses. Some evidence indicates that moderate amounts of novelty seem to be more effective in producing orienting and investigatory responses than high degree of novelty. The variety approach proposes that the "organism attempts to maintain activation at the normal level because large deviations from this level are typi-

---

[2]Play as an exploratory response is not included here as it is not germane to a discussion of the novelty-seeking behavior of consumers.

cally associated with negative affect" (Fiske and Maddi, 1961, p. 271). Thus the need for variation of the organism exists to sustain a normal level of activation. "At any point in time the level of activation is determined by the total impact from various sources of stimulation. If level of activation is higher than normal, exploration of a stimulus having variation should not occur" (Fiske and Maddi, 1961, p. 272). In short, novelty seeking is an attempt made by the human being to satisfy his need for variation by exposing himself to stimuli with variation (novelty).

Individual Differences in Novelty Seeking

It is clear that not only arousal processes, but also the rate of arousal potential that is optimal, can differ widely from individual to individual and from occasion to occasion. Therefore, both Berlyne and Maddi were cognizant of the individual-differences dimension related to exploratory behavior.

Berlyne recognizes that prevailing levels of arousals, minimal levels of arousal, and the magnitude and strength of exploratory and epistemic behavior are all affected by individual differences. A number of personality traits seem to reflect differences in reactions to collative motivation: low and high intolerance of ambiguity, the simplicity-complexity dimension of aesthetic preference, and the "repressors" and "intellectualizers" all seem to be related to some extent with exploratory and epistemic behavior. Persons with high intolerance of ambiguity and persons preferring simplicity and "repressors" seem to favor avoiding or withdrawing from stimulus situations productive of conflict. Those with low intolerance of ambiguity, those that prefer complexity, and the "intellectualizers" seem to favor responses that would make use of exploratory and epistemic behavior. That is, these persons approach the disturbing stimuli to get more information, to become habituated to it, or to engage in some kind of epistemic activity (Berlyne, 1963, p. 347).

Similarly, Maddi (Fiske and Maddi, 1961) considers the *need* for variation as an aspect of personality, and thus individual differences are likely to affect the intensity and quality of variation seeking. Some people will be more disposed toward change, novelty, and the like than other persons. Although the existence of individual differences in variety seeking may be postulated, there is little empirical support at this time. Attempts have been made to measure the need for variation seeking. Garlington and Shimota (1964) developed an instrument to measure the intensity of one's need for changing stimulus impact, called the Change Seeker Index. Kolin, Price, and Zoob (1964) reported the development of a Sensation-Seeking Scale (SSS), designed to measure the optimal stimulation level. Penney and Reinehr (1966) developed a Stimulus Variation Seeking Scale (SVSS) aimed at measuring the amount of stimulus variation seeking customarily sought by an individual. These studies have been concerned with relating need for change seeking and the like to such dependent variables as age, sex, IQ, field independence, hostility, intellectual ability, and authoritarianism. None of these studies related the individual-differences aspect of variation seeking to exposure and exploration of novel items, novel stimuli, or new information and the like. Suffice it to point out then that individual-difference variables are likely to play a major role in the arousal and reduction of novelty-seeking behavior.

ALTERNATIVE EXPLANATIONS

In this section only a brief review of two approaches is provided. Both Hunt's (1963) incongruity-seeking formulation and Driver and Streufert's (1965) general incongruity adaptation are concerned with cognitive motivation mechanisms. Both are intended as integrative cognitive approaches to novelty and complexity seeking. The intent is not to provide complete details of these formulations, but only to sketch them for our understanding of novelty seeking.

Incongruity[3] Theory

Hunt attempted to integrate the cognitive approach to motivation He has tried to use the balance motive in his integrative approach via his cognitive incongruence concept. He assimilates some of Berlyne's (1960) ideas in arriving at optimal arousal. Therefore, Hunt's approach could be viewed as a synthesis of the cognitive-consistency approach and Berlyne's propositions regarding optimal arousal in novelty seeking. The basic premise in Hunt's formulation is that concern with novel stimuli occurs in the absence of any homeostatic need and painful stimulation. Accordingly, drive theories could not account for the seeking of new input. Therefore, he postulated that "motivation inherent in information processing," which is a cognitive motive, tends to reduce incongruity. Novelty, by definition, is considered a type of incongruity.

Hunt's explanations for novelty seeking are as follows: anytime there is an incongruity between an incoming stimulus (novelty) and some standard within the organism, this incongruity instigates (arouses) the motivation inherent in information processing to start operations or activities aimed at reducing the incongruity, that is, until congruity appears. In other words, the operations continue and the organism searches for additional information to match the input with existing standards, and this may well involve continued scrutiny of novel objects. The theoretical explanation is that there exists a motive to reduce incongruity which is inherent in incongruity. Detection of incongruity by the organism instigates behavior, and congruity terminates the activities.

Incongruence is dissimilarity from the standard. The standard is a function

---

[3]The term *incongruity* as used by Hunt (1963) is all encompassing and includes the terms or tendencies known as imbalance, incongruity (of Osgood and Tannenbaum, 1955), inconsistency, and even dissonance.

of past experience and similar to the concept of adaptation level[4] proposed by Helson (1959). Thus familiar objects seen in unfamiliar guise could well be perceived as incongruous. Two types of incongruities are distinguished by Hunt: short-term incongruity and long-term incongruity. Sudden change of input constitutes short-term incongruity. Arousal in such a situation leads to information-seeking orienting reflex, which could serve as a means of reducing incongruity by gathering more information on the novel object. Long-term incongruity arises from failure of new inputs to match expectations derived from past experience. These long-term expectations or standards include beliefs, attitudes, and the like. Thus "by attributing all long-term incongruity reduction to one basic motive Hunt has attempted to unite all of the diverse 'balance' theories" (Driver and Streufert, 1965, p. 36).

So far, the formulation of Hunt's parallel cognitive-consistency theory is that the organism is engaged in reducing incongruity to congruity. Where Hunt parts company with the consistency school is in suggesting that the organism's approach to or avoidance of incongruous stimuli seems to be a function of an optimum, based on past experience, of either arousal or incongruity. Adopting Berlyne's (1960) position, Hunt has suggested that the relationship between incongruity level and arousal is U-shaped, thereby indicating that there is an optimal level of arousal (see Figure 2). This has led him to the "expectation that when the organism's level of arousal happens to be below the optimum, it would prefer greater degrees of incongruity than it would prefer when the level of arousal should happen to be above the optimum and vice versa" (Hunt, 1963, pp. 76-77). In Berlyne's formulation (see Figure 1) arousal potential is based on the collative variables (including novelty) and variations in arousal are related to variations in arousal potential. Thus the direction of behavior is determined by the amount of arousal. From the standpoint of incongruity, "arousal may be increased by either too little or too much incongruity, but it is incongruity that probably determines the direction of behavior. Arousal may commonly be associated with either too little or too much incongruity but it is neither a necessary nor a sufficient basis for approach or avoidance" (Hunt, 1963, p. 79). Context becomes an important factor in incongruity seeking, for it is postulated that the organism might prefer mildly incongruous circumstances; or, to state it differently, mildly novel stimuli might be preferred to extreme novelty (new but not too new). At low levels of incongruous situations, such as the homogeneous, unchanging, and completely familiar, incongruity seeking will take place. Finally, with respect to novel objects incongruous information may also have

---

[4]According to Helson's (1959) adaptation-level theory, all human behavior centers about the adaptation level (AL) or psychological equilibrium of the organism. The particular level of adaptation depends upon the interaction between the stimuli which confront the organism at that particular time. In other words, in each area of stimulation specific adaptation levels are developed by the human organism, which makes adjustments so that behavior becomes relative to the present state of the organism.

FIGURE 2.   Incongruity and Arousal Relationship

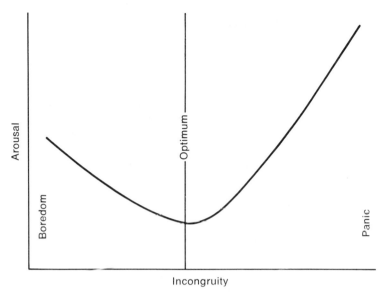

After Hunt (1963), p. 79.

positive hedonic value, tending to produce approach responses in human beings. The fact that they look longer at novel objects than simple or common objects is presented as evidence attesting to this reasoning.

General Incongruity Adaptation Level Hypothesis

Driver and Streufert (1965) felt that Hunt (1963) did not integrate the complexity-level theory within his framework of incongruity reduction and that Hunt's framework did not adequately explain how "standards" were formed or how they changed. Therefore, an attempt was made by them to integrate the complexity level of the organism and the congruity theory as proposed by Hunt; their formulations are known as the general incongruity adaptation level hypothesis.

Driver and Streufert basically adopt Hunt's view that the reaction to optimal incongruity stems from the basic motive to reduce incongruity. However, they view the optimum itself as a standard, and thus deviations from it are viewed as incongruous and the attainment of this optimum thereby reduces incongruity. They postulate that since the organism has had experience with deviations from adaptation level in each area where adaptation level occurs, organisms form expectations regarding the probable amount of incongruity they will encounter in each area. Furthermore, human beings are capable of pooling and averaging "their experiences of incongruity in specific areas into a more global general incongruity experience. By 'general incongruity' is meant the total amount of novelty, imbalance, dissonance, inconsistency, disagreement, failure and conflict an organism encounters summed over all specific adaptation levels" (Driver and Streufert, 1965, p. 50). Thus expectations can be formed concerning the "normal" amount of general incongruity to be expected in the environment. This is termed GIAL (general incongruity adaptation level); GIAL defines the optimal incongruity level within an organism, and any deviation from it is expected to lead to cognitive activity. The attainment of GIAL produces congruencies, and consequently the termination of activities. Thus novelty seeking is explained as follows:

> It is proposed that as incongruity falls below the optimum, cognitive action will produce more input (e.g., exploration, novelty seeking, etc). As incongruity increases beyond the optimum, cognitive action will attempt to reduce or simplify input (as in dissonance reduction) (Driver and Streufert, 1965, p. 59).

Reprise

It is tempting to cast novelty seeking, particularly in the context of consumer behavior, in the cognitive-consistency framework and derive satisfaction from having resurrected the "rationalizing" man. Dissonance theory may even look appealing for this prospect, since both the incongruity model of Osgood and Tannenbaum (1955) and the Heiderian (1958) balance model, as reviewed earlier, do not seem to be amenable to the same type of explanations in the novelty-seeking area. In this section a brief analysis is made of these prospects, and Berlyne's (1960, 1968) collative approach is recommended for viewing novelty seeking in consumer behavior.

It can be argued that when an organism is confronted with a novel stimulus, it is likely to experience dissonance with its previous concept, if there is one. One mode of dissonance reduction will be the exploration of the novel stimulus so as to fit it in with old concepts. Festinger (1957) has indicated that it is more likely that it is the stored concepts that would shift if the organism is in a state of dissonance, and that means that there is no need for exploration. Since dissonance is an unpleasant state, why would anyone seek novelty that might tend to increase dissonance? There are two plausible explanations based on dissonance experiments so far; at times, an individual will expose himself to dissonant information if it is deemed useful, or seek dissonant information so as to refute it (see Driver and Streufert, 1965, p. 18, for a detailed explanation). There are two reasons why this line of reasoning will not be fruitful for our inquiries. First, the latter explanation would mean that dissonance is at times not unpleasant. Second, *how* this exposure to novel stimuli takes place in the first place is not explained. Dissonance-based explanations of exploration of the novel or its usefulness only answer part of the question "what to do when exposed to novel stimuli"; but how we got there in the first place remains unexplained.

If we look at novelty seeking and collecting information about it, or exploration behavior in general, as gathering relevant cognitions with implications for future actions, Festinger (1964) would tend to place novelty seeking in the predecision phase, since conflict resolution takes place in this phase; but dissonance starts only after a choice is made, which indicates that commitment and consequences are expected to flow from the decision. One could argue, as Collins (1968) does so effectively, that limiting conflict processes to predecision and dissonance to postdecision is arbitrary and idiosyncratic. The two experiments upon which these pre- and postdecision process distinctions are made by Festinger (1964) have been questioned on the basis of methodology employed and ambiguity in the experimental designs (Zajonc, 1968, p. 365). With respect to commitment, although it may be an important aspect of dissonance theory, it is viewed as not necessary for the arousal of dissonance (Aronson, 1968, p. 466). The question of *how* one comes to be exposed to novelty will still remain unexplained, even if the distinctions between pre- and postdecision phases are eliminated, and even if a commitment or choice is not involved in the situation.

The variation-seeking formulations (Maddi, 1968) of an organism that at times seeks consistency and at other times needs variation is a romantic one. Although this approach may seem highly relevant, the available empirical evidence is limited; it would appear Berlyne's framework not only has the support of empirical findings, but his elegant formulations are more appealing from the viewpoint of parsimony and fuller explanations of novelty seeking in consumer behavior.

Hunt's (1963) incongruity approach encompasses all the balance models and is much more extensive than Festinger's dissonance theory. However, his concept of incongruity is more of a perceptual nature, and the notion of deviation from a standard (adaptation level) would imply awareness of these standards or their independent existence. It is doubtful that standards of adaptation levels for each product category or brand do exist in consumers' minds, or would they generally be aware of such standards in exploration of novelty. Hunt's optimal concept is a useful one, but it is not different from Berlyne's formulations. Similarly, the concept of the general incongruity adaptation level hypothesis, involving an overall adaptation level (generalized AL), would have difficulty finding parallels in the area of generalized adaptation level for consumers among products or symbolic representations. Second, the GIAL concept might conceivably be more relevant to complexity seeking than novelty, if one could argue that not all complex situations are novel ones.

Berlyne's collative approach appears more suited to the explanations of novelty seeking in consumer behavior, as the very definition of collative properties includes the stimulus properties that others have considered important in the determination of novelty-seeking behavior. Second, the concepts of specific and diversive exploration behavior do seem more relevant in the context of buyer behavior. Third, the concepts of complete novelty and short-term novelty encompass most of the situations involving new products or switching brands after a period of being loyal to them. Finally, Berlyne's formulation has been adapted and emphasized even by others whose formulations deviated considerably (Driver and Streufert, 1965; Maddi, 1968). Optimal arousal and the idea of seeking to maintain this optimal arousal through arousal potential of the collative variables provide plausible explanations for the observable manifestations of consumers with respect to novelty seeking. Such an optimum lying at some intermediate point, implying nonmonotonic functions between the variables, has appealing theoretical and empirical possibilities. In short, Berlyne's formulations appear to contain almost everything needed to explain novelty seeking and much more.

NOVELTY SEEKING IN CONSUMER BEHAVIOR

A logical place to start to find the types of theoretical explanation of novelty seeking in consumer behavior is the area of new-product adoption or what has come to be known as the *diffusion of innovations*. However, the explanations have emphasized the aggregate behavior (see Robertson, 1970, for an excellent summary), and the studies of the process have been in the flow of information, categories of adopters over time, and differences between adopter and nonadopter categories. Some recognition of individual differences is evident in some studies, and such personality factors as *venturesomeness*, risk perception, and attitude toward change (Robertson, 1970) have been investigated. It appears that the diffusion literature is reflective of the concerns of *how the novel item is spread among groups of consumers over time*. They have not been concerned, for the most part, with the cognitive motivations, processes, or with internal variables that might tend to provide basic explanations of the psychological mechanism involved. However, recently there seems to have been some interest in the explanations for novelty seeking. Arndt (1967) speculated that cognitive clarity may have something to do with new-product adoption and word-of-mouth communications related to it. Robertson (1970) suggested that variety theories might provide better explanations for consumers' actions which introduce variety and novelty into their style of life. In a peripheral way, Maloney (1962) has suggested that, at least in the advertising context, to be effective advertising messages for new products (brands) must elicit *curiosity* about the product or brand. His reasoning was that buyers do have stable cognitions and to change them in order to lead to new cognitions must involve an intermediary step of dissonant nonbelief (curiosity), whose components appear to be a moderate amount of nonbelief and low-to-medium amount of uncertainty. This formulation, although based on a cognitive-consistency approach, comes parallel to Berlyne's notion of the conceptual conflict that underlies epistemic curiosity, which is expected to lead to information-seeking activities. It is clear from Maloney's formulation that novelty seeking need not be limited to new products, and there appears to be a growing awareness that novelty seeking or seeking of new products and newness by consumers needs to be explained in some systematic way. Brief theoretical explanations for the underlying mechanism are found in Howard and Sheth (1969) and Hansen (1972). Their formulations, in this area, though brief, are based on Berlyne's approach reviewed earlier.

In order to simplify Berlyne's concepts for their exposition, Howard and Sheth refer to all the collative properties of the stimulus as *stimulus ambiguity*. Thus, in their framework, stimulus ambiguity elicits arousal and arousal leads to exploratory and epistemic behavior by buyers. This behavior will take the form of attention and overt search. Two types of exploratory behavior, specific and diversive exploration, are related to arousal-ambiguity relationships. Howard and Sheth postulate that the consumer tends to routinize his buying decision by reducing the complexities in the situation, and this phase is referred to as *psychology of simplication*. The attainment of this routinization, although helpful, eventually leads to feelings of monotony and of boredom, and thus the buyer is expected to engage in diversive exploration activities. The relationship between stimulus ambiguity and arousal is seen by them as U-shaped and involving an optimum. Thus in this phase the stimulus ambiguity is likely to be getting below the optimum level. On the other hand, when the buyer complicates his buying situation by considering new brands, he is said to be in the *psychology of complication* phase. In this phase, problem-solving behavior with respect to the new brand will come to the fore, resulting in specific exploration. By virtue of its newness, the new brand being considered will likely be more ambiguous than optimal. Thus in the psychology of simplication phase the buyer is likely to find himself in a situation with virtually little stimulus ambiguity leading to arousal and looking for more stimulation; on the other hand, newness having provided more ambiguity will result in activities to lessen the stimulus ambiguity. Thus both phases lead to exploratory activities aimed at reaching the optimal. They indicate that below the optimal level exploration takes the form of diversive exploration, and above the optimum it takes the form of specific exploration.

Hansen's (1972) formulations do not relate specifically to novelty seeking. He views the entire choice processes of consumer behavior as consisting of two types of activities, *exploration* and *deliberation*. Exploration, involving the three steps of orienting behavior, locomotor exploration, and investigatory exploration, is used, in his view, to obtain information in the course of the choice process in general. In his formulation the various aspects of the environment are capable of generating different amounts of arousal. Novelty, change, surprise, and incongruity are aspects of perceived environmental situation. Hansen also subscribes to the concept of maintaining an optimal level of arousal.

Since arousal and its reduction in the choice process entail conflict, Hansen reasoned that uncertainty and importance are both necessary and sufficient conditions for conflict to occur. Such a view recognizes the connection between arousal, exploration, and the concept of perceived risk (Bauer, 1960). Perceived risk involves uncertainty and consequences. Consequently, Hansen argues that although consumers may reduce risk by avoiding risky alternatives, "there is a possible risk associated with not obtaining the advantages inherent in a new product which really is superior. This formulation conforms too with arousal theory since the quest for an intermediate level of arousal will secure a strategy which balances the two counteracting 'risks' " (Hansen, 1972, p. 131).

Theoretical Perspective.   Novelty seeking in consumer behavior can be expected to relate to exposure, attention, and awareness of a new stimulus (new product, new ad, etc.). The next step might be that the novel stimulus is chosen or preferred to the more familiar one by the consumer. Therefore, any theoretical framework aimed at understanding and explaining novelty-seeking behavior can deal with the former; the latter belongs perhaps, to the bailiwick of the diffusion process. The reason for such bifurcation is that adoption of a new product or novelty implies use and continued use of the new item, whereas explanations of novelty seeking will be sufficient if the conditions and the factors that produce this behavior are examined. From a novelty standpoint, continued exposure and use will no longer classify the item as novel or new. The difficulty becomes much more apparent when one considers the meaning of novelty employed in the context of consumer behavior.

Novelty.   What is novelty? At least in the area of new-product diffusion, a range of "newness" is recognized. Effect on established patterns of consumption is the sole criterion used, and, accordingly, three types of innovations (new products or newness) are distinguished: continuous innovation, dynamically continuous innovation, and discontinuous innovation. Disruption of the established patterns of consumers is very low because of the adoption of the first category of innovation; disruption ranges to very high in the case of discontinuous innovations. Most new products introduced to the market, and the study of their adoptions, seem to fit in the first category; a very limited number of them fall into the dynamically continuous category, and only a few products in the long history of new-product introductions to the consumer can be classified as discontinuous. Thus novelty in the sense of newness can be viewed with respect to an organism's *total experience* (completely novel or discontinuous innovations) and with respect to its *recent experience* (short-term novelty or continuous innovations). In the context of consumer behavior rarely, if ever, is there absolute novelty; much of it is "relative novelty." So for purposes of our understanding of novelty-seeking behavior, newness or novelty can range from short-term novelty to complete novelty, with most items or stimuli expected to fall in the intermediate categories of novelty.

Studies of consumer perceptions have indicated that certain stimulus properties and patterns, such as size, intensity, and color, are able to capture consumers' attention. The point to be made is that properties of the stimuli which are external to the consumer have been determinants, among other factors, of perception of products and their attributes. Thus it can be stated that novelty as a stimulus property is a component of some outstanding stimulus properties of importance. They have been referred to earlier as the *collative properties*. Novelty as one of the constituents of collative properties can be expected to capture the attention of the consumer. Although the collative properties relate to the stimulus side, any action by the consumer implies that concern should also be with the relations of these properties with the properties of the organism, and the context in which the stimulus appears.

The collative variables (novelty, ambiguity, surprisingness, incongruity, and power to induce uncertainty) do not directly affect arousal; they relate to arousal via the arousal potential of the collative properties. The distinction between arousal and arousal potential is important for our understanding of the novelty-seeking behavior of consumers. Arousal potential refers to all those properties of the incoming stimuli with power to affect arousal. Although arousal may vary directly with the collative properties, arousal and arousal potential are related in a curvilinear fashion—generally a U-shaped relation. Such a relationship implies an optimum lying at some intermediate point. The novel aspect of a new product or a new stimulus for the consumer usually does not appear alone. It is accompanied sometimes by surprisingness, and being new appears incongruous or ambiguous and induces uncertainty, since it provides very little information to the buyer. In the buying context, then, the collative properties are expected to occur in correlation with one another, although it should be recognized that any one of these properties can appear alone without any other. Since the relationship is postulated as U-shaped, very low and very high amounts of arousal potential will lead to a high level of arousal. So, very close to the absence of newness or novelty in new products, and highly novel items, such as a dynamically continuous innovation, are likely to lead, through arousal potential, to high levels of arousal. However, completely novel or what we have called extremely discontinuous innovation may lead to decline at the upper extreme of arousal potential due to supramaximal inhibition (see Figure 3). (It may be noted here that dissonance formulations suggesting avoidance of novelty might be viewing this type of situation involving a high degree of novelty.) The theoretical implication here is that the consumer, who generally has a choice as to whether or not he wants to seek novelty, may select (what is to him) the right amount of novelty by either leaving novelties that are too dull

FIGURE 3. Stimulus Ambiguity-Arousal Relation

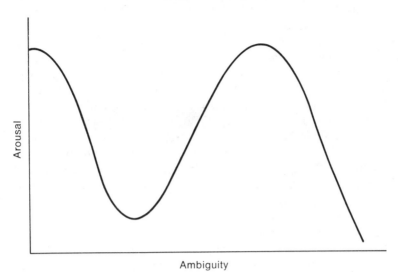

After Howard and Sheth (1969), p. 161.

or avoiding the ones that are too exciting. It is also apparent that to maintain the optimal level moderate amounts of novelty will be sought, or even preferred, over nonnovel or extremely novel items.

The low end of the arousal potential reflects situations in which the consumer has become extremely familiar (habituation) with the product and it is no longer new (surprising, ambiguous, etc.). Brand loyalty over a period of time might indicate the buyer is approaching this situation. This highly predictable buying behavior (brand choice) in these circumstances is also the boring humdrum behavior. Monotony being unpleasant, the continued use of the nonnovel is expected to result in a rise in arousal. On the other side, an unfamiliar item, being novel, induces ambiguity, subjective uncertainty, and may even appear incongruous. The new product, generally, may be unfamiliar but seldom would be completely novel—that is, newness in the consumer context clearly would mean that the new stimulus differs only in degree from other known stimuli (products, brands, etc.). Such collative properties, being productive of high arousal potential, give rise to high arousal, and a conflict situation ensues.

What happens when the consumer is aroused? An aroused state means a tension-producing state, and to reduce this tension the consumer is expected to engage in exploratory behavior. The initial response, on the onset of arousal, is likely to be the *orientation reaction* (attention) by the consumer. Such manifested reactions or responses as turning one's eyes or head toward the source of stimulation, or overt receptor-adjusting responses, have been classified as the orientation reaction. It is suggested that *attention* (orientation reaction) to the novel stimulus is the first basic exploratory response that emanates from the consumer on the onset of arousal. This seems to be a necessary condition for seeking novelty by consumers. Once attention is given to the novel stimulus, the subsequent response is likely to be *investigatory* in nature, such as looking (longer) at the new product, lifting it, physically examining it (if possible), manipulating it, and other such responses to get some information from the novel item so as to classify it in the perceptual system. There may be situations in which orientation reaction may be the only response. But anyone who has observed persons who get interested in the "model house" because of the sign advertising it, and who upon entering the premises go about looking, touching, tilting, and generally manipulating novel items will come to the conclusion that as far as consumers are concerned both of these responses, that is, orientation reaction and investigatory responses, will constitute consumers' exploratory behavior.

If the arousal is the result of routinized choice and the ensuing boredom and monotony, novelty will be sought. Some have suggested that this will take the form of diversive exploration, implying any stimuli with collative properties will be sought. This appears to be a limitation not intended by Berlyne's classification of diversive exploration. For the consumer, in the monotonous situation in particular (and in general), not only the collative properties (including novelty) determine the arousal but the state of the organism, which contains the traces of past experiences, determines the arousal. Thus a particular brand that had been in use for a period of time might result in arousal because of the monotony involved; but in such a case novelty seeking does not mean the selection of a novel item that has not been considered before; one of the other existing brands in that product class, which may even have been considered earlier, now becomes novel simply because *it is new with respect to this consumer's recent experience.* However, the response can take the form of specific exploration, if only one stimulus is being considered, or it can be diversive and need not necessarily be restricted to one mode or the other. In general, we can conclude that consumers engaged in exploratory behavior have both modes of exploration (specific and diversive) and which one is chosen will depend upon the "new" stimulus under consideration and personal and situational factors.

So far the explanations have dealt with arousal and exploratory behavior related to physical perception (attention) of the new product and the explanation implied perceptual conflict aroused by the novelty. Since much of the information for buyers comes from symbols, any explanation of novelty-seeking behavior cannot be limited only to new products, but should look at symbolic response tendencies, such as information seeking or knowledge acquisition, as a way of reducing curiosity generated by the symbols. Thus newness might instigate conflict between symbolic response tendencies and such conceptual conflict is expected to lead to epistemic curiosity, a motivation for seeking information, and epistemic (knowledge-seeking) behavior will ensue. It would appear that epistemic responses can also be a way of reducing conflict in this aroused state. In fact, one can view the exploratory and epistemic behaviors as the response tendencies of consumers faced with some degree of newness in their buying situations, whether they involve significates or symbols. Consumers can be viewed as engaging in orientation reaction (attention) to the new stimuli, then in investigatory responses and information seeking. Diversive exploration, as a response tendency, in this sense may even include overt search and deliberate seeking of information from personal and nonpersonal sources regarding new stimulus situations. Viewed in this framework, all dimensions of newness in the consumer context, such as new products, new advertising (appeals, medium, etc.), and new promotional devices (such as familiar products in unfamiliar surroundings), can be viewed as new stimuli subject to the processes and mechanisms postulated in this section. A comprehensive diagrammatic representation of the theoretical perspective is provided in Figure 4.

FIGURE 4.   **Novelty Seeking in Consumer Behavior: A Theoretical Framework**

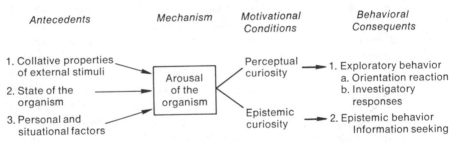

Empirical Evidence

There are no empirical findings in the consumer-behavior literature related to testing any of the hypotheses that can be generated from the new theoretical formulations of Berlyne (1960, 1968), Maddi (1968), Hunt (1963), or others.

The only study dealing with Berlyne's formulation in a buying-behavior context is that of Copley and Callom (1971). This study was concerned with industrial search behavior and attempted to relate perceived risk in the stimulus-ambiguity sense. Subjects for this study were purchasing managers. The hypothesis that a small amount of stimulus ambiguity increases the search behavior of the industrial buyer due to the curiosity motivation (to relieve the monotony of continually using the same source of supply) appears to be supported by the results obtained.

Howard and Sheth (1969) cite the findings from Katz and Lazarsfeld (1955) to indicate that those who bought a new product in that study did so for one of two reasons: dissatisfaction or wanting a change. In the study about two-thirds of those who had changed to the new product indicated that they did so because of their dissatisfaction with their present brand and one third changed to the new product merely because they wanted a change, although they were satisfied with their present brand. These results, at least, may be supportive of the monotony hypothesis advanced earlier. It is recognized that other interpretations, such as Maddi's (1968) variety seeking, are also plausible.

In a study on why people purchase new products Haines (1966) reported that 15 percent of the respondents had bought a new product because it was new. A sidelight of interest in the study was that some people had been persuaded to purchase a new product by information about the new product in advertising. His following conclusion is more relevant for the theoretical perspective provided earlier:

> The introduction of these new products merely altered brand buying behavior within a product class. Perhaps this type of new product is quite different in how people behave toward it compared to a new product which attracts people to use a product class for the first time (Haines, 1966, pp. 692-93).

Cox (1967) in explaining perceived risk and information handling in consumer behavior cited some of his observations regarding brand switching by women and offered the following explanation, which is pertinent for our framework:

> I have found women justify brand switching in product category similar to shampoo on the grounds that they had become "immune" to the brand they had been using. It no longer "did anything" for them and they deliberately tried a brand with which they had not had any (or recent) experience (Cox, 1967, p. 9).

An explanation offered by him was that uncertain or high-risk purchases may have been a way of relieving boredom by these women.

In a study to test his "curiosity" hypothesis with respect to a new test advertisement, Maloney (1962) exposed housewives to an experimental ad, the responses to which were classified as curiosity or disbelief. He concluded that curiosity responses were predictive of enhanced consumer intent to interact with the new product advertised in the test ad. Suffice it to point out that curiosity arousal is related to consumers' interest in engaging in further exploratory behavior.

In a study dealing with comparison of information-processing models of consumer-choice processes, Bettman (1971) suggested that for explaining exploratory behavior or novelty seeking the GIAL model (Driver and Streufert, 1965) could be more relevant. His study did not contain any empirical findings relating to novelty seeking.

None of the studies cited, with the exception of Copley and Callom (1971), specifically tests hypotheses that can be generated from theoretical perspectives; however, their findings amply demonstrate that there may be psychological processes uniquely relevant to novelty seeking, and it appears that these findings can be interpreted in the light of the framework presented in this paper.

Some of the findings relating individual differences or personality variables to new-product adoption are highly relevant to the individual-differences aspect of novelty-seeking behavior. Rogers (1957) found that a trait he identified as *innovative proneness* is related to new-product adoption. Robertson (1970) reported that *venturesomeness* was the most important personality factor related to the adoption of a new product (in this case, touch telephone). Recently, Jacoby (1971) has found that the personality variable of dogmatism was related to innovation proneness. His finding was that low dogmatic individuals were found to be more likely to be the innovators. No attempt has so far been made to relate Cattell's exploration erg, or other personality variables such as intolerance of ambiguity, simplicity-complexity dimensions, and so forth, to new-product adoptions. Although the findings cited may not conclusively establish the relationships between personality variables and new-product adoption, individual differences need to be explored in novelty-seeking behavior.

Although theoretical perspectives have been wanting and empirical findings were unavailable, this does not seem to have deterred the practitioners from indicating marketing strategies and offering practical advice. For example, Myers and Reynolds (1967) have pointed out that one marketing strategy has been to claim "new" (and "improved") features for a product or service. Ogilvy (1963, p. 13) has offered this practical counsel: "Always try to inject news into your headlines, because the consumer is always on the lookout for new products or new ways to use an old product or new improvements in an old product."

Some Directions for Research

The diffusion of innovation models in consumer behavior have generally assumed that the process is started by persons who want to try the new products because they are new. No theoretical interest seems to have motivated their formulations. Since theoretical formulations are now forthcoming [e.g., Howard and Sheth (1969)] and since there is no empirical research relevant to consumer behavior in the novelty-seeking area, some suggestions are offered for the direction of research efforts.

One major criticism of the studies based on cognitive consistency theories has been that they dealt with motivation in a perfunctory manner (Singer, 1966, p. 54). The collative approach to novelty seeking as presented in this paper is amenable to demonstrating some of the physiological indices presumed to be related to arousal (e.g., pupillary measures, GSR tests, etc.). Second, measures of conflict (degree of conflict) can be obtained through reaction times, confusion measures, strength-of-response tendencies, and the like. Third, the collative variables themselves are amenable for quantitative measurements, although problems associated with assigning numerical values in the contexts of consumers' novelty-seeking behavior may prove difficult if not insurmountable. Novelty dimensions appear to be scalable, and there are ways of independently classifying novelty, such as the use of established categories developed by the diffusion of innovation researchers.

What is needed is systematic, empirical research with rigor and unambiguous experimental designs and unassailable and uncomplicated measures. Laboratory experimentation seems to be eminently suited for investigating the processes and properties of the novelty-seeking behavior of consumers. For those who still are partial to real-world studies and experiments in consumer behavior, quasi-experimental designs can be usefully employed in consumer panel methodology and can obtain real-world data from even Dayton, Ohio, the middle-America. Introduction of new products in selected locations, testing of campaigns for new products in selected cities and media, and the like are amenable to controlled experiments in field settings. The important task is to generate hypotheses based on theoretical perspectives and test them so as to fully understand and explain novelty-seeking behavior of consumers.

CONCLUSIONS

After a review of cognitive-consistency theories and their relevance to novelty-seeking behavior, Berlyne's collative approach was advocated as the most suitable for our purposes of understanding this behavior. The reasoning was that this approach can explain the total behavior of consumers with respect to newness. The framework itself is capable of explaining both the purposeful and the manifest behavior of consumers when it comes to seeking varying degrees of novelty and the activities that ensue. The framework provided can even be viewed in terms of the cognitive-consistency approach; that is, people may find total consistency unpleasant and might seek inconsistency up to an optimal level of inconsistency (consistency to an optimal standard). Conceptual conflict can even be viewed in terms of cognitive consistency, whereas perceptual conflict may be seen as a situation in which inconsistency is motivating under certain circumstances. Since conflict and dissonance are not very different, according to Collins (1968), the conflict-reduction framework is claimed by some (Maddi, 1968) as really a consistency-theory viewpoint. For our purposes, the elegant and rich explanations of the collative approach are capable of offering complete explanations for the total behavior, and cognitive-consistency theories have no counterpart for them, at least for the present.

REFERENCES

Anderson, L. K., J. R. Taylor, and R. J. Holloway, "The Consumer and His Alternatives: An Experimental Approach," *Journal of Marketing Research*, 3 (1966), 62-67.

Arndt, Johan, *Word of Mouth Advertising.* New York: Advertising Research Foundation, Inc., 1967.

Aronson, Eliot, "Dissonance Theory: Progress and Problems," in *Theories of Cognitive Consistency: A Sourcebook,* ed. R. P. Abelson and others. Skokie, Ill.: Rand McNally & Company, 1968, 5-27.

Bauer , R. A., "Consumer Behavior as Risk Taking," in *Dynamic Marketing for a Changing World,* ed. R. S. Hancock. Chicago: American Marketing Association, 1960, 389-98.

Bell, G. D., "The Automobile Buyer After the Purchase," *Journal of Marketing,* 31 (1967), 12-16.

Berlyne, D. E., *Conflict, Arousal, and Curiosity.* New York: McGraw-Hill Book Company, 1960.

Berlyne, D. E., "Motivational Problems Raised by Exploratory and Epistemic Behavior," in *Psychology: A Study of Science,* ed. S. Koch. Vol. 5. New York: McGraw-Hill Book Company, 1963.

Berlyne, D. E., "Curiosity and Exploration," *Science,* 153 (1966), 25-33.

Berlyne, D. E., "The Motivational Significance of Collative Variables and Conflict," in *Theories of Cognitive Consistency: A Sourcebook,* ed. R. P. Abelson and others. Skokie, Ill.: Rand McNally & Company, 1968, 257-66.

Bettman, J. R., "The Structure of Information Processing in Consumer Choice Processes," *Journal of Marketing Research,* 8 (November 1971).

Cannon, L. K., "Self-Confidence and Selective Exposure to Information," in *Conflict, Decision and Dissonance,* ed. L. Festinger. Stanford, Calif.: Stanford University Press, 1964, 83-96.

Cardozo, R. N., "An Experimental Study of Consumer Effort, Expectation, and Satisfaction," *Journal of Marketing Research,* 2 (1965), 244-49.

Cartwright, D., and F. Harary, "Structural Balance: A Generalization of Heider's Theory," *Psychological Review,* 63 (1956), 277-93.

Cohen, J. B., and M. E. Goldberg, "Factors Relevant to the Adequacy of the Dissonance Model in Post-Decision Product Evaluation." Mimeographed report, 1970.

Collins, B. E., "Behavior Theory," in ed. *Theories of Cognitive Consistency: A Sourcebook,* ed. R. P. Abelson and others. Skokie, Ill.: Rand McNally & Company, 1968, 240-45.

Copley, T. P., and F. Callom, "Industrial Search Behavior and Perceived Risk." Personal Communication, 1971.

Cox, D. F., ed., *Risk Taking and Information Handling in Consumer Behavior.* Graduate School of Business Administration, Harvard University, Boston, 1967.

Deutsch, M., "Field Theory in Social Psychology," in *Handbook of Social Psychology,* ed. G. Lindzey and E. Aronson. Reading, Mass.: Addison-Wesley Publishing Company, Inc., 1968, 412-87.

Driver, M. J., and S. Streufert, *The "General Incongruity Adaptation Level" (GIAL) Hypothesis: An Analysis and Integration of Cognitive Approaches to Motivation,* Paper No. 114, Institute for Research in the Behavioral, Economic and Management Sciences, Herman C. Krannert Graduate School of Industrial Administration, Purdue University, Lafayette, Indiana, 1965.

Engel, J. F., "The Psychological Consequences of a Major Purchase Decision," in *Marketing in Transition,* ed. W. S. Decker. Chicago: American Marketing Association, 1963, 462-75.

Festinger, L., *A Theory of Cognitive Dissonance.* Evanston, Ill.: Harper & Row, Inc., 1957.

Festinger, L., *Conflict, Decision, and Dissonance.* Stanford, Calif.: Stanford University Press, 1964.

Fiske, D. W., and S. R. Maddi, *Functions of Varied Experience.* Homewood, Ill.: Dorsey Press, Inc., 1961.

Garlington, W. K., and H. E. Shimota, "The Change Seeker Index: A Measure of the Need for Variable Stimulus Input," *Psychological Reports,* 14 (1964), 919-24.

Haines, G. H., "A Study of Why People Purchase New Products," in *Science, Technology and Marketing,* ed. R. M. Hass. Chicago: American Marketing Association (1966 Fall Conference Proceedings), 1966, 685-97.

Hansen, F., *Consumer Choice Behavior: A Cognitive Theory.* New York: The Free Press, 1972.

Heider, F., *The Psychology of Interpersonal Relations.* New York: John Wiley & Sons, Inc., 1958.

Helson, H., "Adaptation Level Theory," in *Psychology: A Study of Science,* ed. S. Koch, Vol. 1. New York: McGraw-Hill Book Company, 1959, 565-621.

Holloway, R. J., "An Experiment on Consumer Dissonance," *Journal of Marketing,* 31 (1967), 39-43.

Howard, J. A., and J. N. Sheth, *The Theory of Buyer Behavior.* New York: John Wiley & Sons, Inc., 1969.

Hunt, J. M., "Motivation Inherent in Information Processing and Action," in *Motivation and Social Interaction–Cognitive Determinants,* ed. O. J. Harvey. New York: The Ronald Press Company, 1963, 35-94.

Hunt, S. D., "Post-Transaction Communications and Dissonance Reduction," *Journal of Marketing,* 34 (1970), 46-51.

Jacoby, J., "Exploring the Potential of Negative Sources: An Application of Heider's Balance Model," Paper No. 110, Purdue Papers on Consumer Psychology, 1970.

Jacoby, J., "Personality and Innovation Proneness," *Journal of Marketing Research,* 8 (1971), 244-47.

Jecker, J. D., "The Cognitive Effects of Conflict and Dissonance," in *Conflict, Decision and Dissonance,* ed. L. Festinger. Stanford, Calif.: Stanford University Press, 1964, 21-32.

Kassarjian, H. H., and J. B. Cohen, "Cognitive Dissonance and Consumer Behavior," *California Management Review,* 8 (Fall 1965), 55-64.

Katz, E., and P. F. Lazarsfeld, *Personal Influence.* New York: The Free Press, 1955.

Kolin, E. A., L. Price, and I. Zoob, "Development of a Sensation-Seeking Scale," *Journal of Consulting Psychology,* 28, 6 (1964), 477-482.

LoSciuto, L. A., and R. Perloff, "Influence of Product Preference on Dissonance Reduction," *Journal of Marketing Research,* 4 (August 1967), 286-90.

Maddi, S. R., "The Pursuit of Consistency and Variety," in *Theories of Cognitive Consistency: A Sourcebook,* ed. R. P. Abelson and others. Skokie, Ill.: Rand McNally & Company, 1968, 267-74.

Maloney, J. C., "Curiosity Versus Disbelief in Advertising," *Journal of Advertising Research,* 2 (1962), 2-8.

McGuire, W. J., "The Current Status of Cognitive Consistency Theories," in *Cognitive Consistency,* ed. Shel Feldman. New York: Academic Press, Inc., 1966, 1-46.

McGuire, W. J., "Selective Exposure: A Summing-Up," in *Theories of Cognitive Consistency: A Sourcebook,* ed. R. P. Abelson and others. Skokie, Ill.: Rand McNally & Company, 1968, 797-800.

Mittelstaedt, R., "A Dissonance Approach to Repeat Purchasing Behavior," *Journal of Marketing Research,* 6 (November 1969), 444-47.

Myers, J. H., and W. H. Reynolds, *Consumer Behavior and Marketing Management.* Boston: Houghton Mifflin Company, 1967.

Newcomb, T. M., "An Approach to the Study of Communicative Acts," *Psychological Review,* 60 (1953), 393-404.

Newcomb, T. M., "Interpersonal Balance," in *Theories of Cognitive Consistency: A Sourcebook,* ed. R. P. Abelson and others. Skokie, Ill.: Rand McNally & Company, 1968, 28-51.

Ogilvy, D., *Confessions of an Advertising Man.* New York: Atheneum Publishers, 1963.

Osgood, C. E., and P. H. Tannenbaum, "The Principle of Congruity in the Prediction of Attitude Change," *Psychology Review,* 62 (1955), 42-45.

Penney, R. K., and R. C. Reinehr, "Development of a Stimulus-Variation Seeking Scale for Adults," *Psychological Reports,* 18 (1966), 631-38.

Robertson, T. S., *Consumer Behavior.* Glenview, Ill.: Scott, Foresman and Company, 1970.

Rogers, E. M., "Personality Correlates of the Adoption of Technological Practices," *Rural Sociology,* 22 (1957), 267-68.

Sheth, J. N., "Cognitive Dissonance, Brand Preference and Product Familiarity," in *Insights Into Consumer Behavior,* ed. J. Arndt. Boston: Allyn and Bacon, Inc., 1968, 41-54.

Sheth, J. N., "Are There Differences in Dissonance Reduction Behavior Between Students and Housewives?" *Journal of Marketing Research,* 7 (May 1970), 243-45.

Singer, J. P., "Motivation for Consistency," in *Cognitive Consistency,* ed. Shel Feldman. New York: Academic Press, Inc., 1966, 48-73.

Tannenbaum, P. H., "The Congruity Principle: Retrospective Reflections and Recent Research," in *Theories of Cognitive Consistency: A Sourcebook,* ed. R. P. Abelson and others. Skokie, Ill.: Rand McNally & Company, 1968, 52-71.

Venkatesan, M., "Cognitive Dissonance," in *Handbook of Marketing Research,* ed. R. Ferber. New York: McGraw-Hill Book Company (in press).

Zajonc, R. B., "Cognitive Theories in Social Psychology," in *Handbook of Social Psychology,* ed. G. Lindzey and E. Aronson. Reading, Mass.: Addison-Wesley Publishing Company, Inc., 1968.

10

Consumer Decisions and Information Use

Steven H. Chaffee and Jack M. McLeod
University of Wisconsin

INTRODUCTION

Information Ignored. Information Distorted. Lack of Involvement. Risk. The Study of Information Use.

THE MODEL

Decision Matrix. Products and Brands. Information Availability. Information Needs. Involvement and Discrimination. Complex Consumer Decisions. Stages in Decision Making. Processes in Decision Making. Uses of the Model. Salience of Brands and Attributes. Information as Psychological Uncertainty.

METHODOLOGICAL PROBLEMS

Self-Report Data. Concept of Cost. Measurement. Observing Communication.

RESEARCH ON INFORMATION PROCESSES

Predecisional Cognizance. Evaluation. Postdecisional Cognizance.

MARKETING COMMUNICATION STRATEGIES

REFERENCES

INTRODUCTION

The concept of information should be an attractive one for students of consumer behavior and communication. To begin with, information is a highly marketable commodity in itself. Machlup's (1962) estimate indicates that nearly one third of total GNP in the United States is accounted for by the "knowledge production" industry, broadly defined. More particularly, information would intuitively seem to be an important component of most (in a sense, all) consumer decisions. This suggests that an understanding of principles of information use would be highly important for marketing strategists. Such information inputs as advertising and retail store displays are "controllable" (LeGrand and Udell, 1964) or "marketer-dominated" (Engel, Kollat, and Blackwell 1968), in that they can be manipulated to maximize marketing gains.

Information Ignored

Empirical studies of consumer behavior do not, however, offer strong encouragement for this view. For example, Bucklin (1965) found that only about one shopper in ten checked advertisements before shopping for shoes or personal accessories. Even for costly and heavily advertised purchases such as appliances, auto accessories, and furniture, scarcely half the sample reported checking ads before shopping. LeGrand and Udell (1964) found that major family purchases (television sets and furniture) were made almost one third of

The authors are especially grateful to Steven E. Scharbach for the information and insights he has contributed to this paper.

the time by one spouse without consulting the other, and without visiting more than one store. In another study, purchasers of small appliances typically visited only one store, made their buying decisions within a week of coming to a tentative decision, and relied on their own experience with a brand far more than on advertisements or catalogs (Udell, 1966).

This disinclination to seek out information should by no means be dismissed as evidence of "irrational" behavior on the part of consumers. Gathering and processing information adds substantially to the total cost of the purchase (Bender, 1964; Engel, Kollat, and Blackwell, 1968). Trips to stores, or even studying advertisements and catalogs, can take time and cost money. Furthermore, these activities postpone the purchase of items that may be needed, or at least desired, immediately. And finally, the total volume of information from a thorough search could be so confusing that the consumer might well decide he would have been as well off without it.

Even when information is easily available, the consumer may consider it wiser to ignore (or even distort) it than to attempt to cope with it by carefully calculated reasoning. Often purchases are simply not worth the effort. In a study of impulse buying, Kollat (1966) noted that many consumers who were exposed to information sources nevertheless said that this gave them "no useful information." He proposes a "customer-commitment hypothesis" that the consumer is unwilling (or unable) to make the effort of completely spelling out purchase plans.

Information Distorted

Distortion of information, although difficult to demonstrate empirically in marketing studies, is a well-established principle in the semiconsumer field of voting and political information. In their study of voters in Elmira, New York, in the 1948 presidential campaign, Berelson, Lazarsfeld, and McPhee (1954) found tendencies toward both selective exposure to campaign information and selective patterns of misperception of the candidates' stands on major issues. Selective exposure in this case consisted of Democrats hearing or reading more information favorable to President Truman, and Republicans being similarly over-exposed to information favorable to their party's challenger, Governor Thomas Dewey. Distortion consisted of attributing to one's own candidate a position opposite to the stand he had taken in the campaign, when his position was opposed to the voter's own opinion. For example, despite Truman's veto of the Taft-Hartley Labor Law and his many speeches against it, four of every ten Democrats who favored this law said they thought the President did also. (This error was made by only 10 percent of the Democrats who agreed with Truman in opposing the law.) Similarly, 43 percent of the Republicans who opposed Taft-Hartley thought Truman was for it, an error that was made by only 27 percent of pro-Taft-Hartley Republicans.

Analogous examples of errors in consumer perceptions of complex products might well be demonstrated by careful research. But the point is probably not as important as it would appear at first blush. What appear to an outside observer to be damning examples of "irrationality" and "distortion" probably carry much less import in the consumer's mind. Voting, despite its collective importance to the political system, is not a particularly consequential act for most voters; electoral behavior tends to be highly predictable and consistent from one election to the next, just as most consumer brand choice is somewhat consistent from one purchase to the next (Campbell, et al., 1960; Engel, Kollat, and Blackwell, 1968). This, coupled with the frequent neglect of potential information by consumers, suggests that many purchases are made with as little personal intellectual investment as goes into many votes for candidates. Voters could be said to be party-loyal, and consumers brand-loyal, to a considerable extent; but it would probably be more accurate to say that they are often uninvolved in the vote or purchase, and hence behave repetitively, because it is the easiest thing to do.

But to say that is merely to describe the kind of behavior we are *not* concerned with in this article. Our interest is in the search for and use of information. It is clear that this does not occur in every instance of a consumer purchase or vote, and in some areas it may not occur very frequently at all. But when it does, it is of particular interest both from an academic standpoint and in the pragmatic view of a marketing strategist. If campaign information can account for "only" 10 or 15 percent of the vote, a candidate will surely not ignore this factor; elections are often won by only a few percentage points, and the campaign can make *all* the difference if it means winning instead of losing. Similarly, even if "only" 15 or 20 percent of the market for a product can be reached by consumer information, in many cases this will mean that millions of dollars are at stake. (These figures are hypothetical examples, not real estimates of the relative importance of information in decisional behavior.)

Although the notion of "brand loyalty" may seem a satisfactory label to apply to the frequent observation of consistencies in purchasing, it is a dangerous misnomer. It is a misnomer because it implies that a consumer's main objective is to remain loyal to a particular brand, which is hardly a reasonable characterization of the usual case; it is dangerous because it focuses attention on the outcomes of consumer decisions, rather than on the process by which they are achieved (Seggev, 1970). Here we shall try to lay a groundwork for analyzing that process from the perspective of the communication of information.

Risk

One key organizing variable in marketing research in recent years has been the concept of *risk* (Bauer, 1960). The general approach has been to see the consumer as entering the marketplace faced with certain potential dangers: a poor purchase decision could cost him time, money, the benefits that the product was supposed to provide, and even a social "loss of face" if others recognize his mistake. His search for and handling of information will be directed toward minimizing these potential risks; when, by contrast, they pose little or no threat, it would be perfectly reasonable for him to ignore "information" entirely—however relevant that information might appear in the eyes of a marketer or researcher.

Since its introduction into the field, the risk-handling or risk-reduction approach has generated a variety of experimental and field studies of consumer behavior (e.g., Cox, 1967; Sheth and Venkatesan, 1968; Roselius, 1971). Without attempting to review that literature here, we can observe that the perception of risk is an empirical definition of the general concept of involvement that we have alluded to above as a precondition for information use by consumers. Although risk appears clearly a sufficient condition for involvement, it is problematic whether it is a necessary one. There would seem to be a number of more positive sources of involvement, such as rewards inherent in the product after purchase.

Study of Information Use

It has been typical to study information as an adjunct to a detailed analysis of some other phenomenon. For example, when a sociologist analyzes the diffusion of technological information, his goal is to elaborate a theory of social diffusion. Or when a psychologist tests the persuasive power of messages containing greater versus lesser amounts of consumer information, his work is designed to advance attitude-change theory. In either case information remains very loosely conceptualized, a sort of "given" that is treated only in a commonsense fashion.

The central purpose of this chapter is to suggest ways in which information can be used as a focal organizing concept in the analysis of consumer behavior. Two major classes of behavior are involved: decisions and communication. We shall set out a conceptual matrix or "map" for the analysis of consumer decisions, and a model of stages in the decision process. This framework will enable us to define several different types of consumer information. Communication will be treated at some points as an independent or *causal* variable, and in other situations as a dependent variable or *effect*. We approach the topic of information from our special viewpoint as students of communication processes, not as specialists in consumer behavior.

As noted above, we do not assume here that a consumer is always involved, nor that his behavior will conform to some external standard of rationality. But we do assume that *under certain conditions* he is especially likely to process information rationally, in the sense that he will use whatever information (right or wrong) is available to him. Similarly, we assume that there are conditions under which he will be motivated to increase the amount and accuracy of information available to him. Our first job here will be to specify what those conditions are and to discuss how a researcher might empirically determine when they are met. We shall also consider the kinds of communication that should be expected of consumers under these varying conditions, again in terms of the ways a researcher might observe these behaviors. Our attack on these questions will differ from the cost-benefit approach to information search summarized by Engel, Kollat, and Blackwell (1968). These two formulations should be considered complementary, not mutually exclusive.

In summary, this is an outline for an approach to behavioral research on consumer information use in the decision-making context. Although it is intended primarily for those who might be planning research, it should also provide a helpful model for interpretation of existing research findings for those who are devising consumer-information campaign strategies.

THE MODEL

Decision Matrix

Since we want to conceive of the consumer as both an information processor and a decision maker, we need a psychological model of information that corresponds to the major dimensions of decisions. The decision matrix that we shall employ is diagrammed schematically in Table 1. Its major dimensions are called *objects* and *attributes,* a distinction that has proven useful in social psychology (see e.g., Zajonc, 1960; Carter, 1965; Chaffee, et al., 1969). In Table 1, we have arrayed objects along the horizontal axis, and attributes along the vertical. The entries in the cells of this matrix are the *values* that are associated with each object, in terms of each specific attribute. An *object* is defined quite broadly as any element of the environment that exists psychologically for the person. An *attribute* is a dimension of judgment on which two or more objects can be compared (Carter, 1965).

The objects in Table 1 are designated by letters: $A, B, \ldots, Z$. The attributes are numbered $1, 2, \ldots, n$. There must be at least two objects (A and B) and at least one attribute for a decision to take place. The information in the matrix would, in this minimal case, consist of the values A_1 and B_1 of the two objects on the attribute, as compared to one another. If the consumer finds that his two alternatives differ, he can decide in favor of the object that has the higher value on the attribute.

Of course most decisions are more complicated in that they involve more than one comparison among more than two alternatives. As Figure 1 indicates, a complete decision matrix would identify all the alternative objects, all the relevant attributes, and a value for each of the cells in the matrix.

TABLE 1. Schematic General Model of a Decision Matrix (Cell Entries Are Relative Object Values)

Alternative Objects (Brands or Products)

	Object A	Object B	. . .	Object Z
Attribute 1	A_1	B_1	. . .	Z_1
Attribute 2	A_2	B_2	. . .	Z_2
. . .				
Attribute n	A_n	B_n	. . .	Z_n

A decision matrix in which all this information is available to the consumer is a theoretical goal that is rarely, if ever, found in real life. A moment's reflection should convince the reader that he rarely makes decisions on the basis of such complete information. As we have mentioned, the "failure" to inform oneself fully about alternatives and attributes is commonplace. But it is only partly due to the various costs of information search. It can also be attributed in part to inadequacies in the communication systems that service consumers with information. It is remarkably uncommon to find information packaged along the general lines of a decision matrix. We can best illustrate this deficiency in our information systems by tying our concepts to the real world of the consumer.

Products and Brands

Our vague definition of an object as something that "exists psychologically" can be greatly clarified for a discussion of consumer behavior. The relevant objects can be roughly divided into two categories, which are conventionally called products and brands. We will reserve the term *product* to refer to *classes* of commodities. For example, automobiles comprise one product class, news magazines a second, and perhaps presidential candidates a third. The term *brand* indicates a specific alternative *within a product class* (e.g., Fords versus Volkswagens).

Although this product-brand distinction is commonplace terminologically, its implications for the analysis of decisions and information use are not always followed. First, we should assume that a product decision must necessarily precede a brand decision. That is, before a consumer chooses between a Ford and a Volkswagen, he must decide whether to buy a car or not. The range of brand alternatives is normally restricted to very few varieties of a product, whereas the list of product alternatives is practically infinite. And whereas competing brands differ only slightly in price or other attributes, competing products often differ enormously.

Information Availability

It is a paradox, perhaps, that consumer-information sources stress between-brands comparisons much more than those between products, even though the need for information is much greater in the latter case. There is, however, an intermediate level that might be called *subproduct* information, which is fairly common but not specifically related to brands. An example is the "Take Tea and See" advertising campaign that challenged coffee at the product level. A less obvious instance would be the promotion of a "mild" filter cigarette, which implicitly argues for this general class of cigarettes against the subproduct category of strong unfiltered varieties—even though the advertisement seems overtly devoted to a particular brand.

Generally, products are more difficult to compare than brands, because the attributes are so rarely the same. (Should a quart of soup cost more, or less, than a pound of nuts?) But even at the brand level, the most carefully packaged information tells the consumer less than he needs to know. For example, *Consumer Reports* compares available brands on many specific attributes, but cannot tell the consumer which attributes would be most important to him. At best, the job of collecting and assessing information is not simple.

Information Needs

Product decisions are often forced on the consumer, in a sense. That is, the need to purchase a particular product frequently arises simply because one's supply has been depleted and must be replaced (Kollat, 1966). In voting the situation is similar; considerably more people vote than express interest in an election—perhaps because they consider it their civic duty to vote (Berelson, Lazarsfeld, and McPhee, 1954). In such situations it may be preferable to make *any* brand decision than to make none. Sheth and Venkatesan (1968) have shown experimentally that information search is greatly reduced when well-known brands are available; apparently consumers lump these name brands into a "safe" or low-risk category on the basis of familiarity.

The informational value of advertising extends well beyond mere familiarity with a product. Bucklin (1965) has found that ads are more likely to be consulted when the product is costly, when it has not been purchased recently, and when the consumer has no "favorite" store in mind. There is also evidence that those who check advertisements know more about the attributes of the various brands, including price.

As might be expected, price is one of the most common types of information sought by consumers, and to find out about it the consumer usually consults "controllable" information sources, such as ads, or visits the store itself (LeGrand and Udell, 1964). However, price turns out to be a less important factor in the brand decision, and price-reduction bears no clear relationship to brand choice (Seggev, 1970). Indeed, price seems to be used as an indicator of brand quality, which is the most common type of information sought (LeGrand and Udell, 1964). There is a tendency to choose the high-priced brand, especially when there is a great deal of between-brand variation in quality, and when the risks involved in choosing an unsatisfactory brand are great (Lambert, 1970). It should be noted, however, that the influence of price may be underrated due to methodological problems. Banks (1950) found, for example, that price was a better predictor of purchase than of brand preference.

Involvement and Discrimination

A lower-limit example of consumer-information use can be found in the purchase of table salt. The product decision is forced (salt is necessary), brand names are available, prices are about equivalent, and there are really no essential differences in brand quality (salt is simply sodium chloride) beyond a few minor variations in additives or packaging. A situation of this sort is said to be characterized by low *product involvement* and lack of *discriminating attributes*.

Product involvement is essentially a motivational concept rather closely related to perceived risk. It refers to the degree to which the consumer "cares about" his brand decision. As suggested in our discussion of risk, factors such as cost, importance of the product to the person, previous experience with the product, and differences between brands account for differences in product involvement.

An experiment by Bowen (1970) indicates that readers of advertisements are sensitive to the rationality of a sales appeal only when a high-involvement product is being considered. In the case of low-involvement products, rationality is a negligible factor. For example, an ad for an economy car that brings out many product-relevant attributes that favor that brand is likely to be more effective than a less informative appeal. The same holds true for other products that involve a high cost (e.g., diamond rings) or a lot of information (e.g., stereo phonographs). But the difference in effectiveness between highly rational appeals and other, less rational, ads is much less when product involvement is low—as in the case of cigarettes, sun-tan lotions, or camera flash cubes, for example. The consumer simply lacks the motivation to process a great deal of information in preparation for such inconsequential brand decisions.

The principle of the discriminating attribute is a cognitive concept introduced by Chaffee and Tipton (1969). In hypothetical decision situations, consumers expressed a strong preference for additional information regarding attributes on which the alternative choices differed. But if the alternatives were known to be identical insofar as a particular attribute was concerned, there was relatively little interest in finding out more about that attribute—regardless of its seeming intrinsic importance. Information preference also favored attributes on which the alternatives *could be* compared, but on which no values were yet known, apparently because this was seen as possibly a discriminating attribute. Information-seeking indices for discriminating attributes—that is, those attributes on which the alternatives differed, or might differ—were considerably higher than similar measures of information seeking about the alternatives themselves. This demonstrates that it is the attribute, not the brand or product itself, that is the central factor in decisional information processing. But the principle does not extend to nondiscriminating attributes; they cannot aid in decision making, and so in a sense (to be discussed later) do not provide information at all.

A similar concept can be found in Cox's (1967) "sorting rule" model, in which he proposes that the probability that a consumer will use a given "cue" in reaching a decision is partly determined by the cue's "confidence value." This comes down, roughly, to the cue's capacity to indicate a clear choice between alternatives—that is, the extent to which it constitutes a discriminating attribute. He presents some evidence to suggest that a dichotomous "go-no go" decision is made as to whether to apply a given attribute, based on the consumer's confidence in his ability to discriminate between brands on that attribute.

The reader should recognize that we are using the term *attribute* in a somewhat unusual fashion. In common language people often talk of "the attributes of brand X"; but we stipulate here that an attribute must apply to *both* brands (or products) to be relevant to a decision. That is, each alternative must have "it" to some identifiable degree (from zero on up), or "it" cannot affect the consumer's decision. Furthermore, the consumer must know (or be able to estimate) the value of each brand on the attribute, or it fails to meet the requirements of our model—which deals with both information and decision.

Complex Consumer Decisions

If a consumer's involvement in a purchasing decision were great enough, he might go to the effort of gathering a good deal of pertinent information. Beyond this, it would be necessary to organize and summarize the information in the decision matrix—an activity that is generally referred to as information processing. Once all this is done, a decision would seem practically automatic. But of course it is a rare case, since involvement is rarely so strong as to stimulate such a mental effort.

There should be instances of this extensive information processing, however, or the model we have proposed would be empirically moot. One likely example is the purchase of an automobile. There are many brands and subproduct categories. Involvement should be high because of price, of the risk of buying a car that will be costly to maintain, and of the social prestige that is often at stake. There are many discriminating attributes involved, and only extremely knowledgable specialists can keep track of more than a few of them. Even so, car owners who are fairly satisfied with the performance of their present model are quite likely to purchase the same make again (May, 1969).

Car purchases have provided the topic for empirical demonstrations of subtle principles of consumer communication behavior following a brand decision (e.g., Ehrlich, et al., 1957; Guerrero, 1969). Our point here is not that the automobile provides an ideal object for analysis of consumer decisions. Rather it demonstrates that our model can be applied to a product for which our assumptions hold. We would expect the same to be true of other high-involvement products, and we consider these an interesting and important subset of all consumer decisions. The model is inappropriate for analyzing other forms of consumer behavior, which fall outside the information-use area.

Stages in Decision Making

It should be obvious by now that consumer decision making is not a simple story that has a beginning, a middle, and an end. We shall attempt here to sort out the major stages and processes that are involved, so that differences between them can be explained. Figure 1 illustrates our model in the fashion of a flow chart.

Our model does have a beginning, which we have labeled the *inceptive* stage. It is one of three stages in the model, the others indicating the points at which the product and brand decisions have been made. The importance of these stages is that they can be identified for research purposes. That is, it is possible to

FIGURE 1.   **Decision Stages and Intervening Information Processes**

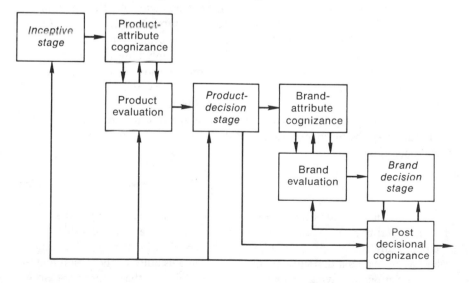

determine (often simply by asking) whether a consumer has made a brand decision. If he has not, he may have at least made a product decision. Failing that, he should be considered at the inceptive stage. Note that the researcher should work backward across the flow chart until he locates the last stage the consumer has reached. If the consumer has decided which brand of soap to buy, he has obviously also made the product decision to buy soap. It is important that the consumer be located at the proper stage in the model, so that his behavior regarding information processing will not be misinterpreted. In field studies this can be determined by a few questions, or by intercepting consumers at identifiable points in the decision process. Both methods have been widely used.

As we indicated earlier, we think of the product-decision stage as more complex in several ways than the brand-decision stage. Whereas brand decision is essentially a matter of "Should I buy brand *A* or brand *B*?", product decision is not necessarily the analogous "Should I buy product *X* or product *Y*?" As Carter (1965) points out, it is inherent in information processing that the person may *decide not to do anything.* For example, McPhee (1963) incorporates a "no-vote" outcome in his computer simulation model of voting behavior. A good many potential voters fail to reach the polls, apparently because of low involvement, lack of discriminating attributes, or conflicting information from different attributes; thus they make no "brand choice" between candidates (see Berelson, Lazarsfeld, and McPhee, 1954). If a person decides, in this sense, not to be a consumer, the model ceases to apply. We are making a teleological assumption that the consumer is moving toward an eventual brand decision. It is usually possible (and always advisable) to determine whether this major assumption holds in each person's case (e.g., by asking respondents in a field survey).

The model has no end. Its latest point, a process called *postdecisional cognizance,* leads backward to the several stages and evaluation processes within the model, and forward to an undefined state that simply indicates a cessation of cognitive involvement in the decision under consideration. Research and theory on postdecisional cognizance have been dominated by the intriguing psychological principle of cognitive dissonance (Festinger, 1957). We shall return to that topic more fully later. At the moment we must turn our attention to the principal processes of cognizance and evaluation that occur prior to product and brand decisions.

Processes in Decision Making

In focusing on cognitive processes we do not intend to imply that these factors determine all consumer behavior. On the contrary, we consider social factors highly important, particularly at the postdecisional stage. A consumer who has purchased a particular brand, for example, is quite likely to find himself in the position of having to explain that decision to other consumers. So his postdecisional cognitive needs are partly socially determined. Bearing in mind that social interaction constantly bears upon consumer behavior, let us concentrate our attention for the moment on the purely internal cognitive factors in order to spell out Figure 1.

Our model specifies that two distinguishable kinds of information processing precede a decision between two or more objects. The first process we call *object-attribute cognizance*. It consists, conceptually speaking, of building a matrix of the type indicated in Table 1 by laying out the objects and attributes to be considered. The second process, which is necessarily intertwined with cognizance, we call *object evaluation;* this consists, in effect, of "filling in" a decision matrix like Table 1 with values for each object on each attribute, and arriving at summary values for each object across all attributes. Given these summary values, the decision follows and the person moves to the next stage in the model.

In Figure 1 this sequence of events is shown schematically twice, once for products and then again for brands. The general theory is the same in the two cases, but the specifics of information processing are, of course, quite different. As our earlier discussion suggests, product-attribute cognizance is very difficult, for two reasons. First, the many product alternatives cannot be easily listed. Second, it is not obvious what attributes should be considered. Often one must make product evaluations on visceral, even mystic, feelings. Brand-attribute cognizance, by contrast, can seem rather simple. Certainly, a reasonably adequate list of alternative brands can be compiled for most product classes.

Since brand cognizance is rarely a matter of great difficulty, we should expect to find brand information seeking directed mostly at discriminating attributes. To our knowledge, no research has been done to demonstrate structural differences in the type of information sought prior to brand decisions versus product decisions, but it appears to be a promising field for empirical work. Our general hypothesis would be that brand decisions are preceded by efforts at getting attribute information, whereas information seeking prior to product decisions would concentrate more on objects (i.e., products) than attributes. This difference would not be due to any inherent structural distinction between the two kinds of decision, but would result from the fact that brands tend more often (through advertising) to present themselves to the consumer with little or no effort on his part.

Product- and brand-evaluation processes are also theoretically identical, but in practical experience they doubtless differ a great deal. Perhaps the greatest single difference is in the degree to which they occur at all. Evaluation is work, as is all mental activity, so it may not take place. As we indicated earlier, for example, brand evaluation is less likely for low-involvement products or when there are few discriminating attributes. The consumer will probably decide that it is not worth the effort to bother himself with overly rational evaluation of trivial and marginally differentiated brands. In the case of products, by contrast, careful evaluation may well be abandoned because the consumer finds the situation *too* complex and *too* involving. More important perhaps, he may find that although his decision concerns highly complex products, this provides him with very few pertinent attributes because the products are simply not comparable. A man with an afternoon free may consider going to a baseball game versus reading a novel. When he tries to evaluate the ball game as an alternative, he thinks in terms of attributes such as weather, probable starting pitchers, importance of today's game in the pennant race, and so forth. These attributes are rather difficult to apply to a novel. If our consumer attempted to make a rational choice in the sense of Figure 1, he would be reduced to the consideration of minor attributes, such as dollars and cents, that have little to do with his original motivation. Under such conditions, a product decision made with little, if any, information processing would be understandable behavior on the consumer's part; for purposes of explaining consumer behavior, however, it leaves the researcher without much to analyze if he has to assume a rational model such as our Table 1. This sort of example, which may be more the rule than the exception, must be relegated to a category outside the scope of our model, along with brand loyalty.

Uses of the Model

Without denying that all consumer behavior may be logical in the sense that the consumer weighs the usefulness of information against its costs, we have seen that a great many consumer decisions are made on a nonrational basis—by which we mean that potentially available information is not used. Why, then, should we want to develop a model for analyzing rational consideration of information by the consumer? The question can be given both an academic answer and a pragmatic one. For purposes of academic research, a rational model can produce fairly clear-cut hypotheses that lend themselves to empirical demonstration and can be incorporated into rather interesting theories. Mystical explanations of consumer behavior, by contrast, are necessarily vague and amorphous, and generally beyond the scope of empirical research; and explanations based on concepts of habit (e.g., brand loyalty) seem simply too dull to sustain any significant degree of research interest. The pragmatic attraction to rational models lies in the fact that this kind of theory can tell us something about how we might act more effectively, either as consumers or as professional marketing communicators. It enables us, for example, to conceive and test a new type of advertising or promotional campaign. It implies that changes in consumer behavior *can* occur, and gives us clues about the conditions that will facilitate or impede change.

We have noted, for example, that advertising directed at product decisions is rather rare, because the marketing industry is mainly organized by brands. When a product class is advertised, it is usually pitted against an obvious competing product that dominates the market and that shares many discriminating attributes with it. We have noted the example of advertising tea as a product; its dominant competitor, coffee, is advertised by brand, however. This difference suggests that different stages in the decision process are addressed by the two products.

Similarly, the consumer information movement has been organized almost entirely on a brand- rather than a product-evaluation basis. A consumer can study analyses by governmental laboratories or read *Consumer Reports* to help decide which brand is his best buy. But he can only do so after he has made his product decision—on his own. These deficiencies in consumer-information sources are no one's "fault." They are unavoidable, because only pertinent information can be gathered, organized, and communicated. It staggers the imagination to conceive of a consumer-information industry that would provide value estimates for all possible products on all the possible attributes that a very heterogeneous nation of consumers might consider relevant.

Salience of Brands and Attributes

It is often observed that many advertisements contain no information that could be pertinent to a rational decision (as outlined in Table 1), and yet these ads seem to be quite effective in influencing consumer behavior. Preston (1968) calls these "non-rational" ads, but points out that decisions based on them may be quite rational from the consumer's viewpoint. In part the success of such ads is simply a matter of sustaining brand-inertia, especially for low-involvement products. But these minimal-information ads can also be relevant to our model.

Consider the extreme case of the pure brand-recognition advertisement, in which only the name of the brand, or perhaps the shape of its insignia or container, is brought to the consumer's attention. Such an ad, although information-free in the sense of Table 1, increases the likelihood of brand cognizance, which is an important feature of Figure 1. When new items are introduced into the market, this kind of advertising is obviously highly advisable. It is necessary to get consumers thinking about one's product or brand before they can evaluate it. Political "unknowns" face the same problem when they challenge an incumbent.

There is also evidence that familiarity with an object is in itself an important component of value. Carter (1965) calls this factor the "salience" of an object, which is conceptually independent of the "pertinence" values based on attributes. Generally speaking, it seems that the more experience a person has had with an object, the better he will like it—although his evaluation is also influenced by specific pertinent details of his experience with it, too (Chaffee, 1967; Zajonc, 1968). This principle is sometimes expressed as a folk preference for "the Devil we know," when faced with the alternative of "the Devil we don't know." *Any* advertisement for a brand could be expected to increase its salience—and, of more direct interest to the advertiser, its sales. The techniques by which the salience-building power of ads might be increased—e.g., humor, novelty, art—constitute an important subfield of marketing research. Sheer volume of advertising is, of course, an effective "persuader" (LoSciuto, Strassmann, and Wells, 1967). Generally, salience should be a relatively more important determinant of consumer decisions when few relevant attributes are involved. This means that salience will tend to dominate product decisions even more than brand decisions, since it is so difficult to make pertinent comparisons between product alternatives.

When there are a number of pertinent attributes, salience comes into play in a different fashion. Just as objects differ in their salience for the person, so do attributes. Again, the weight or value assigned to a given attribute by a consumer will be a major factor in determining his overall decision. Following our previous reasoning, we would expect attribute salience to be a more important factor in brand evaluation than in product evaluation, because there are few pertinent attributes in the latter case. Hansen (1969) has proposed a general formula for brand choice based centrally on variations in the salience of attributes. Experiments showed this approach predicts outcomes better than measures of attitudes (salience) toward the objects themselves. A pioneering study by Banks (1950) developed a preliminary method for ascertaining the effect of attribute salience on both brand preference and purchase, using multiple regression analysis.

Attribute salience can be viewed as the basis for reduction of the total information matrix (Table 1) to a decision. There are several different ways in which the consumer can reach his decision by applying attribute salience values. For purposes of illustration, we shall limit ourselves here to examples of brand decisions between automobiles.

The simplest method of decision making is to focus on the single most salient attribute. The brand that is superior in that respect would be chosen. For example, let us say that a consumer has narrowed his choices down to a Ford versus a Volkswagen (an unlikely situation, but imagine it for now). His decision will be determined by his choice of attributes. The Volkswagen salesman will, in all likelihood, stress economy. If that attribute remains the most salient, we should expect our consumer to buy the VW. But economy may not be as salient to him as, say, engine power or body styling. Those attributes, which a Ford salesman would doubtless stress, would incline him toward the Ford. Guerrero (1969) has found less postdecisional avoidance of messages attacking the *brand* of car purchased than of messages attacking the *attribute* on which that decision was based. This indicates again the key role of attributes in consumer information processing.

Now let us take a more complicated example. Suppose that several attributes were salient for a consumer. Going back to the Ford-VW choice, what happens if economy, power, and styling are all considered? If each attribute is weighted equally, then Ford would seem to have the edge because of superiority on two of the three attributes (power and styling). Note that journalistic analyses of two-sided issues tend to treat all attributes as of equal weight, as does *Consumer Reports* in its attribute-by-attribute analysis of competing brands.

But equal weighting is probably very rare for an individual, except perhaps for an unusual consumer who might habitually structure his thinking in this manner. For many of us, some attributes are more important than others. In the Ford-VW decision, for example, economy may not be the only pertinent attribute, but it is so highly salient that the Ford would need many points of superiority before it would be preferred over the economical VW. Now obviously auto buying is complex enough that there are many Fords *and* VWs on the road, presumably mostly with satisfied owners. This indicates the essential point that attribute salience structures vary tremendously from one consumer to another.

Indeed, attribute saliences are probably far more variable than are brand saliences. This can be demonstrated by a famous example in consumer-behavior annals. For many years the toothpaste market had remained pretty static, with Colgate at the top of the list. Crest, a relatively new brand, was well down the list, in about sixth place. Students of habitual behavior would have thought of toothpaste buyers as highly brand loyal. Then, in the early 1960s, Crest jumped to first on the list in about half a year. This was the result of the introduction of a new attribute into an otherwise stable situation. Crest had won an endorsement from the American Dental Association. With an advertising campaign keyed almost entirely to this endorsement, Crest in effect sold itself by selling a single attribute. (Previously, this had not been a discriminating attribute because no toothpaste had been singled out for special praise by the ADA.) It is likely that most, even all, product classes are open to this sort of restructuring *if new discriminating attributes can be made salient.* If not, brand-inertia will tend to maintain itself, and the competing brands will fight the battle for consumer attention with salience-oriented advertisements, yielding minimal results in terms of overall net change.

Information As Psychological Uncertainty

To this point we have used the term "information" rather loosely to refer to entries in the decision matrix (Table 1). But the concept has a rigorous scientific meaning that should be considered here, because it has many points of similarity with our usage—and some important differences.

The key concept in what is called Information Theory (Shannon and Weaver, 1949) as applied to social psychology is *uncertainty* (Garner, 1962). In the specific consumer-decision context that concerns us here, we can limit our consideration to the consumer's psychological uncertainty about which brand (or product) to purchase. Information Theory assumes that uncertainty always tends to decrease over time, so that it would be maximal at the inceptive stage of our model (Figure 1) and minimal (zero, in fact) at the brand-decision stage. Between those two points a cognitive input (i.e., an entry into the decision matrix of Table 1) would consist of information only to the extent that it reduced the consumer's uncertainty.

The reader should sense at once that applying this approach to consumer decisions will not square very well with reality. The very important information-search activities of object and attribute cognizance consist of *increasing uncertainty* by expanding the cognitive matrix of Table 1. It has been found, for example, that information processing changes in several ways when there are more alternative brands under consideration (Anderson, Taylor, and Holloway, 1966). Even though consumers typically consider only a small subset of available brands (Seggev, 1970), we should not care much for a definition of information that would not allow that subset to expand. The root of the problem is that Shannon's definition of information as uncertainty-reduction assumes that a *closed system* is under analysis. It is this limitation that has rendered Information Theory much less applicable to biological, social, and psychological research than had been anticipated by those who had hoped to see a general systems theory develop that would eventually embrace all the sciences (e.g., von Bertalanffy, 1968).

Moreover, it is obvious that many consumer decisions are made despite considerable uncertainty. Bauer (1960) points out that different consumers will handle a highly uncertain decision in different ways, and that this will partly depend on other factors in the situation. It would seem from the frequency of unplanned "impulse" purchases (Kollat, 1966), and the many consumer decisions that are made without considering even easily available information, that at least some high-uncertainty situations are resolved by making immediate "snap" consumer decisions. We would expect this to be most likely when risk is low (Sheth and Venkatesan, 1968). Whatever the precise merits of this argument, it is clear that we should not adopt a model that implies that uncertainty should be totally eliminated before information search ceases; that would scarcely be "rational" consumer behavior by any reasonable definition, given the added costs of search.

There is evidence from studies of political behavior that very high uncertainty is likely to lead to "nonbehavior" rather than to increased search. For example, citizens who are subject to "cross pressures" because they are members of social groups with conflicting voting norms delay their voting decisions longer and are less likely to vote than are those whose social allegiances reinforce one another politically (Berelson and Steiner, 1964). Similarly, discussion of school finance elections is low among voters who think of themselves strongly in the conflicting roles of parent and taxpayer (Carter, 1963). It appears that too-high uncertainty can suppress, rather than stimulate, information seeking and decision making. At the other extreme, too, very low uncertainty would seem to provide little motivation for information seeking. So our key communication variable is probably a *curvilinear* function of uncertainty, whereas Information Theory would suggest that uncertainty produces a linear or monotonic mathematical function.

Nevertheless, there is an intuitively appealing element to the concept of uncertainty that commends it to us in outlining a model of information use. It appears to fit well in the product-evaluation and brand-evaluation cells of Figure 1, since these processes take the total decision matrix as their starting point, and work toward a decision stage.

A more likely overall conception of consumer decisions would take a more probabilistic Bayesian approach, assuming that consumers play an "uncertainty game" in which the perceived risk of making the wrong decision is balanced against the perceived risk of building a decision matrix that is too complicated and confusing to comprehend. And again, this very interesting kind of cognitive behavior should be distinguished from the low-involvement situation in which the consumer makes "any old decision" because he has little interest in it or information about it. This too means that the researcher must be careful in his assumptions about the consumer's general orientation to the decision, and if possible should try to test those assumptions against some kind of evidence.

To this point we have taken most entirely a theoretical approach, outlining a general model, generating a variety of hypotheses from it, and discussing it in terms of existing bodies of theory and data. Let us now turn to a discussion of a few of the difficulties that will be faced by the researcher who attempts to study consumer-information use.

Self-Report Data

Ever since Freud began to point out the many ways in which humans deceive themselves and one another, there has been a natural disinclination to accept introspection and self-report as valid data in behavioral research. Not only do we sublimate, rationalize, and ego-defend; what is worse from a clinical standpoint, we do so knowingly. It is entirely reasonable, too, that we assume that others do the same. What faith, then, can we place in data based on a person's self-report about his own thinking or behavior?

As researchers, it turns out, we must place a great deal of faith in such data—our own misgivings and Freudian theory notwithstanding. The reason for this faith is grounded not in evidence, but in necessity. There is no pragmatic alternative for many purposes. If we want to know whether a person has made a brand choice or a product choice, it is often necessary to ask him. If we want to know what alternative brands or products he has been considering, we must also ask him about that. If we want to know on what attributes he has been comparing objects, we must ask him again. Indeed, nearly every assumption we have to this point suggested checking out "empirically" can be approached by direct questioning—and usually by no other means.

An alternative method might be *projective* tests, which have been popular among motivational researchers. However, we would not advise projective tests ordinarily, since they share all the procedural faults of direct self-report, and require more untestable assumptions regarding both the respondent and the researcher.

There are alternative procedures, but these are difficult to set up and should only be used when there is serious reason to doubt self-report data. We can assume a brand decision has been made, of course, when the consumer has been *forced* to choose. This can be done in experimental studies, and it may also occur naturally in field situations. However, there is some difficulty in generalizing results from forced decisions to the more usual consumer situation, when the "decision not to decide" is also a possibility.

Quite often, then, the researcher is forced to trade off validity in the decision situation (is it forced?) against validity in measurement of the person's cognitive state. The issue often comes down to a choice between a laboratory versus a field study, or an experiment versus a survey. Generally, there is a presumption in favor of the experiment and the field study (Campbell, 1957), but those also tend to be mutually exclusive alternatives in practice. For the kinds of data we have been discussing in this chapter, we lean toward accepting self-report data, with all their recognized imperfections. Such data could be better, but the alternatives are probably even less valid (see, however, some suggestions in Webb, et al., 1966).

In asking a consumer to reconstruct the mental events that led to his decision, the researcher should bear in mind that this may not be possible. Once having thought through a decision, the economic mind can be expected to forget the prior steps and retain only the decision itself.

Assuming that research will normally have to be built around real-life field decisions and self-report data, we would recommend that the measures be made as soon after the decision as possible. It is often possible to determine that this is the case when large numbers of persons have faced the same decision. A good example is a political voting decision. As soon as Election Day has passed, the researcher can assume that most citizens will be at the postdecisional cognizance point in our model, and can organize his questioning accordingly. If he waits too long to question them, the decision may fade into cognitive irrelevance. For the more usual types of consumer research, there are often records available that will indicate whether a given person has made a required decision or not. These materials can provide the basis for sampling procedures. Occasionally, the researchers may even find a situation in which a controlled field experiment can be set up, especially when he is directly associated with a marketing agency.

Concept of Cost

In our theoretical discussions we have treated the factor of cost as if it were just another attribute in the person's cognitive structure. Obviously, it is more than that. Often the price of a brand is *the* determining factor in a consumer decision. Certainly it is almost always weighed by the consumer. It is common to talk of "cost-benefit analysis" as if all other attributes can be lumped together as "benefits"; this approach obscures the fact that Brand A may offer greater benefits in terms of one attribute, while Brand B is superior in some other ways.

Several methods can be used to handle the overriding matter of cost, when the goal is to study more subtle comparisons among positive attributes. One procedure is to hold cost constant, which is not an unusual field situation; competing brands are normally priced very similarly. In some cases price information can be withheld from the decision maker; this also implies that, cognitively, cost is constant across brands. Still another possibility is to analyze situations in which "price is no object." This might be true for very rich consumers, or for very cheap products, or (more likely) when the quality of benefit is truly the central consideration, as in the case of medical care for an acutely ill person.

A general theory of consumer-information use would hold regardless of the factor of cost. Research directed toward that goal should involve replication of critical experiments across consumer decisions that involve benefits only (no cost), costs and benefits, and costs only (no benefits). Pure cost-free and benefit-free cases probably do not exist in field situations, but there are some remarkably close approximations to them.

Voting is pretty much a cost-free decision, especially when local administrative offices or judgeships are concerned, or local referenda. (Time and effort are minimal, and balanced by the social cost of being a "poor citizen" if you do not vote.) Voters are often bewildered because they cannot develop any personal cost-orientation toward these minor ballot issues. In such situations other attributes can come powerfully into play, and the voter will be extremely suggestible. Still, his use of information should follow the same patterns as in the more usual cost-benefit case; it will just be harder for him to test the value component of such information as he can find.

At the other extreme, donations to charity can be looked on as benefit-free costs. Here, again, we would intuitively guess that the "consumer" is often highly susceptible to suggestion and likely to be an "impulse-giver." This is probably not so much because he is unable to evaluate information comparing different charities (i.e., brands), as it is due to the fact that little or no comparative information is available to him (Cutlip, 1965). There is also a great deal of habitual annual giving, or charity loyalty.

In discussing costs we should not emphasize price to the exclusion of other factors. As we have implied earlier, expenditures of time, effort, and convenience are additional costs that the consumer can be expected to give some weight to. Furthermore, there is the cost of information processing itself. At some point, thinking becomes more work than it is worth. This probably accounts for the risk-taking behavior of making a decision despite harboring some uncertainty about it.

Measurement

For the kinds of research we are suggesting here, it is usually necessary to gather a great many measures on each consumer, asking him about a number of brands and attributes. If the attribute dimensions are carefully explicated and pretested, they can normally be adequately represented in the form of semantic differential scales (Osgood, Suci, and Tannenbaum, 1957). A respondent can work through several pages, rating each brand on each scale, quite rapidly. It should be remembered, though, that his ability to mark a semantic differential scale is no guarantee that he had previously considered the attribute that the scale represents. Thus the process of data collection can seriously interfere with consumer information processing, the very thing it is supposed to measure. It is sometimes advisable to let the respondent search his own mind for attributes—although this procedure too can force him into more rational modes of thought than would be the case if he had been left to his own cognitive devices. A compromise procedure is to pretest a number of attribute scales on one sample, allowing them to ignore any scale they ordinarily would not use. The small list of surviving "useful" scales can then be applied to a different sample in the main study with fairly good confidence in its validity (Carter, Ruggels, and Chaffee, 1968-1969.) There are many other potentially useful measuring devices as well, which the reader can find described in any textbook on social-research methods.

Many of the attributes on which brands (and especially products) differ are binary in nature and therefore cannot be properly represented by multilevel measures. For example, if one car has a radio and the other does not, that difference can hardly be described by marking a seven-point differential scale. Unfortunately for the researcher, complex object-attribute structures tend to involve a mix of binary and multilevel types of information, making measurement something of a hodgepodge.

Part of this operational problem can be resolved if it is borne in mind that it is the *value* component of a pertinent comparison that is cognitively operative for the consumer. That is, although the presence or absence of a car radio is a binary question, the extent to which that affects the potential buyer's evaluation of the two cars *is* a matter of degree. Some consumers consider a car radio essential; others see it as a very minor consideration.

This points up an additional measurement problem: in many cases it will be necessary to gather two pieces of data for each pertinent comparison. First, the consumer must be asked what difference he perceives between the alternative brands, and then he must be asked what value he attaches to that difference. A theoretical basis for this procedure is discussed in Fishbein (1963). This is sometimes handled by asking him to describe his "ideal" brand on the same scales that he is also using to describe each of the real brands; the difference between each brand and the ideal is assumed to indicate the degree of negative evaluation of that brand on that attribute.

Often one of these two measures can be omitted. For example, the difference between the brands may be so obvious that there can be no doubt that the consumer perceives it, and to ask him about it would in fact be mildly insulting. Or the attribute may be one on which the direction of value is clear-cut. (But the researcher who feels sure of his ability to make such assumptions in the absence of evidence may be sobered by reflecting on the fact that even price is not a clear-cut indicator of direction of value. For some types of socially conspicuous products, many consumers will prefer the higher-priced brand—even when other attributes are equal.)

Observing Communication

We have been discussing communication and research as if it were a simple matter to study communication. At the risk of startling the reader, we shall now suggest that it is probably impossible to observe communication—in the sense of cognitive transactions between persons. To accomplish that, it would first be necessary to observe the symbols that are transmitted between the two; this obviously can be done, although it is rarer than one unschooled in the communication-research literature would suppose. But it would also be necessary, to satisfy any adequate definition of communication, to get some evidence about the perceptions and evaluations occurring within the two persons as they communicate. Obviously this is no simple task. What is worse, the act of gathering data on mental events (for which we normally rely on self-report) is incompatible with the act of observing symbol transmission. That is, the researcher cannot do both these things at once, if only because a respondent who is describing his mental state cannot simultaneously take part in some other ongoing communication situation.

Communication is not the only important process that defies direct observation and analysis because the research techniques would interrupt the process. Indeed, most life processes are incapable of direct study for very similar reasons. Yet biology moves along, making close approaches to observing life. So too may we work toward near approximations to the observation of communication.

One way of simplifying the problem is to assume that only one person (the consumer) need be studied at one time. This relieves the researcher of the need to match the cognitions of two interacting communicators. We should point out, however, that some of the most interesting aspects of consumer behavior are highly social in nature, including the exchange of information. So there will be times when more than one consumer's cognitions should be assessed simultaneously.

Another useful procedure is to stretch the study out over time. First, the consumer's cognitive state regarding the decision can be assessed. At some later time, his communication behavior can be observed in some fashion. Finally, his cognitive state can be remeasured, so that changes in it can be associated with intervening communication behavior. Obviously, the greater the degree of control over extraneous factors (i.e., the more "experimental" the study), the more faith one can place in the results.

In this connection it should also be noted that purely self-report data are of more dubious validity than a mixture of self-report and other kinds of observation. For example, if the measures of cognitive states are made by self-administered questionnaires, it would be preferable to gather data about the person's intervening communication by some other means.

RESEARCH ON INFORMATION PROCESSES

Let us return to the matter of research hypotheses, now that we have reviewed some of the major pitfalls that await the researcher. Figure 1 indicates five different kinds of information processes: product-attribute cognizance, product evaluation, brand-attribute cognizance, brand evaluation, and post-decisional cognizance. We shall lump the first and third, and the second and fourth, of these for discussion.

Predecisional Cognizance

Whether a product decision has been made or not, the object-attribute cognizance process should be studied in terms of *increases* in uncertainty. Figure 1 can be taken as a general model for this kind of analysis. The key communication behavior is information seeking, focusing on the identification of alternative brands (or products) and relevant attributes and the search for data that would fill the cells of the general decision matrix.

As we have indicated earlier, this will be difficult for the consumer who has not yet made a product decision. The researcher who attempts to apply our model at that point may find little to study. Brand-attribute cognizance, however, can account for a good deal of consumer information seeking, particularly regarding attributes. Information Theory would not be applicable to this process, since it assumes a closed cognitive system and the reduction of uncertainty.

Evaluation

Whereas cognizance refers to the expansion and filling in of the decision matrix, evaluation consists of the reduction of that total matrix to an evaluation that indicates the superiority of one brand or product over the other(s). That summary evaluation is the basis for the subsequent decision.

Reduction of the decision matrix can be thought of as a decrease in the uncertainty of a bounded cognitive system. Hence the assumptions and mathematical procedures of Information Theory are applicable to this process. The major events are of a "black-box" nature, purely mental, and so a good deal of research ingenuity is called for. Since Information Theory refers to *changes* in the state of a system, it is essential that repeated measures of the evaluative matrix be made—preferably before and after other events that the researcher presumes are critical to the consumer's decision.

The shift from evaluation to decision can involve some degree of risk taking, which we have defined as making a decision with greater than zero evaluative uncertainty. Note that risk taking occurs as part of a process that is conceptually distinct from information seeking, but these two behaviors can either precede or follow one another in a cycle of cognitive behavior (see Figure 1).

More generally, evaluation processes can lead back to cognizance processes, particularly in the situation where no decision can be made. This is usually called *cognitive conflict* (Chaffee, et al., 1969). If the consumer wants to make a decision, but his evaluations do not indicate any difference among the brands, we should expect him to seek information to expand his brand-attribute cognizance matrix. This communication behavior will probably involve new attributes, mostly. In the case of product evaluation, information is likely to be so incomplete that *some* decision will be made, although theoretically information seeking is at least plausible behavior in that situation too. Berlyne (1960) has suggested that there is some degree of conflict in any behavioral situation. It may not, however, be great enough to motivate a consumer to seek and process information, given the costs inherent in that activity.

Postdecisional Cognizance

More research has been done on postdecisional than predecisional situations, although the latter have more direct implications for consumer-behavior research. In particular, the study of information can be, by definition, limited to predecisional processes. Nevertheless, consumers who have made decisions have available to them much of the same information that is available to predecisional consumers. What do they do with such communications, and why? The answers that are most often given are *selective exposure* and *cognitive dissonance,* respectively.

Dissonance can be simply defined here as a discrepancy between a consumer decision and a prior evaluation. This will suffice for our limited purposes, although a great deal has been written on the topic since its introduction by Festinger (1957). Although there is some dispute about the necessity for the concept (Bem, 1970), it has generated a great deal of research on postdecisional cognizance (see especially Festinger, 1964).

It is easy to see how dissonance might arise and why it has been suggested that *any* decision involves some degree of dissonance. (As Figure 1 indicates, this includes both product and brand decisions, but we shall discuss mainly the latter here.) As we have said, decisions are normally made despite some remaining evaluative uncertainty (risk taking). The consumer, of course, knows this. To the extent that the decision is not consistent with some of the evaluations in the brand-attribute matrix, there is hypothetically some dissonance—and the consumer is presumably motivated to alleviate this unpleasant cognitive condition.

There are several ways of resolving dissonance, but two will particularly concern us here: changing evaluations and adding cognitive elements.

Evaluations can be changed in several ways. But if we go back to the brand-attribute cognizance stage and the general decision matrix (Table 1), it appears that the basic mechanism would be to reevaluate the attributes, not the objects. For example, if the consumer has purchased brand A, even though it was inferior to brand B insofar as attribute Q was concerned, we should expect attribute Q to be considered less important in postdecisional information processing. A nice experimental demonstration of this hypothesis would be to show that attribute Q carries less weight in some subsequent decision involving brands X and Z than it does in a "control group" that had not made the brand-A-over-brand-B decision. The consumer cannot reasonably reevaluate the objects directly without denying his previous perceptions. It would seem that reevaluation of attributes is a more direct and less ego-threatening route to dissonance reduction.

To change cognitive elements, the consumer can either forget dissonant facts that he knew, or arrange his subsequent communication so that he will add to his mental store of evaluations consistent with his decision. These hypotheses are called selective retention and selective exposure. The latter can be attributed to either avoidance or seeking of specific communication content. Avoidance in particular has proven difficult to demonstrate (Carter, Pyszka, and Guerrero, 1969).

"Selective information seeking" would be a contradiction in terms, since we have specified that information is predecisional, whereas the selective communication processes are postdecisional. Freedman and Sears (1965) have argued that the research record does not always show selective exposure, and that the remaining cases can plausibly be attributed to the greater availability of consonant communications to most people most of the time. A rather careful experiment by Atkin (1969), however, indicates that availability alone cannot account for all the selectivity found in postdecisional communication. The hypothesis remains a useful one for research, whether it can be attributed to dissonance or some simpler process.

Another source of postdecisional "discomfort" might be the realization that there are attributes that the consumer should have considered, but did not. If this cognition is coupled with dissonance, the outcome would probably be to revert to a predecisional cognizance stage, if possible. If the decision is irrevocable, this will not be possible—and the total dissonance may be greater.

Some authors have attempted to explain away mass communication "effects" on the basis of the selective-exposure hypothesis (e.g., Klapper, 1960). This approach ignores the entire predecisional phase of consumer behavior, in which the most important uses of information take place. As we have noted earlier, however, consumers do not make decisions, in the sense we are describing here, nearly so often as might be imagined. Much of consumer behavior takes place without any serious attempt at information processing, and is practically impervious to mass-media information sources. We would argue that the more important cases for research and theory are those in which communication does provide information that the consumer can use in reaching a decision, rather than the more numerous cases in which "nothing happens."

MARKETING COMMUNICATION STRATEGIES

Our purpose here has been to outline a model and some related methods and hypotheses for research. Our analysis of consumer-information uses also has some implications for the reader whose primary interest lies in planning marketing communication, rather than formal study.

We can assume that the general goal of a professional communicator is to influence the consumer's decision. (Of course, he wants to influence it in a particular direction, but first things first.) The key to having *any* influence lies in designing the communication so that it is relevant to the consumer's information processing.

For example, if one brand dominates the market and you are planning advertising for it, your client can only lose if you introduce new attributes (to say nothing of other brands) into the situation. By contrast, if your client is one of the other brands, you not only should try to bring out new attributes, you also have nothing much to lose by comparing your brand explicitly to the dominant one. These principles seem to be rather well understood by professional advertisers, in that many examples could be found to demonstrate both points. The old rule that competing brands should never be mentioned has been broken in recent years—but not by the leading brand within a product category.

In terms of our model, the introduction of new attributes is a method of encouraging the consumer to shift back from postdecisional cognizance to brand-attribute cognizance. That would in turn imply a new brand evaluation, and conceivably a new brand decision. The latter is the basic goal of the advertiser.

Advertising strategies should also be geared to the level of involvement of the consumer with the product. For low-involvement products, ads designed to create salience value will probably be more effective than ads that give complicated details on various attributes. When a high-involvement product is at stake, however, more "rational" ads are advisable. Again, current practices in professional advertising seem to reflect adherence to this principle.

Not all consumer information is packaged so cleverly, however. We have referred earlier to voting and charity donating as two types of "consumer" behavior that are particularly needful of information. Charities, having no direct "benefits" to offer the giver, advertise strictly according to salience-value principles. Both their ads and the news stories devoted to promoting them imply that there are no other charities to compare. From the consumer's viewpoint, of course, this is not so. But he is not given information that will help him make rational choices between competing charities.

In voting the situation is probably equally unfortunate for that rare citizen whose interest is high but whose precommitment to one party or ideology is low. Here is a true decision maker, yet the mass media seem to consider him a trivial case. (In a sense he is, because he is so rare; but here we are concerned less with the usual than with the cognitively active.) Media reports on candidates are rarely explicitly comparative. Often they report on some attributes for one candidate and other attributes for his opponent. The voter is left with a number of empty spaces in his cognitive matrix.

A similar information deficit was demonstrated by Groot (1970) in a study of agricultural extension publications in the Philippines. He found *some* information on many different varieties of rice, and descriptions of *some* attributes for each variety. But no farmer, even if he were to search through all the available governmental publications, would have been able to fill in more than half the possible cells in a decision matrix (Figure 1) defined by all varieties (objects) and all attributes on which at least some information was available.

We would suggest that deficiencies in informational systems can to a great extent be traced to a failure to conceive of the consumer as a decision maker, and to gather and organize information for him accordingly. That general conclusion should be taken tentatively, however, since many of the assumptions and principles we have introduced here have not yet been examined in any coherent program of research. Empirical testing should precede any extensive attempts to apply these principles to professional practice.

REFERENCES

Anderson, L. K., J. R. Taylor, and R. J. Holloway, "The Consumer and His Alternatives: An Experimental Approach," *Journal of Marketing Research,* 3 (1966), 62-67.

Atkin, C. K., "Relative Availability and Exposure to Information." Paper presented to Communication Theory and Methodology Division, Association for Education in Journalism, Berkeley, Calif., 1969.

Banks, S., "The Relationships of Brand Preference to Brand Purchase," *Journal of Marketing,* 15 (1950), 145-57.

Bauer, R. A., "Consumer Behavior as Risk Taking," in *Proceedings American Marketing Association,* ed. R. S. Hancock, 1960, 389-98. Also in Cox (1967).

Bem, D. J., *Beliefs, Attitudes, and Human Affairs.* Belmont, Calif.: Wadsworth Publishing Company, Inc., 1970.

Bender, W. C., "Consumer Purchase-Costs–Do Retailers Recognize Them?" *Journal of Retailing,* 40 (1964), 1-8, 52.

Berelson, B. R., P. F. Lazarsfeld, and W. N. McPhee, *Voting.* Chicago: University of Chicago Press, 1954.

Berelson, B. R., and G. A. Steiner, *Human Behavior.* New York: Harcourt Brace Jovanovich, Inc., 1964.

Berlyne, D. E., *Conflict, Arousal and Curiosity.* New York: McGraw-Hill Book Company, 1960.

Bowen, L., "The Effects of Product Involvement on the Evaluation of Rational and Non-rational Advertising Appeals." Unpublished Master's thesis, University of Wisconsin, 1970.

Bucklin, L. P., "The Informative Role of Advertising, " *Journal of Advertising Research,* 5 (1965), 11-15.

Campbell, A., P. E. Converse, W. E. Miller, and D. S. Stokes, *The American Voter.* New York: John Wiley & Sons, Inc., 1960.

Campbell, D. T., "Factors Relevant to the Validity of Experiments in Social Settings," *Psychological Bulletin,* 54, 4 (1957), 297-312.

Carter, R. F., "Multiple Reference Groups," Colloquium presented to Department of Communication, Stanford University, 1963.

Carter R. F., "Communication and Affective Relations," *Journalism Quarterly,* 42 (1965), 203-12.

Carter, R. F., R. H. Pyszka, and J. L. Guerrero, "Dissonance and Exposure to Aversive Information," *Journalism Quarterly,* 46 (1969), 37-42.

Carter, R. F., W. L. Ruggels, and S. H. Chaffee, "The Semantic Differential in Opinion Measurement," *Public Opinion Quarterly,* 32 (1968-69), 666-74.

Chaffee, S. H., "Salience and Pertinence as Sources of Value Change," *Journal of Communication,* 17 (1967), 25-38.

Chaffee, S. H., K. R. Stamm, J. L. Guerrero, and L. P. Tipton, "Experiments on Cognitive Discrepancies and Communication," *Journalism Monographs,* No. 14, 1969.

Chaffee, S. H., and L. P. Tipton, "Conflict, Information-seeking and the Discriminating Attribute," in Chaffee, et al. (1969).

Cox, D. F., ed., *Risk-Taking and Information Handling in Consumer Behavior.* Graduate School of Business Administration, Harvard University, Boston, 1967.

Cutlip, S. M., *Fund Raising in the United States.* New Brunswick, N.J.: Rutgers University Press, 1965.

Ehrlich, D., I. Guttman, P. M. Schonbach, and J. R. Mills, "Postdecision Exposure to Relevant Information," *Journal of Abnormal and Social Psychology,* 54 (1957), 98-102.

Engel, J. F., D. T. Kollat, and R. D. Blackwell, *Consumer Behavior.* New York: Holt, Rinehart and Winston, Inc., 1968.

Festinger, L., *A Theory of Cognitive Dissonance.* Evanston: Harper & Row, Inc., 1957.

Festinger, L., *Conflict, Decision and Dissonance.* Stanford, Calif.: Stanford University Press, 1964.

Fishbein, M., "An Investigation of the Relationships between Beliefs about an Object and the Attitude toward the Object." *Human Relations,* 16 (1963), 233-40.

Freedman, J. L., and D. O. Sears, "Selective Exposure," in *Advances in Social Psychology,* ed. L. Berkowitz, Vol. 2. New York: Academic Press, Inc. 1965.

Garner, W. R., *Uncertainty and Structure as Psychological Concepts.* New York: John Wiley & Sons, Inc., 1962.

Groot, H. C., "Coorientation and Technological Change: Communication Variables in Perceptions of 'Miracle Rice' in the Philippines." Unpublished Ph.D. dissertation, University of Wisconsin, 1970.

Guerrero, J. L., "Avoidance, Relevance and Exposure to Discrepant Information," in Chaffee et al. (1969).

Hansen, F., "Consumer Choice Behavior: An Experimental Approach," *Journal of Marketing Research,* 6 (1969), 436-43.

Klapper, J. T., *The Effects of Mass Communication.* New York: The Free Press, 1960.

Kollat, D. T., "A Decision-Process Approach to Impulse Purchasing," in *Science, Technology and Marketing,* ed. R. M. Haas. Chicago: American Marketing Association, 1966.

Lambert, Z. V., "Product Perception: An Important Variable in Price Strategy," *Journal of Marketing,* 34 (1970), 68-76.

LeGrand, B., and J. G. Udell, "Consumer Behavior in the Market Place," *Journal of Retailing,* 40 (1964), 32-40, 47.

LoSciuto, L. A., L. H. Strassmann, and W. D. Wells, "Advertising Weight and the Reward Value of the Brand," *Journal of Advertising Research,* 7 (1967), 34-38.

Machlup, F., *The Production and Distribution of Knowledge in the United States.* Princeton, N.J.: Princeton University Press, 1962.

May, F. E., Adaptive Behavior in Automobile Brand Choices," *Journal of Marketing Research,* 6 (1969), 62-65.

McPhee, W. N., *Formal Theories of Mass Behavior.* New York: The Free Press, 1963.

Osgood, C. D., G. J. Suci, and P. H. Tannenbaum, *The Measurement of Meaning.* Urbana, Ill.: University of Illinois Press, 1957.

Preston, I. L., "Relationships among Emotional, Intellectual and Rational Appeals in Advertising," *Speech Monographs,* 35 (1968), No. 4,504-11.

Roselius, T., "Consumer Rankings of Risk Reduction Methods," *Journal of Marketing,* 35 (1971), 56-61.

Seggev, E., "Brand Assortment and Consumer Brand Choice," *Journal of Marketing,* 34 (1970), 18-24.

Shannon, C. E., and W. Weaver, *The Mathematical Theory of Communication.*

Sheth, J. N., and M. Venkatesan, "Risk-reduction Processes in Repetitive Consumer Behavior," *Journal of Marketing Research,* 5 (1968), 307-10.

Udell, J. G., "Prepurchase Behavior of Buyers of Small Electrical Appliances," *Journal of Marketing,* 30 (1966), 50-52.

von Bertalanffy, L., *General Systems Theory.* New York: George Braziller, Inc., 1968.

Webb, E. J., D. T. Campbell, R. D. Schwartz, and L. Sechrest, *Unobtrusive Measures: Nonreactive Research in the Social Sciences.* Skokie, Ill.: Rand McNally & Company, 1966.

Zajonc, R. B., "The Process of Cognitive Tuning in Communication," *Journal of Abnormal and Social Psychology,* 61 (1960), 159-67.

Zajonc, R. B., "Attitudinal Effects of Mere Exposure," *Journal of Personality and Social Psychology Monograph Supplement,* 9 (1968), Pt. 2, 1-27.

11

Theories of Diffusion

Gerald Zaltman
Northwestern University

Ronald Stiff
Illinois Institute of Technology

ELEMENTS OF SOCIAL CHANGE

Social Change and Marketing. Social Change Defined. Social
Change Paradigm.

METHODOLOGICAL PERSPECTIVES ON THE STUDY OF THE
DIFFUSION OF INNOVATIONS

Criteria for a Useful Diffusion Theory for Consumer Behavior.
Research Methods Required for the Development of Useful
Theories of Diffusion and Consumer Behavior.

IMPLICATIONS OF RECENT ADVANCES IN DIFFUSION RESEARCH
AND THEORY FOR THE STUDY OF CONSUMER BEHAVIOR

Innovation. Adopting Units. Channels of Communication. Acceptance Process. Diffusion over Time and Space.

SYSTEM MODELS, MATHEMATICAL MODELS, AND SIMULATION
OF DIFFUSION IN MARKETING

Use of Observations for Grounding Parameters and Relationships in Simulation Models. Examples of Diffusion of Innovation Simulations—Any Luck?

CONCLUSION

REFERENCES

This chapter presents theoretical perspectives on the adoption and diffusion of innovations with emphasis on consumer behavior. The adoption of innovations refers to the processes whereby an innovation comes to be the most acceptable alternative available at that time. Should other things remain constant, and the same need or desire develops again, the same item would be employed once more (see Zaltman, 1965; Rogers and Shoemaker, 1971). The diffusion process is the process whereby an innovation is disseminated and accepted among individuals or other adopting units. Adoption occurs at a micro level, whereas diffusion occurs at a macro level. As an introduction to this subject we take a brief look at the more general process of social change, particularly planned social change, of which adoption and diffusion processes are essential dynamic parts. After our treatment of social change, we focus attention on consumer behavior and the adoption and diffusion processes.

ELEMENTS OF SOCIAL CHANGE

Social Change and Marketing

The tempo of social change in most parts of the world is unparalleled in the history of man. In many societies this change is taking place exponentially. Marketing is playing a key role in this change process. This is not often acknowledged. More significantly, however, marketing has a still greater potential role to play in fostering planned social change. This has been noted recently by several authors close to both marketing and the social sciences (Simon, 1968; Ziegler, 1970; Kotler and Zaltman, 1971; Zaltman, Kotler, and Kaufman, 1972). This association between marketing and social change is a dynamic one. Marketing activities are both a causal force in social change and a consequence of social change as well.

Social Change Defined

A good working definition of social change is provided by Rogers (1969, p. 3). Social change is "the process by which alteration occurs in the structure and function of a social system. . . . The structure of a social system is provided by the various individual and group statuses of which it is composed. The functioning element within this structure of status is a role, or the actual behavior of the individual in a given status."

Structural or functional change may be unplanned or planned. When a problem arises, social mechanisms, for example, norms or behavior rules, may automatically work to solve the problem, or new mechanisms may develop through normal processes to deal with the problem, or there may be factors external to the system that help the system react to the problem. In all instances here the problem and reaction concern unplanned spontaneous change. Although marketing must react to spontaneous change creatively and quickly with new goods and services and plans, it is also sometimes concerned with planned social change. Planned social change will be used here to mean any change having its origin in a decision by an individual or marketing organization to make a deliberate effort to alter the structure and/or function of a social system.

Social Change Paradigm

Figure 1 is a summary paradigm of social change. It is a mixture of microanalytic concepts (at the beginning) and macroanalytic concepts (at the end). Of ultimate interest for this chapter are the micro process of adoption and the macro process of diffusion. It is through the process components that marketing and social change experience mutual enhancement. Briefly, the paradigm in Figure 1 states that there exists some impetus or stimulus causing a change in wants which may lead to an incentive to innovate. This incentive triggers creative cognitive processes (so called because a restructuring of attitudes, behavioral intentions, and cognitions is likely to occur) in which for the first time there is an interaction between the attributes of the innovation itself and certain attributes of the adopting unit (e.g., personality or group decision-making processes). The innovation decision is the next element. It involves a process of empathy or identification. At this point the individual imagines himself to be using the innovation; he projects himself psychologically into situations in which he has

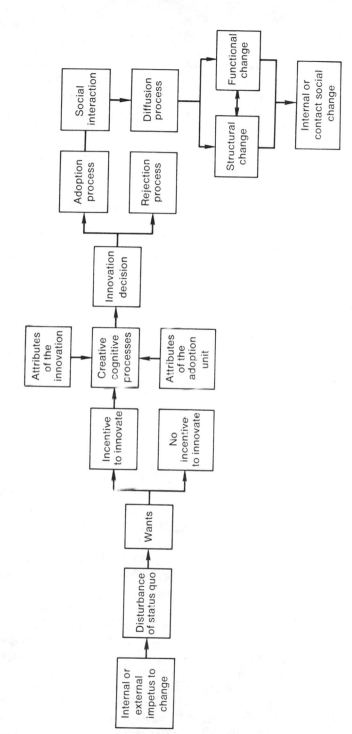

FIGURE 1. Summary Paradigm of Social Change

Adapted from Zaltman and Lin (1971).

adopted the innovation and assesses the probable experience. Depending upon the nature of the innovation, he may actually try it out. The innovation decision is a process of persuasion. If, as a result of the innovation decision, the individual decides to commit himself to the innovation on a more or less permanent basis, then adoption is said to occur.

The adoption of an innovation by an individual or other relevant adoption unit such as a family (Grambois, 1966), city (Crain, 1966), or state (Walker, 1969) represents one half of the dynamic core of social change. It is the fruition of a decision-making process often influenced by deliberate plans or strategies made by others (change agents), affected by personality and creative ability, basic wants, and so forth. The diffusion process is the other half of the dynamic core of social change. It is a phenomenon that emerges (Blau, 1964) from the adoption of an innovation by several adopter units, and is usually a partial result of social interaction among these units. Thus it is something more than the simple summation of many individual adoption decisions. It involves the additional phenomenon of patterned interaction among potential adopter and adopter units throughout the social structure. Often the result of the adoption and diffusion process is a change in the structure and/or function of the relevant social system. Depending upon the origin of the original impetus to change, the resulting social change may be called internal social change (coming from within the system) or contact social change (coming from outside the system).

Social interactions are important for they bridge the two processes of adoption and diffusion with which this chapter is primarily concerned. Also, the two processes bridged are the most dynamic part of social change, and it is therefore important that the linking mechanism be considered.

The diffusion process is more than the simple summation of individual adoption processes. Lippitt, Wabon, and Westley (1958) have specified three kinds of forcing phenomena. First they hypothesize a need for closure, that is, a need to complete a task which has begun. This is especially likely if there has been some previous investment in the change program. They note that "up to a certain critical point an individual or group may show strong resistance to starting on a sequence of activities. Once this point has been passed and the system has acquired some investment in the process, there is a dramatic reversal. Forces which were once opposed to change come to its support." This situation would lead to a rapid and widespread dissemination of the innovation as previous nonadopters embrace the change. A second change force is rooted in the relationship between client system and change agent. The client system will gradually if not immediately learn that the change agent has certain expectations of this client, and knowledge of these expectations will constitute an additional force in disseminating or diffusing innovations. In short, it is argued that people in one or another role will come to do what is expected of them in that role (see Chapter 6). The influence of outside expectations on personal behavior is the emergent phenomenon in this case. A third change force is an awareness by the client that he is the subject of a change effort. When a client system acquires insight into the change force to which it is subjected, it is better able to respond. This response of course can be adoptive or rejective. It is not possible to appraise the theoretical perspectives of this planned social change paradigm without considering the methodological foundations for theory development.

METHODOLOGICAL PERSPECTIVES ON THE STUDY OF THE DIFFUSION OF INNOVATIONS

Methodology in the behavioral sciences has been assigned a broad definition as those steps required for the evolution of social inquiry. Wallace (1969) views methodology as an ongoing and interactive process of making observations, building theory through empirical generalizations, using this theory to develop testable propositions, and in turn testing these propositions through new observations. It is apparent that theory and methods of making observations interact significantly in the process of social inquiry. Often theory or observations may predominate, when a more balanced approach would have provided more powerful insights. Denzin (1970), in a symbolic interaction approach to the research act suggests that each type of theory requires a special set of methods. We take a view that past theory and observations in diffusion and innovation interacted strongly. It is not possible to consider future diffusion theory without consideration of this interaction of theory and method in the inquiry process. Therefore, we consider the likely form of a useful diffusion theory and the methods most useful for developing such a theory. This discussion provides a perspective for reviewing the recent advances in diffusion research and theory.

Criteria for a Useful Diffusion Theory for Consumer Behavior

We consider a theory to be any organizing scheme for what would otherwise be a large number of unlinked empirical studies related to a substantive area such as the diffusion of innovations. Some types of theory have the potential for greater usefulness. *Descriptive theory,* or a simple framework for organizing empirical results, is of limited value. A more powerful level of theory would be theory that *predicts* future events from past events. Prediction may come from projections, hunches, intuition, or insight without any ability to explain why the predictions are successful or why they fail. The strongest theory provides *explanations* that, in principle, allow the prediction and control of future events. The most useful theory will be an organizing scheme that permits explanation of the various phenomena related to the diffusion of innovations. There are additional criteria that increase the usefulness of explanatory theory. A marketing and diffusion-relevant discussion of such criteria can be found in Zaltman, Angelmar, and Pinson (1971).

Homans (1964) and Blalock (1969) make strong arguments in support of deductive theories. Such theory would contain sets of propositions which are interrelated in a deductive system that allows the deduction of lower-order propositions from more powerful higher-order propositions. The derived lower-order propositions should, through stating covariances and temporal sequences, make testable predictions. A deductive system of this sort would be very powerful and efficient as an organizing scheme for diffusion research. Meehan (1968) feels that the deductive paradigm is extremely limited for the purposes of explanation. The natural world does not tend to fit itself into the slots required in deductive theory, and a partial deductive system is often quite useless. Meehan proposes that we revise our approach from a deductive paradigm to a system paradigm which creates a network of expectations that can be matched against the empirical situation. The systems paradigm permits partial and incomplete explanations that combine what we know into a logical structure. Diffusion theory as it currently exists is more suited to Meehan's systems paradigm than to a deductive paradigm.

If a theory is ever to gain great acceptance by the researchers and practitioners in marketing, it must be testable. Any theory will become more persuasive the more times it is tested and the stronger the test used. In order to be testable we must observe different states of the variables, some of these must covary, there must be a causal or temporal direction, and we must minimize the possibility of alternative or spuriousness variables causing or effecting our observations (Stinchcombe, 1968).

We conclude that the general structure of a diffusion theory for consumer behavior should be a system of interrelated propositions which provide at least a partial explanation of the diffusion of innovations. The system should allow prediction and thereby be testable. The types of propositions necessary for diffusion theory are suggested by Katz, Levin, and Hamilton's (1963) definition of the process of diffusion: "as the (1) acceptance, (2) over time, (3) of some specific item—an idea or practice, (4) by individuals, groups or other adopting units, linked to, (5) specific channels of communication, (6) to a social structure, and (7) to a given system of values, or culture." Acceptance implies that diffusion theory must contain behavioral propositions. Over time implies the need for dynamic propositions expressing absolute level or rates of change. By individuals indicates the need for psychological propositions, as suggested by Homans (1964). Psychological propositions may potentially provide more generalizable explanations than propositions about groups or societies.[1] Specific channels of communications suggest the need to include propositions relating to the structure and functioning of human communications networks. The other factors in the process of diffusion, including some specific item, social structure,

[1] Sociological variables, however, may be more useful in marketing decision making directed to aggregate market segments.

and a given system of values or culture, are not propositions in a specific theory of diffusion but affect how generalizable a given theory will be across innovations, social systems, and cultures. It is still not known under what conditions a theory of diffusion may be applied across specific items, social structures, and cultures. For a theory of diffusion to be both powerful in providing explanations and also generalizable, propositions including these factors are required.

In addition to these propositions for a general theory to explain the diffusion of innovations, a useful theory should contain propositions that relate directly or closely to the marketing-mix instruments under the control of marketing managers and analysts. Although it may help to explain diffusion to know that early adopters are more cosmopolitan than later adopters, such information by itself is not necessarily useful in formulating marketing decisions. It is quite possible to develop a consumer behavior theory of the diffusion of innovations without approximating or including marketing decision-making variables, but the value of such theory to the marketing decision maker is limited.

Research Methods Required for the Development of Useful Theories of Diffusion and Consumer Behavior

Cross-sectional methods including one-shot interviews or written instrument surveys are useful for measuring symbolic or actual acceptance of an innovation and characteristics of individual adopters and nonadopters. In fact, a great deal is known about these variables in the consumer behavior process. Additionally, surveys can define the specific item of innovation and the specific cultures in which it is evaluated. However, these variables and propositions are not sufficient to develop a complete theory of diffusion. Additional observations of the adoption process over time by individuals linked to specific channels of communications within a social structure are necessary. Specific responses to marketing decision variables must also be considered. These observations are not revealed by the one-shot survey. Multiple observations over time of social units are required to develop these propositions.

Observations over time may occur through experimental designs (Campbell and Stanley, 1963), multiple survey observations, panel studies (Pelz and Andrews, 1964), or a combination of these designs, which in total are generally referred to as longitudinal studies. Kollat, Engel, and Blackwell (1970) stress the need for greater use of longitudinal studies in consumer behavior research, and these methods are especially powerful in the study of a process as dynamic as the diffusion of innovations. Dynamic measures or multiple measures over time provide an observational framework of which static methods, such as the one-shot survey, represent a special case. When reviewing the results of one-shot surveys, it should be kept in mind that they are snapshots of an ongoing process which may be measured any number of times. Conflicting results between such surveys may be a result of measuring the same changing process at different points in time.

Observations across communications networks or social structures require methods such as Coleman's relational analysis (1958). Relational analysis includes snowball sampling in which networks are revealed by using sociometric questions to move from one member of the study population to another. Another relational approach is to interview everyone within the relevant social structure, as Coleman, Katz, and Menzel did in their study of the adoption of drugs by physicians (1966). Cluster sampling of populations may enable definition of interrelationships between units if the clusters are quite dense. Multistage sampling is yet another approach.

In summary, useful theory would consist of an interrelated set of testable propositions including

1. Behavioral propositions.
2. Dynamic propositions.
3. Propositions relating to the structure and functioning of human communications networks.
4. Propositions relating to the innovation, social structure, and culture if generalizable theory is desired.
5. Propositions that relate directly or closely to the marketing-mix instruments under the control of marketing managers.

The methods required to obtain the theory would place an emphasis on multiple observations over time and adopting units including

1. Experimental and quasi-experimental designs.
2. Multiple survey observations.
3. Panel studies.
4. Relational analysis.

The next section reviews advances in diffusion research and theory. It is useful to keep these methodological considerations in mind when appraising the contributions of research and theory.

IMPLICATIONS OF RECENT ADVANCES IN DIFFUSION RESEARCH AND THEORY FOR THE STUDY OF CONSUMER BEHAVIOR

The recent literature of both a theoretical and empirical research nature relating to the consumer behavior aspects of the diffusion of innovations will be reviewed. New directions for building theory and directing empirical inquiries will be suggested, and we consider how this research has the potential for suggesting decision-making strategies for marketing managers.

A reorganization of the Katz, Levin, and Hamilton (1963) diffusion scheme will be used to structure the discussion in this section. This new version of their scheme is presented in paradigm form in Figure 2. Briefly, the revised system

FIGURE 2. **Model of the Diffusion of Innovations**

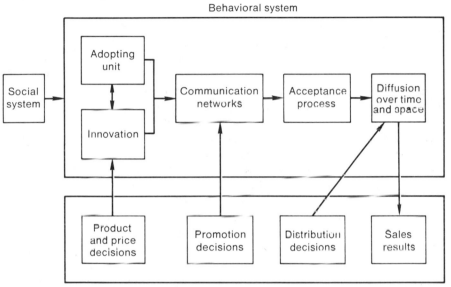

views the social structure as an exogenous variable affecting all subsequent elements in the adoption and diffusion processes. Within the social structure there must then exist both an adopting unit and an innovation. The inherent characteristics of the innovation generally define the particular type(s) of adopting units. To the extent that marketers are concerned with unmet consumer needs and respond with new goods and services, then the adopting unit, via the marketing organization, influences the existence and character of the innovation. Communication processes come into play next, linking cognitively and/or physically adopter units with innovations. This triggers decision making or acceptance processes into action. Acceptance processes both within adopter units and among adopter units take place over time and space. The marketing organization can intervene in this overall process at the innovation, communication, and time and space points. Intervention takes the form of product, price, promotion, and distribution policies. One caution to the reader is necessary. The model in Figure 2 is not to be interpreted as being causal. The sequence is a temporal one only. There is reciprocal causation among all elements shown. Each component of the behavioral system will be developed in detail.

Innovation[2]

Given the centrality of an innovation in the process of marketing, it is vital that we understand some of its possible dimensions. Before doing this we shall consider first various attempts to define just what an innovation is and then elaborate somewhat on our definition.

Barnett (1953) views an innovation broadly by emphasizing objectively measurable qualitative differences. According to Barnett, an innovation is "any thought, behavior or thing that is new because it is qualitatively different from existing forms." He goes on to emphasize the distinction between thought, behavior, and thing. "Strictly speaking, every innovation is an idea, or a constellation of ideas; but some innovations by their nature must remain mental organizations only, whereas others may be given overt and tangible expression."

The Federal Trade Commission has emphasized Barnett's definition in an advisory opinion in stating that consumer and industrial products can be called "new" only when they are "either entirely new or have been changed in a functionally significant and substantial respect" (Federal Trade Commission, 1967). Others have defined as innovations only those ideas, products, or services which have not yet secured more than 10 percent acceptance within the target population (Bell, 1963). Robertson (1971) has suggested that the critical factor in defining an item as an innovation should be its effect upon established patterns of consumption or behavior. He suggests three possible patterns of effect. An innovation that has little disruptive impact on behavior patterns is called a continuous innovation; flouride toothpaste would be an example. In this case the item constitutes only slight alteration of a current practice or product. Next are dynamically continuous innovations, which have a moderate impact on behavior patterns (e.g., electric toothbrushes). Finally, there are discontinuous innovations that involve the establishment of new behavior patterns. This generally involves the creation of previously unknown items. A preventive tooth decay pill is an example of this type of innovation.

In this chapter we shall consider as an innovation *any idea, practice, or material artifact perceived to be new by the relevant* adopting unit.[3] The adopting unit may vary from a single individual or single family to a city (Crain, 1966) or state legislature (Walker, 1969). This position is very similar to the

---

[2]Discussion in this section is adapted from Zaltman and Lin (1971).

[3]Since innovations can only be defined from the viewpoint of the potential adopter, and potential adopters will have different levels of awareness and attitudes toward the innovation. marketing decision makers may choose to segment the target population by perceptions about the product (see Zaltman and Dubois, 1971).

stance taken by Rogers and Shoemaker (1971): "An innovation is an idea, practice, or object perceived as new by the individual. It matters little, as far as human behavior is concerned, whether or not an idea is 'objectively' new as measured by the lapse of time since its first use or discovery . . . If the idea seems new and different to the individual, it is an innovation." Our definition differs from Rogers primarily in allowing for the possibility that the adopting unit may be larger than an individual. This in turn allows the possibility that not all members of a multimember adopting unit may perceive the item as an innovation.

One caveat to be added here concerning the use of the perception of the unit of adoption as a criterion for defining innovativeness is that perception will vary according to the physiological state of the individual and according to the different contextual situations for the adopting unit. Perception may also vary over time during the acceptance process. For example, when a person has only limited knowledge of an item, he may not perceive it as an innovation. (Of course, the reverse may also be true.) As additional information is accumulated and attitudes toward the object are formed or changed, the individual may develop a new perception in which the object is cast as an innovation. Ostlund (1969) found perception to be a better predictor of adoption than personal characteristics.

Caution is suggested by one study of several characteristics of innovations (divisibility, communicability, relative advantage, compatibility, and complexity) originally proposed by Rogers (1962). A panel of educators were asked to rate each of six widespread educational innovations by applying the five characteristics to the six innovations (Carlson, 1968). The result was little agreement among panel members in their ratings.[4] This suggests caution in utilizing the various innovation characteristics indiscriminately in different contexts. Another caveat must be mentioned. The relevance of a particular attribute may depend upon the perspective from which it is viewed. A manufacturer may define the relevant aspects of an innovation in a totally dissimilar way than the consumer. The manufacturer may view a new product as a major labor-saving device and develop his marketing strategy accordingly. Consumers, however, may not perceive the time saved as significant and thus reject the new product; or they adopt it for other reasons, such as the desire for social approval, ease of operation, low cost, and so on.

There are many dimensions of innovations that are made implicit or explicit in the literature. There are also several relevant dimensions that have received little attention, if any. In the following discussion various dimensions of

---

[4]Chin (1963) has characterized education innovations as involving substitution (e.g., one textbook for another), alteration (e.g., a minor change such as lengthening the school day by a few minutes), perturbation (e.g., moving class to a mobile classroom), restructuring (e.g., adopting team teaching), and value orientation (e.g., replacing the teacher by self-administered simulation games).

innovations will be presented and their importance noted. While this list will be extensive, it will not be exhaustive. Furthermore, all attributes will not pertain to all possible innovations. Some characteristics are uniquely associated with particular innovations. Once again, perception is important.

The following attributes of innovations are among the many that have been widely discussed in the literature (Rogers and Shoemaker, 1971; Fliegel and Kivlin, 1966). The particular dimensions selected here are those which seem to have relevance for a wide array of innovations found in different contexts. It is important to add one caveat: much of the existing "knowledge" rests more on discussion and speculation rather than on research evidence.

One of the most obvious dimensions is *cost*. One type of cost is *financial* in nature. This involves both initial and continuing costs of implementing an innovation. Initial financial cost, in a study by Fliegel and Kivlin (1966) was found to have a positive partial correlation with the adoption rate, whereas continuing cost and the adoption rate had a negative partial correlation. One explanation is that there is a cost-quality relationship which states that the more expensive an innovation is, the higher its perceived quality. This would seem to apply primarily to durable industrial and consumer goods that are purchased infrequently and are expected to have a long life. Thus the perceived extra cost of a particular durable-good innovation is, in a psychological sense and in an accounting sense, prorated over a long period of time, thus making the incremental cost appear small.

Social cost is another form of expense. Social cost may come in the form of ridicule, ostracism, or even exclusion or expulsion from some relevant reference group. Social position within a group influences the degree to which such a cost may occur and how serious the individual may perceive this cost (Homans, 1961). The marginal member of a group may have little to lose by innovating, and therefore even in the presence of considerable disapproval he may proceed to adopt an innovation. There is always the possibility that the decision might prove to be a wise one and he may gain stature as a consequence (Becker, 1970). A high-status member of a group may also adopt, even in the presence of potential or actual ridicule. The high-status person can do so because he will generally have an inventory of goodwill or social credit upon which he may draw, and will suffer little if the innovation does not succeed.

A second dimension concerns the *returns to the investment*. This is of special significance among consumers who have little tolerance for situations in which a deferral of gratification is necessary. This deferral of gratification varies according to culture and within cultures according to class, education, income, achievement motivation, and cosmopolitaness. Consumers having lower levels of education, achievement, motivation, and income will be less apt to adopt innovations having no immediate and substantial rewards.

The *efficiency* of an innovation in terms of (1) time saving and (2) the avoidance of discomfort is another important factor. In fact, some of the most basic wants acting as a stimulus for change are relief and avoidance wants (Barnett, 1953). These represent the desire for nonexistent or not presently possessed means or goals and appear in both industrial and consumer marketing contexts. The time factor and avoidance of discomfort factor are important dimensions for innovations dealing with household operation and maintenance.

The *risk* associated with innovations is also an important factor. The relevance of perceived risk will vary across social sectors. For some, the consequence of a wrongly (out of fashion, poor quality, etc.) chosen wardrobe is much less severe than that of selecting the wrong physician or even that of a physician prescribing an inappropriate drug.

The *communicability* of an innovation is of considerable importance in the adoption and diffusion process. First, the ease and effectiveness with which the results of the innovation can be disseminated to others constitutes a major force in the diffusion process (Rogers, 1962). Linked with this is the *clarity of results* of an innovation. Often innovations are introduced into dynamic situations involving the operation of several factors and where there are not effective controls over those other factors. It then becomes difficult to ascribe or attribute to the innovation any changes that may occur after the innovation has been introduced. There is clearly a need for much more work on research techniques in such instances, although some recent advances have already been made (Campbell, 1969; Sonquist, 1970).

Compatibility concerns the similarity of the innovation to an existing product, which it may eventually supplement, complement, or replace (Rogers, 1962). This assumes that an innovation is perceived in a particular context, and the perceived relationship between the innovation and other elements in the context influences the adoption and diffusion of the innovation. The *pervasiveness* or degree to which an innovation relates to and requires changes or adjustments on the part of other elements in the social situation influences the speed of acceptance (Barnett, 1953). The greater the pervasiveness of an innovation, the slower will be its acceptance.

The *complexity* of the innovation clearly has a bearing on its acceptance. Generally, the more complex an innovation is in terms of operating it, the less rapid its acceptance will be. Complexity may become manifest on two levels. First, the innovation may contain complex ideas. Second, the actual implementation of the innovation may be complex. We might hypothesize that an innovation which is easy to use but whose essential idea is complex is more likely to be adopted than an innovation which is difficult to use but whose essential idea or concept is readily understood.

The *perceived relative advantage* the innovation has over other alternatives including current practice is important. Those things the innovation does that other alternatives do not do are its critical attributes. The larger the number of critical attributes and the greater their magnitude, the more likely it is that the innovation will be adopted. The *visibility* or salience of the relative advantage is important. The more obvious the innovation, the more likely it is to be adopted. This suggests still another factor. The more amenable to *demonstration* the innovation is, the more visible its advantages will be, and thus the more likely it is to be adopted.

An understanding of the salient aspects of innovations as perceived by the adopting unit is essential (Ostlund, 1969). This section has presented some of the dimensions of innovations most likely to be perceived as relevant by adopter units. Strategies and tactics of marketing intervention must consider explicitly the nature of innovations. To the extent that attributes of innovations can be manipulated, they are important to the marketer as entry points into the social-change process. Thus two steps are involved. The first is to determine current or most probable perceptions of the innovation. The next step is, when necessary, to alter the attributes of the innovation or revise communications programs to improve the perception of these attributes. In doing so, the change agent is controlling the most fundamental element in the social-change process, the innovation.

Adopting Units

The adopting unit is that individual or group of individuals that participate in the acceptance decision-making process leading to potential adoption of an innovation. Alternatively, it is that entity whose authority or acquiescence is a necessary (although alone not always sufficient) prerequisite for the implementation of an innovation. It is most commonly assumed that the adoption unit is an individual. For consumer behavior the family is frequently the adopting unit for many products. In fact, the characteristics of the innovation, as considered in the previous section, are generally determinants of the adopting unit. The family will be the major adopting unit for some innovations, such as food products. In other instances, such as clothing, the individual may be the adopting unit, although still influenced by friends and family members. The acceptance process is considerably more complex when the adopting unit is the family rather than the individual.

There are, of course, even more complex adopting units than the family. In fact, there is almost an infinite array of possible units of adoption, varying in part according to the characteristics of the innovation, its outward function, and the social structure. Multimember units other than the family which have been studied include cities (Crain, 1966), state legislatures (Walker, 1969), complex organizations (Myers and Marquis, 1969; Allvine, 1968; Appel, 1970; Knight, 1967; Shepard, 1967), industries (Webster, 1969), universities (Evans, 1970), and scientific societies (Crane, 1972; Zaltman and Koehler, 1972; Garvey, Lin, and Nelson, 1970). Katz, Levin, and Hamilton have attempted to sum up all possible units of adoption by placing them in one of three distinguishable categories: the individual, informal group or collectivity, and formal organizations. Although consideration of organizations and communities as adopting units is highly relevant to industrial and governmental marketing, these adopting units are of less interest to consumer marketers than individual consumers and families.

Characteristics of Individuals as Adopting Units. A definition of adopter categories as ideal types includes innovators, early adopters, early majority, late majority, and laggards. The innovators are viewed as venturesome and risk taking, composing about the first 3 percent of those to adopt the innovation. Early adopters, who are the next 13 percent to adopt, command respect from their peers and are more integrated into their social system than others, especially more than the innovators, who are often at the isolated boundaries of a social system. The early majority are likely to be deliberate and represent 34 percent of the adopting population. Late majority and laggards comprise the remaining 50 percent of the individual adopting units and are either skeptical or traditional about the innovation and may adopt only after rather strong social pressure or vivid demonstration of the relative advantage of the innovation over other products or services. These classes are ideal definitions rather than concepts inferred through research. They serve as a guide to research in determining the characteristics of the adopting unit.

Rogers and Stanfield (1968) specify several characteristics relating to innovativeness in agricultural contexts. These include more education, higher income, higher level of living, higher achievement motivation, greater educational aspirations, more mass-media exposure, and more active participation in group activities. Age has not been a good discriminator of innovative behavior.

In studying innovators of the Community Antenna Television system (CATV), Boone (1970) discovered many of the same characteristics mentioned by Rogers and Stanfield. Use of the California Personality Inventory revealed greater self-confidence, acceptance of newness, and more leadership ability for innovators than for later adopters of CATV.

Fashion innovators hold a critical position in the success of a change of fashion due to the short period of a fashion season. King (1964) has found that fashion innovators for women's millinery are more concerned with hair care, more involved in social visiting, older, and have more education and higher family income than later adopters. King (1963) concludes that fashion adoption does not "trickle down" from an upper-class fashion elite to the middle and lower classes, but trickles across each social class. Summers (1970) has shown that women's fashion opinion leaders are distinctly different from nonleaders on a wide variety of characteristics and are likely to represent a critical market segment.

Robertson (1967) has studied characteristics of innovative adopters of Touch-Tone telephones. He found these innovators are more venturesome, more socially integrated, socially mobile, financially privileged, and less cosmopolitan than noninnovators. Early adopters of color television have been shown to have higher incomes, more group memberships, and more likely to be involved in professional or managerial occupations (Gorman and Moore, 1968).

Laggards as market segments have received little research, which seems unusual in the light of the importance of late-adopting market segments. The cause may well be that researchers prefer to undertake more "positive" studies. Uhl, Andrus, and Poulsen (1970) have studied laggards for acceptance of new food products. Laggards of food products had lower family income than innovators. They were older and had smaller families. As might be expected, the laggards are more brand loyal than innovators. The researchers consider this segment important, since once they adopt an innovation they may continue adoption beyond the time the earlier adopters have moved on.

Personality characteristics have an intuitive appeal for explaining adopter types. However, personality constructs have proved to be quite disappointing in much of the research. This situation is no different in the study of the diffusion of consumer innovations. Robertson and Myers (1969) cast doubt on postulated relationships of personality variables with innovative behavior. They find only weak relationships between opinion leadership, innovativeness, and the scales on the California Personality Inventory. Personality research is at its early stages, and negative findings at this time should not be taken to mean that personality research will not contribute to the understanding of innovative behavior in the future.

Those doing research in consumer behavior have most frequently employed personality inventories combining many measures of personality dimensions. Single-dimension personality constructs, such as dogmatism ("mental inflexibility"), applied in a precise manner may be more productive than the use of personality inventories. For example, dogmatism has been shown to be positively related to the adoption of new (but not too novel) products and negatively related to the adoption of novel new products. Blake, Perloff, and Heslin (1970) tested this relationship for 35 products and found those high in dogmatism would be earlier adopters of new products promoted with authoritative communications. Use of a personality inventory rather than a specific dogmatism scale could have hidden this relationship (see Chapter 4 for more detail on personality theories).

Studies of demographic and predispositional factors (personality and attitudes) have failed to provide consistent relationships with innovative behavior. Ostlund (1969) proposes that consideration of the perceived characteristics of the innovation might explain the inconsistencies in these findings. For example, Randoe (1968) suggests that opinion leaders will be more cosmopolitan than average when the product has cosmopolitan features, such as interior decoration. However, early adopters for detergents and baby food may not be cosmopolitan at all.

Once having located and defined innovators, early adopters, and later adopters, it is of interest to determine if the adoption process is different for each group. If it is different, how can these differences be utilized in formulating more effective marketing strategies? Robertson (1968) found that innovators and noninnovators respond differently at later stages in the acceptance process. The noninnovators are less likely to reach later stages of the acceptance process. Marketers may encourage adoption by helping noninnovators through the acceptance process by stressing "social correctness" of the innovation. Testimonial appeals may be effective in gaining legitimation of the innovation by noninnovators.

Robertson's findings were based on a study of adoption of the Touch-Tone telephone. Engel, Blackwell, and Kegerreis (1969), when studying the adoption of automotive diagnostic centers, found more information-seeking activity by the innovators than the noninnovators during the early stages of the acceptance process. The difference in their findings and Robertson's is likely to be a function of the differences in risk involved in the adoption of a Touch-Tone telephone and an automotive diagnostic center. It seems likely the automotive diagnostic centers are both more difficult to comprehend and involve more risk than the Touch-Tone telephone, since most consumers are unaware of the effectiveness of a complex new service.

Families As Adopting Units. Rogers and Shoemaker (1971) make brief consideration of the family as an adopting unit in a discussion of collective innovation decisions. They suggest that a more cosmopolitan member of the family brings information into the acceptance process.

Without a tradition of studying the family as an adopting unit, the researcher must turn to secondary sources regarding the family. Robertson (1971) has reviewed some literature on the family. We need to determine exactly what role the members of the family play in the stages of the acceptance process. Role specialization may lead to some members playing a more important role at some stages of the decision-making process. Those members with greater numbers of contacts outside the family may play a larger role in the early stages of the acceptance process. As the later stages of the acceptance process are reached, participation by greater numbers of the family is likely.

Ostlund (Chapter 6) reviews the literature of family decision making. He concludes that little has been done in this area, and those conclusions that have been reached are often amusingly obvious. A consideration of husband and wife dominance may provide some help in understanding the acceptance process by linking variables explaining the acceptance process. Much research remains to be done in considering the family as the adopting unit.

Social Structure Consideration. There are several perspectives from which one could view the adopter units within the social structure. Although some degree of similarity and overlap exists among the perspectives, each has a unique contribution of its own. The first of these concerns a *tiering* of adopter units. As indicated earlier, the most frequent approach followed in the study of the adoption and diffusion processes is to focus on a single unit of adoption, regardless of its composition. Yet in fact there may often be tiers of adoption units within a given social structure and for a specific innovation. To some degree this is implicit in discussions of innovators or early adopters, gatekeepers, and opinion leaders. Gatekeepers and opinion leaders may or may not adopt an innovation in order to perform their functions. If they do adopt (as opposed to solely supplying information) an innovation, they become the first and second tiers, respectively, whereas those who follow their lead become a third tier. Here we are assuming that the tiers are structurally related; that is, there is interaction among them. This type of tier is to be distinguished from another form concerning ideal-type adopter units, (i.e., innovators, early majority, etc., mentioned earlier). As far as the requirement is concerned for the collectivity, it consists of individuals each of whom makes more or less voluntary decisions to join or not to join the group; for the formal organization the decision, however it is reached, is binding upon all members (Olson, 1965).

The next consideration concerns the *composition of the adopter unit.* The adopter unit may be a single-member unit, as may be the case of a state legislator acting upon an abortion bill or other legislation or a family deciding how to use leisure time. In some cases the very nature of the innovation may require or dictate the specific adopter unit. Team teaching when it is voluntary on the part of teachers requires acceptance by at least two teachers. When it is not voluntary among teachers, it requires adoption by the department chairman or school principal, or possibly the superintendent of schools. The social structure of the particular school system will determine where the authority is likely to reside. Thus there may be a tiering of adopter units within the school system. Also, product characteristics are important. For the marketing of inexpensive academic innovations the individual teacher is likely to be the unit of adoption, regardless of the social structure.

The multimember unit of adoption may consist of a system of undifferentiated roles, or it may be composed of functionally different roles. When voting in a referendum on the issue of fluoridation of the city water supply, all voters have equal status and homogeneous functions, although this is unlikely to be true prior to the referendum. The concept of a social-action management team, suggested recently by Zaltman and Vertinsky (1971), is an illustration of an adopter unit consisting of three functionally different but carefully orchestrated roles. The three roles (monitor, strategist-tactician, and implementer) collectively and in concert determine the action the marketing program takes.

Another consideration is the *location* in the social structure of the adopter unit. This has been alluded to above. What is interesting is that there may be a *nesting* of tiers. For example, in a legislature there are committees which exert strong influence as gatekeepers and as decision makers. These committees often have sufficient authority to strongly influence the implementation or non-implementation of the piece of legislation. The nature of the innovation may also prescribe one unit rather than another, depending upon the norms of a group.

There is an important distinction to be made between the adopter unit and the implementation of the adoption decision. In many cases in the marketing sphere the relevant adopter unit is the individual and sometimes the family. Although the peer group is an important source of influence, especially as a source of legitimation in the decision-making process by consumers, it is not often the adopter unit. In some instances, not uncommon to marketing, when the decision to adopt is made by one individual and implemented by another, it can be argued that the adopter unit is actually a dyad. This argument is most convincing when the implementer has considerable latitude or discretion in determining how the acceptance decision is to be carried out. There are also instances when the decision maker is not the ultimate user. The physician prescribing drugs for a patient is an illustration. A parent's decision to buy only enriched cereals is more or less binding on the children who would be its main users.

Channels ot Communication

An individual has two main channels of information regarding innovations available. The mass media of television, radio, magazines, and newspapers provide great quantities of impersonal information sponsored by the marketing organization promoting the innovation and neutral sources such as the news content of the mass media. These impersonal channels are used in conjunction with the personal sources available to the individual. Impersonal and inter-personal channels serve different, and often complementary, functions during the adoption process. Recently developed communications models have recognized this complementary function.

The first models of the effects of mass communications developed out of the growth of radio in the 1930s. These models pictured the media as having a direct and relatively immediate effect on an atomized audience. Although the total effects occasionally seemed quite impressive, the average direct effects of the media on the population reached was and still is quite small. The supporting role of interpersonal communications in the spread of ideas was first studied in the 1940s in election studies by Lazarsfeld and his associates. These studies are summarized in *Personal Influence* (Katz and Lazarsfeld, 1955). They lead to the argument for the two-step flow model of mass communications. The two-step flow model recognizes the mass audience as interacting individuals. The media are viewed as providing messages to opinion leaders in the audience who, in turn, act to spread the messages to other members of the audience. This model also may be used to explain the stimulation of word-of-mouth advertising. In a study of the diffusion of a new brand of a frequently purchased food product, Arndt

(1967b) found general support for a number of hypotheses or predictions derived from the two-step flow hypothesis. Influence did appear to flow from impersonal sources to opinion leaders. He also found that leaders are more active in the word-of-mouth communication process as both givers and receivers of information. This latter observation, that leaders are both transmitters and receivers, supports the opinion sharing (rather than opinion giving) findings by Trodahl and Van Dam. The Arndt data also reinforced the basic two-step flow model in that opinion leaders were found not only to be relayers of information from impersonal sources, but also transmitted personal evaluations about the object of communication. Moreover, these evaluations were influential in the decision-making process of the receiver. "Those receiving favorable word-of-mouth communications were three times as likely to buy the new product as were those receiving unfavorable word-of-mouth" (p. 465).

There have also been a number of studies whose findings conflict with or call for the modification of the basic two-step flow of communication hypothesis (Trodahl and Van Dam, 1965; Van Den Ban, 1964; Trodahl, 1966; Deutschmann and Danielson, 1960).

The two-step flow model was a pioneering attempt to relate the interaction of mass communications and interpersonal communications. As such, it served to stimulate a great deal of research to replicate and strengthen the two-step model or to develop extended models recognizing a more complicated multiple-step model. This research has revealed a number of complications in relating interpersonal and impersonal communications, including difficulties in locating opinion leaders with consistent characteristics, finding that communication networks are often nonexistent or incomplete, and that different networks exist for different groups within the social structure.

Rogers (1972) notes six limitations of the two-step flow model.

1. It implies a passive audience and active, information-seeking opinion leaders who provide the main thrust in initiating the communication flow. Rather, opinion leaders may not be active seekers of information and may be passive in communicating to followers.

2. The two-step flow masks multistage communication processes or, in the other direction, may underestimate the direct impact the mass media may have on a very large audience.

3. The two-step flow overemphasizes the importance of the mass media for the opinion leader. "The specific channels utilized by opinion leaders depend on such considerations as the nature of the message, its origin, and the social location of the opinion leaders in the social structure."

4. The basic study (Lazarsfeld, 1940) preceding the two-step flow concept (and some of the follow-up studies) did not take into account the time of knowing a new idea. That is, opinion leaders may simply be early knowers of ideas. Other people—the interpersonal channels—because they are unaware of the idea may not be capable of functioning as a source of

information, thus increasing the relative importance of the mass media for early knowers.

5. The two-step flow hypothesis, at least as originally formulated, ignored the time dimension involved in decision making. Subsequent diffusion studies (particularly in rural sociology and consumer behavior) have demonstrated that knowledge and persuasion acceptance stages (among others) exist for opinion leaders and followers and that for both groups the mass media are important at the persuasion stage. "Thus it is not only the opinion leaders who use mass media channels as the original statement of the two-step flow model seems to imply".

6. The implied dichotomy of opinion leaders versus followers (Katz, 1957) is misleading. First, opinion leadership is a continuous variable. Second, nonleaders are not necessarily followers.

Lin (1971) has suggested two important reasons for the inconsistent findings concerning the two-step flow hypothesis. One is the failure of researchers to distinguish between two types of communication events, _information flow_ and _influence_. The second reason is the lack of focus on the individual's decision-making process in association with the communication of information and influence. Time is an important element here. First, the decision-making process occurs over time, ranging in duration from what Lin calls instantaneous to protracted to infinite. Second, information flow is most likely to be high near the initial point of the decision making process and influence a more critical factor near the terminal point of the decision-making process.

The opinion leadership concept is an appealing one for those managing the diffusion of innovations. If opinion leaders exist and can be located, they represent a point of communication leverage or multiplication in promoting the innovation. Yadav and Rogers (1966) cite references showing opinion leadership to be positively related to the degree of conformity to social system norms, the degree of formal organization leadership, innovativeness, cosmopolitaness, cosmopolite social relationships, mass-media exposure, perceived competence, prestige accorded to a certain position, perceived social accessibility, spatial accessibility, social perceptiveness, low dogmatism, empathy, achievement motivation, political knowledgeability, functional literacy, education, and younger age. King and Summers (1970), using a broad definition of opinion leadership, found about 70 percent of their study population qualified as opinion leaders for at least one of six consumer product categories and concluded that high overlap in leadership across categories suggests the existence of generalized opinion leaders. Montgomery and Silk (1969) also found high overlap across most categories of consumer products they studied. Most of these studies have used a self-designating opinion-leadership scale to determine opinion leadership. This scale is similar in most studies, consisting of six or seven written items asking people if they are regarded as good sources of information regarding a specific product or innovation. It seems likely that this self-designating opinion-leadership scale is correlated highly with self-esteem, and may in fact be a measure of self-esteem rather than opinion leadership. Arndt (1967b) has found those high in self-esteem are more likely to be exposed to interpersonal communications. We suggest that the self-designating opinion-leadership scale measures a combination of self-esteem and the quantity of interpersonal communications an individual receives rather than actual opinion leadership. These studies probably reveal two distinct communications networks in which the opinion leaders are communicating with each other and the "followers" are isolated and are not communicating with anyone a great deal. One group feels a need for interpersonal communications; the other does not.

A study of opinion leadership for food and household products in the United Kingdom found opinion leaders and followers to be quite similar. As a group the leaders and followers differed from both "discussers" (those who talk about marketing but are not active seekers or "givers of advice") and "silenters" (those who neither give nor take advice) (Gross, 1971). This study does not support the Katz and Lazarsfeld two-step flow hypothesis. It suggests a population with segments that differ in their needs for information. There is not necessarily a flow between segments. Rather there are flows within each segment.

Engel, Kegerreis, and Blackwell (1969) found innovators for automotive diagnostic services to be more active users as well as more active disseminators of word-of-mouth communications compared to the general population. It is not possible to determine to whom these innovators were communicating. The communications may have been mainly between innovators. If the innovators acted as opinion leaders for the general population, they may have greatly influenced the rate of adoption of automotive diagnostic services. If they only talked among themselves, their effects on the later adopters were small.

Opinion leadership may then be an artifact created by the use of surveys applied to individuals and subsequent failure to measure the interpersonal communications networks. The written survey is a limited instrument and is probably insufficient to the task asked of it. It may create the appearance of communications when none exist through the use of forced-choice questions. More complicated methods, such as those described by Coleman (1958), including snowball sampling in which communications networks are traced from individual to individual or saturation sampling, may be required to provide strong explanations for the flow of interpersonal communications. Coleman, Katz, and Menzel (1966) used saturation sampling to study the flow of communications regarding new drugs among physicians. This study revealed two communications networks: one for the more socially integrated set of doctors and a separate nonnetwork for the isolated doctors. Innovative drugs were adopted more rapidly through the network of integrated doctors than through the isolated doctors who were not receiving a great deal of professional interpersonal communications. It seems likely that a self-designating opinion-leadership scale applied to these doctors would reveal the integrated doctors to be high in opinion leadership and the isolates to be low in opinion leadership.

The two- or multistep flow of communications model is possibly the result of using cross-sectional research methods in attempting to reveal the dynamic acceptance process. Impersonal and interpersonal communications seem to serve different functions at the various stages of the acceptance process. Awareness of an innovation may be created as effectively by either impersonal or interpersonal communications channels. The mass-media channels often serve the awareness function in a modern society in which their reach is very large. Attitude and behavior change during the acceptance process are likely to require interpersonal communications to legitimize and effectively describe the use of the innovation in a persuasive and risk-reducing manner. The mass media are unlikely to be able to accomplish this function with the majority of potential adopters.

Impersonal communications, including product advertising, are best viewed as input into the variety of communications networks that exist within a social structure. These inputs may serve to stimulate interpersonal communications whenever they provide new or inconsistent information requiring a restructuring of attitudes or behavior. In most cases interpersonal communications are likely to be obtained through casual conversation, which is not in any one direction of flow, but shared by the participants. Only in situations where strong inconsistencies or high risk is perceived are people likely to seek out their "opinion leaders" (Van Den Ban, 1964; Trodahl, 1966). The person most likely to be sought for advice is first a person who is most like the information seeker ("homophily" as defined by Rogers, 1969) and, second, one who is likely to be able to provide the information needed. It seems probable that in most cases someone who is known to be a high media user, possesses associates inside the local communications network, or is an adopter of the innovation is the more favored source of advice. Not surprisingly, research has borne this out (Rogers, 1962). The majority of interpersonal communications are likely to be casual and two directional; they may, however, be occurring within relatively closed but overlapping series of communications networks. This is suggested by Coleman, Katz, and Menzel (1966) for physicians and by King (1963), who proposes that independent communications networks exist within social classes for women's millinery.

More effective diffusion theory may be developed if we define the varieties of communications networks and their characteristics. If an interpersonal word-of-mouth communication can be started within a communications network, it may flow without the stimulus of the opinion leader through established channels, except in high-risk and inconsistency situations. In these cases there may be some persons who serve an opinion-leadership role. The important need is not to locate the opinion leader but to locate the networks of interpersonal communication.

Pareek and Singh (1969) have located different communications networks at different stages of the adoption of three agricultural innovations in India. Communications through these networks increased, in general, with the more advanced stages of the acceptance process. Coleman, Katz, and Menzel (1966) discovered different networks among physicians, and these operated differently through the acceptance process. Storer (1966) has located "invisible colleges" or systems of informal communications between scientists that vary as a function of the product and the audience for the discipline.[5] Arndt (1967b) found those higher in self-esteem to be more likely to use interpersonal communications networks. Consumer adoption units are likely to make use of a variety of interpersonal communications networks, including occupational, personal, family, and professional networks for husband, wife, and children. These networks are likely to be different by social class, age, life cycle, and other traditionally demographic market-segmenting variables. It is likely that the traditional market-segmenting variables can be used to locate the various interpersonal communications networks. This strategy may be more useful in planning promotion policies for innovative products than the location of the more diffuse and difficult to define opinion leaders who may not exist. Even if they do, they may only be useful for risky products or inconsistency-producing campaigns.

We do not imply that finding the appropriate communications networks is an easy undertaking. There has not been much research designed to determine the distinguishing characteristics of interpersonal communications networks. It is likely that communications networks are developed as a function of the social structure of a culture. Once interpersonal networks are located the determination of how to communicate through the media to these networks will become more a marketing research problem for the individual firm than a behavioral research problem. If a substantial number of interpersonal communications networks do not exist, the innovation may be diffused incompletely through the social structure and fail to complete a substantial diffusion process. The innovation may be adopted by a single subculture (see Chapter 12). The diffusion process might be quite irregular as new interpersonal networks begin discussion regarding the innovation. There may be flat spots in the diffusion curve such as with the book *Games People Play*, which was published many years before its rapid diffusion to a small but substantial segment mainly through a combination of interpersonal and mass-media communications. It is not always apparent which networks will be efficient in generating interpersonal communications networks. If we can locate these networks we can begin to react to this aspect of the social structure. Cox (1967) has suggested that once located we should develop methods to monitor the flow of information in the interpersonal networks and determine ways to provide the consumer with information he desires but is not currently receiving through these channels. There have been

---

[5]See Crane (1972) for additional discussion of invisible colleges.

reports of even more aggressive attempts to stimulate these interpersonal networks through paid word-of-mouth communicators (Arndt, 1967a).

The next steps in studying the channels of communication in the diffusion of consumer products require the use of the more powerful research methods necessary to reveal the structure of interpersonal communications networks and how a given social structure produces its variety of interpersonal networks. Once these networks are specified structurally we can begin to study how information flows within them and determine if the concept of opinion leaders has any usefulness. The amount of independence and overlap of these networks may suggest valid criteria for market segmentation. Promotional programs could then be planned both in advance of the word-of-mouth effects and later in reaction and concert to these effects. Such research is likely to lead to more adaptive media communications policies when encouraging the diffusion of an innovation.

Acceptance Process

The acceptance process leads to the adoption of the innovation, the dependent variable in the diffusion process. The behavioral variable of adoption (and the time of adoption) is also a major marketing management variable, sales. The acceptance process is recognized as being far more complex than the simple act of adoption. The stages of the acceptance process from awareness to adoption, or equally important the failure to ever adopt (rejection or ignorance), are receiving a great deal of attention. Models of the acceptance process have been developed by researchers in rural sociology (Rogers, 1962), advertising (Lavidge and Steiner, 1961), and consumer behavior (Howard and Sheth, 1969). Figure 3 outlines the stages involved in these models. A more comprehensive model attempting to synthesize the three models has been suggested by Robertson (1971).

Robertson's Acceptance-Decision Process Model. Robertson's acceptance-decision model is shown in Figure 4. The stages are:

1. *Problem-perception stage.* There is initially a want or need such as those suggested by Barnett (1958), creating an inconsistency in the individual and probably stimulating processes of selective perception. Before any effective or systematic action can be taken to satisfy a need or motive, the basic problem or nature of this need or motive must be perceived and defined.

2. *Awareness stage.* At this stage the existence of the innovation becomes known, but the individual lacks significant information about the innovation and does not possess strong attitudes about it.

3. *Comprehension stage.* "Comprehension is based on knowledge and represents the consumer's conception of what the product is and what functions it can perform" (Robertson, 1971). Together with the awareness stage the comprehension stage is the information-processing stage and comprises the cognitive field of the purchase-decision process.

FIGURE 3.   **Stages of Three Proposed Acceptance Processes**

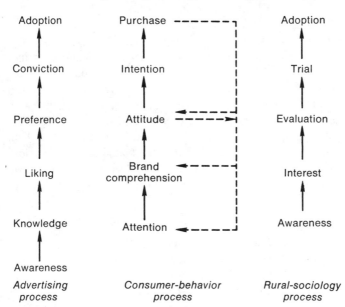

4. *Attitude stage.* The attitude stage consists of the development of a favorable or unfavorable behavioral disposition by the individual toward the innovation. Unless the outcome of this stage is believed favorable toward the innovation, the adoption process is likely to terminate.

5. *Legitimation stage.* At this stage the individual becomes convinced that the adoption of the innovation is the appropriate course of action. The critical attributes of the innovation are likely to be perceived favorably.

6. *Trial stage.* The decision to test or try the innovation is a result of legitimation while in the attitude field. The trial may simply be cognitive (symbolic adoption), in which case the individual projects himself vicariously into a hypothetical situation of using the innovation, or he may actually, but temporarily, put the innovation to use (in part or in total depending upon the nature of the innovation). The reevaluation of the innovation on the basis of this new information (experience) may result in (a) rejection (incomplete acceptance process), (b) continued information gathering, or (c) adoption.

7. *Adoption stage.* At this stage the individual decides and acts to implement the innovation on a full scale on a more or less permanent basis. The idea or product ceases to be an innovation for the individual, and processes of brand switching become more important to the continued acceptance of the innovation.

The first three stages of Robertson's model are the information-processing stages. "They comprise the cognitive field on the purchase decision process.

Comprehension overlaps with the attitude stage since knowledge, defined in terms of beliefs, is recognized as an attitude component . . . The comprehension, attitude, and legitimation stages may be considered to comprise the attitude field of the adoption decision process . . . The legitimation, trial, and adoption stages comprise the behavior field in the adoption decision process" (1971). Dissonance or cognitive inconsistency may occur as another stage if the consumer is attracted to alternative decisions that were preempted by the adoption of the specific innovation. Robertson's proposed cognitive field, attitude field, and behavior field will be used as a conceptual scheme to detail the acceptance process.

Other features of the Robertson model are the provisions for skipped stages in the acceptance process, regression from one stage to a previous one, and the possibility of incompleted acceptance processes or failure to adopt the innovation. Robertson omits the interest and evaluation stages proposed by Rogers (1962) from his acceptance process model, since interest is considered the prerequisite motivation to move from any stage to another, and evaluation is a

FIGURE 4. Summary Acceptance-Decision Process Model

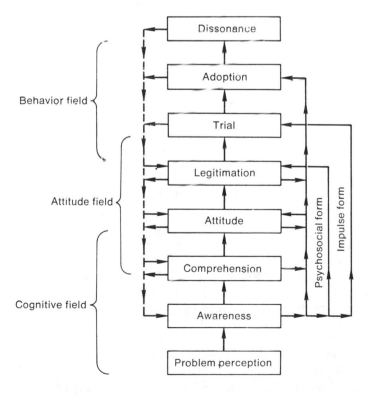

From Robertson (1971).

process that occurs at each stage of the acceptance process. Ozanne and Churchill (1968) had difficulties in defining the evaluation stage in the acceptance of machine tools. Studies of the acceptance process of birth-control devices and methods (Palmore, 1968) and for farming innovations in India (Sawhney, 1967) have not revealed clear-cut interest and evaluation stages.

Cognitive Field. The cognitive field consists of the problem perception, awareness, and comprehension stages of the acceptance process. Problem perception occurs if the felt want or need for seeking an innovative solution precedes exposure and awareness of the innovation. When the innovation is perceived in advance of any perceived problem, awareness is the first stage in the acceptance process.

Diffusion researchers have observed that awareness of an innovation is likely to be produced by impersonal communications, either media, change agent, or salesman (Rogers, 1962, 1969). The source of these communications is less important than mere exposure for creating awareness. Personal communications would probably be equally or more effective but are much less likely to occur, and personal communication is not an easily controllable marketing instrument. Mass media or interpersonal communications may be assumed equally effective for creating awareness, assuming equal opportunity for exposure. Findings that innovators and early adopters name impersonal sources for awareness communications more often than later adopters is not unexpected, since there is a low likelihood of opportunities for any personal communications at the early stages of diffusion. An important issue is do individuals actively seek or avoid exposure to those information sources providing an awareness of innovation?

Avoidance of exposure to information regarding a specific innovation seems nearly impossible, since an individual does not know what he should avoid. An individual may, however, choose to avoid those general sources which would be more likely to create awareness of classes of innovations. For example, tradition-bound doctors may not find time to talk with detail men, read journals, or even talk with peers. Katz (1957) reports this behavior is more likely to occur among later adopters. Whether avoidance of awareness sources for innovation is a result of any purposeful behavior or a chance occurrence during the acceptance process is not clear. Even if it is purposeful behavior, selective avoidance of awareness is not especially important to the acceptance process, because awareness can be forced by change agents and other members of the social system much more readily than the stages following awareness in the adoption process. Most advertising managers know that creating awareness is not the most difficult barrier to product adoption.

Aggressive seeking of exposure to innovative information sources is more vital to the acceptance process, since behavior of this type may accelerate the diffusion process by leading to earlier adoption of the innovation across the population. Newcomb (1962) has suggested that people select environments supportive of their value and attitude structure. If this is so, some individuals may seek exposure to innovation awareness sources to satisfy some felt need or motive. McGuire (1969, p. 218) states, "The positive aspect of the postulate (seeking of supportive information) has received a fair amount of experimental support." The reasons for seeking supportive environments are not clear, but it is likely that learning theory may offer some insight to this process (see Chapter 2). Complexity and variety theory predicts seeking of novel, surprising, and unpredicted information for individual needs, but it may be that social needs are greater and people also seek innovation if this behavior is accepted in groups to which they aspire (see Chapter 9 for more detail on the need for variety).

The comprehension stage is included in both the attitude field and the cognitive field. It will be considered in the attitude-field discussion since it represents the vital link between awareness and the formation of effective and behavioral attitudes regarding the innovation.

Attitude Field. Robertson includes the stages of comprehension, attitude, and legitimation as comprising the attitude field of the acceptance process. These stages are quite similar to McGuire's (1969, p. 173) stochastic process of attitude change including (1) attention, (2) comprehension, (3) yielding, (4) retention, and (5) action. If we roughly equate attitude and legitimation with yielding and retention, the processes are identical. The stages of attitude formation and retention are influenced by several classes of variables including (1) source, (2) message, (3) channel, (4) receiver, and (5) destination (exact type of change desired) (McGuire, 1969). Many of these factors are considered in Day's chapter on attitude structure and change in this volume. We see no need to repeat this discussion since most of these factors interact in similar ways in many consumer decision processes and are not specific to the diffusion of innovations. There are, however, some unique aspects of channel effects on the adoption and diffusion processes that were considered in the communications section of this chapter, and there are unique aspects of receiver factors in relation to innovations. These will be considered next.

The attitude field of the acceptance process is a particularly murky area, since measurements of the process dynamics of change to an individual's attitude field must be inferred through observation of his verbal behavior (opinions). Most diffusion researchers feel sufficiently uneasy about this area to ignore or gloss over the cognitive processes. Although the stages of this field are not well defined, the goal of the process is the acquisition of persistent behavioral dispositions in such a way as to produce initial and continued adoption of the innovation.

Comprehension of the innovation may not be a difficult process, as we have suggested previously. Legitimation or yielding and retention beliefs are, however, more central and salient to the consumer than awareness and comprehension beliefs. Simple verbal instruction about the characteristics of the innovation may be sufficient for awareness and comprehension, but a greater variety of communications may be required to increase the probability of movement through the attitude field. That is, advertising may be insufficient and an actual demonstration may be required. The attitude field is much more complex than simple attitude formation and change, including the additional requirements of legitimation and retention over time so that action may eventually occur.

It has been demonstrated that legitimation and retention may depend more on the person's cognitive work regarding a message than on remembering specific message details (Greenwald, 1968; McGuire, 1969). Watts (1967) found that active improvisation of a persuasive message produces greater attitude retention than reading a message. Elms (1966) and Mann and Janis (1968) found role playing more effective than passive acquisition for retention of a message. In addition to these studies of individual cognitive work and active acquisition, retention seems to be greater when attitudes are acquired in group situations. Maccoby, et al. (1962), found that retention is greater for persons talking to like-minded others. Studies of hysteria in groups have revealed persistent attitudes (Kerckhoff and Back, 1968). Freedman and Fraser's (1966) "foot-in-the-door" experiments suggest that prior compliance to low-cost requests leads to an increased probability of later acceptance of higher-cost requests.

These findings are a limited set available from the literature of retention following attitude change. They are biased to select propositions that have something to offer in explaining the acceptance process, and there are other experiments that do not offer confirmation of these propositions by failing to show retention. The ideas suggested by these propositions include

1. Active improvision of arguments.
2. Active involvement or role playing.
3. Cognitive work
4. Presence of a group.

These are not independent concepts relating to the process of legitimation and retention during the attitude-field process. This research suggests that some communications situations are more powerful in producing persistent attitude change.

The implications of these findings to a marketing manager or to a change agent are that during the legitimation, yielding, and retention stages of the attitude field, communications should be designed so that potential adopters will directly experience or directly perceive the rewards for adopting the innovation and the means of acquiring the innovation. This is congruent with the finding that adoption is an accelerating process, since, as more persons acquire the innovation, the more active modes of communications have more chance to occur. The innovation can be viewed directly and tried either directly or mentally. Demonstration of the empirical validity of these findings to consumer behavior could provide a strong argument for providing real or "near real" samples of innovations through the population so that the more powerful modes of communications are more likely to occur. This research could provide a theoretical grounding for the policy of providing free samples of innovative products.

These findings have much in common with theories of learning through exposure to a model or "vicarious learning" (Berger and Lambert, 1968; also see Ray's chapter on learning theory in this volume). Unfortunately, the majority of research on vicarious learning and modeling deals with the acquisition of rather simple behavioral dispositions. Also the models consider directly measurable behavioral variables and do not consider changes in a person's attitude field.

We propose that the consumer forms a model within his attitude structure regarding adoption and use of the innovation through stimuli received through exploration, perception, and verbal instruction. Some of these modes of acquisition may be more effective in developing models than others. It seems that the vicarious cognitive modeling, symbolic adoption, or cognitive work an individual performs prior to the adoption of an innovation is a useful concept for developing change strategies, but it requires a great deal of additional development and testing.

Behavior Field. The behavior field, including the stages of trial and adoption, is linked to the stages of legitimation preceding behavior and dissonance following behavior. Diffusion research has concentrated on observation of the adoption behavior of individuals and largely ignored linking these processes with legitimation and dissonance. When considering the trial-and-adoption behavior, our primary concern is adoption by whom, when, and what is his role within groups. We know that early adopters

1. Are more socially integrated than later adopters.
2. Try innovation on a smaller scale than later adopters.
3. Have greater contact with the outside world than later adopters.
4. Are heavy users of products or behavior similar to the innovation or products or behavior replaced by the innovation (Rogers, 1962).

Specific personality and socioeconomic characteristics of early adopters have been found, but these are less consistent across studies than the above four characteristics.

These descriptions of early adopters are congruent with the findings reviewed in the previous section. Greater social integration provides the early adopter with a greater opportunity to discuss the acquisition and use of innovations, calling upon the processes of role playing and cognitive work. Trial of the innovation on a small scale provides an antecedent behavior very close to consequent adoption. Greater contact with the outside world increases the probability that the early adopter will make use of demonstrations relating to the acquisition and use of the innovation. As heavy users of products and behaviors similar to the innovation, the existing behavior of early adopters is more closely related to the behavior required to acquire and use the innovation than for later adopters. In short, the early adopters have many more early opportunities for significant *vicarious cognitive modeling (symbolic adoption)* than later adopters.

If vicarious cognitive modeling is the process leading to adoption, does it help to explain differences between early and later adopters? Two possible hypotheses are

1. Early adopters are more *efficient* in constructing vicarious cognitive models of the acquisition and use of the innovation than later adopters.

2. Early adopters do not construct vicarious cognitive models any more efficiently than later adopters. Pure *frequency* and *variety* of exposure to communications regarding the innovation are greater for early adopters than later adopters.

Frequency of communications effects have not been measured in diffusion research, and we cannot tell if the differences between early and late adopters are a result of individual differences or a result of communications frequency and variety. The implications of this question are vital to the adoption process, since the first hypothesis implies the way to effectively reach the later adopter is to assure rapid adoption by the early adopters, and the second hypothesis implies that the way to effectively reach the later adopters is by taking more pains to communicate to later adopters directly and more frequently. For the marketing manager or change agent with a fixed budget the answer to this question would influence his free sampling and communications mix, if he had some knowledge of who the early and later adopters were likely to be and how he could reach these market segments.

Acceptance Processes with Skipped Stages. Robertson, as well as most other researchers who have proposed acceptance processes, recognizes that under some conditions stages may be skipped in the process. The impulse-purchase form of acceptance process would move directly from awareness to trial, either skipping the intermediate stages or moving through too rapidly for them to be measured. Compliance to innovations that have been adopted by substantial numbers of an individual's peers may lead to the psychosocial form of the acceptance process in which legitimation occurs concurrently with awareness.

Skipped stages, it is argued, will be a function of "(1) the importance of the decision, (2) the extent of meaningful product differentiation, (3) the extent of product conspicuousness, (4) the extent to which the consumer can take risks, and (5) the decision-making ability of the consumer" (Robertson, 1971).

Campbell (1966) proposes additional criteria for skipped stages. "Non-rational" acceptance processes occur when the evaluation stage is skipped. This definition provides little insight if evaluation is considered to occur at all stages with the opportunity to measure it as a distinctive stage unlikely. Campbell explains the absence of the interest stage when the problem perception overlaps and precedes awareness. If the innovation is perceived in the absence of any perceived problem, the interest stage will still be likely to occur.

Allvine (1968) found the trial stage preceding evaluation missing in the adoption of consumer games by supermarket chains. Kelly (1967) found evaluation following trial in the adoption of a retail dairy store. It seems more reasonable that evaluation occurred in all stages of the acceptance process but was more important to continuation of the process after the trial stage.

The critics of the skipped-stages notion fall into one of two camps. First is the position that the acceptance process simply takes place at such a rapid pace and in such a condensed form that certain stages are methodologically difficult or impossible to detect, but that they are there nevertheless. Another stance assumed maintains that the acceptance process or some part of it may actually have taken place at some prior point in time, and all that was lacking was the opportunity to implement the decision or, in the case of the incomplete decision process, all that was lacking was the added stimulus to complete the acceptance process. Thus although the acceptance of a given innovation may appear impulsive because of the lack of any manifest decision-making activity immediately prior to the innovation exposure, the decision-making process was actually performed earlier in time.

Incomplete Acceptance Processes. The acceptance process may be incomplete for an individual. The result of incomplete processes is the failure of the innovation to be adopted. Given the very high rate of commercial failure for new products and new practices, it is curious that the great majority of published reports on innovations concern successful ventures. Certainly we stand to gain valuable insight into factors influencing a completed adoption process by also looking at the incompleted process. One should be able to learn from these incomplete processes how to better manage and stimulate completed acceptance processes.

A number of factors may lead to incompleted acceptance processes. Not all advocated changes are necessarily functional within whatever framework one used in judging their effectiveness. Resistance to change tends to protect the status quo, which maintains some order and equilibrium in society. This is not to say that it is in the interests of society to maintain absolute stability; rather, for any given individual, group, or other unit of society there may be a maximum rate of change that can be absorbed. Klein (1969) has suggested that "a necessary prerequisite of successful change involves the mobilization of forces against it." It is important that the marketing manager identify sources of resistance and apathy and study their characteristics.

Watson (1971) has identified two basic sources of resistance to change; one resistance is personality, the other source being embedded in the social system. Briefly, sources of resistance in personality come in the form of homeostasis or complacency; habit and ritual; the processes of selective exposure, selective perception, and selective retention; the process of socialization, which created early in life a dependence on the existing order of things; the superego, which imposes behavioral constraints; self-distrust, which dampens curiosity and experimentation; and insecurity and regression.

Resistance to change in the social system also manifests itself in several ways: peer-group pressure may strengthen compliance to noninnovative norms; systemic and cultural coherence, which stresses the interdependence of elements in a social system such that when one element changes pressure is exerted by the other elements to bring the deviant element back into line; vested interests may actively militate against change, (e.g., detergent manufacturers may resist reduction of phosphates in their products); certain parts of society are sacrosanct; and a normal tendency born of suspicion to reject outsiders.

The acceptance process may remain incomplete at any of its stages. The incompleted acceptance process may be caused by either the marketing organization or by the consumers. Some potential causes of incompleted processes are given in Table 1. Even successful innovations encounter incompleted acceptance processes with large numbers of adopting units. Innovations deemed "successful" merely minimize, rather than eliminate, incompleted acceptance processes. This is generally the result of careful planning by the engineering, manufacturing, and marketing organization sponsoring the innovation.

This section has considered the acceptance process as an individual process. As previously discussed, for many innovations the acceptance decision involves adopting units larger than an individual. Their decisions may include families, organizations, or communities. The role of these larger adopting units is important to the adoption of many innovations. There has been no research on the acceptance process for adopting units more complex than individuals. The product of numerous acceptance processes of diffusion is discussed in the next section.

Diffusion over Time and Space[6]

The acceptance process alone is of less interest to marketing managers than the accumulation of individual acceptance processes over time and space. Diffusion results in the spread of the innovation through some segments of a target population. The success of the innovation is generally measured by the

---

[6]When considering time it is very important to keep in mind the warning by Zaltman and Dubois (1971, p. 418): "Defining groups on the basis of relative time of adoption is very misleading. *Time is merely a proxy variable* serving as a convenient operational measure of a more complex set of variables" (italics added).

TABLE 1. Potential Causes of Incompleted Acceptance Process

Acceptance Process Stage	Marketing Organization Causes of Incompleted Processes	Consumer Causes of Incompleted Processes
Dissonance	Innovation attributes incorrectly communicated	Innovation fails to meet expectations
Adoption	Failure to develop new products and improve old products	Replaced by another innovation
Trial	Behavioral response not specified in communications Poor distribution system	Alternative equally as good Innovation not available
Legitimation	Poor source effect of communications	Peer-group pressure against adoption Laws regulating use of innovation
Attitude	Communication not persuasive	Complacency Suspended judgment
Comprehension	Communication difficult to understand	Selective retention
Awareness	Poorly used or too little communication	Selective exposure Selective perception
Problem perception	Poor marketing research	Lack of problem

degree of diffusion throughout the population more than any other single criterion. The diffusion process begins when the first member of the population becomes aware of the innovation and continues until the innovation is no longer being adopted, either because of total adoption by the population or non-adoption by some segments of the population. The time period of the diffusion process is partly dependent on the time period of the individual adoption process, although it is probably not a simple linear function (Rogers, 1962). The time period of the acceptance process is likely to be different for those who are first to adopt an innovation than for those who are later to adopt, adding complexity to the diffusion process.

Time and the number of adopters are easily quantifiable variables, and the opportunity to build mathematical models of the diffusion process has not gone unnoticed. Diffusion curves provide useful predictors of the future success of innovations. If diffusion curves are constructed from propositions regarding the underlying process of acceptance diffusion curves, they provide a test of these propositions. Research has not, in general, related the microbehavioral propositions of acceptance with the macro-parameters of diffusion curves, as the following discussion reveals.

The most accepted assumption regarding the shape of the diffusion curve is that the acceptance process follows a normal (bell-shaped) curve over time. When plotted on a cumulative acceptance basis of the percentage of the population accepting as a function of time, an S-shaped curve results. Although only rough empirical matches to this curve have been found, the curve is most often logically defended as the combination of the individual adoption processes plus the effects of interactions between adopters and nonadopters. Initially, the innovation is rather slow to be accepted. Then as it begins to be accepted and the number of adopters increases the probability of interpersonal interactions regarding the innovation increases, leading to more rapid spread through the population. As the diffusion process nears total adoption, it becomes increasingly hard to gain acceptance and the diffusion process slows down. Since it is much easier to obtain data during the early part of the diffusion process when the innovation is being accepted for the first time by generally well-defined populations, we know much more about the shape of the initial part of the diffusion process than the later part. Toward the end of the diffusion process the data usually become quite messy. Frequently, the diffusion process is still occurring when the curve is estimated and the later stages are still unknown (DeFleur, 1966; Bass, 1969).

Matching and comparison of specified mathematical models of diffusion with empirical data has seldom been attempted. A major problem is the collection of data on the diffusion process over time. Such studies often rely on human recall of acceptance, incomplete records of the time of acceptance, inferences from other variables, or less frequently on actual observations over time. Only one of these means has proved to be reliable in obtaining data that help to explain the diffusion process; making actual observations over time and space. Coleman, Katz, and Menzel (1966) used pharmacists' records to define doctors by the time of their adoption of innovative drugs. They used this information to locate doctors to be interviewed in an attempt to explain the diffusion process. This complex procedure of obtaining data allowed them to reveal two different diffusion curves where a less complex data-collection procedure would have revealed only a single curve. A single-curve model of diffusion in this study would have been almost of no value to a marketing manager for a drug company. When decomposed into two curves, two different market segments were revealed, suggesting the differential strategies of personal selling to doctors with large numbers of interpersonal contacts and mass mailing to less socially integrated doctors. Mathematical models of the diffusion process have neither been good matches to the empirical data for the diffusion process, nor do they generally provide sufficient data about the process to allow reasonable managerial action to be taken. The likely causes against close fits of the diffusion process to empirical data are often the result of variables that can be most influenced by marketing managers or work in favor of the marketing manager. These causes against consistent and regular mathematical models of the diffusion process include failure to consider incomplete communications networks, population changes, and failure to consider distribution centers and advertising in the diffusion process.

A simplifying assumption made in nearly all the models of diffusion is that all people in the process have equal numbers of contacts with others. Therefore, as each person adopts an innovation he will be equally effective in demonstrating the value of the innovation to other people both in quality and quantity of personal contacts. This is a rather ideal assumption that in reality may only be true to a very limited extent, and may be quite dependent on the nature of the innovation and whether it is likely to be talked about to a great extent by any segments of the target population. Coleman (1964) has developed mathematical models of the diffusion process through incomplete social networks assuming small separate groups and partially interacting groups. These models have not been tested with empirical data.

Diffusion theories generally assume a constant target population. Since diffusion of innovations usually takes place over years and at times over generations, the target populations actually exhibit quite high turnover rates, and many new members enter the population and many old members leave before the innovation can diffuse throughout a significant part of the population. In fact, increasing populations may create situations in which the innovation will never reach "total" acceptance at any specific point in time. Bennett (1969) distinguishes between the processes of innovativeness, or how soon a population member accepts an innovation after it appears, and precocity, or how soon after a person becomes a member of the target population he accepts an already existing innovation. These new members of the population enter as a "cohort," which experienced many of the same events and may be quite different from the original "fixed" innovation target population. Each entering cohort or entering age group may represent different market segments exhibiting different acceptance processes and different responses to marketing instruments under the control of a marketing manager. Motion pictures in the 1960s were greatly influenced by the combined effects of innovativeness and precocity.

Another problem with current macromathematical formulations of the diffusion process is the failure to account for diffusion of the innovation over space. If an innovation is not being actively marketed, diffusion occurs through the interaction of adopters and nonadopters and is limited to the travel patterns of the adopters and the probability that they will encounter a nonadopter. Natural barriers such as mountains and rivers may limit the diffusion process and lead to incomplete acceptance. Geographers have considered this process in the study of spatial diffusion of innovations (Hagerstrand, 1967). When innovations are not being marketed, one of the most powerful factors in the diffusion process is the migration of adopters across natural boundaries. History provides many examples.

Brown (1968) has been one of the few theorists to combine the study of diffusion with the effects of distribution policies. The major variables in Brown's model of the acceptance of innovations are the distribution decision of those interested in marketing the innovation and the shopping-trip behavior of potential adopters. The model also allows the simultaneous operation of personal and nonpersonal influence factors, and does not assume discrete steps in the flow of communications (such as the two-step flow model).

It is obvious that management decisions regarding the mix of marketing instruments can play a great role in shaping the diffusion curve. As has been previously noted, mass communications are the most powerful means of assuring awareness of the innovation. Interpersonal communications may be required to move through the attitude field; however, distribution decisions exert a very direct control over the adoption of the innovation and hence the shape of the diffusion curve over space, and therefore over time.

Care must be taken not to confuse a firm's sales response curve over time with the traditional diffusion curve.[7] The diffusion curve represents adoption of the innovation for the first time by individuals of a generic innovation. The summation of individual first-purchase sales curve over time and space for the generic innovation is a close approximation to the diffusion curve. In general, sales data do not allow a determination of whether the sale was an adoption or a repeat purchase, which we consider to be a different behavior than the initial purchase. The sales curve comes close to approximating the first-purchase curve for products that are only purchased once or that have long lives such as consumer durables. Bass (1969) has developed diffusion curves for consumer durables assuming that the time of a person's initial purchase is a function of the number of previous buyers (interpersonal communications effect). The model assumes exponential decay. The model was quite good in predicting the time and quantity of the peak of the diffusion curve.

Mathematical models of the diffusion curves over time and space have concentrated on using the structural variables, such as geographical features or the structure of interpersonal communications networks and past adoptions, to predict future adoptions. As such they can only predict the diffusion process, and provide little in the way of explanation. This should seem especially bothersome to the marketing manager who has some belief that his pricing, advertising, promotion, product development, and distribution decisions can have an effect on the shape of the diffusion curve. When several firms are marketing an innovation, the diffusion curve often may be approximated by definable mathematical function, although individual sales curves may be quite different and

---

[7]See Kotler (1967, p. 291) for a discussion of the stages in the product life cycle.

irregular as a result of the differing abilities, timing of decisions, and resources of the competing firms. Decomposition of the diffusion curve into its component explanations (sales curves) is no easier than decomposing any marketing-mix problem into its individual components. To do so will surely require a systems approach, such as discussed by Kotler (1971). To test such theoretical systems models it seems likely that we shall be forced to turn to computer-simulation methods.

SYSTEM MODELS, MATHEMATICAL MODELS, AND SIMULATION OF DIFFUSION IN MARKETING

The theories and empirical observations from the diffusion tradition have often been quite diffuse and lacking in integration. One alternative to the apparent lack of rigor and integration in diffusion theory is to adopt the view that society is a complex adaptive system, that many of the processes in society behave as adaptive subsystems, and that the diffusion of innovations is one of these subsystems. We are then faced squarely with determining what Kaplan (1964) calls the "explanatory shell," or those variables that compose a necessary and sufficient "isolated system" for explaining the events and processes in the diffusion of innovations. Ideally, we would like to discover a closed system of variables explaining the diffusion of innovations completely. This is more a goal than a possibility, since behavioral systems are open or contain error terms as surrogates for unexplained variance and unobserved variables. Adaptive systems must, in fact, be open to avoid running down (the entropy problem) (Buckley, 1968). It seems unlikely that explanations of successful diffusions can be represented as closed systems, although failures of innovations to diffuse widely may be just that.

In an adaptive system the relationship between variables is a process over time and is likely to be nonlinear and developmental. The effects are likely to be partial and stochastic rather than total and deterministic; additionally, there are likely to be multiple variables interacting through several, perhaps nested, feedback loops, resulting in a quite complex system. Complex systems possess a number of important characteristics considered by Forrester (1969). The complexity of these systems is likely to lead to behavior that is counterintuitive and not obvious from the observation of isolated subsystems, which ignore important feedback loops. The complexity of the system may make the system as a whole generally insensitive to parameter change, although there may be several influence points in the system to which the system is quite sensitive and that will create widespread changes if they are varied (sensitivity). These points are usually not obvious, but are only revealed through careful study of the entire system. Additionally, the short-run responses of a complex system may be quite different than the long-run responses to a variable change. This characteristic has significant implications for marketing policy based on systems theories, since the success of marketing programs is frequently measured by short-run sales.

Blalock (1969) proposes a method that simplifies the construction and testing of adaptive systems theory. If systems can be divided into smaller recursive blocks, each block may be studied in a more manageable way. A recursive block may output exogenous variables to another block and, in turn, receive exogenous variables as input variables. An experiment may be regarded as the simplest form of a block-recursive system in which the initial observation determines the state of the input exogenous variables, the treatment is the endogenous variable (independent variable), and the posttreatment observation determines the state of the output exogenous variables (dependent variable change). A block-recursive system is open to division of labor if agreement upon defining blocks and variables can be reached. In regard to this Bonjean, Hill, and McLemore (1967) have documented the fact that few attitude and personality scales are used more than once. This implies that block-recursive systems, which require even greater acceptance of others' concepts and operations, do not seem likely to gain a great deal of acceptance by researchers of consumer behavior.

A dilemma is created in that the search for methods sufficiently powerful to represent the processes of complex adaptive systems may require mathematics that are too complex to be open to solution. This also provides a strong argument, although usually not explicitly realized, for not learning a great deal of mathematics. The solution to this dilemma has only recently been developed through the computer or information-processing machine with its ability to process information (numeric *and* alphabetic) in less restrictive and formal ways than those permitted by mathematics. The construction of computer models is a useful way to build theory of the diffusion of innovations that provides the patterns required of systems theory. Computer simulations permit consideration of threshold effects, discontinuities, and a variety of levels of measurement, which are problems not conveniently handled through the techniques of mathematics. Therefore, if the diffusion of innovations is viewed theoretically as a complex adaptive system, it may be that the most efficient way to represent this system is through simulation models on the computer. The simulation model is an adaptive one in that the parameters of the simulation may be adjusted to reflect new observations of the diffusion process. To do this the traditional methods of observations in behavioral science become more powerful than they seemed without the simulation model.

Use of Observations for Grounding Parameters and Relationships in Simulation Models. If we view the diffusion process as an adaptive system that consists of complex behavioral variables and communications networks acting dynamically, it is obvious that there are no known methods of observation which will reveal the whole process in a suitable manner. At best we can obtain snapshots of the ongoing process and attempt to reconcile these with our model of the process.

As such it becomes impossible to make closed observations of the actual diffusion process. When we attempt to create closed observations through controlled experiments, we run the risk of cutting a feedback loop that was fundamental to an understanding of the process. Even if we do not do this, we should make multiple observations to assure that the system has stabilized after our treatment (e.g., the sleeper effect in attitude research). It is probably more reasonable to conduct open (field) experiments than closed (laboratory) experiments and to expect them to give one of several possible outcomes (system states) rather than a single outcome, since not all the relevant variables can be controlled. The simulation model should suggest a set of possible outcomes for any given experiment, and when the field experiment does not result in the predicted outcome over repeated trials, we tend to become suspect of the model's parameters. With new information we can adjust them to the new parameters or at least adjust them through a Bayesian weighing process to reflect the likelihood that a new value comes closer to fitting the pattern of the diffusion process.

The power of a well-developed adaptive simulation lies in the fact that any method of making observations should provide partial information for confirming or adapting the model. There is no crucial test for such a model, nor is it testable in total. Simulation as a route to theory requires caution, since the researcher may create theory that is not grounded through empirical observation (Glaser and Strauss, 1967). In fact, simulation models can be designed to create their own observations, and the entire inquiry process can occur within the logic of the computer without the necessity for grounding the parameters through tests with empirical patterns of data. The failure to ground the simulation may result in premature closure (Kaplan, 1964) and overconfidence in using the model. The danger in being seduced with the richness of the simulated observations, which avoid the problem of messy data, is great. Forrester's *Urban Dynamics* (1969) is a fascinating case of just such a trap. Many possible ungrounded solutions to urban problems are proposed. However, this may be a bit unfair to Forrester, since, as Feldt (1970) points out, the work is, in general, methodological in intent rather than theoretical or for policy planning. As such Forrester has much to offer on the methodology of simulation as a route to theory building.

When empirical data are available, the actual grounding process is primarily a statistical procedure. The flexibility of simulation creates a difficulty, since the observations it generates are usually continuous and ratio scaled. These must be matched against empirical data, which are more likely to be less than ratio scaled and discrete (see Siegal, 1956, for a detailed discussion of measurement.) To assume the simulation can contain any more information than its grounding data presents an inductive dilemma similar to generalization from any behavioral research. Usually parsimony in nature must be assumed in order to fill the spaces.

Examples of Diffusion of Innovation Simulations—Any Luck?

Kotler and Schultz (1970) describe a simulation model created by Alba for the Touch-Tone telephone. The variables in Alba's model consist of seven individual traits, individual sources of information, and the date of adoption. Empirical data on these variables were available from a survey of 100 residents of Deerfield, Illinois. The model fit to the data was quite poor. The fault is probably a result of not gathering data on the dynamics of interpersonal and media communications, processes that were assumed but not tested within the simulation. Observations of these process variables may have greatly improved the Alba model.

Another simulation of the diffusion of innovations is described by Rogers (1969). A simulation of the diffusion through a Colombian village resulted in a linear diffusion curve, whereas survey data revealed an S-shaped curve. The problem was believed to be the representation of the communications process as two stage (Katz and Lazarsfeld, 1955) when in reality it was multistage. In a footnote written after the chapter was completed the problem was discovered to be a computer programming error in the simulation, which when corrected brought the simulation and survey data quite close together. Simulation on the computer creates such new threats to validity as programming error.

Geographers have developed a number of spatial diffusion simulations. Hagerstrand's (1967) Monte Carlo simulation does not make use of any behavioral or marketing variables and seems limited in explanatory value. Brown (1968) has quantified both shopping behavior and the interpersonal communication-persuasion process in a very complex model. The model, although very elegant, has not been grounded through testing with observations.

Bass and King (1968) developed a mathematical model predicting the total number of first purchases of a *new product*. The underlying assumption of their model is "the probability of first purchase at any time is a function of the number of previous buyers" (p. 272). They conclude that their model produces "good descriptions of the growth of first purchases" for appliances, cleaners and polishers, drugs, and several other types of products. Bass (1969) later expanded this model and made a detailed analysis of color television sales. These models forecast total effects and do not recognize the effects an individual company can have on the diffusion of a product through effective use of marketing instruments. The model also does not account for population growth and turnover.

Simulations may be thought of as consisting of several block-recursive subsystems. The simulations reviewed here were grounded on the basis of the output of these subsystems represented only by the diffusion curve. Without grounding the individual subsystems, such as the innovation, adopting unit, and interpersonal communications processes, the simulation does not offer an explanation, but only a prediction for the diffusion curve. Explanatory simulations must be grounded throughout rather than just in the predictions of their exogenous output.

Prediction, rather than explanation, is usually sufficient for market forecasting purposes. Day (1970) shows how data from panel or longitudinal designs allow the monitoring of new-product introductions. Knowledge of the sample populations, word-of-mouth communications, media exposure, and product use allow prediction of rates of attitude formation and change. This information allows modification of marketing programs to create or reinforce attitudes relating to the product. Day tested his model with two new branded convenience food products. Other methods of using consumer-panel data to predict market share for new products utilize the sales results of market tests (Ah1, 1970). The stochastic evolutionary adoption model (STEAM), developed by Massy (1969), also makes use of parameter estimates from panel data.

The majority of new-product models fail to recognize the influence of marketing variables on the sales of the new product. Instead the models forecast future sales based on panel data obtained in a test market. Claycamp and Liddy (1969) have proposed a model predicting initial purchase levels based on controllable and uncontrollable marketing variables. These factors do not specifically allow distinctions between a new product and an innovation, and like most new-product models their model is more likely to be successful in forecasting new-product sales for products that are not truly innovative.

For true innovations it seems desirable to utilize a combination of market tests with a staged new-product forecasting model. Such a model guides decisions among making market tests, cost studies, channel tests, advertising studies, dropping the product, or going to a full marketing program. Each decision is guided by the results of past decisions. Several models to accomplish this are reviewed by Montgomery and Urban (1969, p. 312) including the DEMON and SPRINTER models. These models are too complex for discussion here.

CONCLUSION

It is not possible within the scope of this chapter nor is it the intent of this chapter to espouse a particular theory of diffusion. This is largely the result of the general absence in the published literature of an acceptable overall theory of the diffusion process. However, there are certainly many useful concepts, hypotheses, and subtheories concerning particular components of the diffusion process developed in the existing literature. The authors of this chapter have attempted to present the most relevant and promising of these. Considerably more integration of research in such diverse areas as science and technology, education, health and family planning, marketing, and organizational behavior is necessary before a truly representative diffusion theory can be evolved. Moreover, in the process of integrating diverse research it will be necessary to consider the interrelationships among the several components (adopting unit, the innovation, social structure, etc.) of the diffusion process. That is, a viable diffusion theory will have to consist of a set of linked or interrelated hypotheses involving the most relevant concepts concerning the major components of the diffusion process.

Although it is premature to present a functional comprehensive middle-range theory, it is possible to indicate some of the characteristics such a theory should have. A good theory should provide explanation, allow testability, and contain propositions dynamically relating behavioral components of the diffusion process. To date researchers have seldom gone beyond descriptive theory for any of the five components of the diffusion paradigm: adopting unit, innovation, communication networks, the acceptance process, and diffusion over time and space. Development of more powerful explanatory theories for the diffusion of innovations is dependent upon utilization of more complex methodologies than the frequently used one-shot surveys.

Designs that are significant elaborations of the one-shot survey are generally quite expensive and quite demanding on the intellectual and administrative abilities of the researcher. We seem to be nearing the point in the development of a diffusion theory in consumer behavior where significant advances may well require such efforts. Even assuming researchers are willing to undertake the more elaborate methods of design and data collection, the analysis of these data poses quite severe problems. The more elaborate data will almost always require a mathematical analysis of change (Coleman, 1968). The diffusion process has continuous variables interacting over continuous time in a stochastic way. Analysis may occasionally require differential equations, which may be further complicated by feedback or reciprocal causation.[8]

There are few researchers who are able to cope with meaningful analysis utilizing complex mathematical structures, and there may be a great deal of anxiety in collecting data that are only open to this type of formal analysis. The computer, however, offers an alternative means of analysis. Differential equations are a good deal easier to understand when treated as difference equations solved by iteration methods on the computer. Many of the complex relationships and observations of diffusion research are open to analysis through the building of predictive models on the computer. These may be tested through empirical observations. Such models may be far more complex than current paper-and-pencil theories without the need for the more formal aspects of mathematics. Computer models can allow relationships that are not possible in the formal language of mathematics, such as complicated threshold effects. These models are similar in intent to the systems paradigm of interrelated sets of propositions proposed by Meehan (1968). The parameters of these models may

---

[8]For elaboration of these needs, see Blalock (1969).

be estimated through observation of the diffusion process and adapted, perhaps in a Bayesian way, as new data become available. This would provide an adaptive model of consumer behavior for the diffusion of innovations that would provide a paradigm for researchers in the field.

Adaptive systems models of the diffusion process would be a theoretical equivalent to the adaptive marketing decision-making models described by Montgomery and Urban (1969). The link between the more general theory of diffusion, which is of concern here, and adaptive decision-making models would be those propositions in diffusion theory that relate closely or directly to the marketing-mix variables in the specific adaptive decision-making model for a firm. The parameters of a firm's adaptive model would be revised by either the firm's marketing research or the result of theoretically directed inquiry into the diffusion of innovations by the researchers in the field.

Advancing the theory of a process as complex as the diffusion of innovations will not be an easy enterprise. Equally difficult is the translation of theoretical advances into applied marketing decision making. We believe that these challenges and the equivalent potentially high returns make the study of the diffusion of innovations an intriguing problem.

REFERENCES

Ahl, D. H., "New Product Forecasting Using Consumer Panels," *Journal of Marketing Research,* 7 (1970), No. 2, 160-67.

Allen, I. L., "Social Relations and the Two-Step Flow," *Journalism Quarterly,* 46 (1969), No. 3, 492-98.

Allvine, F. C., "Diffusion of a Competitive Innovation," in *Proceedings of the Fall Conference of the American Marketing Association,* 1968, 341-51.

Appel, D. L. "Market Segmentation—A Response to Retail Innovation," *Journal of Marketing,* 34 (1970), No. 2 64-67.

Arndt, Johan, "Word of Mouth Advertising and Informal Communication," *Risk Taking and Information Handling in Consumer Behavior,* ed. D. F. Cox. Graduate School of Business Administration, Harvard University, Boston, 1967a, 188-239.

Arndt, Johan, "Perceived Risk, Sociometric Integration, and Word of Mouth in the Adoption of a New Food Product," in *Risk Taking and Information Handling in Consumer Behavior,* ed. D. F. Cox. Graduate School of Business Administration, Harvard University, Boston, 1967b, 289-316.

Barnett, H. G., *Innovation: The Basis of Cultural Change.* New York: McGraw-Hill Book Company, 1953.

Bass, F. M., and C. W. King, "The Theory of First Purchase of New Products," in *Proceedings of the Spring Conference of the American Marketing Association,* 1968, 263-72.

Bass, F. M., "A New Product Growth Model for Consumer Durables," *Management Science,* January 1969.

Becker, M. H., "Sociometric Location and Innovativeness: Reformulation and Extension of the Diffusion Model," *American Sociological Review,* 35 (1970), No. 2, 267-82.

Bell, William, "Consumer Innovators: A Unique Market for Newness," in *Proceedings of the American Marketing Association,* 1963, 85-95.

Bennett, C. F., "Diffusion Within Dynamic Populations," *Human Organization,* 28 (1969), No. 3, 243-47.

Berger, S. M., and W. W. Lambert, "Stimulus-Response Theory in Contemporary Social Psychology," in *Handbook of Social Psychology* (2nd ed.) ed. G. Lindzey and E. Aronson, Vol. 2. Reading, Mass.: Addison-Wesley Publishing Company, Inc., 1968.

Blake, Brian, Robert Perloff, and Richard Heslin, "Dogmatism and Acceptance of New Products," *Journal of Marketing Research,* 7 (1970), No. 4, 483-86.

Blalock, H. M., *Theory Construction: From Verbal to Mathematical Formulations.* Englewood Cliffs, N.J.: Prentice-Hall, Inc., 1969.

Blau, Peter, *Exchange and Power in Social Life.* New York: John Wiley & Sons, Inc., 1964.

Bonjean, C. M., R. J. Hill, and S. D. McLemore, *Sociological Measurement.* San Francisco: Chandler Publishing Company, 1967.

Boone, L. E., "The Search for the Consumer Innovator," *The Journal of Business,* 43 (1970), No. 2, 135-40.

Brown, Lawrence, *Diffusion Dynamics.* Lund, Sweden: Lund Studies in Geography, 1968.

Buckley, W., *Modern Systems Research for the Behavioral Scientist.* Chicago: Aldine-Atherton, Inc., 1968.

Campbell, D. T., "Reforms as Experiments," *American Psychologist,* 24 (1969), 409-29.

Campbell, D. T., and J. C. Stanley, *Experimental and Quasi-Experimental Designs for Research.* Skokie, Ill.: Rand McNally & Company, 1963.

Campbell, R. R., "A Suggested Paradigm of the Individual Adoption Process," *Rural Sociology,* 31 (1966), No. 4, 458-66.

Carlson, R. O., "Summary and Critique of Educational Diffusion Research," *Research Implications for Educational Diffusion.* Michigan Department of Education, 1968.

Chin, Robert, "Models and Ideas about Changing," in *Identifying Techniques and Principles for Gaining Acceptance of Research Results,* ed. W. C. Meierhenry. Lincoln, Neb.: University of Nebraska Press, 1963

Claycamp, H. J., and L. F. Liddy, "Prediction of New Product Performance: An Analytical Approach," *Journal of Marketing Research,* 6 (1969), No. 4, 414-20.

Coleman, J. S., E. Katz, and H. Menzel, *Medical Innovation: A Diffusion Study.* Indianapolis: The Bobbs-Merrill Company, Inc., 1966.

Coleman, J. S., "Relational Analysis: The Study of Social Organizations with Survey Methods," *Human Organization,* 16 (1958), 28-36.

Coleman, J. S. *An Introduction to Mathematical Sociology.* New York: The Free Press, 1964.

Coleman, J. S., "The Mathematical Study of Change," in *Methodology in Social Research*, ed. H. M. Blalock and A. B. Blalock. New York: McGraw-Hill Book Company, 1968, 428-78.

Cox, D. F., "The Audience as Communicators," in *Risk Taking and Information Handling in Consumer Behavior*, ed. D. F. Cox. Graduate School of Business Administration, Harvard University Boston, 1967, 172-87.

Crain, Robert, "Fluoridation: The Diffusion of an Innovation Among Cities," *Social Forces*, 44 (1966), No. 4, 467-76.

Crane, Diana, *Invisible Colleges*, Chicago: University of Chicago Press, 1972.

Day, S., "Using Attitude Change Measures to Evaluate New Product Introductions," *Journal of Marketing Research*, 7 (1970), No. 4, 474-82.

DeFleur, M., "Mass Communications and Social Change," *Social Forces*, 44 (1966), 314-26.

Denzin, N. K., *The Research Act*. Chicago: Aldine-Atherton, Inc., 1970.

Deutschmann, P. J., and Wayne Danielson, "Diffusion of Knowledge of the Major News Study," *Journalism Quarterly*, Summer 1960, 345-55.

Elms, A. C., "Influence of Fantasy Ability on Attitude Change Through Role Playing," *Journal of Personality and Social Psychology*, 4 (1966), 36-43.

Engel, J. F., D. Blackwell, and R. J. Kegerreis, "How Information is Used to Adopt an Innovation," *Journal of Advertising Research*, 9 (1969), No. 4, 3-10.

Engel, J. F., R. J. Kegerreis, and R. D. Blackwell, "Word of Mouth Communication by the Innovator," *Journal of Marketing*, 33, No. 3 (1969), 15-19.

Evans, R. I., *Resistance to Innovation in Higher Education*. San Francisco. Jossey-Bass, Inc., Publishers, 1970.

Federal Trade Commission, "Permissible Period of Time During Which New Products May Be Described as 'New,' " *Advisory Opinion Digest*, No. 20 (April 15, 1967).

Feldt, A. G., "Review of Urban Dynamics," *American Sociological Review*, 35 (1970), No. 2, 364-65.

Fliegel, F. C., and J. E. Kivlin, "Attributes of Innovations As Factors in Diffusion," *American Journal of Sociology*, 72 (1966), 235-48.

Forrester, J., *Urban Dynamics*. Cambridge, Mass.: The MIT Press, 1969.

Freedman, J. L., and S. C. Fraser, "Compliance without Pressure: The Foot-in-the Door Technique," *Journal of Personality and Social Psychology*, 4, (1966), 195-202.

Garvey, W. D., Nan Lin, and C. E. Nelson, "Communication in the Physical and Social Sciences," *Science*, 170 (1970), 1166-73.

Glaser, B. G., and A. L. Strauss, *The Discovery of Grounded Theory: Strategies for Qualitative Research*. Chicago: Aldine-Atherton, Inc., 1967.

Gorman, W. D., and C. T. Moore, "The Early Diffusion of Color Television Receivers Into a Fringe Area Market," *Journal of Retailing*, 44 (1968), No. 3, 46-56.

Graham, A., "Is Opinion Leader and Opinion Follower Identical Persons?" *ESOMAR Congress Papers*, 1968, 133-47.

Grambois, D. H., "The Role of Communication in the Family Decision-Making Process," in *Proceedings of the American Marketing Association,* 1966.

Greenwald, A. G., "Cognitive Learning, Cognitive Response to Persuasion and Attitude Change," in *Psychological Foundations of Attitudes,* ed. A. G. Greenwald. New York: Academic Press, Inc., 1968.

Gross, E. J., "Book Review of *Opinion Leaders, A Study in Communication* (London: ATV House), *Journal of Marketing Research,* 8 (1971), No. 1, 131-32.

Hagerstrand, T., *Innovation Diffusion or a Spatial Process.* Chicago: University of Chicago Press, 1967.

Homans, G. C., *The Human Group.* New York: Harcourt Brace Jovanovich, Inc., 1961.

Homans, G. C., "Contemporary Theory in Sociology," in *Handbook of Modern Sociology,* ed. R. E. L. Faris. Skokie, Ill.: Rand McNally & Company, 1964. 951-77.

Howard, J. A., and Jagdish Sheth, *The Theory of Buyer Behavior.* New York: John Wiley & Sons, Inc., 1969.

Kaplan, A., *The Conduct of Inquiry.* San Francisco: Chandler Publishing Company, 1964.

Katz, Elihu, "The Two-Step Flow of Communication: An Up-to-Date Report on an Hypothesis," *Public Opinion Quarterly,* 1957, 61-78.

Katz, Elihu and P. F. Lazarsfeld, *Personal Influence.* New York: The Free Press, 1955.

Katz, Elihu, M. L. Levin, and Herbert Hamilton, "Traditions of Research on the Diffusion of Innovation," *American Sociological Review,* 28, (1963), 237-52.

Kelly, R. F., (1963), "The Role of Information in the Patronage Decision: A Diffusion Phenomenon," in *Proceedings of the American Marketing Association,* June 1967, 119-29.

Kerckhoff, A. C., and K. W. Back, *The June Bug: A Study in Hysterical Contagion.* New York: Appleton-Century-Crofts, 1968.

King, C. W., "Fashion Adoption: A Rebuttal to the 'Trickle Down' Theory," in *Proceedings of the Winter Conference of the American Marketing Association,* 1963, 108-25.

King, C. W., "The Innovator in the Fashion Adoption Process," in *Proceedings of the Winter Conference of the American Marketing Association,* 1964, 324-39.

King, C. W., and J. O. Summers, "Dynamics of Interpersonal Communications: The Interaction Dyad," in *Risk Taking and Information Handling in Consumer Behavior,* ed. D. F. Cox. Graduate School of Business Administration, Harvard University Press, Boston, 1967.

King, C. W., and J. O. Summers, "Overlap of Opinion Leadership Across Consumer Product Categories," *Journal of Marketing Research,* 7 (1970), 43-50.

Klein, Donald, "Some Notes on the Dynamics of Resistance to Change: The Defender Role," in *The Planning of Change,* ed. W. G. Bennis, K. D. Benne, and R. Chin. New York: Holt, Rinehart and Winston, Inc., 1969, 498-507.

Knight, K., "A Descriptive Model of the Intra-Firm Innovation Process," *Journal of Business*, 40 (1967), No. 4, 478-96.

Kollat, D. T., J. F. Engel, and R. D. Blackwell, "Current Problems in Consumer Behavior Research," *Journal of Marketing Research*, 7 (August 1970), 327-32.

Kotler, Philip, *Marketing Management.* Englewood Cliffs, N.J.: Prentice-Hall, Inc., 1967.

Kotler, Philip, *Marketing Decision Making.* New York: Holt, Rinehart and Winston, Inc., 1971.

Kotler, Philip, and R. L. Schultz, "Marketing Simulations: Review and Prospects," *The Journal of Business*, 43 (1970), No. 3, 237-95.

Kotler, Philip, and Gerald Zaltman, "Social Marketing: An Approach to Planned Social Change," *Journal of Marketing*, 35 (1971).

Lavidge, R. J., and G. A. Steiner, "A Model for Predictive Measurements of Advertising Effectiveness," *Journal of Marketing*, 25 (1961).

Lazarsfeld, P. F., *Radio and the Printed Page.* New York: Duell, Sloan & Pearce, 1940.

Lerner, Daniel, *The Passing of Traditional Society.* The Free Press, 1958.

Lin, Nan, "Information Flow, Influence Flow and the Decision-Making Process," *Journalism Quarterly*, 1971, 33-40.

Lippitt, Ronald, Jeanne Wabon, and Bruce Westley, *The Dynamics of Planned Change.* New York: Harcourt Brace Jovanovich, Inc., 1958.

Maccoby, N., E. E. Maccoby, A. K. Romney, and Adams, *Critical Periods in Seeking and Accepting Information*, Paris-Stanford Studies in Communication, Institute for Communications Research, Stanford, Calif., 1962.

Mann, C., and I. L. Janis, "A Follow-Up Study on the Long Term Effects of Emotional Role Playing," *Journal of Personality and Social Psychology*, 9 (1968), 322-28.

Massy, W. F., "Forecasting the Demand for New Convenience Products," *Journal of Marketing Research*, 6 (1969), No. 4, 405-12.

McGuire, W. J., "The Nature of Attitudes and Attitude Change," *The Handbook of Social Psychology*, (2nd ed.), ed. G. Lindzey and E. Aronson, Vol. 3. Reading, Mass.: Addison-Wesley Publishing Company, Inc., 1969, 136-314.

Meehan, E. J., *Explanation in Social Science: A System Paradigm.* Homewood, Ill.: Dorsey Press, Inc., 1968.

Montgomery, D. B., and A. J. Silk, "Patterns of Overlap in Opinion Leadership and Interest for Selected Categories of Purchasing Activities," in *Proceedings of the Fall Conference of the American Marketing Association*, ed. P. R. McDonald, 1969, 377-86.

Montgomery, D. B., and G. L. Urban, *Management Science in Marketing.* Englewood Cliffs, N.J.: Prentice-Hall, Inc., 1969.

Myers, Sumner, and D. G. Marquis, *Successful Industrial Innovations*, National Science Foundation NSF69-17, 1969.

Newcomb, T. M., "Persistence and Regression of Changed Attitudes: Long Range Studies," *Journal of Social Issues*, 4 (1962), 3-13.

Olson, Mancur, *The Logic of Collective Action.* Cambridge, Mass.: Harvard University Press, 1965.

Olson, Mancur, "Preliminary Thoughts about the Causes of Harmony and Conflict." Mimeographed report, 1970.

Ostlund, L. E., "The Role of Product Perceptions in Innovative Behavior," in *Proceedings of the Fall Conference of the American Marketing Association,* ed. P. R. McDonald. Chicago, 1969.

Ozanne, U. B., and Gilbert Churchill, "Adoption Research: Information Sources in the Industrial Purchasing Decision," in *Proceedings of the American Marketing Association,* 1968, 352-59.

Palmore, J. A., "Awareness Sources and Stages in the Adoption of Specific Contraceptives," *Demography,* 5 (1968), Pt. 2, 960-72.

Pareek, U., and Y. P. Singh, "Communication Nets in the Sequential Adoption Process," *Indian Journal of Psychology,* 46 (1969), 33-55.

Pelz, D. C., and F. M. Andrews, "Detecting Causal Priorities in Panel Study Data," *American Sociological Review,* 29 (1964), 836-48.

Randoe, G. J., "Some Notes on the Application of a General Diffusion of Innovations on Household Decision Making," *ESOMAR Congress Papers,* 1968, 93-131.

Robertson, T. R., and J. H. Myers, "Personality Correlates of Opinion Leadership and Innovative Buying Behavior," *Journal of Marketing Research,* 6 (1969), No. 2, 164-68.

Robertson, T. S., "Determinants of Innovative Behavior," in *Proceedings of the American Marketing Association,* ed. Reed Moyer. Chicago: American Marketing Association, 1967. 328-32.

Robertson, T. S., "Purchase Sequence Responses: Innovators vs. Non-Innovators," *Journal of Advertising Research,* 8 (1968), No. 1, 47-54.

Robertson, T. S., *Innovative Behavior and Communication.* New York: Holt, Rinehart and Winston, Inc., 1971.

Rogers, E. M., *Diffusion of Innovations.* New York: The Free Press, 1962.

Rogers, E. M., and J. D. Stanfield, "Adoption and Diffusion of New Products," in *Applications of the Sciences in Marketing Management,* eds. F. Bass, C. King, and E. Pessemier. New York: John Wiley & Sons, Inc., 1968.

Rogers, E. M. *Modernization Among Peasants.* New York: Holt, Rinehart and Winston, Inc., 1969.

Rogers, E. M., "Mass Media and Interpersonal Communication," *Handbook of Communication,* ed. W. Schramm. Skokie, Ill.: Rand McNally & Company, 1972.

Rogers, E. M., and Floyd Shoemaker, *The Communication of Innovations.* New York: The Free Press, 1971.

Roper, Elmo, *New Trends in the Public's Measure of Television and Other Media.* New York: Television Information Office, 1964.

Sawhney, M. M., "Farm Practice Adoption and the Use of Information Sources and Media in a Rural Community in India," *Rural Sociology,* 32 (1967), 310-23.

Shepard, H. A., "Innovation-Resisting and Innovation-Producing Organizations," *Journal of Business,* 30 (1967), No. 4.

Sherif, M., and H. Cantril, *The Psychology of Ego-Involvements*. New York: John Wiley & Sons, Inc., 1947.

Siegal, Sidney, *Nonparametric Statistics for the Behavioral Sciences*. New York: McGraw-Hill Book Company, 1956.

Simon, Julian, "A Huge Marketing Research Task—Birth Control," *Journal of Marketing Research*, 5 (1968), 21-27.

Sonquist, J. A., *Multivariate Model Building*. Institute for Social Research, University of Michigan, Ann Arbor, 1970.

Stinchcombe, Arthur, *Constructing Social Theories*. New York: Harcourt Brace Jovanovich, Inc., 1968.

Storer, N., *The Social System of Science*, New York: Holt, Rinehart and Winston, Inc., 1966.

Summers, J. O., "The Identity of Women's Clothing Fashion Opinion Leaders," *Journal of Marketing Research*, 7 (1970), No. 2, 178-85.

Taylor, J., "Introducing Social Innovation," *Journal of Applied Behavioral Science*, 6 (1970), 69-77.

Trodahl, V. C., "A Field Test of a Modified 'Two-Step Flow of Communication' Model," *Public Opinion Quarterly* (Winter 1966-67).

Trodahl, V. C., and Robert Van Dam, "Face-to-Face Communication About Major Topics in the News," *Public Opinion Quarterly*, 29 (1965-66), No. 4, 626-34.

Uhl, Kenneth, Roman Andrus, and Lance Poulsen, "How Are Laggards Different? An Empirical Inquiry," *Journal of Marketing Research*, 7 (1970), No. 1, 51-54.

Van Den Ban, A. W., "A Revision of the Two Step Flow of Communications Hypothesis," *Gazette*, X (1964), No. 3, 237-49.

Walker, J. L., "The Diffusion of Innovations Among the American States," *The American Political Science Review*, 63 (1969), 880-99.

Wallace, W. L., *Sociological Theory*. Chicago: Aldine-Atherton, Inc., 1969.

Watson, Goodwin, "Resistance to Change," *American Behavioral Scientist* 1971.

Watts, W. A., "Relative Persistence of Opinion Change Induced by Active Compared to Passive Participation," *Journal of Personality and Social Psychology*, 5 (1967), 4-15.

Webster, Fred, "New Product Adoption in Industrial Markets: A Framework for Analysis," *Journal of Marketing*, 33 (1969), No. 3, 35-39.

Yadav, D. P., and E. M. Rogers, "Interpersonal Communication in Innovation Diffusion," Working Paper Number 5 AID Diffusion Project, Department of Communications, Michigan State University, East Lansing, 1966.

Zaltman, Gerald, *Marketing: Contributions from the Behavioral Sciences*. New York: Harcourt Brace Jovanovich, Inc., 1965.

Zaltman, Gerald, Reinhard Angelmar, and Christian Pinson, "Metatheory in Consumer Behavior Research," *Proceedings of the Second Annual Conference of the Association for Consumer Research*, ed. D. M. Gardner, 1971.

Zaltman, Gerald, and Bernard Dubois, "New Conceptual Approaches in the Study of Innovations," *Proceedings of the Second Annual Conference of the Association for Consumer Research*, ed. D. M. Gardner, 1971.

Zaltman, Gerald, and B. P. Koehler, "Transaction Flows and Diffusion in an International Scientific Community," *Journal of the American Society of Information Sciences* (August 1972).

Zaltman, Gerald, Philip Kotler, and Ira Kaufman, *Creating Social Change*. New York: Holt, Rinehart and Winston, Inc., 1972.

Zaltman, Gerald, and Nan Lin, "On the Nature of Innovations," *American Behavioral Scientist* (May-June 1971).

Zaltman, Gerald, and I. Vertinsky, "Health Marketing: A Suggested Model," *Journal of Marketing,* 35 (1971).

Zeigler, John, "Social Change Through Issue Advertising," *Sociological Enquiry,* 1970, 159-65.

12

Subculture Theory: Poverty, Minorities, and Marketing

Frederick D. Sturdivant
The Ohio State University

THE MEANING OF CULTURE
SUBCULTURES
SUBCULTURES AND MARKETING
   Low-Income Black Consumer
MARKETING RESEARCH AND SUBCULTURES
CONCLUSION
REFERENCES

The field of marketing was by no means immune to the influences of the social revolution that struck American society in the 1960s. One of the consequences of this revolution was that students of marketing began to turn their attention to questions of the interrelationships between the market system and the poor. The level of understanding, based on research to date, is still relatively primitive. The relationships are, of course, complex, and thus the analysis must begin at a very fundamental level. The beginning point is an understanding of culture. The purpose of this chapter, therefore, is to add to the literature of consumer behavior a systematic treatment of the concept of culture as it related to the analysis of the poor and minorities.

In the early 1960s, W. T. Tucker wrote *The Social Context of Economic Behavior,* which focused on the role of class, group, and culture as the three principal sociological structures that influence individual behavior. Tucker noted that "Almost everyone is aware of group pressures, no matter how unthoughtful or untutored he is. Almost everyone is similarly aware of class distinctions, although he may be relatively unaware of the ways in which his thinking and behavior are different from those of other classes." However, when it came to the third concept Tucker concluded that "Most of us are naive about culture" (p. 22). This is not to suggest that students of marketing have now drawn on the concept of culture in their analyses of human behavior. The concept is fundamental to the literature treating diffusion of innovation and plays a central role in much that has been written about personality theory, group influence, and social stratification. Generally, however, these studies have drawn on selected components rather than the total concept of culture.

This partial treatment of the concept in the literature may in large measure be explained by the fact that the effect of culture on human behavior is less visible—more abstract—than is the case with class or group. In addition, the social scientists who employ culture as an analytical device in studies of complex, urban societies have generally ignored the marketplace as a vital milieu within which to observe the behavior of their subjects. Although Riesman has written about consumer behavior within the framework of his other-directed and inner-directed scheme (1961) and Lerner has suggested that the United States is a "consumer's culture" (Vol. II, 1957), most students of American culture have restricted their observations to marriage, child rearing, peer groups, religion, language, and the like. This is a strange omission in view of the fact that a noted anthropologist has suggested that "A humble cooking pot is as much a cultural product as a Beethoven sonata" (Kluckhohn, 1949a, p. 17). One might also assume that the decision to acquire the cooking pot and the process by which it and myriad other goods and services are accumulated would also be of vital interest to the student of culture.

In suggesting that the consumer is culture bound, Tucker has noted that "The culture always provides approved specific goal objects for any generalized human want. A reasonably cosmopolitan culture provides a host of alternatives serving the same general end, and in an economically mature culture most of the alternatives imply products" (1964, p. 37).

> Even those of us who pride ourselves on our individualism follow most of the time a pattern not of our own making. We brush our teeth on arising. We put on pants—not a loincloth or a grass skirt. We eat three meals a day not four or five or two. We sleep in a bed—not in a hammock or on a sheep pelt (Kluckhohn, 1949a, p. 18).

An understanding of culture, therefore, is vital to the study of consumer actions as well as any other form of human behavior.

MEANING OF CULTURE

What, then, is culture? How does it develop and what are its essential characteristics? It should first be noted that there is something less than universal agreement to the answers to these questions, as evidenced by the fact that one book treats 164 definitions of culture (Kroeber and Kluckhohn, 1963). Nevertheless, the original and classic definition of the concept can serve as the basis for the remaining discussion: ". . . that complex whole which includes knowledge, belief, art, morals, law, custom, and any other capabilities and habits acquired by man as a member of society" (Tyler, 1891, p. 1).

Culture is thus a pervasive force that has evolved in different ways throughout the world for thousands of years. According to Dewey, culture is, in fact, essential to the existence of societies. "Society exists through a process of transmission, quite as much as biological life. This transmission occurs by means of communication of habits of doing, thinking, feeling from the older to the younger. Without this communication of ideas, hopes, expectations, standards, opinions from members of society who are passing out of the group life to those who are coming into it, social life could not survive" (1916, pp. 10-11).

This communication of culture is heavily dependent on the use of symbols. "Man can be defined as a symbol-using animal at least as well as he can be defined in any other way; and social relationships can be traced effectively on the basis of the network of symbols and communications in society" (Ross, 1957, p. 155). Indeed, the symbolic aspects of culture have been emphasized by White:

> Culture is an organization of phenomena-acts (patterns of behavior), objects (tools; things made with tools), ideas (belief, knowledge), and sentiments (attitudes, "values")—that is dependent upon the use of symbols. Culture began when man as an articulate, symbol-using primate, began. Because of its symbolic character, which has its most important expression in articulate speech, culture is easily and readily transmitted from one human organism to another. Since its elements are readily transmitted culture becomes a continuum; it flows down through the ages from one generation to another and laterally from one people to another. The culture process is also cumulative; new elements enter the stream from time to time and swell the total. The culture process is progressive in the sense that it moves toward greater control over the forces of nature, toward greater security of life for man. Culture is, therefore, a symbolic, continuous, cumulative, and progressive process (1949a, pp. 139-40).

Culture thus represents a unifying concept that enables one to understand the totality of a social system. It provides a common framework and acts as a social bond. "Bonds may restrain, like chains on a slave, or they may sustain, like the climber's rope" (Ross, 1957, p. 172). Culture does both. One thing cultures do not do, however, is respond uniformly to environmental forces. For many years the environment was assigned a role akin to that of biological determinism. In fact, the environment should be viewed as an enabling as well as a restricting agent. The physical properties of the North American continent were the same for the American Indian as they were for the Spanish, French, Dutch, and English settlers, and yet each group responded to that environment differently. Had the Chinese established North American colonies during the same period, a quite different culture would have been present on the continent. The diversity of cultures that emerges in relatively similar environments is explained by the fact that "culture acts as a set of blinders, or series of lenses, through which men view their environments" (Kluckhohn and Murray, 1949, p. 45).

Before turning to a discussion of the dominant culture that has emerged in the United States, it might be useful to note briefly the distinguishing characteristics of culture in general. This analysis is adapted from a discussion of the nature of culture by Murdock (1940).

1. Learned Quality of Culture. Culture is made up of both conscious and subconscious elements that are learned rather than being physiologically or biologically determined. "For the most part, it is learned early in life and invested with a good deal of emotion. Deviations from the going culture usually cost something in comfort, status, peace of mind, or safety" (Berelson and Steiner, 1964, p. 14). The learned quality of culture is perhaps best understood by viewing the interaction between biological, physiological, and cultural influences.

> Cultural determinism is as one-sided as biological determinism. The two factors are interdependent. Culture arises out of human nature, and its forms are restricted both by man's biology and by natural laws. It is equally true that culture channels biological processes—vomiting, weeping, fainting, sneezing, the daily habits of food intake and waste elimination. When a man eats, he is reacting to an internal "drive," namely, hunger contractions consequent upon the lowering of blood sugar, but his precise reaction to these internal stimuli cannot be predicted by physiological knowledge alone . . . *What* he eats is of course limited by availability, but is also partly regulated by culture . . . Emotions are physiological events. Certain situations will evoke fear in people from any culture. But sensations of pleasure, anger, and lust may be stimulated by cultural cues that would leave unmoved someone who has been reared in a different social tradition (Kluckhohn, 1949a, p. 21).

2. Transmissive Quality of Culture. Margaret Mead has stressed the importance of child rearing in shaping the values and perceptions of people growing up in a given culture. "In every culture, in Samoa, in Germany, in Iceland, in Bali, and in the United States of America, we will find consistencies and regularities in the way in which new-born babies grow up and assume the attitudes and behavior patterns of their elders—and this we may call 'character formation'" (1942, p. 20). Park emphasizes that the influences on the shaping of the children's character are, of course, much broader than merely the parents. The point can be established by considering the experience of children of immigrants. "Children do not inherit the cultural complexes of their parents, and when children of immigrants grow up in the country of their adoption they inevitably take over all the accents, the inflections, the local cultural idioms of the native population" (1964, p. 26). Thus parents and other members of the culture transmit the symbols, attitudes, and behavior patterns of the culture. This quality means that, unlike animals, man not only learns but has the capability of building on the experiences of successive generations.

3. Social Quality of Culture. The habits and patterns of behavior transmitted from one generation to the next include social practices that facilitate social interaction between members of the same culture. In sum, the "rules" of social intercourse are a vital part of the culture. Hall has illustrated this point rather dramatically by contrasting perceptions of *time* between cultures.

> As a rule, Americans think of time as a road or a ribbon stretching into the future, along which one progresses. The road has segments or compartments which are kept discrete ("one thing at a time"). People who cannot schedule time are looked down upon as impractical. In at least some parts of Latin America, the North American (their term for us) finds himself annoyed when he has made an appointment with somebody, only to find a lot of other things going on at the same time ... The American concept of the discreteness of time and the necessity for scheduling is at variance with this amiable and seemingly confusing Latin system (1959, pp. 19-20).

4. Ideational Quality of Culture. "To a considerable extent, the group habits of which culture consists are conceptualized (or verbalized) as ideal norms or patterns of behavior" (Murdock, 1940, p. 365). Considerable disparity exists, of course, between the ideal and actual practices, but the more strongly held a given value, the greater the risk of group sanction for those who would violate it. Thus although an important cultural symbol such as a flag may be "mildly" violated through improper use (as in an advertising brochure) without strong negative reaction, a flagrant violation of its status may well lead to arrest or physical attack. As another illustration, the American cultural ideal of egalitarianism, though often violated, has retained its position as a dominant ideal to which individuals are supposed to conform.

5. Gratifying Quality of Culture. A viable culture satisfies biological and social human needs. The persistence of a given cultural trait or behavior pattern depends on its ability to satisfy innate or acquired drives. Failure to bring such satisfaction would lead to the disappearance of the trait or ultimately the culture itself. It would not be at all difficult to conceive of the dramatic impact a sudden decline in the gratifying quality of materialism would have on the American culture. A mass conversion to the traditionally nonmaterialistic values of the Zuni Indians of New Mexico would produce social shock waves that would dwarf the physical threat of the San Andreas Fault.

6. Adaptive Quality of Culture. That such dramatic shifts do not occur is attributable to the fact that culture possesses an adaptive quality. That is not to say that cultures are endowed with eternal life, but they *may* adapt to changing needs and environments. Culture is not static. Especially in our time cultural change is comparatively rapid. But a rapid cultural change is unbelievably slow. It took women 80 years to get the right to vote after they first began to press for that reform. "Today," Tucker notes, "the excitement, the threats of catastrophe, the promises of utopia that attended that long effort seem ridiculous" (1964, p. 23).

> The most obvious form of adaptation of culture occurs in connection with the geographical environment, as when persons bearing the culture adapt their social patterns to the exigencies of the jungle or the frozen north. This does not mean that the geographical environment *determines* the development of culture, but merely that the culture adjusts to the geographical necessities on the basis of the degree of cultural advancement. Culture must also constantly adapt to itself, in the sense that its different aspects are constantly changing and necessitating changes in other and related parts of the culture. This last statement is equivalent to saying that man makes use of culture and that man is the most adaptive of all the animals (Merrill and Eldredge, 1952, p. 47).

7. **Integrative Quality of Culture.** Given the slowness with which cultural change normally takes place, the integrative quality of culture should be readily apparent. Indeed, the phrase "cultural pattern" suggests a consistent or characteristic arrangement of behavior. This quality is most apparent in relatively isolated and simple cultures, but even in heterogeneous cultures there is a strong *central tendency.* In a very general sense, this centripetal force can be thought of as producing a cultural personality.[1] Linton has observed that although individuals who make up a culture belong to a variety of subgroups (such as age, sex, occupation) with quite distinct personality norms, "every society has its own basic personality type and its own series of status personalities differing in some respects from those of any other society" (Linton, 1945, p. 130).

> It is a fact of experience that if a Russian baby is brought to the United States he will, as an adult, act and think like an American—not like a Russian. . . . The process of becoming a representative member of any group involves a molding of raw human nature. Presumably the newborn infants of any society are more like other infants anywhere in the world than like older individuals in their own group. But the finished products of each group show certain resemblances. The great contribution of anthropology has consisted in calling attention to the variety of these styles of behavior . . . (Kluckhohn, 1949a, p. 172).

---

[1] For an excellent discussion of the concept of national character as approached by historians and behavioral scientists, see Potter (1954). It is rather interesting to observe the inconsistencies as well as the common traits of the "American character" as suggested by a host of observers. The following list is by no means exhaustive: Horney (1937); Brogan (1944); Myrdal (1944); Laski (1948); Kluckhohn and Murray (1949); de Tocqueville (1954); Lerner (Vol. 1, 1957); Commager (1959); and Riesman (1961).

SUBCULTURES

The question of integration and diversity within a culture is an important issue for students and practitioners of marketing. Perhaps its significance has been most apparent in the literature treating international marketing in which the implications of cultural differences have been quite pronounced. Less apparent and less well understood have been the implications of subgroups *within* a given culture. Especially in a country such as the United States, comprised largely of immigrants and descendants of immigrants from throughout the world, careful consideration must be given to the relevance of subcultures for marketing strategies. Clearly, the integrative pattern of the culture is not sufficiently strong to warrant the assumption that responses to advertising and product offerings will be uniform throughout the society.

A question arises, therefore, concerning the meaning of subculture and the utility of that concept in analyzing consumer behavior. It is a complex concept, one that is not easily delineated or understood. Anthropologists, sociologists, social psychologists, and others have used and misused the concept to the point that considerable confusion exists in the literature. In fact, Valentine has suggested that it has become "intellectually stylish to discover 'cultures' everywhere in national and international life" (1968, p. 104).

Valentine developed a partial inventory of social categories that are often labeled as subcultures.

> The list only begins with (1) socioeconomic strata—such as the lower class or the poor. It goes on to include (2) ethnic collectives—e.g., Negroes, Jews; (3) regional populations—Southerners, Midwesterners; (4) age grades—adolescents, youth; (5) community types—urban, rural; (6) institutional complexes—education, penal establishments; (7) occupational groupings—various professions; (8) religious bodies— Catholics, Muslims, and even (9) political entities—revolutionary groups, for example. Yet this does not exhaust the catalog, for one also finds (10) genera of intellectual orientation, such as "scientists" and "intellectuals"; (11) units that are really behavioral classes, mainly various kinds of "deviants"; and (12) what are categories of moral evaluation, ranging from "respectables" to the "disreputable" and the "unworthy" poor (1968, p. 105).

To varying degrees marketers have drawn upon these classifications in identifying market segments for their products and services. The most commonly utilized probably have been socioeconomic, regional, age, occupational categories, and one notable omission from the above list—sex. In recent years increasing attention has been given to race, ethnicity, and poverty as determinants of unique attitudes and behavior. For example, numerous books and articles have been published about the Negro culture or the Negro market. Yet most of the authors have failed to treat the topic systematically or in depth. Too many questions remain unanswered. Is the behavior which is described attributable to the fact that the subjects are black or is it because they are poor, or Southern, or urban, or young? Indeed, the question may be posed as to whether researchers have not been guilty of focusing on a limited number of unique differences rather than the many common characteristics that are shared with the dominant society. In sum, because of methodological problems, including the failure to isolate the presumed causal factor (race, religion, and so forth), heavy reliance on survey data, and the almost complete absence of comparative analyses, marketing literature on subcultures presents a largely confused picture—a trait that it shares with much of the literature in the behavioral sciences.

This chapter will attempt not only to identify the methodological problems associated with using the subcultural concept as an analytical device, but also to establish a framework for structuring the analyses of extant literature. The primary focus will be on research related to lower-income minority groups residing in urban areas.

Much of the confusion surrounding the subculture concept could be eliminated if researchers and writers would stress the complementary nature of subcultures vis-a-vis the total culture. This relationship was, in fact, emphasized in the literature on American anthropology in the 1930s and 1940s when the subculture concept first became established. Linton emphasized this point in *The Cultural Background of Personality* (1945) by noting that the overall cultural system is composed of a variety of subsystems, and every member of society has a place in several of these systems. Thus a person has a place in the age-sex system, the occupational-location system, and so forth. Yet he stressed that the components did not stand separately from the total culture, but instead complemented that system and shared its dominant values. Kroeber summarized this notion as follows:

> [E]ach class in a society exhibits a more or less distinct phase, a sub-culture of the total culture carried by the society; just as geographical segments of the society manifest regional aspects of the culture. This principle extends further: to age levels and the sexes. Men do not practice the specific habits of the women in their culture, and vice versa [but] the culture is not felt complete without both components. The same thing holds, incidentally, for the class phases, and often for the regional phases of well integrated culture. Scavengers and bankers will be recognized in such cultures as quite properly following diverse strains of life and making diverse contributions, but their coherence within the body politic of culture and society is felt to outweigh the separateness. They are both organs within the same body, like the patricians and plebians in the old Roman fable about the stomach and the limbs (1948, p. 274).

It should be clear, therefore, that an effective analysis of consumer behavior within subcultures must recognize the overlapping influences acting upon the behavior of individuals and that many values will be shared among the subgroups within the overall culture. It also suggests the complexity of the analysis and the dangers of generalizing about *the* Mexican-American market or *the* black consumer. How is it possible to ascribe homogeneity to groups composed of 8 and 20 million individuals, respectively—individuals of differing ages, incomes, occupations, and the like? In recognition of these complexities Arnold has defined a subculture as

> a concept used to refer to a subdivision of a national culture, composed of a combination of factorable situations such as class status, ethnic background, regional or rural residence and religious affiliation, but *forming* in their combination a functioning unity which has an integrated impact on the participating individual (1970, p. 17).

Given the large number of variables that can contribute to the formation of a "functioning unity," it is perhaps essential to establish a somewhat simplified framework for viewing subcultures. The key elements of the framework are acculturation, assimilation, and social class.

Acculturation refers to the process of learning a culture that differs from the one in which an individual was raised. The middle-aged or elderly Italian immigrant to the United States may learn relatively little of the new culture because he is deeply rooted in the Italian culture. In addition, it is likely that he will settle in a neighborhood or community populated by other Italian immigrants, and thus his exposure to the dominant culture will be "screened" by his participation in the Italian-American community. Whereas the first generation of immigrants tends to cling to its cultural heritage, the second generation generally discards the culture of its parents and absorbs the American culture. A more secure third generation tends to reevaluate its ethnic origins and embrace the more appealing features of it (Herberg, 1955). In fact, the generational effect on acculturation is so pronounced among Japanese-Americans that "the Japanese have a special terminology for each generation: *Issei* refers to the first-generation immigrant born in Japan, *Nisei* refers to the second generation born in the United States to Issei parents; and *Sansei* to the third generation . . ." (Kitano, 1969, p. 5).[2] The concept of acculturation also applies to people moving from one region of the country to another. Thus the dust bowl migrants who left Kansas, Oklahoma, and Texas for California in the 1930s and the steady stream of rural blacks fleeing to New York, Chicago, Washington, D.C., and other major cities have experienced a similar process of acculturation.

---

[2]Discussion of the "generation gap" and the existence of a youthful "counterculture" during the 1960s and 1970s has suggested that a generational effect is present among middle-class families as well as immigrants and migrants. It has been suggested that many college students from middle-class families are rejecting the cultural values of their parents just as takes place among immigrant families; for example, see Keniston (1968), Goodman (1960), Draper (1965), Roszak (1969), Farber (1970), and Reich (1970). For a treatment of generations within the Mexican-American subculture see Alvarez (1971).

Acculturation may be thought of as a continuum along which a new entrant to a culture moves. At one extreme is the totally unacculturated and the other end is represented by those who have internalized the norms of the culture. The "standard" norms of the United States would be those of the middle class.

Middle-class norms also play a key role in assessing the degree of assimilation enjoyed by an outsider. The concept refers to the process of acceptance by the dominant society. "The fact is that people can become acculturated without being assimilated, and they can be assimilated without being acculturated. For example, in the United States it is probably fair to say that the Amish are more assimilated than acculturated, whereas the Northern Negro is more acculturated than assimilated" (Berelson and Steiner, 1964, pp. 16-17).[3] Gordon (1964) has identified several types of assimilation to reflect that groups may not be accepted at the same rate in all aspects of life. For instance, structural assimilation (occupational or residential patterns) may well show advances before marital assimilation. It should also be noted that the willingness of the dominant society to accept certain groups directly affects the rate of acculturation of those groups. In short, the two processes are interactive.

The third dimension of the framework for viewing subcultures is social class.[4] In their introduction to *Blacks in the United States* (1969), Glenn and Bonjean have observed that

> In recent years a prevalent belief among liberal whites has been that there is no black subculture in the United States and that black-white differences in attitudes and behavior are totally "social class" and regional differences, explained by differences in education, occupation, income, region of residence, and region of origin . . . Since the mid-1960s, a convincing array of empirical evidence has been published that rather conclusively refutes this point of view . . . However, it is still important to keep in mind that differences in socioeconomic standing and region of residence and origin *do* account for a substantial portion (and possibly most) of all the attitudinal and behavioral differences between blacks and whites in the United States (p. 18).

Later in this chapter, material will be reviewed that treats differences in subculture consumer behavior. For the present, however, the focus will be on social class as the construct that is most useful in analyzing the marketplace behavior

---

[3]One of the strangest cases of acculturation and assimilation is represented by the Chinese families originally brought to the Mississippi delta to replace emancipated blacks. For many years they were classed as "black," but are now viewed as essentially white (Loewen, 1971).

[4]Gordon (1964) develops a much more complex model utilizing the variables of ethnicity, rural versus urban, and geographical location as well as social class. In addition, he stratifies by means of two other dimensions: social status (economic-political power) and race-nationality-religion. Gordon notes the interaction of these variables with behavior. It should also be recalled that Kitano (1969) found it necessary to add the generation variable in his study of Japanese-Americans.

among lower-income urban residents. What follows is not offered as an in-depth treatment of social class. Instead, some basic concepts will be established, various social classes briefly described, and these ideas related to subculture theory.

Social class refers to the stratification of the members of a society into a hierarchy. The ranking may be based on a number of variables. The key concepts in understanding social class are social prestige and interaction. The most commonly accepted variables used for operational definitions are occupation, house type, dwelling area, income, source of income, and institutional memberships (Warner, Meeker, and Eells, 1949). The very concept of a hierarchy of social status suggests vertical mobility. Mobility, in turn, may be viewed as an opportunity (upward) or a threat (downward). Thus the accumulation of certain products and services that can serve as *symbols* of class position suggests one of the relationships between class and consumer behavior.[5] At different levels the symbols of social status will differ and the relative importance of given products and services will vary (kind of automobile, private school for the children, bowling club membership, size and location of house, church membership, and so forth).

Although it should be recognized that classes are not neat compartments into which all people are easily fitted and that rather wide ranges of behavior are exhibited within classes, some generalizations can be made. Kahl (1956) has discussed ideal types in treating the various classes.

1. Upper Class: Graceful Living. These families are the most powerful, richest, exclusive members of the community. Although often divided into the "old families" and the self-made newcomers, there is generally an emphasis on spending one's money properly—art, antiques, travel. Relative to other classes it is a small and cohesive group as opposed to a statistical classification. In effect, they are the "society" of the community. They are the Mellons, the Rockefellers, J. Paul Getty, and Jackie Onassis.

2. Upper Middle Class: Career. These are the people who make things happen. They are the top managers, professionals, and intellectual elite. As Kahl notes, "they do not have jobs, they occupy positions; they do not work, they pursue careers" (1956, p. 191). Among the older and declining segment of this stratum are the entrepreneurs and independents of the business, agricultural, and professional worlds. The fast-growing newcomers are the salaried men who fill the middle and upper echelons of the nation's burgeoning bureaucracies. They are mostly white, American-born residents of the better urban apartments and suburbs. The husband's career is the critical determinant of the family's status and high income, and thus they are competitive, mobile, industrious, and very concerned about the education and career plans of their children.

[5]For a detailed and insightful treatment of symbolism in consumer behavior, see Levy (1959), Boyd and Levy (1963), and Levy (1971).

3. Lower Middle Class: Respectability.   Unlike their upper-middle-class counterparts, most people in this class fail to get very high in their organizations in spite of their industriousness. Most have a high-school education or even some college or special training. They are on the fence in that they know they are not "big" people and yet they know they are superior to others. They cannot focus too intently on their dead-end jobs, so they emphasize respectability in their work and life styles. "Sure, I could have had that promotion but I wasn't willing to play politics to get it." Home ownership, family solidarity, high moral standards often including a highly active religious orientation, and the strong desire to see their children get a college education and a good job tend to highlight their lives.

Estimates of the percentage of the population represented by these three classes vary somewhat and, of course, the situation is not static. Estimates of the upper class average around 4 percent, whereas upper middle class is generally estimated at 10 percent and lower middle class at 30 percent. In short, these oversimplified, highly condensed descriptions of Kahl's ideal types that have thus far been reviewed represent less than half the population. The other half, the working and lower classes, will receive detailed treatment.

At this point it should be noted that both culture and class are constructs, that is, moderately sophisticated terms made to subsume various behaviors or social relationships, creating broad categories. The term *culture* implies no specific techniques for determining the edges of a culture. Which people are in what culture is a question that has no good theoretical or empirical answer. The underlying assumption is that people who have undergone common experiences behave in limited ways that are somewhat predictable. On the other hand, social class theory has a specific method for stating the sense in which people are likely to have had more or less common experiences—their position in the social hierarchy. However, neither concept should ever be thought of as causal. Causal events are interactions between the biological animal and the events of his life. When middle-class blacks behave more like middle-class whites than they behave like lower-class blacks, it would make little sense to say that social class provides the better explanation. Culture theory would probably stress the fact that those aspects of the culture passed on through various events to the middle-class blacks were more like those of the middle-class whites than those of the lower-class blacks.

Up to this point, the acculturation-assimilation-social class framework would suggest the following about subcultures:

1. The extent to which members of a given subculture have learned and adopted the norms of the dominant culture is measured by its acculturation. Given the number of variables at work that influence behavior, it is important to recognize that acculturation to the point of attaining some ideal stereotype is impossible. There is a danger, therefore, of analyzing sub-

cultures in terms of their differences while ignoring the behavior they share with others in the culture.

2. The notion of assimilation suggests that a subculture may become highly acculturated and still not be "accepted" by the dominant groups within a culture. It would be a mistake, therefore, to assume that minorities which create their own institutions or display life styles which differ from those of the dominant society are acting out distinct subcultural responses. Liebow notes that "There is, fortunately, a growing suspicion that 'culture' and 'historical continuity' may not be the most useful constructs for dealing with lower-class behavior. Hylan Lewis, for example, suggests that 'It is probably more fruitful to think of lower class families reacting to the facts of their position and to relative isolation rather than to the imperatives of a lower class culture.' " (1967, p. 208).

3. Social class provides an important basis for understanding behavior in the marketplace. It has been noted that "class distinctions are of tremendous importance to individuals of all classes [because] almost no one has learned the lessons of his class perfectly or can keep up with its changing values. Since loss of social position may attend serious evaluative mistakes and since even small losses in status or prestige are regarded as serious, class limits on choices become persistent and intense factors in the hierarchy of personal wants" (Tucker, 1964, p. 44). Or, as Tucker stressed later, "Class realities remain useful variables in the prediction of behavior" (1967, p. 15).

The relevance of social class as the principal construct for understanding behavior within subcultures was central to Gans's thoughtful analysis of a working-class community of Italian-Americans in Boston's West End.

> One of the initial purposes of this study was to compare a low-income population such as the West Enders to the middle class, and, if possible, to isolate some of the basic differences between them. The relative stability of the social structure across generations from Southern Italy to the West End . . . would seem to suggest that there might be an Italian way of life. This idea in turn would support the hypothesis that the peer group society [a major characteristic of the West End community] is an ethnic phenomenon and that the principal differences between the West Enders and the middle class are ethnic ones.
>
> An alternative hypothesis, however—that the peer group society is a working class phenomenon and that class differences separate the West Enders from the middle class—is more justified (1962, p. 229).

Gans continues this argument by noting that "The hypothesis is further supported by studies of other working-class populations which have shown that these, too, exhibit many characteristics of the peer group society . . . Consequently, the class hypothesis offers a better explanation than the ethnic one" (p. 230).

He concluded the point by suggesting that "The characteristics that West Enders share with other working-class groups can be conceived as forming a working-class subculture, which differs considerably from both lower- and middle-class subcultures" (p. 230). Thus, unlike Glenn and Bonjean, Gans would conclude that social class is virtually synonymous with subculture.

It is important to describe, at least briefly, the characteristics of working- and lower-class members. Too often researchers treating a given ethnic or racial group will ascribe "unique" characteristics to that group when, in fact, they are common to most groups within the same social class. This problem has been especially acute with respect to studies of blacks. According to Valentine,

> These authors devote much discussion to broad socioeconomic characteristics that actually are associated with low income regardless of ethnic status. Yet they tend very much to treat these characteristics as if they were attributes of the ethnic minority without reference to other dimensions. Thus, in spite of occasional disclaimers, we find that many statements about "the Negro family" are not true of high-income Negro households but are true of a high percentage of poor non-Negro families. This amounts to representing what are really class characteristics as if they were racial or ethnic features (pp. 122-23).

4. Working Class. Family relationships and other forms of peer-group behavior, as well as attitudes toward work are among the most distinctive features of the working class. Among the lives of these semiskilled workers, who generally did not complete high school, the family circle plays a dominant role. The extended family provides the participants for most social activities. Gans found that "Adult West Enders [spent] almost as much time with siblings, in-laws, and cousins—that is, with relatives of the same sex and age as with their spouses, and more time than with parents, aunts, and uncles" (p. 37). This pattern of peer-group relationships begins in childhood and continues throughout the lives of the working class. Feagin (1968) and other researchers have found similar patterns in other racial and ethnic working-class communities.[6] "Thus, each of the marriage partners is pulled out *centrifugally* toward his or her peers, as compared with the middle-class family in which a *centripetal* push brings husband and wife close together" (Gans, p. 39).

The other major distinguishing characteristics of the working class are attitudes toward work. Kahl (1956, pp. 205-15) has described this attitude as "get by." Employment is seen as a source of insecurity because of periodic layoffs and strikes. Since they occupy "lower" positions, they do not express

[6]For examples of peer-group patterns in other working-class communities, see Dotson (1951), Kiser (1952), Blumberg and Bell (1959), Rainwater, Coleman, and Handel (1959), Berger (1960), and Meadow (1962). For parallels in the British experience, see Mogey (1956) and Young and Willmott (1957).

the same pride in their jobs as the lower middle class nor the total career commitment of the upper middle class. They express negative attitudes toward supervisors (Young and Willmott, p. 14) and resent authority possessed by bosses. The detachment from work is understandable given the limited skills and occupational alternatives. However, education is seen to some extent as a route to occupational success for their children (Archibald, 1953; Hyman, 1953).

Among the other important traits of the working class is their high level of absorption of selected forms of mass media—especially action-oriented television programs (Glick and Levy, 1962); their hostility toward and suspicion of the "outside" world (Gans, 1962); a strong skepticism toward institutions and individuals offering them service—caretakers (Padilla, 1958); and a particularly high level of satisfaction derived from the amount of their earnings (Kahl, 1956).

5. Lower Class. This class is often described by such adjectives as apathetic, ignorant, alienated, and inferior. They are the "defeated" at the "lowest level" of society's hierarchy. The pejorative tone of much of the literature on the lower class tends to cloud the distinction between *permanent* and *temporary* response to environmental conditions.

The distinction is an important one for marketers as well as those concerned with public policy. The central question is whether low-income people share the basic norms of the larger culture or if they represent a separate subculture—termed "culture of poverty" by Oscar Lewis (1959). If the former is the case, then the distinctive traits of the lower class can be traced to their lack of money, their marginality in the job market, their inadequate educational background, and their physical disadvantages traceable to poor diets, inadequate medical care, and substandard housing. Lewis (1966) stresses the other view.

> As an anthropologist I have tried to understand poverty and its asso-
> ciated traits as a culture, or, more accurately, as a subculture with its
> own structure and rationale, as a way of life which is passed down from
> generation to generation along family lines. This view directs attention
> to the fact that the culture of poverty in modern nations is not only a
> matter of economic deprivation, of disorganization or of the absence of
> something. It is also something positive and provides some rewards
> without which the poor could hardly carry on (p. xliii).

Lewis notes that "the culture of poverty is both an adaptation and reaction of the poor to their marginal position in a class-stratified, highly individuated, capitalistic society" (1966, p. xliv). However, he ascribes a permanence and self-renewing trait to the subculture that would distinguish it from a purely class phenomenon.

> Once it comes into existence it tends to perpetuate itself from genera-
> tion to generation because of its effect on the children. By the time
> slum children are age six or seven they have usually absorbed the basic

values and attitudes of their subculture and are not psychologically geared to take advantage of changing conditions or increased opportunities which may occur in their lifetime (1966, p. xlv).

In the view of Liebow, by contrast, the world of the poor "does not appear as a self-contained, self-generating, self-sustaining system or even subsystem with clear boundaries marking it off from the larger world around it" (1967, p. 209). Liebow's analysis was based on an in-depth study of a group of lower-class black men who passed much of their time on a given corner in a Washington, D.C., slum. Liebow studied the streetcorner men for over a year. His findings centered on employment and interpersonal relations. In exploring these topics he finds underlying values and attitudes shared with the dominant society that are often obscured by less thoughtful observers. Supported by the experiences of the streetcorner men from his study, Liebow challenges a number of widely accepted stereotypes of the poor. With respect to jobs, for example, he found that

> A crucial factor in the streetcorner man's lack of job commitment is the overall value he places on the job. *For his part, the streetcorner man puts no lower value on the job than does the larger society around him.* He knows the social value of the job by the amount of money the employer is willing to pay him for doing it. In a real sense, every pay day, he counts in dollars and cents the value placed on the job by society at large (p. 57).

Liebow concludes that so far as employment is concerned

> The streetcorner man is under continuous assault by his job experiences and job fears. His experiences and fears feed on one another. The kind of job he can get—and frequently only after fighting for it—steadily confirms his fears, depresses his self-confidence and self-esteem until finally, terrified of an opportunity even if one presents itself, he stands defeated by his experiences, his belief in his own self-worth destroyed and his fears a confirmed reality (p. 71).

In contrast to the findings that the poor are unable to defer gratification and thus are "present-time oriented," Liebow suggests

> But from the inside looking out, what appears as a "present-time" orientation to the outside observer is, to the man experiencing it, as much a future orientation as that of his middle-class counterpart. The difference between the two men lies not so much in their different orientations to time as in their different orientations to future time or, more specifically, to their different futures . . . Living on the edge of both economic and psychological subsistence, the streetcorner man [in contrast to the middle-class man] is obliged to expend all his resources on maintaining himself from moment to moment (pp. 64-65).

Liebow's conclusions about the lack of stability in marriages have a similar theme:

> Thus, marriage is an occasion of failure. To stay married is to live with your failure, to be confronted by it day in and day out. It is to live in a world whose standards of manliness are forever beyond one's reach, where one is continuously tested and challenged and continually found wanting. In self-defense, the husband retreats to the streetcorner. Here, where the measure of man is considerably smaller, and where weaknesses are somehow turned upside down and almost magically transformed into strengths, he can be, once again, a man among men (pp. 135-36).

In sum, Liebow suggests that the world of the lower-class black man is not a self-supporting, social system with a separate value system. Indeed, it is a world largely shaped by its commitment to the values of the larger society.

> From this perspective, the streetcorner man does not appear as a carrier of an independent cultural tradition. His behavior appears not so much as a way of realizing the distinctive goals and values of his own subculture, or of conforming to its models, but rather as his way of trying to achieve many of the goals and values of the larger society, of failing to do this, and of concealing his failure from others and from himself as best he can (p. 222).

The conflicting conclusions of Lewis and Liebow suggest that even with an understanding of acculturation, assimilation, and social class the researcher's task in identifying and analyzing a subculture is a complex one. While Liebow concludes that much of the lower-class black male's behavior can be understood only in terms of his failure to achieve middle-class goals, Lewis argues that "People with a culture of poverty are aware of middle-class values, talk about them and even claim some of them as their own, but on the whole they do not live by them" (Lewis, 1966, p. xlvi).

This issue, which clearly is not going to be resolved here, is more than a mere academic debate.[7] It has significant implications for marketing practitioners as well as those concerned with public policy. In essence, Liebow's position would suggest that improvements in the economic condition of the lower class would lead to the adoption of a life style similar to that of the middle class. Once the sources of failure were removed the lower class could fulfill their middle-class values. If Lewis's culture-of-poverty concept is, in fact, correct, then a distinct value system is so deeply rooted that mere alteration of economic conditions would not dramatically change the life style. Such a change would be gradual, accomplished only through the slow process of acculturation.

It should also be kept in mind that Glenn and Bonjean (1969, p. 18) have

---

[7]For a detailed criticism of the concept of a culture of poverty, see Leacock (1971).

suggested that a distinct black subculture exists regardless of social class position. In his study of the blues singer and his audience, Keil suggests that blacks have a unique outlook on life because of "a dearly bought wisdom, a 'perspective by incongruity' " (1966, p. 170). Glazer and Moynihan have argued that "the Negro is only an American, and nothing else. He has no values and culture to guard and protect" (1963, p. 53). However, Blauner has developed a persuasive case for a black subculture (1970). He maintains that a more complex model is required to understand the black subculture than for ethnic groups. In short, he contends that "poverty is only one source of black culture. . . . Among the other sources . . . are Africa, slavery, the South, Emancipation and northern migration, and above all, *racism*" (p. 352). The key to his premise about racism is that it "blocked the participation of Negroes in the dominant culture so that unfilled needs for symbols, meaning, and value had to be met elsewhere" (p. 356). In sum,

> Negro American culture is an ethnic as well as a class culture because the history of black people *in the United States* has produced a residue of shared collective memories and frames of reference. It is because black Americans have undergone unique experiences in America, experiences that no other national or racial minority or lower-class groups have shared, that a *distinctive* ethnic culture has evolved (p. 352).

SUBCULTURES AND MARKETING

The issue of to what extent the low-income minority groups in the United States share the values of the dominant society with respect to consumer behavior is one that, as has been noted earlier, has received relatively scant attention. Especially is this true of ethnographic and participant-observation studies conducted by anthropologists and sociologists. With the notable exception of Gans, who devotes an entire chapter to "Consumer Goods and the Mass Media" in *The Urban Villagers,* most of the studies ignore this aspect of their subjects' lives. Yet it is these methodological techniques which hold the greatest promise of resolving the underlying issue of the similarities and differences in values among these groups vis-à-vis the rest of society.

Those researchers who have studied the marketplace of the nation's ghettos and the behavior of its participants have come largely from the fields of marketing and economics. The research methodologies employed have been primarily survey techniques or laboratory experiments. To the extent that these studies have taken into account the income levels and marketplace environment of their subjects, they have provided useful insights into the consumer behavior of various racial and ethnic low-income groups. To date, however, these studies have left unanswered the question of how deeply rooted these patterns of behavior may be. Having stated this important limitation of the research findings, the balance of this chapter will focus largely on the literature treating the most thoroughly studied of the groups—the low-income Negro. This review of the literature will be followed by a consideration of a variety of research methodologies appropriate for the extension of the inquiry into this topic.

Low-Income Black Consumer

Enough has been said about the learned and transmissive qualities of culture to suggest that any analysis of the low-income black consumer cannot ignore the historical roots of the black experience in the United States. Over a period of nearly 400 years some 15 million black slaves were transported to the Western Hemisphere. Although the first slaves to arrive on what was to become the mainland of the United States were probably brought by Lucas Vásquez de Ayllón in 1526 to a site near Jamestown, Virginia, and other black slaves were to be found in various North American Spanish settlements, slave trade did not begin in the English colonies until 1619 (Mannix and Cowley, 1962, p. 54). As Mannix and Cowley note,

> That nameless Dutch vessel which arrived a year before the *Mayflower* was hardly less important in American history. She carried not only twenty Negroes but, for the future, everything those Negroes and their successors would contribute to American wealth and culture, including Carolina rice, Louisiana cane, and the Cotton Kingdom. She carried, or announced, the maritime trade of New England and the training of the first sailors in the United States Navy; then the plantation system, the Abolition Society, the Missouri Compromise, and the Civil War; then Reconstruction, the Solid South, Jim Crow, and the struggle for integration. She carried the spirituals, jazz, the researches of such Negro scientists as George Washington Carver, the contributions to American culture of . . . musicians, statesmen, scholars, writers . . . (1962, p. 55).

The important question which this quotation does not pose is what of the African culture known by these people before they were enslaved? The slaves came from established cultures, and it is intriguing to search for links between those African cultures and the black population of the United States. The English, who began their slave trade in the early seventeenth century, some 100 years after the Portuguese and Spanish, were fascinated not only with the blackness of the Africans, but also with their ways of living. "Africans were *different* from Englishmen in so many ways: in their clothing, huts, farming, warfare, language, government, morals, and (not least important) in their table manners. Englishmen were fully aware that Negroes living at different parts of the coast were not all alike [but] no matter how great the actual and observed differences among Negroes, though, none of these black men seemed to live like Englishmen" (Jordan, 1969, pp. 24-25). As will be seen, these racial and cultural differences caused the black Africans to be viewed as savages, and thus was established the intellectual, moral, and legal "justification" for the enslavement of these people. As for the cultural links, Frazier pieced together "scraps of memories, which form only an insignificant part of the growing body of traditions in Negro families, [and these] are what remains of the African heritage. Probably never before in history has a people been so nearly completely stripped of its social heritage as the Negroes who were brought to America" (1966, p. 15). It is not difficult to comprehend the near destruction of the cultures. Many villages were sacked with only remnants of the community carried away. Others died as members of slave coffles, which were often forced to march in chains for hundreds of miles from the interior to the West African Coast (Elkins, 1963, pp. 89-98). Once on board ship, an English Privy Council in 1789 estimated that 12.5 percent would die in Middle Passage (Mannix and Cowley, p. 123). From this point on the account is even more depressingly familiar: slave auctions, the separation of the few families that had together survived the earlier steps, and finally, in what must be a classic understatement, the difficulty of finding in their new home "a congenial milieu in which to perpetuate the old way of life" (Frazier, p. 7).[8]

Although a brief review of the nature of the slave trade may help to explain the very limited transmission of the African cultures to the United States, it does not explain the irony that Handlin suggests: "Only a few, like St. George Tucker and Thomas Jefferson, perceived that here were the roots of a horrible tragedy that would someday destroy them all" (1957, p. 22). And at the heart of this irony lies a key to the understanding of the cultural role of blacks in the United States. That key is the attitudes of whites toward blacks. Those attitudes not only shaped the institution of slavery but the lives and institutions of contemporary black Americans.

The origins of these attitudes may well be rooted in the intensely negative meanings associated with the word black, which predated the English encounter with black people. As Jordan notes in his excellent work on American attitudes toward blacks,

> No other color except white conveyed so much emotional impact. As described by the *Oxford English Dictionary,* the meaning of *black* before the sixteenth century included, "Deeply stained with dirt; soiled, dirty, foul . . . Having dark or deadly purposes, malignant; pertaining to or involving death, deadly; baneful, disastrous, sinister . . . Foul, iniquitous, atrocious, horrible, wicked . . . Indicating disgrace, censure, liability to punishment, etc." Black was an emotionally partisan color, the handmaid and symbol of baseness and evil, a sign of danger and repulsion (p. 7).

[8]In his classic study on this topic, Herskovitz (1941) contends that blacks did retain much of their cultural heritage. However, more recent evidence gives greater weight to Frazier's position. For a fascinating account of one black American's efforts to trace his family's African roots, see Haley (1972).

Although the English had no traditions or institutions based on slavery, they nonetheless did possess a concept of slavery. Thus the preconceptions of blackness, the view of the African cultures as uncivilized or savage, the superior power of the English, and the attractive financial rewards of joining the slave trade combined to overcome whatever moral barriers might have prevented them from engaging in such a shameful enterprise.

Similar motivations could be attributed to the American slavers, slave holders, and the consenting public. In addition, the perpetuation of slavery and abuses and degradation of blacks after the slaves were granted their "freedom" were associated with the whites' fear of retaliation by blacks, the sexual exploitation of blacks by their white "masters," and the deeply rooted hatred which grew out of these fears. Jordan concludes that this tragedy rests in a perpetual duel within the white man, a struggle between his higher and lower natures.

> His cultural conscience—his Christianity, his humanitarianism, his ideology of liberty and equality—demanded that he regard and treat the Negro as his brother and his countryman, as his equal. At the same moment, however, many of his most profound urges, especially his yearning to maintain the identity of his folk, his passion for domination, his sheer avarice, and his sexual desire, impelled him toward conceiving and treating the Negro as inferior to himself, as an American leper. At closer view, though, the duel appears more complex than a conflict between the best and worst in the white man's nature, for in a variety of ways, the white man translated his "worst" into his "best." Raw sexual aggression became retention of purity, and brutal domination became faithful maintenance of civilized restraints . . . In fearfully hoping to escape the animal within himself the white man debased the Negro, surely, but at the same time he debased himself. . . . Conceivably, there was and is a way out from the vicious cycle of degradation, an opening of better hope demanding an unprecedented and perhaps impossible measure of courage, honesty, and sheer nerve . . . Common charity and his special faith demanded that he make the attempt. But there was little in his historical experience to indicate that he would succeed (pp. 581-82).

There is ample evidence that only the most painfully slow progress has been made by the dominant society in correcting the injustices to blacks. In short, whites did not show an abundance of "courage, honesty, and sheer nerve." And this environment of hostility, discrimination, and injustice perpetuated the widespread problems of poverty that have plagued black people in the United States. It is not possible here to trace the innumerable forces unleashed by the dominant society and analyze their impact on blacks, but an effort will be made to look systematically at the consumer behavior of low-income urban blacks. Although the focus of the discussion necessarily narrows at this point, it is critical that the reader keep in mind the broader societal context.

1. Ghetto Marketplace. It is important to look at least briefly at the setting within which the low-income urban black acts out his role as a consumer. The Bureau of the Census reported in 1969 that 70 percent of the blacks in the United States lived in metropolitan areas. The comparable figure for whites was 64 percent. The figures for the two groups in 1950 had been 56 and 60 percent, respectively. In spite of the apparent similarities in the locational patterns for blacks and whites, a major difference is noted when metropolitan area is divided into central cities and suburbs. In 1969, 55 percent of all blacks lived in central cities versus 15 percent in the suburbs. The breakdown for whites was 26 percent versus 38 percent (Bureau of the Census, 1969, pp. 5-6).

Since the majority of blacks reside in the central cities, they generally rely on the marketplaces of those cities for their goods and services. The principal marketplace for the poor is easily distinguished from the "downtown" shopping district or from the typical suburban shopping center. As one writer has noted,

> One of the cruelest ironies of our economic system is that the disadvantaged are generally served by the least efficient segments of the business community. The spacious, well-stocked, and efficiently managed stores characteristic of America's highly advanced distribution system are rarely present in the ghetto. The marvels of mass merchandising and its benefits for consumers normally are not shared with the low-income families. Instead their shopping districts are dotted with small, inefficient "mom and pop" establishments more closely related to stores in underdeveloped countries than to the sophisticated network of retail institutions dominant in most of the U.S. economy (Sturdivant, 1968, p. 132).

Systematic studies of the retail structure of ghetto areas have been undertaken. An early research effort in Chicago by Berry found that the major determinants of the structure of a commercial district were population and median family income (1963).[9] Based on studies in Buffalo, New York, Andreasen has suggested that ghetto business structures should be analyzed using a four-stage developmental model that accounts for changes in the racial and economic composition of the area. The four stages are:

1. White equilibrium.
2. White-to-black transition.
3. Major economic decline (a period of reconsolidation).
4. Black equilibrium.

[9]Although this is not the appropriate place for a detailed discussion of models of commercial structures in ghetto areas, sources of information on this growing body of literature should be noted: Pred (1963), K. Cox (1969), W. Cox (1970), Haines, Simon, and Alexis (1970), and Sengstock (1968). For more general works treating the characteristics of low-income-area retailing see Caplovitz (1967) and Sturdivant (1969a).

According to Andreasen, "Whether the area continues to decline economically depends on whether there is net black out-migration and/or whether average incomes in the area continue to decline. In part, in some areas this is a function of whether policies can be developed to arrest and reverse the decay process of the third stage" (1971, p. 23).

Among the conclusions reached by Andreasen are two that have been critical factors in the analysis of ghetto markets.

> The exodus of white businessmen and their mass merchandise outlets and the relatively slow rate of entry of black businessmen results in considerable hardship for residents in transitional communities in terms of the quality and quantity of outlets available to them . . . Frictions involved in the transition from white to black business ownership may well contribute significantly to inner city racial tensions (1971, p. 28).

These conclusions point to the relationship between the structure of a retail market and its performance. Sturdivant has suggested that these two factors plus the conduct of the merchants in such communities provide an important framework for analyzing ghetto retail communities (1970). The interrelationship of structure, conduct, and performance can perhaps be summarized by a finding from the Federal Trade Commission study of food-chain practices in Washington, D.C., and San Francisco.

> The distribution system performs less satisfactorily in low-income areas of our inner cities than in suburban areas. Many food stores serving low-income, inner city areas are small, less efficient, and have higher prices. Consumers in these areas are frequently sold lower quality merchandise and are provided fewer services than in other areas. Moreover, the retail facilities of low-income areas are often old and in a shabby state of upkeep (1969, p. 3).

2. Where Do the Ghetto Poor Shop?   If the commercial districts that are closest to the residences of the low-income urban blacks represent "a shopping situation that generally offers them higher prices, inferior merchandise, high-pressure selling, hidden and inflated interest charges, and a degrading shopping environment" (Sturdivant, 1968, p. 131), do they, in fact, shop in such areas? The evidence is mixed. Caplovitz, in his pioneering study of low-income consumers of major durables in New York City during the early 1960s, had difficulty answering the question because of a questionnaire design problem. His 464 respondents (median income was $3500, 29 percent of the sample was black) were asked to classify purchases as "in neighborhood" or "out of neighborhood." Caplovitz noted that for a number of reasons "[i]t would be a mistake . . . to interpret 'out of neighborhood' as referring only to the large down-town stores" (p. 52).

In spite of the problems associated with classification of responses, Caplovitz was able to devise an "index of shopping scope" and found the following:

> Various characteristics of families are associated with the breadth of their shopping scope: family income, age of household head, the extent of his education, the length of time the family has lived in New York City, and race. The higher the family income, the greater the education of the head, and the younger his age, the greater the tendency of the family to shop out of the neighborhood. Families that have been living in New York City for a long time, or where the head grew up in a city, also have wider shopping horizons. Puerto Rican families restrict their shopping to neighborhood stores more frequently than either white or Negro families; Negroes in the sample, since they tend to be younger than whites, are oriented most of all to the stores outside the neighborhood (p. 55).

Sturdivant also found differences in mobility among low-income groups in Los Angeles. Less than half the households studied in Watts had automobiles and the public transportation facilities serving the south-central section of Los Angeles were inadequate at best. There was heavy reliance on neighborhood stores. By contrast, in east Los Angeles the Mexican-Americans had greater mobility; 73 percent of the households had automobiles and the bus services were better than in Watts. The Chicano community was also in relative proximity to downtown and other major shopping facilities. Nonetheless, the study concluded that the Mexican-Americans were also "trapped," but in their case by "the need for cultural reinforcement in the marketplace" where there was a "Spanish-speaking atmosphere [and where] a variety of Mexican goods was offered" (1969b, p. 75). Thus although mobility differed between the two groups, both concentrated their shopping in local stores.

In their analysis of 1962 data collected in Chicago (sample size was 1000 with 760 white and 240 black respondents), Feldman and Star found that 81 percent of the whites and 78 percent of the nonwhites sometimes traveled more than 30 minutes to shop for nonfood items (1968). They found "a strong relation between income and the percentage of respondents who sometimes travel more than 30 minutes to shop" (p. 219). They reported no statistically significant difference between races at any income range between $0 and $9999.

Although the finding that a high percentage of blacks in Chicago "sometimes" traveled more than 30 minutes to shop for nonfood items might not lead one to the conclusion that the respondents were highly mobile, a study in Pittsburgh reached exactly that conclusion. The findings by Gensch and Staelin (based on 455 personal interviews with blacks in an area where half the families had incomes of less than $6000) were as follows:

> In general the residents were extremely mobile in terms of the number of shopping areas used even though 45 percent of the families reported

they did not own a car. Over 90 percent of the families indicated that they regularly used three or more shopping areas for their nondurable goods . . . Food shopping was the only activity in which families not owning cars seemed to alter their shopping behavior and rely more on the convenience of the ghetto neighborhood (1972, p. 54).

Even the evidence on food shopping is somewhat mixed. Most such studies report dependence on the ghetto marketplace for most food purchases. For example, Mason and Madden in reporting on a study of low-income blacks in a Southern community of 100,000 population (196 randomly selected households with a median annual income of $2765) found that

Even though 44 percent of the respondents utilized a private auto for purposes of making their major food purchases . . . less than 8 percent made shopping trips outside the study area. The 8 percent shopping outside the study area possessed the highest median incomes, highest levels of education, spent the least average amount for food, and based their decision on where to shop in terms of the availability of specials. The 14 percent of the respondents who patronized the "mom and pop" outlets, in addition to having the lowest median levels of income and education, shopped these outlets primarily because they were close and featured credit (1971, p. 9).

Goodman, on the other hand, concluded from a study in West Philadelphia (520 randomly selected households, 96 percent black and median income $4000 to $5000) that "local convenience stores are used entirely as supplementary sources of emergency items or for frequently purchased perishables such as bread and milk" (1968, p. 23). It might be important to note, however, that the food stores designated "outside" by Goodman were no more than one-half mile from the study area (p. 19).

If there are conclusions to be drawn from the available studies, it would seem that income, automobile ownership, and local circumstances influence the shopping scope of consumers. It should also be noted that little evidence is available of significant differences between low-income blacks and whites in this regard.

3. Consumption Patterns. A number of researchers have attempted to deal with the issue of whether or not there is a distinct market comprised of blacks by doing comparative analyses of consumption patterns of whites and blacks *of similar income.* One section of the literature treats consumption within broad categories (e.g., food, recreation, and saving). Other researchers have pushed their analysis into specific generic classifications and even brands within product groupings.

A comprehensive survey of the literature treating the issue of black and white consumption differences was developed by Alexis (1962). He collected budget data from several sources "to determine if there is any basis for the contention that Negro and white consumers with comparable means allocate their income differently to the following budget items: savings, food, housing, clothing, recreation and leisure, house furnishings and equipment and transportation (nonautomobile and automobile)" (p. 11). According to Alexis,

> When all the data have been digested, the following major findings emerge:
>
> 1. Total consumption expenditures of Negroes are less than for comparable whites, or Negroes save more out of a given income than do whites with the same income.
> 2. Negro consumers spend more for clothing and nonautomobile transportation and less for food, housing, medical care and automobile transportation than do comparable income whites.
> 3. There is no consistent racial difference in expenditures for either recreation and leisure or home furnishing and equipment at comparable income levels (p. 27).

Writing some 8 years later on the same topic, Alexis along with Haines and Simon restated the same three conclusions, but added two more:

> 4. The research which has been done on consumption is remarkable for its lack of policy implications. This, it may be speculated, arises from the use of race as a dummy variable to cover a host of differential cultural and environmental factors which affect consumption. Policy implications could arise from research on differential consumption patterns only if the effect of environmental factors which affect consumption was explicitly measured.
> 5. None of the research surveyed has shown that past differential consumption patterns based on race-income effects can be used to predict future consumption (1970, pp. 24-25).

Based on the findings from his earlier search of the literature (summarized in Table 1), Alexis encouraged economists and marketers to give greater attention to "race as a consumption variable." He also noted that "It is impossible to predict with any accuracy when Negroes shall be accorded all the rights and privileges which whites take for granted. It is very likely, however, that observed differences in consumer behavior will continue to be influenced by differences in the socio-economic environment" (p. 27).

Stafford, Cox, and Higginbotham (1968) made an effort to gain additional information on this issue. The data base was a probability sample of 1546 housewives in the Houston area (1335 whites and 211 blacks). They analyzed five product categories—food, soft drinks, liquor, personal hygiene products, and major home appliances. "A major finding of this study was that, for many household products, consumption-pattern differences were small both in number and magnitude" (p. 628). Where variations did occur, the authors felt that a substantial portion "were explainable more in terms of income or sociodemo-

TABLE 1. Summary Statement of Findings for Studies Covered by Whether Negroes Spent More or Less Than Comparable Whites

Study	Food	Housing	Clothing	Recreation and Leisure	Home Furnishings and Equipment	Medical Care	Auto Transportation	Nonauto Transportation
Edwards (1932)	Less	Less	More	More	Less	-	-[b]	-
Sterner (1943)	Less	More[a]	More	Less	Less	Less	-[b]	-
Bureau of Labor Statistics								
Detroit[c] (1949)	Less	Less	More	More	More	Less	Less	More
Houston[c] (1949)	Less	Less	Less	More	Less	Less	Less	More
Washington (undated)	More	More	More	Less	Less	Less	Less	More
Memphis[d] (1951)	Less	Less	More	Less	Mixed	Less	Less	More
Friend and Kravis (1957)	Less	Less	More	Less	More	Less	Less	More
Fact Finders (1953)	Less	-	-	-	-	-	-	-

Source: Alexis (1962, p. 28).
[a]In Southern villages there was no difference.
[b]Edwards and Sterner discuss transportation, but do not make a breakdown by auto and nonauto.
[c]See Humes (1949).
[d]See Ruark and Mulrany.

graphic variations than by purely 'racial' influences" (p. 629). Nonetheless, they concluded that

> Marketers who assume that product buying in Negro households is roughly a match for that in white families of similar economic circumstances are far from correct. A combination of societal constraints; cultural traditions; and differences in values, preferences, and psychological needs have led Negroes. . .to vary their expenditures across different products and, probably, brands compared with whites (p. 630).

In reviewing Table 2 from their study, Stafford, Cox, and Higginbotham (1968) would remind the reader "that the indications in this study are that the Negro market is not completely homogeneous [because] there has been increasing economic and cultural stratification within the Negro community which, among other things, has led to internal consumption-pattern variations" (footnote 16, p. 630).

Studies of the type conducted by Stafford and his colleagues and reported on by Alexis are numerous[10] and of mixed quality. They have sparked debate over the effect of relative income on saving behavior, the importance of mobility, and so forth. Nonetheless, there are two major points of agreement, at least among the better pieces of research, that are central to this paper: (1) there is a Negro market, and (2) there is great uncertainty over the question of whether blacks in the United States comprise a distinct subculture. Although data such as those presented in Table 2 suggest some interesting differences in expenditures for blacks and whites of the same income, in general it could be argued that blacks represent an identifiable market because of their general low income and because of their geographical concentration in the inner cities, not because of race per se. As early as 1962, Sawyer argued (based on a regression analysis of black-white consumption data from large cities in the north) that

> Although the data examined here do not rule race out as a factor in the determination of consumption patterns, they cast such serious reflections on the hypothesis as to make it, with all charity, useless. There are too many uncontrolled variables to warrant the conclusion that race alone is responsible for the difference in consumption patterns. It has become clear in this study that the concept of race as a factor in the statistical analyses of group economic behavior, such as in the assessment of so-called Negro-white savings and consumption patterns, has no more validity than left-handedness, eye pigmentation, or height (p. 220).

[10]For surveys of this literature, see Alexis (1962), Bauer and Cunningham (1970a), and Bauer and Cunningham (1970b, pp. 1-28), and Kindel (1970, pp. 26-59). For studies of consumption patterns, see Humes (1949), Edwards (1932), Friend and Kravis (1957), Brimmer (1964), Akers (1968), Feldman and Star (1968), Larson (1968), and King and De Manche (1969).

TABLE 2. Percentage of Negroes and Whites Who Had Recently Purchased or Who Owned Various Household Products

| | Annual Family Income ($) | | | | | | | |
| Products | Less than 3,000 | | 3000-5999 | | 6000-7999 | | 8000 or more | |
	Whites	Negroes	Whites	Negroes	Whites	Negroes	Whites	Negroes
Food products[a]								
Butter	6.6	23.3	8.0	31.2	7.7	26.9	14.1	45.4
Margarine	58.3	61.6	63.6	72.7	69.8	57.7	69.5	81.8
Frozen vegetables[b]	30.5	31.4	28.0	50.6	39.6	34.6	47.1	54.6
Canned vegetables[c]	20.5	35.6	35.6	44.5	37.9	40.4	40.6	43.2
Dietary soft drinks	7.3	17.4	11.9	23.4	20.8	23.1	25.5	13.6
Nondietary soft drinks	26.5	60.5	55.5	71.4	62.4	23.1	67.1	45.4
Liquor								
All respondents[d]	15.2	26.7	29.7	39.0	39.3	46.2	56.5	54.6
Scotch[e]	3.3	9.3	4.2	22.1	7.7	34.6	19.7	27.3
Bourbon[e]	7.3	15.1	20.3	23.4	29.2	7.7	40.9	40.9
Personal hygiene products[f]								
Shampoo	42.4	41.9	59.3	52.0	74.5	65.4	72.6	50.0
Deodorant	39.7	65.1	56.8	79.2	74.5	92.3	76.6	81.8
Toothpaste	48.3	76.7	75.0	89.6	86.9	88.5	89.1	86.4
Mouthwash	43.7	61.6	58.5	75.3	56.7	88.5	63.5	86.4
Disinfectants	52.3	69.8	56.4	80.5	70.1	61.5	68.6	86.4
Home appliances[g]								
Auto. washing machine	47.4	19.8	57.6	29.9	78.6	50.0	85.5	72.7
Auto. clothes dryer	12.6	5.8	16.5	7.8	34.2	15.4	54.9	27.3
Auto. dishwasher	2.0	-	5.5	-	14.1	3.8	33.8	-
Black-and-white television	87.4	91.8	89.5	98.7	83.7[h]	97.9[h]	-	-
Color television	3.3	0.6	5.7	1.9	24.3[h]	6.2[h]	-	-
Home ownership								
Own home	68.3	39.5	49.4	57.1	70.8	73.0	81.5	77.3

Source: Stafford, Cox, and Higgenbottom (1968, pp. 626-627).

[a]Purchased within the past 7 days. [b]Includes all types of frozen vegetables. [c]Includes canned corn, peas, green beans, and tomatoes. [d]Percentage of total respondents purchasing some alcoholic beverages within past 12 months. [e]Percentage of Scotch and Bourbon purchases among total respondents. [f]Purchased within past 30 days. [g]Percentage "having" in the home. [h]Last two income classes were combined because of small number of respondents.

498

However interesting it may be, therefore, to compare black-white consumption patterns for men's shoes, Scotch whiskey, automobiles, and the like they do not deal with the difficult question—"Why?" It is an attempt to deal with this question that insights may be gained into the existence and nature of a black subculture.

4. Beyond "Nose Counting." In commenting on his analysis of black consumers in 1961, Bullock noted the limitations of the extant research. "We sought help from existing literature on the Negro market, but found none. Principally all of this literature consists of 'nose-counting' surveys that simply supply facts on population, purchasing power, brand preferences, and, occasionally, accessibility to advertising media" (1961a, p. 91). He also noted that "Although surveys like these identified brands that were momentarily most popular among Negroes, they still failed to meet the problem of '*why*' . . ." (1961a, p. 91).

Unfortunately, Bullock's criticism of the literature continued to be valid. Most of the subsequent research emphasized patterns of shopping and consumption, brand preferences, media utilization and the like with relatively few explanations attempted for the underlying causes of this behavior. Whereas most of the researchers who did comparative analyses of black and white consumers held income reasonably constant, too little attention was paid to the historical, social, and psychological context, the structural characteristics of the respective marketplaces utilized, or the possible differences in values. Bullock made an important beginning in attempting to deal with certain of these issues. His analysis focused on "(1) the needs of both Negroes and Whites to 'belong'— albeit in different ways—and how each race trades to 'belong'; and (2) how insecurities of both races influence their behavior as consumers, and how in each case the consumer trades money and credit for security" (1961a, p. 93).

The study was conducted in Southern cities, principally Houston, but including Atlanta, Birmingham, Memphis, and New Orleans. The sample size was 1643 (1106 blacks and 537 whites) representing a variety of socioeconomic classes. Depth interviews were conducted with 300 respondents (200 blacks and 100 whites). This group of 300 also completed the Minnesota Multiphasic Personality Inventory and a Thematic Apperception Test.

Bullock found what he felt were important differences between whites and blacks in their need to belong and their need for security—differences that would influence consumer behavior. He found that blacks had a stronger need to belong, which he attributed to the tradition of discrimination and rejection by the dominant society coupled with the resultant self-hatred of blacks. "*Both* races feel the pressure to define all things white as 'good' and all things black as 'bad,' and from this contrast conception grows the first significant motivational aspect of racial segregation" (1961a, p. 94). Thus Bullock suggested that blacks and whites enter the marketplace with considerably different self-images, which leads to the following contrast:

Negroes want group identification; whites, feeling that they already have this, want group distinction. More specifically, Negroes want to be identified with the general American society and all its peoples, while whites want to remain generally acceptable but particularly exclusive (1961a, p. 93).

Bullock also found that the need for security helped to explain contrasts in the consumer behavior of the two races. "Some degree of insecurity seems to grow directly out of their respective social-cultural settings, and additional anxieties are apparently fostered by the goal blockages which they encounter in their pursuits of belongingness" (1961a, p. 96). Bullock traced the insecurities of blacks to the instability of their family life, which caused many black children to "enter their adult life with personalities already twisted by the insecurities from which they suffer" (1961a, p. 97). He found that blacks had higher test scores on the MMPI in tendencies toward suspiciousness, oversensitivity, and feelings that people were against them or even out to injure them. The study found that the principal fear of white consumers was their ability to keep up or face the threat of falling down a rung on the social-class ladder. The remainder of the Bullock article and a subsequent piece (1961b) were devoted to an analysis of how these factors influenced the consumer behavior of blacks and whites with respect to credit buying, department-store shopping, salesmen relationships, product attitudes, name brands, and advertising.

The validity of these specific analyses may well be limited when viewed more than a decade later (the data were collected in 1959). It would be important to measure to what extent the black revolution of the 1960s altered blacks' need to belong and need for security. To what extent, for example, were "black is beautiful" and the "natural look" manifestations of profound changes in values related to the need to emulate and belong to the dominant society? Furthermore, not all the limitations of Bullock's research were related to timeliness. A question must be raised about the representativeness of Southern urban blacks and whites. Bullock argued that the findings were generally applicable to Northerners as well as Southerners because any regional differences would be a matter of degree rather than kind. An especially important limitation was the absence of subclassifications by socioeconomic class.[11] Thus the analysis assumed considerable homogeneity within the racial categories. And yet, most of the survey data from earlier studies revealed important differences based on socioeconomic status within racial groups. In spite of whatever methodological problems might exist, the Bullock research established a valuable framework for viewing the consumer behavior of blacks and whites. It was a lead that too few researchers followed.

[11]Though in most cases the findings are not related specifically to consumer behavior, there is a considerable body of literature treating regional and social-class differences among blacks. For example, see Du Bois (1899), Dollard (1937), Lewis (1955), Frazier (1962), Killian and Grigg (1962), Glenn (1963), Pettigrew (1964), and Pinkney (1969).

The basic issue continued to be the question of the extent to which blacks shared the value system of the dominant society and behaved accordingly in the marketplace, given the limitations of economic resources. In short, were subcultural differences demonstrated in the consumer behavior of blacks? According to Bauer, Cunningham, and Wortzel (1965), because of the important symbolic role products and services play in the American culture, the acquisition of these goods and services can be used by blacks to establish their status within society. After noting that the relatively low income status of blacks is the major determinant of their consumer behavior, Bauer, Cunningham, and Wortzel stated their hypothesis: "*the basic dilemma of Negroes is whether to strive against odds to attain these middle-class values (and the goods which come with them), or to give in and live without most of them*" (1965, p. 2).[12] The principal bases for the testing of the hypothesis were a survey of women's shopping practices in New York and Cleveland (Rich and Portis, 1963), and a proprietary study of male Scotch whiskey buyers in Northern urban areas.

Bauer and his associates assumed that blacks shared the dominant society's values. "Certainly it is the consensus of both Negro and white students of the American Negro that Negroes have accepted white middle-class values" (1965, p. 2). They hypothesized that in response to the dilemma stated above, blacks could be segmented into "strivers" (those who make the effort to strive against odds in order to obtain material goods which reflect middle-class values) and "nonstrivers" (those who "give in and live more for the moment") (1965, p. 3). As surrogates for striving they assumed "that Negro women who are high on the scale of fashion-consciousness and Negro men who report they are regular Scotch drinkers are 'strivers' and that others are 'nonstrivers' " (1965, p. 3).

The basic findings of the study were that "[t]he Negro women 'strivers' [compared with white women strivers] are more committed to goods of high symbolic value , , ., more involved with the world outside the family, and show more concern over making shopping decisions" (1965, p. 4). Their conclusions concerning the men were that "Negroes are more likely than whites to report having an established brand preference, and at least as likely to specify a particular brand of Scotch when ordering a drink" (p. 4). They concluded that

> Compared with whites, Negroes show more concern, more anxiety, and more ambivalence over spending money for material goods . . . While some Negroes will become increasingly secure in their status, it is probable that a growing proportion will become strivers as their expectations rise to the point where they work for a full place in

---

[12]It would have been more accurate to have stated that "the basic dilemma of Negroes is whether to strive against odds to attain material symbols of middle-class values, or to give in and live without most of them." Since the authors assumed that blacks and whites share the same values, it would be incorrect to suggest that they were striving to *attain* those values. Rather it would be hypothesized that they were seeking to act out those values in the marketplace by acquiring the symbols of those values.

American life. The proportion of nonstrivers will probably decrease as aspirations rise in general. But until Negroes' opportunities are brought in line with their aspirations, the basic dilemma we have discussed will remain (p. 6).

In an extension of this effort to explain differences in the consumer behavior of blacks and whites with comparable incomes, Bauer and Cunningham (1970b) conducted a study in Baltimore in 1967. The subjects of the study were 200 white and 200 black women. Of the respondents, 96 blacks and 71 whites had incomes of less than $7000 (this income level was used to divide the groups into "high" and "low" income categories). The purpose of the Baltimore study was to analyze two propositions.

> First, if the distinction between striving and nonstriving reflects the sort of basic dilemma for the Negro that we have suggested, then any measure of this phenomenon ought to be associated with greater differences in the market behavior of Negroes than of whites. Second, if the above is true, then the strivers ought to behave more like whites than the nonstrivers (1970b, pp. 34-35).

Rather than rely on fashion consciousness and regularity of Scotch consumption as indicators of striving,[13] Bauer and Cunningham constructed their own index of striving based on responses to four questions contained on their data collection instrument. Even though the median income of blacks in the sample was over $7000, only 39 percent fell into the striver category versus 76 percent of the white women. After classifying respondents as strivers or nonstrivers, questions were asked about a variety of products. The following is an example of the kinds of questions asked.

> In a series of questions, we asked respondents which of two paired items they would prefer over another: a Chevrolet sedan over a Chevrolet convertible; a Lincoln over a Cadillac; a color television set over a vacation; and a vacuum cleaner over new clothes for oneself. Each of these pairings presents one of the issues traditionally associated with the Negro market, an emphasis on display (sedan vs. convertible) and an emphasis on immediate gratification (a vacation) versus something more enduring (color television) (p. 45).

The answers to these questions are shown in Table 3. Bauer and Cunningham note that, with the exception of the Lincoln versus Cadillac question, there are very few differences between white strivers and nonstrivers. However, among

---

[13]Bauer and Cunningham noted in the appendix to their study (1970b, pp. 62-66) the serious limitations of using fashion consciousness as an index of striving. Their Baltimore data presented conflicting evidence which indicated "that fashion consciousness . . . involved two things that are not associated with striving: (1) a desire for display, and (2) possibly a disposition to experience status vicariously, by reading about fashion even though one does not necessarily implement one's desires . . ." (p. 63).

blacks there are greater differences between the two subclassifications. In fact, "[f]rom 79 unselected dependent variables, 48 showed significant differences (at the .15 level) between black strivers and nonstrivers, compared to 14 statistically significant variables for whites" (p. 62).

In sum, Bauer and Cunningham found that "[s]triving involves acceptance of values that are more characteristic of the White community" (p. 62). In addition, the basic dilemma of Negroes is reflected in the greater differences among black strivers and nonstrivers than in their white counterparts. Finally, they found that the market behavior and attitudes of black strivers were closer to those of whites.

In their Chicago-based study, Feldman and Star (1968) (see Table 4) utilized the Bauer-Cunningham "dilemma" in the analysis of the data and concluded that

> We have seen that in only 2 of 11 aspects of shopping behavior was a statistically significant difference observed between whites and Negroes with incomes of $5,000 or more. It is reasonable to infer that Negroes with this level of income tend to resolve their dilemma in favor of middle class values because the level of their income is high enough to permit realistic aspirations for middle class status .... On the other hand, there do appear to be substantial differences between white and Negro shopping behavior for those with incomes less than $5,000, particularly with respect to store shopping behavior. For many Negroes at this level of income, aspiration to the middle class values of the dominant white culture is unrealistic and they have resolved the dilemma (if they ever explicitly confronted it) by engaging in nonstriving be-

TABLE 3.   **Choices among Pairs of Items**

A. Income

Choices	Negro		White	
	High	*Low*	*High*	*Low*
Sedan over convertible	64%[a]	73	86	85
Lincoln over Cadillac	39	42	42	43
Color TV over vacation	16	27	23	35
Vacuum cleaner over clothes	15	11	12	17
N =	(104)	(96)	(124)	(71)

B. Striver Index	Negro		White	
Choices	*Striver*	*Nonstriver*	*Striver*	*Nonstriver*
Sedan over convertible	83	59	86	84
Lincoln over Cadillac	48	36	46	33
Color TV over vacation	37	12	25	33
Vacuum cleaner over clothes	18	10	15	10
N =	(78)	(122)	(149)	(49)

Source: Bauer and Cunningham (1970, p. 46).

[a] Read 64% of high-income Negroes would prefer a sedan over a convertible.

TABLE 4. Pattern of Statistical Significance, Comparison of Whites and Blacks

	Family Income				
	All Respondents	0-2999	3000-4999	5000-6999	7000-9999
Credit at major department store	S[a]	-	-	-	-
Use of phone or mail order	S	S	-	-	-
Catalog purchasers	S	S	-	-	-
Shopping travel time	—	-	-	-	-
Drive to shop	S	-	S	-	-
Number of shopping centers	S	S	S	-	-
Frequency of shopping trips	S	-	-	S	-
Frequency of discount store shopping trips	—	-	S	-	-
Visits to state street department stores	S	-	S	-	-b
shopping attitudes	S	-	S	-	S
Discount vs. department stores	S	-	-	-	-b

Source: Feldman and Star (1968, p. 225).
[a]"S" indicates statistically significant difference beyond $p = .05$.
[b] Significance not testable; expected frequency < 5.

havior. In addition, to the extent that Negroes at the lower levels of income are "first generation" urban immigrants with many of the consumption patterns of the southern rural culture of their origin, these differences in behavior would be exacerbated (p. 226).[14]

Fundamental to the Bauer-Cunningham dilemma is the concept of aspirations and its relationship to product symbolism. In essence, the thrust of their argument is that the behavior of blacks in the marketplace can be explained, at least in part, by classifying black along these two dimensions. In a study of reference-group behavior and relative deprivation Sommers and Bruce (1968) used basically the same dimensions but a quite different methodology in an analysis of black and white housewives. According to Sommers and Bruce, "Those products which individuals use and prefer . . . symbolize their activities (real or idealized) and present an aspect of the culture or subculture to which they belong" (1968, p. 631). They utilized the Q-sort methodology in their analysis of 152 housewives in Austin, Texas (see Table 5 for a profile of the respondents). In explaining the research design, Sommers and Bruce noted that

A person or social category may be relatively deprived: (1) in comparison with an Ideal, however established, or (2) in comparison with some

[14]Feldman and Star, like Bauer and Cunningham, also imply that people go shopping for values, or at least they aspire to them. Furthermore, it should be noted that Bauer and Cunningham found *no* correlation of striving with income among black women in Baltimore in the $5000-$9000 income range.

other reference individual or group. Relative deprivation may be measured: (1) by the disparity between the self-conceptions of different social categories (potential reference points). Products are used to obtain such measurements in this design. Subjects are asked to rank products in a given set on two bases: the first to describe themselves on a current basis (the Self) and the second to describe or symbolize themselves on a future basis (the Ideal). Comparisons then made among the various Selves and Ideals serve to identify reference points and to measure relative deprivation (1968, p. 632).

TABLE 5. **Socioeconomic Characteristics of Subjects**

Characteristics	Lower Stratum		Middle Stratum	
	Black	White	Black	White
Age (mean) in years	34.7	35.0	36.6	35.2
Number of children (mean)	3.1	2.6	3.3	2.8
Husband's occupation	Laborers and other unskilled workers	Craftsman, foreman, and kindred workers	Operative and kindred workers	Sales worker, official, and proprietor
Annual family income ($)	3000-4000	5000-6000	5000-6000	7000-8000

Source. Sommers and Bruce (1968, p. 633).

Therefore, each of the women was presented with a deck of 38 cards with the name of a household product (deodorant, dresses, refrigerator, magazines, books, and so forth) on each card. In the process of examining the deck the housewife was asked to make two separate decks, one for products that she used or owned and one for products that she did not use or own. She was then instructed to select the item from the first deck (items owned or used) that best described her and place it on position 1 of a sorting board containing 38 positions. She was then instructed to continue this process until the first deck had been exhausted. Thus the owned or used products were ranked in decreasing order of their descriptive power. The same procedure was then followed for the deck of products not owned or used. Each of the housewives also sorted the same products with the Ideal frame of reference in mind.

Based on the sorts of the 38 products, eight product profiles were established. These profiles "allow for comparisons between blacks (B) and whites (W) representing 'lower' (L) and 'middle' (M) strata, and between blacks and whites at the two levels and for the frames of reference Self (S) and Ideal (I)" (p. 635). Correlations (r) between pairs are shown in Table 6.

The correlation matrix allows for an almost endless series of comparisons,

TABLE 6. Correlation Matrix of Black and White Self and Ideal Product Arrays by Strata

	BLS	BMS	WLS	WMS	BLI	BMI	WLI	WMI
BLS	1.00							
BMS	.92	1.00						
WLS	.75	.77	1.00					
WMS	.80	.77	.76	1.00				
BLI	.88	.81	.55	.61	1.00			
BMI	.83	.83	.62	.71	.87	1.00		
WLI	.45	.26	.20	.30	.60	.54	1.00	
WMI	.57	.36	.31	.48	.61	.54	.76	1.00

Source: Sommers and Bruce (1968, p. 639).

but there is one set of relationships that is of particular interest. First, both black strata experienced deprivation at nearly the same low level: r (BLS:BLI) = .88 and r (BMS:BMI) = .83. Sommers and Bruce suggested that these high correlations indicated a very low need for achievement "for both of the Black strata insofar as this need is expressed and measured by the products in the test" (p. 639).[15] This is to be contrasted with whites of both strata who experienced much greater deprivation; r (WLS:WLI) = .20 and r (WMS:WMI) = .48 and thus suggests a greater need for achievement.[16] Sommers and Bruce also indicated that "the 'middle' stratum White seems to be a more important reference point for the 'middle' stratum Black than for the 'lower' stratum Black . . ." (p. 639).

There is little point in trying to generalize widely on the findings of these studies. For one reason, the studies were largely exploratory in nature. In addition, they were conducted in different places, at different times, and used substantially different methodologies and sample frames. It would have been of interest, for example, had Sommers and Bruce used the Bauer and Cunningham index of striving as another means of classifying their subjects. In turn, the Q-sort would have been an interesting tool for Bullock as well as Bauer and his associates. Nevertheless, one finding which appears to be consistent among these

[15]For a contrasting view see Gottlieb and Campbell (1968).

[16]When tested for statistical significance the differences were as follows: r(WMS:WMI) = .48 - r(BMS:BMI) = .83 = .45 (p = .03); and r(WLS:WLI) = .20 - r(BLS:BLI) = .88 = .68 (p = .002). These are rather startling findings. On the surface these data say that blacks see much more congruence between what they are and what they would like to be than do whites. To suggest that they have a lower need for achievement may be to put a "white" interpretation on the data.

studies was that higher-income (Feldman and Star), higher-status (Bullock), middle-stratum (Sommers and Bruce), and striving (Bauer, Cunningham, and Wortzel) blacks behave increasingly like their white counterparts. As Sommers and Bruce note, "This finding is consistent with Pettigrew's observation that as status increases, the black community moves toward the white community rather than away from it" (p. 640).

Unfortunately, these limited research efforts represent much of what is known about the *whys* of black consumer behavior. As has been discussed, much of the research on black consumers has focused on patterns of behavior (buying more Scotch and deodorant soaps, spending less on automobile transportation than whites with comparable incomes, and so forth). The other major research focus has been the characteristics and performance of the market systems serving low-income blacks.[17] In addition, there are data on the interest of blacks in fashion (Portis, 1966), information on attitudes toward and purchases of clothing (Kindel, 1970), shopping patterns in mass merchandising stores (Capitman, 1971), and a host of studies related to the use of blacks in advertising.[18] Thus until additional studies are undertaken that analyze the values and underlying motivations of blacks and other minority groups, the issue of the existence of subcultures and their behavior in the marketplace will continue to be unresolved.

MARKETING RESEARCH AND SUBCULTURES

Most of the studies discussed were survey based, and, as has been noted, only a few attempted to analyze the underlying motivations of the black consumers. Such studies have helped to define the parameters of the problem and to suggest hypotheses. It has also been seen that there is a need for more studies to utilize the kinds of in-depth techniques employed in Bullock's research. There are other methodologies that should be employed as well.

One approach that holds promise might be termed cross-subcultural research (Robertson, Dalrymple, and Yoshino, 1968). In a sense, most of the studies noted previously were comparative in nature. That is, they involved comparisons of blacks and whites—generally of similar economic status. However, subcultural comparisons involving more than two groups are relatively rare, and yet they add an important dimension to the study of subcultures. Alexander (1958) in a

[17]In addition to those studies cited earlier, see Groom (1966), Dixon and McLaughlin (1968, 1971), Marcus (1969), Wall (1969), Endo (1970), and Sexton (1971a, b).

[18]Most of these studies treat the issue of the frequency of appearance of black models in advertisements, the status of the roles portrayed, and/or the reaction of blacks and whites to integrated advertising. See Barban and Cundiff (1964); Petrof (1968); Kassarjian (1969, 1971); Cagley and Cardoza (1970); K. Cox (1970); Dominic and Greenberg (1970); Gould, Sigband, and Zoerner (1970); Guest (1970); Roeder (1970); Stafford, Birdwell, and Van Tassel (1970); and Wheatley (1971).

comparative study of black, Puerto Rican, Jewish, and Italian consumers found important differences in food-product adoption among the groups. Based on a study of 150 West Los Angeles area consumers (Japanese-American, black, and white), Robertson, Dalrymple, and Yoshino (1968) concluded that there was some correlation between subcultures and innovativeness for various product categories. Furthermore, they suggested that "the ability to reach a subculture is negatively related to its assimilation level in the broad mix of American society" (p. 75). Robertson and his associates argued strongly for cross-subcultural research as a means of gaining greater understanding of possible subcultures.

Sturdivant (1971) conducted a study of low-income Mexican-American, black, and Anglo-white residents of two small towns (195 families in Paso Robles, California, and Gonzales, Texas). On the basis of the findings in the two towns, an attempt was made to determine the extent to which there were consistencies in attitudes and behavior *within* subgroups *between* the two towns. In short, did the Mexican-Americans in Gonzales behave like their counterparts in Paso Robles or were there significant differences? Each ethnic group was analyzed for degree of uniformity on eight factors (see Table 7). The findings suggest that within the categories analyzed behavior was least consistent between blacks in the two towns. Chicanos, by contrast, were different at a level of statistical significance in only two of the eight categories and Anglo-whites in only one of the eight. A middle-income control group, which was comprised entirely of Anglo-whites, behaved as homogeneously as the Mexican-Americans. These findings might suggest the existence of better-defined cultures for the Chicanos and Anglo-whites than for the blacks.

Cross-subcultural research offers two principal advantages. In the first place, such studies broaden the range of enquiry beyond whites and blacks to include such groups as Japanese-Americans, Puerto Ricans, and Mexican-Americans. Second, they offer the basis for generating hypotheses to be tested by in-depth research techniques.[19]

Ironically, the method that probably offers the greatest promise for understanding consumer behavior within subcultures is ethnography, a method which has had only the most limited application in the study of consumers. Given the wide range of unanswered questions about the consumer behavior of blacks, Chicanos, Indians, Japanese-Americans and other such groups, ethnographic research should be undertaken. According to Valentine, ethnography "is essentially an exploratory enterprise seeking to chart extensive unknowns" (p. 174). Often described under the rubric of participant observation, the approach calls for prolonged and extensive involvement with the group under study. In some cases the researcher lives in the community (Gans and his study of the West Enders in Boston) or in other cases the researcher lives elsewhere but

---

[19]For an example of this kind of research on an international scale, see Katona, Strumpel, and Zahn (1971).

TABLE 7. Comparative Purchasing Practices and Attitudes in Gonzales, Texas, and Paso Robles, California, by Subcultural Classification

	Television Ownership	Use of Credit in Television Purchase	Washing Machine Ownership	Use of Credit in Washing Machine Purchase	Use of Credit in Clothing Purchases	Attitudes Toward the Use of Credit	Total Current Debt ($500 or More vs. $499 or Less)	Total Savings ($101 or More vs. $100 or Less)
Low-income groups								
Negro	p = .57	p = .43	p = .01[a]	p = .40	p = .08[b]	p = .01[a]	p = .01[a]	p = .04[a]
Mexican-American	p = .99	p = .01[a]	p = .39	p = .17	p = .35	p = .40	p = .10[b]	p = .25
Anglo-white	p = .46	p = .03[a]	p = .42	p = .47	p = .55	p = .15	p = .20	p = .52
Middle-income groups	p = .38	p = .24	p = .01[a]	p = .54	p = .46	p = .44	p = .02[a]	p = .50
Total middle-income vs. total low-income	p = .28	p = .02[a]	p = .08[b]	p = .09[b]	p = .01[a]	p = .06[b]	p = .27	p = .01[a]

Source: Sturdivant (1971).

[a]Significant at alpha level of $p \leqslant .05$.

[b]Significant at alpha level of $p \leqslant .10$.

spends many hours each day and many months "visiting" in the area (Liebow in his study of the streetcorner men in Washington, D.C.). Whatever the residential status of the researcher, the objective is to experience the way of life of the subjects and to analyze dispassionately their culture or subculture. Thus, in addition to treating the kinds of issues focused on by survey research, the ethnographer attempts to gain a knowledge of the *processes* by which the consumer acts out his role.

In an appendix to *The Urban Villagers,* Gans (1962) offers what is perhaps the best description available of this research method. In part, he describes six major approaches used in his study.

> 1. *Use of the West End's facilities.* I lived in the area, and used its stores, services, institutions, and other facilities as much as possible. This enabled me to observe my own and other people's behavior as residents of the area.
> 2. *Attendance at meetings, gatherings, and public places.* I attended as many public meetings and gatherings as I could find, mostly as an observant spectator. I also visited area shops and taverns in this role.
> 3. *Informal visiting with neighbors and friends.* My wife and I became friendly with our neighbors and other West Enders, spending much time with them in social activities and conversations that provided valuable data.
> 4. *Formal and informal interviewing of community functionnaires.* I interviewed at least one person in all of the area's agencies and institutions—talking with directors, staff members, officers, and active people in settlement houses, church groups, and other voluntary organizations. I also talked with principals, ministers, social workers, political leaders, government officials—especially those concerned with redevelopment—and store owners.
> 5. *Use of informants.* Some of the people I interviewed became informants, who kept me up to date on those phases of West End life with which they were familiar.
> 6. *Observation.* I kept my eyes and ears open at all times, trying to learn something about as many phases of West End life as possible, and also looking for unexpected leads and ideas on subjects in which I was especially interested (pp. 337-38).

The data collected from these various approaches were kept in a diary of field notes and became the basis for *The Urban Villagers.*

Engel, Kollat, and Blackwell (1968) were early supporters for ethnographic research in consumer behavior. They did note that the approach had two major weaknesses: "(1) they usually do not have a systematic sampling plan, and (2) the presence of the observer as a participant may introduce changes into the culture" (pp. 238-39). They also noted that participant observation is "sometimes criticised for its lack of objectivity and comprehensiveness" (p. 239). In spite of these problems, Engel, Kollat, and Blackwell concluded that "what the anthropologist sacrifices in methodological rigor in his participant-observer field study he makes up for in an approach that is often richer in content, more ramified, and more pertinent to behavior in everyday life settings" (p. 239).

Since anthropologists and sociologists who have conducted ethnographic studies of poor people and minorities in the United States have paid little or no attention to their role as consumers, the extant research data are thin. For example, sociologist David Schulz spent over three years studying ten families in a high-rise, segregated housing project in St. Louis and, although his book *Coming Up Black* (1969) is a fascinating account of patterns of socialization, one gets only glimpses of the people as consumers. At one point Schulz explained the economic performance of the Ethyl Perry household.

> Boyfriends are indispensable. Ethyl remarks: "When I get through paying the house rent and two or three bills—insurance maybe—I don't have enough money left for food . . . My friend buys my groceries every week and things like that. And if I need any extra money, I ask him for it and he'll give it to me." The style of life reflected in the furnishings of the Perry apartment and the newness of the children's clothes testify to Ethyl's skillful manipulation of a series of boyfriends, one of whom bought over half her furniture in addition to her weekly food (1969, p. 11).

In another account he noted the relationship between "face saving" and one's role as a consumer.

> Another important function of the lie in the ghetto is "face saving." The Cadillac, the forty-five dollar shoes, the one hundred and twenty dollar suit tell the world, "I'm a success and I've been around," although the reality is ordinarily quite grim. Gerald Buchanan carried this off quite well in a small way when he remarked at a restaurant that he had tasted all of the twelve or thirteen wines on the wine list except the ruby port which he selected (pp. 79-80).

These insights into the world of the lower-class urban black coupled with Liebow's (1967) confession that when he began his field work he "was not fluent in their language" (p. 252) should underline the importance of more profound approaches to this complex behavior than can be gained from surveys. At the very least, it should signal a warning against ready acceptance of many of the easy generalizations concerning low-income black consumers. And given the heterogeneity of the black population (social classes, ages, locations, and the like), references to "the black consumer" should be seen as a form of shorthand at best and simplemindedness at worst.

There are groups for which the information on consumer behavior is even more sparse. Mexican-Americans are of importance not only because they are the second most populous minority group in the country, but because of their remarkably slow rate of assimilation. The very extensive study by Grebler,

Moore, and Guzman (1970) did not contain any reference to consumer-related topics in its index.[20] Some studies of Mexican-Americans as consumers have been undertaken. Hodges (1969) undertook a study of low- and medium-socioeconomic members of the Mexican-American community in San Antonio and patterned his research after the work of Sommers and Bruce (1968). The purpose of the study was to determine whether or not the degree of acculturation of the participating housewives influenced their perception of product meaning. The two studies by Sturdivant (1969b, 1971) were based on surveys and were quite preliminary and tentative. When it is recognized that even less is known about Puerto Ricans and that the low-income Anglo-white has been largely ignored, it is safe to conclude that the state of the art in subculture theory as it applies to marketing to low-income and minority groups is at a primitive stage of development.

CONCLUSION

This chapter has attempted to establish the concept of culture—or more precisely, subculture—as the appropriate framework for viewing the behavior of low-income and minority consumers in the United States. In using this framework it has been suggested that the crucial elements of the analysis revolve around the processes of acculturation and assimilation as well as social-class position. In short, the relative distinctiveness of the marketplace behavior of poor people or minority groups will be associated with the degree to which they have internalized the values of the dominant society (acculturation) and the extent to which they have been accepted as full participants in the society (assimilation). Thus, even though a group may be highly acculturated, its members may not be assimilated, and many aspects of their lives, including their consumer behavior, may be a function of the resultant adaptive behavior. Hence the fundamental issue is whether or not the group in question shares the values of the dominant society or whether the group has its own rather distinct and reinforcing value system.

One pitfall in conducting this kind of analysis is the propensity to focus on differences rather than the more numerous shared values. From this standpoint the concept of social class represents an important perspective to maintain in viewing the behavior of poor people and minorities. Few people have difficulty in understanding that a society which has many shared values may nevertheless be structured on a hierarchial basis related to status and power. In many respects, therefore, behavior may well be more closely related to social class than

---

[20]The book by Grebler, Moore, and Guzman, *The Mexican-American People* (1970), contains an extensive bibliography. For sharp criticisms of the book by leading Mexican-American scholars see Alvarez (1971), Burma (1971), Chavarria (1971), Glenn (1971), and Rocco (1971).

to the fact that the family happens to be second-generation Italian-American or black.

The brief review of the literature on the consumer behavior of blacks revealed that only a relatively limited number of studies had been undertaken which dealt with issues of values and underlying motivations. Most of the studies have been based on surveys of shopping and buying patterns with efforts to contrast those patterns with whites of comparable incomes. Whether the differences revealed by such studies are a function of local conditions, temporary adaptive behavior, or deeply rooted values is generally ignored. Progress in gaining insights into such questions probably will not be made until in-depth studies utilizing ethnographic or participant-observation techniques are undertaken.

Whereas it might be argued that differences in consumer behavior of blacks are largely a function of social-class position (with the least understood being the lower-class blacks, as is true of any segment of the society), so little is known about such groups as Mexican-Americans and Puerto Ricans that such an argument would be built on a shaky foundation. The proximity to the mother culture, the distinct language, and the complex role of the Catholic religion in their lives suggest that survey data simply will not suffice in coming to an understanding of their behavior in the marketplace.

The need to conduct the kinds of research that will increase the understanding of the poor and racial and ethnic minorities should be clear. The purpose is not to find ways to get them to respond uniformly to appeals to buy a given brand of soap or cigarettes, but rather to develop greater appreciation for their uniqueness and to serve them better in the marketplace.

REFERENCES

Akers, F. C., "Negro and White Auto-Buying Behavior," *Journal of Marketing Research,* 5 (August 1968), 283-89.

Alexander, Milton, "The Significance of Ethnic Groups in Marketing," in *Advancing Marketing Efficiency,* ed. L. H. Stockman. Chicago: American Marketing Association, 1958, 557-61.

Alexis, Marcus, "Some Negro-White Differences in Consumption," *American Journal of Economics and Sociology,* 21 (January 1962), 11-28.

Alexis, Marcus, G. H. Haines, Jr., and L. S. Simon, "Consumption Behavior of Prisoners: The Case of the Inner City Shopper," Working Paper Series No. 7012, Rochester: University of Rochester, 1970.

Alexis, Marcus, Leonard Simon, and Kenneth Smith, "Some Determinants of Food Buying Behavior," in *Empirical Foundations of Marketing,* ed. Marcus Alexis, Robert Holloway, and Robert Hancock. Chicago: Markham Publishing Company, 1969, 20-32.

Alvarez, Rodolfo, "The Unique Psycho-Historical Experience of the Mexican-American People," *Social Science Quarterly,* 52 (June 1971), 15-29.

Andreasen, A. R., "Towards a Model of Structural Dynamics in Inner City Markets." Mimeographed report, Department of Environmental Analysis and Planning, State University of New York, Buffalo, 1971.

Archibald, Katherine, "Status Orientations Among Shipyard Workers," in *Class, Status and Power,* ed. Reinhard Bendix and S. M. Lipset. New York: The Free Press, 1953, 395-403.

Arnold, D. O., *The Sociology of Subcultures.* Berkeley, Calif., Glendasary Press, 1970.

Barban, A. M., and E. W. Cundiff, "Negro and White Responses to Advertising Stimuli," *Journal of Marketing Research,* 1 (November 1964), 53-56.

Bauer, R. A., and S. M. Cunningham, "The Negro Market," *Journal of Advertising Research,* 10 (April 1970a), 3-13.

Bauer, R. A., and S. M. Cunningham, *Studies in the Negro Market.* Cambridge, Mass.: Marketing Science Institute, 1970b.

Bauer, R. A., S. M. Cunningham, and L. H. Wortzel, "The Marketing Dilemma of Negroes," *Journal of Marketing,* 29 (July 1965), 1-6.

Berelson, Bernard, and G. A. Steiner, *Human Behavior: Shorter Edition.* New York: Harcourt Brace Jovanovich, Inc., 1964.

Berger, B. M., *Working-Class Suburb.* Berkeley, Calif.: University of California Press, 1960.

Berry, B. J. L., "Commercial Structure and Commercial Blight," Department of Geography Research Paper No. 85, University of Chicago, 1963.

Blauner, Robert, "Black Culture: Myth or Reality?" in *Afro-American Anthropology,* eds. N. E. Whitten, Jr., and J. F. Szwed. New York: The Free Press, 1970, 347-66.

Blumberg, Leonard, and R. R. Bell, "Urban Migration and Kinship Ties," *Social Problems,* 6 (Spring 1959), 328-33.

Boyd, H. W., Jr., and S. J. Levy, "New Dimensions in Consumer Analysis," *Harvard Business Review* (November-December 1963), 129-40.

Brimmer, A. F., "Economic Trends in the Negro Market," *Marketing Information Guide.* Washington, D.C.: U.S. Department of Commerce, May 1964.

Brogan, D. W., *The American Character.* New York: Alfred A. Knopf, Inc., 1944.

Bullock, H. A., "Consumer Motivations in Black and White—Part I," *Harvard Business Review,* 39 (May-June 1961a), 80-104.

Bullock, H. A., "Consumer Motivations in Black and White—Part II," *Harvard Business Review,* 39 (July-August 1961b), 110-24.

Bureau of the Census and Bureau of Labor Statistics, *The Social and Economic Status of Negroes in the United States.* Washington, D.C.: U.S. Department of Commerce and U.S. Department of Labor, Series P-23, No. 29, 1969.

Burma, J. H., "Another American Dilemma: Finding 'the Unknown Minority,' " *Social Science Quarterly,* 52 (June 1971), 30-34.

Cagley, J. W., and R. N. Cardoza, "White Responses to Integrated Advertising," *Journal of Advertising Research,* 10 (April 1970), 35-39.

Capitman, W. G., "Negro Shopping Patterns in Mass-Merchandising Stores." Working paper, Marketing Science Institute, Cambridge, Mass., June, 1971.

Caplovitz, David, *The Poor Pay More.* New York: The Free Press, 1967.

Chavarria, Jesus, "Professor Grebler's Book: The *Magnum Opus* of a Dying Era of Scholarship," *Social Science Quarterly,* 52 (June 1971), 11-14.

Commager, H. S., *The American Mind.* New Haven, Conn.: Yale University Press, 1959.

Cox, K. K., "Social Effects of Integrated Advertising," *Journal of Advertising Research,* 10 (April 1970), 41-44.

Cox, W. E. Jr., "A Commercial Structure Model for Depressed Neighborhoods," *Journal of Marketing,* 33 (July 1969), 1-9.

Cox, W. E. Jr., "Business Opportunities in the Inner City." Paper presented at the Conference on Improving Inner City Marketing, Buffalo, New York, June 3-6, 1970 (mimeographed).

de Tocqueville, Alexis, *Democracy in America.* New York: Random House, Inc., 1954.

Dewey, John, *Democracy and Education.* New York: The Macmillan Company, 1916.

Dixon, D. F., and D. J. McLaughlin, Jr., "Do the Inner City Poor Pay More for Food?" *Economics and Business Bulletin,* 20 (Spring 1968), 6-12.

Dixon, D. F., and D. J. McLaughlin, Jr., "Shopping Behavior, Expenditure Patterns, and Inner-City Food Prices," *Journal of Marketing Research,* 8 (February 1971), 96-99.

Dollard, John, *Caste and Class in a Southern Town.* New Haven: Yale University Press, 1937.

Dominic, J. R., and B. S. Greenberg, "Three Seasons of Blacks on Television," *Journal of Advertising Research,* 10 (April 1970), 21-27.

Dotson, Floyd, "Patterns of Voluntary Association Among Urban Working Class Families," *American Sociological Review,* 16 (October 1951), 687-93.

Draper, Hal, *The New Student Revolt.* New York: Grove Press, Inc., 1965.

Du Bois, W. E. B., *The Philadelphia Negro.* Philadelphia: University of Pennsylvania Press, 1899.

Edwards, P. K., *The Southern Urban Negro as a Consumer.* Englewood Cliffs, N.J.: Prentice-Hall, Inc., 1932.

Edwards, P. K., "Distinctive Characteristics of Urban Negro Consumption." Unpublished D.C.S. dissertation, Harvard University, 1936.

Elkins, S. M., *Slavery.* New York: The Universal Library, 1963.

Endo, Russell, "Food Stores in the Low-Income Marketplace: A Research Note," *University of Washington Journal of Sociology,* 2 (November 1970), 15-27.

Engel, J. F., D. T. Kollat, and R. D. Blackwell, *Consumer Behavior.* New York: Holt, Rinehart and Winston, Inc., 1968.

Fact Finders Incorporated, *Analysis of 525 Washington, D.C. Negro Families Who Read the Afro-American Compared with 525 White Families Living in Homes of Similar Rent or Value.* Washington, D.C.: Afro-American Newspapers, 1953.

Farber, Jerry, *The Student as Nigger.* New York: Pocket Books, Inc., 1970.

Feagin, J. R., "The Kinship Ties of Negro Urbanites," *Social Science Quarterly,* 49 (December 1968), 660-65.

Federal Trade Commission, *Economic Report on Food Chain Selling Practice in the District of Columbia and San Francisco.* Washington, D.C.: U.S. Government Printing Office, July, 1969.

Feldman, L. P., and A. D. Star, "Racial Factors in Shopping Behavior," in *A New Measure of Responsibility for Marketing,* ed. Keith Cox and Ben Enis. Chicago: American Marketing Association, 1968, 216-26.

Frazier, E. F., *Black Bourgeoisie.* New York: P. F. Collier, Inc., 1962.

Frazier, E. F., *The Negro Family in the United States* (rev. abr. ed.). Chicago: University of Chicago Press, 1966.

Friend, Irwin, and I. B. Kravis, "New Light on Consumer Markets," *Harvard Business Review,* 35 (January-February 1957), 105-16.

Gans, H. J., *The Urban Villagers.* New York: The Free Press, 1962.

Gensch, D. H., and Richard Staelin, "Making Black Retail Outlets Work," *California Management Review,* 15 (Fall 1972), 52-62.

Glazer, Nathan, and D. P. Moynihan, *Beyond the Melting Pot.* Cambridge, Mass.: MIT Press, 1963.

Glenn, N. D., "Negro Prestige Criteria: A Case Study in the Bases of Prestige," *American Journal of Sociology,* 68 (May 1963), 645-57.

Glenn, N. D., "Some Reflections on a Landmark Publication and the Literature on Mexican-Americans," *Social Science Quarterly,* 52 (June 1971), 8-10.

Glenn, N. D., and C. M. Bonjean, *Blacks in the United States.* San Francisco: Chandler Publishing Company, 1969.

Glick, I. O., and S. J. Levy, *Living with Television.* Chicago: Aldine-Atherton, Inc., 1962.

Goodman, C. S., "Do the Poor Pay More?" *Journal of Marketing,* 32 (January 1968), 18-24.

Goodman, Paul, *Growing Up Absurd.* New York: Random House, Inc., 1960.

Gordon, M. M., *Assimilation in American Life.* New York: Oxford University Press, Inc., 1964.

Gottlieb, David, and Jay Campbell, Jr., "Winners and Losers in the Race for the Good Life: A Comparison of Blacks and Whites," *Social Science Quarterly,* 49 (December 1968), 593-602.

Gould, J. W., N. B. Sigband, and C. E. Zoerner, Jr., "Black Consumer Reactions to 'Integrated' Advertising: An Exploratory Study," *Journal of Marketing,* 34 (June 1970), 20-26.

Grebler, Leo, J. W. Moore, and R. C. Guzman, *The Mexican-American People.* New York: The Free Press, 1970.

Groom, Phyllis, "Prices in Poor Neighborhoods," *Monthly Labor Review,* 89 (October 1966), 1085-90.

Guest, Lester, "How Negro Models Affect Company Image," *Journal of Advertising Research,* 10 (April 1970), 29-33.

Haines, G. H., L. S. Simon, and Marcus Alexis, "The Dynamics of Commercial Structure in Central City Areas," Working Paper Series No. 7008, Rochester: University of Rochester, 1970.

Haley, Alex, "My Furthest-Back-Person—'The African' " *The New York Times Magazine* (July 16, 1972), pp. 13-16.

Hall, E. T., *The Silent Language*. Greenwich, Conn.: Fawcett Publications, Inc., 1959.

Handlin, Oscar, *Race and Nationality in American Life*. Garden City, N.Y.: Doubleday & Company, Inc., 1957.

Herberg, Will, *Protestant, Catholic, Jew; An Essay in American Religious Sociology*. Garden City, N.Y.: Doubleday & Company, Inc., 1955.

Hodges, B. S., "Acculturation and Product Meaning." Unpublished Ph.D. dissertation, The University of Texas, 1969.

Horney, Karen, *The Neurotic Personality of Our Time*. New York: W. W. Norton & Company, Inc., 1937.

Humes, H. H., "Family Income and Expenditures in 1947," *Monthly Labor Review,* 68 (April 1949), 389-97.

Hyman, H. H., "The Value System of Different Classes," in Bendix and Lipset (1953), 426-42.

Jordan, W. D., *White over Black: American Attitudes toward the Negro, 1550-1812*. Baltimore: Penguin Books, Inc., 1969.

Kahl, J. A., *The American Class Structure*. New York: Holt, Rinehart and Winston, Inc., 1956.

Kassarjian, H. H., "The Negro and American Advertising, 1946-1965," *Journal of Marketing Research,* 6 (February 1969), 29-39.

Kassarjian, H. H., "Blacks in Advertising: A Further Comment," *Journal of Marketing Research,* 8 (August 1971), 392-93.

Katona, George, Burkhard Strumpel, and Ernest Zahn, *Aspirations and Affluence*. New York: McGraw-Hill Book Company, 1971.

Keil, Charles, *Urban Blues*. Chicago: University of Chicago Press, 1966.

Keniston, Kenneth, *Young Radicals*. New York: Harcourt Brace Jovanovich, Inc., 1968.

Killian, L. M., and C. M. Grigg, "Urbanism, Race and Anomia," *American Journal of Sociology,* 67 (May 1962), 661-65.

Kindel, T. I., "The Negro Market: The Impact of Race on Economic Behavior." Unpublished Ph.D. dissertation, University of South Carolina, 1970.

King, R. L., and E. R. De Manche, "Comparative Acceptance of Selected Private-Branded Food Products by Low-Income Negro and White Families," in *Marketing Involvement in Society and the Economy*, ed. P. R. McDonald. Chicago: American Marketing Association, 1969, 63-69.

Kiser, C. V., *Sea Island to City: A Study of St. Helena Islanders in Harlem and Other Urban Centers*. New York: Columbia University Press, 1952.

Kitano, H. H. L., *Japanese Americans*. Englewood Cliffs, N.J.: Prentice-Hall, Inc., 1969.

Kluckhohn, Clyde, and H. A. Murray, *Personality in Nature, Society, and Culture*. New York: Alfred A. Knopf, Inc., 1949.

Kroeber, A. L., *Anthropology* (rev. ed.). New York: Harcourt Brace Jovanovich, 1948.

Kroeber, A. L., and Clyde Kluckhohn, *Culture: A Critical Review of Concepts and Definitions*. New York: Random House, Inc., 1963.

Larson, C. M., "Racial Brand Usage and Media Exposure Differentials," in *A New Measure of Responsibility for Marketing,* ed. Keith Cox and Ben Enis. Chicago: American Marketing Association, 1968, 208-15.

Laski, Harold, *The American Democracy.* New York: The Viking Press, Inc., 1948.

Leacock, E. B., ed., *The Culture of Poverty: A Critique.* New York: Simon and Schuster, 1971.

Lerner, Max, *America as a Civilization: The Basic Frame,* Vol. I. New York: Simon and Schuster, 1957.

Levy, S. J., "Symbols for Sale," *Harvard Business Review* (July-August 1959), 117-24.

Levy, S. J., "Symbolism and Life Style," a previously unpublished paper in *Perspectives in Marketing Management,* ed. F. D. Sturdivant, et al. Glenview, Ill.: Scott, Foresman and Company, 1971, 112-18.

Lewis, Hylan, *Blackways of Kent.* Chapel Hill, N.C.: The University of North Carolina Press, 1955.

Lewis, Oscar, *Five Families: Mexican Case Studies in the Culture of Poverty.* New York: Basic Books, Inc., Publishers, 1959.

Lewis, Oscar, *La Vida.* New York: Random House, Inc., 1966.

Liebow, Elliot, *Tally's Corner.* Boston: Little, Brown and Company, 1967.

Linton, Ralph, *The Cultural Background of Personality.* New York: Appleton-Century-Crofts, 1945.

Loewen, J. W., *The Mississippi Chinese.* Cambridge, Mass.: Harvard University Press, 1971.

Mannix, D. P., in collaboration with Malcolm Cowley, *Black Cargoes: A History of the Atlantic Slave Trade.* New York: The Viking Press, Inc., 1962.

Marcus, B. H., "Similarity of Ghetto and Nonghetto Food Costs," *Journal of Marketing Research,* 6 (August 1969), 365-68.

Mason, J. B., and C. S. Madden, "Food Purchases in a Low-Income Negro Neighborhood: The Development of Socio-Economic Behavioral Profile as Related to Movement and Patronage Patterns." The Graduate School of Business, University of Alabama, Conference Paper (mimeographed) 1971.

Mead, Margaret, *And Keep Your Powder Dry.* New York: William Morrow and Company, Inc., 1942.

Meadow, K. P., "Negro-White Differences Among Newcomers to a Transitional Urban Area," *Journal of Intergroup Relations,* 3 (1962), 320-30.

Merrill, F. E., and H. W. Eldredge, *Culture and Society.* Englewood Cliffs, N.J.: Prentice-Hall, Inc., 1952.

Mogey, J. M., *Family and Neighborhood.* London: Oxford University Press, 1956.

Murdock, G. P., "The Cross-Cultural Survey," *American Sociological Review,* 5 (June 1940), 361-70.

Myrdal, Gunnar, *An American Dilemma.* New York: Harper & Row, Inc., 1944.

Padilla, Elena, *Up from Puerto Rico.* New York: Columbia University Press, 1958.

Park, R. E. *Race and Culture.* New York: The Free Press, 1964.

Petrof, John, "Customer Strategy for Negro Retailers," *Journal of Retailing,* 43 (Fall 1967), 30-38.

Petrof, J. V., "Reaching the Negro Market: A Segregated Versus a General Newspaper," *Journal of Advertising Research,* 8 (June 1968), 40-43.

Pettigrew, T. F., *A Profile of the Negro American.* New York: Van Nostrand Reinhold Company, 1964.

Pinkney, Alphonso, *Black Americans,* Englewood Cliffs, N. J.: Prentice-Hall, Inc., 1969.

Portis, Bernard, "Negroes and Fashion Interest," *Journal of Business,* 39 (April 1966), 314-23.

Potter, D. M., *People of Plenty.* Chicago: University of Chicago Press, 1954.

Pred, Allan, "Business Thoroughfares as Expressions of Urban Negro Culture," *Economic Geography,* 39 (July 1963), 217-33.

Rainwater, Lee, Richard Coleman, and G. Handel, *Workingman's Wife.* Dobbs Ferry, N.Y.: Oceana Publications, Inc., 1959.

Reich, C. A., *The Greening of America.* New York: Random House, Inc., 1970.

Rich, S. U., with the assistance of Bernard Portis, Jr., *Shopping Behavior of Department Store Customers.* Boston: Division of Research, Harvard University Graduate School of Business Administration, 1963.

Riesman, David, *The Lonely Crowd.* New Haven, Conn.: Yale University Press, 1961.

Robertson, T. S., D. J. Dalrymple, and M. Y. Yoshino, "Cultural Compatibility in New Product Adoption," in *Marketing Involvement in Society and the Economy,* ed. P. R. McDonald. Chicago: American Marketing Association, 1968, 70-75.

Rocco, R. A., "On the Limitations of an Assimulative Perspective," *Social Science Quarterly,* 52 (June 1971), 35-38.

Roeder, R. A., "Integration in Business Advertising," *The MBA,* 5 (October 1970), 26-29.

Ross, Ralph, *Symbols and Civilization.* New York: Harcourt Brace Jovanovich, Inc., 1957.

Roszak, Theodore, *The Making of a Counter Culture.* Garden City, N.Y.: Doubleday & Company, Inc., 1969.

Ruark, M. C., and G. H. Mulrahy, "Family Spending in Memphis, 1949," *Monthly Labor Review,* 72 (June 1951), 655-61.

Sawyer, B. E., "An Examination of Race as a Factor in Negro-White Consumption Patterns," *The Review of Economics and Statistics,* 44 (May 1962), 217-20.

Schulz, D. A., *Coming Up Black.* Englewood Cliffs, N.J.: Prentice-Hall, Inc., 1969.

Sengstock, M. C., "The Corporation and the Ghetto: An Analysis of the Effects of Corporate Retail Grocery Sales on Ghetto Life," *Journal of Urban Law,* 45 (Spring-Summer 1968), 673-703.

Sexton, D. E., Jr., "Comparing the Costs of Food to Blacks and to Whites; A Survey," *Journal of Marketing,* 35 (July 1971a), 41-46.

Sexton, D. E., Jr., "Do Blacks Pay More?" *Journal of Marketing Research,* 8 (November 1971b), 420-26.

Sommers, Montrose, and G. D. Bruce, "Blacks, Whites, and Products: Relative Deprivation and Reference Group Behavior," *Social Science Quarterly,* 49 (December 1968), 631-42.

Stafford, James, Al Birdwell, and Charles Van Tassel, "Integrated Advertising— White Backlash?" *Journal of Advertising Research,* 10 (April 1970), 15-20.

Stafford, J. E., Keith Cox, and J. B. Higginbotham, "Some Consumption Pattern Differences Between Urban Whites and Negroes," *Social Science Quarterly,* 49 (December 1968), 619-30.

Sterner, Richard, et al., *The Negro's Share.* New York: Harper & Row, Inc., 1943.

Sturdivant, F. D., "Better Deal for Ghetto Shoppers," *Harvard Business Review,* 46 (March-April 1968), 130-39.

Sturdivant, F. D., *The Ghetto Marketplace.* New York: The Free Press, 1969a.

Sturdivant, F. D., "Business and the Mexican-American Community," *California Management Review,* 11 (Spring 1969b), 73-80.

Sturdivant, F. D., "Distribution in American Society: Some Questions of Efficiency and Relevance," in *Vertical Marketing Systems,* ed. L. P. Bucklin. Glenview, Ill.: Scott, Foresman and Company, 1970, 94-113.

Sturdivant, F. D., "Low-Income Shoppers in Small Towns: An Exploratory Study of Subcultural Differences," in *Proceedings,* ed. D. M. Gardner. Urbana, Ill.: Association for Consumer Research, 1971.

Tucker, W. T., *The Social Context of Economic Behavior.* New York: Holt, Rinehart and Winston, Inc., 1964.

Tucker, W. T., *Foundations for a Theory of Consumer Behavior.* New York: Holt, Rinehart and Winston, Inc., 1967.

Tylor, E. B., *Primitive Culture* (3rd English ed.). London: John Murray Publishers, Ltd., 1891.

Valentine, C. A., *Culture and Poverty.* Chicago: University of Chicago Press, 1968.

Wall, K. A., "Marketing to Low-Income Neighborhoods: A Systems Approach," in *Marketing in a Changing World,* ed. B. A. Morin. Chicago: American Marketing Association, 1969, pp. 24-27.

Warner, L. W., Marchia Meeker, and Kenneth Eells, *Social Class in America.* Chicago: Science Research Associates, 1949.

Wheatley, J. J., "The Use of Black Models in Advertising," *Journal of Marketing Research,* 8 (August 1971), 390-93.

White, L. A., *The Science of Culture.* New York: Grove Press, Inc., 1949.

Young, Michael, and Peter Willmott, *Family and Kinship in East London.* Baltimore: Penguin Books, Inc., 1957.

13

Stochastic Models of Consumer Choice Behavior

David B. Montgomery
Stanford University

Adrian B. Ryans
University of Western Ontario

INTRODUCTION

CONSUMER CHOICE BEHAVIOR FROM A STOCHASTIC MODELING VIEWPOINT

Choice Behavior in Marketing. Fundamental Elements of Stochastic Models. Basic Stochastic Choice Models. Problems in Stochastic Modeling of Consumer Behavior.

SOME APPLICATIONS OF STOCHASTIC CHOICE MODELS

Choice Models. Intraconsumer Representation of Brand-Choice Probability. Choice Incidence Models.

UTILIZATION OF STOCHASTIC CHOICE MODELS

Summary Market Measures. Conditional Prediction. Structural Analysis.

SUMMARY AND CONCLUSIONS

An understanding of consumer behavior is undoubtedly the single most important resource a marketing manager can bring to the analysis of any marketing problem. Unfortunately, such an understanding is not gained easily, for consumer behavior is an extremely complex phenomenon, depending, in any particular situation, on individual, group, and sociocultural factors. Models of consumer behavior are clearly necessary if we are to distill from the mass of data information that will be useful to the marketing decision maker.

Although there are several classes of consumer-behavior models, in this chapter we shall only be concerned with the class of stochastic models. In stochastic models of consumer behavior, consumer responses are considered to be the outcome of some probabilistic process. There are several reasons why it is appropriate to have a probabilistic element in a model of consumer behavior. Our present state of knowledge of consumer behavior does not allow us to predict behavior with complete accuracy, and even if we were aware of all the variables that affect behavior in a given situation, we would probably ignore some to reduce the problem to manageable proportions. Thus we incorporate a stochastic element to represent the net effect of all factors not explicitly considered in the model. Since we rarely have completely accurate data with which to work, due to sampling and measurement errors, stochastic elements are also useful for accounting for the discrepancy between actual and predicted behavior.

The problem of describing consumer behavior thus becomes one of specifying a probability law for the behavior of interest. This approach is useful, since it often allows us to represent quite complex behavior with relatively simple models.

In the next section of this chapter consumer choice behavior in marketing is discussed, followed by a discussion of certain fundamental properties of stochastic choice models and the three basic types of stochastic models of choice behavior. This section concludes with a brief discussion of some important issues concerning the evaluation of any given stochastic model.

The third section reviews some applications of stochastic choice and choice incidence models in marketing. This treatment is not intended to be comprehensive, but it does trace the development of stochastic models of choice behavior, and it tends to emphasize the most recent developments in the field. The section ends with a discussion of the empirical comparison of some of the more recent models.

The fourth section is concerned with the utilization of stochastic models of choice behavior for summarizing market activity, for making conditional predictions, and for structural analysis.

The chapter concludes with a section suggesting which areas seem to provide the most fruitful avenues for future research.

CONSUMER CHOICE BEHAVIOR FROM A STOCHASTIC MODELING VIEWPOINT

Understanding the choice behavior of consumers is one of the most difficult tasks facing marketing managers. Yet, if the marketing manager is to allocate his marketing resources effectively, it is essential that he gain a good understanding of the consumer's choice behavior, and that he be able to utilize this understanding to predict consumer response to his company's marketing mix.

In this section we shall briefly outline some of the major aspects of choice behavior in marketing. Following this, certain fundamental properties of stochastic choice models are presented. Since most stochastic choice models have their roots in one of three model types, we next discuss these basic stochastic choice models. This is followed by a consideration of some important issues that need to be understood in order to evaluate any given stochastic model.

Choice Behavior in Marketing

The consumer buying process can be conceptualized most simply as five stages: perception of a need, prepurchase activity, purchase decision, use behavior, and postpurchase evaluation. Consumer choice behavior is of some importance in all stages of the buying process, but it is most important in the first three stages.

In the first two stages, when the consumer perceives a need and engages in prepurchase activity, his media choice decisions are important to the marketing manager who is attempting to expose the consumer to information on his product or service. For example, understanding and prediction of consumer's television channel choice behavior, which is amenable to stochastic modeling, would be of great value to media executives and to the sponsors of advertisements in particular programs.[1]

During the prepurchase-activity and purchase-decision stages, consumer store choice behavior is of importance both to the retailer and to the manufacturer of the product. Where distribution of the product is not complete, store choice can be the critical factor in whether or not a given brand in a product class is considered for purchase.

In the purchase-decision stage the consumer makes a number of choices that are of considerable importance to the marketing manager: he decides whether to purchase on a "deal" or not, he makes a brand-choice decision, and in some instances he may make a package-size decision. Clearly, these decisions are not independent of each other. For example, the decision to take advantage of a deal may determine brand and package size. Rao has shown that there is an interaction between store and brand switching, and that there is a further interaction between the size of package purchased and brand and store switching.[2] For the product he studied, store switching and brand switching were related to a decrease in the package-size purchases.

Clearly, the discussion of brand choice, store choice, and package size is only of use for stochastic modeling purposes when the product is relatively frequently purchased, since the parameters of stochastic models are typically estimated from the past sequences of purchases for a group of consumers. In the case of major durables, such as automobiles and refrigerators, information on the sequence of purchases is usually not available, and, even if it is, it usually stretches over such a long time period that the earlier purchases are of little value, since market conditions will have changed radically in the intervening period. Some manufacturers of major durables, however, do gather panel (longitudinal) data on consumer attitudes toward brands in certain product classes. This has suggested to some researchers that stochastic models should be

[1]The potential applicability of stochastic models to TV channel choice behavior has been discussed briefly by D. A. Aaker, "Using Buyer Behavior Models to Improve Marketing Decisions," *Journal of Marketing,* 34 (July 1970), 52-57. For a discussion of TV show preference based upon a choice model, see D. R. Lehmann, "Television Show Preference: Application of a Choice Model," *Journal of Marketing Research,* 8 (February 1971), 47-55.

[2]T. R. Rao, "Consumer's Purchase Decision Process: Stochastic Models," *Journal of Marketing Research,* 6 (August 1969), 321-29.

applied to attitude data, rather than to purchase data, for infrequently purchased products.[3]

The timing of choice decisions is another dimension of choice behavior of both practical and theoretical significance. Clearly, segments of consumers who are frequent purchasers in a product class represent the greatest potential market, other things being equal (e.g., package size and price). Once again, data constraints and the passage of time have tended to limit most choice timing applications to the class of frequently purchased, branded consumer items.

The response a consumer makes in a given choice situation is often the result of a complex interaction between individual, group, and sociocultural factors and the particular situation. One can imagine stochastic models of consumer behavior being arrayed along a continuum from models of individual behavior to models that attempt to represent the behavior of individuals as they socially interact.[4] Development of this latter type of stochastic model has not occurred to any extent in marketing, perhaps due to the complex form such models would have to take. Another factor that has hindered development is the general lack of marketing data to which stochastic social interaction models could be applied. This indicates the need for new sources of marketing data, if progress is to be made on this front. The work of Davis on husband and wife interaction in automobile and furniture purchase decisions makes it appear that additional effort on this problem will be worthwhile.[5]

Fundamental Elements of Stochastic Models

The basic elements in a stochastic model are the choice probability (probabilities) and/or the time of choice. All stochastic choice models have one or both of these basic elements. By choice probability we mean the probability of choosing a particular alternative, say brand A, at time t, given that a choice is made at time t. We shall denote the choice probability of alternative A by $P(A(t))$, where the fact that this probability is conditional on a choice being made at time t is understood. In contrast, choice incidence models are concerned with the times (t's) at which choices are made.

It is useful to examine some of the factors affecting choice probability. These factors are readily divided into two categories: interconsumer and intra-

[3]For example, see D. A. Aaker, *op. cit.* Day has applied a stochastic model to attitude data for a frequently purchased product class. See G. S. Day, *Buyer Attitudes and Brand Choice Behavior* (New York: Free Press, 1970).

[4]Some work with models of social interaction has been undertaken by mathematical psychologists. For a summary of this work, see Seymour Rosenberg, "Mathematical Models of Social Behavior," in *Handbook of Social Psychology*, ed. G. Lindzey and E. Aronson (Reading, Mass.: Addison-Wesley, 1968), 179-244.

[5]H. L. Davis, "Dimensions of Marital Roles in Consumer Decision Making," *Journal of Marketing Research,* 7 (May 1970), 168-77.

consumer factors. The first relates to the plausible notion that consumers are likely to differ from one another in their choice probabilities. Later discussion in this chapter will illustrate how models which ignore this issue of consumer heterogenity may lead to erroneous behavioral inferences.

All the intraconsumer factors relate to the basic issue of whether or not a particular model postulates a constant or a potentially changing choice probability for the individual consumer over a sequence of choices. A major potential factor that might cause a consumer's choice probability to change between choice occasions is the experience which is gained from the previous choice. For example, a choice of brand A at time t might alter a consumer's probability of purchasing brand A again at $t + 1$ as a result of his use experience with brand A during the interpurchase interval. This feedback from the choice at t upon the choice probability at $t + 1$, $P(A(t + 1))$, will be termed *choice event feedback*. Naturally, there are many other factors besides experience that might tend to alter a consumer's choice probability between choice occasions. For example, changes in the marketing offerings of different brands, the retail outlet in which one makes a choice, the introduction of a new brand, and so on, could all cause changes in an individual's choice probability. A few stochastic choice models build these factors in directly. Others use time as a surrogate for all the external factors that might change the choice probabilities of individual consumers.

Two additional points should be raised concerning the treatment of choice probability at the individual level in stochastic choice models. The first relates to the number of distinct values an individual's choice probability may assume. This varies from models which imply that a consumer's choice probability never changes during the time period of interest to models which allow the choice probability to assume any value between 0 and 1. The second issue is whether a model permits changes in choice probability, which may be either increases or decreases, or whether the model only allows for unidirectional change from a particular value.

The factors discussed in this section are summarized in Table 1 for easier reference later.

Basic Stochastic Choice Models

Most stochastic models of consumer choice behavior that have been developed in marketing have their roots in one or more of three basic types of stochastic models: zero-order, Markov, and linear-learning models.[6] Before delving into the actual models that have been developed, it is appropriate to examine briefly each of these basic models to determine the assumptions upon which each of the formulations is based.

---

[6]This framework was first proposed in D. B. Montgomery, "Stochastic Modeling of the Consumer," *Industrial Management Review,* 8 (Spring 1967), 31-42.

TABLE 1.   **Factors Affecting Choice Probability**

I. Interconsumer

    A. Consumers identical in their choice probabilities.

    B. Consumers heterogeneous in their choice probabilities.

II. Intraconsumer

    A. Choice probability constant (or stationary) over a sequence of choices.

        1. Each individual consumer has only one choice probability value.

        2. Since the choice probability of each individual is constant, the directions in which it may change are zero.

    B. Nonstationary choice probabilities for each consumer.

        1. Choice event feedback.

        2. External factors such as company market actions or changes in economic conditions.

        3. Time effects as a surrogate for external factors.

        4. Values an individual's choice probability may attain (ranges from 1 to the possibility of any value on the 0-1 continuum).

        5. Directions of change in choice probability (1 or 2).

Zero-Order Models. The simplest type of stochastic model is one in which the response probability can change from trial to trial, but in which this change is not affected or altered by the particular sequence of choices the consumer has made. Consider the situation in which the individual consumer is faced with a choice between alternatives A and B at several points in time. The situation might be the purchase of a product, where A represents some brand of interest and B represents a composite of all other brands in the market. If $P(A_t)$ represents the probability of purchasing brand A at purchase occasion t, then in a zero-order model the conditional probability of purchasing A given some history of purchases of A and B can be represented as

$$P(A_t \mid \{\text{some history of purchases of } A \text{ and } B\}) = P(A_t)$$

Thus the history of purchases has no effect on the probability of purchasing A at purchase occasion t.

In behavioral terms the zero-order model suggests there is no feedback from the purchase event. The model is thus only a behaviorally valid representation of the consumer's choice behavior, if we can assume as a first approximation that choosing brand A or brand B does not positively or negatively reinforce the individual consumer. At a first glance this behavioral assumption seems invalid for the majority of consumers in the majority of choice situations. But we must not overlook the fact that in many choice situations the situational factors may be much more important determinants of behavior than the feedback from past experiences resulting from the choice behavior, which are represented in the individual by attitudes and intentions.[7] Thus it is quite possible in many choice situations of interest to marketers that situational influences, such as the limited number of brands stocked by a store, specials, out-of-stock conditions in the case of brand choice, and the handiness of the nearest supermarket in the case of store choice may be the major influences in the choice situation.

The response probability in a zero-order model may be free to change over time, thus allowing the model to represent changes in these situational variables. Therefore, if brand A becomes available in a much greater number of stores, we would expect $P(A_t)$ to rise for many consumers that purchase that product class, all other factors remaining unchanged.

Markov Models. Another type of stochastic model is the Markov model. Here the probability of choosing a given alternative is a function of what the consumer has previously done. In the simplest case the probabilities of choosing each of the various alternatives at choice occasion $t + 1$ are a function only of the choice the consumer made at choice occasion t. This is called a first-order Markov model. By redefining the state space (i.e., the set of alternatives to choose from) of the Markov model, processes in which the choice probabilities at choice occasion t depend on two or more previous choice occasions can be represented as first-order Markov models.

Consider the situation of a market with two brands A and B (again B may be a composite brand), which is assumed to follow a first-order Markov process. This situation can be represented by the following transition matrix:

$$
\begin{array}{cc}
 & \begin{array}{c} \textit{Brand Purchased at} \\ \textit{Choice Occasion } t+1 \end{array} \\
 & \begin{array}{cc} A & \quad B \end{array} \\
\begin{array}{c} \textit{Brand Purchased} \\ \textit{at Choice Occasion } t \end{array}
\begin{array}{c} A \\ B \end{array}
&
\begin{bmatrix} P_{A,A} & P_{A,B} \\ P_{B,A} & P_{B,B} \end{bmatrix}
\end{array}
$$

This matrix indicates, for example, that if the consumer bought brand A at choice occasion t, there is a probability $P_{A,A}$ that he will purchase A, and a probability $P_{A,B}$ that he will purchase B at choice occasion $t + 1$. The Markov model requires that the sum of the probabilities in each row must equal 1; that is, in our simple two-brand example $P_{A,A} + P_{A,B} = 1$ and $P_{B,A} + P_{B,B} = 1$.

Again at first glance, this model may not seem to be a valid representation of

---

[7]It is a common finding in psychological studies that attitudes are relatively poor predictors of behavior. A good discussion of studies relating to this problem can be found in A. W. Wicker, "Attitudes versus Actions: The Relationship of Verbal and Overt Behavioral Responses to Attitude Objects," *Journal of Social Issues,* 25 (1969), 41-78. G. S. Day has also briefly reviewed the subject in Chapter 8 of this book.

any type of consumer choice behavior. It may seem to be unreasonable to assume that the probability of choosing an alternative remains constant whether the consumer has been making the same choice on the last 20 choice occasions or only on the last one. This may not be, however, a bad assumption in many marketing situations in which the consumer either forgets or ignores his previous choices, or where the alternatives he has tried are so similar that the actual trial is neither positively nor negatively reinforcing.

One useful piece of diagnostic information that may be obtained from a Markov model is an indication of the likelihood of each alternative being chosen after a very long sequence of choices. In the case of brand choice this could be long-run market shares. In making such an extrapolation it is implicitly assumed that the transition probabilities (the P_{ij}'s in the transition matrix) remain constant over time, even though consumer preferences and marketing efforts by manufacturers, which presumably change the probabilities, do change. Although future changes in the transition probabilities are to be expected, a Markov model will still yield a useful indication of where a market is heading under current circumstances. Thus, in effect, the Markov extrapolation provides a conditional prediction (conditional upon the circumstances affecting choice probabilities remaining unchanged) as to where the market appears to be headed. Naturally, if such a prognosis for a firm's brand looks bad, the firm will attempt to rectify the situation by positive market actions, which it hopes will alter the unfavorable situation. Hence the diagnostic information from a Markov model may motivate a firm to take actions that will indeed alter the transition probabilities and thereby invalidate the extrapolation.[8] Yet in such cirsumstances the extrapolation is clearly of importance to management.

Linear-Learning Models. One of the earliest types of stochastic models applied to choice behavior was the linear-learning model.[9] The fundamental notion in linear-learning models is that the occurrence of a response increases the probability of the occurrence of that response again in the future. The linear-learning model represents an extreme example of choice occasion feedback, since it assumes that all past choices affect the probability of choosing alternatives at the next choice occasion.

Again let us consider a purchase situation with a market containing two brands, brand A and brand B, where brand A is the brand of primary interest and brand B is a composite of all other brands in the market. Now consider the probability of purchasing A on the next purchase occasion (P_{t+1}). Since brand A or brand B could have been purchased on the last purchase occasion, the

[8]This is similar to the use of macromodels of the economy that may indicate the likelihood of an undesirable result, which in turn will motivate policy makers to attempt to alter the economic picture.

[9]The first published application of the linear-learning model to brand choice was Al Kuehn, "Consumer Brand Choice—A Learning Process?" *Journal of Advertising Research,* 2 (December 1962), 10-17.

probability of purchasing brand A at the next choice occasion can be represented by one of the following equations:

$$P_{t+1}^P = \alpha_1 + \beta_1 P_t = \text{probability of choosing brand } A \text{ at purchase occasion } t + 1, \text{ if brand } A \text{ was purchased at purchase occasion } t;$$

$$P_{t+1}^R = \alpha_0 + \beta_0 P_t = \text{probability of choosing brand } A \text{ at purchase occasion } t + 1, \text{ if some other brand was purchased at purchase occasion } t.$$

These equations are known as the purchase operator and the rejection operator, respectively. The linear-learning model is depicted in Figure 1.

In the case when the probability of purchasing brand A at purchase occasion t is P_0, the probability of purchasing brand A at purchase occasion $t + 1$ is P_1^P or P_1^R, depending on whether or not brand A was purchased at purchase occasion t. Note that if brand A was purchased at purchase occasion t, the probability of purchasing brand A at time $t + 1$ is greater than if some other brand was purchased; that is, $P_1^P > P_1^R$.

In Figure 1 we can see that P_t and P_{t+1} have an upper and lower bound U_A and L_A. That is,

$$L_A \leq P_t \leq U_A \quad \text{and} \quad L_A \leq P_{t+1} \leq U_A.$$

In situations where $L_A > 0$ and/or $U_A < 1$, we have incomplete learning, which represents the situations when the consumer is never completely certain to purchase either brand A or brand B.

As was pointed out above, this model assumes that the consumer's complete purchase history with the product affects the probability of purchase at any purchase occasion. This purchase-history effect at any purchase occasion is, of course, incorporated in the current value of P_t.

The linear-learning stochastic model grew out of early work done by the mathematical psychologists Bush and Mosteller, and it is also similar to some models that grew out of stimulus sampling theory.[10] This model has been found to provide a good fit to experimental data on such things as paired-associated learning by human subjects. But in more crucial experiments designed to test the linear-learning model and all-or-none models in

---

[10] See R. B. Bush and F. Mosteller, *Stochastic Models for Learning* (New York: Wiley, 1955) and E. R. Hilgard and G. H. Bower, *Theories of Learning* (3rd ed.) (New York: Appleton-Century-Crofts, 1966), 338-64.

situations where they made different predictions, the all-or-none models seemed to make better predictions.[11]

FIGURE 1

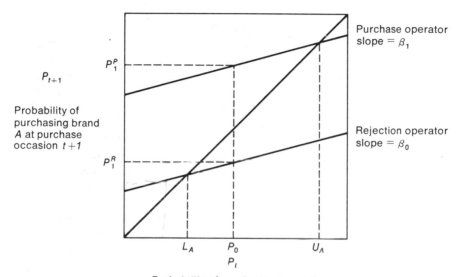

Probability of purchasing brand *A*
at purchase occasion *t*

The linear-learning model makes some behavioral assumptions that may not be particularly valid in many marketing situations. One assumption the model makes is that any time an alternative is chosen the probability of choosing it in the future increases. Yet clearly in many marketing situations the choice occasion feedback may be negatively reinforcing, not positively reinforcing, suggesting that the probability of choosing that alternative in the future will decrease. The simple linear-learning model also implicitly makes the assumption that changes in the levels of marketing variables, such as advertising, promotions, and so forth, do not affect the learning curve, and that the learning curve parameters remain unchanged over time. These are clearly unsatisfactory assumptions in many instances.

It is clear from this review of the basic types of stochastic models which have been used in the study of consumer behavior that only the grossest theoretical considerations have been incorporated into these basic models. This is undoubtedly partly due to the difficulty of reducing behavioral

[11]For a summary and discussion of three of these tests, see Frank Restle and J. G. Greeno, *Introduction to Mathematical Psychology* (Reading, Mass.: Addison-Wesley, 1970), 41-82.

science theoretical notions to a quantifiable form that can be introduced into a stochastic model and that will be mathematically tractable. One point that has emerged from our discussion of the behavioral assumptions underlying the basic stochastic models of consumer behavior is that we may find greater emphasis in the future on using a model in a situation where the behavioral assumptions underlying the model appear to be realistic. For a given data base containing choice behavior information for several consumers at several points in time, any of the basic models may provide a good fit to the data. This is often due to the fact that only short sequences of choice behavior are available for each consumer, and this, coupled with the flexibility of the models to fit the given data, makes it very difficult to determine which is the most appropriate model. This problem is compounded by noise in the system and the fact that different subgroups in the population may actually be behaving in accord with different behavioral theories; for example, in a brand-choice situation, brand-loyal consumers may be actually following a Markov process, while other consumers behave according to some zero-order process. Although different models may fit the data quite well, if their behavioral assumptions are incorrect, the usefulness of the models may be reduced and in fact inferences made from them may be misleading. This is particularly true of inferences made at the individual consumer level. Inferences of aggregate behavior may still be useful, however,

Problems in Stochastic Modeling of Consumer Behavior

It is important that the marketing manager be aware of several issues in the building and testing of stochastic choice models, if he is to be able to intelligently evaluate and utilize these models. These issues are[12]

1. There may be a many-to-one mapping of models into a set of data.
2. The effects of heterogeneity and nonstantionarity of response probability may be confounded.
3. The stochastic process generating the response probabilities may itself undergo change.
4. A combining of classes problem may arise, when an N-alternative market is collapsed into a two-alternative model.

The first issue, mentioned briefly in the last section, refers to the fact that several alternative models with quite different underlying structures may prove to be consistent with the empirical data. Although some work has been done in

---

[12]These issues are discussed in much greater detail with some numerical examples in D. B. Montgomery and G. L. Urban, *Management Science in Marketing* (Englewood Cliffs, N. J.: Prentice-Hall, 1969), 53-82.

the area of developing methods to discriminate among competing models, there is a definite need for much more work in the area.[13] Thus the fact that a particular model fits a given set of data well should not be taken as evidence that it is the most useful model in the particular situation.

The second issue is a much more complex one. Many simple stochastic models assume that the population of consumers is homogeneous, at least with respect to making any one of the alternative responses. By making this assumption of homogeneity, the person utilizing the model may conclude that the behavior exhibited by the consumers in the market is of relatively high order (i.e., the response at one point in time depends to some extent on the ones in several previous periods), when in fact it may be of low (even zero) order. This issue is relatively easy to illustrate mathematically. In the simplest case, if it is assumed that the market is actually composed of two homogeneous segments, who choose brands according to different Bernoulli (zero-order) processes, and if the consumer purchasing behavior at two consecutive purchases is observed, the behavior will appear to follow a homogeneous first-order Markov process.[14] Thus anyone observing this behavior and making the homogeneity assumption could erroneously conclude that purchasing behavior at the second time point is influenced by the previous behavior.

If the underlying probability mechanism is actually nonstationary (i.e., it changes over time), it is again possible to reject the hypothesis that the behavior is Bernoulli, when it is in fact Bernoulli. For example, if in the period of observation a consumer switched from purchasing brand A with probability 0.3 to purchasing brand A with probability 0.8 on any given purchase occasion, it would be quite possible to reject the Bernoulli hypothesis for the complete sequence of purchases. This is because the statistical tests that could be used to test the Bernoulli hypothesis (e.g., the runs test) assume stationarity of the underlying process. Therefore, a discontinuous change in a Bernoulli parameter may lead to the erroneous rejection of a true Bernoulli hypothesis. Thus there is a need for methods that are able to account for heterogeneity, and which assume no more than short-run stationarity.

The third issue, which involves nonstationarity of choice probabilities, may even arise in models that allow the choice probability itself to change. Here changes may occur in the process that generates changes in the choice probabilities. Although changes in the process will generally occur much more slowly than changes in choice probability, this still suggests the need to develop methods that assume only short-run stationarity, even for models that allow the choice probability to change.

[13]For example, see Chapter 2 in W. F. Massy, D. B. Montgomery, and D. G. Morrison, *Stochastic Models of Buyer Behavior* (Cambridge, Mass.: MIT Press, 1970).

[14]A numerical example illustrating this is presented in Montgomery and Urban, *op. cit.* 90-92.

In many models of consumer choice behavior, all brands other than the brand of primary interest are combined into a composite brand. The fourth issue is concerned with this problem. If this combining of all other brands into a composite brand is to leave the structure of the system unchanged, then a stochastic operator on the state space of the system must be of a special form.[15] This issue is thus of some importance in stochastic models of choice behavior. since both Markov and linear-learning models involve stochastic operators. However, this issue does not appear to be as important as the first three mentioned.

It is desirable that models of stochastic choice behavior be designed to satisfactorily handle *as many* of these problems as possible.

SOME APPLICATIONS OF STOCHASTIC CHOICE MODELS

Stochastic choice models of consumer behavior can be divided into two classes: choice models and choice incidence models. In the previous section we discussed the behavioral assumptions underlying stochastic models of consumer choice. In this section we shall discuss specific applications of stochastic models to both the choice itself and the incidence of these choices.

This discussion is not intended to be an exhaustive review of all the models in these areas. We shall attempt to briefly trace the history of progress in these areas, noting significant developments, and to emphasize the most recent advances in the field.[16]

Choice Models

Zero-Order Models. From the earlier discussion it may be recalled that zero-order models are based on the assumption that the probability of choosing a given alternative at choice occasion t is not a function of the previous choices the consumer has made in this choice situation. Any changes in the probabilities of choosing the given alternatives are assumed to be solely a function of changes in the environmental factors that influence the consumer's choice behavior.

The earliest studies of consumer choice behavior were conducted by Brown and Cunningham in the early 1950s.[17] Their work on brand and store loyalty

[15]See Bush and Mosteller, *op. cit.*

[16]A more extensive review of the earlier models can be found in Montgomery and Urban, *op. cit.*, 53-82. Some parts of this section are based on this material.

[17]See G. Brown, "Brand Loyalty—Fact or Fiction?" *Advertising Age*, XXIII (June 9, pp. 53-65; June 30, pp. 45-47; October 6, pp. 82-86; and Dec. 1, 1952, pp. 76-79), and R. M. Cunningham, "Brand Loyalty—What, Where, How Much?" *Harvard Business Review*, XXXIV (Jan.-Feb. 1956), 116-128, and R. M. Cunningham, "Customer Loyalty to Store and Brand," *Harvard Business Review*, XXXIX (Nov.-Dec. 1961), 127-37.

implicitly assumed that consumer choice behavior could be represented by a Bernoulli process, that is, stationary (no change in the probabilities over time) binomial and multinomial choices, which is obviously a zero-order model. Both researchers made use of *Chicago Tribune* panel data, which contained information on the sequence of brand choices and store choices made by a number of consumers for several products classes.

Brown studied the degree of brand loyalty exhibited by consumers purchasing such frequently purchased products as toothpaste, coffee, margarine, soap, and so on. He developed a measure of brand loyalty based upon the number and pattern of purchases of different brands made by these consumers in 1951. He used this measure to classify households into classes based on the degree of brand loyalty they exhibited. Although a later researcher has demonstrated that Brown's measure of brand loyalty was unsatisfactory, Brown's study did indicate that brand loyalty was more prevalent than had been supposed.[18] This finding helped to spur interest in the whole area of consumer choice behavior and brand loyalty.

Cunningham developed an improved measure of brand or store loyalty: the proportion of choices within a product or store class that a household devotes to its favorite or most frequent choice. He then studied the store and brand loyalty of the panel consumers, using as his null hypothesis the hypothesis that neither brand nor store loyalty exists; that is, brand and store choices are made on an equiprobable basis. The major findings that emerged from this study were that a significant degree of brand loyalty does exist within product classes, that store loyalty exists and varies with the type of store, and that brand and store loyalty are not significantly related. He also found that the consumers who were brand loyal varied from product to product (i.e., some consumers do not appear to be loyalty prone), and that consumption of the product class and brand loyalty are unrelated.

Two issues of great importance in the modeling of consumer choice behavior—heterogeneity and aggregation—were discussed in a paper by Frank.[19] He proposed that consumer brand choice could be represented by a zero-order model with a Bernoulli process in which consumers were heterogeneous (i.e., they could differ from one another) with respect to their brand-choice probabilities. The hypothesis that individual households exhibit behavior consistent with a zero-order model was tested using a nonparametric runs test. The behavior of most families was consistent with the zero-order model, although this particular test has certain limitations in this situation, and it thus should not be considered a crucial test of the hypothesis. Frank also raised the

[18]D. G. Morrison, "Stochastic Models for Time Series with Applications in Marketing," Technical Report No. 8, Joint Program in Operations Research, Stanford University.

[19]R. E. Frank, "Brand Choice as a Probability Process," *Journal of Business*, XXXV (Jan. 1962), 43-56.

question of aggregation. He pointed out that if a group of households with heterogeneous brand-choice probabilities is aggregated together, the resultant might show spurious "learning" effects, even when each household is exhibiting zero-order behavior. Recall our discussion of the confounding of heterogeneity and choice event feedback in the previous section.

Another investigation of whether or not consumer choice behavior can be represented as a zero-order process was conducted by Massy and Frank.[20] Their methodology was quite different from that used in Frank's earlier study. For each family they generated simulated purchase sequences of coffee, tea, and beer, assuming zero-order choice processes. For each simulated and actual sequence of purchases within each family they developed 29 summary statistics, such as number of brand runs and number of store runs. These statistics for both the actual and simulated populations were then factor analyzed, and the resulting profiles for the actual and simulated runs were compared. This analysis allowed the authors to conclude that all the brand and store switching behavior for the three products, except for the beer brand switching, was adequately described by a zero-order process. The brand-switching behavior for beer appeared to be a higher-order process. The methodology used in this study, because it was based on statistics for individual families, avoided the aggregation problem Frank had noted earlier. One difficulty with the methodology is that it is not clear to what extent the factor profiles are sensitive to deviations from the zero-order assumption.

In a later study of the regular coffee market, using only those families who had relatively constant (i.e., stationary) brand-choice probabilities and who were frequent purchasers, Massy showed that at the individual-family level the hypothesis of zero-order behavior was tenable for most families.[21] Yet when these same families were aggregated, the zero-order null hypothesis was rejected at a very high level of significance. This provides support to Frank's earlier statement, and emphasizes the danger in making inferences about family-specific processes from aggregate data, since these inferences are very sensitive to the assumptions of stationarity and homogeneity. In this study Massy also found that stationarity is the exception rather than the rule in the regular coffee market. This suggests that if a stochastic brand-choice model is to be a viable representation of consumer behavior in markets like the coffee market, it must allow individual-consumer brand-choice probabilities to vary over choice occasions; that is, it must allow for nonstationarity.

An early heterogeneous zero-order model that does allow for nonsta-

[20]W. F. Massy and R. E. Frank, "The Study of Consumer Purchase Sequences Using Factor Analysis and Simulation," *Proceedings of the Business and Economics Section of the American Statistical Association* (Dec. 1964).

[21]W. F. Massy, "Order and Homogeneity of Family Specific Brand Switching Processes," *Journal of Marketing Research,* 3 (Feb. 1966), 48-54.

tionarity and that may be applied to consumer choice situations has been proposed by Howard.[22] In his model the underlying parameters of the stochastic process that generate observable outcomes are themselves subject to change at times determined by yet another stochastic process. Hence an individual's response probability is nonstationary. The heterogeneity enters when these underlying parameters are themselves randomly distributed according to some distribution function. In essence, then, Howard's model undergoes discrete changes at randomly selected intervals.

Montgomery has proposed another heterogeneous zero-order model that allows nonstationarity of the response probabilities.[23] The model is called a Probability-Diffusion model and is an extension of a class of stochastic response models developed in the mathematical sociology field by Coleman.[24] Although the model is heterogeneous, that is, at any response occasion different respondents may have different response probabilities, the same response probability change process holds for all respondents. This, of course, is true for virtually all stochastic models.

The Probability-Diffusion model when fitted to data yields estimates of the distribution of response probabilities across the population of consumers, the expected equilibrium share for each alternative, the rate at which the market will approach its steady state from any disequilibrium position, and the propensity for the choice probability of a given brand to increase or decrease. The model has been fitted to Market Research Corporation of America's National Consumer Panel data in the dentifrice product class just before and just after the American Dental Association endorsed Crest toothpaste in August 1960. The model provided an excellent fit to the data, both in the normal market prior to the endorsement and in the unstable market that resulted from the endorsement. It is important to note here the problem encountered when one attempts to use a model, such as the Probability-Diffusion model, that is based on response-to-response behavior for such things as market-share estimates, which requires inferences based on real time. The strategy used in this case was to segment the consumers into four groups on the basis of their average interresponse times, and to estimate the parameters for each of these segments separately. This empirical test of this model and some other models will be discussed in greater detail in a later section.

Another heterogeneous, nonstationary, zero-order brand-choice model has

---

[22]R. A. Howard, "Dynamic Inference," *Operations Research* (Sept.-Oct. 1965), 712-33.

[23]D. B. Montgomery, "A Stochastic Response Model with Application to Brand Choice," *Management Science*, 15 (March 1969), 323-37.

[24]J. A. Coleman, *Models of Change and Response Uncertainty* (Englewood Cliffs, N. J.: Prentice-Hall, 1964).

recently been developed by Aaker.[25] The New-Trier model was developed specifically to model the brand-choice behavior of a consumer after he had purchased a brand that was unfamiliar to him; that is, the brand does not necessarily have to be a new brand, only a brand that the consumer has not used before, or that he has used so long ago that he has essentially forgotten it. The model assumes that there is a trial period after the initial purchase, during which the probability of purchasing the brand for that family remains constant. After a number of trial-period purchases, which is assumed to vary from consumer to consumer, the consumer is assumed to reach a decision and thereafter to have a new probability of purchasing the brand. The probabilities of purchasing the new brand during and after the trial period are assumed to be distributed across the population according to independent beta distributions, thus achieving interconsumer heterogeneity. In this form the New-Trier model is somewhat unrealistic, since it has no mechanism to allow the consumer to stop buying the brand at some point in the posttrial period, such as when the consumer tries and adopts a new brand in the product class. To handle this situation, Aaker's model includes an opportunity for the consumer to reject the brand in the posttrial period. The probability of the consumer rejecting the brand is assumed to decrease with time, which seems reasonable, since a new brand would seem to be more vulnerable to rejection in the immediate postdecision period before the purchase of the new brand has become a routinized decision for the consumer. In summary; in the postdecision period the consumer has a constant probability. Once the brand is rejected, the consumer will not purchase it again.

The New-Trier model provides information similar to that yielded by the Probability-Diffusion model, including estimates of the distribution of individual response probabilities across the population of consumers, and estimates of the equilibrium share of the market the new brand will obtain. A discussion of the uses of this model appears in a later section.

This section has traced the development of zero-order models of consumer brand choice over the last two decades. The models have developed from fairly simplistic formulations of limited usefulness to quite sophisticated models incorporating heterogeneity and nonstationarity that have provided a good fit to empirical brand-choice data in certain product classes.

Markov Models. As the reader will recall, Markov models make the assumption that only the respondent's behavior on the last choice occasion will affect his current behavior (as we noted earlier, this assumes the state space is redefined if the process is of higher than first order). The simple Markov model described earlier gives the probability that a consumer who chose alternative i at choice occasion t will choose alternative j at choice occasion $t + 1$. This basic model assumes that all consumers are characterized by the same transition matrix; that

[25]D. A. Aaker, "The New Trier Stochastic Model of Brand Choice," *Management Science,* 17, (April 1971), B-435-50.

is, it assumes the consumers are homogeneous with respect to their transition matrices.

If the user desires, the Markov model may be modified to model real-time (e.g., weekly) behavior, rather than choice occasion to choice occasion behavior, by incorporating an artificial *no-purchase* state to account for those consumers who do not choose an alternative in a given period. This formulation also implicitly assumes that no consumer will make more than one choice response in a given period.

Variants of this simple model applied to consumer brand-choice behavior have been proposed by several authors, including Harary and Lipstein.[26] They avoided some of the problems associated with the assumption of a homogeneous transition matrix by disaggregating their population of consumers into two groups based on the degree of brand loyalty the consumers exhibited toward any of the brands in the product class. The group that exhibited high brand loyalty, which was operationally defined to include those consumers who devoted three quarters or more of their total purchases in a given product class to a single brand, was used to estimate the parameters of one Markov transition matrix. The other group, who exhibited less, or no, brand loyalty, was used to estimate a second Markov transition matrix, thus making each group more internally homogeneous than the entire set of consumers taken together. Harary and Lipstein used these Markov models to gain some insight into what was happening in a market and where it appeared to be heading under the prevailing conditions.

The application of the simple Markov chain model to brand-switching behavior and other consumer choice behavior involves assumptions about the order of the switching process, its stationarity over the data period, and the homogeneity of the transition matrices across consumers. The first analysts to examine these assumptions were Styan and Smith.[27] They used the simple Markov model to analyze product-switching behavior for a panel of British housewives. For a 26-week period each housewife's purchase behavior in the laundry powder market was classified into one of the following four mutually exclusive and collectively exhaustive categories:

1. Bought detergent only in week t.
2. Bought soap powder only in week t.
3. Bought both detergent and soap powder in week t.
4. Bought no laundry powder in week t.

These categories were used to define the state space of the Markov chain analysis.

[26]F. Harary and B. Lipstein, "The Dynamics of Brand Loyalty: A Markov Approach," *Operations Research*, X (Jan.-Feb. 1962), 19-40.

[27]G. P. H. Styan and H. Smith, Jr., "Markov Chains Applied to Marketing," *Journal of Marketing Research*, 1 (Feb. 1964), 50-55.

Using the data in this form, Styan and Smith were able to estimate 25 transition matrices for each pair of consecutive weeks in the 26-week period. These matrices, of course, represent aggregage switching behavior, which implicitly assumes the consumers are homogeneous. Each transition matrix was used to test the hypothesis that the aggregate switching data were from a first-order Markov process; that is, the null hypothesis was that the data were from a zero-order process. It was found that the null hypothesis could be rejected in favor of the alternative hypothesis that the aggregate data were from a first-order Markov process, at a very high level of significance. Ideally, they would have liked to test the first-order hypothesis against second- and higher-order alternatives, but unfortunately there were not sufficient data. It is worth reconsidering at this point Massy's finding (discussed earlier) that aggregation of a sample of households, who individually exhibited zero-order behavior, would give rise to highly significant inferences of a first-order process in the aggregated data. Thus although Styan and Smith's research indicates that the aggregate data from their sample of housewives come from a first- or higher-order Markov chain, this should not be construed to mean that the individual housewife's behavior can be considered as following a first-order Markov process.

Styan and Smith also tested the stationarity of the aggregate transition matrices over the 26-week period and found that the null hypothesis of stationarity could not be rejected, since the significance level of the test was relatively high (over 24 percent). Hence the aggregate data appeared to be consistent with a stationary, first-order Markov chain.

Two interesting new Markov models have been developed by Morrison.[28] In these models Morrison relaxed the assumption of a homogeneous transition matrix for all consumers in the sample under consideration. Harary and Lipstein had relaxed this assumption slightly by assuming that there were two segments with different transition matrices, but they still assumed that each segment contained homogeneous consumers. Morrison simply generalized these previous models to include the case when individual consumers could be heterogeneous with respect to their brand-switching matrices in two-brand markets.

The first of Morrison's two models is called the Brand-Loyal model. The consumer's transition matrix in this model takes the form

		Brand Purchased at Occasion t + 1	
		A	*B*
Brand Purchased at Occasion t	*A*	p	$1 - p$
	B	kp	$1 - kp$

[28]D. G. Morrison, "Testing Brand Switching Models," *Journal of Marketing Research,* 3 (November 1966), 401-9.

where brand A represents the consumer's favorite brand and brand B represents all other brands. Heterogeneity is introduced by assuming that the probability p is distributed across the consumer population according to some probability law. The parameter k is a constant for all families and lies between 0 and 1. Notice that if $k = 1$ the probability of choosing brand A on purchase occasion $t + 1$ is independent of the brand purchased on occasion y, and thus the model has simplified to a heterogeneous, zero-order model. The model is termed the Brand-Loyal model because if p is high for a given consumer, he will be likely to purchase brand A at purchase occasion $t + 1$ even if he purchased brand B at purchase occasion t.

The Last-Purchase-Loyal model, on the other hand, acts in a way opposite to that of the Brand-Loyal model. Here the consumer transition matrix takes the form

		Brand Purchased at Occasion $t + 1$	
		A	B
Brand Purchased at Occasion t	A	p	$1 - p$
	B	$1 - kp$	kp

where p is again distributed across the population of consumers according to some probability law and k lies between 0 and 1. In this model a person with a high p is more loyal to the brand he last purchased than is a person with a low p. Thus, in contrast to the Brand-Loyal model, the Last-Purchase-Loyal model assumes a person's loyalty is directed towards the last brand he purchased, rather than towards a particular brand.

Morrison has developed minimum chi-square procedures for estimating and testing these models. The Brand-Loyal model was found to provide a good fit to data for regular coffee purchases from the *Chicago Tribune* consumer panel, and it also provided some interesting structural insights, which will be discussed later.

All the first-order Markov models discussed have implicitly ignored the effects of marketing variables on consumer behavior. Yet it seems clear that changes in the levels of marketing variables, such as advertising, will affect consumer behavior that is represented by the transition probabilities in the transition matrix. Telser made an early attempt to handle this problem by linking price to the transition probabilities.[29] In this study he used a variant of the Markov brand-switching model to develop estimates of the price elasticities of branded goods. In this type of Markov model the transition probabilities are made functions of the marketing variables (in this case price) that prevail in the

[29]L. G. Telser, "The Demand for Branded Goods as Estimated from Consumer Panel Data," *Review of Economics and Statistics,* XXXXIV (August 1962), 300-24.

market at the time the brand choice is made. The transition probabilities were expressed as

$a_{ii} = f_{ii}(P_{it}, P_{it}^*) =$ conditional probability of repeating the purchase of brand i during period t as a function of P_{it} and P_{it}^*,

$a_{ki} = f_{ki}(P_{it}, P_{it}^*) =$ conditional probability of purchasers shifting to brand i from all other brands during period t as a function of P_{it} and P_{it}^*,

where $P_{it}^* =$ average price of all other brands during period t.

Thus in the variable Markov formulation the brand-switching probabilities are able to change from period to period in response to changes in the competitive activity. In Telser's case one would expect a_{ii} and a_{ki} to become higher, the lower P_{it} is relative to P_{it}^*.

To be able to estimate the effect of competitive prices on the transition probabilities, it was necessary for Telser to further specify the functions f_i (P_{it}, P_{it}^*) and $f_{ki}(P_{it}, P_{it}^*)$. He chose the simplest specification, making the f's linear functions of the difference in price between brand i and the average price of all other brands in each period. In particular he let $p_{it} = P_{it} - P_{it}^*$ be the price variable, and approximately specified the function as

$$a_{ii} \simeq f_{ii}(p_{it}) = c_{ii} + b_i p_{it},$$
$$a_{ki} \simeq f_{ki}(p_{it}) = c_{ki} + b_i^* p_{it}.$$

As we discussed above, a_{ii} and a_{ki} vary inversely with p_{it} for most products, thus resulting in an expectation of negative values for both b_i and b_i^*.

Telser also developed in the same paper a method for estimating the transition probabilities from market share and price data. This method of estimating the transition probabilities also allowed him to estimate the price elasticities for the brands under consideration.

Nakanishi has recently proposed a more complex variable Markov formulation to model the reactions of consumers toward new products.[30] In his model Nakanishi considers the underlying process of consumer acceptance to be divided into three stages: an awareness stage, a trial stage, and an acceptance stage. Each stage is modeled separately by a variable Markov process.

In the awareness-stage model Nakanishi has proposed two alternative specifications; one is based on the assumption that consumers who are once

---

[30]Masao Nakanishi, "A Model of Market Reactions to New Products" (unpublished Ph.D. dissertation, Graduate School of Business Administration, University of California, Los Angeles, 1968).

made aware of the product remain aware of it, and the other is based on the (more reasonable) assumption that consumers may forget. The transition matrix for the memory-loss case is

		State of Awareness in Period $t + 1$	
		Aware	Not aware
State of Awareness in Period t	Aware	$\pi_{PP}(t + 1)$	$1 - \pi_{PP}(t + 1)$
	Not aware	$\pi_{IP}(t + 1)$	$1 - \pi_{IP}(t + 1)$

where $\pi_{PP}(t + 1)$ is the probability that a consumer who is aware of the product at t remains aware during period $t + 1$, and $\pi_{IP}(t + 1)$ is the probability that a consumer who is not aware of the product in period t becomes aware of it in period $t + 1$.

The probabilities $\pi_{PP}(t + 1)$ and $\pi_{IP}(t + 1)$ are not assumed to be constants, but are assumed to be a linear function of such marketing variables as advertising expenditures. The first step in the application of the model is to gather data from which the parameters of the model can be estimated. The data are gathered from test markets or from the early periods after the product has been regularly introduced. Aided or unaided recall questions administered to independent cross sections of consumers (i.e., in each time period a different sample of consumers is randomly selected from the population) are used to estimate the transition probabilities.[31] The parameters of the linear function relating the expenditure on marketing activities to the transition probabilities can then be estimated by the application of multiple regression.

The relationships between the transition probabilities for the trial and acceptance stages and the expenditures in marketing activities can be determined by a conceptually similar procedure. The estimated values of the parameters relating the expenditures on marketing activities and the transition probabilities in the three models can provide interesting insights into the nature of the acceptance process for new products. The models can also be used to generate predictions, conditional on the timing and the amount of expenditures on marketing activities. These uses of stochastic choice models will be discussed in greater detail in a later section.

In the area of Markov models of consumer choice behavior, as in the zero-order model area, there has been a steady progression from relatively naive

---

[31] The estimation problem in the memory-loss specification is not straightforward, since from any independent cross-section data are only available on the proportion of people who are now aware of the product. Thus π_{pp} and $\pi_{ip}(t + 1)$ cannot be directly estimated from the data, since it cannot be determined what proportion of those who are aware in a given period were also aware in the previous period. For details of the method used, see Nakanishi, *op. cit.*, or for the same method in another context see N. G. Telser, "Advertising and Cigarettes," *The Journal of Political Economy*, LXX, (October 1962), 471-99 (especially 488-89).

models to models that can be of significant value to the marketing decision maker.

Linear-Learning Models. In the early discussion of the Linear-Learning model it was emphasized that the basic concept underlying this model is that the appearance of a response (be it the purchase or nonpurchase of a brand of interest) in one period increases the probability that the same response will be repeated at the next choice occasion. The structure implies that the total history of a consumer's choice behavior affects the probability of choosing a given alternative at any given decision point.

Kuehn was the first researcher to attempt to apply learning models to consumer behavior.[32] He used a modified form of Bush and Mosteller's Linear-Learning theory as a model of brand choice. Although he developed the model, Kuehn has not estimated the Linear-Learning model in any of his published work. In his thesis he used factorial analysis to analyze frozen orange juice purchases made by households in the *Chicago Tribune* consumer panel. The factorial analysis was used to determine the influence of the four preceding choices on the choice the consumer made on the fifth purchase occasion. The results are presented in Table 2 where brand A is Snow Crop and brand 0 represents all the brands. These results appear to indicate an increasing effect of the most recent

TABLE 2. **Kuehn's Learning Model Results**

Brand Choice on Four Previous Purchases	Observed Probability of Purchasing Brand A on the Next Trial
AAAA	0.806
OAAA	0.690
AOAA	0.665
AAOA	0.595
AAAO	0.486
OOAA	0.552
AOOA	0.565
OAOA	0.497
AOAO	0.405
OAAO	0.414
AAOO	0.305
OOOA	0.330
OOAO	0.191
OAOO	0.129
AOOO	0.154
OOOO	0.048

Source: Reproduced with permission from A. A. Kuehn, "Consumer Brand Choice—A Learning Process?" *Journal of Advertising Research,* 2 (December, 1962), 10-17.

[32] A. A. Kuehn, "An Analysis of the Dynamics of Consumer Behavior and Its Implications for Marketing Management" (unpublished Ph.D. dissertation, Graduate School of Industrial Administration, Carnegie Institute of Technology, 1958).

purchases, and that the behavior is suggestive of a linear adaptive process. These and other results tend to support the notion that the Linear-Learning model is a reasonable representation of consumer choice behavior in certain product classes. However, since Kuehn assumed a homogeneous population, the "learning" effect in these results may be spurious due to a confounding of heterogeneity and choice event feedback. Recall the Frank results and the Massy results in the earlier discussion of zero-order models.

The first published study that attempted to empirically test the Linear-Learning hypothesis was reported by Carman.[33] The data base used in the study was the dentifrice purchases data from the Market Research Corporation of America (MRCA) consumer panel for the period subsequent to the endorsement of Crest by the American Dental Association in August 1960. Carman felt that the situation in the dentifrice market after the endorsement was somewhat unique in that the conditions in the market were ideal for testing the Linear-Learning hypothesis. One implicit assumption of the model is that competitive marketing activity should stay relatively constant. In the early postendorsement dentifrice market, Carman felt the Crest promotional campaign was so intense that competitive marketing activity would have little effect on consumer purchasing behavior. Another advantage of using the Crest data was the large number of subjects in the market who had an opportunity to "learn" about Crest's attributes, and who probably had a very low probability of purchasing Crest before the endorsement, since Crest in the preendorsement period had a much lower market share than after the endorsement.

Carman tested the special case of the Linear-Learning model in which the slopes of the purchase operator and the rejection operator are constrained to be the same. He generated data for his estimation procedure by using purchase sequence trees on five purchases to generate 15 probability triplets $(P_t, P_{p,t+1}, P_{r,t+1})$, where

P_t = probability of purchasing Crest at time t,

$P_{p,t+1}$ = probability of purchasing Crest at time $t + 1$, given that a purchase of Crest was made at time t,

$P_{r,t+1}$ = probability of purchasing Crest at time $t + 1$, given that a purchase of some other brand was made at time t.

The empirical frequencies from the probability triplets were weighted by the number of consumers generating the triplet, and these data were used to estimate the parameters of the purchase and rejection operators by least-squares regression. These parameters were estimated for relatively homogeneous subgroups of the population, where the subgroups were based on the time interval

---

[33]J. M. Carman, "Brand Switching and Linear Learning Models," *Journal of Advertising Research*, 6 (June 1966), 23-31.

between purchases and the degree of brand loyalty exhibited on three previous purchases. In all subgroups Carman found the linear model provided a good fit to the data, with coefficients of determination in the regressions ranging from 0.67 to 0.99. Thus the Crest data were not inconsistent with the Linear-Learning model.

When Carman used the learning model to determine the projected equilibrium market shares (i.e., the market share when the number of people switching to Crest equals the number of people switching from Crest to other brands), there were some indications that the learning process was nonstationary over time; that is, the parameters of the model a, a_2, and β $(= \beta_1 = \beta_2)$ changed over time. This may have been due to the fact that towards the end of the postendorsement period, competitive reaction to the Crest success may have invalidated the assumption that competitive market activity was relatively constant.

In his empirical test of the Linear-Learning model Carman attempted to minimize the effect of assuming a homogeneous population by disaggregating this sample into somewhat homogeneous subgroups, and then estimating his parameters for each of these subgroups. This method is not entirely satisfactory, and to overcome this problem Massy has developed procedures for estimating the Linear-Learning model when heterogeneity exists.[34] In this formulation the initial response probability is assumed to be distributed over the population of respondents according to some probability law. He presents both a maximum likelihood procedure and a minimum chi-square procedure for estimating the Linear-Learning model.

Haines has used a modified form of the Linear-Learning model to represent market behavior after an innovation.[35] In the development of this model Haines made a major simplifying assumption. Since the model was to apply to innovations, he made the assumption that there were no directly competitive products available in the introductory period that would affect the consumer's probability of purchasing the innovation. This assumption allowed him to modify the rejection operator, so that in the event the consumer did not purchase the innovation on a given trial the probability of purchasing the innovation on the next trial would remain unchanged. Thus

$P_{t+1} = P_t$ if some other brand was purchased at times t (i.e., this is the revised rejection operator).

Haines has applied his model to data from the introductory period of a new product in some 34 regions. He fitted his model to aggregate market-share data

[34]See Massy, Montgomery, and Morrison, *op. cit.,* 157-67.

[35]G. Haines, "A Theory of Market Behavior After Innovation," *Management Science,* 10 (July 1964), 634-58.

for each of the 34 regions to estimate asymptotic market share for the new product and the rate at which this asymptotic value was approached. The model appeared to be consistent with the data, with only 2 of the 34 regions not significant at a type I error probability of 0.10.

In the theory underlying his model Haines proposed that the rate of approach of the market share to the asymptotic value would be a function of price, promotion, advertising, availability, and product characteristics in the initial period following the introduction. The asymptotic market-share value was assumed to be a function of the values of these variables throughout the introductory period. The aggregate market measures were then regressed in turn against the appropriate set of marketing variables, using the data from the 34 different regions. The rate of approach to the asymptotic market share was found to be most significantly related to the prior availability of the product and advertising expenditures in the first two periods. The asymptotic level of market share adjusted for the number of people in each region was found to be significantly related to per capita promotional expenditures in each region.

Haines's approach to this problem was a sound one. He first estimated the parameters of a stochastic model of consumer behavior in a number of different regions, and then used the determined parameters in regressions on important marketing variables. This approach allowed him to estimate the impact of marketing expenditures on different marketing activities. The role of the learning model in this case was to provide summary measures (asymptotic choice share and response rate) of the market dynamics in each region.

Rao has proposed a model of market behavior incorporating brand choice, store selection, and purchase timing.[36] The model assumes that the consumers are heterogeneous in their underlying probabilities of purchasing a specific brand, choosing a given store, or making the choice decision at a given time, even though the model assumes that each consumer's decision is the result of the same interaction process among the three variables. Linear-Learning models are incorporated in the model to represent brand- and store-choice behavior. The store is assumed to act as an intervening variable between a consumer's preference for a brand and choice of a brand; that is, a consumer with an underlying predisposition toward a brand may have a different probability of purchasing the brand depending on the store in which she shops. The relative effectiveness of the store's promotional environment modifies the consumer's underlying probability of purchasing a brand. The consumer's preference toward a given brand is assumed to be affected by the length of time since she last purchased the brand. The interpurchase time is represented by a probability distribution. After the parameters of the model have been estimated for a given product class,

[36]T. R. Rao, "A Model of Market Behavior" (paper presented at the American Meetings of the Institute of Management Sciences—College Sessions on Marketing, Los Angeles, Oct. 19-21, 1970).

the model can be used to simulate the market behavior for that product class. Rao is currently evaluating the simulation model's predictive ability.

Rao has fitted the store-choice linear-learning submodel to data on the purchases of a tissue product from the *Chicago Tribune* consumer panel. Since the store data available from the panel records indicated store ownership, not location, the Linear-Learning model was found to provide a reasonably good fit to the data for six different chains of stores (one of which represented a composite of all stores not in the five major chains). The use of stochastic models to represent certain types of consumer behavior within the framework of a larger model is an important application of these models.

Aaker and Jones have also modeled store-choice behavior with the linear-learning model.[37] They tested the model on *Chicago Tribune* panel data for a paper product, toothpaste, and coffee. As in Rao's case, they were constrained to fitting the model to store-chains or store-type (e.g., discount stores) data, since only ownership of stores was available from the panel. Of the 15 sets of data that were fitted to the model by the chi-square procedure, only four resulted in the model being rejected by a chi-square test at the 0.10 level (the *p* level suggests the probability that a chi-square statistic would equal or exceed the one obtained from the data if the model perfectly represented the underlying structure). In three of the four cases where the model did not fit well, the type of outlet being modeled was a type of store rather than a specific chain. Aaker and Jones suggested that this might indicate that store-type decisions may not have the characteristics of a Linear-Learning model. This type of study has value in that it helps establish the descriptive ability of a model for more than one set of data. This work is necessary if one is to determine in which types of situations a given model is viable.

Dual-Effects Model.   The earlier behavioral discussion indicated that zero-order models and Linear-Learning models assume that very different factors cause changes in choice probabilities. Zero-order models, such as Montgomery's Probability-Diffusion model, assume that the changes are the result of external influences in the marketplace. On the other hand, the Linear-Learning model assumes that choice occasion feedback is the factor affecting the choice probabilities. Jones has proposed a model that allows both external effects and feedback from the choice occasion.[38] The model is called the Dual-Effects model of brand choice.

The Dual-Effects model is essentially an extension of Montgomery's Probability-Diffusion model. In his model Montgomery assumes that at any response occasion there are only two mutually exclusive and collectively

[37]D. A. Aaker and J. M. Jones, "Modeling Store Choice Behavior," *Journal of Marketing Research,* 8 (February 1971), 38-43.

[38]J. M. Jones, "A Dual-Effect Model of Brand Choice," *Journal of Marketing Research,* 7 (November 1970), 458-64. Figure 2 in this section follows closely figures in this article.

exhaustive responses, *A* and *B*. Each respondent is assumed to possess *N* hypothetical response elements, which, at any response occasion *t*, are assumed to be uniquely associated with either response *A* or response *B*. The response elements have some transition intensity (α and β for elements associated with *B* and *A*, respectively) toward becoming associated with the other response. These transition intensities are increased by an amount γ for each element associated with the opposite response. For an individual in state *i*, the element's propensities to change from one response to another are

$$\lambda_i = (\alpha + i\gamma)(N - i), \quad \text{for elements associated with } B,$$

$$\mu_i = [\beta + (N - i)\gamma]i, \quad \text{for elements associated with } A,$$

where *i* is the number of elements associated with *A*.

In a marketing context response *A* could represent the purchase of brand *A* and response *B* the purchase of some other brand. At any point in time *t* the probability of purchasing brand *A* is assumed to be equal to the proportion of elements associated with response *A*; that is, $P(A_t) = i/N$.

In Jones's extension of Montgomery's model, he assumes the transition intensities α and β may change only following the purchases of *A* and *B*, respectively. Thus α changes only when brand *A* is purchased; that is, if there is positive purchase event feedback, α will increase, causing a greater propensity for an element associated with *B* to become associated with *A*.

The Dual-Effects model thus incorporates the effects of both changes in the external environment, which can occur continuously over time, and changes due to purchase event feedback, which occur at discrete points in time. The differences between the Dual-Effects model and the Linear-Learning and Probability-Diffusion models can be illustrated for a consumer in the case when two sequential brand *A* purchases are made at times t_1 and t_2 (see Figure 2).

The Dual-Effects model allows the response probability to vary when one of the effects represented by the Linear-Learning and Probability Diffusion models is absent. In a situation where both effects are operating the model provides a means for estimating the direction and strength of the effects resulting from external factors and purchase event feedback. This might be critical in the case of a heavily advertised new product, when it is very important for the manager to estimate whether the product's sales success is due to the introductory campaign (an external factor) or the product's attributes (purchase event feedback). Clearly, this knowledge is invaluable if the decision maker is to allocate his resources effectively.

Jones has fitted the model to the dentifrice purchase data from the MRCA panel for the period following the American Dental Association's endorsement of Crest in August 1960. Three versions of the model, differing in the specific mechanism by which α and β changed after a purchase, were fitted to the data,

FIGURE 2

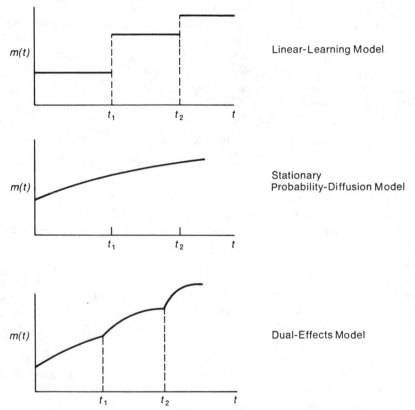

where $m(t) = E(P(t))$ = expected value over the population of the probability of purchasing brand A at time t

Adapted with permission from J. M. Jones, "A Dual-Effects Model of Brand Choice," *Journal of Marketing Research*, 7 (November 1970), 458-64.

which were split into five segments based on the average interpurchase time. Using a one-tailed test, none of the models could be rejected at the 0.05 level, and at the 0.10 level only one of the three formulations was rejected in two segments. Thus the three models provide a reasonably good fit in most of the situations. The fit of these Dual-Effects models, and some of the other models discussed, to the Crest data will be discussed in the next section.

The Dual-Effects model represents a significant advance in the state of the art of building stochastic models of choice behavior, in that it provides a means for separating out and estimating the effects on consumer choice behavior of two different types of factors. Earlier models could only measure and represent either choice occasion feedback or external effects, which in extreme cases might cause decision makers to make invalid inferences about what was happening in the marketplace.

Comparison of the Choice Models. In our discussion a number of fairly sophisticated models of consumer choice behavior have been presented. These models differ in their assumptions and, hence, in the way they represent the brand-choice probability of individual consumers. Before discussing empirical comparisons of some of these models, it is appropriate to briefly review how each represents consumer brand-choice probabilities. Variants of all the models to be discussed in this section allow heterogeneity of brand-choice probability in a consumer population. However, the models differ in their intraconsumer representation of brand-choice probability.

Intraconsumer Representation of Brand-Choice Probability

The following characteristics relate to the representation of brand-choice probability for any individual consumer. Although they were discussed in an earlier section, they are summarized here for convenience.

Nonstationarity. Nonstationarity refers to whether a consumer's brand-choice probability may change between purchase occasions.

Choice Occasion Feedback. Choice occasion feedback (or purchase event feedback in the case of brand choice) represents whether or not the actual choices made influence the brand-choice probability.

Time Effects. Time effects represent a surrogate for all the changes in external factors that may change choice probability.

Values a Consumer's Brand-Choice Probability May Attain. This characteristic indicates the number of distinct values between 0 and 1 that a consumer's brand-choice probability may attain.

Directions in Which a Consumer's Response Probability May Change. If a model assumes nonstationarity, a consumer's response probability can change in either one or two directions.

Table 3 summarizes how several of the previously discussed models represent an individual consumer's brand-choice probability.

Empirical Comparison of the Choice Models. Many of the models discussed have been empirically compared by fitting two or more of them to the same data base, and then comparing their fit.

The fit of the models to the data set is determined by using a chi-square test with the model to be tested as the null hypothesis. From the data set used to estimate the model's parameters, the actual number of consumers making each possible mutually exclusive and collectively exhaustive series of choices can be calculated. The model, after it has been estimated, also generates the expected number of consumers making each of the possible series of choices. The chi-square statistic can be calculated using this information:

TABLE 3. Brand-Choice Probability Representation

Characteristics of Brand-Choice Representation		Model				
	Bernoulli	Zero-Order Probability-Diffusion	New-Trier	Markov Morrison's BL and LPL	Linear-Learning Massy's Heterogeneous	Dual-Effects Jones
Nonstationarity	No	Yes	Yes	Yes	Yes	Yes
Choice occasion feedback	No	No	No	Yes	Yes	Yes
Time effects	No	Yes	No	No	No	Yes
Values it may attain	One	Infinite number	Three[a]	Two	Many	Infinite Number
Directions it may change	No change	Two	Two	One	Two	Two

[a] Including 0.

where:

$$\chi^2 = \sum_{i=1}^{k} \frac{(O_i - E_i)^2}{E_i},$$

i = 1 to k indexes the set of collectively exhaustive and mutually exclusive series of choice responses,

O_i = observed number of consumers making the ith series of choice responses,

E_i = expected number of consumers making the ith series of choice responses (this is a function of the estimated parameters of the model).

The chi-square test statistic will be distributed as a chi-square statistic with k - q - 1 degrees of freedom, where q is the number of parameters of the model estimated from the data.[39] Since the chi-square statistic may have a different number of degrees of freedom for each model (since q may vary), the empirical comparison will be based on the p level of the statistic. The p level represents the probability that the chi-square statistic would be as large as it is, if the model actually generated the data. Thus the closer the p level is to 1, the better is the fit to the data.

A complementary method of evaluating the fit of models to the empirical data is to examine the estimated parameters of the model to see if any of them attain infeasible values; For example, the linear learning slope parameter, β , should have an estimated value of between 0 and 1 ($0 \leqslant \beta \leqslant 1$).

Montgomery and Jones have both fitted a number of models to the MRCA panel data for Crest toothpaste.[40] Montgomery fitted four models, the Brand-Loyal and Last-Purchase-Loyal Markov models, the Linear-Learning model (modified to allow heterogeneity), and the Probability-Diffusion model, to the Crest data before and after the August 1960 ADA endorsement of Crest. The population of consumer households was segmented into four groups on the basis of their average interpurchase interval in the preendorsement period. The models were fitted separately for each segment. The Linear-Learning and Probability-Diffusion models seemed to provide a significantly better overall fit to this data set than the Markov models (see Table 4). The Probability-Diffusion model seemed to be superior to the Linear-Learning model in the very unstable post-endorsement period.

Jones, also using the Crest case, used considerably different criteria for including households in his sample, and classified people into average inter-

[39]For a more detailed discussion of the chi-square test in this context see Massy, Montgomery, and Morrison, *op. cit.*, 33-47.

[40]D. B. Montgomery, "Stochastic Consumer Models: Some Comparative Results," in *Marketing and the New Science of Planning,* ed. R. King (Chicago: American Marketing Association, 1969) and J. M. Jones, "A Comparison of Three Models of Brand Choice," *Journal of Marketing Research,* 7 (November 1970), 466-73.

TABLE 4. Comparison of *p* Levels of Models

Data Source	Group (by average interpurchase interval in days)	Sample Size	BL	LPL	LL	PD	A	DE M	E
MRCA dentifrice	Before[a]								
Data: January 1958	0-30	751	0.37	0.00	0.69	0.54			
to April 1963	31-45	618	0.13	0.01	0.32	0.28			
(Montgomery)	46-60	503	0.30	0.00	0.03	0.04			
	Over 60	1163	0.00	0.00	0.33	0.61			
	After[a]								
	0-30	751	0.01	0.25	0.92	0.76			
	31-45	618	0.04	0.00	0.00	0.66			
	46-60	503	0.33	0.00	0.60	0.94			
	Over 60	1163	0.32	0.01	0.41	0.63			
MRCA dentifrice	After[a]				0.43	0.28	0.19	0.17	0.07
Data: August 1960	0-30	724			0.36	0.38	0.30	0.27	0.19
to April 1963	31-45	670			0.16	0.28	0.21	0.19	0.06
(Jones)[d]	46-60	586			0.72	0.41	0.55	0.37	0.22
	61-75	469			0.71	0.72	0.57	0.53	0.27
	Over 75	1207							

[a]The before and after designate brand purchasing data before and after the ADA endorsement of Crest.

[b]BL—Morrison's heterogeneous Brand-Loyal Markov model
LPL—Morrison's heterogeneous Last-Purchase-Loyal Markov model
LL—Kuehn Linear-Learning Model, as modified by Massy to incorporate heterogeneity
PD—Montgomery's Probability-Diffusion model
DE—Three versions of Jones's Dual-Effects model:
    version A—a and β change according to an additive mechanism after each purchase
    version M—a and β change according to a multiplicative mechanism after each purchase
    version E—a and β change according to an elemental learning mechanism after each purchase

[c]Adapted with permission from D. B. Montgomery, "Stochastic Consumer Models: Some Comparative Results," in *Marketing and the New Science of Planning,* ed. R. King (Chicago: American Marketing Association, 1969).

[d]Adapted with permission from J. M. Jones, "A Comparison of Three Models of Brand Choice," *Journal of Marketing Research,* 7 (November 1970), 466-73.

purchase interval segments on the basis of their postendorsement behavior, in contrast to Montgomery's use of their preendorsement behavior. This resulted in the Linear-Learning model providing a slightly better overall fit. Jones, in the same study, fitted the three versions of his Dual-Effects model to the same Crest data. One version, where the transition intensities change by an additive mechanism, dominated the other two versions for this data base. Even this additive version of the Dual-Effects model was generally dominated by the Linear-Learning and Probability-Diffusion models in most segments. The parameters of the Dual-Effects model did provide, however, some interesting insights into what was happening in the postendorsement market that could not be gleaned from application of the Linear-Learning or Probability-Diffusion models. These insights are discussed in a later section.

The p levels in the after period as estimated by Montgomery and Jones differ for the Linear-Learning and Probability-Diffusion models. This is because Montgomery's average interpurchase interval segments were based on the pre-endorsement period, whereas Jones's segments were based on the postendorsement period. The rules for determining the eligibility of panel members to be included in the data base also were different. The variations in the goodness of fit of the Linear-Learning and Probability-Diffusion models between the Jones and Montgomery studies illustrate a certain amount of sensitivity of the results to the specific households included in an analysis. These variations indicate that researchers should make every attempt to use households representative of the group about which they wish to draw inferences.

Aaker has also empirically compared his New-Trier model and the heterogeneous Linear-Learning model using two sets of panel data on a frequently purchased consumer good product.[41] In both cases the Linear-Learning model provided a better fit to the data, as indicated by the p levels associated with the chi-square goodness-of-fit test (0.54 versus 0.52, and 0.99 versus 0.88). As these p levels indicate, both models provide a good fit to the data. Aaker also used the estimated models to predict the empirical proportions that would purchase the brands on the nth purchase occasion ($n = 1, 2, \ldots, 10$) following the estimation period. In both cases the New-Trier model seemed to make better predictions of the empirical proportions, after the first four or five purchase occasions, than the Linear-Learning model did. This is, of course, by no means a conclusive test even for these products, since market conditions may have changed significantly from the estimation to the prediction period. The New-Trier model also had an advantage in that a five-purchase sequence was used to estimate its parameters, whereas the Linear-Learning model only used a four-purchase sequence.

Care must be taken, when making these empirical comparisons, not to reject a model out of hand when it performs very poorly on one data set. It may perform poorly because the data were generated in a market where the assumptions on which the model is predicated do not hold. Much more empirical comparative work will have to be done before it will be possible to make general statements about the empirical validity of different models or about the situational characteristics that are likely to render one model a more adequate approximation to choice behavior than another.

Choice Incidence Models

The zero-order, Markov, Linear-Learning, and Dual-Effects models discussed were all concerned with modeling consumer choices, and they generally ignored the question of the timing of these choice decisions.

[41]D. A. Aaker, "New Method for Evaluating Stochastic Models of Brand Choice," *Journal of Marketing Research,* 7 (August 1970), 300-306.

Several researchers have suggested the presence of an interaction effect between interresponse time and brand-choice data, found that a consumer's probability of repurchasing the same brand on two successive purchase occasions declined as the interresponse time increased.[42] The probability, in fact, was found to asymptotically approach the brand's market share. Herniter, after analyzing some data, hypothesized that as the interresponse time increases the probability of repurchasing a brand tends toward the brand's advertising share (this does not necessarily conflict with Kuehn's finding, since in many markets market share and advertising share are closely related).[43] Morrison, in an empirical analysis of coffee, did not find a significant change in brand loyalty as the interpurchase time varied.[44] Carman, in his analysis of the Crest data using the Linear-Learning model, also concluded that there was no significant difference between the parameters for frequent and infrequent purchasers.[45] Thus the interaction between interresponse time and brand choice does not appear to be a universal phenomenon, and may be restricted to certain types of products.

Although choice behavior models do not specifically incorporate purchase timing, they may be modified to have some correspondence to real time. The simplest way to do this is to fit the model to several segments, each of which contains consumers who are relatively homogeneous with respect to their interpurchase times. Although such ad hoc procedures can be useful, specialized interpurchase models may be more useful when the decision maker is primarily concerned about making period-by-period predictions. In this section, six such models, which vary greatly in sophistication, will be reviewed.

Fourt and Woodlock's New-Product Model. The objective of Fourt and Woodlock was to develop a model that could use consumer-panel data to make an early prediction of success or failure for frequently purchased, low-price grocery products.[46] In their model they focus on two significant aspects of the new-product introduction: its ability to get people to make an initial purchase of the product (i.e., its penetration), and its ability to hold customers (i.e., its repeat-purchase performance).

Fourt and Woodlock had observed that the annual cumulative penetration curves of numerous new products showed similar patterns; in each successive time period the increment in these curves declined and the cumulative curve asymptotically approached some limiting penetration. The fit to actual pene-

[42] A. A. Kuehn, "Consumer Brand Choice as a Learning Process," *op. cit.,* 10-17.

[43] J. D. Herniter, "Stochastic Market Models and the Analysis of Consumer Brand Data" (paper presented at the 27th National Meeting of the Operations Research Society of America, Boston, May 6-7, 1965).

[44] D.G. Morrison, "Interpurchase Time and Brand Loyalty," *Journal of Marketing Research,* 3 (August 1966), 289-91.

[45] Carman, *op. cit.*

[46] L. A. Fourt and J. W. Woodlock, "Early Prediction of Market Success for New Grocery Products," *Journal of Marketing,* 25 (October 1960), 31-38.

tration data was improved if the penetration ceiling was made a linearly increasing function of time.

A model that has these characteristics is an exponential growth model of the form shown in Figure 3. Fourt and Woodlock have developed a simple empirical rule for estimating k for a new product. It is also possible to obtain efficient estimates of x_0 and $1 - r$ from the early new-product panel data, thus allowing the cumulative penetration curve to be estimated.

FIGURE 3. **New Buyer Penetration As a Function of Time**

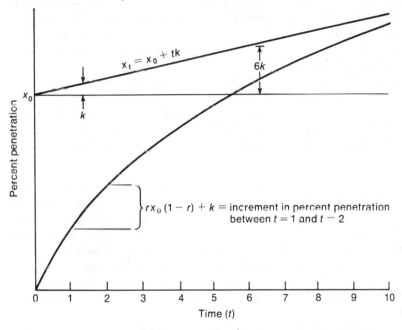

where: % penetration by time $t = kt + \sum\limits_{i=1}^{t} rx_0 (1 - r)^{i - 1}$

k = small positive constant

x_0 = the limiting penetration level at time 0. The limiting penetration level increases by k each period.

r = the proportion of the penetration between the penetration at the beginning of period t and the limiting penetration at the end of t that will be achieved in period t, when k equals 0.

Adapted with permission from L. A. Fourt and J. W. Woodlock, "Early Prediction of Market Success for New Grocery Products," *Journal of Marketing* (October 1960), 31-38.

The repeat-purchase performance is estimated from the observed repeat ratios, that is, the number of households that purchase the product on the $(n + 1)$st occasion after having purchased it on the nth occasion. The empirical repeat ratio must be adjusted upward, since at the end of the observation period there are always people who have not yet had an opportunity to repeat. These repeat ratios are of course equivalent to the transition probabilities in a Markov model. Thus the n to $(n + 1)$st repeat ratio is the probability that a consumer in state n will eventually move to the $(n + 1)$st state. One minus the n to $(n + 1)$st repeat ratio is the probability that a consumer in state n will reject the brand and go to an absorbing rejection state.

By applying the repeat ratio to the cumulative penetration curve it is possible to derive the cumulative first repeat-purchase curve. By applying the appropriate repeat-purchase ratios to the successive repeat-purchase curves, it is possible to obtain the family of such curves. The family of curves combined with some average purchase size can then be used to estimate the sales performance of the product over time. This estimate implicitly assumes that the elements of the company's marketing mix remain relatively stable, and that competitive activity does not change markedly.

This relatively simple model provides marketing managers with some information on the success or failure of a new product, and allows them to make some diagnosis of why it is performing in a certain manner; that is, low repeat ratios may suggest that consumers find the product unsatisfactory. The performance of the model in new-product situations appears to have been quite good.

Parfitt and Collins.   Parfitt and Collins have proposed another relatively simple purchase incidence model, similar to the one described by Fourt and Woodlock.[47] It can be used to predict the brand share of a new product at a time t after the product's introduction and to evaluate the effectiveness of changes in the marketing mix associated with a product. Parfitt and Collins found that prediction is improved if the market is segmented on the basis of when the consumer made his first purchase. The model is then estimated for each segment separately, and the results summed over all segments to obtain the total market forecast.

This conceptually simple model has been found to give quite accurate predictions of the ultimate market share for a wide range of products. The model has also provided interesting data on the effectiveness of price cutting and promotional activity in certain markets. By separating buyers into segments based on time of arrival in the market and by extrapolating past trends, it is possible to estimate the effectiveness of the changes in the marketing mix. Whereas price cutting and promotional activities, in the cases cited by Parfitt and Collins, did increase significantly the number of first-time buyers, the effect on repeat-purchase rates was much more variable. In two cases where price cutting was used, the new buyers attracted to the brand proved to have low repeat-purchase rates, thus resulting in no major long-term improvement in market share. In the promotional cases cited, the repeat-purchase ratios for the new buyers were somewhat higher, resulting in a more significant improvement in the

[47]J. H. Parfitt and B. J. K. Collins, "Use of Consumer Panels for Brand Share Prediction," *Journal of Marketing Research,* 5 (May 1968), 131-45.

long-term market share. These analyses indicate that although it is relatively easy to improve the short-term market share, maintaining it is much more difficult. This model is thus by its nature a useful tool for managers trying to separate the effects of underlying trends in the market from the effects of changes made by the manager in his marketing mix. This is especially important in the case of a new product.

Howard's Semi-Markov Model. Howard proposed the semi-Markov model to avoid what he felt to be an artificial aspect of the simple Markov model: the need for a no-purchase state for consumers who do not purchase any brand in a time interval.[48] In the semi-Markov model the transition probabilities representing brand choice are conditional upon a transition (i.e., a choice) being made. The choices occur at time intervals randomly determined by some underlying probability function. The model allows the distribution of time to the next purchase to be a function of the current state. Thus, in the situation where response *A* represents the purchase of a 2-pound package and response *B* represents the purchase of a 1-pound package, the effect on interpurchase time can be realistically represented by the model.

The model does suffer, however, from certain limitations. In its present form, for example, it does not allow the representation of heterogeneous consumer transition probabilities or interresponse times. The model also requires the development of statistical methods to make it more empirically viable. Even in its present most general form, where the interresponse time is a function of the current state, the model may be an excessive burden on the data base. It may not be possible to reliably estimate and test the model with the purchase-sequence histories that might be available. If the required purchase sequences are too long, it may not be realistic to assume that the transition probabilities and the interresponse time distributions have remained constant. These data-requirement problems would be compounded if an attempt were made to allow consumers to be heterogeneous with respect to interresponse time and transition probabilities, as was suggested previously.

Ehrenberg's Negative Binomial Model. Another early model of consumer behavior that incorporated interpurchase timing was proposed by Ehrenberg.[49] In his model he assumed that the number of purchases made by each consumer per time period would be distributed according to a Poisson distribution. The use of a Poisson distribution to represent the number of purchases per time period implies that the interpurchase intervals are exponentially distributed. It also implies that the purchases occur independently of each other. This assumption will be plausible under two conditions, which can normally be met:

---

[48]R. A. Howard, "Stochastic Process Models of Consumer Behavior," *Journal of Advertising Research,* 3 (September 1963), 35-42.

[49]A. S. C. Ehrenberg, "The Pattern of Consumer Purchases," *Applied Statistics,* VIII (March 1959), 26-46.

1. The successive time periods are of equal length and conform to natural cycles of purchasing activity, such as weeks or months, not days.

2. The time periods are not so short that purchasing activity in one period affects the activity in the next period; that is, for products which the average household consumes in 2 or 3 weeks, 1-week time periods would obviously be too short.

The model incorporates heterogeneity, so that each consumer may be represented by a Poisson distribution with a parameter μ_i representing her own average rate of purchasing. The model assumes that these μ_i are distributed over the population of consumers according to a gamma distribution. This is not a particularly constraining assumption, since the gamma distribution is a relatively flexible distribution. When the assumptions that the individual's purchases per time period follow a Poisson distribution and that the mean values of the individual Poissons are distributed according to a gamma distribution over the population are met, the distribution of consumer purchases in any time period follows a negative binomial distribution. In his development of the model Ehrenberg used a special case of the gamma distribution, the chi-square distribution.

The Ehrenberg model assumes that the Poisson process that generates the purchases of the individual household remains stationary over the period of interest. That is, the μ_i (mean purchase rate) for each individual i remains constant. Although this is a limitation of the model, the model has proved to be empirically viable for some product classes.

In a later paper Chatfield, Ehrenberg, and Goodhardt extended the early model.[50] They demonstrated that if one was willing to ignore those who do not purchase in a given period, the ones who did in fact purchase at least once in the period can be approximately represented by the logarithmic series distribution. This result has two advantages:

1. Since there are consumers who do not purchase in a given period, it obviates the need to specify a priori the population of relevant purchasers.

2. The logarithmic series distribution is a simpler one-parameter distribution that is easier to estimate than the negative binomial distribution.

Another development in the second paper was the introduction of the concept of a joint distribution of the number of units purchased in a period between time periods. This distribution is a multivariate extension of the negative binomial distribution, and it too arises as a consequence of the heterogeneous Poisson process discussed above. From this it can be shown that if all the consumers who made exactly x purchases in period t_1 are selected, the distribution of purchases among this subgroup in period t_2 will be univariate

---

[50]C. Chatfield, A. S. C. Ehrenberg, and G. J. Goodhardt, "Progress on a Simplified Model of Stationary Purchasing Behavior," *Journal of the Royal Statistical Society,* Series A, CXXXIX (1966), 317-67.

normal in period t_2 regardless of the value of x. These results of Chatfield, Ehrenberg, and Goodhardt indicate that the negative binomial distribution is a basic and useful distribution for describing stationary purchase incidence processes.

Empirical results from the application of the model by Ehrenberg and his colleagues to purchase data indicate that the negative binomial distribution fails to fit in the tails of the empirical distribution of purchases. This failure is apparently attributable to the failure of the gamma distribution to fit the tails of the distribution of μ across the population. Nevertheless, Ehrenberg and his colleagues have concluded that the stationary Poisson process is adequate, at least when dealing with established products.

Massy's Stochastic Evolutionary Adoption Model. The work of Fourt and Woodlock, using penetration and repeat-purchase concepts, has been extended in important ways by Massy in his Stochastic Evolutionary Adoption Model (STEAM).[51] The basic objective of STEAM is to utilize disaggregative consumer-panel data, gathered during the early periods after the introduction of a new product or during test markets, to forecast the sales volume of the product after the unstable introductory period is over. STEAM has the advantage over some other choice incidence models in marketing in that there is no need for the user to define a product class to which the new product belongs. In many markets this is not a trivial advantage.

STEAM's basic structure consists of a primary model, which represents the purchasing decisions of individual households, and a series of secondary models, which specify how the parameters of the primary model vary according to the specific individual, time, and situation being modeled. By combining these models a composite probability law for the aggregate new-product adoption process was derived.

As in Ehrenberg's negative binomial model, Massy used the Poisson distribution to represent the number of purchase events per time period, where a purchase event is defined as the purchase of any number of packages of any size at one time. The discussion of this distribution in connection with Ehrenberg's model indicated that it could provide a reasonable approximation to the actual situation for many products. Thus the Poisson distribution is the primary model used to represent the number of purchases made by a given household per period. In the case of STEAM it is more convenient to consider the distribution of the lengths of time between purchases, rather than the number of purchases per period. As pointed out earlier, the waiting times (i.e., the times between purchases) for a homogeneous Poisson distribution are exponentially distributed. To allow the consumer's propensity to purchase to vary over time, Massy assumed a nonhomogeneous (with respect to time) Poisson model in which the

[51] The most detailed exposition of STEAM can be found in Massy, Montgomery, and Morrison, *op. cit.,* 325-443.

parameters of the primary model can vary with time. The waiting-time distribution for the nonhomogeneous Poisson can then be defined.

The first secondary model deals with the changes in the purchase propensity over time. A variety of sources of product information, such as advertising promotions, and word-of-mouth communications may change the purchase propensity, as might the forgetting effect due to the passage of time since the last purchase. Massy assumed that the purchase propensity would vary as a geometric function of the time since the last purchase of the new product. That is,

$$\mu(t) = \mu_0 t^\lambda \quad \text{for } t \geq t_0 = 1,$$

where μ_0 represents a household's propensity to consume the new product right after the last purchase, which is assumed to have occurred at $t_0 = 1$ (i.e., the time origin in this model is 1, not 0). Note that $\mu(t)$ can follow a variety of paths over time depending on the value of μ.

A second secondary model deals with population heterogeneity. Since it is extremely unlikely that families will all have the same preference for the new product and will use it at the same rate, it is necessary for the parameter of the process to be distributed over the population. As the reader will recall, Ehrenberg, when faced with this same situation, used a special case of the gamma distribution, the chi-square distribution. However, when the resulting negative binomial model was applied to the data, it failed to fit the tails of the empirical frequency distribution. Massy hypothesized that this problem was caused by the fact that the gamma distribution is unimodal. Thus if a large proportion of the households have very low purchase propensities, the peak of the gamma will be at 0, preventing it from having a peak at $\mu > 0$. Therefore, Massy proposed that the gamma distribution should only be fitted to the relevant population, that is, those who have a μ_0 greater than 0. Thus the probability density function would have two peaks, one at 0, and one at some value of $\mu > 0$ (see Figure 4). Summarizing;

$Pr[\mu_0 > 0] = M$ where M is the "relevant population" (i.e., the proportion of the population that will eventually make another purchase),

$f(\mu_0 \,|\, \mu_0 > 0) = $ gamma (α, β).

As the earlier discussion in this chapter indicated, purchase event feedback may be a significant factor affecting choice behavior in many product classes. Although the purchase of any related product may affect the propensity to purchase the new product (i.e., it changes the relative propensities), it is likely, if the new product is significantly different, that the learning effects from this new experience will swamp those of the older related products. Thus Massy felt it was a reasonable simplification to ignore the learning effects of other products in the same general product class. Since the effects of experience with a new

FIGURE 4. Probability Density Function

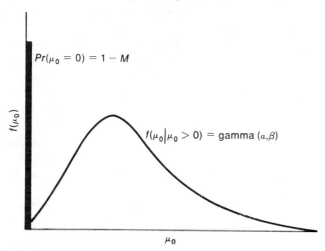

Adapted with permission from W. F. Massy, D. B. Montgomery, and D. G. Morrison, *Stochastic Models of Buying Behavior* (Cambridge, Mass.: MIT Press, 1970).

product could be significantly nonmonotonic, Massy proposed that the learning effect be handled by assuming that different prior distributions of μ exist for households who have made different numbers of purchases of the new product. Thus the parameters of the gamma distribution, a and β, would be estimated separately for each depth of trial class (i.e., for each group of households that had made the same number of purchases).

A final secondary model in STEAM deals with the effects that the timing of the previous purchases of the product might have on μ_0. One would expect that the first few who reach a given depth of trial class would have a larger value of μ than those who arrive much later. Massy proposed that this effect be incorporated by making the α parameter of the gamma distribution a function of Υ, the time at which a given household enters the current depth of trial class. Υ is usually taken to be relative to a time origin, such as the time the depth of trial class would be entered if a household purchased the product immediately after introduction and continued to repurchase it thereafter as soon as it was consumed. The particular function proposed by Massy is

$$\alpha = \alpha_0 \Upsilon^\gamma,$$

where a_0 and γ are new parameters to be estimated from the data.

To summarize, STEAM consists of a primary model for the interpurchase times based on a nonhomogeneous Poisson distribution and a series of secondary models that incorporate the effects of time changes in purchase propensity, time of conversion to a depth of trial class, and population heterogeneity on the purchase propensities. Learning effects from experience with the new product are incorporated into STEAM by estimating all the parameters of the model for each depth of trial class separately. The parameters of STEAM (i.e., a, β, γ, λ, and M) are estimated by the method of maximum likelihood.

Once the parameters of the model have been estimated, STEAM can be used as a forecasting tool. Due to the complexity of STEAM, forecasting by analytical methods is difficult, if not impossible. To circumvent this problem, Massy has developed a microanalytic stochastic projection simulation. The projection is microanalytic in the sense that each household is individually Monte Carlo simulated over time. In actual practice, the purchase history of each individual household may be simulated more than once, if the sample size in a depth of trial class is small, so that the stability of the simulation will be improved. The aggregate forecast is developed by summarizing the purchasing behavior of the individual families.

Massy has reported two empirical applications of STEAM to new products.[52] In both instances the model was used to project market perform-

TABLE 5. **Comparison of Actual Versus STEAM Projections by Depth of Trial Class (Product A)**

Depth of Trial Class	Penetration in Period 46 Projected by STEAM Based on Periods 1-13	Actual Penetration in Period 46
0	0.15	0.22
1	0.42	0.52
2	0.63	0.69
3	0.84	0.76
4	0.77	0.82
5	0.85	0.85

ance in the future on the basis of early results. In Table 5 we present the results for the first product, product A. The actual results for penetration by depth of trial class for the forty-sixty data period are given along with the projected results on data available up to the thirteenth period. By depth of trial class we mean the number of purchases of product A which have been made. Hence, depth of trial class 0 represents nonpurchasers, whereas depth of trial class 5 represents those who have purchased product A five times. The entries in the table are the proportion of the households in a given depth of trial class that make at least one more purchase by period 46. From Table 5 we see that by period 46, 22 percent of all households had actually tried the new product. The STEAM projection of this penetration was 15 percent. Similarly, STEAM projected that 85 percent of the households that had purchased product A five times would purchase it at least one more time by period 46. The actual result was also 85 percent. In sum, Table 5 indicates that the STEAM projections by

[52]*Ibid.*, Chapter 10.

FIGURE 5.   Actual Versus STEAM Projected Sales (Product *B*)

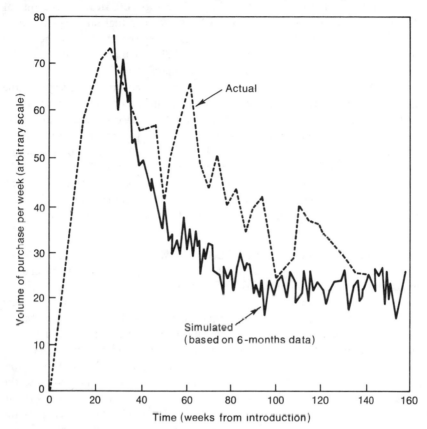

Adapted with permission from W. F. Massy, D. B. Montgomery, and D. G. Morrison, *Stochastic Models of Buying Behavior* (Cambridge, Mass.: MIT Press, 1970).

depth of trial class, although less than perfect, give a reasonably good idea of what management can expect from product *A*.

In the second application, product *B*, the STEAM parameters were estimated based upon the first 6 months of data after the product was introduced. The parameters were then used in a Monte Carlo projection of the results that might be anticipated over the first 3 years or so after introduction. The simulated and actual results are presented in Figure 5. From the figure the early sales results seemed to indicate a rosy future for the product. However, STEAM's processing of the repeat rates at different depth of trial classes indicated that the product seemed headed for trouble. When the actual sales dropped considerably by week 50, management attempted to prop up the product with an intensive promotional campaign. This, of course, was not taken into account in the STEAM projections and is the primary reason for the divergence of the STEAM results from the actual sales results from weeks 50 to 100. However, in spite of management's efforts to keep the project "alive," the actual sales had fallen to the level projected by STEAM by week 140. It appears as though the heavy promotional prop simply postponed the inevitable, which was predicted by projecting the repeat rates via the STEAM machinery.

STEAM is a very sophisticated model that incorporates many of the phenomena that appear to be important factors in the new-product situation. The reported empirical applications of the model suggest it is empirically viable, and that it can provide extremely useful information to new-product managers. Massy has also extended the theoretical development of STEAM to incorporate the effects on a household's purchasing propensities of such factors as the purchase of substitute or complement products, changes in the level of marketing variables, and differences in description variables among the households in the sample.[53] No attempt has yet been made to empirically test this theoretical extension.

Herniter's Purchase-Timing and Brand-Selection Model. Herniter has developed a stochastic model of consumer purchase behavior for frequently purchased, low-cost products that combines both brand selection and purchase timing.[54]

For his purchase-timing model Herniter has proposed that the interpurchase time be represented by an Erlang density function, with the average purchase frequence (λ) distributed over the population according to a functional form that appears appropriate for the product class under consideration. Herniter has proposed a functional form (with parameters q and μ) that divides the population into two segments, the fraction q of the population who purchase the product, and hence have a positive value for λ, and the fraction 1 - q who do not purchase the product and have a λ value of 0. The parameter μ is the inverse of the average value of λ for the population. The parameters of the interpurchase time model can be readily estimated from empirical data.

In his paper Herniter used a homogeneous first-order Markov model for the brand-selection model, but he has noted that more complex nth-order Markov models could be developed.

The purchase-timing and brand-selection models are combined by assuming that these two aspects of consumer behavior are independent. As the discussion earlier in this section indicated, this assumption may not be reasonable for some product classes. Herniter has reported, however, some encouraging results with this simple model. Both the purchase-timing model and the combined purchase-timing- and brand-selection model provided a reasonably good empirical fit to data on at least two products.

---

[53]For a detailed discussion of the extensions of STEAM, see *ibid.*, 414-43.

[54]Jerome Herniter, "A Probabilistic Market Model of Purchase Timing and Brand Selection," *Management Science: Professional Issue—Marketing Management Models*, ed. D. B. Montgomery (December 1971).

This continuous-time Markov model is a special case of the semi-Markov model discussed earlier, since Herniter's model makes a simplification by assuming the independence of the two submodels. Herniter's model does go further than Howard's proposed model in allowing the distribution of inter-response times to vary over the consumers, but it does not make the additional step, suggested in the earlier section on Howard's semi-Markov model, of allowing consumers to be heterogeneous with respect to their transition probabilities.

In this section six choice incidence models have been discussed that can provide marketing managers with information on the total demand for their product over time. Before leaving the subject of choice incidence models, it is worthwhile to point out their usefulness in situations when use of a brand-choice model might appear to be more appropriate. The successful application of brand-choice models depends on the ability of the model builder to define the relevant product class for the product. In some situations this can be very difficult, and it may only be feasible to model the timing of the purchases of the particular brand being studied, if this will provide some of the desired information. Application of a brand-choice model to situations in which the product is ambiguous, where different people may use it as a member of different product classes, may lead to erroneous interpretations of the model parameters and reduce the fit of the model to the data.

This lengthy discussion of the development of a large number of stochastic choice and choice incidence models of consumer behavior points to the importance marketing has attached to this area. It is not appropriate to consider how these models can be used to improve marketing decisions.

UTILIZATION OF STOCHASTIC CHOICE MODELS

The utilization of stochastic choice models may usefully be broken down into three distinct, albeit interrelated, categories: summary market measures, conditional prediction, and structural analysis. Each category will be discussed in turn with examples drawn from the applications presented in the preceding section.

Summary Market Measures

Stochastic models of choice behavior provide summary measures of market activity, which can aid the marketing manager in understanding and interpreting the vast amounts of disaggregative data available to him from such sources as the MRCA consumer panel.[55] To illustrate the manager's need for help in this area,

---

[55]See R. E. Frank and W. F. Massy, *Computer Programs for the Analysis of Consumer Panel Data,* Graduate School of Business, Stanford University, August 1965, for computer programs to assist in the processing of such vast arrays of data.

consider the fact that in 1 year MRCA-panel households generate on the order of 200,000 records of purchases in the product class of coffee alone. Furthermore each purchase record contains such information as date of purchase, brand of purchase, store of purchase, amount, cost, and type of special deal, if any. This further magnifies the volume of data available for analysis. With household-by-household data available on this scale, the manager clearly needs help if he is to transform this plethora of raw data into management information.

In this context stochastic choice models may be used as constructs for organizing and interpreting market data. The use of constructs by managers and market researchers is, of course, nothing new, even though their use may not be recognized as such. Consider, for example, the case of monthly market-share data, which may be obtained from consumer-panel data. These data are aggregates of raw choice data and are often used for comparative purposes between months. But consider how little information is actually conveyed by a rise or a drop in market share between months, other than just a signal that "something has perhaps happened." Such a signal, although potentially useful, yields little information about what has happened, where, and why; nor do these data provide a very useful picture of what is likely to happen if present conditions persist. In sum, simple constructs, such as market-share computations, do not exploit very fully the information available from consumer-panel data.[56]

A useful step in more fully exploiting panel data is to perform a gain-loss analysis or one of its extensions suggested by Rohloff.[57] Gain-loss analysis addresses the question of where a brand's business is coming from, whether it is coming from repeat purchases or from other brands. Furthermore, it is concerned with which brands are taking purchases away from the brand of interest. The juxtaposition of the time trend of such measures with market promotions may often yield insight into the dynamics of a market.

Stochastic models of choice behavior offer a variety of summary measures that may help the marketing manager. Nearly all such models will provide estimates of the long-run choice share for a given alternative if present conditions persist. This measure, which we denote by $S(\infty)$ to indicate the long-run choice share for an alternative of interest, provides an indication of where a market seems to be heading from its present position. Clearly, a product manager who finds his product heading from a share of 15 toward 20 percent is in a very different position from the manager whose product is at 15 percent

---

[56]In a recent report on a survey of users of consumer-panel data by Market Facts, Inc., the authors stated that it appeared that consumer purchase panels were used principally for relatively unsophisticated monitoring of trends in market share or volume, rather than for studying the dynamics of consumer purchasing and the economics of promotional activity, for which they felt this disaggregative data are more suitable (the present authors agree). See D. K. Hardin and R. M. Johnson, "Patterns of Use of Consumer Purchase Panels," *Journal of Marketing Research*, 8 (August 1971) 364-67.

[57]A. C. Rohloff, "Brand Switching Theory and Application" (mimeographed, October 1966).

headed toward 10. Consequently, the long-run choice share that may be inferred from a stochastic model may be of considerable diagnostic interest to a product manager.

Another measure that may be inferred from most stochastic models is the rate, R, at which the market appears to be moving from its current position toward its long-run position $S(\infty)$. Again, this rate is conditional upon present circumstances prevailing; but even so the signal as to what's likely to happen if nothing changes is often of import to management.

Other summary measures are also available from some stochastic models. The Probability-Diffusion model, for example, can provide an indication of the distribution of choice probability in a population of consumers for each choice occasion in a sequence of choices. Marked shifts in this distribution may be indicative of the nature of response to external events. The situation is clearly different if consumers are tending to polarize in their choice probabilities (i.e., concentrate at 0 and 1) than if they are clustering about some intermediate value. Other models, such as the Markov model, provide estimates of brand-switching probabilities; others, such as STEAM, provide inferences concerning the time between purchases for different depth of trial classes. Aaker has suggested the use of his New-Trier model to develop a measure of brand health that would provide an indication as to whether a brand appears to be worth promotional support.[58]

The above discussion serves to illustrate the fact that stochastic choice models provide a measurement framework within which large quantities of data may be distilled into key summary measures of market activity and dynamics.

Once a given stochastic model has been tested on many products and brands and found to be a good approximation to the choice process, the opportunity presents itself to use the summary measures available from these tests as base lines in analyzing future cases. For example, if STEAM were to be applied to a wide variety of products and the subsequent market performance assessed in each case, analysis of a new case might be compared to these results to see, for instance, if the interpurchase time for second-repeat buyers appeared to be in line with previous successful products.[59] If not, management might consider promotions designed to shorten the repeat interval. Such use of stochastic choice models is in the spirit of some of Ehrenberg's work, which also yields base-case

---

[58]D. A. Aaker, "A Measure of Brand Acceptance" (Working Paper No. 55, Institute of Business and Economic Research, Berkeley, Calif.).

[59]If one had such base data from stochastic models of consumer choice behavior on a sufficient number of successful and unsuccessful products, it might be worthwhile to apply product profile analysis to the data. Product profile analysis in the context of screening new product possibilities is discussed in J. T. O'Meara, "Selecting Profitable Products," *Harvard Business Review* (Jan.-Feb. 1966), 83-89, and M. Freimer and L. Simon, "The Evaluation of Potential New Product Alternatives," *Management Science,* 13 (February 1967), B-279-92.

guidelines as standards of comparison for new cases.[60] Such guidelines provide the basis for exception reporting to management.

Conditional Prediction

Some of the measures discussed in the previous section may be used as conditional predictions. That is, they are indicators of where a market is headed if circumstances do not change. For example, $S(\infty)$ is the choice share expected in the long run if the present situation continues. Models of the choice incidence variety are often used for prediction. Such models usually attempt to predict ultimate sales from early sales results in either test market or in national distribution.

One of the simplest models used to make conditional predictions is the simple Markov model. The mathematics of Markov chains provides a method whereby the long-run choice shares of a set of alternatives may be calculated.[61] In a brand-choice context if the alternatives of interest are defined to include the no-purchase state, then the long-run choice shares will be the market shares for the brands.

In some markets, such as the automobile and some major durable markets, the marketing manager is seldom fortunate enough to have information on the consumer's history of brand choices. In the typical situation he might have information on the consumer's current choice and his previous choice (e.g., the make of automobile traded in by the consumer). From this information an aggregate Markov transition matrix can be estimated, which may itself represent no significant segment in the market. Here it would also be useful to calculate the conditional steady-state market-share values. The question immediately arises as to whether or not the steady-state estimates from the aggregate matrix are reasonable estimates of the true values for the heterogeneous population from which the homogeneous aggregate matrix was estimated. Recall our earlier discussion of the problems associated with heterogeneity of consumers. Morrison, Massy, and Silverman have examined this problem using Monte Carlo methods and have found that the steady-state solution from the aggregate transition matrix for a variety of heterogeneous populations will provide a result very close to that of the true value (usually within 1 or 2 percent).[62] The adequacy of the long-run estimate from the aggregate transition matrix held even when their heterogeneity distributions were quite extreme.

As was indicated previously, conditional predictions from choice incidence models are generally oriented toward predicting sales and choice shares in

[60]See the papers by Ehrenberg and his associates referenced in this chapter.

[61]J. Keming and J. L. Snell, *Finite Markov Chains* (Princeton, N.J.: Van Nostrand, 1960).

[62]D. G. Morrison, W. F. Massy, and F. N. Silverman, "The Effect of Non Homogeneous Populations on Markov Steady State Probabilities," *Journal of the American Statistical Association*, 66 (June 1971), 268-74.

new-product situations. The focus of attention has been upon utilizing sales and choice share results from early periods in a product's introduction to attempt to gain a picture of what the product's ultimate success might be. Even so simplistic a formulation as the early Fourt and Woodlock trial and repeat penetration model (discussed earlier) has proved useful.

The somewhat more sophisticated model of Parfitt and Collins has been tested for ability to project monthly market shares for new brands after introduction. The tests were performed using data for 24 successful new-brand introductions in a variety of product classes. In each of these cases the model was used to project ultimate market share using data from the first few months after introduction. These projections of ultimate market share were then compared to the actual market share 12 to 18 months after introduction. In each of the 24 cases the market-share projection was within the range of actual monthly observations for the twelfth through the eighteenth month. It thus appears that the model is able to provide rather good projections from early market results.

Recall that Parfitt and Collins have made another conditional prediction use of their model. They used the model projection to provide an estimate of what would have happened if certain price cuts and promotions had not occurred. That is, they made a projection conditional on no change. This then provides a base line for evaluating the market impact of such price and promotional activities. Without such a base line, evaluation is extremely difficult. The model, used as a device for conditional prediction, thereby enables inferences to be made about incremental payoffs.

As additional examples of the use of choice incidence models for conditional prediction, recall the discussion of Massy's applications of STEAM to products *A* and *B*. In both instances, using only early information, the model provided quite good insight into the direction a market was heading.

Furthermore, the asymptotic or steady-state share of consumer choices can be calculated separately for various segments in the market.[63] The conditional predictions of asymptotic market or choice share can be used as a criterion variable for evaluating the success of the product and its marketing program in various market segments. The conditional predictions of asymptotic market share in different geographical areas can also be used as one criterion variable in marketing experiments designed to test the effectiveness of different promotional programs. As discussed earlier, such an approach has been used by Haines to estimate the impact of marketing expenditures in different marketing activities during the introductory campaign for an innovative product. For example, he found that the ultimate sales level of the product was most affected by per capita promotion expenditures. Haines also used as a criterion variable the rate at which the model expects the market to approach the steady state,

[63]D. A. Aaker, "Using Buyer Behavior Models to Improve Marketing Decisions," *op. cit.*

which is also a variable of considerable interest to the marketing decision maker. He found that advertising expenditures during the first 2 months of the introduction and prior availability most affected the response rate of the market.

Structural Analysis

Structural analysis is the other broad area in which stochastic models of consumer behavior can be of assistance to marketing decision makers. Several examples exist in which stochastic models have provided important insights into consumer behavior in certain markets.

For example, Morrison has fitted his Brand-Loyal and Last-Purchase-Loyal models to data for regular coffee purchases from the *Chicago Tribune* consumer panel. He found that for all segments of the market the Brand-Loyal model provided a better fit to the data, but that the value of the k parameter was close to 1, indicating (as the reader will recall from our earlier discussion) that the purchasing behavior in this market was quite close to being zero order.[64] This result is consistent with Massy and Frank's earlier finding for the regular coffee market. This indicates that in some situations examination of the estimated parameters of a model in a given application may indicate that the model can be replaced by a simpler model. In another analysis of Morrison's models, the heterogeneous Linear-Learning model and the Probability-Diffusion model, Montgomery found that the latter two appeared to be better structural approximations to brand-choice data, with some advantage for the Diffusion model in an extremely unstable market.

To illustrate the kind of insights into consumer behavior that can be gained from stochastic models of consumer behavior, it is worth briefly considering the more complex behavior exhibited by consumers in the dentifrice market following the endorsement of Crest by the American Dental Association. Here we shall limit ourselves to discussing the results of fitting the heterogeneous Linear-Learning model, Montgomery's Probability-Diffusion model, and Jones's Dual-Effects model.[65]

Examination of the parameters in the Probability-Diffusion model indicated that the endorsement of Crest (the change in the market environment) enhanced the likelihood that an individual's probability of purchasing Crest would increase, but more surprisingly it indicated that if this probability did increase it would be very unlikely that it would then decrease from this new high level. Thus the

---

[64]D. G. Morrison, "New Models of Consumer Behavior: Aids to Selling and Evaluating Marketing Plans" (paper presented at the American Marketing Association 1965 Fall Conference, Sept. 1-3, 1965).

[65]The following section is based on the discussions in Massy, Montgomery, and Morrison, *op. cit.*, 265-67, and Jones, "A Comparison of Three Models of Brand Choice," *op. cit.*, 469-73.

endorsement had a much greater effect on the retentive capacity of Crest than on its attractive capacity.

The Linear-Learning model indicated the presence of positive purchase event feedback. The more general Dual-Effects model indicated, however, that in most segments there was negative purchase event feedback; that is, the feedback from the purchase and use of Crest did not seem to be a factor in the rapid rise in Crest sales. The influence of the ADA endorsement was presumably so overwhelming that it swamped the negative feedback. In this instance the Linear-Learning model erroneously ascribes the over time effects of an external event to purchase event feedback. The negative feedback indicated in three out of five segments by the Dual-Effects model is supported by some reports at the time that Crest had a taste disadvantage. Thus the Dual-Effects model, with its ability to represent both purchase event feedback and external effects, was able to provide insights into the structure of the dentifrice market that could not be obtained from models able to represent only one mechanism.

As our earlier discussion indicated, some stochastic models of consumer choice behavior directly incorporate marketing variables into their structure. The variable Markov formulations used by Telser and Nakanishi are examples of this. In the Nakanishi model, where the acceptance process for new products by consumers is divided into three stages, the user of the model is able to get direct estimates of the effects of expenditures on the different marketing activities in each stage. In applying his model to two new grocery products, Nakanishi found that consumer behavior in the awareness and trial stages was influenced by advertising, but that advertising appeared to have little effect in the acceptance stage. Such information is of course invaluable to a manager trying to decide how to allocate scarce marketing resources. As Nakanishi has also demonstrated, his model allows a marginal analysis of the effectiveness of expenditures in different marketing activities. The model can also be used to evaluate different marketing plans over time, thus allowing the manager to determine an optimal marketing plan for his product for the market situation represented by the model.

In another context Aaker developed some interesting market insights from empirical application of his New-Trier stochastic model.[66] For example, he found that consumers seem to have a constant number of alternative brands in their consideration set. If a brand a consumer has not been using is to be adopted, it appears that it would have to displace some other brand in the consumer's consideration set. Aaker concludes that a new brand in a product class must dislodge an existing brand in consumers' minds. As a consequence, he suggests that new brands require more aggressive introductions than would be required if the consumer's consideration set were more elastic. It would be most informative to examine a broad range of applications of the new-trier model in different

[66]D. A. Aaker, "Using Buyer Behavior Models to Improve Marketing Decisions," *op. cit.*

product contexts in order to ascertain the extent to which product classes differ in the number of brands in the evoked set. Should substantial differences be found, it would then be worthwhile to attempt to identify market factors relating to the size of the evoked set.

Aaker also used the New-Trier model to examine the effects of consumer deals on New-Trier brand acceptance. Dissonance theory would suggest that if the first purchase were made on a deal, the likelihood of ultimate brand acceptance would be reduced. However, he found that deals had little effect on brand acceptance. Lawrence has also empirically examined this question for toothpaste purchases in the period January 1959 to June 1962.[67] Lawrence operationally defined conversion to a new brand as a switch followed by three consecutive purchases of the brand. Of the nondeal switchers, 13.9 percent continued buying the new brand (i.e., were converted) compared to only 9.6 percent of the deal-pack switchers. Thus the phenomenon does not appear to be a universal one, and it may be at least partly a function of the product class.

The above examples serve to illustrate the fact that stochastic choice models can suggest interesting and useful behavioral insights into the structure of market response. Such insights and the coupling of marketing and segmentation variables to stochastic models (either directly as in the variable Markov formulation or indirectly as in Haines's analysis) can serve to help managers learn systematically and correctly about the nature of market response. This in turn should foster the development of better judgmental inputs to market analysis, as well as more decision-relevant models.

In sum, this brief discussion of some of the uses of stochastic models of consumer behavior has pointed out the variety of ways they can be of assistance to the marketing manager in evaluating his position in the market, in planning his future actions, and in improving his understanding of the consumers in the market.

SUMMARY AND CONCLUSIONS

This chapter first examined consumer choice behavior from a stochastic modeling viewpoint. Attention then was turned to an examination of a wide range of applications to choice and the incidence of choice. Emphasis was given to recent developments. Finally, the utilization of stochastic models was illustrated by several examples. In the remainder of this chapter we shall attempt to provide a partial blueprint for future research.

One major problem with research to date is the fact that most of the models have only been applied to one or two products. The principal exceptions are the work of Parfitt and Collins and Ehrenberg. Although this situation is, perhaps,

---

[67]R. J. Lawrence, "Patterns of Buyer Behavior Time for a New Approach?" *Journal of Marketing Research,* 6 (May 1969), 137-44.

understandable in view of the relatively short history of stochastic models in marketing, it is to be hoped that it will be rectified in the not too distant future. Application of the models to many product classes should provide useful base lines from which to assess future applications. Furthermore, it would be useful to develop a taxonomy of products, market segments, and other competitive circumstances that render one structural approximation better than another.

More work is required to develop new models that incorporate multiple effects. The work of Jones in incorporating both choice event feedback and external effects and the work of Rao incorporating both brand and store choice exemplify what is needed. Herniter's incorporation of both choice and choice timing is another case in point. One main limitation of the Probability-Diffusion model and the Linear-Learning model (at least in its published accounts) is the need to reduce the set of choice alternatives to two. Work is needed to extend these models or their future variants to handle such cases.[68] An advantage of Markov models, of course, is that they generally allow for more than two alternatives.

New developments in model structure are also needed, especially in terms of providing direct linkage to marketing policy variables. Some beginnings here are exemplified by the variable Markov work of Telser and Nakanishi and Massy's extended STEAM.[69] Normative use of such models seems promising. For example, an extremely efficient algorithm exists for optimizing policy in a variable Markov process.[70]

Another important aspect of model structure is the provision of a mass point at choice probability zero to represent consumers who may never make the choice in question. Several models such as STEAM, the New-Trier model, and Herniter's model incorporate this feature. Jones has recently presented some empirical evidence indicating the importance of the mass point at zero.[71]

Another promising area for application to infrequently purchased products is the application of the stochastic choice models to attitude data rather than choice data. This should expand the useful scope of stochastic models beyond frequently purchased, branded consumer items.

Finally, there is a clear need for better methods of discriminating among

---

[68]For some partial results relating to multialternative extensions of the probability-diffusion model, see D. B. Montgomery, "Note on a Limit Distribution Arising in Certain Stochastic Response Models," Research Paper No. 23, Graduate School of Business, Stanford University, July 1971.

[69]See Massy, Montgomery, and Morrison, *op. cit.,* Chapter 11.

[70]R. A. Howard, *Dynamic Programming and Markov Processes,* (Cambridge, Mass.: MIT Press, 1962). For a marketing application of this algorithm see L. M. Lodish, D. B. Montgomery, and F. E. Webster, Jr., "A Dynamic Sales Call Policy Model," Working Paper 339-68, Sloan School of Management, MIT, 1968.

[71]J. M. Jones, "Distributions of Probability of Purchase in Models of Consumer Brand Choice Behavior," dittoed paper, Western Management Science Institute, U.C.L.A., May 1971.

models. As the reader will recall, several very different models may all provide relatively good fits to a given set of data. Although some work has been done on this problem, more and better tests are needed.[72]

In conclusion, choice models now have a reasonably good foundation in marketing. The future should see many refinements in theory and application.

[72]See R. C. Atkinson, G. H. Bower, and E. J. Crothers, *An Introduction to Mathematical Learning Theory* (New York: Wiley, 1965), 395 for a proposed pseudo-F test. See Aaker, *op. cit.* (August 1970), for a proposed predictive test. In a simulation test D. E. Schendel, J. O. Summers, and D. L. Weiss, "Simulation and Model Testing," in *Marketing and the New Science of Planning* ed. R. King (Chicago: American Marketing Association, 1968), 416-30, found that a linear-learning model could only be distinguished from a constant probability model when the two were extremely dissimilar.